THE STANDARD BIBLE COMMENTARY

Thessalonians, Corinthians, Galatians and Romans

By
J. W. McGARVEY, LL.D., and
PHILIP Y. PENDLETON, A.M.

WIPF & STOCK · Eugene, Oregon

Wipf and Stock Publishers
199 W 8th Ave, Suite 3
Eugene, OR 97401

Thessalonians, Corinthians, Galatians and Romans
By McGarvey, J. W. and Pendleton, Philip Y.
Softcover ISBN-13: 978-1-7252-8176-9
Hardcover ISBN-13: 978-1-7252-8174-5
eBook ISBN-13: 978-1-7252-8178-3
Publication date 5/26/2020
Previously published by Standard Publishing Foundation, 1916

This edition is a scanned facsimile of the original edition published in 1916.

INTRODUCTION

In presenting this third volume of THE STANDARD BIBLE COMMENTARY to the public we feel that little need be said by way of introduction.

The same painstaking care and laborious research which were given to THE FOURFOLD GOSPEL have also been used in preparing this volume. It is true nearly double the number of volumes were consulted in preparing the former work, but numbers do not tell the whole story. The text of Paul's Epistles presents such a wilderness of exegetical difficulties that the Gospels seem a smooth and well-worked road in comparison. Moreover, the difficulties of the text are always reflected in the comments thereon, and therefore the comments on Paul's writings are longer and more intricate than those employed in expounding the Gospels.

Again, it should be noted that while the original element in THE FOURFOLD GOSPEL is large, that of this work is, of necessity, very much larger, for it was a common occurrence to find no satisfactory explanation, even after every available authority had been consulted, thus compelling original work. We have tried never to dodge, but always to explain, and the public owes a debt of gratitude to our publishers who made the financial sacrifice which permitted us to take the time needful for such carefulness.

If the exegetical scholar finds his trained and sensitive ear offended by a roundabout rhetoric which uses many simple words where a single technical term would have better satisfied him, we beseech him to remember that this series of commentaries is written for Sunday-school workers. It is therefore void of all rhetorical ambitions, not to say vanities, and seeks only to be plain and practical—a simple exposition for busy people. Over thirty years ago Russell Errett directed our attention to the need of such a commentary, so we gratefully acknowledge that the idea did not originate with us.

Numberless kind words and commendations which appeared in the press, and which came to us by mail, have encouraged us greatly, though we have been too busy to acknowledge them.

It is our hope that this volume may be as helpful as the others seem to have been.

PHILIP Y. PENDLETON.

CONTENTS

PAGE.

FIRST EPISTLE TO THE THESSALONIANS

INTRODUCTION 1

PART FIRST.

PERSONAL RELATIONS, AFFECTIONATE DESIRES AND PRAYERS.

I. Salutation and Thanks for the Faith of the Thessalonians 3
II. How the Word was Preached and How Received..... 7
III. Reasons for Sending Timothy, and Joy over the Report He Brought.. 11

PART SECOND.

EXHORTATIONS, INSTRUCTION AS TO THE LORD'S COMING, FINAL EXHORTATIONS, PRAYER AND BENEDICTION.

I. Sundry Exhortations 15
II. The Resurrection and the Lord's Coming............. 19
III. Closing Admonitions, Prayer and Benediction......... 24

SECOND EPISTLE TO THE THESSALONIANS

INTRODUCTION 28
I. Thanksgiving and Prayer for the Church—God's Impartial Judgment 30
II. The Coming of Christ and of Antichrist.............. 33
III. Thanksgiving, Prayer, Exhortation and Benediction... 43

FIRST EPISTLE TO THE CORINTHIANS

INTRODUCTION 48

PART FIRST.

APOSTOLIC RELATIONS, AND ASSERTIONS OF AUTHORITY.

I. Greeting, Thanksgiving, Reproof of Divisions, Vanity of Philosophy 50

CONTENTS

	PAGE.
II. The Gospel versus Philosophy	58
III. Supremacy of God and the Church	62
IV. Apostolic Stewardship and Authority	67

PART SECOND.

Apostolic Responses and Conclusions.

I. Response to Report of Incest	71
II. Response to Rumors of Litigation, etc.	74
III. Response as to Marriage	78
IV. Fourth Response—Concerning Idolatrous Meat	85
V. Fifth Response—As to His Apostolicity	88
VI. Renewal of Response concerning Idolatrous Meat	97
VII. Sixth Response—Concerning Head Costume	108
VIII. Seventh Response—As to the Lord's Supper	114
IX. Eighth Response—As to Spiritual Gifts	119
X. As to the Supremacy of Love	127
XI. Spiritual Gifts Concluded	133
XII. Ninth Response—As to the Resurrection	145
XIII. Concerning the Collection, Personal Matters, Salutations and Benediction	160

SECOND EPISTLE TO THE CORINTHIANS

Introduction 167

PART FIRST.

Paul's Maintenance of his Apostleship.

I. Thanks for Comfort—Defense as to Change of Plans	169
II. Explanation as to Change of Plans—As to the Incestuous Person—A Pean of Joy	176
III. Apostleship above Human Commendation, and the Ministry of Moses	181
IV. The Hope of Future Glory Sustains in Present Trials	187
V. Reconciliation, and the Ministry of Reconciliation	194
VI. Introduction to a Warning, and the Warning	199
VII. An Appeal to be Accepted	204

CONTENTS

PART SECOND.

CONCERNING THE COLLECTION FOR THE JERUSALEM CHURCH.

I. The Collection and the Messengers in Charge of it.... 210
II. Exhortation to Have His Boasting Sustained......... 215

PART THIRD.

PAUL MEASURES OR COMPARES HIMSELF WITH HIS CHIEF OPPOSERS OR OTHER DETRACTORS.

I. Foes, Weapons and Measurements................... 220
II. Apology for Self-condemnation, Denial of Charges and Laying of Counter Charges........................ 225
III. A Comparison of Labor, Signs, etc.................. 229
IV. The Third Visit—Conclusion....................... 237

EPISTLE TO THE GALATIANS

INTRODUCTION 245

PART FIRST.

ARGUMENTS SUSTAINING PAUL'S GOSPEL AND APOSTOLIC OFFICE.

I. Paul's Gospel and Apostleship Divinely Derived...... 248
II. Paul's Gospel Apostolically Approved—His Equality with Peter 256

PART SECOND.

BIBLE TEACHING AS TO FAITH.

I. Justification by Faith in Christ Biblically Vindicated.. 264
II. Childhood and Manhood—Sarah and Hagar.......... 271

PART THIRD.

EXHORTATIONS TO STEADFASTNESS IN FREEDOM AND TO FAITHFULNESS.

I. Exhortation to Maintain Freedom without License, and to Abstain from Legalism........................ 279
II. Exhortations to Mutual Helpfulness—Right and Wrong Glorying 284

CONTENTS

EPISTLE TO THE ROMANS

PAGE.

INTRODUCTION 289

PART FIRST.

DOCTRINAL: THE UNIVERSAL NEED OF RIGHTEOUSNESS SATISFIED BY THE GOSPEL.

Subdivision A.

I. Salutation and Personal Explanations................ 295
II. Righteousness by the Gospel......................... 301

Subdivision B.

I. Need of Righteousness by the Gentiles............... 302
II. Need of Righteousness by the Jews................... 307
III. Jewish Privilege Does Not Diminish Guilt—Scriptures Include both Jew and Gentile Alike under Sin...... 316

Subdivision C.

I. Neither Jew nor Greek Can Obtain Righteousness otherwise than by the Gospel....................... 320
II. The Gospel Method of Justification must be Applied both to the Literal and Spiritual Seed of Abraham.. 324

Subdivision D.

I. Results of the Justification Wrought by Christ; viz., Peace, Hope, Love and Reconciliation.............. 330
II. Adam, the Trespasser unto Death, Contrasted with Christ, the Righteous unto Life.................... 333

Subdivision E.

I. Justification Brought about by Such Relation to Christ as Creates Obligation to be Dead to Sin and Alive to Righteousness 341
II. Justification Results in Change from Service of Law and Sin to Service of Grace and Righteousness..... 346
III. Change of Relationship from Law to Christ Illustrated 349

CONTENTS

IV. Sense of Bondage Which Comes through Law Prepares Soul to Seek Deliverance through Christ...... 352
V. New Relationship to Christ Changes Mind from Carnal to Spiritual 357
VI. New Relationship to Christ Results in Adoption, Spirit of Adoption and Heirship......................... 360
VII. New Relationship Results in Aid of Spirit, and Assurance of Salvation because Divinely Decreed...... 364

PART SECOND.

EXPLANATORY: THE DOCTRINE OF RIGHTEOUSNESS BY FAITH RECONCILED.

I. Since Doctrine Results in Condemnation of Israel, Paul Shows This is Contrary to Personal Wish.......... 373
II. Rejection of Israel Not Inconsistent with God's Promise 383
III. Rejection of Israel Not Inconsistent with Justice of God 393
IV. God's Absolute Power Asserted...................... 401
V. The Grand Conclusion and Its Explanations.......... 412

Subdivision A.

The Conclusion of the Argument Reached............ 412

Subdivision B.

Five Explanations of the Grand Conclusion, and Ascriptions of Praise.................................. 418

I. First Explanation—Jews Responsible for Their Rejection 418
II. Second Explanation—Universality of Gospel Demands its World-wide Extension......................... 430
III. Third Explanation—Casting off of Israel Is but Partial. 442
IV. Fourth Explanation—Salutary Results of Israel's Temporal Fall and Future Rise....................... 453
V. Fifth Explanation—A Like Mercy to be Shown Jews and Gentiles 470
VI. Concluding Ascriptions of Praise to God............. 478

CONTENTS

PART THIRD.

PAGE.

HORTATORY APPLICATION—VARIOUS PHASES OF FAITH-LIFE OF BELIEVER IN CHRIST.

I. Basis of Faith-life Defined—It Is Sacrificial and Sanctified 484
II. Faith-life Operating in Church Affairs in Humility.... 490
III. Faith-life Operating in Church and Social Affairs in Love and Other Virtues........................... 496
IV. Faith-life Discharging Civil Duties................... 505
V. Faith-life Recognizing Just Rights of Others.......... 513
VI. Faith-life Finds Its Motives in Ever-impending Coming of the Lord................................... 517
VII. Faith-life Operating in Mutual Forbearance.......... 523

PART FOURTH.

EPISTOLARY CONCLUSION, CONTAINING PLANS, REQUESTS, ETC.

I. The Apostle's Ministry and Plans—A Request for Prayers 536
II. Commendation of Phœbe—Salutations—Warnings—Benediction 544

FIRST EPISTLE TO THE THESSALONIANS.

INTRODUCTION.

On his second missionary journey Paul founded the first European church at Philippi. Continuing his journey one hundred miles farther, he came to Thessalonica, which was the capital of the second Roman district of the province of Macedonia. It was a large and important commercial city, containing much wealth and learning. To this day it is the second city in European Turkey, ranking next to Constantinople, and has between 75,000 and 100,000 inhabitants. It is now called Saloniki. When Paul entered it, A. D. 52, the Greek element preponderated, and Roman colonists were next in number. The Jews also were there, and had at least one synagogue. In this synagogue Paul and Silas and Timothy began their work, but after three Sabbaths they were apparently ejected from that place of worship. Then an uproar was raised by the Jews, and Paul and Silas were led out of the city by night, and conducted by brethren to Berœa. It is not unlikely that Paul was in Thessalonica longer than three weeks, for he succeeded in founding a church there before persecution compelled him to retire. Immediately south of Thessalonica were the snowclad slopes of Mount Olympus, the supposed seat of the mythical gods of Greece. The infant church was therefore not only endangered by the opposition of the Jews, but was also liable to assault on the part of the pagans, being so near one of their geographical centers. As might be expected, Paul felt keenly the perils of this small band of raw, half-instructed Christians, and (probably while in Berœa) he twice tried to return to them, but was hindered by Satan. Then trouble broke out in Berœa, and Paul was hurried off alone to Athens. Timothy, either after his arrival in Athens, or probably before he left Berœa, was ordered by Paul to go and visit the church at Thessalonica, and bring him word as to its condition. From Athens Paul came to Corinth, and here was joined by Silas and Timothy, the latter bringing the apostle a fairly good report of the church at Thessalonica. Timothy, however, seems to have reported that the Thessalonians had not wholly forsaken the sensuality and covetousness which had characterized them as pagans, and Paul exhorts them to forsake these sins. Then, too, the Thessalonians had a wrong view of the second coming of the Lord. They expected it to take place in the near future, and had gotten the notion that only those who were alive at the Lord's coming would participate in the glories and joys of that hour. Paul corrects this idea also by showing that the resurrection of Jesus guarantees the resurrection of those who believe in him. The doctrines of the Epistle are simple and practical, for the Judaizing questions discussed in Galatians and Romans, and the Gnostic errors handled in Colossians and Ephesians, had not yet been raised. As a whole, the Epistle may be taken as an argument tending to confirm the faith of the Thessalonians in the divine origin of the gospel. That the gospel is of God is shown in four ways: 1. It had been attested by miracles. 2. It had been preached to the disadvantage of its ministers and despite bitter opposition. 3. It set forth precepts the sanctity of which were worthy of heaven. 4. Its author was divine, having risen from the dead and become the author of the resurrection. On his third journey Paul must have visited Thessalonica frequently, and these visits, together with his Epistles, were not without their fruits, for Thessalonica was for centuries the bulwark of Christian faith in the East, and long resisted the invading forces of the Mohammedans. When word went forth in A. D. 1430 that Thessalonica had fallen, all Christendom was dismayed.

PAUL'S FIRST EPISTLE TO THE THESSALONIANS

PART FIRST

1: 1-3: 13

PERSONAL RELATIONS, AFFECTIONATE DESIRES AND PRAYERS

I.

SALUTATION AND THANKS FOR THE FAITH OF THE THESSALONIANS

1: 1-10

1 **Paul, and Silvanus, and Timothy, unto the church of the Thessalonians in God the Father and the Lord Jesus Christ: Grace to you and peace.** [In this salutation Silas and Timothy are united with Paul because they had aided Paul in founding the church at Thessalonica. The account of the founding of this church will be found in Acts 17. Silas is mentioned before Timothy because he is older, both in years and in service. Compare Acts 15: 22, 32, 40 with Acts 16: 1-3. Silvanus is the full name, and Silas the abbreviation. The name is Roman, and Silas was a Roman citizen (Acts 16: 37). Silas was now at Corinth with Paul, and Paul mentions his services there (2 Cor. 1: 9). Much of the opening part of this letter embraces Silas and Timothy in its thought, but in chap. 2: 18 Paul distinguishes himself from them, and from that time on the letter is wholly his. Neither in this Epistle nor in that to the Philippians does Paul speak of himself as an apostle. In other Epistles he affirms his apostleship because, in the case of the Epistle to the Romans, he wrote to strangers, and in other cases his apostle-

ship had been challenged. As to Thessalonica, see the Introduction. The church is spoken of as being in God and in Christ because in this respect it differs from all other organizations. It is its privilege to dwell in fellowship with God, so that it may be, as it were, ensphered and encircled by him. *Grace* was the Greek and *peace* the Hebrew salutation; Paul here combines them. Grace indicates the favor of God and all the gifts which flow from it, while peace represents tranquility and prosperity, either inward or outward.] **2 We give thanks to God always for you all, making mention *of you* in our prayers; 3 remembering without ceasing your work of faith and labor of love and patience of hope in our Lord Jesus Christ, before our God and Father** [Paul thanked God for the church at Thessalonica for its evidences of Christian life mentioned in the remainder of this section. In the words before us he sets forth their relations to the three cardinal Christian graces, or faith, hope and love (1 Thess. 5: 8; Col. 1: 4, 5; 1 Cor. 13: 13). Their faith was not formal, barren and dead (Jas. 2: 20, 26); but it actively worked, bringing their wills into obedience to the will of God (Rom. 1: 5; 16: 26); their love was not idle, but caused them to employ themselves in heartfelt toil for the welfare of others; and their hope in Christ sustained their souls, so that they endured all trials and persecutions, and were unyielding in their conflict with temptation and doubt. Thus, each in its own way, the three graces manifested themselves, and in such a way that it was evident that these graces were centered in, inspired by, and renewed of Christ, and viewed with approval by the Father]; **4 knowing, brethren beloved of God, your election, 5 how that our gospel** [ours not by right of authorship, but of proclamation] **came not unto you in word only, but also in power, and in the Holy Spirit, and *in* much assurance; even as ye know what manner of men we showed ourselves toward you for your sake. 6 And ye became imitators of us** [1 Cor. 11: 1], **and of the Lord, having received the word in much affliction** [Acts 17: 4-10], **with joy of the Holy**

PERSONAL RELATIONS

Spirit; **7 so that ye became an ensample to all that believe in Macedonia and in Achaia.** [Continuing, Paul gives thanks that he has so much evidence of the election of the Thessalonians that it amounts to a practical knowledge of that election. This evidence is threefold: 1. The power with which he and his companions had felt endued when they preached the gospel in Thessalonica, for they had come not as vain "babblers" of empty words (Acts 17: 18, 32), but as messengers of God speaking truth powerful in itself, and additionally supplemented by the power of the Spirit. 2. The undaunted way in which the Thessalonians had received the gospel, despite the swiftness with which they had fallen a prey to persecution. 3. The prompt manner in which the gospel had brought forth fruit in their lives. But what does Paul mean by election? Not that rigid, arbitrary choice of God first promulgated by Augustine, and afterwards emphasized by Calvin, for such doctrine was not then known. Such an absolute, unchangeable thing as Calvinistic election could only have been *fittingly* made known to an apostle by direct revelation, but Paul knew the election here spoken of by mere sensuous evidence. To elect means to choose, and the choosings of God do not annul the free will or agency of man. Thus Israel is chosen (Deut. 7: 6); yet afterwards cast off because of unbelief (Matt. 8: 11, 12). Election is not made absolute by God; on the contrary, the choosing of God requires that we ourselves make our calling and election sure (2 Pet. 1: 10); it does not make our salvation sure, for as supplemental to it we ourselves must still work out our own salvation with fear and trembling (Rom. 9: 11). We may make shipwreck of the faith to which we have been called or chosen (1 Tim. 1: 20), and Paul's exhortations suggest that some of these elect in Thessalonica were in danger of doing this—Thess. 4: 1-8.] **8 For from you hath sounded forth** [as the sonorous, soul-stirring blast of a trumpet] **the word of the Lord, not only in Macedonia and Achaia** [after its subjection by the Romans, all Greece was divided into two parts, of which Macedonia was the northern, and Achaia the southern], **but in every place** your faith to God-ward is gone forth; so that we need not to speak anything. [Thessalonica, being a seaport, had intercourse with all Greece, and with much of the then known world. News of the church in that place, and of the peculiar virtues that characterized it, soon spread through all Greece, and was borne by believers, and those interested in carrying such news, to the more remote parts of the earth. Though Paul had not been beyond the confines of Greece since his departure from Thessalonica, yet his experience in Greece leads him to speak by way of anticipation of parts as yet unvisited, and to represent the good news of the faith, etc., of the Thessalonians to have preceded him so that he had no need to say anything about it.] 9 For they themselves [those to whom Paul came] report concerning us what manner of entering in we had unto you; and how ye turned unto God from idols, to serve a living and true God, 10 and to wait for his Son from heaven, whom he raised from the dead, *even* Jesus, who delivereth us from the wrath to come. [Paul had gone from Thessalonica to Athens, and from Athens to Corinth. He may have done considerable missionary work in the smaller villages about Corinth. Now, as he went about through Corinth and through these villages he found that instead of being permitted to tell of the good work which he had done at Corinth, he himself had to become a listener while strangers told him how he had preached the gospel there, and how those who had been for generations worshipers of dead idols had turned unto the living God, and those whose fathers had for centuries worshiped the imaginary gods of that Mount Olympus under whose shadow they dwelt, had suddenly become worshipers of the true God as revealed in Christ: thus becoming disciples of a religion which taught that Jesus was the Son of God, that he had been raised from the dead, that he had ascended to heaven, from whence he had promised to return to his waiting disciples, whom he keeps in a constant state of justification, so that they are delivered from every manifestation of the wrath of God, either now present or to be revealed at the last judgment.]

II.

HOW THE WORD WAS PREACHED AND HOW RECEIVED.

2: 1-16.

[In this section, Paul amplifies two statements made in the previous section. In verses 1-13, he enlarges upon the facts set forth in verse 5 above, and verses 13-16 are a similar enlargement of the matter contained in verse 6.] **1 For yourselves** [as distinguished from those above mentioned who carried or repeated the news of the work at Thessalonica], **brethren, know our entering in unto you, that it hath not been found vain** [that Paul's coming to Thessalonica had not been vain or fruitless was proved by the fact that in this pagan city a church of Christ was now found]: **2 but having suffered before and been shamefully treated, as ye know, at Philippi, we waxed bold in our God to speak unto you the gospel of God in much conflict.** [The Thessalonians remembered how Paul and Silas had come to them fresh from Philippi, with the evidences of persecution yet apparent on their bodies—a persecution which was indeed shameful because it was wholly undeserved and contrary to law—but they also remembered that they were in no way terrified or deterred either by these present tokens of past suffering, or by the storm of persecution which threatened their speedy repetition, from preaching the gospel boldly.] **3 For our exhortation** *is* **not of error, nor of uncleanness, nor in guile** [The word "exhortation" has a double significance—it includes the idea of rousing the slothful, and also that of comforting the sorrowful. Paul here begins to contrast his teaching with that of false teachers with whom the world abounded, and with whom the Thessalonians had been long familiar. The instruction of these teachers, being founded on myths, fables and delusions, was full of error. The purpose of the instruction was to introduce lascivious mysteries and unhallowed rites such as the Bacchic, Isiac, Mythraic, etc.; the manner of the instruction was full of trickery and guile (Acts 8: 9; 13: 6-10). Paul had not roused the indifferent by proclaiming *false* dangers, nor comforted the despairing by wakening *vain* hopes]: **4 but even as we have been approved of God to be intrusted with the gospel, so we speak; not as pleasing men, but God who proveth our hearts.** [Instead of preaching the old falsehoods which had so long pleased the wicked of Thessalonica, Paul had come as a trustee of God commissioned to preach the gospel, and he had preached it realizing his accountability as to the trust imposed upon him.] **5 For neither at any time were we found using words of flattery, as ye know, nor a cloak of covetousness, God is witness** [As to his *outward* conduct (that it was without flattery) he calls the Thessalonians to witness, and as to his *inward* desires (that they were without covetousness) he calls God to witness. Self-seeking and flattery were the besetting sins of false teachers (Rom. 16: 18). Paul had spoken plainly of the sins of his hearers, and had demanded immediate and thorough repentance]; **6 nor seeking glory of men, neither from you nor from others, when we might have claimed authority as apostles of Christ.** [As the apostle had not preached for money, neither had he preached for fame. Though he might have stood upon his dignity, and magnified his office as an ambassador of God, yet he had not done even this. He had not preached the gospel because he held high office in the kingdom, and so would be exalted by its enlargement; but he had preached to save souls. Not only at Thessalonica had he done this, but everywhere else.] **7 But we were gentle in the midst of you, as when a nurse** [nourisher; *i. e.*, nursing mother] **cherisheth her own children: 8 even so, being affectionately desirous of you** [not yours, but you], **we were well pleased to impart unto you, not the gospel of God only** [as the sincere milk of the Word], **but also** [as mothers often do for their new-born babes] **our own souls** [lives—1 John 3: 16], **because ye were become very** dear to us. **9 For ye remember, brethren, our labor and travail: working night and day** [the Hebrew order—Gen. 1:5], **that we might not burden any of you, we preached unto you the gospel of God.** [The apostle was so intent upon blessing the Thessalonians with the gospel of God that he toiled at night to make up the time spent in teaching them by day.] **10 Ye are witnesses, and God** *also,* **how holily** [toward God] **and righteously** [toward man] **and unblamably** [either toward God or man] **we behaved ourselves toward you·that believe** [Paul here claims not perfection, but consistency of life]: **11 as ye know how we** *dealt with* **each one of you** [individually, and without partiality], **as a father** [as patiently, tenderly and earnestly as a father] **with his own children, exhorting you, and encouraging** *you,* **and testifying, 12 to the end that ye should walk worthily of God, who calleth you into his own kingdom and glory.** [As those who are called to an honor owe it to the one calling them to walk worthy of the honor, so the Thessalonians, being called to have part in the present kingdom and future glory of God, needed to walk circumspectly. Having thus rehearsed the ministry at Thessalonica step by step, from the day he entered the city until he departed from it, Paul now turns to tell the effects of that ministry upon the Thessalonians.] **13 And for this cause we also thank God without ceasing** [without ever failing to mention it in our prayers], **that, when ye received from us the word of the message,** *even the word* **of God, ye accepted** *it* **not** *as* **the word of men, but, as it is in truth, the word of God, which also worketh in you that believe.** [The word is the good seed of the kingdom which the heart receives, and from which it brings forth fruit with patience—Luke 8: 11-15.] **14 For ye, brethren, became imitators of the churches of God which are in Judaea in Christ Jesus: for ye also suffered the same things of your own countrymen, even as they did of the Jews** [their countrymen]; **15 who both killed the Lord Jesus and the prophets,** and drove out us, and please not God, and are contrary to all men; 16 forbidding us to speak to the Gentiles that they may be saved; to fill up their sins always [Gen. 15: 16; Matt. 23: 32]: **but the wrath is come upon them to the uttermost.** [While narrating the course of events at Thessalonica, Paul notes the similarity between the history of the Thessalonian church and that of the Judæan churches, and reviews the latter history for the encouragement of the Thessalonians. Surely the opposition of their pagan countrymen ought not to cause these Thessalonian Christians to doubt that God favored or approved them, for such opposition was to be expected. Even the Jews, though professedly the people of God, had killed God's prophets and Christ their Lord, and had driven out the apostles and evangelists. Though the Jews were God's people, their conduct in rejecting God's Son showed that they did not please God; and that they were haters of their fellow-men was very apparent, for they even forbade Christ's apostles to attempt to save the Gentiles by preaching the gospel to them. Their opposition to churches either in Judæa or Greece was therefore no evidence that God disapproved these churches: on the contrary, God patiently permitted them to do all this, that their wickedness might be fully ripened and exposed, so that a full and notable punishment might be meted out to them—a punishment which began just before the siege of Jerusalem, and continues to this day. Wrath unto the uttermost, or unto the end, signifies a wrath which fully expends itself in executing judgment. It does not mean wrath unto the end of the world—Rom. 11: 15, 25, 26.]

III.

REASONS FOR SENDING TIMOTHY, AND JOY OVER THE REPORT HE BROUGHT.

2: 17-20 ; 3: 1-13.

17 **But we, brethren, being bereaved of you for a short season** [about six months], **in presence not in heart** [Col. 2: 5], **endeavored the more exceedingly to see your face with great desire** [Paul had been torn rudely from the Thessalonians by the hand of persecution, so he speaks of being "bereaved" of them, thus using a strong word which indicates both the separation and the sense of desolation which arose from it. Though he had been but about six months absent from them, his heart was filled with desires to return to them]: 18 **because we would fain have come unto you, I Paul once and again** [emphatic way of saying twice]; **and Satan hindered us.** [How Satan hindered, we are not told, but we find that his emissaries had so little disposition to let Paul return that they drove him from Berœa *onward* to Athens.] 19 **For what is our hope, or joy, or crown of glorying? Are not even ye, before our Lord Jesus at his coming?** 20 **For ye are our glory and our joy.** [Paul also calls the Philippians his joy and crown (Phil. 4: 1), and expresses, as here, a hope of glorying hereafter both in them and in the Corinthians (Phil. 2: 16; 2 Cor. 1: 14). Paul usually employs the word "crown" in a figurative sense, the figure being derived from the wreath or chaplets worn by athletes in the Grecian games (1 Cor. 9: 24-27; 2 Tim. 4: 7, 8), and it is fair to suppose that he does so here. The full thought, then, is this: As an athlete, who, in the absence of his king, had entered the contest, competed for, and won the crown, would, on the king's appearing, rejoice to lay his trophy at the king's feet; so Paul, having won the Thessalonians for Christ, hoped that he might joyfully present them to Christ at his coming. The passage is a beau-

tiful but effectual rebuke to the idle fears of some Christians that they will not recognize their friends in the hereafter. If Paul could not recognize the Thessalonians, how could he present them as his crown, or glory in them?]

III. 1 Wherefore when we [by this plural Paul means himself only] **could no longer forbear, we thought it good to be left behind at Athens alone; 2 and sent Timothy, our brother and God's minister in the gospel of Christ, to establish you, and to comfort** *you* **concerning your faith** [fearful lest the infant church should succumb to temptation or to persecution, and unable longer to endure his want of information concerning it, Paul had sent Timothy, from Athens, that he might visit the Thessalonians, and bring him word as to their spiritual condition; though in so doing he had deprived himself of all brotherly fellowship and ministerial assistance in Athens, the seat of idolatry and vain philosophy]; **3 that no man** [of you] **be moved by these afflictions; for yourselves know that hereunto we are appointed.** ["We" refers to all Christians, and Theophylact sagely remarks, "Let all Christians hear this." As to the doctrine, see Matt. 13: 21; Mark 10: 30; John 15: 18; 16: 33; Acts 4: 22.] **4 For verily, when we were with you, we told you beforehand that we are to suffer affliction; even as it came to pass, and ye know.** [As to the affliction which Paul foretold and which came upon them, see Acts 17: 5-9.] **5 For this cause** [because he feared that persecution might cause them to apostatize] **I also, when I could no longer forbear** [resuming the thought of verse 1], **sent that I might know your faith, lest by any means** [and Satan has many] **the tempter had tempted you, and our labor should be in vain.** [It is sad to lose spiritual labor, but sadder still to lose the souls which are the results of it. But we should not leave this passage without observing that if Paul had had Calvinism in mind, and had wished to assert that the elect might fall from grace and be lost despite their election, he could hardly have stated his point more clearly, for these

REASONS FOR SENDING TIMOTHY

words are addressed to those whom he has just pronounced elect.] **6 But when Timothy came even now** [suggesting that Paul wrote on the day of Timothy's arrival, or very soon after] **unto us from you, and brought us glad tidings of your faith and love, and that ye have good remembrance of us always, longing to see us, even as we also** *to see* **you; 7 for this cause, brethren, we were comforted over you in all our distress and affliction through your faith** [Since Paul would be comforted as to the Thessalonians by the good news of their condition brought by Timothy, the "distress and affliction" must have referred to other matters which disturbed the apostle's rest. These were doubtless the failure at Athens, and the troubles which he had at Corinth before the negative protection afforded him by Gallio, when that official refused to interfere, either to aid or hinder him (Acts 18: 6-12). Thus the good news from Thessalonica lightened the apostle's burdens at Corinth]: **8 for now we live, if ye stand fast in the Lord.** [The good news made Paul relish and enjoy life, just as his afflictions and distress had been to him a kind of death. Comp. 1 Cor. 15: 31.] **9 For what thanksgiving can we render again unto God for you, for all the joy wherewith we joy for your sakes before our God** [Paul felt that he could not be thankful enough for the joy which the faith of the Thessalonians gave him; not a joy arising from worldly or personal pride in them, but a joy so pure and holy that it could be displayed before the searching eye of God]; **10 night and day praying exceedingly that we may see your face, and may perfect that which is lacking in your faith?** ["Night," says Joseph de Maistre, "is a great chapter in the Psalms, to which David often recurs." Paul, like David, employed much of the night in meditation and prayer. At such times he remembered the brevity and sudden termination of his ministry in Thessalonica, and realized that his converts were not fully instructed in many items of faith and doctrine; he therefore prayed that he might return and complete his instruction. After three or four years his prayer was answered (Acts 20: 1, 2), and some ten years after that it was again answered—1 Tim. 1: 3.] 11 Now may our God and Father himself, and our Lord Jesus, direct our way unto you: 12 and the Lord make you to increase and abound in love one toward another, and toward all men, even as we also *do* toward you; 13 to the end he may establish your hearts unblamable in holiness before our God and Father, at the coming of our Lord Jesus with all his saints. [The "you" of verse 12 is emphatic, and stands in contrast with "our" of verse 11, as though Paul said "the Lord direct *our* way to you, but whether he does so or not, may he prosper *you*, causing your love to grow and abound, even as we grow in love toward you, that by love (though ye may lack somewhat of instruction) ye may be so established that no one can lay anything to your charge when the Lord Jesus comes." The Epistles to the Thessalonians have many such brief prayers (1 Thess. 3: 11; 5: 23; 2 Thess. 1: 11; 2: 16; 3: 5-16). In verse 11, and also at 2 Thess. 2: 16, 17, while we have God and Jesus for nominatives, yet the accompanying verb is in the *singular*, thus showing the oneness or unity of God. The love which Paul here asks for is Christian love. "This," says Theophylact, "is the character of divine love to comprehend all; whereas human love hath respect to one man, and not to another." Since the word "saints" (literally, holy ones) is used in the Old Testament to include angels, it is likely that they are included here, for Paul's words are, no doubt, an indirect quotation of Zech. 14: 5.]

PART SECOND.

EXHORTATIONS, INSTRUCTION AS TO THE LORD'S COMING, FINAL EXHORTATIONS, PRAYER AND BENEDICTION.

4: 1-5: 28.

I.

SUNDRY EXHORTATIONS.

4: 1-12.

1 Finally then, brethren, we beseech and exhort you in the Lord Jesus, that, as ye received of us how ye ought to walk and to please God, even as ye do walk,—that ye abound more and more. [The first part of this Epistle was retrospective and historical. In it Paul fully revived the spirit of love which had existed between him and these Thessalonians. This he did that this second part, which is prospective and hortatory, might be made more effective. "Finally" is the word with which Paul customarily introduces the closing part of his Epistles (2 Cor. 13: 1; Eph. 6: 10; Phil. 4: 8; 2 Thess. 3: 1). The word "then" connects this chapter with the close of the third chapter, showing that what Paul now says is spoken that the Thessalonians may be blameless at the Lord's coming. "In the Lord Jesus" shows that Paul wrote as the organ or instrument of the Lord. In the phrase "ye do walk" Paul concedes their virtue that he may water it and increase it.] **2 For ye know what charge we gave you through the Lord Jesus.** [The commandments were given by Paul through the inspiration of the Spirit sent of Jesus. Throughout this chapter Paul asserts his inspiration.] **3 For this is the will of God, even your sanctification, that ye abstain from forni-**

cation; 4 that each one of you know how to possess himself of his own vessel in sanctification and honor, 5 not in the passion of lust, even as the Gentiles who know not God [By "will of God" Paul means the divine desire. Not an absolute desire, but one which human perversity may frustrate. "Sanctification" means holiness in its general sense. In all his Epistles to the Gentile churches Paul introduces exhortations to purity of life. He was at this time in Corinth, whose patron goddess was Venus, and where social impurity abounded. "Heathenism," says Whedon, "had made the crime trivial, jocular, rather smart, and even religious and right. All this must Christianity reverse, and place it among the most heinous sins, and subject to the most fearful penalties." There has been much discussion over the phrase "possess himself of his own vessel," some asserting that it means to acquire a wife, and others that it means to control the body and its desires. The problem is surely a difficult one. The verb "possess" is commonly used to indicate the winning or acquiring of a wife, and 1 Pet. 3: 7 is cited to prove that the word "vessel" is used to indicate a wife. One other citation is given from the Talmud, where Ahasuerus is represented as calling his wife his "vessel." But the Talmud does not prove Hebrew usage in Paul's day, being written many centuries later, and the citation from Peter proves nothing, for the word "vessel" is there used to indicate the human body, the man's being the stronger, and the woman's the weaker. The human body or personality is elsewhere called a vessel in the Bible (Acts 9: 15; Rom. 9: 21-23; 2 Cor. 4: 7; 2 Tim. 2: 21; 1 Sam. 21: 5). This Biblical use of the word is strongly against the idea that it could mean a wife. The word "vessel," then, favors the idea that Paul is talking about the *body*. On the other hand, it is urged that the verb "possess" here used simply means to win or acquire, and never has that ethical use (to possess morally, to subdue, or control) which is claimed for it here. It is true that no classical or Biblical citations can be given of such a use, but that *it is used so here is unquestionable*, whichever interpretation we put upon "vessel"; for the full phrase is "possess in sanctification and honor," etc., introduced by the phrase "know how." Conceding that Paul is talking about a wife, he certainly does not mean to say that each man should know how to win or acquire a wife; there is nothing moral or spiritual about such knowledge. What he does say is that a man should know how to hold or possess (either his wife or his body) in sanctification and in honor; *i. e.*, in moral cleanliness. We take it that Paul here urges bodily self-control, and that the passage is a parallel rather to Rom. 6: 19 than to 1 Cor. 7: 2]; **6 that no man transgress** [literally, overreach], **and wrong his brother in the matter** [Because the word "overreach" is usually associated with bargaining, trading, and other business transactions, able commentators have thought that Paul here introduced covetousness, that it might be rebuked together with lust. But Paul's language is not to be so contorted. The thought flows smoothly on to the end of verse 8. Lust has its deceptions, its overreachings, its covetousness, as well as commercialism. "Thou shalt not covet thy neighbor's wife"]: **because the Lord is an avenger in all these things, as also we forewarned you and testified.** [God punishes all such crimes—Rom. 13: 4; Eph. 5: 5, 6; Col. 3: 6.] **7 For God called us not for uncleanness, but in sanctification.** [" God has not called us under the law that we should be impure, since, indeed, the very cause and condition of our calling is that we should cease to be what we once were."— *Erasmus.*] **8 Therefore he that rejecteth, rejecteth not man, but God, who giveth his Holy Spirit unto you.** [The "rejecteth" of this verse refers to the forewarning and testifying of verse 6. Those who did not heed the warning and testimony were not rejecting the counsel of Paul, but the counsel of God himself (Luke 13: 16; Acts 5: 4), and if they were Christians they were doubly guilty, it being sin enough to reject God's warnings even if he had not given his Holy Spirit to strengthen and encourage in heeding those warnings. The Holy Spirit makes us temples not to be defiled. Here again Paul asserts the divine authority of the teaching which came through him.] **9 But concerning love of the brethren ye have no need that one write unto you** [having spoken of that false, unclean, lustful thing which the world called love, and which made them give the title "goddess of love" to Venus, Paul here turns to discuss the true love which Christians bear to Christians—Heb. 13: 1 ; 1 John 3: 14]: **for ye yourselves are taught of God to love one another** [Concerning this love the whole gospel had instructed the Thessalonians, for when they were born of God by it they became children of God's household, and brethren unto each other. The very framework and structure of Christianity inculcated principles of love and affection]; **10 for indeed ye do it toward all the brethren that are in all Macedonia. But we exhort you, brethren, that ye abound more and more** [Though their love already reached beyond the large confines of Thessalonica, and took in all Macedonia, Paul exhorts them to extend it to even a larger compass. Christian love must embrace the world]; **11 and that ye study to be quiet** [The Greeks were naturally mercurial and restless. How much they needed this advice to be quiet, or steady, will be seen in Paul's second Epistle, where he reproves them for their wild fanaticism, built upon false hopes of Christ's immediate coming], **and to do your own business** [without being meddlesome], **and to work with your hands, even as we charged you; 12 that ye may walk becomingly toward them that are without, and may have need of nothing.** [Instead of spending their time in restless gadding about or idle meddling with other people's affairs, Paul expected them to heed his warning, and earn their own living. These Thessalonians were mostly of the laboring class. If they were idle, they would quickly be reduced to dependence or beggary, and the unbelieving world without (Col. 4: 5) would quickly say of the new religion that it made men idle and worthless. Paul therefore counsels them to that industry that would make them independent, self-respecting and respected.]

II.

THE RESURRECTION AND THE LORD'S COMING.

4: 13-5: 11.

13 But we would not have you ignorant [This is Paul's habitual formula, used either negatively or positively, with which to start a new topic (Rom. 1: 13; 11: 25; Col. 2: 1; 1 Cor. 10: 1; 11: 3; 12: 1; 2 Cor. 1: 8; Phil. 1: 12). It shows us that what he is now about to say has no connection with what precedes. It seems that Timothy brought Paul word that many Thessalonians entertained the crude notion that only the living would participate in the joys of Christ's coming, and that all those who were so unfortunate as to die before that event, would thereby forfeit their share in it. It is not strange that such a doctrine should spring up among those who had been so hastily instructed as the Thessalonians, especially when we may safely surmise that many new converts had been added to their number since Paul's departure], **brethren, concerning them that fall asleep; that ye sorrow not, even as the rest** [the pagans], **who have no hope.** [Paul speaks of the dead as sleeping, employing the beautiful New Testament metaphor (John 11: 11; Acts 7: 16; 1 Cor. 15: 18, 51), in which the grave becomes a couch wherein the body rests until it is wakened at the resurrection. Those grossly pervert the metaphor who use it to prove that the soul also slumbers. The apostle does not forbid sorrow over our departed (Acts 8: 2; John 11: 35), but that despairing grief which characterized the pagan of that day who had no hope of a resurrection. Alford gives such quotations as these from pagan writers. Theocritus: "Hope goes with life; all hopeless are the dead." Æschylus: "Once dead there is no resurrection more." Cetullus: "Suns may set and may return; we, when once our brief life wanes, have eternal night to sleep." Lucretius: "None ever wake again whom the cold pause of life hath overtaken." To these might be added the pathetic lines of Moschus: "We shall sleep the long, limitless, unawakable slumber," and the citation of Jowett as to "the sad complaints of Cicero and Quintilian over the loss of their children, and the dreary hope of an immortality of fame in Tacitus and Thucydides." The Christian should stand in contrast to all this, assuaging his sorrow by a blessed hope.] **14 For if we believe that Jesus died and rose again, even so them also that are fallen asleep in Jesus will God bring with him.** [Paul here founds an affirmation on the intimate relation which exists between Christ and his people; a relation which he elsewhere likens to the union between the head and the body (Eph. 4: 15, 16); the argument being that if the head enjoys a resurrection, the body must likewise share in it. "With him" does not here mean that Jesus will bring the disembodied spirits from *heaven* to the resurrection, but that God, who brought Jesus from the grave, will also bring from the *grave*, in conjunction with Jesus, all those who entered it with their lives spiritually united with Jesus. But the bringing from heaven is taught at 1 Thess. 3: 13.] **15 For this we say unto you by the word of the Lord, that we that are alive, that are left unto the coming of the Lord, shall in no wise precede them that are fallen asleep.** [The facts here set forth were revealed to the apostle by direct revelation, as at 1 Kings 20: 35, and he had many such revelations (1 Cor. 11: 23; Gal. 1: 11, 12; 2: 2; Eph. 3: 3; 2 Cor. 12: 1). Paul declares that the living shall not go before the dead to meet the coming Lord. The "we" in this verse has led many to think that Paul expected to be alive when Jesus came, but conversely the "us" at 2 Cor. 4: 14 proves that he expected to be then dead, and the schedule of events which at 2 Thess. 2: 1-5 he says must take place before the coming, favors the latter view. The truth is, Paul uses "we" as a mere word of classification, as we might do in a sentence like this: "We of the United States now number eighty odd million; a century from now *we* will number—" etc. This would not imply that the writer expected to be then alive.

THE RESURRECTION

16 For the Lord himself shall descend from heaven, with a shout, with the voice of the archangel, and with the trump of God ["Himself" shows that the Lord will not come by messenger, or by representative, but in person. Paul does not describe any of the convulsions of nature which accompany the advent (2 Pet. 3: 10; Rev. 20: 11); but he mentions three sounds which will accompany it, for these have to do with the resurrection which he now has under discussion. The shout of Christ the King is the signal that the awful moment has arrived. Immediately after it the voice of the archangel is heard summoning the other angels to the performance of their duty; viz.: the gathering of the saints (Matt. 24: 31; Mark 13: 27), which are just being roused from the slumber of death by the trumpet of God. The word "archangel" is also used at Jude 9, where we are told that the archangel's name is Michael. It is used nowhere else in Scripture, and there is no hint that there is an order or class of archangels. Michael is the chief or ruler of all the angels (Rev. 12: 7). The trumpet is called "trump of God," because it heralds the approach of God, and summons the people to meet him (Ex. 19: 16-19). There is no hint as to who blows this trumpet, though it is mentioned several times —1 Cor. 15: 52]: **and the dead in Christ shall rise first; 17 then we that are alive, that are left, shall together with them be caught up in the clouds, to meet the Lord in the air: and so shall we ever be with the Lord.** [Some, mistaking the spiritual resurrection mentioned at Rev. 20: 4, 5, for a literal one, have thought that there are two resurrections, one for the righteous (the first resurrection) and one for the wicked (the second resurrection). Of course such a doctrine is abhorrent to the idea of a single hour of judgment, with the saved upon the right hand and the lost upon the left, but it shall be fully discussed in its own place. Those who hold this theory appeal to this passage in proof of it, reading it thus: "The dead in Christ shall rise first, and the dead out of Christ shall rise second." But in order to make it read thus they have *supplied* a correlative clause which is totally foreign to the context, and which crowds out the correlative which Paul himself has given; for "shall rise *first*" is correlative with "*then* shall be caught up." The apostle has been drawing a comparison, not between the righteous dead and the unrighteous dead, but between the dead and the living at the hour of the advent. He began this comparison at verse 15, and he here completes it by showing that the supposition that the living would precede the dead is so contrary to the facts that, on the contrary, the dead will be raised *before* any ascension is allowed the living, and *then* after the resurrection of the dead, the living and the dead shall be caught up together to meet the Lord. That glorious change, wherein the mortal puts on the immortal, as indicated at 1 Cor. 15: 51, 55, will no doubt be simultaneous with the resurrection of the dead. The phrase "caught up" implies the sudden and irresistible power of God. We are not to understand that we are to be caught up with clouds, but that we will meet him who comes with clouds (Dan. 7:13; Rev. 1:7; Matt. 24: 30). He makes the clouds his chariot (Ps. 104: 3). The term "air" is used generally for the region above the earth. No doubt we will be caught up far beyond our atmosphere into the realm of pure space—Eph. 1: 3; 2: 2.] **18 Wherefore comfort one another with these words.** [Thus are we commanded to tell all Christians who mourn that they will meet their lost in Christ on the day that Christ appears, and that in sweet union and communion they will ever be with him.]

V. 1 But concerning the times and the seasons, brethren, ye have no need that aught be written unto you. [When Christian hopes are thus vividly pictured forth, our human nature naturally asks, "When?" (Luke 21: 7). The Thessalonians had been fully taught by Paul that the time of the Lord's coming was unrevealed (Matt. 24: 36; Acts 1: 7), and that therefore Paul could not enlighten them on this point. The term "times" indicates long eras, and "seasons" the briefer epochs into which they are divided.] **2 For yourselves know perfectly that the day of the Lord**

THE RESURRECTION

so cometh as a thief in the night. [Here is an echo from the lips of Jesus (Matt. 24: 36-51 ; Luke 12: 39, 40). See also 2 Pet. 3: 10; Rev. 3: 3. The coming of the thief implies our loss, if he catches us asleep and unprepared. How fearful our loss if we are not prepared for the coming of the Lord— Heb. 10: 31.] **3 When they** [the thoughtless and careless] **are saying, Peace and safety** [*i. e.*, there is no ground for apprehension], **then sudden destruction cometh upon them, as travail upon a woman with child ; and they shall in no wise escape. 4 But ye, brethren, are not in darkness, that that day should overtake** [surprise] **you as a thief : 5 for ye are all sons of light, and sons of the day : we are not of the night, nor of darkness ; 6 so then let us not sleep, as do the rest** [the pagans], **but let us watch and be sober. 7 For they that sleep sleep in the night; and they that are drunken are drunken in the night. 8 But let us, since we are of the day, be sober, putting on the breastplate of faith and love ; and for a helmet, the hope of salvation.** [The idea that the thief comes in the night as set forth in verse 2 suggests the thought that those that live in the night must find it hard to guard against him. But those who live in a perpetual day are not easily surprised by a thief. Now, the Christians, being enlightened as to the Lord's coming, lived in such a perpetual day ; in fact, to use a Hebraism, they were "sons" of the light and of the day ; *i. e.*, they belonged to the day. There was no need, therefore, that their spiritual faculties should be asleep. Day is no time for such sleep, and those that dwelt in it should find it easy to watch and be sober and wear their armor as good soldiers, while those who dwelt in the night would find it hard to keep awake, to keep sober, or to wear armor. It was common in the East for people to be drunken in the night-time, as they were ashamed to be seen intoxicated in the daylight (Acts 2: 15). The nights of the Greeks and Romans were given to revelry, and it was counted an especial mark of profligacy to be drunken in the daytime (2 Pet. 2: 13). Polybius emphasized the abandoned condition of a drunkard by **saying, "Even by day he was often conspicuous to his friends, drunk."**] **9 For God appointed us not unto wrath, but unto the obtaining of salvation through our Lord Jesus Christ, 10 who died for us, that, whether we wake or sleep** [live or die before his coming], **we should live together with him.** [This verse is suggested by the word "salvation" which precedes it. The hope of salvation may well defend us in the hour of temptation, and it should be strong enough to do so, for God has not appointed us to be lost, but to be saved, and has given his Son to die that we might be saved; and so, whether we remain alive unto his coming, or pass to our rest before that day, we may be assured that we shall live in one company with him.] **11 Wherefore exhort one another, and build each other up, even as also ye do.** [As Paul closed his main teaching about his Lord's coming with an injunction that the Thessalonians comfort each other with it (chap. 4: 18), so he closes this afterpiece to it with a similar injunction that because of it they should exhort and strengthen one another.]

III.

CLOSING ADMONITIONS, PRAYER AND BENEDICTION.

5: 12-28.

12 But we beseech you, brethren, to know them that labor among you, and are over you in the Lord, and admonish you; 13 and to esteem them exceeding highly in love for their work's sake. [Paul here admonishes the church as to how it shall treat its elders. He bids the church recognize their leadership, respect them, and hold them in affection because of the blessed and divine work which they were discharging, the work being that enjoined by the third term of the great commission; viz.: admonishing or teaching the church to observe all things whatsoever Jesus commanded (Matt. 28: 20). Such teaching is an essential duty of an elder (1 Tim. 3: 2; 2 Tim. 2: 24; Tit. 1: 9). This section is closely connected with the last verse of the preceding one, the instruction of the elders being the chief means of effecting the edification there mentioned.] **Be at peace among yourselves.** [Mark 9: 50. Contempt for the instruction and authority of the elders is the first step toward that strife and faction which is here reproved.] **14 And we exhort you, brethren, admonish the disorderly, encourage the fainthearted, support the weak, be longsuffering toward all.** [The word "disorderly" describes the soldier who does not remain in the ranks; it is the following out of the military figure introduced at verse 8. The whole is an admonition against a too strictly disciplinarian spirit. The disorderly are not to be too hastily considered apostates, nor are the fainthearted to be regarded as cowards, nor the weak called backsliders, nor are any to be hastily cast out; but the church, being slow to condemn, is to bear with offenders, and seek to reclaim them.] **15 See that none render unto any one evil for evil** [Christians are repeatedly bidden to return good for evil (Matt. 5: 38-48; Rom. 12: 19-21; 1 Pet. 2: 18-25). "See that" puts the Thessalonians on notice that the practice of retaliation or revenge was apt to creep in unawares, and so it was, for persecution wakens revenge as fire kindles fire, thus making two wrongs out of one]**; but always follow after that which is good, one toward another, and toward all.** ["Make," says the Cambridge Bible, "the good of your fellow-men your constant pursuit, and let no injury or unworthiness on their part turn you aside from it. Revenge must be cherished neither toward those within nor those without the church, but good must be rendered to all—Gal. 6: 10.] **16 Rejoice always** [A short time previous to Paul's letter the Thessalonian Christians had all been pagans, and as such, under similar conditions of distress and persecutions, would have been apt to seek escape from their troubles by suicide; but now they are bidden to make their sufferings for Christ a source of new joy, as Jesus had commanded (Matt. 5: 10-12), and as Paul, who practiced this teaching, had so often enjoined (Rom. 5: 3-5; 2 Cor. 12: 10). Confidence in the good providence of God made such joy possible—Rom. 8: 28]; **17 pray without ceasing** [This not only means to observe habitual seasons of prayer, and to cultivate a disposition to pray, but to be ever in a prayerful spirit, to have constantly a subconsciousness of the presence of God. Compare 1:9; 12:12; Eph. 6:18; Col. 4:2]; **18 in everything give thanks** [not for peace and prosperity only, but also for affliction and persecution (Acts 5: 41), and as did Paul and Silas at Philippi—Acts 16: 25]: **for this** [the discharge of the three duties just named] **is the will** [desire] **of God in Christ Jesus to you-ward. 19 Quench not the Spirit** [as fire may be smothered out by overwhelming it with noncombustible matter, so the Spirit of God in the breast of a man may be quenched by overloading the life with worldly cares]; **20 despise not prophesyings** [Prophesyings were instructions given through inspired men, and included moral and spiritual precepts as well as predictions as to the future. Such instructors stood next in rank to the apostles (1 Cor. 12: 28). Compare also Eph. 2: 20; 1 Cor. 14: 1-5, 39. They were neither to neglect to hear nor refuse to obey prophecy]; **21 prove all things; hold fast that which is good** [Sift the bad from the good (1 John 4: 1-13), and cherish the good. To this corresponds the "unwritten saying" attributed to Jesus, "Show yourselves approved money-changers;" *i. e.*, distinguish between the true coin and the counterfeit. Surely such advice has always been pertinent, when false teaching of every kind abounds]; **22 abstain from every form of evil.** [These words close the sentence; the full thought is this: despise no prophecy, but prove it; if it is good, hold fast to it, but abstain from every form of evil teaching or practice.] **23 And the God of peace himself sanctify you wholly; and may your spirit and soul and body be preserved entire, without blame at the coming of our Lord Jesus Christ.** [May God, who makes peace between himself and mankind, himself prepare

CLOSING ADMONITIONS

you for his judgment-day, making your entire being, in all its threefold nature, fit to be preserved, and wholly above all censure.] **24 Faithful is he that calleth you, who will also do it.** [If God were not thus faithful to sanctify and preserve blameless, it would be useless for him to call us; for it is certain that left to ourselves we can not keep ourselves from sin and evil-doing. This faithfulness is elsewhere noted (1 Cor. 1: 8, 9; 10: 13; 2 Thess. 3: 3; 1 John 1: 9); and is the basis of the glorious and sublime confidence expressed at Rom. 8: 31-39.] **25 Brethren, pray for us.** [It was Paul's habit to ask for the prayers of those to whom he wrote (Rom. 15: 30; 2 Cor. 1: 11; Eph. 6: 19; Col. 4: 3; 2 Thess. 3: 1). Compare Heb. 13: 18. **26 Salute all the brethren with a holy kiss.** [In the East, a kiss was and still is a common salutation among kindred and near friends. Paul did not, by this command, create a church ordinance or ceremony; nor did he even create a new custom. He merely injected a spiritual virtue into an old-established, time-honored custom. This custom never prevailed among the nations of the West, and we feel that we obey Paul when we shake hands with holiness; *i. e.*, with cordial sincerity and honest good-will. The Bible was not written as a work on etiquette, nor was it intended in this case that the Syrian and Grecian custom should become universal.] **27 I adjure you by the Lord that this epistle be read unto all the brethren.** [The importance of the Epistle is shown by the solemnity of the adjuration. The command in this, the first of the Epistles, is fittingly echoed in the last written of the New Testament books. See Rev. 1: 3. They suggest that the New Testament writings were to be read in the churches, and by all the people, just as the Old Testament was read in the synagogues. " What Paul *commands* with an adjuration," says Bengel, "Rome *forbids* under a curse."] **28 The grace of our Lord Jesus Christ be with you.** [This is the benediction with which Paul closes most of his Epistles. It is a prayer that they may have all the blessings which the loving favor of God can bestow.]

SECOND EPISTLE TO THE THESSALONIANS

INTRODUCTION.

That the second Epistle to the Thessalonians was written very soon after the first is apparent from the fact that the two Epistles show that practically the same conditions existed in that church, and also from the fact that Silas and Timothy join with Paul in both letters; and it can not be shown that these three men were ever together after the earlier part of Paul's ministry in Corinth. We would therefore date this letter in the latter part of A. D. 52 or the early part of A. D. 53. Jesus had left the world about twenty-three years before, promising to return at an indefinite date. This indefiniteness gave free scope to the conjectures of his early followers, until the clear teaching of his apostles brought about a better understanding. There are evidences in the first Epistle that the Lord's coming was a subject of great interest to the Thessalonians. It seems likely that at the date of that Epistle the disciples there were expecting the Lord's return in the near future; for they were grieving over the thought that their loved ones who died would thereby be cut off from all participation in the joys of that coming—a joy which those still living fully expected to realize. In correcting this false view as to the dead, Paul had not thought it needful to specify that all would likely die before the Lord came, since in his teaching while in Thessalonica he had shown that the events which God had decreed should intervene before the coming of the Lord, were of such a nature as to necessarily require much time. Thus the idea that the Lord's return would take place in the near future remained uncorrected by him, for he was not really aware that it prevailed. Moreover, certain passages in his first Epistle could be, and evidently were, misconstrued to favor the idea, and were used to foster and strengthen it. See 1 Thess. 4: 15, 17; 5: 4, 6. Again, traditional sayings of the apostle were appealed to in confirmation of this erroneous notion, and, as a consequence of all this, the church was excited and troubled. The design, therefore, of this second Epistle was to correct the error as to the Lord's coming, and thus restore tranquility to the church. To do this the apostle reminds them of his former instruction, wherein he showed that the rise and fall of the man of sin must precede the coming of the Lord. Having corrected the doctrinal error, he closes his Epistle, as usual, with prayer and admonitions and a benediction.

EXPOSITION OF SECOND THESSALONIANS.

I.

THANKSGIVING AND PRAYER FOR THE CHURCH. GOD'S IMPARTIAL JUDGMENT.

I: 1-12.

1 Paul, and Silvanus, and Timothy, unto the church of the Thessalonians in God our Father and the Lord Jesus Christ; 2 Grace to you and peace from God the Father and the Lord Jesus Christ. [For a similar salutation, see I Thess. 1: 1.] **3 We are bound to give thanks to God always for you, brethren, even as it is meet** [just], **for that your faith groweth exceedingly, and the love of each one of you all toward one another aboundeth** [Paul acknowledged himself obliged to give thanks because his prayer at 1 Thess. 9: 13 had been answered by the Thessalonians doing the things which he prayed they might do. Thus he very forcefully recognizes the good in his converts that he may be listened to with patience when he begins to correct their faults]; **4 so that we ourselves glory in you in the churches of God for your patience and faith in all your persecutions and in the afflictions which ye endure** [The faith and love of the Thessalonians were such that, spontaneously, of their own accord, Paul and his companions delighted to tell of it to the churches at Corinth, Cenchreæ and in other parts of Achaia. Though the persecutions which arose while Paul was in Thessalonica were still continuing, yet they neither exhausted the patience of the Christians so as to drive them to forsake God, nor their faith so as to lead them to mistrust God. We should

THANKSGIVING AND PRAYER

observe that the churches are commonly called, by Paul, as here, churches of God, though sometimes churches of Christ]; 5 *which is* a manifest token of the righteous judgment of God; to the end that ye may be counted worthy of the kingdom of God, for which ye also suffer: 6 if so be that it is a righteous thing with God to recompense affliction to them that afflict you, 7 and to you that are afflicted rest with us, at the revelation of the Lord Jesus from heaven with the angels of his power in flaming fire, 8 rendering vengeance to them that know not God, and to them that obey not the gospel of our Lord Jesus [The patience and faith of the Thessalonians were a manifest token (*i. e.*, pledge, proof or demonstration) of that coming day wherein God will disclose the righteousness of his judgments, and wherein all apparent violations of justice shall be rectified (Eccl. 3: 16, 17; Phil. 1: 28). The purpose of this judgment will be that those who suffer for the kingdom of God may graciously be counted worthy of the heavenly joys of that kingdom, and that the wicked may be punished. If it is indeed a righteous thing (and who can doubt it?) for God to recompense evil for evil, so that those who afflict the righteous shall themselves be afflicted, and those who have suffered affliction for righteousness' sake may find rest with their fellow-Christians when Jesus, who is now hidden from their sight in heaven, reveals himself to human vision with the angels which display his power, and with that flaming fire which at once shows forth his glory and consumes his enemies (Heb. 10: 27; 12: 29), rendering vengeance as a great judge, not as a resentful potentate, to them that willfully know not God—Ex. 5: 2; Rom. 1: 28; Luke 12: 47, 48; Rom. 2: 14, 15 (principally Gentiles), and them that obey not the gospel (principally Jews)—Rom. 10: 3, 16. In verse 6 Paul draws a comparison between the law which forbids retaliation to the individual (Rom. 12: 17), and that which accords it to all government, especially the government of God himself, under whose rule unforgiven iniquity never escapes punishment (Heb. 2: 2;

Rev. 20: 12). He does this to show that God is under the second and not under the first law. In verse 7 we are reminded that the negative happiness of heaven is rest from all afflictions, sorrows, pains, persecutions, etc. (Heb. 4: 9; Rev. 14: 13; 21: 4). It is the quiet haven of the storm-tossed bark. Continuing the thought, Paul says further of the objects of God's vengeance—]: **9 who shall suffer punishment,** *even* **eternal destruction from the face of the Lord and from the glory of his might, 10 when he shall come to be glorified in his saints, and to be marvelled at in all them that believed (because our testimony unto you was believed) in that day.** [In that day when Jesus comes to be glorified, those who refuse to know God, and those who disobey the gospel, shall receive a punishment which is here clearly described as eternal. The word "destruction" imports the wreck or dissolution of the organism, but not the annihilation of the essence. The rest of the sentence implies banishment and separation from the presence of the Lord with all its joys, and from all participation in that manifestation of his power which will show itself in the glorification of his redeemed (Matt. 25: 41; Col. 3: 4). The latter thought is expanded by Paul throughout the remainder of the chapter. In that day Jesus shall be "marvelled at in all them that believe," because they shall reflect his glory as a mirror gives back the radiance of the sun (2 Cor. 3: 18). The parenthesis ("because," etc.) is injected into the thought for the purpose of identifying the Thessalonians with the believers, and so with the glorification promised to believers.] **11 To which end** [*i. e.*, with a view to this glorious consummation; viz.: of being glorified in Christ] **we also pray always for you, that our God may count you worthy of your calling, and fulfil every desire of goodness and** *every* **work of faith, with power; 12 that the name of our Lord Jesus may be glorified in you, and ye in him, according to the grace of our God and the Lord Jesus Christ.** [Paul prays that the Thessalonians may be counted worthy of the gospel invitation, so that they may receive, according to the fullness of God's limitless power, all the blessings to which they have been invited; viz.: all the graces and glories that ever the goodness of God desired to bestow, and every aspiration or heavenly ideal for which their own faith prompted them to strive; that thus their lives might glorify Christ, and be glorified by Christ, according to the gracious purposes of God in Christ. Jesus is glorified in his saints by their reflection, and the saints are glorified in Jesus by his impartation of his divine excellencies.]

II.

THE COMING OF CHRIST AND OF ANTICHRIST.

2: 1-12.

The section before us expresses the principal object of this Epistle, which was to correct the misapprehension that the Lord was about to come at once. Without professing to set forth all the events which would intervene between the date of his Epistle and the Lord's coming, the apostle enumerates three: 1. A great apostasy. 2. The removal of that power which hindered the manifestation of the lawless one. 3. The manifestation of the lawless one, and his reign. Since Paul gives us only a bird's-eye view of events, which covers a very extended range of history, it would be injudicious to fill in his outlines with elaborate details. The full outline of prophecy covering the Christian dispensation is given in Revelation, and will be discussed when that book is reached.

II. 1 **Now we beseech you, brethren** [having just prayed *for* the Thessalonians, Paul now passes to entreaties *to* them], **touching the coming of our Lord Jesus Christ, and our gathering together unto him** [the final gathering (1 Thess. 4: 17). He entreats them to be soberminded both as to the coming and the gathering, for each of these events had been used to generate error and fanaticism—1 Thess. 4: 13; 2 Thess. 3: 11]; **2 to the end that ye be not quickly shaken from your mind** [Shaken is a figurative expression taken from waves agitated by a storm. The minds of the Thessalonians having been instructed by Paul, and having a thorough apprehension of the entire subject, ought not to have been so readily, and with such small reason, confused—Eph. 4: 14], **nor yet be troubled, either by spirit, or by word, or by epistle as from us, as that** [as teaching that] **the day of the Lord is just at hand** [Paul here enumerates the three forces which had produced the fanatical unrest at Thessalonica. The first was probably the cause of this unrest, and the second and third were more likely used to excuse or justify it. Some highly wrought souls, laboring under morbid excitement, had delivered exhortations or discourses which were professedly inspired. While these men ought not to have been despised without due consideration, neither ought they to have been believed without being thoroughly tested (1 Thess. 5: 20, 21; 1 John 4: 1). The Thessalonians, however, despite the apostle's warning, had imprudently accepted both the prophet and the prophecy, and had permitted, and perhaps aided and encouraged, the justification of the prophecy. The prophecy was justified by "words," by which we may understand misapplications or misquotations either of the apostle's own teaching while he was with them, or of the words of Christ orally communicated by him to them, as, for instance, the sayings at Matt. 16: 28; 24: 34.. It was also justified by a misuse of certain phrases in Paul's first Epistle, as for instance the passages cited in our introduction. Commentators almost universally contend that by the phrase "epistle as from us" Paul means a spurious or *forged* epistle which had been palmed off upon the church as if it had come from him. In support of this notion it is urged that if Paul had referred to his first Epistle he would not have disowned it, but would have explained it. But to this it may be answered that Paul does explain his first Epistle by thus tersely and emphatically disowning the misconstruction placed upon it. Against the idea of forgery, four points may be considered: 1. Ought any of the church at Thessalonica to be lightly accused of such a fraud? 2. Was there any sufficient inducement for their committing such a fraud? 3. Was such an event likely to be made the subject of fraud? 4. Would Paul have passed over such a sacrilegious outrage without a syllable of rebuke, while in verse 5 he even rebukes their forgetfulness, and in verse 14 he orders the excommunication of any man who fails to give heed to his Epistle? Had there been a forgery we would reasonably have expected some such language as that of Gal. 1: 6-12. Moreover, had there been a forgery Paul could not have repudiated *it* without explanation, else his repudiation might have been shrewdly used by the forgers to cast discredit upon his first Epistle. Paul taught that the day of the Lord was at hand (Rom. 13: 12; Phil. 4: 5), as did other of the apostles (1 Pet. 4: 7; Rev. 1: 3), John using a very strong expression (John 2: 18); but the phrase "just at hand" is stronger still; it denotes an imminence nothing short of the actual appearing of the Lord the next instant—an imminence answering to the fanaticism of the Thessalonians, and one which Paul had not taught. In teaching us to be always prepared for the Lord's coming, the Scripture nowhere justifies or excuses us in letting the thoughts of his coming absorb our mind, or the expectation of his coming interfere with the most trivial duty]; **3 let no man beguile you in any wise: for *it will not be*, except the falling away come first** [Paul uses the article "the" because this apostasy was well known to the church, its coming having been announced by Jesus (Matt. 24: 10-12), and reiterated by Paul while at Thessalonica. This apostasy, or falling away, may be defined to be a desertion of the true religion and the true God], **and the man of sin be revealed, the son of perdition** [Literally, son of perishing. The man of sin is identical with the antichrist of 1 John 2: 18. Though he is distinguished from Satan in verse 9, yet is he in a sense an incarnation of Satan, for as Satan entered into the heart of Judas (John 13: 27), who was the first great apostate and son of perdition (John 17: 12), so he shall enter into the heart of this second apostate and son of perdition, who shall be a man made up of sin, a veritable manifestation of concrete wickedness, and thus self-fitted for perdition. The language clearly shows that he is a person, but there is nothing to forbid us from regarding him as an official rather than an individual personality, as, for instance, a line of popes rather than an individual pope. Those who have denied the right to thus construe his personality, have for the most part straightway fallen into the solecism of interpreting the phrase "one that restraineth," of verse 7, so as to make it mean a line of emperors, or succeeding generations of rulers in our human polity, or some other official personality that existed in Paul's day and long afterward, though the assertion of personality is as strong in verse 7 as it is in verse 3. Antichrist does not cause the apostasy, but is rather the cap-sheaf of it, being revealed in connection with it, and exalted by it], **4 he that opposeth and exalteth himself against all that is called God or that is worshipped; so that he sitteth in the temple of God, setting himself forth as God.** [The antichrist will be antagonistic to God, and will exalt himself as a rival to everything that is worshiped, whether it be king or emperor, mythical god or true God, even entering, not only into the outer courts of the temple, but penetrating to the inner sanctuary, and taking his seat where God alone has a right to rest, and there making an arrogant display of himself as an object of worship (comp. Acts 12: 21-23). The Greek word for "worship" is *sebasma :* from it came *Sebastus* or Augustus (*i. e.*, the Worshipful), which was the title of the Roman emperors. A man of that age could hardly see this word in such a connection without thinking that Paul meant to convey the idea that the antichrist would arrogate to himself all the reverence then claimed by the great civil lords of the earth, such as emperors, kings, etc. The temple is Paul's favorite metaphor for the church—1 Cor. 16: 17; 2 Cor. 6: 16; Eph. 2: 21.] **5 Remember ye not, that, when I was yet with you, I told you these things?** [Literally, was telling. He had repeated the instruction often, and now reproves the Thessalonians for forgetting what he did say, and being agitated by false reports of what he did not say.] **6 And now ye know** [because Paul had told them verbally] **that which restraineth** [*i. e.*, retards and delays the antichrist], **to the end that he may be revealed in**

his own season. [And not prematurely. Thus we see that the Thessalonians had a key to Paul's prophecy that we do not possess. His probable reason for withholding from his Epistle that which he freely stated verbally will be given later.] **7 For the mystery of lawlessness doth already work: only *there is* one that restraineth now, until he be taken out of the way.** [In verse 6 we have a *thing* ("that which") restraining the *person* of antichrist, and in this verse we have the *thing* ("mystery of lawlessness") which would produce the antichrist restrained by a *person*. This nicety of expression is important, and should be noted. The traces of that spirit which overrules God's laws and substitutes its own were abundant in the church. It showed itself in attempts to engraft both Judaism and paganism into Christianity, thus paving the way for an apostasy, with a great head apostate. Romans and Galatians were written to correct Judaizing tendencies, and the Epistle to the Hebrews was an attempt to wean weak Christians from the sensuous ritualism of Moses. Tendencies to lapse into paganism are also frequently reproved. See especially Col. 2: 16-23; 1 Cor. 5: 1-8.] **8 And then shall be revealed the lawless one whom the Lord Jesus shall slay with the breath of his mouth, and bring to nought by the manifestation of his coming** [After the removal of the hinderer, the vague spirit or mystery of lawlessness will become an embodied personality—a Christ-rival. At the mere thought of his thus being revealed, Paul, in his fervent zeal for Christ, at once announces the triumph of the Lord over this adversary, though he has not yet finished describing him. In the next verse we shall find the apostle returning to tell what manner of ruler the antichrist was to be, and the quality and destiny of those who should follow him. "Breath," etc., does not mean that Jesus shall slay antichrist by converting, and thus cutting off, his followers; for "breath" does not signify God's truth or instruction, but the execution of his judgment (2 Sam. 22: 16; Job 4: 9; 15: 30; Isa. 11: 4; 30: 27-33). The manifestation (Greek, *epiphany*) of his coming is undoubtedly the divine excellency, radiance, glory and sublimity of the revealed Godhead; for the word "epiphany" conveys this idea (Tit. 2: 13; 1 Tim. 6: 14-16; comp. Rev. 20: 11). The destruction of antichrist will be caused by the judgment of God, and be effected by the appearing of God. The manifestation of the real and perfect will stand in awful, consuming contrast to the revelation of the sham and lie]; **9 *even he*, whose coming is according to the working of Satan with all power and signs and lying wonders** [To give full force to the Greek we should here translate "all lying power, all lying signs, all lying wonders." Antichrist shall employ the methods of Satan, and shall prove his claims by false miracles, like those of Jannes and Jambres—Ex. 7: 10-13; 2 Tim. 3: 1-8], **10 and with all deceit of unrighteousness for them that perish; because they received not the love of the truth, that they might be saved.** [Antichrist comes with lies, to those who love not the truth as to right and wrong, etc., that they may be saved by it; but sentence themselves to perish by preferring that deception leading to unrighteousness —which makes unrighteousness appear the better course.] **11 And for this cause God sendeth them a working of error** [the threefold working of error mentioned in verse 9], **that they should believe a lie: 12 that they all might be judged who believed not the truth, but had pleasure in unrighteousness.** [God permits Satan to present lies to those who, because of their love for sin, desire to be deceived (Deut. 13: 1-5). Having given our exposition of the above passage, we should like also to give a history of its exposition, but must content ourselves with referring the reader to those given by Newton, Lunemann, Alford, Gloag, etc. We should like also to discuss the theory of most commentators who identify the man of sin with the beast at Rev. 13, and the Roman Empire with the red dragon at Rev. 11 and 12, and who find in the Antiochus of Daniel the prototype of this lawless one. See Newton on the Prophecies, Dissertation 22. But we will content ourselves with the presentation of the antichrist, and remarks on this prophecy. The term "antichrist" conveys not only the idea of one who is *opposed* to Christ, but

THE COMING OF CHRIST

also of one who is the *antithesis* of Christ. This latter idea has been touched upon, but not fully developed. The antichrist is a counterfeit or caricature of Christ, and his life is an elaborate parody of that part of the Christ life which may be so contradicted, contorted and adapted so as to comport with worldly ambition. The antichrist is the personification of sin (verse 3), whereas Christ is the incarnation of righteousness (Acts 3: 14). He is the son of perdition (verse 3), just as Jesus is the Prince of life (Acts 3: 14). He opposes his will against God, and exalts himself against God, and enthrones himself in the temple of God, and displays himself as God (verse 4), while Jesus resigned himself to the Father's will (Luke 22: 42) and humbled himself in complete obedience (Phil. 2: 5-8), and, though truly claiming to be divine (John 14: 8-11), waited until he was exalted of God (Phil. 2: 9), when he sat down at the right hand of the majesty in the true temple on high, because he was divine (Heb. 1: 3-5; 8: 1, 2). Antichrist has a season or time for revelation (verse 6), just as Jesus had (Gal. 4: 4), and still has a proper time for revealing himself (Acts 1: 6, 7). He first exists as a mystery, and then has his open revelation (Greek, *apocalypse*)—verses 7, and 2, 6, 8; and so also did Jesus (Rom. 16: 25, 26). Moreover, as a mystery the antichrist existed as lawlessness, and finally came forth the lawless one, while Jesus was first concealed in the mysterious types of the law (John 5: 46; Rom. 3: 21, 22), and was born under the law (Gal. 4: 4) and was the very incarnation of law (Rom. 10: 4; Matt. 5: 17, 18), and is the mystery of godliness (1 Tim. 3: 16). He has a coming (Greek, *parousia*) —verse 9, just as Christ has (verse 8). His coming is according to the working of Satan with lying power, signs and wonders (verse 9), while Jesus came after the working of God (John 5: 19, 20; Eph. 1: 19, 20), with God's real powers, signs and wonders—Acts 2: 22 ("powers" being translated "mighty works"). With these lying miracles he established an antigospel, formed in the deceit of unrighteousness and producing death (verse 10); while Jesus, as is shown by the same verse, brought the gospel of truth that men might be saved. And finally, his kingdom rests on belief—the belief of a lie (verse 11)—just as Christ's rests upon the belief of the truth. Thus, step by step, the antichrist parodies the glories, but not the humiliations of the Christ, but he fails to rise to the last step, for he has no manifestation (Greek, *epiphany*) answering to that which Christ has, as shown by verse 8. That is to say, he has no divinity to subdue all things by the outburst of its glory. He can assume the figure of Christ, but can not rival Christ *transfigured*. In interpreting this passage commentators divide themselves into three parties: 1. Those who think the prophecy long since fulfilled. 2. Those who regard it as in process of fulfillment. 3. Those who look upon it as yet to be fulfilled in the future. The first class fail to note that the antichrist is to be destroyed by the epiphany of Christ's coming. Hence antichrist can not have come and gone, since this epiphany is yet to take place. The great body of Protestant commentators are found in the second class, who look upon the long line of popes as the antichrist, and the church of Rome as the apostasy. The third class, of whom Alford and Olshausen are exponents, look upon the pope as a prefiguration or forerunner of the antichrist, having many of his characteristics, but not filling up all the Scripture details by which he is described; Olshausen urging that the pope can not be antichrist, because, contrary to John 2:22, he confesses that Jesus is the Christ; and Alford objecting on the two grounds that the pope does not oppose God, and exalt himself above God, according to verse 4, for the pope is found to be very worshipful; and because the Papacy has existed for some fifteen hundred years, and Christ has not yet come, though the revelation of the antichrist is to *immediately* precede the coming of Christ. Taking up these three objections in their order, we would note, first, that a mere verbal, formal or ceremonial confession of Christ certainly will not relieve any one from being charged by the Spirit with having denied Christ. To really confess Jesus as Christ, is to look to him as the supreme Priest, to be guided by him as the all-authoritative Prophet or Teacher, to be ruled by him utterly as the divine and absolute King. Does the pope's confession answer to this? Secondly, the language of verse 4 should not be so strained as to make it stronger than it is. It must be borne in mind that antichrist is a *man*, and not a deity, and hence his opposition to God, exaltation of self against God, etc., must be such as is possible to man. Alford so construes verse 4 as to demand not only one who lifts himself against God, but even *above* God, so as to make himself the sole object of worship. But Whedon justly remarks, "If this prophecy is to wait for a being who literally exalts himself *above* the Omnipresent and Omnipotent, it waits for an impossibility." Moreover, in permitting the worship of saints and of the virgin, the pope does not avoid the charge of opposing all that is worshiped, for it must be borne in mind that the very spirit of worship demands an *unseen element*. If the pope should entirely deny all the unseen, then worship itself would be at an end. Since he must permit some continuance of this unseen element or defeat his own purposes, he contents himself with dictating as to it, deciding for himself in what it shall consist. Too rigorous a denial of all worship would destroy that which he seeks to parody, and obliterate his title as antichrist. Lastly, the third objection, that the Papacy has existed for fifteen hundred years, carries no weight; for the word "immediately," on which Alford founds it, is neither in the text nor in the thought, and prophecy has very little perspective at best. It is sufficient that the Papacy still exists, and if it *continues to exist* till the Lord comes, and is brought to naught by that event, it will fulfill that part of the prophecy under consideration. In short, while we will not attempt to say that the final form of antichrist, Papal or otherwise, may not exceed in wickedness all that we have yet seen (for prophecies are certainly iterative), yet we are constrained to contend that if no other form appears, the Papacy has already fulfilled the prophecy, for it agrees in all the points, as follows: 1. It has one official man ever at its head, and the arrogancy of its claims are centered in him. 2. That man came with and out of an apostasy, and the very kind of an apostasy which Paul elsewhere describes (1 Tim. 4: 1-3; 2 Tim. 3: 1-9). Can that

apostacy exist for all these centuries, and antichrist be still
unborn of it? 3. The spiritual pride and lawlessness which
worked and would have produced antichrist in Paul's day, was
curbed by the person of the Cæsar whose superior spiritual
pride and lawlessness restrained that of the church by contempt and persecution. 4. When, notwithstanding the over-
shadowing emperor, the bishops of Rome began to assert
themselves *spiritually*, they were still checked and restrained
from revealing themselves as *earthly potentates* by the temporal power of the empire, just as the language of verses
6 and 7 so carefully distinguishes. 5. When the power
of the Roman Empire was taken away, the pope appeared,
and has since been unceasingly in evidence. Paul's readers
could readily see how the emperor and the empire would
check the antichrist; but Paul could not openly write that
emperor and empire were to fall, for, had he done so, the
Romans would have appealed to his words as affording a just
cause for persecuting the church. So thought Tertullian
(A. D. 150-240), Cyril of Jerusalem (315-386), Ambrose
(340-397), Jerome (342-420), Chrysostom (347-407), Augustine
(354-430), etc. 6. The pope is careful to keep up his line of
succession, so as to establish his identity and claims; and
arising out of the fall of Rome and the apostasy of the
church, which accompanied that event, he has continued for
centuries with little change, and certainly none for the better.
7. He exalts himself against God and Christ, calling himself
the vicar, or infallible substitute for Christ, and permitting and
encouraging his followers to speak of him thus: "Our Lord
God the Pope, another God upon earth . . . doeth whatsoever
he listeth, even things unlawful, and is more than God."
Under these titles he presumes to set aside divine laws in
favor of his own. Thus as a substitute person he makes substitute laws, and arrogates to himself divine power, as did
Pope Clement VI. when he commanded the angels to admit
certain souls to paradise. 8. He sits in the temple of God,
i. e., he has his sphere of dominion in the church, and the
temple or church which he occupies is still a temple erected to

God, albeit the Spirit and presence of God may have long since departed from it. 9. He proves his supreme claims by fraudulent miracles, signs and wonders; of which cures effected by relics and shrines and pictures; prayers, made effectual by blessed beads; indulgences; souls prayed out of purgatory for money; absolution, and transubstantiation are fair samples.]

III.

THANKSGIVING, PRAYER, EXHORTATION AND BENEDICTION.

2: 13-3: 18.

13 But we are bound to give thanks to God always for you, brethren beloved of the Lord, for that God chose you from the beginning unto salvation in sanctification of the Spirit and belief of the truth [From the sad picture of those who, through love of unrighteousness, were given over to the working of error unto perishing, Paul turns to give thanks for the Thessalonians, who were chosen from the beginning (though Gentiles) unto salvation—a salvation which is worked out on the divine side in the sanctification of the Spirit, and on the human side in the belief of the truth. From the beginning God had determined that the Gentiles should be saved, and had arranged his plans to that end— Rom. 9: 23-26; Eph. 3: 5, 6]: **14 whereunto he called you through our gospel, to the obtaining of the glory of our Lord Jesus Christ.** [To this working of salvation God had called the Thessalonians, not by an arbitrary election, but by the gospel which Paul had preached to them, and he had called them that they might be possessors, or sharers, in the glory of Christ—"joint heirs" with him—Rom. 8: 17.] **15 So then, brethren, stand fast** [in contrast to being shaken, as stated in verse 2], **and hold the traditions which ye were taught, whether by word, or by epistle of ours.** [God was doing his part in calling and in sanctifying, and so the Thessalonians are here exhorted to do their part in firmly adhering to the truth which they had believed. For if one would hold the gospel salvation he must hold the gospel truths. These truths are here called traditions; for, though inspired truths, they were as yet falling from the lips of living men, and were not yet reduced to writing, though we see by these two epistles of Paul that the New Testament record was in process of construction.] **16 Now our Lord Jesus Christ himself, and God our Father who loved us and gave us eternal comfort and good hope through grace, 17 comfort your hearts and establish them in every good work and word.** [Paul, as a minister of Christ, was endeavoring to comfort and establish the Thessalonians in their words and deeds, and he here prays that Christ himself and God the Father may thus comfort and establish them; and he describes the Father as one who loved them (John 3: 16), and through mere grace had given them the means of never failing consolation, and a good hope of a final salvation, which is more than consolation.]

III. **1 Finally, brethren, pray for us, that the word of the Lord may run and be glorified, even as also** *it is* **with you** [Here, as elsewhere, Paul asks for the prayers of the disciples (1 Thess. 5: 25; Eph. 6: 9; the request at Col. 4: 2, 3, being very similar. The unselfishness of his request should be noted. He asks nothing for himself, but desires that the truth may prosper in his hands elsewhere, as it was now prospering in Thessalonica. He speaks of the Word as a thing of life (comp. Ps. 19: 5; 147: 15; 2 Tim. 2: 9); for the Word, being energized of God, approaches a living personality. The Word is glorified when it saves souls (Acts 13: 48). Possibly there is here an allusion to the applause of the people when a racer wins his race]; **2 and that we may be delivered from unreasonable and evil men; for all have not faith.** [*i. e.*, all professed Christians are not really such. A phrase answering to that at Rom. 9: 6.] **3 But the Lord is faithful, who shall establish you, and guard you from the evil** *one*. [Evidently Paul, while at Corinth, met with some of the false brethren of whom he speaks (2 Cor. 11: 13, 26). These refused

THANKSGIVING AND PRAYER 45

to be moved by argument or persuasion, and were evil and without faith; that is, faithless, insincere, as the word means at Matt. 23: 23; Tit. 2: 10. These false brethren no doubt added greatly to Paul's distress, though he was already suffering, or about to suffer, persecution at the hands of the Jews (Acts 18: 12). In asking prayers for deliverance from these, Paul joyfully pauses to contrast this his fellowship with false brethren, with the condition of the Thessalonians who were in the fellowship of that faithful God who would establish them and guard them from the evil one.] **4 And we have confidence in the Lord touching you, that ye both do and will do the things which we command.** [The faithfulness of God to supply power and protection gave the apostle confidence that the Thessalonians were living in obedience to his instructions, and would continue to so live.] **5 And the Lord direct your hearts into the love of God, and into the patience of Christ.** [From expressions of confidence in God, Paul easily passes to prayer to him, that the Thessalonians may be led to love him, and to exercise in their trials and persecutions the patience which Christ exhibited under unparalleled suffering. To love God, together with the brotherly love which they already possessed (1 Thess. 4: 9, 10), constituted a fulfillment of the law (Matt. 22: 37-40; Rom. 13: 10), and hence led to acceptable obedience.] **6 Now we command you** [because confident, as we have just said, that you will obey], **brethren** [not the officers, but the whole church], **in the name of** [by the authority of] **our Lord Jesus Christ, that ye withdraw yourselves from** [abstain from your habitual fellowship with] **every brother that walketh disorderly, and not after the tradition** [Christian rules of life] **which they received of us.** [Paul does not specify any particular disorder, but the next verse shows that he had a special reference to parasitical idleness.] **7 For yourselves know how ye ought to imitate us: for we behaved not ourselves disorderly among you; 8 neither did we eat bread for nought** [gratis, without compensation] **at any man's hand, but in labor and travail, working night** and day, that we might not burden any of you [1 Thess. 2: 9]: **9 not because we have not the right** [to demand support while preaching—Luke 10: 7; 1 Cor. 9: 1-18], **but to make ourselves an ensample unto you, that ye should imitate us.** [Many of the Thessalonian converts were from the laboring classes. Now, laborers in that day were brought into competition with slave-labor, and hence were disposed to look upon all manual work as degrading. This false view of life was the main influence which produced that vast multitude of parasites that then swarmed in every large city of the empire. To correct this mistaken pride, and to restore labor to its just dignity, Paul had made tents and supported himself by his hands while at Thessalonica. For these and other reasons he had also waived his right to support and had sustained himself while at Corinth (Acts 18: 3; 2 Cor. 11: 9) and at Ephesus (Acts 20: 34). But notwithstanding his example and instruction, and despite his written rebuke (1 Thess. 4: 11, 12), idleness appears to have increased rather than diminished; so the apostle here devotes some space to it.] **10 For even when we were with you** [and so even before we wrote you our first epistle], **this we commanded you, If any will not work, neither let him eat.** [This precept is founded on Gen. 3: 19. It forbids the Christian to exercise that false charity which genders beggary and becomes the parent of manifold crime.] **11 For we hear** [probably by the returning messenger who carried his first epistle] **of some that walk among you disorderly, that work not at all, but are busybodies.** [A *paranomasia*, or play on words; "work" and "busybodies" being cognate; so it may be translated, "who have no business, and yet are busy with everybody's business"—such as lead a lounging, gadding, gossiping, meddlesome life.] **12 Now them that are such we command and exhort** [mixing entreaty with authority] **in the Lord Jesus Christ, that with quietness they work, and eat their own** [this word is emphatic] **bread. 13 But ye** [who stand in contrast to the disorderly], **brethren, be not weary** [lose not heart] **in well-doing.** [A general exhortation as to all well-doing. As applied to the parasites, it might mean that disgust at them should not discourage true charity. The great body of commentators, including the ablest, attribute this idleness to the erroneous notion that the Lord was about to come; but there is no hint of this in the text; and we find the idleness existing when Paul wrote them his first Epistle, though there was then no such exciting expectation. Moreover, such expectations as to the Lord's coming have often been repeated in history, and have not been found to be very productive of idleness, and certainly not in that "busybody" form which is here rebuked. On the whole, it is best to suppose that the Christian spirit of love opened the hearts of the wealthy to liberal charities, and the parasitical tendency, always strong, took advantage of it.] **14 And if any man obeyeth not our word by this epistle, note that man, that ye have no company** [fellowship] **with him, to the end that he may be ashamed.** [By noting your moral indignation, and seeing his conduct repudiated by the church.] **15 And** *yet* **count him not as an enemy, but admonish him as a brother.** [They were not to give him the complete estrangement of Matt. 18: 17. The purpose of discipline is to save (1 Cor. 5: 5). It is medicine for curing, not poison for killing; it is not to gratify the hatred of the judge, but to admonish the offender who is judged (Gal. 6: 1). Yet the safety of the church sometimes demands complete excommunication.] **16 Now the Lord of peace himself give you peace at all times in all ways.** [Peace outward and inward, for time and for eternity.] **The Lord be with you all. 17 The salutation of me Paul with mine own hand, which is the token in every epistle: so I write.** [*I. e.*, this is my penmanship.] **18 The grace of our Lord Jesus Christ be with you all.** [This, like most of Paul's Epistles, was dictated. Verses 17 and 18 were writtten by Paul's own hand, this being a guarantee of the Epistle's genuineness, just as our signatures are to-day. With some slight variation of form, "grace" closes all Paul's Epistles, and the Epistle to the Hebrews.]

FIRST EPISTLE TO THE CORINTHIANS.

INTRODUCTION.

The Corinth of Paul's day was a comparatively new city, with a population of about 400,000. The old Corinth, so famous and powerful in the days of the Peloponnesian war, had been burned by the Roman consul, L. Mummius, B. C. 146, and, having lain a desolation for a century, had been rebuilt by Julius Cæsar, A. D. 46, as a token of respect to Venus, its patron goddess; for Cæsar claimed a mythical descent from her. He had colonized it largely with Roman freemen, so that its population was very heterogeneous; though the Greeks stamped their character upon the inhabitants generally, and Corinth became the Vanity Fair of the Roman Empire, its citizens being dishonest, voluptuous, litigious, speculative, suspicious, factious, volatile and excessively egotistic. The chastity of our age wisely forbids us to unveil the profligacy and licentiousness of this hotbed of vice, with its richly endowed temple of Venus, supporting a thousand priestesses dedicated to harlotry, so that even in that dark age Corinth had a bad name. Discouraging as the field was, Paul entered it alone, and was there for three months before Silas and Timothy joined him. However, he found there Aquila and Priscilla, and their companionship strengthened him greatly. Paul reasoned in the Jewish synagogue until Silas and Timothy came, after which the hostility of the Jews drove him to the house of Justus, and afterwards arraigned him before Gallio. After a year and a half of labor in Corinth, an account of which will be found at Acts 18: 1-17, Paul returned to Antioch by way of Jerusalem, and setting out on his third missionary journey, came to Ephesus, where he sojourned for three years, during which time he probably visited Corinth

INTRODUCTION

once, and wrote an Epistle which is now lost, and which is older than this which we call his first Epistle. Before Paul's arrival at Ephesus, the eloquent Apollos, having been there more fully instructed by Aquila and Priscilla, came to Corinth, gained great popularity, and gathered many converts. Then Apollos joined Paul at Ephesus, and after his departure the church at Corinth divided into factions, some claiming to be followers of Paul, and others of Apollos, and others of Peter, and others of Christ. The Petrine faction was likely formed by Judaizers who habitually exalted Peter to disparage Paul. These may have been added to the church by letter (2 Cor. 3: 1). But it is possible that Peter himself may have been at Corinth, for Dionysius, the bishop of Corinth, in a letter written to the church at Rome about A. D. 170, claims that Peter visited and labored in Corinth (Eusebius, Book 2, chap. 25). In addition to this evil and factious spirit, the licentiousness, for which the city was noted, appeared in the church in a most flagrant form, and the spiritual tone of the church became so sadly lowered that even the Lord's table took the form of a secular banquet, and became a scene of envy and disorder. To remedy matters, Paul sent Timothy and Erastus to Corinth. Before their return the church at Corinth sent Fortunatus, Achaicus and Stephanas, bearing a letter from the Pauline (or largest) party, asking the apostle for instructions in many matters, such as marriages, the eating of idolatrous meat, the attire of women, relative value of spiritual gifts, the resurrection, and the collection for the poor at Jerusalem. Responding to all these reasons for a letter, the apostle wrote this that we call the first Epistle to the Corinthians. It was written, as we see, from Ephesus in the spring, or a little before Pentecost, A. D. 57 (1 Cor. 16: 8).

FIRST EPISTLE TO THE CORINTHIANS

EXPOSITION

PART FIRST

APOSTOLIC RELATIONS, AND ASSERTIONS OF AUTHORITY

1: 1-4: 21

I.

GREETING, THANKSGIVING, REPROOF OF DIVISIONS, VANITY OF PHILOSOPHY

1: 1-31

1 Paul, called *to be* **an apostle of Jesus Christ through the will of God, and Sosthenes our brother** [Paul does not here call himself the slave of Christ as he afterwards did when he wrote to the Romans, for he now needed to assert the divinity of his apostleship because certain Judaizers had affirmed in Corinth that he was not divinely called, as were the twelve. See 1 Cor. 9: 1; 2 Cor. 12: 12. His apostleship was not the result of his own choice, nor yet the choice of any church, but of the will of God. Who Sosthenes was is not known. It is not unlikely that he was Paul's amanuensis, as was Tertius (Rom. 16: 22). The speed with which the apostle uses the pronoun "I" (verse 4) shows how little Sosthenes had to do with the Epistle. It is highly improbable that he is the same man mentioned at Acts 18: 17], **2 unto the church of God which is at Corinth,** *even* **them that are sanctified in Christ Jesus, called** *to be* **saints, with all that call upon the name of our Lord Jesus Christ in every place,**

GREETING, THANKSGIVING, ETC.

their *Lord* and ours [All Christians are sanctified, *i. e.*, set apart from the world and consecrated to God, and in the New Testament Scriptures they are all called saints, which means "holy ones" (Rom. 15: 23 ; 1 Cor. 6: 1, 2; Eph. 1: 1, 18; Phil. 1: 1 ; Col. 1: 2). Into this saintship they were called by the Holy Spirit through the agency of preachers like Paul and Apollos, etc. Unto the saints at Corinth, together with all others who showed themselves saints by calling upon or praying (Acts 7: 51; 9: 14; Rom. 10: 3), in the name of Jesus, who is Lord over all Christians everywhere, Paul addresses his letter, and gives the greeting which follows in verse 3]: **3 Grace to you and peace from God our Father and the Lord Jesus Christ.** [See note at 1 Thess. 1: 1.] **4 I thank my God always concerning you, for the grace of God which was given you in Christ Jesus ; 5 that in everything** [in every respect] **ye were enriched in him, in all utterance** [so that they were able to preach, teach, prophesy, and speak with tongues (1 Cor. 12: 8-10 ; 2 Cor. 8: 7 ; 11: 6] **and all knowledge** [so that they had perception of doctrine, discerning of spirits, and interpretation of tongues] ; **6 even as the testimony of** [about] **Christ was confirmed in you** [Paul here asserts that the miraculous gifts of the Spirit which characterized the times when he preached to them and converted them, were still equally manifest among them]: **7 so that** [causing that] **ye come behind** [other churches] **in no gift** [or miracle-working power of the Spirit]; **waiting for the revelation of our Lord Jesus Christ** [Christ taught all his followers to be constantly ready for his coming, and the Corinthians were conforming to this rule] ; **8 who shall also confirm you** [assuming that they earnestly desired and labored to be confirmed, or kept stedfast] **unto the end** [*i. e.*, unto the coming of Christ], *that ye be* unreprovable [unimpeachable, because forgiven (Col. 1: 22 ; 1 Tim. 3: 18; Tit. 1: 6] **in the day** [judgment day] **of our Lord Jesus Christ. 9 God is faithful, through whom ye were called into the fellowship of his Son Jesus Christ our Lord.** [The faithfulness of God insured that it would be no fault of his if the Corinthians failed to attain fellowship with Jesus; *i. e.*, a close intimacy with him in the present, and an association with him in glory in the future. In these nine verses with which the apostle opens his Epistle he follows his usual course of putting his commendation before his reproof. But the quality of his commendation should be carefully noted. He praises them for their spiritual endowments, and not for their private virtues. There is no commendation for moral advance, as is accorded to the Thessalonians and Philippians. Moreover, he deftly concludes by noting how God had brought them into fellowship and union with Christ, that this unifying act of God might stand in sharp contrast with the schisms and factions into which they had divided themselves, and for which he is just now going to reprove them.] **10 Now I beseech you** [a voice of entreaty], **brethren, through the name of our Lord Jesus Christ** [a voice of authority, enforced by threatened judgment (1 Cor. 4: 21). In this Epistle Paul has already used the name of Jesus nine times, thus emphasizing its virtue before he uses it as the symbol of supreme authority: as Chrysostom says, "he nails them to this name"], **that ye all speak the same thing, and** *that* **there be no divisions among you; but** *that* **ye be perfected together in the same mind and in the same judgment.** [The pride of Corinth showed itself largely in philosophical conceit, and the citizens who vaunted their superior intelligence were divided into sects, of whom Aristotle, Plato, Zeno, Epicurus, and later philosophers, were the heads. The church became inflated with this same intellectual vanity, and apparently sought to make Christianity the rival of philosophy by exalting her humble teachers to be heads of religio-philosophical sects, and rivals of Christ himself. As to this sinful condition the apostle gives an injunction, covering three points: 1. Unity of speech. 2. Unity of organization. 3. Unity of mind and judgment. They may be treated in their order as follows: 1. Paul first strikes at their speech, because then, as now, speculative discourses, philosophical dissertations, unscriptural reasonings, vapid dialectics for display's sake, etc., had become a fruitful **cause of**

GREETING, THANKSGIVING, ETC.

division. It is this speculative, argumentative spirit which genders confessions and creeds. 2. He strikes next at the divisions themselves, as the finished, completed evil complained of. But the divisions which he censures were mere parties in the church, not sects disrupting it, nor organized denominations professing to be "branches of the church." These greater divisions, and hence greater evils, came centuries later. 3. He proposes unity of mind and judgment as the ideal condition—the condition in which he had left them, and to which he would now restore them. The "mind" represents the inner state, the "judgment" the outward exhibition of it in action. In all this, Paul bespeaks not a partial, but a perfect, unity. "Perfected together" is a very suggestive phrase. Perfection of knowledge brings unity of thought and action, but defective understanding results in division. If one body of men, therefore, grows in truth faster than another, the tardiness of the latter tends to divide. All should grow and be perfected together. Hence, it becomes the duty of the growing disciple to impart his knowledge, and the correlative duty of the ignorant disciple to freely receive it.] **11 For it hath been signified** [made known] **unto me concerning you, my brethren** [as they indeed were, despite their shortcomings], **by them** *that are of the household* **of Chloe** [no doubt one of their number], **that there are contentions among you. 12 Now this I mean, that each one of you saith, I am of Paul; and I of Apollos; and I of Cephas; and I of Christ. 13 Is Christ divided?** [the church is called the "body of Christ" (1 Cor. 12: 12, 13, 27), and Paul asks if that body can be cut in pieces and parceled out to human leaders] **was Paul crucified for you? or were ye baptized into the name of Paul?** [Paul shows the disinterestedness of his rebuke by centering it more especially upon those who had honored him as their leader, thus showing, as Bengel says, that "he disliked Paulinists as much as he did Petrinists." Jesus became the Author of our salvation, and the head of the church through suffering upon the cross (Heb. 2: 10), and Paul, in order to be his rival, should not only have been crucified for his followers, but his sacrifice should have been as efficacious for the cleansing of sin and the procuring of salvation as was Christ's. This was, of course, preposterous. Again, if *Paul* was incompetent as the head of a religious body, his *followers* also had not properly qualified themselves as his disciples, for they had not been baptized into Paul's name, but being baptized into Christ they had put on Christ (Gal. 3: 27), and, becoming thus members of Christ, how could they belong to Paul? What Paul thus spoke of himself could be said with equal force of either Apollos or Cephas.] **14 I thank God** [who, foreseeing the future, prevented him from making such a mistake] **that I baptized none of you, save Crispus** [the ruler of the synagogue—Acts 18: 8] **and Gaius** [from whose house Paul wrote his Epistle to the Romans—Rom. 16: 23]; **15 lest any man should say that ye were baptized into my name.** [Paul knew that they would think it unreasonable that he should be accused of baptizing in his own name, but it was equally unreasonable in them to suppose that he was making disciples in his own name. Though many converts were made at Corinth, they appear to have been baptized by Paul's assistants, Silas and Timothy, and the few whom he baptized with his own hand were no doubt converts made before Paul's two friends arrived from Thessalonica. We should note how inseparably connected in Paul's thought were the sacrifice of the cross and the baptism which makes us partakers in its benefits—Rom. 6: 3-11.] **16 And I baptized also the household of Stephanas** [this man, being then present with Paul in Ephesus, probably reminded the apostle of his baptism]**: besides, I know not whether I baptized any other.** [Inspiration did not make the apostle remember such matters.] **17 For Christ sent me not to baptize, but to preach the gospel: not in wisdom of words, lest the cross of Christ should be made void.** [A baptism is part of the commission (Matt. 28: 19). Paul was sent to baptize; but it was not necessary that the apostle should administer the rite in person. It sufficed if he saw to it that it was done (John

4: 2). Paul does not here mean to assert that he preached without study or forethought. His words must be construed in the light of the context, which show that he intends to deny that he encumbered the gospel message with any philosophical reasoning.] **18 For the word of the cross is to them that perish foolishness; but unto us who are saved it is the power of God.** [From this point Paul proceeds to contrast the "words," or message of the cross, with the "wisdom of words," or worldly wisdom, *i. e.*, the philosophical messages or schemes of men, of which he has just spoken; having particularly in mind those of the two leading classes; viz.: Greeks and Jews. He first notes that the word of the cross is differently viewed by two different classes; those who, whether as disciples of Greek philosophers or of Jewish scribes, have dulled their moral perception by following worldly wisdom, and leading a worldly, perishing life, look upon it as foolishness; while those who have quickened their apprehension by leading a godly life, look upon it as God's saving power.] **19 For it is written, I will destroy the wisdom of the wise, And the discernment of the discerning will I bring to nought. 20 Where is the wise? where is the scribe? where is the disputer of this world?** [triumphant questions, as at Isa. 36: 19] **hath not God made foolish the wisdom of the world? 21 For seeing that in the wisdom of God the world through its wisdom knew not God, it was God's good pleasure through the foolishness of the preaching to save them that believe.** [Here Paul quotes Isa. 24: 14 to show that God had foretold how he would make foolish and useless all kinds of worldly wisdom, Grecian or Jewish, by making the gospel the only means of salvation, and how he had carried out the prophecy; for in his wisdom, or plan of operation, he had frustrated the efforts of wise men to find or know him by their coldblooded, philosophical research, or speculative reasoning (Acts 17: 23), and showed that it was his good pleasure to reveal himself and his salvation through this (to them) foolish preaching, and save **them** who believe the preaching. Where, then, asked the apostle in triumph, are these men of worldly wisdom, be they scribes or philosophical dialecticians? What have they done in comparison with that gospel which reveals their efforts as foolish and useless? What place, then, has a wise Paul or a disputing Apollos in the church, which, having the gospel, has this superior, saving wisdom of God? and why should the Corinthians leave the leadership of God in Christ and return to fools?] **22 Seeing that Jews ask for signs, and Greeks seek after wisdom: 23 but we preach Christ crucified, unto Jews a stumblingblock, and unto Gentiles foolishness; 24 but unto them that are called, both Jews and Greeks, Christ the power of God, and the wisdom of God. 25 Because the foolishness of God is wiser than men; and the weakness of God is stronger than men.** [The apostle here enlarges the thought of verse 18, and describes the two methods by which worldly wisdom sought to be led to God, or to know him when he revealed himself as he did in Christ. The Jews looked for him to prove his claims by miracles of power, such as signs from heaven (Matt. 12: 38; 16:1; John 2: 18; 4: 48); and the Greeks required that he transcend all their philosophers before they gave him their allegiance. But God revealed himself in his crucified Son, and so was rejected by both classes of wiseacres, the one stumbling at a crucified Messiah, whom they regarded as an accursed one (Deut. 21: 23; Gal. 3: 13), when they expected a regal and victorious Messiah (Rom. 9: 33; comp. Isa. 8: 14); the other, looking upon crucifixion as a slave's death, regarded salvation by such a one as absurd. But believing Jews saw in Jesus a power of God far transcending all their dreams of an earthly Messiah, and believing Greeks found in him a divine wisdom higher than all their ideals of truth, goodness and holiness. Thus God vindicated his so-called foolishness as wiser than all man's wisdom, and his so-called weakness in Christ as stronger than all the conceptions of an earthly Messiah—yet the Corinthians were leaving this transcendent sign and incarnate truth to return to their old worldly wisdom with its human leaders.] **26 For behold your calling** [the "principle God has followed in calling you"—Beza; a principle whereby "God," as Augustine says, "caught orators by fishermen, not fishermen by orators"], **brethren, that not many wise after the flesh, not many mighty, not many noble,** *are called* [The wise were moved by conceit to reject the gospel invitation: see the case of Gallio (Acts 18: 12-17). The corruptness of Roman politics kept the mighty aloof from the purity of Christianity, and the pride of noble birth felt repugnance at the lowly fellowship of the early church. A brief catalogue will record all the distinguished names brought into the church during its first thirty years, viz.: Joseph of Arimathea, perhaps Nicodemus, Saul of Tarsus, Sergius Paulus and Dionysius the Areopagite]: **27 but God chose the foolish things of the world, that he might put to shame them that are wise; and God chose the weak things of the world** [Ps. 8: 2; John 2: 5], **that he might put to shame the things that are strong; 28 and the base things of the world, and the things that are despised, did God choose,** *yea* **and the things that are not** [the people whom the world called "nobodies"], **that he might bring to nought the things that are: 29 that no flesh** [no minister or other instrument of his] **should glory** [take pride in himself, and aspire to be head of a faction] **before God.** [The Corinthians in endeavoring to exalt their leaders were running counter to the counsels of God, who had rejected as his instruments all those who had worldly wisdom and power, and had chosen those utterly deficient in those things, that the triumph of his gospel might be manifestly due to his own power, and not to any excellency residing in the instruments or ministers whom he chanced to employ (2 Cor. 4: 7.] **30 But of him are ye in Christ Jesus, who was made unto us wisdom from God, and righteousness and sanctification, and redemption: 31 that, according as it is written** [Jer. 9: 24], **He that glorieth, let him glory in the Lord.** [By the power of God, therefore, and not by the human wisdom of preachers, were the Corinthians brought into Christ, in whom they had found a wisdom of God superior to all worldly wisdom, and also the blessings of righteousness and sanctification and redemption, which no philosophy could obtain for them; so that every one who gloried in being a Christian was properly directed by the Scripture to glory in the Author of his salvation, and not in the humble nobody whom God had used as a messenger of grace. Glorying in men is even more sinful in us than it was in the Corinthians, for we have more light.]

II.
THE GOSPEL VERSUS PHILOSOPHY.
2: 1-16.

In the last section Paul showed that it was God's plan to overthrow the vain wisdom of the world by those weak and lowly ones whom the world despised. He now proceeds to show that the church at Corinth was founded by him as a weak and lowly one, in accordance with God's plan.] **And I, brethren, when I came unto you, came not with excellency of speech** [as an orator] **or of wisdom** [as a philosopher], **proclaiming to you the testimony of** [about] **God.** [Though Paul was educated at Tarsus, which Strabo preferred as a school of learning to Athens or Alexandria, yet he made no display of his learning, and hence his enemies spoke of his speech as contemptible or no account (2 Cor. 10: 10). He quotes from Aratus at Acts 17: 28, and Epimenides at Tit. 1: 12, and Menander at 1 Cor. 15: 33. But Paul counted all such polite learning as mere dross in comparison with the excellency of the knowledge of Christ—Phil. 3: 8.] **2 For I determined not to know anything among you, save Jesus Christ, and him crucified.** [Paul here asserts that the subject-matter of his preaching was selected from choice, or fixed design. He does not mean to say that every sermon was a description of the crucifixion of our Lord, but that all his teaching and preaching related to the atonement wrought by Christ upon the cross. This atonement, through

THE GOSPEL VERSUS PHILOSOPHY

the sacrifice of our Lord, was recognized by Paul as the foundation of the Christian system, and he here means to say that he handled no doctrine or theme at Corinth without remembering and recognizing its relation to that foundation.] **3 And I was with you in weakness, and in fear, and in much trembling.** [Paul frequently asserts his tendency to physical weakness and depression (1 Cor. 4: 7-12; Gal. 4: 13; 2 Cor. 10: 1, 10; 12: 7). This sense of weakness was accentuated by his recent semi-failure at Athens, by frequent persecution, and by the absence of his companions, Silas and Timothy, till Paul's sense of timidity amounted to actual fear (Acts 18: 9). He was also out of money and had to work for Aquila. The slight admixture of philosophy which he had used in addressing the Athenians (Acts 17: 22-34) had thoroughly convinced the apostle that it was of no use, or benefit, in the presentation of the gospel.] **4 And my speech** [discourse on doctrine] **and my preaching** [announcement of facts] **were not in persuasive words of wisdom, but in demonstration of the Spirit and of power** [1 Cor. 1: 5. He relied upon the divine aid, rather than upon the aid of human learning]: **5 that your faith should not stand in** [should not be based upon] **the wisdom of men, but in the power of God. 6 We** [as an inspired apostle] **speak wisdom, however, among them that are fullgrown: yet a wisdom not of this world, nor of the rulers of this world, who are coming to nought** [Paul here begins to correct the impression which his semi-ironical lauguage about the foolishness of God might have made, and proceeds to show that the gospel is the highest wisdom—a wisdom which he had not yet been able to impart to the Corinthians because it could only be comprehended by mature Christians, and so was above the receptive powers ot the Corinthians who as yet were mere babes in Christ (1 Cor. 3: 1). But if the Corinthians who were developing in spiritual manhood could not receive this heavenly wisdom, much less could the world-rulers who were moving backward, crab-fashion, into nothingness, in accordance with the plan of God outlined in the last section. Thus the apostle reveals the startling fact that progression in philosophical and political worldliness is retrogression as to the kingdom of God, so that the Corinthians in seeking to better their religious condition by bringing these worldly elements into the church, were not only retarding their spiritual growth, but were actually associating themselves with those who were shrinking and shriveling toward the vanishing point]: **7 but we speak God's wisdom in a mystery,** *even* **the** *wisdom* **that hath been hidden, which God foreordained before the worlds unto our glory** [Paul often speaks of Christ and his gospel as a mystery (Rom. 16: 25; Eph. 3: 4-9; Col. 1: 26; 1 Tim. 3: 16, 17). God's purpose to give his Son for the salvation of the world was a mystery long hidden, but now revealed, but still hidden from those who wickedly refused to receive it (Matt. 11: 25; 13: 10-13), to which class Paul proceeds to relegate the world-rulers]: **8 which none of the rulers of this world hath known: for had they known it, they would not have crucified the Lord of glory** [their conduct proved their ignorance even as Jesus asserted—Luke 23: 34]: **9 but as it is written, Things which eye saw not, and ear heard not, And** *which* **entered not into the heart of man, Whatsoever things God prepared for them that love him.** [This passage is taken from Isa. 64: 4; but it is an exposition, and not a verbatim quotation. The words form an unfinished sentence, and, as is not infrequent with Paul's quotations, do not fit nicely into the general structure of his discourse. To understand them we should supply the words "we speak" from verse 7; *i. e.*, we fulfill the prophecy by telling those things which God prepared for those that love him (the mystery of the gospel), but which no uninspired man ever in any way surmised or anticipated. The prophecy includes the unseen glories of heaven.] **10 But unto us** [inspired apostles] **God revealed** *them* **through the Spirit** [Here the defective knowledge gained by the world-rulers through their wisdom or philosophy stands in sharp contrast to the heavenly and perfect knowledge which the apostles had by revelation of the Spirit. Paul proceeds to discuss the perfec-

THE GOSPEL VERSUS PHILOSOPHY 61

tion of this inspired knowledge] : **for the Spirit searcheth all things; yea, the deep things** [Rom. 11: 33] **of God. 11 For who among men knoweth the things of a man, save the spirit of the man, which is in him? even so the things of God none knoweth, save the Spirit of God. 12 But we received, not the spirit of the world, but the spirit which is from God ; that we might know the things that were freely given to us of God.** [As a man alone knows himself, so God alone knows himself. As the thoughts and intentions of a man are best known by his own spirit, so also are the divine counsels of God best known by the Spirit of God. If a man's knowledge of himself surpasses that of his neighbor who knows him well, much more must the revelation of the unseen God by his Spirit far surpass all the speculations of mankind with regard to him. But this revelation of God the apostles enjoyed, through the Spirit of God, who guided them into all truth (John 13: 16). How superior, then, was their knowledge to that of worldly philosophy, even if it embraced the collective knowledge of all men.] **13 Which things also we speak, not in words which man's wisdom teacheth, but which the Spirit teacheth ; combining spiritual things with spiritual *words*.** [Here again we have a clear claim to inspiration, and not only so, but *verbal* inspiration. Paul did not reason after the manner of worldly philosophers, but imparted his truth under the guidance of the Spirit, who taught him the words to use, so that he taught spiritual truths with spiritual words, a fitting combination. The leaders of our current Reformation did well in conforming to this rule, by seeking to express Bible thoughts in Bible language. To Paul the terms and phrases of theology would have been as distasteful as those of philosophy, because equally man-made and unspiritual.] **14 Now the natural man receiveth not the things of the Spirit of God: for they are foolishness unto him; and he cannot know them, because they are spiritually judged.** [As sound is perceived by the ear, and not by the eye, so the spirit of man perceives spiritual things which can not be comprehended by his psychic nature. But a man who has lived on the low psychic plane—a carnal, sensuous victim to bodily appetites—has, by neglect, let his spiritual faculties become so torpid, and by sin so deadened them, that the spiritual things of God become as foolishness to him, despite their worthiness—1 Tim. 1: 15.] **15 But he that is spiritual judgeth all things, and he himself is judged of no man. 16 For who hath known the mind of the Lord, that he should instruct him? But we have the mind of Christ** [A spiritual man, helped by the indwelling Spirit of God, is enabled to judge of things divine, and much more of things human. But he himself can not be judged of carnal men, because they have no knowledge of those things by which they should weigh or estimate him. Could a man know God so as to instruct him? Surely not. No more, then, could a man counsel, judge or instruct a man who, by the inspiring power of the Spirit, thinks the thoughts and has the mind of Christ. Jesus revealed his mind to the apostles (John 15: 15), and also to Paul as one of them—Gal. 1: 11, 12.]

III.

SUPREMACY OF GOD AND THE CHURCH.

3: 1-23.

1 And I, brethren, could not speak unto you as unto spiritual, but as unto carnal, as unto babes in Christ. [The simplicity of Paul's instruction had given occasion to the false apostles (2 Cor. 11: 12-15) to criticize him as a shallow teacher (2 Cor. 10: 10), rather than as one who had "the mind of Christ." To this the apostle replies that their own immature condition up to the time when he left them, rendered them incapable of any fuller instruction; for, far from being mature disciples (ch. 2: 8 : Eph. 4: 13), they were still swayed by the prejudices and passions of the unregenerate life out of which they had been but lately born, and to which they were not wholly dead.] **2 I fed you with milk, not with meat, for**

ye were not yet able *to bear it* [he had merely grounded them in first principles, and had not enlightened them as to those higher doctrines which lead on to perfection, because they could not grasp them. Comp. Heb. 5: 11–6: 2; 1 Pet. 2: 2; Mark 4: 33; John 16: 12]: **nay, not even now are ye able; 3 for ye are yet carnal** [showing undue reverence for men, etc.]: **for whereas there is among you jealousy and strife, are ye not carnal** [Gal. 5: 19, 20; Jas. 3: 16], **and do ye not walk after the manner of men? 4 For when one saith, I am of Paul; and another, I am of Apollos; are ye not men?** [Surely the Corinthians had no ground to argue with Paul as to their condition when he was among them, for their present condition was no better, since they were still swayed by the same prejudices and passions, and were showing themselves worldlings, rather than Spirit-led Christians—Gal. 5: 25.] **5 What** [the neuter of disparagement] **then is Apollos? and what is Paul? Ministers** [literally, deacons, *i. e.*, servitors—Acts 6: 2; Col. 1: 7; not leaders—Luke 22: 25, 26] **through whom** ["not in whom"—Bengel] **ye believed; and each as the Lord gave to him.** [*i. e.*, gave spiritual gifts (Rom. 12: 6); and success.] **6 I planted, Apollos watered; but God gave the increase. 7 So then neither is he that planteth anything** [in himself, without Christ—2 Cor. 12: 12; John 5: 4, 5, 16], **neither he that watereth; but God that giveth the increase.** [Paul brought them into the vineyard or kingdom, Apollos instructed them; but God gave the results, causing them to live and grow, and so to God alone was due the honor and praise (Ps. 115: 1). Paul regarded it as his especial duty because of his apostleship to tarry in no territory already occupied, but to press into new fields and plant churches, leaving others to help water them—Rom. 15: 20; 2 Cor. 10: 15, 16.] **8 Now he that planteth and he that watereth are one** [with respect to their purposes, or the ends for which they labor: hence, not rivals]: **but each shall receive his own reward according to his own labor.** [Since God gives the increase, the reward will be proportioned to fidelity, etc., rather than to results.] **9 For we are God's fellow-workers: ye are God's husbandry, God's building** [The supreme ownership of God is here emphasized, as is shown by the three possessives. Paul and Apollos were not fellow-workers with God, but fellow-workers with each other under God. The Corinthians were God's field in which they labored, or his building which they reared; but workers, field and building all belonged to God.] **10 According to the grace** [apostleship with its attendant gifts—Rom. 1: 5; Gal. 1: 15, 16; Eph. 3: 8] **of God which was given unto me, as a wise masterbuilder I laid a foundation** [In Corinth Paul had preached Christ as the foundation of the church and of each individual Christian, and this foundation admitted no mixture of philosophy and no perversion which could produce sects (Gal. 1: 9). All this Paul asserts without any shadow of boasting, for the skill or wisdom by which he had done it had been imparted to him by God]; **and another buildeth thereon. But let each man take heed how he buildeth thereon. 11 For other foundation can no man lay than that which is laid** [of or by God the Father (1 Pet. 2: 6); God laid him by gift, Paul by preaching], **which is Jesus Christ.** [Paul had laid Christ as the foundation (Matt. 16: 18; Acts 4: 11, 12; Eph. 2: 20); and others (each being individually responsible, hence the singular) had been building carnal, worldly-minded factions upon it, and these are warned that the superstructure should comport with the foundation, for so worthy a foundation should have a correspondingly worthy structure.] **12 But if any man buildeth on the foundation gold, silver, costly stones, wood, hay, stubble; 13 each man's work shall be made manifest: for the day** [the judgment day] **shall declare it, because it is revealed in fire** [as to its quality]; **and the fire itself shall prove each man's work of what sort it is.** [All of the building materials here mentioned were familiar in Corinth. The first three kinds were found in their fireproof temples—material worthy of sacred structures, and the latter three were used in their frail, combustible huts which were in no way dedicated

SUPREMACY OF GOD

to divinity. The argument is that Corinthian Christians should build the spiritual temple of God, the church, with as good spiritual material as the relative earthly material employed by their fathers in constructing idolatrous shrines. The church should be built of true Christians, the proper material; and not of worldly-minded hypocrites, or those who estimate the oracles of God as on a par with the philosophies of men. The day of judgment will reveal the true character of all who are in the church, as a fire reveals the character of the material in a temple structure. The Roman Catholic doctrine of purgatory is in some measure founded on this passage; but the context shows a purging of all evil men from the church as an entirety. There is no hint that the evil in the *individual* is purged by fire, leaving a residuum of righteousness. Our sins are not purged by fire, but by the blood of Christ, and without the shedding of blood there is no remission—Heb. 9: 22.] **14 If any man's work shall abide which he built thereon, he shall receive a reward. 15 If any man's work shall be burned, he shall suffer loss** [if a teacher's disciples endure the test of judgment, he shall receive a reward, of which his converts will be at least a part (1 Thess. 2: 19; Phil. 2: 16); but if his disciples do not stand that test, he shall of course lose whatever property he had in them, and perhaps more—2 John 8]: **but he himself shall be saved; yet so as through fire.** [The teacher may of course be saved independently of his disciples, for salvation is a gift and not a reward; but he will be saved as a steward who has lost the things of his stewardship; as a tenant who has had his harvest burned, or as a contractor whose structure has gone up in flames: see verse 9.] **16 Know ye not** [a touch of amazement at their ignorance] **that ye are a temple of God, and that the Spirit of God dwelleth in you?** [In verse 9 he had called them God's building; he now reminds them of what kind the building was, and how exalted were its uses. The Jerusalem temple was honored by the Shechinah, but the church by the very Spirit of God.] **17 If any man destroyeth the temple of God, him shall God destroy; for the** temple of God is holy, and such are ye. [The factions are here plainly made aware of the magnitude of their sin, and the severity of their punishment. They were destroying the church by their divisions (Eph. 5: 27), maiming and dismembering it by their discordant factions—2 Pet. 2:1.] **18 Let no man deceive himself.** [By thinking himself wise enough to amend or modify God's truth.] **If any man thinketh that he is wise among you in this world, let him become a fool, that he may become wise.** [Let such a one become a fool in the world's sight, as Paul was (Acts 26: 24; ch. 4: 10), that by preaching the so-called foolishness of God he may learn the real wisdom of it.] **19 For the wisdom of this world is foolishness with God. For it is written** [Job 5: 13], **He that taketh the wise in their craftiness: 20 and again** [Ps. 94: 11], **The Lord knoweth the reasonings of the wise, that they are vain.** [Alford interprets the passage thus: "If God uses the craftiness of the wise as a net to catch them in, such wisdom is in his sight folly, since he turns it to their own confusion." How foolish to modify or adapt the gospel to make it palatable and acceptable to sectarian spirits or worldly minds! Man is to be adjusted to God, not God to man, for he is unchangeable —Jas. 1: 17; Heb. 13: 8.] **21 Wherefore let no one glory in men.** [A returning upon the thought at ch. 1:31.] **For all things are yours** [why, then, grasp a paltry part and forego the glorious whole?]; **22 whether Paul, or Apollos, or Cephas, or the world** [Matt. 5: 5; Mark 10: 29, 30], **or life** [with its possibilities], **or death** [with its gain—Phil. 1: 21], **or things present, or things to come** [Rev. 21: 5-27]; **all are yours** [This is a positive, as Rom. 8: 38, 39 is a negative side of the truth at Rom. 8: 28. All things further, and nothing hinders the saint's prosperity]; **23 and ye are Christ's** [and hence not the property of his servants]; **and Christ is God's.** [These words are an echo of the prayer of the Master at John 17: 21-23. The church must have perfect unity in Christ that Christ may maintain his unity with God. Christ must of necessity quiet all contention between the members of his body (1 Cor. 12: 12); for if he is at variance with himself, how can he have unity with the Father? Variance is an infallible proof of imperfection, and imperfection can not have unity with God, who is perfection—Matt. 5: 48.]

IV.
APOSTOLIC STEWARDSHIP AND AUTHORITY.
4: 1-21.

1 Let a man so account of us, as of ministers of Christ, and stewards of the mysteries of God. [Paul here gives the rule by which apostles and evangelists are to be estimated. They are not to be magnified, for they are servants, nor are they to be deprecated because of the value and importance of that which is entrusted to them as stewards. The term "ministers" here means literally *under-rowers*. The church is a ship, or galley; Christ is the chief navigator, or *magisterium;* and all the evangelists and teachers are mere oarsmen with no ambition to be leaders. In the second figure the church is a household, God is the householder, the gospel truths are the food and other provisions which are dispensed by the evangelists or stewards.] **2 Here, moreover, it is required in stewards, that a man be found faithful.** [It was not expected of the steward that he would procure or provide; he was merely to distribute that which was provided by the master. The apostles were not philosophers burdened with the discovery and invention of truth, but were mere dispensers of truth revealed to them by God—truth which must be thus revealed because it can not be discovered by any process of ratiocination. If the apostles faithfully rehearsed that which was revealed, nothing more could be asked of them.] **3 But with me it is a very small thing that I should be judged of you, or of man's judgment: yea, I judge not mine own self. 4 For I know nothing against myself; yet am I not hereby justified: but he that judgeth me is the Lord.** [Paul is not arrogantly vaunting himself as disdaining the good or bad opinion of the Corinthians, but pointing out the inadequacy of all human judgment, even his own, to decide that which God alone can decide. God gave the office and fixed the manner in which its duties should be discharged, and so God alone can judge the officer (Rom. 14: 4). One might do wrong unconsciously, and yet justify himself—Ps. 19: 12; 1 John 3: 20.] **5 Wherefore judge nothing before the time, until the Lord come, who will both bring to light the hidden things of darkness, and make manifest the counsels of the hearts; and then shall each man have his praise from God.** [The revelation or manifestation of things which shall accompany the Lord's coming, was mentioned in our last section. In the light of that hour, not only the deeds of men will be manifest, but even the motives which prompted the deeds. The Corinthians, having no adequate means of telling whether Paul spoke less or more than was revealed, would have to wait until that hour of revelation before they could judge him accurately and absolutely. If he was then approved, he would receive not only their praise, but the praise of God—Matt. 25: 21.] **6 Now these things, brethren, I have in a figure transferred to myself and Apollos for your sakes; that in us ye might learn not *to go* beyond the things which are written; that no one of you be puffed up for the one against the other.** [Though neither Paul nor Apollos had headed a faction in Corinth, Paul has spoken in this Epistle as though they had done this, and that he might spare the feelings of the real leaders in faction he had put himself and Apollos in their places, and had shown the heinousness of their supposed conduct as reproved by many passages of Scripture. He had done this that the Corinthians, seeing the evil of such a thing even in an apostle, might see it more plainly in their little local party leaders, and might not boast themselves of any one leader to the disparagement of another. We may be sure that those who were puffing themselves up in one, were correspondingly busy traducing the other.] **7 For who maketh thee to differ? and what** hast thou that thou didst not receive? but if thou didst receive it, why dost thou glory as if thou hadst not received it? [God had made them to differ both in natural and in spiritual gifts (Rom. 12: 3-8). If, then, one had more subtle reasoning faculties than another, what ground had he for boasting, since his superiority was due to the grace of God in bestowing it, and not to himself in acquiring it?] **8 Already ye are filled** [with self-satisfaction], **already ye are become rich** [with intellectual pride], **ye have come to reign without us** [Ye have so exalted yourselves that we poor apostles have become quite needless to your lordly independence. The inflated self-esteem of the Corinthians was like that of the Laodiceans some twoscore years later—Rev. 3: 17, 18] : **yea and I would that ye did reign, that we also might reign with you.** [Here, moved by his ardent affection, the apostle passes instantly from biting sarcasm to a divinely tender yearning for their welfare. He wishes that they possessed in reality that eminence which existed only in their conceit. How different, then, would be his own condition. Their true development was his joy, their real elevation his exaltation, and their final triumph in Christ his crown of glorying (1 Thess. 2: 19; 9: 23). From the brilliant picture thus raised before his imagination, Paul turns to depict his true condition, in all its unenviable details.] **9 For, I think, God hath set forth us the apostles last of all, as men doomed to death: for we are made a spectacle unto the world, both to angels and men.** [As, after the end of the performance, condemned criminals were brought into the amphitheater and made a gazing-stock to the populace before their execution, so the apostles seemed to be exhibited to public contempt.] **10 We are fools for Christ's sake, but ye are wise in Christ; we are weak, but ye are strong; ye have glory, but we have dishonor.** [In this verse Paul resumes his satire, contrasting the vain imaginations of the Corinthians with the real condition of the apostles, himself in particular.] **11 Even unto this present hour we both hunger, and thirst, and are naked, and are buffeted** [smitten with the clenched fist], **and have no certain dwelling-place** [Matt. 8: 20; 10: 23]; **12 and we toil, working with our own hands: being reviled, we bless** [Luke 6: 27; 1 Pet. 2: 23]; **being persecuted, we endure; 13 being defamed, we entreat** [Matt. 5: 44] **: we are made as the filth of the world, the offscouring of all things, even until now.** ["Filth" indicates either rubbish swept up, or such foulness as is cleansed by washing. "Offscouring" indicates dirt removed by scraping or scouring. Each neighborhood to which the apostles came hastened to be cleansed of their presence.] **14 I write not these things to shame you** [to make you feel how contemptible you are in adding to my many sorrows and burdens], **but to admonish you as my beloved children.** [As to the foolishness of your conceit.] **15 Though ye have ten thousand tutors** [literally, pedagogues: the large number rebukes their itch for teachers] **in Christ, yet** *have ye* **not many fathers** [they had but one—Paul]**; for in Christ Jesus I begat you through the gospel.** [In the first, or highest, sense disciples are begotten by the will of God (John 1: 13); but in a secondary sense they are begotten by the teacher of gospel truths (Jas. 1: 18). The Corinthians had many builders, but one founder; many waterers, but one planter; many tutors, but one father. He had rights, therefore, which could never be rivaled.] **16 I beseech you therefore, be ye imitators of me.** [Again, in the highest sense we can only be imitators of God (Eph. 5: 1); but in a secondary sense the Corinthians could imitate Paul—his humility, faithfulness, self-sacrifice and industry, as did the Thessalonians—1 Thess. 1: 6.] **17 For this cause have I sent unto you Timothy, who is my beloved and faithful child in the Lord, who shall put you in remembrance of my ways which are in Christ, even as I teach everywhere in every church.** [To aid you in imitating me, I have sent Timothy. He can tell you how I teach, not accommodating the gospel to the prejudices and foibles of any locality; and he can, as my spiritual son, aid you by his own manner of life to remember mine. Paul knew that as soon as they heard of this sending of Timothy, his enemies would conclude that he had sent a messenger because he was afraid to face the church himself. Instantly, therefore, he proceeds to counteract this conclusion.] **18 Now some are puffed up, as though I were not coming to you. 19 But I will come to you shortly** [as he did], **if the Lord will** [Jas. 4: 15]; **and I will know, not the word of them that are puffed up, but the power.** [I will test not their rhetorical ability, but their power, whether they can stand against that which I possess as an apostle.] **20 For the kingdom of God is not in word, but in power. 21 What will ye?** [which do you choose or prefer?] **shall I come unto you with a rod** [to punish you], **or in love and a spirit of gentleness?** [Because ye will have repented of your factious spirit.]

PART SECOND.
APOSTOLIC RESPONSES AND CONCLUSIONS.
5:1-16: 24.

I.
RESPONSE TO REPORT OF INCEST.
5: 1-13.

1 It is actually reported that there is fornication among you, and such fornication as is not even among the Gentiles, that one *of you* **hath his father's wife.** [*i. e.*, his step-mother. She was probably a pagan, and hence is not rebuked. The offense of the Corinthians had been magnified in that they had let Paul find out their sin by public gossip. Though they had written to him seeking light on other matters (ch. 7: 1), they had not even mentioned this deplorable wickedness. Such incest was of course condemned by the Jewish law (Lev. 18: 8; Deut. 27: 20). But even Corinth, moral cesspool that it was, would be scandalized by such a crime, for it was condemned alike by Greeks and Romans. See the Œdipus of Sophocles, the Hippolytus of Euripides, and Cicero's Pro Cluentio, 5. As to such a case Cicero uses these words: "Oh, incredible wickedness, and—except in this woman's case—unheard in all experience!"] **2 And ye are puffed up, and did not rather mourn, that he that had done this deed might be taken away from among you.** [Our last section shows in what manner they had been puffed up. Had they been mourning over their real sinfulness, instead of priding themselves in their philosophical knowledge, this offender would have been taken away by excommunication.] **3 For I verily, being absent in body but present in spirit, have already as though I were present judged him that hath so wrought this thing** [The swiftness of Paul's judgment stands in sharp contrast with the tardiness and toleration of the Corinthians. The broken structure of this verse and the one which follows it, shows Paul's deep emotion. "The passage is, as it were, written with sobs."—*Wordsworth*], **4 in the name of our Lord Jesus, ye being gathered together, and my spirit, with the power of our Lord Jesus, 5 to deliver such a one unto Satan for the destruction of the flesh, that the spirit may be saved in the day of the Lord Jesus.** [The full assembly of the church was required, for the discipline was to be administered by the entire body. The marked way in which Paul assured them of his presence, and the peculiar punishment which he directs to be administered, have led many to believe that he promises to be present in some miraculous spiritual manner (Col. 2: 5; comp. 2 Kings 5: 26); so as to use his miraculous power to smite the offender with sickness, or some bodily infirmity, as the phrase "deliver . . . unto Satan" is taken to mean, Acts 5: 1-11; 13: 11; 1 Tim. 1: 20, being cited to sustain this meaning. The argument is very flimsy, and is not sustained by the facts recorded in this case. The meaning is that Paul, having commanded the condemnation of the culprit, will be spiritually present to aid the church in that condemnation. The offender, being excluded from the kingdom of God, is to be thrust back into the kingdom of Satan, that the sense of his loneliness, shame and lost condition may cause him to repent, and mortify or subdue his flesh, *i. e.*, his lust, after which his spirit, being thus delivered, might be saved. The sequel of the case comports with this interpretation, and there is no hint that the man ever suffered any corporeal punishment. See 2 Cor. 2: 5-8.] **6 Your glorying is not good.** [Their glorying was sinful enough at best, but much more so when it was so inopportune.] **Know ye not that a little leaven leaveneth the whole lump? 7 Purge out the old leaven, that ye may be a new lump, even as ye are unleavened. For our passover also hath been sacrificed,** *even* **Christ: 8 wherefore let us keep the feast, not with old leaven, neither with the leaven of malice and wickedness, but with the unleavened bread of sincerity and truth.** [Verses 6-8 form an enlargement of verse 2. The reference to the passover was probably suggested by the season of the year (ch. 16: 8), and was very apropos. Leaven is a type of evil, illustrating the hidden constant way in which it spreads. To the Jew it was a symbol of the corruption of Egypt, and he was directed just before the passover to search for it diligently in every part of his house, and remove it (Ex. 12: 15). But to the Christian Christ is a perpetual sacrifice, an ever-present paschal Lamb, demanding and enforcing constant vigilance and unceasing cleanliness. The individual must put away every sinful habit of the old life. The church must purge itself of all whose lives are sources of corruption.] **9 I wrote unto you in my epistle** [see introduction] **to have no company with fornicators; 10 not at all** *meaning* **with the fornicators of this world, or with the covetous and extortioners, or with idolaters; for then must ye needs go out of this world** [In this earlier Epistle the apostle had directed that fornicators and other backsliders *inside* the church, should be treated as outcasts, since they were so regarded of God (Eph. 5: 5; Gal. 5: 19-21). But he had been misunderstood, and had been thought to say that fornicators, etc., *outside* the church were to be wholly avoided; a very impractical precept, which could only be obeyed by migrating to another planet, since this world is steeped in sin—comp. John 17: 15]: **11 but as it is, I wrote unto you not to keep company, if any man that is named a brother be a fornicator, or covetous, or an idolater** [Col. 3: 5], **or a reviler, or a drunkard, or an extortioner; with such a one no, not to eat.** [Have no interchange of hospitality which would imply brotherly recognition, lest the church should thereby not only be disgraced, but corrupted—1 Cor. 15: 33.] **12 For what have I to do with judging them that are without? Do not ye judge them that are within? 13 But them that are without God judgeth.** [These facts showed that the apostle had referred to those within the church; the discipline of those without is exclusively in the hands of God.] **Put away the wicked man from among yourselves.** [A summary command as to him and other wicked men.]

II.

RESPONSE TO RUMORS OF LITIGATION, ETC.

6: 1-20.

1 Dare any of you, having a matter against his neighbor, go to law before the unrighteous, and not before the saints? [1. Division, 2. Incest, 3. Litigation: such is the order of Paul's rebukes. With reckless audacity the Corinthians, by indulging in litigation and submitting their causes to pagan tribunals, were not only disobeying the Lord's command (Matt. 18: 15-17), but were also committing treason against their present brotherhood and their future status as judges. It appears that even the Jews refused to sue each other before pagan tribunals—Josephus Ant. 14: 10-17.] **2 Or know ye not that the saints shall judge the world? and if the world is judged by you, are ye unworthy to judge the smallest matters? 3 Know ye not that we shall judge angels? how much more, things that**

RESPONSE TO RUMORS, ETC.   75

pertain to this life? [They were permitting themselves to be judged by those whom they were appointed to judge. To prove that the saints will participate with Christ in the final judgment, the following passages are often cited (Ps. 49: 14; Dan. 7: 22-27; Matt. 19: 28; 20: 23; Jude 6; Rev. 2: 26; 3: 21; 20: 4). It is doubtful if any of these are applicable; the manner of our participation is nowhere explained. Barrow suggested that in the order of the judgments the saints would be justified *first* (Matt. 25: 41), after which they would sit with Christ as assessors, or associate judges, in the condemnation of the wicked and the evil angels, and his view is pretty generally received. But it is more probable that the saints will only participate as mystically united with Christ the judge, just as, by mystical union, they are kings and priests, though in no sense exercising these offices literally. The church shall judge the world in Christ her head. But the point made by Paul is that those whom God honors by association in so important a judicature may well be entrusted to judge trivial matters; for the weightiest matter of earth is light compared with the questions of eternal destiny decided on that day.] **4 If then ye have to judge things pertaining to this life, do ye set them to judge who are of no account in the church? 5 I say *this* to move you to shame.** [If called on as a church to judge any matter, would you choose its simpletons and numbskulls as judges? I ask this to make you ashamed, for ye do even more foolishly when you submit your cases to worldlings, who are even less competent judges.] **What, cannot there be *found* among you one wise man who shall be able to decide between his brethren, 6 but brother goeth to law with brother, and that before unbelievers?** [This question is a crushing rebuke to their vaunted pride as learned sages. The rebuke is intensified by the phrase "know ye not," which is used six times in this chapter, four times in the rest of his writing to the Corinthians, and only twice by him elsewhere—Rom. 6: 16; 11: 2; comp. Matt. 12: 3.] **7 Nay, already** [before ye even begin civil action] **it is altogether a defect in you, that ye have lawsuits** [more correctly, matter worthy of litigation] **one with another.** [Here Paul emphasizes the ripened state of their criminality by condemning even its germinal stage as a defect.] **Why not rather take wrong? why not rather be defrauded? 8 Nay, but ye yourselves do wrong, and defraud, and that** *your* **brethren.** [Far from enduring wrong and obeying Christ (Matt. 5: 40; 1 Pet. 2: 22; comp. Prov. 20: 22), they were actually perpetrating wrong upon their brethren. In view of this flagrant wickedness Paul proceeds to warn them of the results of wickedness, and of their professed repentance as to it.] **9 Or know ye not that the unrighteous shall not inherit the kingdom of God?** [That glorious celestial kingdom of which the church is the earthly type.] **Be not deceived** [so as to think sin will not result in punishment —Gal. 6: 7]**: neither fornicators, nor idolaters, nor adulterers, nor effeminate** [catamites]**, nor abusers of themselves with men** [Rom. 1: 26, 27]**, 10 nor thieves, nor covetous, nor drunkards, nor revilers, nor extortioners, shall inherit the kingdom of God.** [Paul here accords with James that faith without works is dead (Jas. 2: 17). Our highest privileges may be abrogated by sin.] **11 And such were some of you** [they had been true Corinthians]**: but ye were washed** [Acts 22: 16; Eph. 5: 26; Tit. 3: 5; Heb. 10: 22]**, but ye were sanctified** [set apart to God's uses]**, but ye were justified in the name of the Lord Jesus Christ** [counted righteous after the remission of your sins]**, and in the Spirit of our God.** [The work being consummated by the Holy Spirit—Acts 2: 38.] **12 All things are lawful for me; but not all things are expedient.** [The abruptness here suggests that, in palliation of their undue laxity and toleration, they had in their letter (7: 1) urged this rule; which they had doubtless learned from Paul (ch. 10: 23; Gal. 5: 23). Hence Paul takes up the rule to show that it does not avoid the disinheriting of which he has just spoken.] **All things are lawful** [literally, within my power] **for me; but I will not be brought under the power of any.** [They **had** erred in taking the rule as to things indifferent, such **as** natural appetites, and so applying it as to make it cover not only sinful things, but even those grossly so, such as sensuous lusts (comp. 1 Pet. 2: 16). The rule is properly applied by the apostle at ch. 8: 8-10. He here refutes their ideas as to the rule by showing that their application of it would gender bondage, as excess of freedom invariably does.] **13 Meats for the belly, and the belly for meats: but God shall bring to nought both it and them. But the body is not for fornication, but for the Lord; and the Lord for the body: 14 and God both raised the Lord, and will raise up us through his power. 15 Know ye not that your bodies are members of Christ?** [parts of his body (ch. 12: 27; Eph. 5: 30); branches of the Vine—John 15: 5] **shall I then take away the members of Christ, and make them members of a harlot? God forbid.** [Literally, let it never be; a phrase often used by Paul when indignantly rejecting a false conclusion.] **16 Or know ye not that he that is joined to a harlot is one body?** [as if in Satanic marriage] **for, The twain, saith he** [Gen. 2: 24; Matt. 19: 5; Eph. 5: 31], **shall become one flesh. 17 But he that is joined unto the Lord is one spirit.** [Having closest spiritual union with Christ—Gal. 2: 20; 3: 27; Col. 3: 17.] **18 Flee fornication.** [As Joseph did—Gen. 39: 12.] **Every sin that a man doeth is without the body; but he that committeth fornication sinneth against his own body.** [Paul notes the mutual adaptation or correlation between the belly and food, but asserts that this correlation is transient, and will be demolished by death. A *subservient* correlation also exists between husband and wife, for they twain become one flesh, and the innocency of their union does not interfere with the relation of either to God, which is the body's *supreme* correlation. But there is no lawful correlation between the body of the Christian and that of the harlot, and such a correlation can not be subservient to the body's supreme correlation, but is repugnant to it. The correlation between the stomach and food is transient, ending at death; but that between the body and the Lord is made eternal by the resurrection. Now, other sins, even drunkenness and gluttony, are sins *without* the body; *i. e.*, sins against those parts of the body that shall not inhere to it in the future state (Rev. 7: 16), and hence do not strike directly at that future state; but fornication joins the whole body in sinful union to a body of death, so that it becomes one flesh with the condemned harlot, thereby wholly severing itself from the mystical body of life in Christ, and thus it does strike directly at the body's future state. **19 Or know ye not that your body is a temple of the Holy Spirit which is in you, which ye have from God?** [as the whole church is a temple (ch. 3: 16; Rom. 14: 8), so also the body of each individual Christian is likewise a temple] **and ye are not your own; 20 for ye were bought with a price** [sold to sin (1 Kings 21: 20; Rom. 7: 14), we have been redeemed by the blood of Christ—Acts 20: 28; Rom. 6: 16-22; Heb. 9: 12; 1 Pet. 1: 18, 19; Rev. 5: 9]: **glorify God therefore in your body.** [Since our bodies belong to God, they should be used to glorify him. The whole passage confutes the slander of those materialists who contend that Christianity depreciates the body.]

III.

RESPONSE AS TO MARRIAGE.

7: 1-40.

1 Now concerning the things whereof ye wrote [Hitherto Paul has written concerning things which he learned by common report; he now begins to reply to questions which they had asked him in their letter. As we come to the several answers we will state the probable form of the question, as an aid to interpretation. All of the apostle's answers, however, have reference to then existing conditions, which were very stringent and threatening. His advice is therefore to be wisely and conscientiously applied by modern Christians after weighing differences between present conditions and those which then existed. First question: *Is marriage to be desired or avoided* *by Christians?* Paul answers]: **It is good** [advisable, proper] **for a man not to touch** [marry] **a woman. 2 But, because of fornications, let each man have his own wife, and let each woman have her own husband.** [Paul does not discourage marriage, much less forbid it (1 Tim. 4: 3; Heb. 13: 4). Moreover, while he begins by counseling the Corinthians to abstain from it under their present conditions (verse 26), he tempers and practically countermands his counsel because of the prevalent licentiousness in Corinth, against which matrimony, being man's normal state, was a great safeguard.] **3 Let the husband render unto the wife her due: and likewise also the wife unto the husband. 4 The wife hath not power over her own body, but the husband: and likewise also the husband hath not power over his own body, but the wife. 5 Defraud** [deprive] **ye not one the other, except it be by consent for a season, that ye may give yourselves unto prayer, and may be together again, that Satan tempt you not because of your incontinency. 6 But this I say by way of concession, not of commandment.** [That his readers may understand his counsel, Paul discusses the marriage state, and shows that the reciprocal rights of the parties thereto forbid abstinence to either husband or wife, save in cases where one wishes to devote a season to prayer; but even here the abstinence must be by mutual consent, and the apostle does not enjoin it, but merely concedes or permits it at such times, because the higher duty of prayer may for a season suspend conjugal duty. But here again caution must be observed, lest too prolonged abstinence might work temptation to either party, especially the prayerless one.] **7 Yet I would that all men were even as I myself. Howbeit each man hath his own gift from God, one after this manner, and another after that. 8 But I say to the unmarried and to widows, It is good for them if they abide even as I. 9 But if they have not continency, let them marry: for it is better to marry than to burn.** [In contrast with the enforced indulgence of matrimony, Paul sets up his own life of abstinence as preferable, but only to such as have with him a gift of absolute self-control. But all have not this gift, for God's gifts are infinitely various. He therefore advises the unmarried who have the gift of self-control to remain unmarried, but those lacking it should avoid unlawful lusts by marriage. In short, then, the single state is preferable in troublous times to such as have Paul's continence. Second question: Is marriage to be dissolved when one party believes, and the other does not? It is likely that this question was raised by the Judaizers, for while the original law given by Moses only forbade marriage with the seven Canaanitish nations (Deut. 7: 1-3), yet the prophets and rulers so interpreted the law as to make it include Egyptians and Edomites (1 Kings 11: 1, 2; Ez. 9: 1, 2), and at last it came to be understood that Jews were forbidden to marry outside their own nation (Josephus Ant. VIII. 7: 5; XI. 5: 4; XI. 7: 2; XI. 8: 2; XII. 4: 6), and the children of such marriages were regarded as illegitimate—Ez. 10: 3.] **10 But unto the married I give charge,** *yea* **not I, but the Lord** [by his own lips—Matt. 5: 31, 32; 19: 3-12; Mark 10: 12], **That the wife depart not from her husband 11 (but should she depart, let her remain unmarried, or else be reconciled to her husband); and that the husband leave not his wife. 12 But to the rest** [the further application of the law or principle] **say I** [as an inspired apostle], **not the Lord** [with his own lips]: **If any brother hath an unbelieving wife, and she is content to dwell with him, let him not leave her. 13 And the woman that hath an unbelieving husband, and he is content to dwell with her, let her not leave her husband. 14 For the unbelieving husband is sanctified in the wife** [The word "sanctified" is here used in the Jewish sense of being not *unclean*, and therefore not to be touched], **and the unbelieving wife is sanctified in the brother** [her husband]: **else were your children unclean; but now are they holy.** [Holy is contrasted with *unclean*, and means the same as "sanctified."] **15 Yet if the unbelieving departeth, let him depart: the brother or the** sister is not under bondage in such *cases*: but God hath called us in peace. 16 For how knowest thou, O wife, whether thou shalt save thy husband? or how knowest thou, O husband, whether thou shalt save thy wife? 17 Only, as the Lord hath distributed to each man, as God hath called each, so let him walk. And so ordain I in all the churches. [Paul first answers generally that under no conditions are the husband and wife to separate (the single exception (Matt. 19: 9) not being given, because not a point in controversy). This law, however, rests not on Paul's authority alone (which some of the Judaizers might question), but on that of the Lord himself, who plainly propounded it, repealing the ordinances of Moses which were contrary to it (see "Fourfold Gospel," p. 242). As an inspired apostle, Paul applies this law to the case of Christians united in wedlock with unbelievers, and declares that such should not separate on account of their faith; for the law of Christ so reverses that of Moses that the Christian sanctifies or removes the uncleanness of the unbelieving partner, and of the children. But such unequal marriages are not favored by God (2 Cor. 6: 14), and therefore if the unbeliever be so intolerant as to refuse to live with a converted partner, then the partner is not under bondage to the unbeliever. But God calls the believer to a life of peace which forbids any such discordant acts as tend to induce or drive the unbeliever to dissolve the marriage, for by the exercise of Christian gentleness and forbearance the believer may convert and save the unbeliever (1 Pet. 3: 1, 2). As a summary rule for all things of a smaller nature, the apostle says that each man must rest content to walk in the lot which God has apportioned to him, not making his new religion an excuse for unwarranted changes. As this rule applied to all churches, it worked no especial hardship to the Corinthians.] **18 Was any man called** [converted] **being circumcised? let him not become uncircumcised.** [1 Macc. 1: 15.] **Hath any been called in uncircumcision? let him not be circumcised. 19 Circumcision is nothing, and uncircumcision is nothing; but the keeping of the commandments of God. [is, in this connection, everything.] 20 Let each man abide in that calling [trade or social condition] wherein he was called. 21 Wast thou called being a bondservant? care not for it: nay, even if ["nay, even if" should read "but if"] thou canst become free, use it [*i. e.*, freedom] rather. 22 For he that was called in the Lord being a bondservant, is the Lord's freedman: likewise he that was called being free, is Christ's bondservant. 23 Ye were bought with a price; become not bondservants of men. 24 Brethren, let each man, wherein he was called, therein abide with God. [*i. e.*, abide with God in the calling wherein he was called. Taking up the rule of verse 17, Paul shows by way of illustration its application to other matters. Christianity does not require that Jews or Greeks change their nationality, for nationality has nought to do with salvation, which rests wholly on obedience to the law of Christ. Again, Christianity does not demand that a man change his vocation or calling, if honest and clean (comp. Luke 3: 12-14). Taking up the extreme case of slavery, Paul counsels that a change is not to be feverishly sought. If, however, freedom can be obtained, it is to be preferred, and where master and slave are both Christians it should be *bestowed*, for the slave is exalted to be Christ's freedman (Luke 1: 52), and the master is humbled in Christ to be a servant (Matt. 20: 25-28). Acting under these principles, Paul asked Philemon to free Onesimus. The price which the Lord paid for his own when he gave his precious blood as their ransom, so far exceeds that paid for them as slaves that it nullifies slavery. Third question: *Is celibacy or virginity preferable to marriage?* Paul answers:] 25 Now concerning virgins I have no commandment of the Lord: but I give my judgment, as one that hath obtained mercy of the Lord to be trustworthy. 26 I think therefore that this is good by reason of the distress that is upon us, *namely*, that it is good for a man to be as he is. 27 Art thou bound unto a wife? seek not to be loosed. Art thou loosed from a wife? seek not a wife. 28 But shouldest thou marry, thou hast not sinned; and if a virgin marry, she hath not sinned. Yet such shall have tribulation, in the flesh: and I would spare you. [the pains and sufferings which will arise by reason of your marriage ties.] 29 But this I say, brethren, the time is shortened, that henceforth both those that have wives may be as though they had none; 30 and those that weep, as though they wept not; and those that rejoice, as though they rejoiced not; and those that buy, as though they possessed not; 31 and those that use the world, as not using it to the full: for the fashion of this world passeth away. [At the time of Paul's writing, a great social convulsion was expected. The persecutions under Nero and his successors, and the destruction of Jerusalem, were sufficient of themselves to form the burden of many an awe-inspiring prophecy, and such were no doubt plentiful. Because of the nearness of the impending crisis Paul counsels each one to stay as he is, and refrain from entangling himself with new ties and obligations; for the trials of the hour would require stoical fortitude of every disciple. He gives this advice and that which follows simply as a Christian, and not as an inspired apostle.] 32 But I would have you to be free from cares. He that is unmarried is careful for the things of the Lord, how he may please the Lord: 33 but he that is married is careful for the things of the world, how he may please his wife, 34 and is divided. *So* also the woman that is unmarried and the virgin is careful for the things of the Lord, that she may be holy both in body and in spirit: but she that is married is careful for the things of the world, how she may please her husband. 35 And this I say for your own profit; not that I may cast a snare upon you, but for that which is seemly, and that ye may attend upon the Lord without distraction. [The less the Christian is entangled with social ties, the freer he is to perform the Lord's service. Those who have no desire to marry have larger liberty to do church work if they remain single.

But the apostle warns us not to turn his counsel into a snare by construing it as a prohibition of marriage. Paul saw no peculiar holiness in celibacy, for with him marriage was holy (1 Cor. 11: 13; Eph. 5: 25-32; comp. Rev. 4: 4; 21: 2). He merely states that unmarried people are less encumbered.] **36 But if any man thinketh that he behaveth himself unseemly toward his virgin *daughter*, if she be past the flower of her age, and if need so requireth, let him do what he will; he sinneth not; let them** [such daughters] **marry. 37 But he that standeth stedfast in his heart, having no necessity, but hath power as touching his own will, and hath determined this in his own heart, to keep his own virgin *daughter*, shall do well. 38 So then both he that giveth his own virgin *daughter* in marriage doeth well; and he that giveth her not in marriage shall do better.** [Marriages in the East were then, as now, arranged by the parents. If a parent saw fit to marry his daughter he had a perfect right to do so and was guilty of no sin, but if he heeded the apostle's warning as to the coming trials and kept his daughter free from alliances he acted more wisely. Fourth question: *Should widows remarry?* is answered thus:] **39 A wife is bound for so long time as her husband liveth; but if the husband be dead, she is free to be married to whom she will; only in the Lord.** [*i. e*, to a Christian.] **40 But she is happier if she abide as she is, after my judgment: and I think that I also have the spirit of God.**

IV.

FOURTH RESPONSE, CONCERNING IDOLATROUS MEAT.

8: 1-13.

[The question which Paul here answers may be stated thus: "*Have not Christians perfect liberty to eat meat that has been sacrificed to idols?*" To this question the Corinthians seem to have added a line or two of argument, that they might obtain an affirmative answer, as appears by the apostle's reply.] **1 Now concerning things sacrificed to idols: We know** [ye say] **that we all have knowledge. Knowledge** [I reply] **puffeth up, but love edifieth.** [literally, buildeth up.] **2 If any man thinketh that he knoweth anything, he knoweth not yet as he ought to know** [for humility precedes true knowledge]; **3 but if any man loveth God, the same** [*i. e.*, God] **is known by him.** [*i. e.*, the lover of God (1 John 4: 7). Before replying to the question, Paul deals with the argument which accompanied it, pointing out the fact that their boasted knowledge was confessedly without love, and being such it was puffing instead of building them up. But the man who loves God, knows God; and in the richness and fullness of that knowledge is able to deal with such questions as that which they ask. He now resumes answering their question.] **4 Concerning therefore the eating of things sacrificed to idols, we know that no idol is *anything* in the world** [Isa. 44: 9-20], **and that there is no God but one. 5 For though there be that are called gods, whether in heaven** [as celestial bodies, or as myths] **or on earth** [as idols]; **as there are gods many** [the Greek cities had pantheons and temples filled with them], **and lords many** [the Roman emperors, and even lesser dignitaries, demanded that divine honors be paid them]; **6 yet to us there is one God, the Father** [contradicting the many], **of whom are all things** [whose creatorship undeifies all other beings, reducing them to mere creatures], **and we unto him** [created as his peculiar treasure and possession, and hence exalted far above the idols which we once worshiped]; **and one Lord** [also contradicting the many], **Jesus Christ, through whom are all things** [as the Father's creative executive—John 1: 3; Heb. 1: 2], **and we through him.** [regenerated and reconciled to the Father.] **7 Howbeit there is not in all men that knowledge** [the apostle limits and corrects their statement found in verse 1]: **but some, being used until now** [being but recently converted from paganism] **to the idol, eat as** *of* **a thing sacrificed to an idol; and their conscience being weak is defiled. 8 But food will not commend us to God: neither, if we eat not, are we the worse; nor, if we eat, are we the better.** [There is no inherent virtue either in eating or fasting.] **9 But take heed lest by any means this liberty of yours become a stumblingblock to the weak. 10 For if a man see thee who hast knowledge sitting at meat in an idol's temple** [Literally, *idoleum,* or idol-house; a term coined by the Jews to avoid desecrating the word "temple" by applying it to seats of idolatry. The idol temples were frequently used as banqueting-houses; but for a Christian to feast in such a place was a reckless abuse of liberty], **will not his conscience, if he is weak, be emboldened** [literally, built up, as at verse 1—built up in evil, not in Christ] **to eat things sacrificed to idols?** [will he not eat as a worshiper, and not sinless as you do?] **11 For through thy knowledge he that is weak perisheth, the brother for whose sake Christ died.** [Paul here presents a new appeal, of unapproachable pathos and power. The world had never before heard any such reason why mercy should be shown to the weak.] **12 And thus, sinning against the brethren, and wounding their conscience when it is weak, ye sin against Christ.** [who suffers with the very least of his servants (Matt. 18: 6; 25: 40, 45). Corinth was full of temples, and sacrifices were daily and abundant. Part of the meat of these sacrifices went to the priests, part was burnt on the altar, and part was returned to the worshiper.

The priests' and the worshiper's parts were frequently sold to the butchers, who in turn vended the same in the public markets. Such sacrificial meat was so plentiful, and was so indistinguishably mingled with other meats, that a Christian could hardly avoid using it unless he refrained from meat altogether. He could not attend any of the public banquets, nor dine with his pagan friends or relatives, without being almost sure to eat such meat. The Jews illustrated the difficulty, for wherever they lived they required a butcher of their own who certified the meat which he sold by affixing to it a leaden seal, on which was engraved the word *kashar*— "lawful." Under such circumstances the strong-minded made bold to eat such sacrificial meat, contending that the idol, being a nonentity, could in no way contaminate it. But there were others having less knowledge, and weaker consciences, who could not shake off the power of old habits, thoughts and associations, and who therefore could not free themselves from their former reverence for the idol, but looked upon it as really representing *something*—a false something, but still a reality. To such the sacrificial meat was part of a real sacrifice, and was contaminating. In answering, therefore, Paul states the correctness of the position that the idol, being nothing, does not contaminate meat sacrificed to it, and urges that the Christian's knowledge of God and relationship to him preclude all thought of reality in idols. But, nevertheless, because it is a cruel sin against Christ to wound those already weak in conscience, he pleads that the strong use forbearance, not privilege; love, not knowledge, lest they make the death of Christ of none effect as to such weaklings. The principle may be applied to many modern amusements and indulgences which the strong regard as harmless, but which they should rejoice to sacrifice rather than endanger weaker lives.] **13 Wherefore, if meat causeth my brother to stumble, I will eat no flesh for evermore, that I cause not my brother to stumble.** [To the Corinthians Paul says "take heed" (v. 9); but for himself he proposes a sublime consecration and perpetual self-sacrifice. The apostle would not make the weak brother a tyrant, as he is often disposed to become. He clearly defines him as being wrong, but pleads that his errors may be humored for mercy's sake.]

V.

FIFTH RESPONSE, AS TO HIS APOSTOLICITY

9: 1-27

[False or factional teachers coming to Corinth expected to be supported by the church according to the usual custom, but were hampered by the example of Paul, who had taken nothing for his services. To justify themselves and to discredit Paul, some of them appear to have gone so far as to deny Paul's appointment as an apostle, and to use his failure to demand wages as an evidence of their assertion. They argued that he knew he was not an apostle, and so forbore through shame to ask an apostle's pay. To settle this controversy, the Corinthians asked some such question as this: "Explain why, being an apostle, you did not take the wages due you as such." Paul begins his answer with four questions which show both surprise and indignation.] **1 Am I not free?** [All free men were entitled to wages for work done. Only slaves worked without compensation. See verse 19.] **Am I not an apostle?** [and so more entitled to wages than an ordinary, less approved Christian teacher.] **Have I not seen Jesus our Lord?** [Apostles were to be witnesses of Jesus' resurrection (Acts 1: 22; 2: 32; 10: 4), and so it was necessary that they should have seen the risen Christ. But Paul had seen more; on the way to Damascus, not only the risen, but the glorified, Christ had appeared to him. This was Paul's first proof of apostleship.] **Are not ye my work in the Lord?** [The presence of a church in Corinth, having in it Christians converted by Paul and living in the Lord, was the second proof of his apostleship. Such work could not be done by impostors—Matt. 7: 15-20.] **2 If to others I am not an apos-**

AS TO HIS APOSTOLICITY 89

tle, yet at least I am to you; for the seal of mine apostleship are ye in the Lord. [An *argumentum ad hominem*. Whatever Paul might be in the estimation of Judaizers and enemies, he must still be held as an apostle by those who owed their spiritual life to him, for if he were no apostle, they were no Christians, and *vice versa*. As the seal vouched for the genuineness and validity of the document to which it was attached, so these Corinthian converts by their existence vouched for Paul's apostleship.] **3 My defence to them that examine me is this.** [This verse refers to what precedes it. It means that when called to defend his apostleship, Paul would point to the presence of a church of his established in Corinth as his answer. A similar answer had satisfied the other apostles (Gal. 2: 6-10.) Thus having proved his apostleship, Paul proceeds to discuss the rights and privileges appurtenant to it.] **4 Have we no right to eat and to drink?** [are we not entitled to be fed by the church?] **5 Have we no right to lead about** [in our constant journeyings] **a wife that is a believer** [*i. e.*, a lawful wife; it was unlawful to marry an unbeliever—2 Cor. 6: 14-16], **even as the rest of the apostles** [this passage creates a fair presumption that at least the majority of the apostles were married], **and the brethren of the Lord** [For their names see Matt. 13: 55. For their relation to Jesus, see "Fourfold Gospel," pp. 119, 224-226], **and Cephas?** [This apostle was married (Matt. 8: 14); yet Catholics claim him as the first pope. If all these apostles were allowed maintenance for themselves and their wives, Paul had equal right to demand that the church support his wife had he chosen to marry.] **6 Or I only and Barnabas** [Though not one of the twelve, he is called an apostle (Acts 14: 14), for he was a messenger or apostle of the Holy Spirit, and of the church at Antioch (Acts 13: 2,) and was associated with Paul (Gal. 2: 9). His name was illustrious enough at Corinth to give countenance to Paul's course. If Barnabas and Paul wrought out their self-support to be nobly independent, did their voluntary sacrifice of rights abolish those rights, or prove that they never existed? This late reference to Barnabas is interesting, for it shows that he was still at work and was still loved of Paul despite their disagreement concerning John Mark. Having thus proved his right to maintenance by the *example* of other church leaders, Paul now goes on to give an argument in six heads showing that the practice of these leaders was wholly lawful and proper. First argument: Wages for service is the rule in all employment; in proof of this, three instances are cited, the soldier, the vine-dresser, the shepherd], **have we not a right to forbear working? 7 What soldier ever serveth at his own charges? who planteth a vineyard, and eateth not the fruit thereof? or who feedeth a flock, and eateth not of the milk of the flock?** [In the East, vine-dressers and shepherds are still thus paid in kind. Work without wages would foster rascality, and it is therefore an unhealthy principle to use in church matters. Second argument: The law of Moses allowed wages for work.] **8 Do I speak these things after the manner of men? or saith not the law also the same?** [Paul asks these two questions to show that while he has appealed to human authority, he has also divine authority for the principle which he asserts.] **9 For it is written in the law of Moses** [Deut. 25: 4], **Thou shalt not muzzle the ox when he treadeth out the corn.** [Grain in the East has never been threshed by machinery. Though flails are used, it is usually threshed out by oxen. These are driven over it to tramp out the grain, and they sometimes draw a small sled or threshing instrument after them. The law forbade the muzzling of an ox thus employed, and in the East this law is still obeyed.] **Is it for the oxen that God careth, 10 or saith he it assuredly for our sake? Yea, for our sake it was written: because he that ploweth ought to plow in hope, and he that thresheth,** *to thresh* **in hope of partaking.** [Those fond of carping and caviling have attempted to use this passage to prove that Paul asserts that God does not care for animals. Such a view is abundantly contradicted by Scripture (Job 38: 41; Ps. 147: 9; Matt. 6: 26; Luke 12: 24). Paul's meaning is clear. In giving the law, God's *proximate* design was to care for oxen, but his *ultimate* design was to enforce the principle that labor should not go unrewarded; that each workman might discharge his task in cheerful expectation that he would receive wages for his employment. Paul asserts that God does not legislate for oxen and forget men. It is an argument *a minori ad magus*, such as Christ himself employed (Matt. 6: 26-30.) Third argument: The law of exchange demands an equivalent for value received.] **11 If we sowed unto you spiritual things, is it a great matter if we shall reap your carnal things?** [What was earthly support in comparison with the riches of the gospel? If Paul had demanded his full carnal recompense, it would have been a meager compensation for blessings and benefits which can never be weighed in dollars and cents. Fourth argument: The concessions which you have made in supporting others having inferior claims debar you from thus denying apostolic claims.] **12 If others partake of *this* right over you, do not we yet more? Nevertheless we did not use this right; but we bear all things, that we may cause no hindrance to the gospel of Christ.** [Since Paul had left Corinth, other teachers had been supported by the church, and this stopped them from denying Paul's right to support. The apostle had not used this right, for to do so would have hindered him in planting the church. It would retard the progress of any movement to demand salaries under it before demonstrating that it was either beneficent or necessary. To have demanded maintenance subsequently would have given Paul's enemies a chance to impugn his motives, and say that he labored for earthly gain. Fifth argument: Priests, whose office, like the apostolic, is purely sacred, are universally maintained by sharing in the sacrifices which they offer.] **13 Know ye not that they that minister about sacred things eat *of* the things of the temple** [the offerings, etc.], ***and* they that wait upon the altar have their portion with the altar?** [Num. 18: 8-13; Deut. 8: 1. Sixth argument: Christ himself ordained that ministers should be supported by those whom they serve.] **14 Even so did the Lord ordain that they** that proclaim the gospel should live of the gospel. [Matt. 10: 10; Luke 10: 7. This precept was all which Paul needed to urge. He no doubt elaborated this argument that the Corinthians might be fully convinced that he was perfectly aware of his rights at the time when he waived them. The apostle next sets forth more fully why he preferred to support himself rather than receive compensation from the churches.] **15 But I have used none of these things** [*i. e.*, these rights]**: and I write not these things that it may be so done in my case** [Paul had a right to receive wages for his labor, and this right was guaranteed both by the customs of the people and the law of Moses; he also had a right to some recompense as an equivalent for the blessings which he bestowed. Moreover, he had a right to receive as fair treatment as that bestowed upon others. Again, he had a right as a man engaged in sacred affairs to be paid by those who enjoyed his services, and lastly as a minister of Christ, the law of Christ, demanded that he be supported. Paul had urged none of these rights, nor did he now assert them that he might shame the Corinthians for their neglect or prepare them to change their conduct toward him when he visited them as he intended]**; for** *it were* **good for me rather to die, than that any man should make my glorying void.** [So far from desiring pay from the Corinthians, he preferred to die rather than receive it, for to do so would deprive him of the glory and joy of preaching the gospel without earthly reward. By denying himself wages, Paul obtained free access to all men, and could found new churches. He gloried in the salvation of souls and in the honoring of Christ.] **16 For if I preach the gospel, I have nothing to glory of; for necessity is laid upon me; for woe is unto me, if I preach not the gospel. 17 For if I do this of mine own will, I have a reward: but if not of mine own will, I have a stewardship intrusted to me.** [He was commanded to preach the gospel. He could not glory therefore in doing it, for he did not do it of his own free will or choice (however cheerfully and willingly he might do it), but because it was a stewardship which he was

AS TO HIS APOSTOLICITY

obliged to discharge (Luke 17: 10). Had he been free to preach the gospel or not, he might have gloried in preaching it. But as it was, he had to seek glory elsewhere.] **18 What then is my reward? That, when I preach the gospel, I may make the gospel without charge, so as not to use to the full my right in the gospel.** [He found his reward in the happiness of preaching the gospel without charge, and in the feeling that as a steward he had not used his privileges to the full, and so was far from abusing them. Paul so loved those whom Christ called that he counted it a privilege to be permitted to serve them gratuitously. But such a course is not without danger to the church—2 Cor. 12: 13.] **19 For though I was free from all** *men* [and therefore had a right to demand wages of them and ignore their prejudices], **I brought myself under bondage to all, that I might gain the more.** [Here was yet another joy which he found in preaching a free gospel. His spirit of self-sacrifice won the confidence of the people, and enabled him to make a larger number of converts. Though entitled to wages as a free man he preferred to work as a slave for nothing, accounting the additional disciples which he thus made as a more acceptable hire than his maintenance. Moreover, after the manner of a slave, he had adjusted himself to the prejudices and idiosyncrasies of each class which he served as far as he innocently could; that, by having a larger measure of their confidence and good-will, he might be able to win a larger number to Christ. He now describes this part of his service.] **20 And to the Jews I became as a Jew** [not a Jew, but *like* one], **that I might gain Jews** [Paul observed the Jewish distinction as to meat (ch. 8: 13); and performed their rites as to vows (Acts 21: 26); and honored their feasts (Acts 20: 16); and classed himself among their Pharisees (Acts 23: 6); and even had circumcision administered (Acts 12: 3), where it did not interfere with the liberty of Gentiles (Gal. 2: 3-5). All these were innocent concessions to and harmless compliances with the law. Though Paul was under no obligation to conform his conduct to the prejudices of others, he

waived his own predeliction in all matters that were indifferent;
but his unbending, unyielding loyalty in all matters of principle
was so well known that he does not deem it necessary to state
that he never surrendered or sacrificed a single truth or right
for any cause]; **to them that are under the law** [This
expression includes proselytes as well as Jews. To these also
Paul made harmless concessions], **as under the law, not
being myself under the law, that I might gain them
that are under the law; 21 to them that are without
law** [pagans and Gentiles—Rom. 2: 12], **as without law**
[Rom. 6: 14. He did not seek to enforce the laws of Moses
among the Gentiles, as did the Jews, and he refrained from
insulting heathens in their beliefs (Acts 19: 37), and dealt
gently with their prejudices—Acts 17: 30], **not being without law to God** [for the Gentiles themselves were not
wholly without such law—Rom. 2: 14, 15], **but under law
to Christ** [Paul did not forget his obligations to the moral
law, nor his duty to the will of Christ. Though behaving himself as a Jew in Jerusalem in things indifferent, he rebuked
Peter openly for playing the Jew in Antioch in matters of
principle (Gal. 2: 11-21). Peter knew better—Acts 15: 10],
**that I might gain them that are without law. 22 To
the weak I became weak, that I might gain the weak**
[The preceding chapter is the best comment on this passage.
Paul was uniformly self-sacrificing and patient with those who
were overscrupulous]: **I am become all things to all men,
that I may by all means save some.** [With untiring
zeal for the salvation of souls, Paul accommodated himself to all
the shapes and forms of character which he met, if he could
do so without sin—ch. 10: 33; 2 Tim. 2: 10.] **23 And I do
all things for the gospel's sake, that I may be a joint
partaker thereof.** [He made every sacrifice for the success
of the gospel, that he might share with other successful apostles and evangelists in its triumphs and blessings (John 4: 36).
He recommends to others a like spirit of abstinence and sacrifice, and to illustrate the necessity and utility of such a course he
draws some comparisons between those who run the Christian

AS TO HIS APOSTOLICITY

race, and the athletes who competed for the prizes in the Grecian games. The Corinthians were familiar with the ways and customs of these athletes, for one of the great racecourses lay in the immediate vicinity of Corinth, and at this time it was the most noted in Greece, having even surpassed the Olympic in its popularity. It was held triennially. Parts of its stadium are still seen as one goes from Corinth to Athens.] **24 Know ye not that they that run in a race run all, but one receiveth the prize?** [Phil. 3: 12-14.] **Even so run; that ye may attain.** [In the Greek contests there was but one prize for each group of contestants, and that was awarded to the winner. But the Christian race is not competitive: each may win a prize, but he does so by contending with his own sinful nature. He must run faithfully, earnestly and continuously if he would win in the race against his lower self.] **25 And every man that striveth in the games exerciseth self-control in all things.** [As Paul denied himself that the gospel might not be hindered, so each athlete, whether he intended to run, wrestle or fight, pursued a course of training and abstinence that was painful, protracted and severe, in order that no fatty tissues or depleted muscles might hinder him in his struggle for victory.] **Now they *do it* to receive a corruptible crown; but we an incorruptible.** For this worthless, withering symbol of victory, men made measureless sacrifice. For the incomparably better and fadeless crown of eternal life, how cheerfully Christians should deny and discipline themselves— 1 Pet. 5: 4.] **26 I therefore** [realizing the value of that for which I contend] **so run, as not uncertainly** [without doubt or hesitation. Paul felt sure of the course which led to the goal, and certain as to the reward which he would attain when the race was over—2 Tim. 1: 12; 4: 8]; **so fight I, as not beating the air** [The allusion here is to the boxer who, in blind confusion, strikes wide of the mark, and misses his antagonist. For an instance of vain effort similarly expressed, see ch. 14: 9; Virgil's Æneid 5: 446]: **27 but I buffet my body, and bring it into bondage** [The body, being, as it is in part, the seat and organ of sin, has become the Biblical term to express our whole sinful nature (Rom. 8: 13). Paul found in this old sinful man with its corrupt affections an ever-present antagonist. He ran no uncertain race with his body, realizing that God would give him the victory if he ran his best. He fought no uncertain fight with it, but so smote it as to bring it into subjection. By smiting he does not mean literal flagellation, self-torture or even fasting, but he means that he subdues his nature by denying its lusts (Col. 3: 5), and that he employed his body in noble labor, with all self-denial and self-sacrifice, for the good of others—2 Cor. 6: 4, 5 ; 10: 23-33]: **lest by any means, after that I have preached to others, I myself should be rejected.** [The word translated "preached" means literally to "proclaim as a herald." It is the word used in the New Testament to describe the preaching of the gospel, and so the reader is at liberty to follow the English version, and drop the metaphor of which Paul has been making use. If he does this, then Paul tells him literally that even he had fears that he might fall from grace, and therefore daily worked out his own salvation with fear and trembling (Phil. 2: 12.) But if "preached" be translated "acted or proclaimed as herald," then Paul conveys to us the same thought metaphorically. It was the duty of the herald to move up and down the lists and proclaim aloud the laws of the contests, the names of the contestants, victors, etc. These laws said in brief that no slave, thief, or man of bad morals, would be admitted as a contestant. Thus construed, Paul expresses a fear lest having laid down the gospel terms of salvation to others, he himself should be rejected for having failed to comply with the very rules which his own mouth had proclaimed (Luke 19: 22; Rom. 2: 1-3. While it was not customary for heralds to be contestants, such a thing was not impossible, for the emperor Nero once played both parts. He was combatant, victor, and herald to proclaim his own triumphs. The metaphors of Paul, like the parables of Jesus, caused the scenes of daily life to suggest great spiritual truths to those who beheld them.

VI.

RENEWAL OF RESPONSE CONCERNING IDOLATROUS MEAT.

10: 1-11: 1.

[In chapter 8 Paul had answered the question of the Corinthians concerning idolatrous meat. In chapter 9 he answered their inquiries concerning his apostleship, and closed with a description of the self-denial which he exercised in order to secure his crown, and a statement that despite all his efforts there was a possibility of his becoming a castaway. Now, the necessity for self-control and the danger of apostasy were the two principal ideas involved in the discussion of eating idolatrous meat, and so the apostle's mind swings back to that subject, and he again treats of it, illustrating it by analogies drawn from the history of Israel.] **1 For I would not, brethren, have you ignorant** [see comment on 1 Thess. 4: 13], **that our fathers were all under the cloud, and all passed through the sea; 2 and were all baptized unto Moses in the cloud and in the sea** [Paul speaks of the fathers of the Jewish race as "our fathers," though addressing Gentiles. The patriarchs of Israel were the spiritual fathers of Gentile Christians (Gal. 3: 7, 8, 29). Moreover, the patriarchal and Mosaic dispensations were preparatory to Christianity, and so, in a certain sense, fathered it. The passage through the Red Sea by the Israelites was in many ways analogous to Christian baptism. 1. It stood at the beginning of a journey undertaken by a divine call, and which led from a life and kingdom of bondage to a land of promise, which should be a land of liberty and an everlasting possession. 2. Baptism is a burial (Rom. 6: 4). With a wall of water on each side and a cloud over them, the Israelites were buried from the sight of the Egyptians, or any others who stood upon the shores of the sea. Relying on the statement at Ex. 14: 19-21 that the cloud was between the Egyptians and the Israelites, and hence *behind* the Israelites part of the night, zealous paidobaptists have argued that at no part of the night were the Israelites under the cloud, their purpose being to avoid the idea of a burial. But in their zeal they have contradicted Paul, who says "under the cloud," "in the cloud," and who elsewhere speaks of baptism as a burial. Paul's language here implies that the children of Israel were between the walls of water while the cloud was still in front of them, and so they were under it and in it as it passed to their rear.   3. Baptism is a resurrection (Rom. 6: 5). "The two phrases, 'were under the cloud,' and 'passed through the sea,' seem to prefigure the double process of *submersion* and *emersion* in baptism" (*Canon Cook*). The baptism of the Red Sea was to Israel a death to Egypt, and a birth to a new covenant. 4. Baptism is the final seal of discipleship (Matt. 28: 19; Gal. 3: 28; chap. 1: 13). The passage of the Red Sea led Israel to fully accept Moses as their master and leader under God—Ex. 14: 31]; **3 and did all eat the same spiritual food; 4 and did all drink the same spiritual drink: for they drank of a spiritual rock that followed them: and the rock was Christ.** [As Israel had an experience answering to baptism, so it also enjoyed privileges similar to the two parts of the Lord's Supper; viz.: the manna (Ex. 16: 13-22), which lasted throughout the wilderness journey (Josh. 5: 12), and which answered to the loaf; and water from the rock, which was given at least twice (Ex. 17: 5-7; Num. 20: 7-13), and which answered to the wine. Some think that the manna and the water are called spiritual because they had a spiritual origin, being produced of God directly, and not by the ordinary means of nature; and others think that they are thus described because they were typical of Christ. But neither of these views is suited to the context, for Paul is here speaking of *benefits* enjoyed by the children of Israel which ministered to their spiritual strength, and which should have kept them from falling. But miraculous food is, of itself, no more strengthening to the spirit than ordinary food (John 6: 26, 27, 49); and a type confers no benefit upon those who do not understand it and are not conscious of it. The true idea is that the manna and the water were so miraculously and providentially supplied that the people could scarcely fail to see the presence and the goodness of God in them, and hence they were spiritual food and drink to the people because they would waken such thoughts, thanksgivings and aspirations as would give spiritual strength. Paul does not assert that the literal rock or the literal water followed the children of Israel on their journey, and hence there is no occasion for saying, as do Alford and others, that Paul even referred to, much less accepted, Jewish fables and traditions to that effect. The fact that water was twice supplied by Christ at different periods would be sufficient to suggest his continual presence (Ex. 33: 14), and thus continually revive their thirsty souls. The Catholics assert that there are seven sacraments, but Paul knew only two ordinances. "The whole passage," says Alford, "is a standing testimony, incidentally, but *most providentially*, given by the great apostle to the *importance* of the *Christian sacraments, as necessary to membership* of Christ, and *not mere signs or remembrances:* and an inspired protest against those who, whether as individuals or sects, would lower their dignity, or deny their necessity." But Paul also guards against that other extreme which trusts to mere ordinances for salvation.] **5 Howbeit with most of them God was not well pleased: for they were overthrown** [literally, strewn in heaps] **in the wilderness.** [In verse 24 of the preceding chapter Paul enforces the lesson of self-control by showing that though all run, yet but one receives the prize. This law, which the Greeks applied to a mere handful of racers, was applied of God with like rigor and stringency to the millions of Israel, a fact which Paul emphasizes by the repeated use of the word "all." Though *all* were under the cloud and *all* passed through the sea and *all* were baptized and *all* ate and drank of spiritual provision, yet only two, Caleb and Joshua, entered the promised land (Deut. 1: 34-38; Num. 26: 64, 65). What was true of racers and true of Israel may also be true of Christians if they fail to exercise self-control.] **6 Now these things were our examples, to the intent we should not lust after evil things, as they also lusted.** [Having shown that the Israelites lost their inheritance despite the fact that they were prepared, sustained and strengthened by the same Christ and practically the same ordinances enjoyed by the Christian, Paul proceeds to show their perfectness as examples to the Corinthians in that they fell by the five sins, viz.: lust, idolatry, fornication, tempting Christ, murmuring, which were the besetting sins of the Corinthians—and of all succeeding generations. In the case of Israel the punishment was directly and visibly connected with the sin, that their history might be used to instruct future generations; for in this life punishment is not, as a rule, summarily and immediately meted out to sinners. In fact, if we judge by appearances only, we might sometimes even think that God rewarded crime and set a premium on sin. The Scripture records show that such appearances are deceptive, and that God's punishments are sure, though they may be long delayed. Israel lusted for what God withheld and murmured at what he provided (Num. 11: 4, 33, 34). As Israel looked back with regret on the flesh and the fish, the cucumbers, melons, leeks, onions and garlic which they had left behind in Egypt, so the Corinthians were disposed to go back into the old life and heap up to themselves philosophical teachers, attend idolatrous feasts, etc.] **7 Neither be ye idolaters, as were some of them; as it is written, The people sat down to eat and drink, and rose up to play.** [Israel worshiped the golden calf, Moloch, Remphan, Baal-peor, etc. The "playing" which Paul refers to (Ex. 32: 3-6, 19, 25) was familiar to the Corinthians, who had indulged in such licentious sportfulness in the worship of Bacchus and Venus. Dancing was the common accompaniment of idolatry (Horace 2: 12-19). Eating at the feast of idols was the very privilege for which the Corinthians were contending.] **8 Neither let us commit fornication, as some of them committed, and fell in one day three and twenty thousand.** [Num. 25: 1-9. While Paul gives the number as twenty-three thousand, Moses gives it as twenty-four. Alford and Kling think the discrepancy is due to a failure in Paul's memory, but why should the Spirit of God let him thus forget? Grotius says that a thousand were slain by Phinehas and his followers, and the rest were destroyed by the plague. Kitto varies this a little by saying that Paul gives the number that fell on one day, as his words show, while Moses gives the full number that perished on both days. But Bengel's solution is a sufficient one. The Hebrews habitually dealt in round numbers, so that a number between twenty-three and twenty-four thousand could be correctly stated by either figure. Moses gave the maximum and Paul the minimum. The sin mentioned was not only an ordinary accompaniment of idolatry, but often a consecrated part of it, as in the rites of Baal-peor among the Moabites and those of Venus among the Corinthians. Sins are gregarious.] **9 Neither let us make trial of the Lord, as some of them made trial, and perished by the serpents.** [Num. 21: 4-6. Compare John 3: 14, 15. To "tempt" here means to try beyond all patience or endurance. Israel tempted God in the case referred to, by its spirit of unbelieving discontent. Compare also Ex. 17: 2-7; Num. 14: 22. As Israel became discontented under the hardships of the wilderness, so the Corinthians were liable to a like discontent because of the severe persecutions brought upon them by ungodly men. Chrysostom, Theodoret and Œcuminius think that Paul warns the Corinthians against tempting God by asking for signs. But this was not the besetting sin of the Greeks (ch. 1: 22), nor is there any evidence that the Christians at Corinth were at all addicted to this sin. Besides, it is at variance with the analogy which Paul has cited. As a matter of fact, men tempt God by putting his fidelity, patience or power to unnecessary tests—Matt. 4: 7; Acts 5: 9; Heb. 3: 9.] **10 Neither murmur ye, as some of them murmured, and perished by the destroyer.** [Num. 14: 2, 29; 16: 41-49. The Israelites murmured against God by rebelling against and rejecting his servants; and the Corinthians were at this time murmuring against Paul, the servant of Christ. They were also liable to complain of their separation from the pagan world, just as many to-day speak resentfully when the pulpit proclaims those Christian principles which are restrictive of worldly excesses. The angel of death is called the destroyer (Ex. 12: 23; 2 Sam. 24: 16). The Jews commonly called this angel Sammael. The "all" of grace and privilege, found in verses 1-4, stands in sad contrast to the "some of them" of deflection and apostasy found in verses 7-10. God showed mercy to all, but some disobeyed in one way and some in another until almost all had proved unworthy of his mercy.] **11 Now these things happened unto them by way of example; and they were written for our admonition, upon whom the ends of the ages are come.** [The facts of the past become examples for the present, because God rules by unchanging principles (Rom. 15: 4). The Christian dispensation is called "the ends of the ages" because it is the last and final dispensation (1 John 2: 18; Heb. 9: 26; Matt. 13: 38, 39; 1 Pet. 4: 7). The Christian is the heir of all the past, but none shall inherit after him.] **12 Wherefore let him that thinketh he standeth take heed lest he fall.** [The weaknesses of saints in former days, notwithstanding their privileges, should warn us of our own frailty lest we presume to dally with temptation, and so fall. This verse is a stumbling-block to those who hold the doctrine "once in grace, always in grace." Whedon aptly says of the Israelites: "If they never truly stood, they never fell; and if they fell, they once stood. If their fault and ruin was in actually *falling*, then their salvation would have been in actually standing—standing just as they were." Their history does not show the mere possibility of apostasy, but demonstrates its actual reality, and the sad prevalence of it. But the apostle, well aware that so weighty and forceful an argument would breed a spirit of hopelessness and despair in the breasts of the Corinthians, now sets himself to show that the temptations so fatal to Israel need not prove similarly disastrous to them if they were not presumptuous, but looked to God to aid them in escaping such temptations.] **13 There hath no temptation taken you but such as man can bear: but God is faith-**

ful, who will not suffer you to be tempted above tha ye are able; but will with the temptation make also th(way of escape, that ye may be able to endure it. [Th(temptations which befell the Corinthians were such as men ha(resisted and could resist. The temptations which had over come some of the Israelites had been resisted by others o their number. The faithfulness of God who called them woul(give them strength for the journey which he required of then (2 Pet. 2: 9; 2 Thess. 3: 3; 1 Thess. 5: 23, 24). God shows hi: faithfulness by providing an opportunity of escape, and we must show our faithfulness by seizing the opportunity when i! presents itself. As temptations vary, so the means of escape also vary. God permits temptation for our strengthening, no! for our destruction.] **14 Wherefore, my beloved, flee from idolatry. 15 I speak as to wise men; judge ye what I say.** [As idolatry had proved the mother of sins in Israel, so had it also in Corinth. Paul, therefore, in exhorting his readers to flee from it, appeals to their own past experience. They were wise men in this respect, and could, out of an abundant personal knowledge, judge as to the wisdom of his counsel when he thus told them to shun all that pertained to it. Idolatry was so interwoven with lust, drunkenness, reveling, etc., that it practically included them, and it was not to be dallied with. If we go to the verge of what is allowable, we make it easy for Satan to draw us over the line into what is sinful.] **16 The cup of blessing which we bless** [Not the cup which brings blessing (though it does that), but the cup over which blessing is spoken, the cup consecrated by benediction. Wine becomes a symbol of the blood of Christ by such a consecration, and even ordinary food is sanctified by prayer (1 Tim. 4: 4, 5. Compare Matt. 26: 26; Luke 9: 16). But the plural "we" used in this paragraph shows that the blessing and breaking were not the acts of the minister exercising priestly functions, but were the acts of the whole congregation through the minister as their representative. Sacerdotal consecration of the elements is not found here nor anywhere else in the New Testament], **is it not a communion**

of [a participation in or common ownership of] **the blood of Christ? The bread which we break, is it not a communion of the body of Christ?** [See John 6: 41-59.] **17 seeing that we, who are many, are one bread, one body: for we all partake of the one bread.** [Paul here points out the nature of the Lord's Supper, showing how it unites us with each other and with the Lord. We all partake of the loaf and thereby become qualitatively, as it were, a part of it, as it of us; and even thus we all become members of Christ's one body which it represents and Christ becomes part of us. Such is the unity of the church: Paul had no conception of a divided church. Though there may be more than one loaf at the communion, yet the bread is one in substance, and is one emblem.] **18 Behold Israel after the flesh: have not they that eat the sacrifices communion with the altar?** [In Paul's eyes the church was the true Israel, and the Jews were Israel after the flesh. Part of the Jewish sacrifice was eaten by the worshiper as an act of worship (Deut. 12: 18), and part was consumed upon the altar as a sacrifice to God; that is, as God's part. Thus the worshiper had communion with the altar, or, more accurately speaking, with God, who owned the altar; a portion of the meat of sacrifice entering his body and becoming part of him, and a portion of it typically entering and becoming part of the Lord. Having thus given two instances showing that sacrificial feasts establish a relationship between the worshiper and the object worshiped, Paul proceeds to make his application of them to idol feasts, and begins by anticipating an objection which the quick-witted Corinthians, seeing the drift of his argument, would begin at once to urge.] **19 What say I then? that a thing sacrificed to idols is anything, or that an idol is anything?** ["But, Paul," say the Corinthians, "your reasoning can not apply to feasts or sacrificial meat offered to idols; for you have already admitted (ch. 8: 4) that an idol is a nonentity. By sacrifice a man may establish a communal relationship with God, for God is; but he can establish no such relationship with an idol, for an idol is not—it has no existence." The under-

CONCERNING IDOLATROUS MEAT

standing of the Corinthians with regard to idols was true, but it was not the whole truth, for there was some reality back of the idol.] **20 But *I say*, that the things which the Gentiles sacrifice, they sacrifice to demons, and not to God: and I would not that ye should have communion with demons.** [It was true that the idol was nothing, but it represented a reality, and it was well established both among Jews and Greeks that that reality was a demon. Among Jews and Christians this word represented an evil spirit (Deut. 32: 17; Lev. 17: 7; 2 Chron. 11: 5; Ps. 96: 5; 106: 39; Matt. 25: 41; Rev. 9: 20; Eph. 6: 12). Among the Greeks the word had a broader significance. With them it meant a demi-god or minor deity—a being between God and men. One part of them were spirits of dead men, mainly dead kings or heroes who had been deified and honored with idols and worship. Another part were regarded as having a supernatural origin, and were like angels. These might be good or evil. Thus Socrates regarded himself as under the care and influence of a good demon. Thus at the core idolatry was demon-worship, and if the Christian who ate the Lord's Supper communed with the Lord, and the Jew who ate the sacrifice of the altar communed with the God of the altar; so the man, be he pagan or Christian, who partook of the idol sacrifice, communed with the demon who appropriated the worship offered to the idol.] **21 Ye cannot drink the cup of the Lord, and the cup of demons: ye cannot partake of the table of the Lord, and of the table of demons.** [At the sacrificial feasts of the pagans the provisions and wine were both blessed in the name of the idol, and thereby consecrated to him. Part of the festal cup was poured out as a libation to the idol, after which the guests drank of the cup and thus had fellowship with the idol. See Æneid 8: 273. Outwardly, Christians might partake of both feasts, but it was a moral impossibility for them to do so inwardly and spiritually. We can not be wicked and holy any more than we can be black and white at the same time. We may also note that there were tables in the temples of the idols on which feasts were prepared.] **22 Or do we** provoke the Lord to jealousy? are we stronger than he? [God does not permit a division of his worship (Matt. 6: 24). Any attempt to do this is said to arouse his jealousy, that passion which arises from wounded love (Isa. 54: 5; Eph. 5: 23-32; Ex. 20: 5). Paul doubtless has in mind the passage at Lev. 32: 17-26, which shows the necessity of obedience on the part of those not able to resist.] **23 All things are lawful; but not all things are expedient. All things are lawful; but not all things edify.** [See comment on ch. 6: 12.] **24 Let no man seek his own, but *each* his neighbor's *good*.** [As to eating idolatrous meat and all similar questions of liberty, be more careful to think of the interests of others than to assert your own rights.] **25 Whatsoever is sold in the shambles, eat, asking no question for conscience' sake; 26 for the earth is the Lord's, and the fulness thereof.** [Ps. 20: 1; 50: 12. Meat sold in the public market might be bought and used by the Christian without stopping to make investigation or to consult his conscience, for when thus sold it was wholly disassociated from the rites of idolatrous sacrifice, and one so using it could not be suspected of doing so as an act of worship. Moreover, all meat was pure, since it had come from the Lord. Being part of the furniture of the earth, it was to be eaten without scruple—Rom. 14: 14, 20; 1 Tim. 4: 4, 5; Acts 10: 15.] **27 If one of them that believe not biddeth you *to a feast*, and ye are disposed to go; whatsoever is set before you, eat, asking no question for conscience' sake. 28 But if any man say unto you, This hath been offered in sacrifice, eat not, for his sake that showed it, and for conscience' sake: 29 conscience, I say, not thine own, but the other's; for why is my liberty judged by another conscience?** [Christianity did not forbid a man to retain his friendships among pagans, nor did it prohibit fellowship with them. If such a friend should ask a Christian to a meal in a private house and not to a sacrificial feast in an idol temple, the Christian need not trouble himself to ask whether the meat that was served was part of an idol sacrifice, for such

CONCERNING IDOLATROUS MEAT

a dining was in no sense an act of worship. If, however, some scrupulous Christian or half-converted person should point out that the meat was idolatrous, then it was not to be eaten, for the sake of the man who regarded it as idolatrous. But so far as the real question of liberty was concerned, each man's liberty is finally judged by his own conscience and not by that of another. Liberty may be waived for the sake of another's conscience, but it is never thus surrendered. Paul's teaching, therefore, is that food is not tainted, and so it is always right to eat it *as food*, but all the rites of idolatry are tainted, and the Christian must do nothing which gives countenance to those rites, and for the sake of others he must abstain from seeming to countenance them even when his own conscience acquits him of so doing.] **30 If I partake with thankfulness, why am I evil spoken of for that for which I give thanks?** [The conscience of another man does not make it wrong for me to do that which I am not only permitted to do by my own conscience, but which I even do in a spirit of prayerful thankfulness. Nor does my doing such a thing give him, or any other, a right to speak evil of me, for I do not have to change my conscience to suit the judgment of others. In theory Paul sided with the strong, but in sympathy he was one with the weak; yet he did not permit them to exercise a vexatious tyranny over him because of their scruples.] **31 Whether therefore ye eat, or drink, or whatsoever ye do, do all to the glory of God.** [All eating should be with thanksgiving to God and should not dishonor God by injuring the consciences of weak men—comp. Col. 3: 17; 1 Pet. 4: 11.] **32 Give no occasion of stumbling** [Mark 9: 42], **either to Jews, or to Greeks, or to the church of God: 33 even as I also please all men in all things** [indifferent or permissible], **not seeking mine own profit, but the *profit* of the many, that they may be saved. XI. 1 Be ye imitators of me, even as I also am of Christ.** [In all matters that were indifferent Paul pleased others, rather than himself (ch. 9: 19, 22; Rom. 15: 2). He did not needlessly trample upon the prejudices of any, whether in the church or out, and he counseled the Corinthians to follow his example in this, as he himself followed the example of Christ in thus showing mercy and consideration—Rom: 15:1-3.]

VII.

SIXTH RESPONSE. CONCERNING HEAD COSTUME.

11: 2-16.

[Paul has been discussing the disorderly conduct of individual Christians. He now proceeds to discuss more general disorders; *i. e.*, those which took place in the meetings of the congregation, and in which the whole church participated. We may conceive him as answering the question, *"Ought men to have their heads covered, or may women have their heads uncovered when they are prophesying in public?"*] **2 Now I praise you that ye remember me in all things, and hold fast the traditions, even as I delivered them to you.** [By "traditions" Paul means the precepts, ordinances and doctrines which he had taught them orally. The traditions of God, given through inspired men, are to be accepted without addition or alteration (ch. 15: 3; 2 Thess. 2: 15; Rev. 22: 18), but the traditions of men should be weighed carefully, and summarily rejected if they conflict with the teaching of God (Matt. 15: 1-9). Since Paul has already censured the Corinthians for departing from his teaching, and since, in the next breath, he points out further departures on their part from his teaching, it is evident that what he says here is a quotation taken from a part of their letter where they were expressing their loyalty to him. Having thus quoted their words in which they committed themselves to his teaching, he points out what the teaching really was, that they may make good their boast by obeying it.] **3 But I would have you know, that the head of every man is Christ; and the head of the woman is the man; and the head of Christ** is God. [Paul settles the humblest difficulties by appealing to the loftiest principles: thus he makes the headship of Christ over man the basis, or principle, on which he decides that the man has headship over the woman, and as we shall see further on, he makes the headship of the man over the woman the principle by which he determines the question as to whether men should worship with uncovered, and women with covered heads; for the uncovered head was the symbol of royalty and dominion, and the covered head of subjection and submission. The order in which he states the several headships is peculiar. We would expect him to begin with God and descend by the regular steps, thus: God, Christ, man, woman. But the order is thus: Christ, man; man, woman; God, Christ. Subtle distinctions are to be made with caution, but it is not improbable that Paul's order in this case is determined by the delicate nature of the subject which he handles. Dominion is fruitful of tyranny, and so it is well, before giving man dominion, to remind him that he also is a servant (Matt. 18: 21-35; 5: 7). Again, the arrangement makes the headship of the man over the woman parallel to the headship of God over Christ, and suggests that there should be between husband and wife a unity of will and purpose similar to that which exists between the Father and the Son. The unquestioned, immediate and absolute submission and concurrence of the Son leave no room for the exercise of authority on the part of the Father, and the infinite and unsearchable wisdom, love, benevolence and good-will on the part of the Father take from the Son every occasion of unwillingness or even hesitation. All Christian husbands and wives should mutually remember this parallel. Jesus the Incarnate, the Son of man and the Son of God, is subject to the Father, by reason of his humanity and his mediatorial kingdom (ch. 3: 23; 15: 24-28; John 14: 28). As to the subjection of the Logos or the eternal Word to the Father we are not informed—comp. Phil. 2: 6.] **4 Every man praying or prophesying** [speaking by divine inspiration], **having his head covered, dishonoreth his head. 5 But every woman praying or prophesying with her**

head unveiled dishonoreth her head [Corinth was made up of Greeks, Romans and Jews, and all these three elements of her population were found in the church to which Paul wrote. The Jew and the Roman worshiped with covered, and the Greek with uncovered, head. Naturally a dispute would arise as to which custom was right. Moreover, as the women were beyond all doubt acquainted with the principle that there is neither male nor female in the spiritual realm (Gal. 3: 28), they seem to have added to the confusion by taking sides in the controversy, so that some of them asserted the right to worship with uncovered heads after the fashion of the Greeks. Now, in the East in Paul's day, all women went into public assemblies with their heads veiled, and this peplum, or veil, was regarded as a badge of subordination, a sign that the woman was under the power of the man. Thus Chardin, the traveler, says that the women of Persia wear a veil in sign that they are "under subjection," a fact which Paul also asserts in this chapter. Now, the symbolic significance of a woman's head-dress became the determining factor in this dispute. For a man to worship with a covered head was an act of effeminacy, a disgrace to his head, and for a woman to worship with uncovered head was likewise disgraceful, for it would at once be looked upon as a bold assertion of unwarranted independence, a sign that she had laid aside her modesty and removed from her sphere. From this passage it is plain that it was not intended that Christianity should needlessly vary from the national customs of the day. For Christians to introduce needless innovations would be to add to the misconceptions which already subjected them to persecution. One who follows Christ will find himself conspicuously different from the world, without practicing any tricks of singularity]; **for it is one and the same thing as if she were shaven. 6 For if a woman is not veiled, let her also be shorn: but if it is a shame to a woman to be shorn** [with shears] **or shaven** [with a razor], **let her be veiled.** [Paul does not *command* that unveiled women be shorn, but he *demands* it as a logical consistency, as a scornful *reductio ad absurdum*. For a woman to wantonly lay aside her veil was an open repudiation of the authority of her husband, and such a repudiation lowered her to the level of the courtesan, who, according to Elsner, showed her shamelessness by her shorn head, and likewise to the level of the adulteress, whose penalty, according to Wetstein and Meyer, was to have her head shaved. Paul, therefore, demands that those who voluntarily seek a low level, consent to wear *all* the signs and badges of that level that they may be shamed into rising above it. Having thus deduced a law from human custom, Paul now shows that the same law rests upon divine and creative relationships.] **7 For a man indeed ought not to have his head veiled, forasmuch as he is the image and glory of God** [Man has no created superior (Gen. 1:27; Ps. 8:6), and, in addition to the glory which is his by reason of the nature of his creation, his estate has been further dignified and glorified by the incarnation of the Son of God (Heb. 1:2, 3), so that, because of his fellowship with Christ, he may stand unveiled in the presence of the Father. Therefore, by covering his head while at worship, man symbolically forfeits his right to share in the glory of Christ, and thus dishonors himself. We are no longer slaves, but sons (Gal. 4:7). "We Christians," says Tertullian, "pray with *outspread hands*, as harmless; with *uncovered heads*, as unashamed; *without a prompter*, as from the heart"]: **but the woman is the glory of the man. 8 For the man is not of the woman; but the woman of the man: 9 for neither was the man created for the woman; but the woman for the man** [Gen. 2:18, 21, 22]: **10 for this cause ought the woman to have *a sign of* authority on her head, because of the angels.** [The argument here runs thus: The rule which I have given you rests upon symbolism—the symbol of the wife's subjection. But this symbolism is correct, for, as man proceeded from God, being fashioned as a minor representative of God, so also woman proceeded from man as a minor representative of man, and her minor state is apparent from the fact that she was created for the man, and not the man for her. Hence, women ought not to do away with the veil while in places of worship, because of the symbolism; and they can not do away with the subordination which it symbolizes, because it rests on the unalterable facts of creation. To abandon this justifiable and well-established symbol of subordination would be a shock to the submissive and obedient spirit of the ministering angels (Isa. 6: 2) who, though unseen, are always present with you in your places of worship" (Matt. 18: 10-31; Ps. 138: 1; 1 Tim. 5: 21; ch. 4: 9; Eccles. 5: 6). Here we find Paul not only vindicating the religious truths of the Old Testament, but authenticating its historical facts as well.] **11 Nevertheless, neither is the woman without the man, nor the man without the woman, in the Lord.** ["In the Lord" means by divine appointment.] **12 For as the woman is of the man, so is the man also by the woman; but all things are of God.** [Lest any man should be inflated with pride by the statement in verse 7, fancying that there was some degree of *proportion* between the exaltation of God over man and of man over woman, Paul adds these words to show that men and women are mutually dependent, and hence nearly equals, but that God, as Creator, is exalted over all. The idea of proportion, therefore, is utterly misleading. To the two reasons already given for the covering of a woman's and the uncovering of a man's head, Paul adds two more.] **13 Judge ye in yourselves** [he appealed to their own sense of propriety, as governed by the light of nature]: **is it seemly that a woman pray unto God unveiled? 14 Doth not even nature itself teach you, that, if a man have long hair, it is a dishonor to him? 15 But if a woman have long hair, it is a glory to her: for her hair is given her for a covering.** [Instinct should teach us that the head of a woman is more properly covered than that of a man, for nature grants it a greater abundance of hair. In Paul's time the hair of a man, unless he was under some vow, such as that of the Nazarite, was uniformly cut short. Long hair in a man betokened base and lewd effeminacy, and we find those who wore it ridiculed by Juvenal. Since nature gives a woman more covering than man, her will should accord with nature, and *vice versa*. Masculine women and effeminate men are alike objectionable. Let each sex keep its place. And in point of attire it is still disgraceful for men and women to appear in public in each other's garments.] **16 But if any man seemeth to be** [a mild way of saying, "if any man is"] **contentious, we have no such custom, neither the churches of God.** [Knowing the argumentative spirit of the Greeks, and being conscious that it was likely that some would even yet want to dispute the matter, despite his three reasons to the contrary, Paul takes it entirely out of the realm of discussion into that of precedent. The settled and established practice of the church had from the beginning followed the course outlined by Paul, which showed that other apostles beside himself had either established it by rule, or endorsed it in practice. In this appeal for uniformity Paul makes it clear that all churches should strive to make their practices uniform, not variant. Paul is here discussing how men and women should be attired when they take a leading part in public worship. He will speak later as to whether or not women should take any such part at all in public worship (ch. 14: 34, 35; 1 Tim. 2: 12). We to-day as males worship with uncovered heads in consequence of Paul's *instruction;* but not for his *reasons.* It is now an expression of reverence, which the Jew then expressed by taking off his sandals. "Holland," says Stanley, "is the only exception. In Dutch congregations, men uncover their heads during the psalmody only." In Western countries a woman's hat has never had any symbolism whatever. We see nothing in Paul's argument which requires us to make it symbolic. The problem in Western assemblies is how best to persuade women to take their hats off, not how to prevail upon them to keep them on. The principle, however, still holds good that the woman is subordinate to the man, and should not make any unseemly, immodest, vaunting display of an independence which she does not possess.

VIII.

SEVENTH RESPONSE. AS TO THE LORD'S SUPPER.

11: 17-34.

17 But in giving you this charge, I praise you not, that ye come together not for the better but for the worse. [Their church services, which were intended for their development, had become so corrupted that they tended to retard and to dwarf their natural growth. Farrar makes the words "this charge" refer back to verse 2; but it is more natural and easy to refer them to what he is about to say.] **18 For first of all** [Paul was not careful as to his divisions, and so his "secondly" is not clearly stated. Olshausen, Ewald, Winer and others think it begins at verse 20, and thus the apostle first censures the factions, and next the evils which resulted from the factions. But as Paul includes both these in one rebuke, it is best with Meyer, Fausset and others to find the "secondly" beginning at ch. 12: 1; so that the first rebuke is directed at their misbehavior at the love-feast and the Lord's Supper, and the second at their misapplication of the gifts of the Spirit], **when ye come together in the church** [*i. e.*, in the *congregation*, for as yet they doubtless had no *building* (Acts 18: 7), and in this latter sense the word is nowhere used in the New Testament], **I hear that divisions exist among you; and I partly believe it.** [Evidently the divisions rebuked in chapter 1 manifested themselves in the meetings of the congregation, and the Pauline, Petrine and other parties gathered in separate groups. Paul was distressed to hear this, and Alford interprets him thus: "I am unwilling to believe all I hear, but some I can not help believing."] **19 For there must be** [Luke 17: 1; Matt. 18: 7; 10: 11] **also factions among you, that they that are approved may be made manifest among you.** [A carnal spirit tends to division (ch. 3: 1-4; 1 John 2: 18, 19). The divisive spirit in the perverse and carnal, manifests, by contrast, the loving, united spirit of the obedient and spiritual, which is approved. "Approved" is the cognate opposite of "rejected" found at ch. 9: 27. The word "division" used in the verse above was a milder term than "factions" found here. The former represented parties separated by *present* or at least very recent dissensions, while the latter described *matured* separations and looked toward permanent organizations. If the former might be regarded as a war of secession, the latter would describe that condition when the war was practically ended, and the two parties were almost ready to establish themselves as separate, independent and rival governments. But factions did not thus mature in Paul's time, nor does Clement's epistle written forty years later indicate that they had matured in his time. No doubt, this epistle of Paul's had much to do in checking their development.] **20 When therefore ye assemble yourselves together, it is not possible to eat the Lord's supper** [The Lord's Supper is a spiritual feast. It is a feast of love, union and communion in and with Christ, and so can not be eaten by those who have already glutted themselves with hatred, factiousness and partyism]: **21 for in your eating each one taketh before** *other* **his own supper; and one is hungry, and another is drunken.** [This verse is an indictment with three counts. There could be no communion supper when: 1. The parties did not eat at the same time, but some before and some after; 2. when each ate his own meal, instead of sharing in "the one bread" (ch. 10: 17); 3. when some ate to the full and others ate nothing at all, because there was nothing left. It is likely that "drunken" indicates a state of partial intoxication. Grotius gives "drunken" the milder, and Meyer the stronger, sense. But the context suggests that one had more than was good for him, and the other less, and there is a subtle innuendo in the crossing of the terms, so that *overdrinking* stands in contrast to *undereating*, for overdrinking is greater debauchery than overeating.] **22 What, have ye not houses to eat and to drink in? or despise ye the church of God, and put**

them to shame that have not? What shall I say to
you? shall I praise you? In this I praise you not.
[Litotes for "I condemn you." The context here makes it
evident that the abuses of the Lord's Supper grew out of the
Agapæ, or love-feast, which was associated with it. As the
feast of the Passover immediately preceded the Lord's Supper,
the early church thought it expedient to have a preliminary
feast as a substitute for the Passover, thinking that the Lord's
Supper would thus have its proper setting. They called this
preliminary meal a "love-feast" (Greek, *Agapai*—Jude 12).
This Agapæ was a club-feast; *i. e.*, one to which each was supposed to contribute his share. But the factious spirit in Corinth
caused the church to eat in different parties and at different
times; and may have, to a large degree, caused each to selfishly eat what he himself had brought. Hence, the apostle
declares that a feast so devoid of all spirit of communion might
just as well be eaten at home. They were mere carnal feasts
of appetite and not spiritual feasts of love. Paul does not,
however, mention the Agapæ, for, being a human and not a
sacred feast, it could not be profaned. But the things which
were a disgrace to it became a profanation and a sin when they
passed from it into the Lord's Supper. Paul shows his sense
of astonishment at the unseemly conduct of the Corinthians by
a "lively succession of questions." His meaning may be paraphrased thus: "Private feasts should be eaten in your own
private houses, or is it possible that you do not own any houses?
Surely you do. Why, then, do you meet in a public assembly to
eat your private meal? Is it because you despise the church of
God, and wish to show your contempt for it by exposing the
poverty of those who have no houses (nor anything else), making a parade of your wealth before them, and publishing the
fact that you do not consider them fit to eat with you?" The
evil spirit of which Paul speaks still exists; but it shows itself
to-day by a parade of dress, and not of victuals. From the
perverted feast of the Corinthians Paul now turns to show the
nature of the true Lord's Supper.] **23 For I received of the
Lord** [Paul did not receive his knowledge as to the supper

AS TO THE LORD'S SUPPER 117

from the apostles or other witnesses (comp. Gal. 1: 11, 12). To be truly an apostle and witness (Acts 1: 8), it was fitting that Paul should have his knowledge from the fountain source. For a comparison of Paul's account with the three others, and comments upon verses 23-26, see "Fourfold Gospel," p. 657] **that which also I delivered unto you, that the Lord Jesus in the night in which he was betrayed** [the solemn and affecting circumstances under which the supper was instituted, as well as the sacred nature of the ordinance itself, should have impressed upon the Corinthians how unbecoming it was to celebrate the memorial of it in a spirit of pride, revelry and disorder] **took bread; 24 and when he had given thanks, he brake it, and said, This is my body, which is for you: this do in remembrance of me.** [The Greek word for giving thanks is *eucharistia*, and from it many call the Lord's Supper the Eucharist. But the "Lord's supper" and the "Lord's table" (ch. 10: 21) and the "communion" (ch. 10: 16) are three Bible terms for it. Many ancient authorities read: "This is my body, which is broken for you" etc. Some regard this as a contradiction of John's assertion that no bone of him was broken (John 19: 36). But the word differs from that used by John, which may be properly translated "crushed." "Broken" is involved in the phrase "he brake it," used here, and in the three other accounts of the supper, and hence they err who use the unbroken wafer.] **25 In like manner also the cup, after supper** [Paul here inserts the entering wedge of reform. The Lord's Supper came *after* the Passover, and was no part of it; hence it was no part of the Agapæ which was substituted for the Passover. As therefore the Agapæ was fruitful of disorder, would it not be well to separate it from the communion? By the end of the first century it was so separated, and at last it was formally prohibited by the Council of Carthage. See Poole's synopsis on Matt. 26: 26], **saying, This cup is the new covenant in my blood: this do, as often as ye drink it, in remembrance of me.** [*Diatheke* may be translated "testament" (Heb. 9: 16), or "covenant." The latter is the meaning here, for wills or testaments were not sealed with blood, as were covenants. The cup is the symbol of Christ's blood, which ratified the gospel covenant.] **26 For as often as ye eat this bread, and drink the cup, ye proclaim** [inwardly and outwardly] **the Lord's death till he come.** [Thus the supper looks forward, as well as backward. The constant observance of this feast through the centuries is one of the strongest of the external evidences of the truth of gospel history. By a chain of weekly links it will connect the first and second comings of our Lord; after which there will be no further need of symbols.] **27 Wherefore whosoever shall eat the bread or drink the cup of the Lord in an unworthy manner, shall be guilty of the body and the blood of the Lord.** [It is possible to partake of either emblem unworthily, and so be guilty as to both (Jas. 2: 10). Though we may be unworthy, we may still *eat* worthily, *i.e.*, in a prayerful, reverent, repentant spirit; but if we eat unworthily, we profane not only the symbols, but the Lord who is symbolized—comp. Heb. 10: 29.] **28 But let a man prove** [test] **himself, and so let him eat of the bread, and drink of the cup.** [A Christian confronting the communion should first test his sincerity (2 Cor. 13: 5), his state of heart (Matt. 5: 22-24), etc., to see if he can eat in a submissive spirit, and in loving remembrance of his Lord.] **29 For he that eateth and drinketh, eateth and drinketh judgment unto himself, if he discern not the body.** [The Corinthians were eating the supper in a spirit of levity, as though it were common food; not keeping in mind what it memorialized.] **30 For this cause many among you are weak and sickly, and not a few sleep.** ["Not a few" indicates a larger number than the preceding "many." It is generally accepted that Paul here refers to physical weakness, ill health and death, and that he asserts that these things came upon the Corinthians as a "judgment" for their abuse of the Lord's Supper (comp. John 5: 14). But the word "sleep" indicates peaceful repose, rather than the violence of the death penalty; and suggests that the Corinthians were condemned to be spiritually unhealthy and sleepy—comp. Matt. 13: 12-15.]

AS TO THE LORD'S SUPPER

31 But if we discerned ourselves, we should not be judged. 32 But when we are judged, we are chastened of the Lord, that we may not be condemned with the world. [If we examined and corrected ourselves, we would escape the correction of God; but, as it is, his judgments are visited upon us, so that we may not finally be condemned with the world (Ps. 94: 12; Heb. 12: 5-12). Verses 28 and 31 call for self-judgment, but there is no Biblical authority for the practice of those who take it upon themselves to judge as to the fitness of other professing Christians to commune (comp. Rom. 14: 4). Moreover, these verses, in giving the true rule of practice, expose the departure of the Romish Church, which calls for no self-examination, but makes confession and priestly absolution the preparation for communion.] **33 Wherefore** [if you wish to remedy matters], **my brethren, when ye come together to eat, wait one for another. 34 If any man is hungry, let him eat at home; that your coming together be not unto judgment.** [By waiting they would eat together, and eat of the same symbolic bread; by eating at home, and taking the edge off their appetites, they would not devour all, and so exclude others from the communion.] **And the rest will I set in order whensoever I come.** [The spiritual ill health of the church had delayed his coming, but when he arrived he would adjust any lesser irregularities which might need attention.]

IX.

EIGHTH RESPONSE.   AS TO SPIRITUAL GIFTS.

12: 1-31.

To avoid confusion in our classification of the subjects handled, we have called this section a *response*, but it is such as to information received, rather than as to questions asked. In the early church the Spirit of God, fulfilling the predictions of prophecy (Joel 2: 28 ff.; Acts 2: 17-21), and the promise of the Lord (Mark 16: 17, 18; Acts 8: 1), begin-

120 FIRST EPISTLE TO THE CORINTHIANS

ning on the day of Pentecost, endowed certain members with miraculous gifts. These were needful in that day: 1. They aided the evangelists and missionaries to propagate the faith in new fields with greater speed. 2. They assured weak converts that God was indeed in that church for which they had abandoned their former religions. 3. They edified the church, and gave it that body of perfect revealed truth which has been preserved and made permanent in the New Testament. But as different gifts were bestowed on different individuals, some of them became a source of pride and envy. Some who had showy gifts made a boastful display of them, and thus vaunted themselves as superior to those who had powers of a less dazzling nature; and those who had the humbler gifts envied the more richly endowed. To correct all this, Paul wrote the three chapters which follow.] **1 Now concerning spiritual *gifts*, brethren, I would not have you ignorant. 2 Ye know that when ye were Gentiles *ye were* led away unto those dumb idols, howsoever ye might be led. 3 Wherefore I make known unto you, that no man speaking in the Spirit of God saith, Jesus is anathema** [devoted to destruction, hence accursed]; **and no man can say, Jesus is Lord, but in the Holy Spirit.** [The previous idolatrous life of the Corinthians left them not only ignorant as to the ways of God's Spirit, but also tended to mislead them. Paul therefore begins their instruction with the elementary principles which concern inspiration and revelation; thus: 1. An idol reveals no truth; it is dumb. 2. Idols are many, but God is one. 3. The pretended revelations and oracles of idols or idol priests and other impostors, may be tested by what their authors say of Jesus, for they will speak evil of him. 4. The true prophets and revealers may also be so tested. They will assert the claims of Jesus, which no man is moved to do save by the Holy Spirit (1 John 4: 2, 3; 2: 22; 5: 1). Treating these four points in their order, we need to note that: 1. Dumb idols were often made to speak by priests concealed in or behind them, who made use of speaking-tubes which led to the parted lips of the idol. Hence, converts from

AS TO SPIRITUAL GIFTS 121

paganism needed to be reminded that idols were indeed dumb, as a safeguard against such fraud. No spiritual truth came from the oracles of idols. 2. As each realm of nature had its god, idolaters were drawn about from shrine to shrine and temple to temple, seeking one blessing from one god to-day, and another blessing from another god to-morrow. Hence, saturated as they were with polytheism, diverse gifts were with them instinctively associated with diverse gods. But the diverse gifts of Christianity were not to be attributed to different deities, or even to different subordinate spiritual beings, such as angels, etc., for they were all from one God, as Paul affirms in this chapter, reasserting it ten times in the next ten verses by way of emphasis. 3. Elymas affords a picture of one pretending to speak oracles—a false prophet. 4. The conflict between Paul and Elymas shows the blasphemy of the false and the confession of the true prophet (Acts 13: 6-12). The oracle of Delphi was near by, and contentions between idolatry and Christianity were, we may be sure, matters of daily occurrence in Corinth, and the ideas of new converts would be easily confused. The third verse shows that the test of a teacher is not his apostolic succession, but the soundness of his doctrine—comp. Gal. 1: 8.] **4 Now there are diversities of gifts, but the same Spirit. 5 And there are diversities of ministrations, and the same Lord. 6 And there are diversities of workings, but the same God, who worketh all things in all.** [Though the gifts were the immediate impartation of the Spirit, yet it was a mistake to think that the Spirit acted as an independent deity in this giving. Hence Paul begins by showing that all the Godhead participated in the bestowal, and that each sustained his own relation to these miraculous manifestations. In relation to the Spirit, they were, as we have seen, gifts; in relation to Jesus, they were means whereby he ministered to the church (Eph. 4: 11, 12; Rom. 12: 6, 7; 1 Pet. 4: 10, 11), and to the world through the church (Mark 16: 20); in relation to the Father, they were workings, or manifestations of power, whereby he sanctioned the church and kingdom of Jesus as proceeding from himself, approved by him, and part of his universal field of operation—John 8: 28, 29; 14: 10, 11.] **7 But to each one is given the manifestation of the Spirit to profit withal.** [Each of the gifted ones had some power which manifested that the Spirit of God was with him, and this power was not given to him for his own profit, but for the good of the church and of the world.] **8 For to one is given through the Spirit the word of wisdom; and to another the word of knowledge, according to the same Spirit: 9 to another faith, in the same Spirit; and to another gifts of healings, in the one Spirit; 10 and to another workings of miracles; and to another prophecy; and to another discernings of spirits: to another *divers* kinds of tongues; and to another the interpretation of tongues: 11 but all these worketh the one and the same Spirit, dividing to each one severally even as he will.** [Paul here sets forth fully the diversity of the gifts, but checks any tendency to boastful comparison by showing that the gifts emanate from a common source, and are operated by a common will, and are bestowed according to the pleasure of the Spirit, and not because of any inferiority or superiority on the part of the recipients. The nine gifts spoken of may be described as follows: 1. The "word of wisdom" was the ability to reveal divine truth which was possessed by the apostles and partially by prophets. 2. The "word of knowledge" was the ability to teach the truth thus revealed. Paul emphasizes that the second gift was as much a work of the Spirit as the first. 3. Faith, in this connection, is more than that which comes by hearing. It is that energy of faith which carries with it divine power (Matt. 17: 19, 20; ch. 13: 2). 4. "Gifts of healing" was the power to supernaturally restore the sick (Acts 5: 15, 16; Jas. 5: 14, 15). This gift may have been separated from the one next named, because some had their miraculous power limited to this field. 5. "Workings of miracles" was larger than the one which preceded it, for it included acts of judgment as well as mercy. It was exercised by Paul in striking Elymas blind, and by Peter in the punishment of Ananias and Sapphira. Paul here names healing first.

AS TO SPIRITUAL GIFTS

possibly because those who are called upon to exercise God's mercy stand higher in his esteem than those who execute his judgment, for pagans and unbelievers have often been used by him to mete out punishment. But in verse 28 he reverses the order, for the greater includes the less. 6. The "gift of prophecy" enabled one to speak the truth under the unerring guidance of the Holy Spirit. In the Old Testament this gift was a very important one; but in the New, the "word of wisdom," which embraced all the larger scope of prophecy, seems to have been mainly confined to the apostles, and so we find New Testament prophets merely foretelling things of a temporary or personal nature, as in the case of Agabus (Acts 11: 28; 21: 9-11). 7. "Discernings of spirits" was the power to recognize the difference between the utterances of genuine inspiration and those of a demoniacal or an unaided human spirit. 8. There has been much dispute as to what is meant by "kinds of tongues." Some modern commentators have attempted to show that the gift of tongues mentioned in the Epistles was entirely different from the ability to speak foreign languages manifested on the day of Pentecost. The weakness of those who take this position is fully exposed by Hodge *in loco*. Speaking with tongues was not an incoherent, meaningless jargon uttered by the speaker in ecstatic rhapsody, nor was it "spiritual language unknown to man, uttered in ecstacy." The second chapter of the Book of Acts shows us clearly what it was, and the New Testament never explains it as being anything less or different. 9. "Interpretation of tongues" was the ability to interpret what was said by the one who spoke with tongues. The gifts of speaking and interpreting were sometimes given to the same person (14: 13), and sometimes to different persons.] **12 For as the body is one, and hath many members, and all the members of the body, being many, are one body; so also is Christ.** [Paul here strikes a fatal blow at that pride which animated those who held superior gifts. Can there be pride in one member of the body, as to the other members of which it is only an organic part? But all Christians, no matter how they differ in gifts, are parts of the body of Christ. Jesus illustrated the organic unity between himself and the church under the figure of the vine and the branches; and the apostles, carrying the figure forward so as to include the unity existing between Christians, spoke of Christ as the head and the church as the body, or Christ as the building and the church as the stones. All organism supposes both unity and diversity.] **13 For in one Spirit were we all baptized into one body, whether Jews or Greeks, whether bond or free; and were all made to drink of one Spirit.** [Paul here proves the unity of the church by the method of its creation. One Spirit, acting through the apostles and all other evangelists and ministers (1 Thess. 1: 5), had begotten people of different races and nationalities and conditions (John 3: 5), and had caused them to be baptized into the one church, and had bestowed itself upon them after they had been thus baptized (Acts 2: 38). Thus it had made them one organism. Paul speaks of the bestowal of the Spirit under the figure of the living water used by Jesus (John 7: 37). As the spirit of a man keeps up the organic unity of the body, so the Spirit of God had vivified and organized the church.] **14 For the body is not one member, but many. 15 If the foot shall say, Because I am not the hand, I am not of the body; it is not therefore not of the body. 16 And if the ear shall say, Because I am not the eye, I am not of the body; it is not therefore not of the body.** [This passage exposes the folly of those who were belittling themselves in the presence of their fellow-Christians. Being in the church, they were organically united to the entire church body. If they felt that their inferiority in gifts excluded them, they were not thereby excluded. Their false views and false assertions did not alter their true condition. Paul associates the members of action (foot and hand) and the members of sensation (eye and ear), and represents each as complaining against the other, because men are apt to be envious and to disparage themselves as to those who have superior gifts similar to their own. We are not envious of those whose gifts are dissimilar. It is the foot and not the eye that envies the hand.] **17 If the whole body were an eye, where were the hearing? If the whole were hearing, where were the smelling?** 18 But now [(as things actually are)] **hath God set the members each one of them in the body, even as it pleased him. 19 And if they were all one member, where were the body? 20 But now they are many members, but one body.** [The necessity for diversity is here shown. If all the church were teachers, who could be taught? If all were healers, who could receive healing? If all were preachers, who could listen? The glory of all organism is its diversity, and the more diverse its functions, the higher it ranks in the scale of life.] **21 And the eye cannot say to the hand, I have no need of thee: or again the head to the feet, I have no need of you.** [The interdependence of the members is here shown. If, as we have seen above, the humbly envious one felt as if he were not included in the church, the proudly superior member felt as if the humbler one should be excluded. Here we find the eye and hand associated contrary to the usage in verses 15 and 16. Those who are puffed up with some great gift do not see the need of any other gifts save their own. But they tolerate those who have their gift in less degree, for such form a background to show off their excellencies. We have seen vain singers who esteemed the preaching as of very little importance, and *vice versa*. Paul continues to discuss this interdependence.] **22 Nay, much rather, those members of the body which seem to be more feeble are necessary: 23 and those** *parts* **of the body, which we think to be less honorable, upon these we bestow more abundant honor; and our uncomely** *parts* **have more abundant comeliness; 24 whereas our comely** *parts* **have no need: but God tempered the body together, giving more abundant honor to that** *part* **which lacked; 25 that there should be no schism in the body; but that the members should have the same care one for another. 26 And whether one member suffereth, all the members suffer with it; or** *one* **member is honored,** all the members rejoice with it. **27 Now ye are the body of Christ, and severally members thereof.** [The hands and face have no need of adornment, but the rest of the body, being less comely, is made beautiful with clothing, so that a state of equilibrium is established, and the whole body is acceptable to the indwelling Spirit as its home. If any part of the body lacks in beauty, the attention of the whole body is drawn to it, and employed to better its condition. Moreover, the parts suffer or rejoice as a whole. Now, God intends that the church shall look upon itself as such an organic whole, and shall feel this lively concern for each of those who lack, feeling that the lack of one is the lack of all. "When a thorn," says Chrysostom, "enters the heel, the whole body feels it, and is concerned: the back bends, the fore part of the body contracts itself, the hands come forward and draw out the thorn, the head stoops, the eyes regard the affected member with intense gaze. When the head is crowned, the whole man feels honored, the mouth expresses and the eyes look gladness."] **28 And God hath set some in the church, first apostles, secondly prophets, thirdly teachers, then miracles, then gifts of healings, helps, governments,** *divers* **kinds of tongues. 29 Are all apostles? are all prophets? are all teachers? are all** *workers of* **miracles? 30 have all gifts of healings? do all speak with tongues? do all interpret?** [Paul here completes his analogy by showing that the gifts bestowed upon individuals in the church are as diverse and variant as the faculties bestowed upon the various members of the body. As the apostle has named nine spiritual gifts, so he here names nine positions in the church. These may be defined thus: 1. The "apostles" were those who possessed plenary inspiration. They could at all times and on all subjects declare the will of God. 2. "Prophets" had occasional inspiration, which was then usually of a very limited nature. 3. "Teachers" were uninspired men that were gifted in teaching and explaining the historic truths of the gospel and the doctrinal truths which came through inspiration, for those having prophetic gifts did not always fully understand the import of

AS TO SPIRITUAL GIFTS 127

their own words (1 Pet. 1:11, 12). 4 and 5. Those who worked miracles and had the gift of healing have been spoken of above. 6. "Helps" means the same as helpers. In our land domestic and other helpers are often provincially called "help." It here refers to those who had a sympathetic nature or a generous spirit, etc. (Rom. 12:8). 7. "Governments." This refers to those possessing powers of leadership and organization, those having administrative ability, such as the elders. 8 and 9. "Divers kinds of tongues" and the power to interpret the same, have already been described. These appear to have been ranked first in importance by the Corinthians, because most showy, and they are here placed last by the apostles because they added but little to edification, and were of small practical value.] **31 But desire earnestly the greater gifts.** [Though these powers were bestowed as gifts by the Spirit, yet they were not bestowed blindly. They were apt to be conferred upon those who strove to be worthy of them.] **And moreover a most excellent way show I unto you.** [This may mean that I show you a most excellent way to attain unto the best gifts; or, I show you a way of love to which all may attain, and which far exceeds any gift or position. This way of love will be fully described in the next chapter.]

X.

AS TO THE SUPREMACY OF LOVE.

13: 1-13.

[This chapter has been admired by all ages, but, unfortunately, it has been practiced by none. In it Paul shows that love is superior to all extraordinary gifts, both by reason of its inherent excellency and its perpetuity. Also that it surpasses all other graces.] **1 If I speak with the tongues of men and of angels, but have not love, I am become sounding brass, or a clanging cymbal.** [The apostle first compares love with that gift of tongues in which the Corinthians took so much pride. The comparison shows that speaking with tongues, even if it were exercised in an unexampled manner, is utter emptiness unless accompanied by love. The gift of tongues, even when it attained its highest conceivable development, is inferior to the language of angels; but even if one spoke with all the gifts of language *human* or *divine*, his word, if loveless, would be but a vainglorious noise, or sounds without soul or feeling; such as come from pounding on some brazen gong or basin, or from cymbals, which are the lowest, most monotonous, least expressive of all musical instruments. It is suggestive that Paul had doubtless heard the language of angels (2 Cor. 12: 4). Corinthian brass was a mixture of gold and silver, and was famous for its resonance when made into trumpets, etc.] **2 And if I have *the gift of* prophecy, and know all mysteries and all knowledge; and if I have all faith, so as to remove mountains, but have not love, I am nothing.** [Love is next compared with the gifts of prophecy and miracle-working faith mentioned in the last chapter. The gift of prophecy manifested itself in two ways: 1. Ability to receive revelations of those counsels of God which were either not revealed at all, or else concealed in mystery (Matt. 13: 11; Rom. 16: 27; ch. 2: 17; Eph. 3: 3, 9; Col. 1: 26). 2. Ability to fully understand the revelations in all their bearings upon present and future life, former revelations, dispensations, etc. This latter Paul calls "knowledge." The phrase "I would not have you ignorant," so familiar in his writings, shows how frequently he used this knowledge to impart the full truth to others. The fate of those who exercised the gift of prophecy and miracles without love is described at Matt. 27: 21-23. Balaam, Judas and Caiaphas may be taken as examples, and Satan himself is partially such. To say that one possessed of such gifts was "nothing"—a spiritual cipher—was a crushing blow to the pride and vanity of the Corinthians. We see that Paul agrees with James that faith which does not work in love is profitless—Jas. 2: 26; comp. Gal. 5: 6; 1 Thess. 1: 2.] **3 And if I bestow all my goods to feed *the poor*, and if I give my body to be burned, but have not love, it prof-**

iteth me nothing. [Love is here contrasted with those works of charity and self-sacrifice which are included under the term "helps;" so that in his comparison Paul practically exhausts the whole catalogue of gifts described in the last chapter, and shows the entire supremacy of love over all of them. The word translated "bestow to feed," means to dole away in mouthfuls, and suggests that though the giving was entire and exhaustive, yet the manner of giving was so parsimonious and grudging as to emphasize the lack of love. From giving goods Paul passes to that higher order of giving in which the body is presented as a sacrifice to God, either by martyrdom, or as a daily offering (Rom. 12: 1; ch. 15: 31; 2 Cor. 12: 15; 11: 29). It has been urged that Paul could not refer to martyrdom, for, though Christians were burned by fire in great numbers some ten years later, yet there is no account of any such form of martyrdom when Paul wrote. But the mere silence of history proves nothing; besides, the case of the three Hebrews is precedent enough (Dan. 3: 23, 28; comp. Heb. 11: 34). See also 2 Macc. 7. Willingness to fight and die for Christianity will not take the place of loving obedience to Christ. Having shown the supremacy of love when compared with miraculous gifts, Paul now enters upon a discussion of the intrinsic merits of love, thus preparing his hearers to grasp the superiority of love over the other two graces. He gives nine negative and six, or rather eight, positive qualities of love. All seventeen qualities will be found beautifully exemplified in the life of our Lord. The Corinthians were conspicuously lacking in the four which head Paul's catalogue, as will be shown by comparing them with ch. 6: 7; 12: 15, 21, 26; 4: 6, 18, 19.] 4 **Love suffereth long,** *and* **is kind** [In this catalogue the first and last negative qualities are coupled with their corresponding positives, suggesting a like coupling throughout. Love suffers evil and confers blessing, and seeks to thus overcome evil with good —Rom. 12: 21; Matt. 23: 37; Luke 22: 48, 50, 51]; **love envieth not** [Is not jealous of the gifts, goods or fortune of another, nor of his spiritual prosperity, as was Cain (Gen. 4: 3-8). Love excludes this feeling; the parent does not envy the child (Rev. 3: 21). Moses was free from envy (Num. 11: 26-29), and so also was John the Baptist—John 3: 26-30]; **love vaunteth not itself** [does not parade itself—Matt. 6: 1; Acts 8: 9; Matt. 11: 29; 12: 19, 38, 39; 21: 5], **is not puffed up** [is not inflated with pride or arrogance, because of wealth, knowledge, power, etc.—Acts 12: 20-23; John 13: 1-5], **5 doth not behave itself unseemly** [Self-love betrays its lack of sympathy by vulgar indecorum, and cares not how offensive its conduct is towards others. Manners often give the measure of the man (Luke 7: 44-47; 23: 11; John 13: 14, 15). Christians should manifest a courteous spirit—1 Pet. 3: 8, 9; Luke 2: 51, 52], **seeketh not its own** [Love is unselfish and disinterested, and is happy in the happiness of others (Rom. 12: 10; 15: 1-3; Phil. 2: 4; Matt. 8: 20; 20: 28). Self-love is grasping and productive of evil—ch. 10: 24-33; Luke 12: 13-21], **is not provoked** [It does not lose its temper; is not easily roused to resentment. The same word is used for the "sharp contention" between Paul and Barnabas (Acts 15: 39). Love curbs exasperation—Isa. 53: 7; Matt. 26: 62, 63; 1 Pet. 2: 23; Heb. 12: 3], **taketh not account of evil** [Is not suspicious of evil, is not careful to retain the memory of it, and does not keep a record of it for the purpose of returning it. It continues its blessing despite rebuffs—John 10: 32]; **6 rejoiceth not in unrighteousness, but rejoiceth with the truth** [It does not rejoice in seeing sin committed nor in the downfall of those who are overcome by it (Rom. 1: 32; 2 Thess. 2: 12; comp. John 8: 3-11), but is glad when truth puts down iniquity (2 John 4; Acts 11: 23; Luke 10: 17-21; comp. 2 Tim. 3: 8). Possibly the verse also includes that malignant joy which many feel at the mishaps or misfortunes of others. It certainly condemns that false charity which compromises truth—Prov. 17: 15; Gal. 1: 9; 2: 5, 11]; **7 beareth all things** [it endures wrongs without complaint, and bears the adversities, troubles and vexations of life without murmuring (Matt. 17: 24-27), and often without divulging its needy condition—ch. 9: 12; Phil. 4: 11, 12], **believeth all things** [It takes the kindest views of men's actions and circumstances. It sees things in their

AS TO SUPREMACY OF LOVE

brightest, not their darkest, colors; and, as far as it consistently can, puts the best construction on conduct—Prov. 10: 12; 1 Pet. 4: 8; Gen. 45: 5; Luke 23: 34], **hopeth all things** [though the object loved is confessedly sinful to-day, yet this supreme grace looks with eager, hopeful expectation for its repentance on the morrow—ch. 3: 2, 3; Luke 13: 6-9; 15: 20; 20: 9-13], **endureth all things.** [The word "*hupomenoo*," translated "endureth," is a military term, and means to sustain an assault; hence it has reference to heavier afflictions than those sustained by the "beareth" of verse 7. It refers to gross ill-treatment, violence and persecution, and such grievances as provoke resistance, strife, etc. (2 Tim. 2: 10, 24; Heb. 10: 32; 12: 2; Matt. 5: 39; comp. John 18: 22, 23, with Acts 23: 2-5). The enduring is not simply that dogged persistency which bears up despite adversity, it is an endurance which forgives offense (Luke 17: 4). From love as it manifests itself in daily life Paul now rises to speak of love in its essence.] **8 Love never faileth: but whether *there be* prophecies, they shall be done away; whether *there be* tongues, they shall cease; whether *there be* knowledge, it shall be done away. 9 For we know in part, and we prophesy in part; 10 but when that which is perfect is come, that which is in part shall be done away. 11 When I was a child, I spake as a child, I felt as a child, I thought as a child: now that I am become a man, I have put away childish things. 12 For now we see in a mirror, darkly; but then face to face: now I know in part; but then shall I know fully even as also I was fully known.** [The superlative excellence of love is here shown in that it survives all things with which it may be compared, and reveals its close relation to God whose name is love (1 John 3: 8), by its eternal, imperishable nature. Prophecies, tongues and knowledge—three supernatural gifts though they were—were mortals compared with the divine spirit of love. They were needful in developing the infant church, but as that institution passed onward toward maturity and perfection (Heb. 5: 12-14; 6: 1; Eph. 3: 14-21; 4: 11-16), they were outgrown and discontinued, because from them had been developed the clear, steady light of the recorded Word, and the mature thoughtfulness and assurance of a well-instructed church. They were thrown aside, therefore, as the wheat stalk which has matured its grain; or, to use Paul's own figure, put away as the speech, feeling and judgment of childhood when they have produced their corresponding faculties in manhood. Though the triplet of child-faculties—speech, feeling, thought, do not form a close parallel with the triplet of gifts—tongues, prophecies, knowledge, yet they were alike in that to both, the child and the church, they seemed severally all-important. All Christians who mistakenly yearn for a renewal of these spiritual gifts, should note the clear import of these words of the apostle, which show that their presence in the church would be an evidence of immaturity and weakness, rather than of fully developed power and seasoned strength. But if the *gifts* have passed from the church as transient and ephemeral, shall not that which they have produced abide? Assuredly they shall, until that which is perfect is come; *i. e.*, until the coming of Christ. Then prophecy shall be merged into fulfillment, and the dim light of revelation shall be broadened into the perfect day. We to-day see the reflection of truth, rather than the truth itself. It has come to us through the medium of minds which, though divinely illuminated, were yet finite, and it has modified itself, though essentially spiritual, so as to be clothed in earthly words; and it is grasped and comprehended by us through the use of our material brains. Thus, though perfect after its kind, and true as far as it goes, our present knowledge of heavenly things is perhaps as far from the full reality as is the child's conception of earthly things (John 3: 12). And so our present knowledge may well merge, as will prophecy, into a higher order of perfection, wherein both the means of manifestation (2 Cor. 5: 7) and of comprehension (1 John 3: 2) will be wholly perfect. So, though at present we may indeed know God, yet our knowledge is more that received by description, than that which is received by direct, clear sight, and personal acquaintance; but hereafter we shall know God in some sense

AS TO SUPREMACY OF LOVE

as he knows us, and know the beings of the heavenly land as thoroughly as they now know us. Mirrors were then made of polished silver or brass, and were far more indistinct than our present glasses; so that to see a reflection in one of them was far less satisfactory than to see the reality.] **13 But now** [in this present state] **abideth faith, hope, love, these three; and the greatest of these is love.** [If we give the phrase "but now" its other sense, as though the apostle said "But to sum things up, to give the net results," then we have him saying that faith, hope and love are eternal. While it is true that faith in the sense of trust and confidence, and hope in the sense of unclouded expectation, shall abide in heaven, yet, in their large, general meaning, faith shall be lost in sight, and hope in fruition (Rom. 8: 24, 25). It therefore seems more consistent to understand the apostle as asserting that the three graces shall abide while the earth stands; in contrast with miraculous gifts, which, according to his own prophetic statement, have ceased. He does not explain the superior excellence of love when compared with faith and hope, but the points of superiority are not hard to find. 1. If all three are eternal, the other two shall be greatly diminished as graces by the Lord's coming, while love shall be infinitely enlarged. 2. Love is the basis of faith and hope, for we only fully believe in and hope for that which we love. 3. Faith and hope are human, but God himself is love. 4. Faith and hope can only properly work by love, and are worthless without it. But here the superiority is not so clear, for the three graces go hand in hand.

XI.

SPIRITUAL GIFTS CONCLUDED.

14: 1-40.

1 Follow after love; yet desire earnestly spiritual gifts, but rather that ye may prophesy. [From the discussion of spiritual gifts Paul turned aside in the last chapter to show that love is superior to all gifts. Having finished his digression, he now resumes the subject of gifts, and proceeds to show that the pursuit of love, as of supreme importance, does not exclude the desire of gifts, as of secondary importance. Having thus brought the subject of gifts again into discussion, he asserts that prophecy is superior to the gift of tongues, and proves his assertion by showing that it is the more useful in the edification of the church. Incidentally his argument shows that though the Spirit gave the gift of tongues to men, that men abused the gift; and so the Spirit, through Paul as its instrument, reproves and corrects this abuse. Prophecy, as here discussed, means preaching under divine guidance, and the gift of tongues was not a gift of the knowledge of, but of the use of, foreign languages. The one having it could declare God's will in a foreign tongue, and could sometimes even interpret what he had declared; but he could not use the language for business conversation, or any personal or worldly purpose.] **2 For he that speaketh in a tongue speaketh not unto men, but unto God; for no man understandeth; but in the spirit he speaketh mysteries. 3 But he that prophesieth speaketh unto men edification, and exhortation, and consolation. 4 He that speaketh in a tongue edifieth himself; but he that prophesieth edifieth the church.** [The apostle here lays the groundwork of his argument. Prophecy is superior to the gift of tongues, because more profitable. The speaker with tongues, exercising his spiritual gift (Rev. 1:10), might indeed speak the divine truths or mysteries of God; but, speaking them in a foreign language, he would be understood only by God and himself, and so would only edify, etc., himself. On the other hand, the prophet, declaring the same or kindred mysteries in the vernacular, would be understood by all present, and thus he would transform the mysteries into revelations, which would benefit the church, either edifying it, so as to enlighten its ignorance; or rousing its latent energies, so as to dispel its sluggishness; or comforting it, so as to remove its sorrows. In short, tongues might excite wonder (Acts 2:12), but preaching **brought** forth fruit (Acts 2: 36-42) and the Corinthian church had need to be more fruitful, since it was not eminent for its holiness or its works. Paul does not mean to say that no man living could understand the tongues, or that they were mere jargon. He means that no man present in the usual Corinthian assemblies understood them. Had speaking with tongues been mere hysterical "orgiastic" jargon, it certainly would not have bodied forth the mysteries of God, nor would it have edified the one speaking, nor could it have been interpreted by him or by others as Paul directs. Those who belittle the gift by construing it as a mere jargon approach dangerously near making Paul (and themselves likewise) criticize the Holy Spirit for giving such a senseless, abnormal gift. But those who read Paul correctly find that he is only censuring the *abuse* of the gift and not the nature of it. It was useful to the church while engaged in missionary work in foreign fields. But it became a source of vanity and vainglorious display when used by a church sitting idly at home. To the missionary it was a splendid addition to the gift of prophecy; but to the Corinthian preachers exhorting in their home church, it was a sad subtraction from that gift. The fruits of the Spirit in the Christian life are far enough from being "orgiastic"—Gal. 5: 22.] **5 Now I would have you all speak with tongues, but rather that ye should prophesy: and greater [because more profitable] is he that prophesieth than he that speaketh with tongues, except he interpret, that the church may receive edifying. 6 But now, brethren, if I come unto you speaking with tongues, what shall I profit you, unless I speak to you either by way of revelation, or of knowledge, or of prophesying, or of teaching?** [The gift of tongues had a subordinate use in the church of God, as an evidence of the presence of the Spirit of God. Moreover, it was a reserve of power, liable to be brought into active use at any time by the scattering of the church through persecution. For these reasons, and also to show that he writes in a spirit of generous good-will, Paul expresses a wish that all the churches in Corinth might be endowed with this gift. But, as a more practical wish, he prefers that they shall be able to prophesy, since the church would not be edified by the use of the gift of tongues, unless the foreign language used was interpreted. If Paul came to them as a visitor or missionary, his profit to them would not lie in his speaking with tongues (even though he, a Jew, spake to them miraculously in their own Greek language); but it would lie in the subject-matter of his utterance, in the edification which he conveyed. Paul names the four ways in which men may be edified by the use of words, and all these four manners were as much at the command of prophecy as they were at that of the gift of tongues. Revelation is the unveiling of divine truth to a prophet, and prophecy is the impartation of that truth to others. Knowledge is the divine illumination of the mind as to the bearing and significance of a truth, and doctrine is the impartation to another of the truth thus grasped. These are all matters of sense, and not of sound only. But speaking with tongues in the presence of those not understanding the language spoken, is sound without sense, and fails to convey any prophecy, doctrine, etc. Paul goes on to show that sound without sense is not only profitless, but may even be baneful.] 7 **Even things without life, giving a voice, whether pipe or harp, if they give not a distinction in the sounds, how shall it be known what is piped or harped? 8 For if the trumpet give an uncertain voice, who shall prepare himself for war? 9 So also ye, unless ye utter by the tongue speech easy to be understood, how shall it be known what is spoken? for ye will be speaking into the air. 10 There are, it may be, so many kinds of voices in the world, and no** *kind* **is without signification. 11 If then I know not the meaning of the voice, I shall be to him that speaketh a barbarian** [a foreigner—Acts 28: 2], **and he that speaketh will be a barbarian unto me. 12 So also ye, since ye are zealous of spiritual** *gifts,* **seek that ye may abound unto the edifying of the church.** [If there be any place where sound without sense is apparently valuable, or profitable, argues Paul, it will be found in the

SPIRITUAL GIFTS CONCLUDED

use of musical instruments. But even here there are laws of cadence, modulation, harmony, etc., which form a veritable grammar of tongue-language, which, when obeyed, give to music what we may call a tone-sense, analogous to the intellectual sense embodied in language. Hence one may play an instrument so as to make it meaningless, and if he does he makes it profitless. Moreover, some instruments, such as the trumpet, because of the fixed and established laws of tone, are used to convey a language as well defined and unmistakable as that of the voice. Thus certain notes on the trumpet command a charge, others the joining of battle, and yet others the retreat, etc. Now, if the trumpet or trumpeter fails to produce this tone-language intelligibly, the army is thrown into confusion. Spiritual guidance uttered in an unknown tongue was like a blare of the trumpet which gave no order. Both disappointed the expectation of the listener. Both spoke idly into the air, instead of profitably into the ear. There are many sounds in the world, but they only become voices when they convey some form of sense. Thus we speak properly enough of the "voice of the trumpet," when it is blown, but no one speaks of the voice of the boiler when it is being riveted. Sense, meaning, signification, are the very essence of voice—the qualities which distinguish it from mere sound. If you use your voice to speak a foreign, and hence a meaningless, language, you degrade it, so that to your hearer it becomes a mere profitless sound. This you should not do. Since you earnestly seek gifts, you should seek them for practical purposes; viz.: for the abundant edification of the church.] **13 Wherefore let him that speaketh in a tongue pray that he may interpret. 14 For if I pray in a tongue, my spirit prayeth, but my understanding is unfruitful. 15 What is it then?** [What is the conclusion of the argument?] **I will pray with the spirit, and I will pray with the understanding also: I will sing with the spirit, and I will sing with the understanding also. 16 Else if thou bless with the spirit, how shall he that filleth the place of the unlearned say the Amen at thy giving of thanks, seeing he knoweth**

138 FIRST EPISTLE TO THE CORINTHIANS

not what thou sayest? 17 For thou verily givest thanks well, but the other is not edified. [The one who was so under the influence of the Spirit of God as to speak with tongues, produced words and sentences with little or no intellectual effort. His spirit, being in accord with the Spirit of God, uttered the exhortation or the prayer with his spirit rather than with his understanding. Therefore, taking the case of prayer as an example, Paul advises that the understanding be kept as active as the spirit, and that a man so control the flow of prayer as to pause from time to time that he might interpret it, thus making his understanding as fruitful as his spirit. If he does not do this, he prays with his tongue indeed, but his understanding bears no fruit in the congregation where he prays. For this reason the apostle made it his rule to pray with his spirit and interpret with his understanding, and to sing also in like manner. If the speaker did not do this, how could one who was not gifted to interpret say Amen to the petition offered, seeing that he knew not what it was? Thus, no matter how ably the gifted one might pray, the ungifted one would not be edified. Amen was then, as now, the word of ratification or assent to an expression of prayer or praise, of blessing or cursing (Deut. 27: 15; Neh. 5: 13; Rev. 5: 14). Justin Martyr (Ap., c. 65, 67) describes the use of the Amen, after the prayer at the communion service. It is to that or some similar use that Paul refers. Doddridge justly says that this passage is decisive against the ridiculous practice of the church of Rome of praying and praising in Latin, which is not only a foreign, but a dead, tongue. Moreover, it shows that prayer is not a vicarious duty done for us by others. We must join in it.] 18 I thank God, I speak with tongues more than you all: 19 howbeit in the church [congregation] I had rather speak five words with my understanding [so as to be understood], that I might instruct others also, than ten thousand words in a tongue. [Paul was thankful for the gift of tongues because of its utility, but especially lest any should think that he disparaged the gift because he did not have it, and assigned it a subordinate place from envy. His disparagement is most emphatic. "Rather half of ten of the edifying sort than a thousand times ten of the other," says Besser. "There is a lesson here," says Johnson, "to preachers who are so learned in their utterances that the people can not understand them."] **20 Brethren, be not children in mind: yet in malice be ye babes, but in mind be men.** [The apostle here reiterates the thought at ch. 13: 11. To desire showy and comparatively worthless gifts was to be like children, pleased with toys. But as Paul exhorted them to be wise as men, the words of the Lord seem to have flashed through his mind (Matt. 10: 16) so that he parallels men with serpents and babes with doves. "Yet in malice be ye babes" is a parenthesis added by way of fullness. It has nothing to do with the line of argument, for there was no possible malice in the use of tongues.] **21 In the law it is written, By men of strange tongues and by the lips of strangers will I speak unto this people; and not even thus will they hear me, saith the Lord. 22 Wherefore tongues are for a sign, not to them that believe, but to the unbelieving: but prophesying** *is for a sign*, **not to the unbelieving, but to them that believe.** [The Old Testament generally is often called the Law by New Testament writers (John 10: 34; 12: 34; Rom. 3: 20). Therefore the reference here is not to the Pentateuch, but to Isa. 28: 11, 12. There the prophet tells how Israel murmured at the quality of the teaching which God gave them, and states that as a consequence God would soon teach them by the tongue of foreigners; *i. e.*, the Assyrians would lead them away captive and they should be instructed by the hardships of captivity. When the captivity came, the necessity to understand and speak a strange tongue was a sign that God was teaching them, and yet a sign which they did not heed. From this incident Paul apparently draws several conclusions: 1. It was no especial mark of divine favor to have teachers who spoke an unknown tongue. 2. Tongues were for unbelievers and prophecy for believers. 3. Tongues were a sign that God was teaching, but the teaching itself was better than the sign. 4. Tongues, unless understood, had never been profitable; *i. e.*, had not produced conversion. It must be remembered that Paul has in mind the abuse rather than the proper use of tongues. He illustrates his meaning by a hypothetical case.] **23 If therefore the whole church be assembled together and all speak with tongues, and there come in men unlearned** [not having the gift to interpret tongues, and not being educated in foreign languages] **or unbelieving** [and hence having no faith in the works of the Spirit], **will they not say** [because of the queer and unintelligible sounds which ye are making] **that ye are mad? 24 But if all prophesy, and there come in one unbelieving or unlearned, he is reproved by all, he is judged** [literally, cross-examined] **by all; 25 the secrets of his heart are made manifest** [being exposed by the cleaving sword of the Spirit (Heb. 4: 12; Jas. 1: 23, 24; comp. John 4: 19, 29]; **and so he will fall down on his face** [The Oriental mode of showing deep emotion (Isa. 45: 14; 1 Sam. 19-24). Here it indicates feelings of submission and self-abasement] **and worship God, declaring that God is among you indeed.** [Paul supposes the case of one who dropped into the meeting out of curiosity. If he heard many people speaking at once in an unknown tongue, he would regard the gathering as little better than bedlam (Acts 2: 13), and the more he heard speaking at once, the worse it would be. Therefore the meeting would be to him void of blessing from God, and the sign without any signification, for he would hear his fellow-citizens addressing him in a foreign tongue, which was to him a mere jargon, instead of hearing foreigners address him in his own tongue, similar to the miracle at Pentecost. If, on the other hand, he heard all his fellow-citizens prophesying in his own tongue, he would be reproved by all, and the secrets of his heart would be laid bare as though he had been cross-examined by a skillful attorney. This would lead to his conversion, and so be of profit to him, and would make him a witness to the divine nature of the church, instead of one who looked upon it as a hive of fanatics. Prophetic preaching must **have** had great power to make men feel that they stood face to face with God, for even the faithful preaching of our day lays bare the sinner's heart. He feels that sermons are aimed at him, and is often convinced that some one has been tattling to the preacher because the life is so fully exposed by his words. It should be observed that if truth is more potent than signs, much more is it more efficacious in revivals than mere excitement or pumped-up enthusiasm.] 26 **What is it then, brethren?** [See comment on verse 15.] **When ye come together, each one hath a psalm, hath a teaching, hath a revelation, hath a tongue, hath an interpretation. Let all things be done unto edifying. 27 If any man speaketh in a tongue,** *let it be* **by two, or at the most three, and** *that* **in turn; and let one interpret: 28 but if there be no interpreter, let him keep silence in the church; and let him speak to himself, and to God. 29 And let the prophets speak** *by* **two or three, and let the others discern. 30 But if a revelation be made to another sitting by, let the first keep silence. 31 For ye all can prophesy one by one, that all may learn, and all may be exhorted; 32 and the spirits of the prophets are subject to the prophets; 33 for God is not** *a God* **of confusion, but of peace.** [Since those who spoke with tongues were not understood, they could all speak at once without any loss. Thus confusion was fostered and encouraged, and those who came with other contributions to the service, such as psalms, teachings, revelations, etc., were prevented from conferring any benefit upon the congregation. The apostle, therefore, orders the babel of tongues to be suppressed, that the congregation might be edified by these other contributions. Those who spoke with tongues were not to monopolize the meeting. In a large church like Corinth, where there would be plenty to take part in the exercises with psalms, teachings, interpretations of what had been said in tongues, etc., there was the opportunity for great variety. Hence Paul forbids more than three to speak with tongues in one exercise, and these must not speak all at once, but in turn, and they must pause and let some one gifted as interpreter translate what they had said for the edification of the church. If there was no such interpreter present, then the man gifted with tongues must keep silence, and worship within himself for the edification and benefit of his own soul. Moreover, not more than three prophets must speak in a meeting, and the others present must give heed, especially those competent to discern between true and false prophecies (1 Thess. 5: 20, 21; 1 John 4: 1; 5: 37). If a fresh revelation was given to a prophet while another prophet was speaking, the one speaking was to give place and keep silence, for the reception of a second revelation at such time would indicate authoritatively that the first revelation had been sufficiently explained. Therefore, the one speaking must desist, lest two should speak at a time, which would defeat the ends of instruction and exhortation. To enforce this rule of silence the apostle asserts the truth that prophets can control their spirits while under the prophetic influence. This guarded against the possibility that any speaker should pretend to be so carried away by the prophetic influence as to be unable to stop. God does not so overcome and entrance men as to make them produce confusion and disorder, for he is the God of order and of peace. God has not changed, and hysteria and frenzy, though they may exist in his churches as they may have done in Corinth, are not from him, nor according to his will. Even in the church at Corinth, where men were endowed with the gifts of the Spirit, all disorders were abuses of the spiritual gift and without excuse.] **As in all the churches of the saints, 34 let the women keep silence in the churches: for it is not permitted unto them to speak; but let them be in subjection, as also saith the law.** [Gen. 3: 16; Num. 30: 3-12.] **35 And if they would learn anything, let them ask their own husbands at home: for it is shameful for a woman to speak in the church.** [This is usually regarded as a very difficult passage, but the difficulties are more seeming than real, if we regard it as a general rule. Paul gives two reasons why the women should keep silence: 1. The Old Testament law made her subject to her husband,

SPIRITUAL GIFTS CONCLUDED

and hence not a teacher, but a pupil. 2. The customs of the age made it a shameful thing for a woman to speak in public. Of these, of course, the first is the weightier, and yet we find exceptions to the rule in both dispensations. There were several prophetesses who exercised their gifts in public (Ex. 15: 20; Judg. 4: 4; 2 Kings 22: 14; Isa. 8: 3; Neh. 6: 14; Luke 1: 41, 42; 2: 36-38; Acts 21: 9). Moreover, the fullness of prophetic endowment granted to the New Testament church was matter of prophecy (Acts 2: 17), and Paul himself gives directions as to the attire of women when exercising the prophetic office in the church (ch. 11: 5). Paul's rule, then, admits of exceptions. Some would do away with the rule entirely as obsolete on the ground that in Christ there is neither male nor female (Gal. 3: 28); but this is undoubtedly unwarranted, for while the gospel emancipated woman, it did not change her natural relation so as to make her the equal of man. The powers of woman have become so developed, and her privileges have been so extended in gospel lands, that it is no longer shameful for her to speak in public; but the failing of one reason is not the cessation of both. The Christian conscience has therefore interpreted Paul's rule rightly when it applies it generally, and admits of exceptions. The gift of prophecy no longer exists in the church, but, by the law of analogy, those women who have a marked ability, either for exhortation or instruction, are permitted to speak in the churches. Moreover, the apostle is speaking of the regular, formal meeting of the church; and it is doubtful if his law was ever intended to apply to informal gatherings such as prayer-meetings, etc. There is some weight to the comment that to understand the apostle we should know the ignorance, garrulity and degradation of Oriental women. Again, women are indeed subject to their husbands (Eph. 5: 22; Col. 2: 18; Tit. 2: 5; 1 Pet. 3: 1). The law is permanent, but the application of it may vary. If man universally gives the woman permission to speak, she is free from the law in this respect.] **36 What?** [An exclamation of indignation] **was it from you that the word of God went forth? or came it unto you alone?** [Becoming puffed up by the fullness of their spiritual gifts, the Corinthians were acting as if they were the parent church and only church. They were assuming the right to set precedent and dictate customs, when it was their duty to conform to the precedents and customs established before they came into existence. Their pretensions needed this indignant rebuke. Others were to be considered besides themselves, others who had sounded out the word which they had received (1 Thess. 1: 8). **37 If any man thinketh himself to be a prophet, or spiritual, let him take knowledge of the things which I write unto you, that they are the commandment of the Lord. 38 But if any man is ignorant, let him be ignorant.** [Since Paul's words were dictated by the Spirit of God, any one filled with that Spirit would be guided to recognize his words as of divine authority, for the Spirit would not say one thing to one man and another to another. But if any man was so incorrigibly obstinate as to refuse to be enlightened by what the Spirit spoke through the apostle, there was no further appeal to be made to him (Matt. 15: 14; 1 Tim. 6: 3-5). Paul's test is still of force. Whoso professes to be inspired, yet contradicts what the Spirit of God has already said in the New Testament, is self-convicted. These verses mark the division between Catholics and Protestants. The former say in effect that the Spirit-filled prophets at Corinth could modify, alter, and even deny what was spoken by the Spirit-filled Paul; for they hold that the pope can change the Scriptures to suit himself. But Protestants hold that a man shows himself to be led of the Spirit of God when he assents and conforms to that which has been spoken by men of undoubted inspiration.] **39 Wherefore, my brethren, desire earnestly to prophesy, and forbid not to speak with tongues. 40 But let all things be done decently and in order.** [Paul concludes with a recapitulation. The higher gift is to be sought and the lower gift is not to be prohibited. But as a caution against the abuse of the lower gift, he lays down that rule of order and decorum which the church has too often forgotten to her sorrow.] .

XII.

NINTH RESPONSE. AS TO THE RESURRECTION.

15: 1-58.

[The response in this section also is rather to a condition of the church than to a question. In the eyes of the Greeks the body was the prison-house of the soul, and death was a release of the soul from its captivity. The resurrection of the body, therefore, was regarded by them as a calamity rather than as a blessing, and so contrary to all sound philosophy as to excite ridicule (Acts 17: 32). While Paul was present in Corinth, his firm faith, full understanding, and clear teaching, had held the church firmly to the truth; but in his absence the church had grown forgetful of the precise nature of his teaching, and, attempting to harmonize the gospel doctrine of a resurrection with the theories of their own learned teachers, the Greek Christians of Corinth had many of them come to look upon the resurrection promised to Christians as a mere resurrection of the soul, and hence as one which, as to the dead, was already past (2 Tim. 2: 18). They flatly denied the possibility of a bodily resurrection. The chapter before us is a restatement of the truth as opposed to this error, and a general discussion of the doctrine of a resurrection tending to remove all the erroneous views which the Greeks held with regard to it. This chapter has been read as an antidote to the pain of death at millions of funerals.]
1 Now I make known unto you, brethren, the gospel which I preached unto you, which also ye received, wherein also ye stand, 2 by which also ye are saved, if ye hold fast the word which I preached unto you, except ye believed in vain. [or without cause. In these two verses Paul reminds them of many important facts, as follows: that they had already heard the gospel, weighed, tested and received it, and that they now stood as a church organized under it, and that their hopes of salvation depended

upon their holding fast to it, unless they had believed inconsiderately, under the impulse of a mere fitful admiration. His correlative appeal to them to think more deeply and steadfastly will be found in the last verse of the chapter.] **3 For I delivered unto you first of all** [as a matter of primary importance: see ch. 2: 3, 4] **that which also I received** [and hence no device or invention of my own]: **that Christ died for our sins** [to atone for them—1 John 3: 5; Gal. 1: 4; 2 Cor. 5: 15; Tit. 2: 14] **according to the scriptures** [Isa. 53: 5, 10; Dan. 9: 26; Ps. 22: 1-22; Zech. 12: 10]; **4 and that he was buried** [and this also was according to the Scriptures—Isa. 53: 9]; **and that he hath been raised on the third day according to the scriptures** [Ps. 16: 10; Isa. 53: 10; Hos. 6: 2; Jonah 2: 10. Here the apostle reminds the Corinthians that the message which he delivered to them was one which he had received by divine revelation; that it consisted of three pre-eminent facts, namely, the death, burial and resurrection of the Lord; that of these facts the two which were hard to believe, *i. e.*, the first and the last, were made more easy of belief by having been predicted in the Scriptures, the latter with minuteness, even as to the day. The apostle does not waste time proving the death; it was witnessed by thousands, it had never been denied by friend or enemy, and it was not now called in question by the Corinthians. The third item was the one called in question, and, having first proved it by a witness before the fact (the Scriptures), the apostle proceeds to refresh their minds as to how fully it had been proved by witnesses after the fact (viz.: the apostles and others), thus making them again aware that the resurrection was a literal, historical, objective fact. A fact so important and so difficult of belief demanded a host of witnesses, but Paul had them to produce; this thing was not done in a corner—Acts 26: 26]; **5 and that he appeared to Cephas** [Luke 24: 34]; **then to the twelve** [John 20: 26-29. "The twelve" was an official name for the apostles, though there were but eleven of them at this time]; **6 then he appeared to above five hundred brethren at once, of whom the greater part remain** [among the

AS TO THE RESURRECTION

living] **until now** [and hence are producible as witnesses], **but some are fallen asleep** [Matt. 28: 16]; **7 then he appeared to James** [This was the one called "the brother of our Lord," and "James the Just." Though Paul speaks of him as an apostle (Gal. 1: 19), he was not one of the twelve. But he was prominent in that day as a chief elder at Jerusalem (Acts 15: 13; 21: 18; Gal. 2: 9, 11). He was author of the Epistle which bears his name. The appearance here mentioned evidently converted James, for before the resurrection the brethren of our Lord did not believe on him—comp. John 12: 3-5; Acts 1: 14; 9: 5]; **then to all the apostles** [Acts 1: 3]; **8 and last of all, as to the *child* untimely born, he appeared to me also.** [Acts 9: 5; 22: 14; 26: 16. The abortive child is usually weak, puny and undersized. Paul speaks of himself as such a child in the brotherhoood of the apostles, and does this without mock modesty (comp. 2 Cor. 12: 11; Eph. 3: 8). For comment on this catalogue of appearances, see "Fourfold Gospel," pp. 751, 753, 761, 764, 766. The other apostles had three years and a half filled with instruction, and so were fully developed in their office; while Paul became a disciple in an instant, and received his instructions briefly by revelation.] **9 For I am the least of the apostles, that am not meet to be called an apostle, because I persecuted the church of God.** [Comp. Acts 7: 57; 8: 1-3; 9: 1; 1 Tim. 1: 13; Gal. 1: 13.] **10 But by the grace of God I am what I am: and his grace which was bestowed upon me was not found vain; but I labored more abundantly than they all: yet not I, but the grace of God which was with me.** [Gal. 2: 8; Phil. 2: 13; Col. 1: 29.] **11 Whether then *it be* I or they, so we preach, and so ye believed.** [Paul recognizes the tardiness of his belief on the Lord and the lateness of his vision of him as an evidence of his unworthiness. Though this personal allusion appears on its face to be a digression from his argument, it really lends great force to it. There could be no higher honor known to men than to be chosen as a witness of the resurrection of Christ. For this reason it might be thought that Paul was zealous in establishing the truth of the resurrection because of the *honors* which he enjoyed as a witness to that truth. But he reminds them that the circumstances under which he saw the Lord so emphasized his own *unworthiness* (he being then on his way to persecute the Christians at Damascus) that the memory of the event wakened in him a sense of humiliation rather than exaltation. In fact, he would be exalted rather than dishonored by their unbelief, for he could claim no reverence as a witness when his testimony necessarily involved a confession of his crimes. But having confessed his crime and consequent inferiority, and knowing that this admission would be most strictly construed by those who disparaged him and contended that he was not an apostle, he rehabilitates himself by showing that his own littleness had been made big by the abounding grace of God, so that he had labored more abundantly than any of the apostles. Moreover, those to whom Peter or Apollos were more acceptable, would gain nothing by their partiality and discrimination in respect to this matter, for all who had preached Christ to them had been a unit in proclaiming the resurrection. Christ had never been preached otherwise than as a risen one. Again, this preaching had resulted in their believing, which was the point he did not wish them to lose sight of. Having committed themselves to belief, they did wrong in thus becoming champions of unbelief; *i. e.*, unbelief in the resurrection. It should be observed that in proving the resurrection Paul cites witnesses (1) who were living; (2) who were many of them commonly known by name; (3) who were too familiar with the form, face, voice, manner, life, etc., of Jesus to be deceived by a pretender, if any could have found motive for practicing such a deception. Having shown their folly in abandoning without evidence that which they had believed on competent testimony, the apostle turns to show the consequences of their act.] **12 Now if Christ is preached that he hath been raised from the dead, how say some among you that there is no resurrection of the dead? 13 But if there is no resurrection of the dead, neither hath Christ been raised: 14 and if Christ hath not been raised, then is**

AS TO THE RESURRECTION

our preaching vain, your faith also is vain. [The resurrection of Christ was the very heart of the gospel, the essence of gospel preaching. The Corinthians had not realized how serious a matter it was to admit the impossibility of any resurrection. By so doing they made the resurrection of Jesus a fiction, and if his resurrection was fictitious, then Christian preaching and Christian faith were both empty vanities. Verily the argument of the rationalists had proved too much, causing them to deny the very faith which they professed. The apostle goes on to develop this thought, in connection with another thought—the *nature* of the issue between the rationalists and Christ's ministers. It was not an issue of truth or mistake, but of truth or falsehood—a direct accusation that the apostles and their colleagues were liars—Acts 2: 32; 4: 33; 13: 30.] **15 Yea, and we are found false witnesses of God; because we witnessed of God that he raised up Christ: whom he raised not up, if so be that the dead are not raised. 16 For if the dead are not raised, neither hath Christ been raised: 17 and if Christ hath not been raised, your faith is vain; ye are yet in your sins.** [unjustified—Rom. 4: 25.] **18 Then they also that are fallen asleep in Christ have perished. 19 If we have only hoped in Christ in this life, we are of all men most pitiable.** [2 Cor. 1: 5-9; 11: 23-32; 2 Tim. 3: 12. If, as the rationalists affirmed, there was no such thing as a resurrection, then Christ was not raised from the dead, and if he was not raised, the apostles and others who witnessed as to his resurrection had borne false testimony as to God, accusing him of doing what he had never done. They were also false witnesses as to the Corinthians, having given them a vain faith as to forgiveness and eternal life, when in reality they were yet in their sins, and doomed to receive the wages of sin which is death. They were also false witnesses as to the dead, for, instead of falling asleep in Jesus, the dead had perished. Moreover, they and other witnesses who had done all this, were wholly without excuse; for they had made others miserable without any profit whatever to themselves. If there was **no** resurrection and future reward for these witnesses, they must have testified falsely, hoping for some gain in this present life; but instead of such gain, these witnesses had drawn upon themselves from every quarter such storms of persecution as made their lives most pitiable—miserable enough to induce them to abandon so profitless a falsehood. The absolute self-sacrifice of such a life as Paul's can be explained only by admitting that he believed his own testimony, and truly hoped for a resurrection and blessings in the future state. At this point he ceases to be the persuasive logician, and speaks as the authoritative, inspired prophet. Against the vain and erroneous reasonings of men he places the infallible and unfailing revelations of the Spirit.] **20 But now hath Christ been raised from the dead, the firstfruits of them that are asleep. 21 For since by man** *came* **death, by man** *came* **also the resurrection of the dead. 22 For as in Adam all die** [Gen. 3: 1], **so also in Christ shall all be made alive. 23 But each in his own order** [literally, cohort, regiment, or military division] **: Christ the firstfruits; then they that are Christ's, at his coming.** [After clearly reaffirming his testimony to the resurrection of Christ, he goes on to show the comprehensive, all-inclusive nature of that resurrection. This he does by appeal to Scriptural figure and fact. On the morrow after the Sabbath of the passover a sheaf of barley (the earliest grain to ripen) was waved as firstfruits before the Lord (Lev. 23: 9-14). The firstfruits had to be thus presented before the harvest could be begun, and its presentation was an earnest of the ingathering. Now on this very day after the Sabbath Christ was raised as the firstfruits from the dead, and became the earnest of the general resurrection. Moreover, that which was so clearly shown in the type was written with equal clearness in the history. If the justice of God caused the death of Adam to include in its scope the death of all, so the mercy of God had caused the resurrection of Christ to work the contrary effect of liberating all from the grave. But as the firstfruits preceded the harvest, so the raising of Christ preceded the **resurrection of the race.** But as the firstfruits was part of the

AS TO THE RESURRECTION

harvest, so the resurrection of Christ is a partial resurrection of all humanity. He must be the Omega as well as the Alpha of the resurrection, and must raise all in whom his Spirit dwells. Because Paul states that there shall be order in the resurrection, and because he names but *two* parties in the order—Christ and his disciples, commentators have been deceived into thinking that there will be a third order—the wicked. Thus they have the anomaly of firstfruits followed by *two* harvests. But this is contradicted by the entire trend of Scripture, which speaks of a resurrection, and not of resurrections; of a harvest (Matt. 13: 36-43), and not harvests; and which describes the judgment day in terms which can not be reconciled with two separate resurrections (Matt. 25: 31-46). The only apparent exception is the spiritual or figurative resurrection mentioned in the Apocalypse (Rev. 20: 4-6). The truth is that in this chapter Paul is considering only the resurrection of the righteous, and takes no account of the resurrection of the wicked at all, for to have done so would have involved his readers in endless confusion. The context clearly shows this. There is but one resurrection day for humanity, and but one trumpet to summon them to arise and appear in one common hour of judgment. 24 Then *cometh* the end [the apostle does not mean to say that this end comes immediately after the resurrection, but that it is next in order of great events, so far as humanity is concerned], **when he shall deliver up the kingdom to God, even the Father; when he shall have abolished all rule and all authority and power. 25 For he must reign, till he hath put all his enemies under his feet.** [Eph. 1: 20-22; Matt. 28: 18; 1 Pet. 3: 22.] **26 The last enemy that shall be abolished is death.** [2 Tim. 1: 10; Heb. 2: 14; Rev. 20: 14.] **27 For** [saith the Psalmist], **He put all things in subjection under his feet. But when he saith, All things are put in subjection** [Ps. 8: 6; 110: 1; 2: 6-9], **it is evident that he** [the Father] **is excepted who did subject all things unto him. 28 And when all things have been subjected unto him, then shall the Son also himself be subjected to him that did** subject all things unto him, that God may be all in all. [*i. e.*, that God may have all headship of all creation; complete and absolute supremacy (Col. 3: 11), so that "all things shall say, 'God is all things to me'" (*Bengel*). In verse 23 the apostle, while arguing the reasonableness of the resurrection, is led to mention its relation to the end of the world, but the resurrection presents its reasonableness in another form, being intimately associated with a higher, more transcendent climax than even the termination of this physical universe; for it is an essential preliminary to the culmination of Christ's mediatorial kingdom into the kingdom of the Father. This culmination can not take place until the mediatorial kingdom has attained ripened perfection through the subjugation of all things. But among the enemies to be thus subdued, death stands forth with marked prominence, and the weapon which subdues him is, and can be no other than, the resurrection. Hence the supreme glorification, or, as it were, the crowning of God as all in all, is predicated upon a resurrection as a condition precedent. The chain of Paul's logic is long, but it runs thus: no glorification until the mediatorial kingdom is turned over to God; no turning over of this kingdom until its work is complete; no completion of its work till all its enemies are destroyed; no destruction of all these enemies while death, a chief one, survives; no destruction of death save by the resurrection: therefore no full glorification of God without a resurrection. The logic would hold good for the doctrine of Universalism, were it not that there is a second death which is not looked upon as an enemy to the kingdom of God.] **29 Else** [*i. e.*, if it were otherwise—if baptism were not an all-important factor in God's plan] **what shall they do that are baptized for** [on account of, with reference to. For full discussion of this preposition see Canon Evans' additional note, Speaker's Commentary *in loco*] **the dead? If the dead are not raised at all, why then are they baptized for them?** [The word "baptized" is an imperfect participle, and denotes an act being continually performed. Paul's question, then, is this: If the resurrection is not part of God's plan—if affairs are otherwise,

AS TO THE RESURRECTION

and there is really no resurrection—then what are converts to do, who, under the mistaken notion that there is a resurrection, are now constantly presenting themselves to be buried in baptism on account of the dead? If the dead are not raised, why then are these converts buried in baptism on their account, or with a view to them? Rom. 6: 3-11 makes Paul's meaning in this passage very plain. The dead are a class of whom Christ is the head and firstfruits unto resurrection. By baptism we symbolically *unite* ourselves with that class, and so with Christ, and we do this because of the hope that we shall be raised with that class through the power of Christ (Rom. 6: 5). But if the dead are not raised at all, then why should converts be united with them by a symbolic burial? why should they be baptized on their account, or with reference to them? If there is no resurrection, baptism, which symbolizes it, is meaningless. Commentators belonging to churches which have substituted sprinkling for baptism make sad havoc of this passage. Having lost sight of the symbolic meaning of baptism—that it is a union of the convert with the dead, and especially with the dead and buried Christ as their head and firstfruits unto life—they are at a loss how to interpret the apostle's words, and in despair assert that Christians were in the habit of being baptized vicariously for their friends who died without baptism. Long after Paul wrote, a similar misunderstanding of this passage led the followers both of Marcion and Cerenthus to practice such vicarious baptisms; but the practice *grew out of Paul's words*, instead of his words being called forth by the practice.] **30 why do we also stand in jeopardy every hour? 31 I protest by that glorying in** [concerning] **you, brethren, which I have in Christ Jesus our Lord, I die daily.** [Rom. 8: 36.] **32 If after the manner of men** [as a carnal man, having no future hope] **I fought with beasts at Ephesus, what doth it profit me?** [The tense and words indicate that Paul had become a beast-fighter as a settled occupation. It is conceded that his language was figurative, and that he spoke of contending with beasts in human form (Tit. 1: 12; 2 Tim. 4: 17), rather than to the fighting of actual beasts in the arena. Had Paul been thrown to the lions, Luke could hardly have failed to mention it when recording the events of Paul's ministry at Ephesus. Moreover, Paul's Roman citizenship shielded him from such a punishment. But he does not refer to the tumult in the theater (Acts 20: 19), for it took place after this letter was written. But we may well believe that Paul was in daily danger in Ephesus—2 Cor. 1: 8, 9.] **If the dead are not raised, let us eat and drink, for to-morrow we die.** [This is an Epicurean maxim which had passed into a proverb. "If," says South, "men but persuade themselves that they shall die like beasts, they soon will live like beasts too." In the three verses above, Paul passes from the symbolic death of baptism to consider death literally. In the hope of a resurrection he was enduring daily a living death, his life being hourly in jeopardy. If it was idle folly in converts to be symbolically united with the dead, much more was it gross foolishness for the apostle to live thus continually on the verge of being literally, actually united with them. But the folly in both instances was made wisdom by the fact of a resurrection. Thus to the arguments already adduced Paul adds the additional one that Christianity, in its initial ordinance, and in its daily life-experience, is built upon the hope of a resurrection. Without this hope no sensible man could start to be a Christian, much less continue to live in accordance with his profession.] **33 Be not deceived: Evil companionships corrupt good morals. 34 Awake to soberness righteously, and sin not; for some have no knowledge of God: I speak *this* to move you to shame.** [Do not be deceived by freethinkers and shun those who would corrupt the truth, for right doctrine and right practice stand or fall together. Shake off, therefore, this drunken fit, and keep from those sins in which it has tempted you to indulge. The sentence "Evil," etc., is a quotation taken from the Greek poet Menander. To show the full enormity of the teaching of the rationalists, Paul declares that it is a shame to the Corinthians to have such Christless Christians in the church—men who have so little knowledge of even the *power* of God as to deny his ability to bring to pass

AS TO THE RESURRECTION

so simple a matter as the resurrection. That God gives life is daily apparent; and to give it is infinitely more wonderful than to restore it.] **35 But some one will say, How are the dead raised? and with what manner of body do they come? 36 Thou foolish one, that which thou thyself sowest is not quickened except it die** [comp. John 12: 24] : **37 and that which thou sowest, thou sowest not the body that shall be, but a bare** [naked] **grain, it may chance of wheat, or of some other kind ; 38 but God giveth it a body even as it pleased him** [guided by his sense of fitness and propriety], **and to each seed a body of its own.** [In this paragraph Paul answers the first question of verse 35. The Corinthians, like all materialists, made the resurrection a puzzling problem. They wondered *how* God could restore a body which returned to the dust, passed thence into vegetation, and thence into the bodies of animals and other men. Paul calls the man who thus puzzles himself a foolish one, because he denies that the all-powerful God can do with a human body that which he himself practically does annually with the bodies (grains) of wheat, etc., by merely availing himself of the common course of nature. When he sows a grain of wheat he does not expect it to come up a naked grain as he sowed it, but he knows that it will die, and in its death produce another body, consisting of stalk, blade, head and other grains similar to the one sown. He knows that though the body thus produced bear small outward resemblance to the single grain planted, yet it is the product of the grain's germinal life, and on examination can be absolutely demonstrated to be such. Moreover, by doing this same thing with corn, oats and other grain he finds that each produces a body of its own kind, adapted by the wisdom of God to its needs. With all this before him, how foolish in man to deny that God can cause the dead body to rise in a higher and nobler form, and that he can also cause each man to have a resurrected body true to his individuality, so that Smith shall no more rise in the likeness of Jones than corn come up after the similitude of oats. But the analogy taught by nature is true in another respect; *i. e.*, the body produced by the seed is greater and more excellent than the seed. Paul enlarges and applies this thought.] **39 All flesh is not the same flesh: but there is one *flesh* of men, and another flesh of beasts, and another flesh of birds, and another of fishes. 40 There are also celestial bodies, and bodies terrestrial: but the glory of the celestial is one, and the *glory* of the terrestrial is another. 41 There is one glory of the sun, and another glory of the moon, and another glory of the stars; for one star differeth from another star in glory. 42 So also is the resurrection of the dead.** [Here the apostle answers the second question of verse 35. If a man rises from the dead changed as the grain of wheat is changed, will he not have a *different* body, and so lose his identity? Will he not cease to be man? Paul gives a threefold answer to this question. He shows that there may be diversity, and yet a common ground of identity. There are diverse forms of flesh, yet all these forms are flesh; there may be different forms of bodies having different glories, yet are they all bodies; yea, even the glories may differ in luster and yet may have common identity as glory. Thus also is the resurrection of the dead. The flesh is changed, and yet it is in a sense flesh—humanity; there may be modifications in the form, and yet it will be the same body. There may be great changes in the glory, yet the glory will still be glory, and not essentially different. Thus man may still be man, and yet be vastly improved. In this part of the argument Paul is correcting a cardinal error in Greek thought. They stumbled at the doctrine of a resurrection, because they regarded the body as a clog to the soul; and so the body might indeed be, if God could form *but one kind* of body. But he can form celestial as well as terrestrial bodies, and spiritual bodies adapted to the needs of the spirit, which will not hinder it as does this earthly tabernacle which it now inhabits—bodies which will not only prove no disadvantage, but of infinite assistance, because answering every requirement. This truth is now further exemplified.] **It is sown in corruption** [Eccl. 12: 7]; **it is raised in incorruption** [Luke 20: 35, 36]: **43 it is sown**

AS TO THE RESURRECTION

in dishonor [buried because it is repulsive and will become offensive—John 11: 39]; **it is raised in glory** [Phil. 3: 21]: **it is sown in weakness** [devoid of all ability]; **it is raised in power** [Rev. 3: 21]: **44 it is sown a natural body; it is raised a spiritual body. If there is a natural body, there is also a spiritual** *body*. [This power of God to preserve identity in diversity works out glorious results for man. Our earthly body, when planted in death, will indeed bring forth after its kind, but God, in the fullness of his power and grace, shall cause it to lay aside its terrestrial glory, and assume the celestial. The nature of the change thus effected is illustrated by four contrasts, the corruption, dishonor, weakness and animal nature of the terrestrial body being laid aside for the incorruptible, glorious, powerful and spiritual body of the celestial world. If man owns a natural, or psychical, body, *i. e.*, a body which is sustained and operated by his lower or soul-life, and suited to this world of death; so he also owns a spiritual body, suited to the desires, motions and operations of the spirit and eternal life; a body wherein the soul takes its proper position of subordination to the spirit, according to God's original plan and purpose when he created man in his image. Paul says *"is,"* for such a body already exists, and is occupied by Christ our head—Rev. 1: 18.] **45 So also it is written** [Gen. 2: 7], **The first man Adam became a living soul. The last Adam** *became* **a life-giving spirit. 46 Howbeit that is not first which is spiritual, but that which is natural; then that which is spiritual. 47 The first man is of the earth, earthy: the second man is of heaven. 48 As is the earthy, such are they also that are earthy: and as is the heavenly, such are they also that are heavenly. 49 And as we have borne the image of the earthy, we shall also bear the image of the heavenly.** [Here the two heads of humanity are contrasted. Adam was a quickening soul, and Christ a quickening spirit (comp. Gen. 2: 7, and John 20: 22. See also 2 Cor. 3: 17; Rom. 8: 2, 11; John 7: 38, 39). But of these two heads the natural came first. We are Adam's by generation, and

Christ's by regeneration. The life principle of Adam is soul, and he was formed of the earth: the life principle of Christ is spiritual. He was in heaven (John 1:1) and from thence entered the world and became flesh (John 1:14; 3:13, 21; Phil. 2:6-8; John 1:1-3; Luke 1:35). Now, as the two heads differ, so do the two families, and each resembles its head; the earthly progeny of Adam having earthly natures, and the spiritual progeny of Christ having spiritual and heavenly natures. But in both families the earthly nature comes first, and the spiritual children *wait for their manifestation*, which is the very thing about which the apostle has been talking, for it comes when they are raised from the dead (Rom. 8:29; 1 John 3:2; Rom. 8:22, 23; 2 Cor. 5:1-10). Life is not retrogression, but ascension. Therefore he assures them that as they have borne the image of the earthly Adam, so also are they to bear the image of the heavenly Christ, both of whom have the bodies of men, yet bodies differing vastly in glory, power, etc., for one belongs to the earth, dies and returns to it, while the other belongs to the deathless heaven and forever abides there.] **50 Now this I say, brethren, that flesh and blood cannot inherit the kingdom of God; neither doth corruption inherit incorruption.** [1 Pet. 1:4.] **51 Behold, I tell you a mystery** [a secret not previously revealed]: **We all shall not sleep** [die], **but we shall all be changed, 52 in a moment, in the twinkling of an eye, at the last trump: for the trumpet shall sound, and the dead shall be raised incorruptible, and we shall be changed. 53 For this corruptible must put on incorruption, and this mortal must put on immortality.** [Man in his fleshly nature has no place in heaven, for corruption is antagonistic to incorruption, as light is to darkness. It is essential, therefore, that man must put off the corruption of Adam and the natural body of Adam, and assume the incorruptible, spiritual body of Christ, before he can enter upon his celestial inheritance. Those who are alive at Christ's coming shall not escape this necessary change. If the dead are changed by resurrection (verses 42, 43), the living shall

AS TO THE RESURRECTION

also be changed by transfiguration; but both shall be changed, and the change in each shall take place at the same moment; *i. e.*, when the trumpet shall summon all to appear before God —1 Thess. 4: 6.] **54 But when this corruptible shall have put on incorruption, and this mortal shall have put on immortality, then shall come to pass the saying that is written** [Isa. 25: 8], **Death is swallowed up in victory.** [When the natural body shall be transformed into the spiritual, then shall be fulfilled that prophecy which describes death—the one who has swallowed up the human race, as being himself swallowed up in victory.] **55 O death, where is thy victory? O death, where is thy sting?** [This passage is quoted loosely from Hos. 13: 14. Warmed by the glow and glory of his argument, the apostle bursts forth in this strain of triumphant exultation, which has wakened a corresponding thrill in the heart of the Christian, and has been a solace and comfort to the church through all subsequent centuries.] **56 The sting of death is sin** [Rom. 6: 23]; **and the power of sin is the law** [Rom. 4: 15; 7: 10-12]: **57 but thanks be to God** [Ps. 98: 1], **who giveth us the victory through our Lord Jesus Christ.** [Death is here spoken of under the figure of a serpent. Sin is the bite or sting with which he slays men, and the power or poisonous strength of sin is found in the curse which the law pronounces upon the sinner. By the triple power of law, sin and death, the glory of man was brought to nought; but thanks are due to God, who restored glory to man through Jesus Christ. Christ gave man the victory over the law, for he nailed it to his cross (Col. 2: 14); he gave him victory over sin, for he made atonement for sin (Heb. 7: 27); and he gave him victory over death by his resurrection, which is the earnest of the general resurrection. Wonderful threefold victory!] **58 Wherefore, my beloved brethren, be ye stedfast, unmovable, always abounding in the work of the Lord, forasmuch as ye know that your labor is not vain in the Lord.** [Therefore, since you see that the dead are raised and made capable of enjoying heaven, do not again be moved from your belief in

160 FIRST EPISTLE TO THE CORINTHIANS

these well-proven and established truths, and be careful to abound in the Lord's work, for no matter what your present sufferings and persecutions may be, the Lord will amply reward you in the resurrection, and your labor will not be in vain.]

XIII.

CONCERNING THE COLLECTION, PERSONAL MATTERS, SALUTATIONS AND BENEDICTION.

16: 1-24.

The fraternal communism of the Jerusalem church (Acts 2: 44, 45; 4: 36, 37; 5: 1), together with the political troubles, famines (Acts 11: 28-30) and persecutions (Acts 8: 1-4), all tended to impoverish the church in Judæa. To relieve this poverty and to bring about a more cordial feeling between Jews and Gentiles, Paul had set about gathering an offering in the Gentile churches for the brethren in Judæa. The church at Corinth had consented to make such offering, but had been hindered by their factions, or some other cause, from so doing. In this chapter Paul requests them to begin taking this offering at once. He also speaks of the reasons why he had postponed his visit, tells them when they may expect him, and treats of some other lesser matters.] **1 Now concerning the collection for the saints** [Christians], **as I gave order to the churches of Galatia, so also do ye.** [Very probably he had ordered, or arranged for, this collection on the journey mentioned at Acts 16: 6, and he probably collected it on that mentioned at Acts 18: 23. "Paul," says Bengel, "holds up as an example to the Corinthians the Ga'atians, to the Macedonians the Corinthians (2 Cor. 9: 2), and to the Romans the Macedonians and Corinthians (Rom. 15: 26): great is the force of example." For other references to this collection, see Acts 11: 29, 30; 24: 17; 2 Cor. 8: 1, 2.] **2 Upon the first day of the week let each one of you lay by him in store, as he may prosper, that no collections be made when I**

CONCERNING THE COLLECTION, ETC. 161

come. [The word *"thesaurizoon,"* translated "in store," means, literally, "put into the treasury;" and the phrase *"par' heauto,"* translated "by him," may be taken as the neuter reflexive pronoun, and may be rendered with equal correctness "by itself." Macknight thus renders these two words, and this rendering is to be preferred. If each man had laid by in his own house, all these scattered collections would have had to be gathered after Paul's arrival, which was the very thing that he forbade. Again, had the collection been of such a private nature, it would have been gathered normally at the *end* instead of at the beginning of the week. But the first day of the week was evidently set apart for public worship (John 20: 19-26; Acts 20: 7; Rev. 1: 10), and this offering was part of the service. It was put in the public treasury of the church, but kept by itself as a *separate fund.* The translation of the Revised Version is unfortunate, as it obscures the idea of the weekly service of the church. According to Paul's method of collecting, each rendered a weekly account of his stewardship, and gave more and felt it less than if he had attempted to donate it all at one time. Paul had promised to take such offerings (Gal. 2: 10). As a Christian he tries to relieve that distress which, as a persecutor, he had aided to inflict (Acts 26: 6-10). He wished each one, rich or poor, to contribute to the offering, and he wanted the whole matter disposed of and out of the way when he came, that he might turn his attention to more important matters.] **3 And when I arrive, whomsoever ye shall approve, them will I send with letters to carry your bounty unto Jerusalem: 4 and if it be meet for me to go also, they shall go with me.** [Paul does not ask to be made custodian of the offering. He directs the church to appoint its own messengers to carry it, thus raising himself above all suspicion of misappropriation, and giving the church a new incentive to make a liberal offering, for it would afford the church a new joy and profit to have in its membership those who had been to Jerusalem and seen the apostles. Paul, as an apostle, and as one personally acquainted with the Jerusalem church, promises to give the bearers of the fund letters of introduction and commendation to the apostles and elders at Jerusalem; and, should the greatness of the collection and the dignity of the occasion require it, he agrees to accompany the bounty himself. The collection proved large enough to justify this, and Paul accompanied the delegates. For the names of those who left Greece with Paul, see Acts 20: 4.] **5 But I will come unto you, when I shall have passed through Macedonia; for I** [purpose to] **pass through Macedonia; 6 but with you it may be that I shall abide, or even winter, that ye may set me forward on my journey whithersoever I go. 7 For I do not wish to see you now by the way** [merely as I pass through]; **for I hope to tarry a while with you, if the Lord permit.** [Jas. 4: 15; Acts 18: 1; Heb. 6: 3; ch. 4: 19.] **8 But I will tarry at Ephesus until Pentecost; 9 for a great door** [the common metaphor expressing opportunity (Acts 14: 27; 2 Cor. 2: 12; Col. 4: 3; Rev. 3: 8; Hos. 2: 15] **and effectual is opened unto me, and there are many adversaries.** [For this success and the adversaries which it aroused see Acts 19: 1-20. For the riot which it afterwards stirred up see Acts 19: 23-41. From this paragraph it appears that it had been Paul's plan to visit Corinth, going thither from Ephesus by direct course across the Ægean Sea; and after a brief sojourn there to pass up into Macedonia, and visit Corinth again on the return. This plan he evidently communicated to the Corinthians in that first epistle which is lost (ch. 5: 9). But the evil reports which came to him concerning the conduct of the Corinthian church caused him to change his purpose, and delay his visit, that they might have time to repent, and so escape the severe correction which he would otherwise have felt constrained to administer to them (2 Cor. 1: 23; 2: 1). Moreover, he reversed his route; coming by Macedonia (Acts 19: 21, 22), and intending to depart by sea (Acts 20: 3). To help bring about a state of repentance, he sent Timothy as a forerunner (ch. 4: 16-21), and sent him by way of Macedonia (Acts 19: 22). He now writes that he has thus altered his plans, and that he is coming through Macedonia, and that he will not pay them two cursory visits, but will make them one long one, and probably stay all winter. However, he will not begin this journey until after Pentecost, for the work in Ephesus has become so fruitful as to demand at present all his attention. Paul carried out his plan as here outlined (2 Cor. 2: 13; 8: 1; 9: 2, 4; 12: 14; 13: 1; Acts 20: 3-6). He suggests their forwarding him on his journey, thus showing his confidence in them, that they would give him this customary proof of affection (Rom. 15: 24; Acts 15: 3; 17: 15; Tit. 3: 13); but intimates, by using "whithersoever," that his course beyond them is uncertain. We find later that he was compelled to change his plan—Acts 20: 3.] **10 Now if Timothy come, see that he be with you without fear; for he worketh the work of the Lord, as I also do** [ch. 14: 17] : **11 let no man therefore despise him** [1 Tim. 4: 12]. **But set him forward on his journey in peace, that he may come unto me: for I expect him with the brethren.** [Timothy, as we have seen, went the long route by way of Macedonia, no doubt visiting the churches as he journeyed. Soon after his departure the messengers from Corinth arrived, bringing the letter from that church, and Paul sends this answer to it by Titus. Now, Titus was evidently despatched by the short route across the sea, with instructions to return by way of Macedonia. Therefore Paul uses "if," for he supposes that Titus may reach Corinth, discharge his errand, start through Macedonia, and there intercept Timothy so as to prevent his ever reaching Corinth. And this very thing seems to have happened, for Titus and Timothy, returning, evidently met Paul at Philippi, where he wrote his second Corinthian letter (2 Cor. 1: 1); yet only Titus is spoken of as having brought any report of the condition of affairs at Corinth (2 Cor. 7: 6, 7). The Corinthians, therefore, had no chance to show their love for Paul by their welcome of Timothy. Paul's words with regard to him remind us that he was at that time a young man and liable to be intimidated by the factious, arrogant spirit of the Corinthians. Timothy seems to have been of a diffident and sensitive nature (1 Tim. 5: 21-23; 2 Tim. 1: 6-8). Paul warns them that any unkindness shown to this young man will soon be reported to him, for he expects Timothy to return with Titus, Erastus and those with them—Acts 19: 22; 2 Cor. 12: 17, 18; 8: 18, 23.] **12 But as touching Apollos the brother, I besought him much to come unto you with the brethren [with Titus, etc.]: and it was not at all *his* will to come now; but he will come when he shall have opportunity.** [Apollos first comes to our notice at Ephesus (Acts 18: 24-28), whence he went to Corinth just before Paul came to Ephesus (Acts 19: 1). From Corinth Apollos returned to and was now at Ephesus. The old Latin commentators say that he left Corinth on account of the violence of the factions, and now declined to return because of them, but it is not likely that they knew anything more about the facts than we do. Jerome tells us that after the factious spirit subsided, Apollos returned to Corinth, and became bishop or elder of the church; but he gives us no authority for his statement. Paul's words are important, because they show that neither he nor Apollos gave any countenance or encouragement to the factions. Paul has no fear that Apollos will do wrong intentionally, yet Apollos fears that he may do wrong by his presence unintentionally. It did not seem to Apollos that it was a fit season for him to show himself in Corinth.] **13 Watch ye, stand fast in the faith, quit you like men, be strong. 14 Let all that ye do be done in love.** [In these brief, nervous phrases, Paul sums up the burden of his entire Epistle. The Corinthians were to be wakeful and not asleep (ch. 11: 30; 15: 33). They were to be steadfast, manly and strong (ch. 15: 2, 58); they were to do all things in love (chs. 7, 8, 10, 11, 12 and 14), not show their lack of love in bringing lawsuits, wrangling about marriage, eating things sacrificed to idols, behaving selfishly at the Lord's Supper, and vaunting themselves on account of their gifts.] **15 Now I beseech you, brethren (ye know the house of Stephanas, that it is the firstfruits of Achaia [*i. e.*, my first converts in Greece—ch. 1: 16], and that they have set themselves to minister unto the saints), 16 that ye also be in subjection unto**

CONCERNING THE COLLECTION, ETC.

such, and to every one that helpeth in the work and laboreth. [The apostle asks the Corinthians to be subject to their truly religious teachers, and picks out the family of Stephanas as a sample. This family was the first converted, and, consequently, probably the best instructed in the church.] **17 And I rejoice at the coming of Stephanas and Fortunatus and Achaicus: for that which was lacking on your part they supplied. 18 For they refreshed my spirit and yours: acknowledge ye therefore them that are such.** [These were the messengers which bore the Corinthian letter to Paul. Of them we know nothing more. What Paul says of them here was probably written to keep the Corinthians from showing resentment toward them for having told him the sad condition of the church. The thought seems to be that they refreshed the apostle by partially filling the void caused by the absence of the Corinthians, and they caused Paul to refresh the church at Corinth both by receiving personal messages from him, and causing him to write the letter. He asks that they be received as a refreshment from him, just as he had received them as such from them.] **19 The churches of Asia salute you.** [These were the churches in the Roman province of Asia, of which Ephesus was the capital. Seven churches of this province are mentioned in the opening chapters of the Book of Revelation. They were in the western coast lands of Asia Minor.] **Aquila and Prisca salute you much in the Lord, with the church that is in their house.** [This devoted couple had been with Paul in Corinth, and were now in Ephesus (Acts 18: 1, 2, 18, 26. Soon after we find them in Rome (Rom. 16: 3), where they also had, as here, a church in their house (Rom. 16: 5). It was yet a day of small congregations, worshiping in private houses—Rom. 16: 4, 15; Col. 4: 15; Philem. 2.] **20 All the brethren** [in Ephesus] **salute you. Salute one another with a holy kiss.** [See commentary on Thessalonians, page 27. "He rightly enjoins the kiss of peace upon those who were in danger of being rent to pieces by schisms."—*Grotius*.] **21 The salutation of me Paul with mine own hand.** [All of Paul's letters save Galatians appear to have been written by an amanuensis (Gal. 6: 11). Inspired Scripture was too important to be wanting in authenticity, or to be subjected to suspicion as forgery.] **22 If any man loveth not the Lord, let him be anathema. Marana tha.** [Literally, "Let him be devoted to destruction. O Lord, come!" They were the words with which the Jews began their greatest excommunication. Here Paul pronounces a curse against the man who, professing to be a Christian, had really no love for Christ. Though the church can not always detect and punish such, yet the Lord at his coming will find them out. This, therefore, is Paul's appeal to the Lord to do this thing, and he writes the words with his own hand to show how seriously he meant them. For use of the word "anathema," see Acts 12: 2; 23: 14; Rom. 9: 3; Gal. 1: 8, 9.] **23 The grace** [the reverse of the anathema] **of the Lord Jesus Christ be with you. 24 My love be with you all in Christ Jesus. Amen.** [The apostle closes with this thought, lest any should misconstrue his letter. Though it contained severe rebukes, it was dictated by love, and not by hatred.]

SECOND EPISTLE TO THE CORINTHIANS.

INTRODUCTION.

Having despatched his first Epistle to the Corinthians by their returning messengers (1 Cor. 16: 17, 18), and having, as it appears, sent Titus with them as his own messenger (comp. 1 Cor. 16: 1, 2 and 2 Cor. 8: 6), Paul became exceedingly anxious as to the effect which his letter would have, and, to get earlier news from it, he advanced from Ephesus to the seacoast at Troas, where he expected to meet Titus. But when Titus did not come, though Paul found "a door opened to him" in Troas, his spirits were so intolerably oppressed by forebodings of evil as to the situation at Corinth, that he crossed over the sea into Macedonia to learn what had occurred there. Here, possibly at Philippi, he meets with Titus, and this second Epistle is called forth by the report which Titus brought (2: 12, 13; 7: 5-7). The first Epistle was written from Ephesus in the spring of A. D. 57, and this one from Macedonia, probably in September or October of the same year. It shows that Titus reported that the majority of the church was with Paul, accepted him as an apostle, read his message with fear and trembling, received his rebukes with grief, and sought to obey his instructions with holy zeal, promptly excommunicating the incestuous man (7: 7-14). But there was still a dangerous and defiant minority for Paul to subdue, an evil influence for him to break down, and this second Epistle is written because of this party. This minority, which existed when the first Epistle was written, had apparently been re-enforced by Judaizers, who came from Jerusalem bearing what purported to be letters of commendation from some high authority. This minority denounced Paul with unscrupulous boldness. They accused him of cowardice, in that he had not come to Corinth, insinuating that he preferred to keep at a distance and thunder in his letters, because he knew that he was weak and contemptible if present. With wanton brazenness they struck at his apostolic authority, asserting that he had no authentic commission, and not even commendatory letters from Jerusalem. They accused him of lying in regard to his journeys and visits, and being so vacillating in his statements and purposes as to be wholly untrustworthy. These, and other charges and innuendoes, were so bold in their character, so gross in their nature and so dangerous in their significance that, for the good of the cause, Paul felt impelled to write this defense. Being strongly emotional from end to end, it is in style the most difficult of all Paul's Epistles, and it is also the least systematic; but the following analysis is fairly satisfactory. Part I. The maintenance of his genuine apostleship (chs. 1-7). This part is addressed more particularly to that section of the church which was loyal, or even friendly, in its attitude toward him. It is divisible into two subdivisions: (1) Defense against the charge of being unreliable because he had changed his plans as to the time and direction of his journey to visit them, and had apparently contradicted himself (chs. 1, 2). (2) A discussion of his apostolic office (chs. 3-7). Part II. Exhortations as to the offerings for the Judæan poor (chs. 8, 9). Part III. A measurement of his life, powers, ability, etc., with those who opposed and defamed him (chs. 10-13). This part is addressed more particularly to those who held him in doubt, and those who openly defied him, and may be subdivided as follows: (1) Preliminary suggestions as to the measurement (ch. 10-11: 21). (2) The measurement in detail (ch. 11: 22-13). The Epistle differs very greatly in its tone, passing from the warmest affection to the most startling menace, because the apostle is sometimes addressing the penitent majority, and sometimes the refractory minority.

SECOND EPISTLE TO THE CORINTHIANS.

PART FIRST.
PAUL'S MAINTENANCE OF HIS APOSTLESHIP.

CHS. 1-7.

I.

THANKS FOR COMFORT. DEFENSE AS TO CHANGE OF PLANS.

1: 1-22.

1 Paul, an apostle of Christ Jesus through the will of God, and Timothy our brother, unto the church of God which is at Corinth, with all the saints that are in the whole of Achaia: 2 Grace to you and peace from God our Father and the Lord Jesus Christ. [Since Paul's apostleship was in dispute, and since it seems to have been insinuated that he ought to have had a letter from the apostles or some others, commending him as such (ch. 3: 1), he begins by asserting that he is such through the will of God, and hence needs no human commendation. He joins Timothy with him in the letter, since this young man had assisted in founding the church at Corinth. Anciently Achaia was the northern strip of the Peloponnese, and in this restricted sense Paul appears to have used it at 1 Cor. 16: 15, for he there calls Stephanas the "firstfruits of Achaia." But in the times in which Paul wrote, Achaia was a Roman province embracing all the countries south of Macedonia, and having Corinth as its capital. Since Paul uses the word "whole," it is likely that Paul means this larger Achaia which included Athens, and of which

Dionysius the Areopagite, or some other Athenian, was the "firstfruits" (Acts 17: 34). As Corinth was the political capital of the region, Paul treated it as the religious headquarters, and addressed all the Achaians through it that any who came to the capital might feel a personal interest in his letter, and read or make copies of it.] **3 Blessed *be* the God and Father of our Lord Jesus Christ, the Father** [fountain, source—Ps. 86: 15; Eph. 1: 17] **of mercies and God of all comfort; 4 who comforteth us in all our affliction, that we may be able to comfort them that are in any affliction, through the comfort wherewith we ourselves are comforted of God.** [Paul regarded affliction as a school wherein one who is comforted of God is thereby instructed and fitted to become a dispenser of comfort unto others. He blesses God for such lofty and blessed instruction.] **5 For as the sufferings of Christ abound unto us, even so our comfort also aboundeth through Christ.** [By "sufferings of Christ" Paul means the persecutions, etc., suffered for Christ's sake. As Christ himself suffered while on the earth, so the church, his mystical body, must likewise suffer while in the flesh (Phil. 3: 17; Gal. 2: 20; Heb. 3: 13; 1 Pet. 4: 13; Acts 9: 4). It does this because it lives as he did, and its work is in a sense supplemental to his (Col. 1: 24; John 17: 14; 18: 19, 20). It is comforted by the Holy Spirit (John 14: 16-18), with the sense of the present love of Christ, and assured hope of reward; a sense of increased power to assist and comfort others; a trust that all things are working together for good (ch. 4: 17). The measure of affliction becomes also the measure of comfort.] **6 But whether we are afflicted, it is for your comfort and salvation; or whether we are comforted, it is for your comfort, which worketh in the patient enduring of the same sufferings which we also suffer** [if, therefore, we are afflicted, it is for your comfort and salvation which is accomplished through the influence of our teaching and example; or if we are comforted, the comfort is given to us for your benefit and profit, that you may receive from us that comfort which causes you to endure with

THANKS FOR COMFORT, ETC.

patience the same suffering which we also suffer]: **7 and our hope for you is stedfast; knowing that, as ye are partakers of the sufferings, so also are ye of the comfort.** [And we have a firm hope with regard to you, that if Christ has comforted us in our affliction, so will he comfort you, if you partake of our sufferings. The phrases "same sufferings which we also suffer" and "partakers of the sufferings," suggest that Paul may have meant an identity rather than a similarity of suffering. The loyal part of the Corinthian church which he is now addressing, no doubt had in a large measure an identity of suffering, for, by taking part with the apostle, they exposed themselves to the same detraction, contempt, etc., which the pestilential minority were visiting upon him. As the comfort of Christ enabled him to be stedfast, he had an unwavering hope that this same comfort would enable his friends also to be loyal and stedfast. His own stedfastness had been recently tested to the uttermost, but the comforting help of Christ had caused the test to increase his stedfastness. Of this test, and its resulting influence of faith and confidence, he now tells them.] **8 For we would not have you ignorant, brethren, concerning our affliction which befell *us* in Asia, that we were weighed down exceedingly, beyond our power, insomuch that we despaired even of life: 9 yea, we ourselves have had the sentence** [or answer] **of death within ourselves** [*i. e.*, when we asked ourselves, "Can we possibly live?" we were compelled in our hopelessness to answer, "No; we must die"], **that we should not trust in ourselves, but in God who raiseth the dead: 10 who delivered us out of so great a death, and will deliver: on whom we have set our hope that he will also still deliver us; 11 ye also helping together on our behalf by your supplication; that, for the gift** [of special deliverance] **bestowed upon us by means of many** [who prayed for us], **thanks may be given by many persons on our behalf.** [Your prayers aided to save our life; and our life, thus saved, may save and bless many, and so cause them to glorify God. The troubles to which the apostle here refers as befalling him in Asia, were evidently those which culminated in the riot at Ephesus (Acts 19: 23-41; 20: 1). Since Paul was accustomed to make light of ordinary physical danger, and since he did not go into the theater, and since they find nothing on the face of Luke's record which indicates that Paul suffered any anguish or any other discomfiture at that time, some commentators have sought to find some other danger or distress assailing him, and, failing to find it, they have set about inventing it. This has led to all manner of extravagant and unseemly absurdities, and to assertions that the apostle had cancer, paralysis, epileptic fits, etc. Those learned in books are very often deficient in the knowledge of human nature; but one skilled in the latter knows that no man could pass through Paul's experience at Ephesus without undergoing immense excitement, constant anxieties and most depressing nervous reaction. If Luke makes no mention of such things as part of the incidents at Ephesus, neither does he mention them elsewhere. He busied himself with the external, not with the consequent distresses of the apostle. One searches his writings in vain for most of that long list of hardships which Paul gives in chapter 11. But Paul himself tells of these anxieties and sufferings (Acts 20: 19, 27, 31; 1 Cor. 15: 32 and note). Had it been any sickness he would likely have mentioned it, and he would hardly in that case have used the expression "so great a death" when referring to it. Death by any *natural* means was not sufficiently repugnant to Paul for him to use such language (ch. 5: 2; Phil. 1: 23). That he contents himself with describing his troubles in this general way is itself significant, for it shows that the apostle thought it would be amply sufficient for the information of the Corinthians. The gossip of merchants and travelers would have acquainted Corinth with the great hubbub which had been raised about Diana and idolatry in Ephesus, and it was prudent in Paul to speak of and commit himself as to his part in it in just such indefinite terms; for his letter would be widely circulated. Having spoken of his life as worth saving, he next takes up that thought, and tells why he dares to speak of himself in this apparently boastful or glorifying manner.] **12 For our glorying is this, the testimony of our conscience** [it is often appealed to by Paul—Acts 23: 1; 24: 16; Rom. 9: 1; 1 Cor. 4: 4], **that in holiness and sincerity of God, not in fleshly wisdom but in the grace of God, we behaved ourselves in the world, and more abundantly to you-ward. 13 For we write no other things unto you, than what ye read** [literally, read aloud] **or even acknowledge, and I hope ye will acknowledge unto the end: 14 as also ye did acknowledge us in part, that we are your glorying, even as ye also are ours, in the day of our Lord Jesus.** [1 Cor. 3: 13. If my words sound boastful, my conscience justifies me in using them, since I have manifested the holy and sincere life befitting one who is directed of God, and not the life of one who is moved by worldly policy and wisdom, and is void of principle. Such has been my general conduct, and it has been especially so in my dealings with you. Thus the apostle shows himself conscious of the scrutinizing suspicion with which the Corinthians watched all his actions. He knew that to govern such a people he must walk with more than common circumspection. Therefore, with a careful, guarded spirit he had penned his letters to them so that there was nothing in them of doubtful meaning. If we assume, with Conybeare and Howson, that the apostle had been suspected of sending private letters in which he modified the statements of his public epistles, the reading becomes clear and smooth, and runs thus: "I have written you nothing save what has been read in public and generally acknowledged as authoritatively mine, and I hope you will thus acknowledge my epistles to the end of the world, even as part of you acknowledged me to be an apostle, and gloried in me as your teacher, even as I also gloried in you as disciples, in expectation that I would appear with you before the Lord Jesus (1 Thess. 2: 19, 20; Phil. 2: 16). By thus placing himself on a level with his disciples in mutual glorying, the apostle removes every semblance of unseemly self-glorification. But the meaning of the passage is practically the same if we merely understand the apostle as appealing from the false constructions placed upon his letters, to the text of the letters, and as asserting that he wrote no words which justified the ambiguous meaning placed upon them. We shall now be told about these ambiguous words.] **15 And in this confidence** [*i. e.*, that you gloried in me and I in you, and that we mutually loved each other] **I was minded to come first unto you, that ye might have a second benefit** [this word implies the spiritual gifts which he bestowed on his visits—comp. Rom. 1 11; 15: 29] ; **16 and by you to pass into Macedonia, and again from Macedonia to come unto you, and of you to be set forward on my journey unto Judaea.** [*i. e.*, trusting in our mutual love, it was my intention to visit you before visiting the Macedonians, that you might have two visits or benefits, one before I went into Macedonia and one when I came out; and I also, trusting in your love, looked to you, instead of to others, to forward me on my journey. The apostle had evidently told the Corinthians of this plan in the lost letter which has already been mentioned. See Introduction to 1 Corinthians, page 49; also 1 Cor. 5: 9. And then he had changed his plan, as we see by 1 Cor. 16: 5-7, and note. This change of plan gave Paul's enemies a chance to accuse him of unprincipled equivocation, as though he said : (1) "Yes, I will come to you first: no, I will come to the Macedonians first." (2) "Yes, I will pay you two visits: no, I will pay you only one visit." (3) "Yes, I am coming soon: no, I am not coming soon."] **17 When I therefore was thus minded** [to come to you first, etc.], **did I show fickleness?** [in determining to come to you second, etc.] **or the things that I purpose, do I purpose according to the flesh, that with me there should be the yea yea and the nay nay?** [Do I form and announce my purposes like an unprincipled worldling, who holds his yes and no subservient to his policy or his pleasure; *i. e.*, does as he pleases, without any regard to his pledges or his promises?] **18 But as God is faithful, our word toward you is not yea and nay. 19 For the Son of God, Jesus Christ, who was preached among you by us,** *even* **by me and Silvanus and Timothy** [Paul's fellow-laborers in founding the church at Corinth], **was not yea and nay, but in him is yea.** 20 For how many soever be the promises of God, in him is the yea: wherefore also through him is the Amen, unto the glory of God through us. 21 Now he that establisheth us with you in Christ, and anointed us, is God; 22 who also sealed us, and gave *us* the earnest of the Spirit in our hearts. ["Every one when he is perfected shall be as his teacher," said Jesus (Luke 6: 40). Paul has this truth in mind, and his meaning is as follows: "As God the teacher is a promise-keeper whose yea is absolute, unchangeable and immutable, so also am I, his pupil, a promise-keeper, a yea-man. I showed my approval of promise-keeping, and likewise taught you the value of such a characteristic, in that I, together with my colleagues, preached Christ as he is—a promise-keeper. For God, no matter how varied his promises, is indeed a promise-keeper, so that he has begotten in us that assurance of faith which causes us to say an expectant amen to all his promises, and to glorify him by living as in anticipation of their fulfillment. Such a God could never indorse a promise-breaker, but God has indorsed me. He has established me, with you, in Christ, and by anointing me he has set me apart to the apostolic office, and has sealed me as his own, and has given me the earnest of the Spirit. If I am thus his apostle and still recognized as his, then am I like him, and raised above suspicion of being a pledge-breaker." The seal was then a sign or symbol indicating ownership (Acts 9: 15 ; Eph. 1: 13 ; 4: 30 ; Rev. 7: 3 ; 9: 4). False apostles might attempt to prove their claims by insufficient evidence, such as letters of recommendation, but Paul was truly certified as such by the unction of the Spirit (Acts 9: 17 ; 1 John 2: 20). Earnest money was a partial payment given to bind a contract, or given to a servant to encourage and stimulate his faithfulness. As a servant might exhibit such earnest-money in proof of his employment, so Paul pointed to the power of the Spirit in his life **as an evidence that he was in the** divine service.

II.

EXPLANATION AS TO CHANGE OF PLANS. AS TO THE INCESTUOUS PERSON. A PEAN OF JOY.

1: 23-2: 17.

[Having first argued that he could not be guilty of duplicity because of the very nature of his relationships to the true and faithful God, Paul in this section answers the charge more specifically by giving such an explanation of his actions as clearly demonstrated his sincerity in the entire premises.] **23 But I call God for a witness upon my soul, that to spare you I forbare to come unto Corinth. 24 Not that we have Lordship over your faith, but are helpers of your joy: for in faith ye stand fast.**

II. 1 But I determined this for myself, that I would not come again to you with sorrow. 2 For if I make you sorry, who then is he that maketh me glad but he that is made sorry by me? [But I call God, who knows all things, even the searcher of hearts, to look upon the secret purposes of my soul, and to confirm the truth if I speak it, and to testify against and punish me if I lie (Mal. 3: 5), that I delayed to come to Corinth in order that you might have time to repent, and show your repentance by obedience; for had I come at the time which I first mentioned to you, I would have been compelled to discipline you, and therefore make you sorry (1 Cor. 4: 1). Not that I have lordship over your faith, for in this realm I am only a fellow-helper of your joy by confirming you in your belief (Rom. 15: 13; Phil. 1: 25); for by your faith you stand as free and independent, full-aged children of God (Gal. 3: 23-26; 4: 1-7, 31; 5: 1). But when through lack of faith you fall into sinful practices I must discipline you. But I determined that for my own gladness I would not come speedily so as to bring you sorrow as I did on my last visit. For if I make you sorry, who will make me glad? will I not have made that very people sorry to whom I myself look for gladness?] **3 And I wrote this very thing, lest, when I came, I**

should have sorrow from them of whom I ought to rejoice; having confidence in you all, that my joy is *the joy* of you all. 4 For out of much affliction and anguish of heart I wrote unto you with many tears; not that ye should be made sorry, but that ye might know the love which I have more abundantly unto you. [I wrote this very thing to you (viz.: how my coming endangered your joy, and how you must repent before I came (1 Cor. 4: 21); and how I would delay my coming, and come by the long and not the short route (1 Cor. 16: 5-8), lest when I came I should have sorrow from those to whom I looked for joy. And I do look for joy from you, for I have this confidence in you all, that, though many of you oppose me, yet there is none of you that does not desire my personal happiness. Moreover, my feelings at the time of writing are a witness unto God of the spirit in which I wrote, for I wrote out of much affliction and anguish of heart and with many tears, which shows that I took no pleasure in thus administering correction. I did not correct you to cause you grief, but that you might know the love which I have more abundantly unto you, and which can not keep quiet when it sees you injuring yourself (Ps. 141: 5; Prov. 27: 6). By referring to 1 Cor. 4: 21 and 5: 1, it will be found that the threat of correction at his coming, and the case of the incestuous person, were twin thoughts in the apostle's mind. The punishment of this offender was one of the principal items that Paul wished them to attend to before he came; in fact, the whole subject of visits, delays, corrections, etc., centered in this offender, and very naturally, therefore, while here explaining the causes for his delay, the case of this incestuous person comes to mind, and the apostle uses him to flood the entire situation with light.] 5 But if any [thus delicately does the apostle introduce this sinner] **hath caused sorrow, he hath caused sorrow, not to me, but in part (that I press not too heavily) to you all.** [As I have said, I did not write to cause you sorrow. But if the incestuous person has caused you sorrow, he has caused sorrow not to me, but to a large part of you. I will not weigh him down with a greater

178   *SECOND EPISTLE TO THE CORINTHIANS*

burden of guilt by saying to whom else he has caused sorrow.
The apostle is not to be understood too literally. This sinner
had added to the sorrows which he has just mentioned (verse
4). But the apostle's sorrow was so small compared with the
great grief of the Corinthian church as to not be worth mentioning. Comp. Luke 23: 28.] **6 Sufficient to such a one
is this punishment which was** *inflicted* **by the many;
7 ro that contrariwise ye should rather forgive him
and comfort him, lest by any means such a one should
be swallowed up with his overmuch sorrow.** [Paul's
purpose had been to save this sinner (1 Cor. 5: 5). It seems
that a minority had espoused his cause, but the majority had
excommunicated him according to the apostle's instruction at 1
Cor. 5: 13. The apostle here writes that this punishment has
already proved sufficient, and should not be continued, but that,
on the contrary, the offender should be forgiven, received back
and comforted, lest he should be swallowed up by despair, and
thus the punishment should defeat the very end for which it
was designed. We should note here that excommunication
and restoration are actions of the church, and not of the
officers.] **8 Wherefore I beseech you to confirm** *your*
**love toward him. 9 For to this end also did I write,
that I might know the proof of you, whether ye are
obedient in all things.** [This shows that Paul had made
his instructions concerning the incestuous man a test. If they
obeyed him in this, he could come to them bringing joy: if
they disobeyed, their condition would call for further delay and
more letters on his part. Here, then, is laid bare before the
Corinthians the inner thoughts which were governing the
actions of the apostle at the time when he was penning the
fifth chaper of his first epistle. They could see now for themselves that their own foolish conduct, and not the fickleness of
the apostle, had caused the delay and the change of plan;
that so far as the apostle was concerned, he had always intended
to visit them, and that all his statements about his visits had
been made in good faith. Observe that as the apostle had become the leader in punishment or discipline, he here becomes

the leader in forgiveness.] 10 But to whom ye forgive anything, I *forgive* also: for what I also have forgiven, if I have forgiven anything, for your sakes *have I forgiven it* in the presence of Christ; 11 that no advantage may be gained over us by Satan: for we are not ignorant of his devices. [There is a close correlation between verse 10 and 1 Cor. 5: 3. There Paul identified himself with the church, and, though absent, anticipated its action and acted with it. Here he ratifies beforehand the action which he bids it take. There he acted in the name of the Lord and here he does it in the presence of Christ. He forgives the sinner for the sake of the church, that he may not be lost to the church. When a church, through carelessness in exercising mercy and forgiveness, loses a member, it is permitting Satan to overreach it. Paul was too well versed in Satan's methods to be thus outwitted by that adversary.] **12 Now when I came to Troas for the gospel of Christ** [*i. e.*, intending to preach], **and when a door** [an opportunity—1 Cor. 16: 9 and note] **was opened unto me in the Lord, 13 I had no relief for my spirit** [worrying about you], **because I found not Titus my brother** [who had agreed to bring me word about you, and meet me at Troas]: **but taking my leave of them** [the brethren at Troas], **I went forth into Macedonia.** [hoping to meet Titus there. For fuller details of Paul's movements and intentions see the Introduction. The relief which came to him in Macedonia when he met Titus causes him at this point to break forth into an expression of thanksgiving. But as it does not at this time suit his purpose to give a detailed statement of his reason for thankfulness, he curbs his rising emotion and directs his thought in another channel.] **14 But thanks be unto God, who always leadeth us in triumph in Christ, and maketh manifest through us the savor of his knowledge in every place. 15 For we are a sweet savor of Christ unto God, in them that are saved, and in them that perish; 16 to the one a savor from death unto death; to the other a savor from life unto life. And who is** sufficient for these things? 17 For we are not as the many, corrupting the word of God: but as of sincerity, but as of God, in the sight of God, speak we in Christ. [But thanks be unto God for the relief which we received in Macedonia. And God's leadings are ever thus. He leads us as a bound, anxious, trembling captive in his triumphal procession, but is constantly showing us mercy; for the procession is the triumph of Christ. He leads us in this procession as a priest bearing a censer, of which the gospel is the incense, giving forth, as a sweet-smelling savor, the knowledge of Christ at Ephesus, Troas, Macedonia or every place whither he leads us. Yea, we ourselves (because Christ liveth in us —Phil. 1: 21) are a sweet savor of Christ unto God, both to them that are saved and to them that perish. To the one the incense of our presence is a deadly savor, and to the other a veritable source of life, for we make them all conscious of the triumph of Christ of which they are part. Now in every triumph some captives know that they are being led to death, and others that they are approaching the moment of forgiveness and life, and of these fates the incense keeps them in mind. And who, therefore, is sufficient to the task of being such a warning, despair-dealing, hope-dispensing, life-giving savor? who is able to preach this gospel of life and death befittingly? Realizing our insufficiency to such a task, we nevertheless do our best, for we are not like the many who oppose us ready to adulterate the word of God to make it popular or to suit our own selfish ends; but, discharging our duty in all sincerity as men inspired of God, and laboring in the sight of God, we speak under authority of Christ. It will be remembered that Paul wrote these words in an age when all the world was familiar with the glorious pageantry of a Roman triumph. When L. Mummius had conquered Corinth, the procession in his honor was one of the most splendid which the world had ever seen. In A. D. 51, just a short while before Paul penned these words, the emperor Claudius had celebrated his triumph over the Britons, and their king Caractacus was led in the triumph, but was spared. Ordinarily when the victor reached the capitol it was the signal for the slaying of many of the captives in his honor, and for the forgiveness of others. Thus the incense of the procession which permeated the air, and kept the captives conscious of the nature of the journey on which they marched, was redolent with hope or sorrow, according to the expectations held out to them by their victors. The phrases "from death unto death" and "from life unto life" are regarded by some as mere Hebrew superlatives; but "from" indicates source: the meaning therefore is, the gospel, which arises from Christ and which is preached through us, is to the unbelieving, but the incense arising from one crucified and dead, and so it is to them a savor from the dead and producing death. But to the believing it is a savor from the living, producing life.]

III.

APOSTLESHIP ABOVE HUMAN COMMENDATION, AND THE MINISTRY OF MOSES.

3: 1-18.

[The closing verse of the preceding cnapter was capable of being construed as an outburst of self-laudation, and as the apostle well knew that his enemies at Corinth accused him of this very vice, and hence would make the most of words susceptible of misconstruction, he anticipates their move by discussing not only his words, but the whole subject of this (apparent) self-glorying.] **1 Are we beginning again** [for places where he might be construed as having done so before, see 1 Cor. 2: 6; 4: 3, 4, 14-16; 7: 7; 9: 1-6, 15, 19, 26, 27; 14: 18; 16: 10] **to commend ourselves? or need we, as do some, epistles of commendation to you or from you?** [These questions are cuttingly ironical. Evidently his opponents at Corinth had come thither with letters of commendation, either from brethren of repute, or from churches, and had drawn disparaging contrasts between their own formal, official, letter-proved standing in the church, and what they were pleased to describe as Paul's self-asserted, self-manufactured,

boast-sustained standing. The apostle therefore turns the edge of their own weapon against them, and shows how ridiculous their claims to reverence and respect were in comparison with his own. Such powerless creatures needed letters of commendation—it was all they had to commend them! Without letters they would be utter nobodies. But the letter which was the top of their honor did not rise to the level of the bottom of the apostle's honor. For himself how ridiculous such letters would be! Could he bring a letter to them? it would be like a father seeking introduction and commendation to his own children. Could he ask a letter from them? why, all the knowledge, grace, etc., which made them capable of commending had come from him, their founder, so that their commendation would, after all, be only another form of self-commendation. Could they think that he overpraised himself to them, hoping thus to cozen them into giving him exaggerated, undeserved commendation to others? Very early the churches learned to grant letters of commendation. See Rom. 16: 1; Acts 18: 27; 15: 25; Col. 4: 10; Tit. 3: 13; but such commendation was always fallible, and liable therefore to abuse—Gal. 1: 7; 2: 12.]
2 Ye are our epistle, written in our hearts, known and read of all men; 3 being made manifest that ye are an epistle of Christ, ministered by us, written not with ink, but with the Spirit of the living God; not in tables of stone, but in tables *that are* hearts of flesh. [Do we need an epistle to any one? Surely not while you exist as a church which we have founded, for ye are our epistle copied by the hand of love in our hearts, so that everywhere we go your conversion vouches for us, that we are true messengers of God. For as men learn of you, either by acquaintance with you as the original epistle, or from what our own heart's copy holds recorded about you, it becomes manifest to them that ye are an epistle of which Christ is the author and dictator; of which I am the amanuensis, or earthly penman; of which the fleshly tables of the heart—the very sources of life itself—are that which receives and holds the message; and the Holy Spirit, the means employed to convey, impress, and make

THE CHRISTIAN MINISTRY 183

abiding the message. All men, seeing your transformed lives, read you as such an epistle; and as ye are my fruit in the Lord, so they need no other commendation of me (Matt. 7: 16). The presentation of life under the figure of a writing was familiar to Old Testament readers (Ezek. 36: 26; Jer. 31: 33; Prov. 3: 3; 8: 3). Some have thought that Paul uses the contrast between stone and heart as a reference to Ezek. 36: 26; but his use of the word "tables," and the context, forbids such a reference. Paul has the tables of the law in mind, and introduces the idea here that he may lead up to the comparison which begins at verse 6.] **4 And such confidence have we through Christ to God-ward : 5 not that we are sufficient of ourselves, to account anything as from ourselves ; but our sufficiency is from God ; 6 who also made us sufficient as ministers of a new covenant; not of the letter, but of the spirit** [*i. e.*, not a minister of the old, legal dispensation, but of the new, spiritual dispensation] : **for the letter killeth, but the spirit giveth life.** [And I have such bold assurance through Christ that God will thus consider you to be my epistle. Not that I am sufficient of myself to account myself as having truly done any part of that which makes you an epistle, save as I have received the power from God. The truth which, written in your hearts, has thus transformed you, is wholly of God; so that our ability or sufficiency to write such an epistle as ye are, is all from God, who made us thus sufficient by calling us to be ministers of that new covenant which performs such wonders of regeneration, instead of calling us to be (as my Judaizing opponents ever seek to coerce me to be) a minister of the old covenant. This old covenant was given in letters graven on stone, and hence was a law of letters governing us wholly from without. But the new covenant, though also committed to writing, and hence in a sense external to us, is a code of principles governing us from within, through the power of the Holy Spirit. This law of letters without could only bring upon us condemnation and death (Rom. 7: 7-11 ; 1 Cor. 15: 56); but this law of the spirit within us (verse 2) gives us life (Rom. 2: 27-29; 6: 4, 11;

8: 2, 10, 11; 1 Cor. 15: 45; Gal. 5: 18). The contrast in verse 6 is not between the outward and inward sense of Scripture, but between the outward and inward power of those two great dispensations, Jewish and Christian. That perversion of the passage which gave it the former meaning, has been used to countenance those baneful allegorical interpretations of Scripture which have been the pest of the church from the days of Origen to the present time. Having shown that the minister of the new covenant had a power not enjoyed by that of the old, Paul proceeds to show that he likewise has a glory (and Paul's enemies were criticizing him for glorying) not enjoyed by any minister of the old dispensation; no, not even by Moses himself.] **7 But if the ministration of death, written** [literally, "in letters"], *and* **engraven on stones, came** [was introduced] **with glory, so that the children of Israel could not look stedfastly upon the face of Moses for the glory of his face** [Ex. 34: 29-35]; **which** *glory* **was passing away: 8 how shall not rather the ministration of the spirit be with glory? 9 For if the ministration of condemnation hath glory, much rather doth the ministration of righteousness exceed in glory. 10 For verily that which hath been made glorious hath not been made glorious in this respect, by reason of the glory that surpasseth. 11 For if that which passeth away** *was* **with glory, much more that which remaineth** *is* **in glory.** [If the old covenant which brought death glorified its introducing minister, so that the face of Moses shone as he brought it from God to the people, and glowed so resplendently that the children of Israel could not look steadily at him (though we should note in passing that this glory was of a temporary, evanescent nature); is it not more to be expected that the initiatory ministers of that new covenant which brings life shall be glorified? For if there was glory in ministering under that covenant which brought condemnation, much more is there glory in ministering under that which brings justification through righteousness. For even though the old covenant was made glorious it had no glory in respect to or comparison with the new covenant by reason of the excelling glory of the latter. For if that which was outshone is glorious, much more is that glorious which outshines it and continues to obscure it. Paul's language suggests the rising sun. Before he comes the stars seem glorious, yet they have no glory in comparison with him. If they are glorious, much more is the king of day glorious, who, by his superior brightness, remands all their glittering orbs to darkness.] **12 Having therefore such a hope, we use great boldness of speech, 13 and *are* not as Moses, *who* put a veil upon his face, that the children of Israel should not look stedfastly on the end of that which was passing away: 14 but their minds were hardened: for until this very day at the reading of the old covenant the same veil remaineth, it not being revealed *to them* that it is done away in Christ. 15 But unto this day, whensoever Moses is read, a veil lieth upon their heart. 16 But whensoever it shall turn to the Lord, the veil is taken away.** [The word "end" in verse 13 is the bone of contention in this passage. It has two meanings: (1) The termination or stopping-point. (2) The purpose, design or ultimate result. Macknight, Alford and others give it the first meaning, and construe Paul as saying that Moses covered his face that the children of Israel might not see the termination of the glory, as it faded from his face. But this construction limits the typical concealment to the mere fact that the Mosaic dispensation was to pass away, and is not large enough for Paul's thought, as is shown by the context. Cameron, Barnes, etc., give it the second meaning, which we have embodied in the following paraphrase: "In dealing with the glory of our ministration we do not veil our meaning in types and shadows, as Moses showed that he did with his ministration, when he typically concealed the glory of his face by putting a veil upon it. He concealed the meaning of his ministration that the children of Israel should not look stedfastly on Christ, the end or fulfillment of that dispensation or law which was typically passing away in the fading glory of Moses' face (now, Christ is thus the end of Moses' law—**Rom.**

10: 4); but the true hindrance was not the typical veil worn by Moses, but the real veil on the minds of the people, who were dull of understanding and sinfully hardened, so that from the very beginning they understood not his dispensation, nor do they yet, for even now when the law is read the great truth is not revealed to them that it is all done away, having ended in Christ. But unto this day, whensoever Moses is read, a veil is upon their heart, and they do not see that Moses preaches Christ. But whensoever the Jewish nation shall turn to the Lord, then the veil is taken away, and they see that the end or purpose of the law is to lead to Christ."—Gal. 3: 24.] **17 Now the Lord is the Spirit: and where the Spirit of the Lord is, *there* is liberty. 18 But we all, with unveiled face beholding as in a mirror the glory of the Lord, are transformed into the same image from glory to glory, even as from the Lord the Spirit.** [Now, Jesus is that Spirit or new covenant of which I have been speaking (verses 3, 6, 8); and where that new covenant is, there is liberty, especially the liberty of seeing. Those living under Moses, as I have said, are veiled so that they can not see Christ in their dispensation, but all we who live under the new covenant see the glory of Christ with unveiled faces as he is mirrored in that new covenant—our dispensation; and our faces, like that of Moses, are transformed at the sight, reflecting the glory of what we see even as the glory shines upon us from the Lord, who is indeed the very covenant itself. However, none of the ministers of Christ, not even the apostles (ch. 5: 16), continually beheld Christ glorified as an objective reality, for it is only in our future state that we shall thus look upon him, and that look will fully effect the transformation into his likeness which our knowledge of him in the gospel has been slowly working out within us during our earthly life (John 17: 24; 1 John 3: 2; Col. 3: 3, 4; Rom. 8: 17; Phil. 3: 12-14; Col. 1: 27).]

IV.

THE HOPE OF FUTURE GLORY SUSTAINS IN PRESENT TRIALS.

4: 1–5: 10.

[Having shown that the Christian ministry is superior to the Mosaic, Paul, in this section, enlarges upon the two antithetical phases of that ministry, showing that viewed carnally it leads to the severest suffering and to death, while, viewed spiritually, it leads to ever-increasing life, culminating in celestial and eternal glory. The prospect of this blessed culmination enables the minister to sustain his present distress without fainting.] **1 Therefore seeing we have this ministry, even as we obtain mercy, we faint not** [having been forgiven for prosecuting the church, and having been graciously called to this glorious ministry of the open vision, we are moved and inspired to holy courage and perseverance]: **2 but we have renounced the hidden things of shame, not walking in craftiness, nor handling the word of God deceitfully; but by the manifestation of the truth commending ourselves to every man's conscience in the sight of God.** [This verse contrasts the true Christian ministry with that false form of it employed by Paul's enemies. They, preaching from selfish motives, had sought to undermine Paul's influence by calumny, by crafty perversions of his statements, and by adulterating the gospel with obsolete Judaism. Paul, on the contrary, had practiced nothing which shame would prompt him to hide, had used no crooked or partisan arts, had taught nothing in private which he did not teach in public; and had, by his open, candid frankness in presenting the truth, commended himself to every variety of conscience, behaving himself as in the sight of God.] **3 And even if our gospel is veiled, it is veiled in them that perish: 4 in whom the god of this world hath blinded the minds of the unbelieving, that the light of the gospel of the glory of**

Christ, who is the image of God, should not dawn
upon them. [These words are called out by the word
"every" found in verse 2. The apostle anticipates that some
Jew would challenge his statement, asserting that the gospel
was as much veiled to him and his brethren, as Paul had above
asserted the law to be (3: 7-18). Paul replies that their failure
to acknowledge the truth may indeed form an exception, but
does not weaken his general assertion, since the obscurity lies
in their own bigotry-closed eyes and not in the truth presented
to them. The fault lay, not in the nature of the gospel, but
in their own nature. By unbelief they had fallen into Satan's
power, and he had blinded them (just as, conversely, those
who believe are enlightened by the Spirit). The completeness
and hopelessness of their blindness is made most apparent by
the glorious luminosity of the divine gospel which they failed
to perceive. Some have been needlessly puzzled by this passage, because Paul called Satan a "god." The apostle does
not mean to attribute divinity to the devil. Satan is not a god
properly, but is merely one in reference to those who have sinfully made him such. Paul calls him a god as he would call
an idol a god; it being only such in the eyes of its worshipers.
(Comp. Phil. 3: 19.) The phrase is equivalent to "prince of
this world," found at John 12: 31; 14: 30; 16: 11, though in
John the word *kosmos*, or space-world, is used, while here it is
the word *aioon*, or time-world. He is prince over this world
of space, and prince also over that time-world which began
with the fall of Adam and closes at the second advent. One
of the methods by which Satan blinds the eyes will be found
at John 5: 44. South pithily remarks, "When the malefactor's eyes are covered, he is not far from execution" (Est. 7:
8). 5 **For we preach not ourselves, but Christ Jesus
as Lord, and ourselves as your servants for Jesus'
sake. 6 Seeing it is God, that said, Light shall shine
out of darkness** [Gen. 1: 3; Isa. 60: 1, 2], **who shined in
our hearts, to give the light of the knowledge of the glory
of God in the face of Jesus Christ.** [From such passages
as 1 Cor. 2: 6, 7; 4: 16; 11: 1; 1 Thess. 1: 6; 2: 4; 3: 9; Gal.

4: 12; Phil. 3: 17, Paul might have been accused of preaching himself; but he had preached himself as a servant (1 Cor. 9: 19). Paul's rivals had preached themselves and had sought to make the preaching a contest between him and them. Paul declines this contest, and declares that it is his business to reflect the light of Christ which has shone in his heart; for God sent his Son to be the light of earth's darkness. The apostle here alludes to the glorified face of the Christ which appeared to him on the way to Damascus. After such a vision it was impossible that Paul could look upon himself as any other than a reflector of the true Light which was sent from God. It was also impossible that he should regard the face of Moses as comparable with it. Moreover, the prophecy spoke of but one light, and took no account of Moses.] **7 But we have this treasure in earthen vessels, that the exceeding greatness of the power may be of God, and not from ourselves** [We, in our mortal bodies, hold the divine and heavenly truth. God has thus committed his gospel to men that it may be evident to all that it is from him. The power of the gospel so transcends that of the human agent who preaches it as to make it apparent to all that the preacher is but an agent performing duties which are beyond the compass of his own unaided faculties. Farrar sees in this a reference to the torches of Gideon's pitchers, but the word "treasure" evidently changes the figure, so that Paul no longer speaks of the gospel as a light. Besides, the Gideon incident conveys the idea of concealment, which is not in Paul's thoughts. The apostle is here supposing that some one will object to his high claims for the Christian ministry, asserting that the humiliations and sufferings endured by the apostle refute the idea that he can be an ambassador of God. His answer is that God put the treasure in an earthen vessel in order that the survival of the perishing vessel when subjected to all manner of vicissitudes might prove the value, in the sight of God, of the treasure within it]; **8 we are pressed on every side, yet not straitened; perplexed, yet not unto despair; 9 pursued, yet not forsaken; smitten down, yet not destroyed** [The apostle again changes his figure, and describes the Christian minister as a warrior defending a divine treasure. His enemies press upon him very closely, yet still leave him room to wield his weapons. He is greatly disturbed in mind because of his imperiled position, yet does not lose hope; as the conflict grows more strenuous he seeks refuge in flight, but feels that Providence has not forsaken him; finally the overtaking enemy strikes him down, and would overcome him, did not God deliver him for the sake of the treasure committed to his defense]; **10 always bearing about in the body the dying of Jesus, that the life also of Jesus may be manifested in our body. 11 For we who live are always delivered unto death for Jesus' sake, that the life also of Jesus may be manifested in our mortal flesh. 12 So then death worketh in us, but life in you.** [The apostle has been speaking of having and holding the knowledge of God in a mortal body. But the knowledge of God brings with it the eternal life that is within God, so that to have divine knowledge is to have divine life (1 John 1: 3; 5: 19). The knowledge of verse 6, therefore, gives place in this passage to the life which it produces. The minister of Christ, having in him the life of Christ (Gal. 2: 20), becomes in a large measure a reduplication of the life and experiences of Christ. He is, as it were, constantly dying and being resurrected. With Paul death was a matter of daily experience (1 Cor. 15: 31). But by thus constantly dying and yet continuing to live, Paul typically reenacted the crucifixion and resurrection of the Lord. By surviving so many trials he made it evident to the world that he was sustained by a life other than human, viz.: the life of Jesus. Moreover, the daily sacrifice of the life of Paul, like the sacrifice of Christ, worked out life and blessing for others, notably the Corinthians, to whom he wrote.] **13 But having the same spirit of faith, according to that which is written** [Ps. 116: 10], **I believed, and therefore did I speak; we also believe, and therefore also we speak** [having the same spirit of faith which was in the Psalmist who proclaimed his faith despite his afflictions, we preach right on despite all opposition]; **14 knowing that he that raised up the Lord Jesus shall raise up us also with Jesus, and shall present us with you.** [The daily preservation of his weak body was to the apostle an earnest, as it were, of the final resurrection, and the hope of this resurrection, in company and fellowship with the Corinthians, as the fruit of his labors, encouraged him to speak out and proclaim the gospel despite all forms of persecution.] **15 For all things *are* for your sakes, that the grace, being multiplied through the many, may cause the thanksgiving to abound unto the glory of God.** [The whole gospel ministry is for the sake of the believer, for the believer is the recipient of the grace of God, and the returner of thanks to God. God is glorified in him both by the grace which he bestows upon him and the thanksgiving which he receives from him. It therefore follows that the more believers there are, the more grace there is bestowed and the more thanksgiving there is received, and hence the more God is glorified.] **16 Wherefore** [because each death is followed by a co-ordinate resurrection] **we faint not; but though our outward man is decaying, yet our inward man is renewed day by day.** [The sacrifice of the carnal ever tends to the increase of the spiritual. The apostle knew that the transfiguration described at 3: 18 was perfecting itself daily]. **17 For our light affliction, which is for the moment, worketh for us more and more exceedingly** [Literally, in excess unto excess: a Hebraism: a method of expressing intensity by repetition of the same word. It might well be rendered "an abounding upon an abounding," thus suggesting the idea of progression by upward steps] **an eternal weight of glory; 18 while we look not at the things which are seen, but at the things which are not seen : for the things which are seen are temporal; but the things which are not seen are eternal.** [We have here the same law for the Christian which governed the life of Christ (Phil. 2: 7-11). If afflictions are viewed with regard to temporal affairs, they seem heavy and profitless; but when we look upon them as part of God's

192 SECOND EPISTLE TO THE CORINTHIANS

discipline which prepares us for an unseen world, then they seem light and momentary. In proportion as we keep our eyes upon the future kingdom of God, with its glorious circumstances and modes of existence, our afflictions increase our faith and enlarge our character, and so work out for us a more glorious future. The phrase "eternal weight" suggests a royal garment, richly freighted with ornaments of gold and jewels. Trapp quaintly observes, "For affliction, here's glory; for light affliction, a weight of glory; for momentary affliction, eternal glory."]

V. 1 For we know that if the earthly house of our tabernacle be dissolved, we have a building from God, a house not made with hands, eternal in the heavens. [An allusion to the merging of the tabernacle into the temple of Solomon. As the Spirit of God dwelt in the frail tent during the pilgrimage in the wilderness, and afterwards took up his abode in the substantial and immovable temple in the midst of an established city, so the spirit of man sojourns in a tent-dwelling—a mortal body—while on his journey to the new Jerusalem, but at the journey's end he shall have a "house not made with hands;" *i. e.*, not this present, material body which seems almost within the compass of human construction, but a spiritual body which is utterly beyond it (comp. Mark 14: 58). Hence it is also spoken of as "from heaven," to distinguish it from this present body, the substance of which comes from the earth. The present tense "we have" is used, not because our spiritual bodies now exist in organic form (a mechanical view), but to give vivid expression to the certainty of our receiving such bodies (comp. 2 Tim. 4: 8); and perhaps also to indicate that in divine contemplation and plan our future bodies are growing and taking form according to the daily growth and development of our inner man.] **2 For verily in this we groan** [Rom. 7: 24; 8: 23], **longing to be clothed upon with our habitation which is from heaven: 3 if so be that being clothed we shall not be found naked. 4 For indeed we that are in this tabernacle do groan, being burdened; not for that we would**

be unclothed, but that we would be clothed upon, that what is mortal may be swallowed up of life. [The apostle here expresses two wishes, suited to either contingency which confronted him. If he survived till the Lord's coming, he longed to be clothed with the spiritual body which the redeemed shall then receive; and expressed the hope that if he survived to that day he would be found clothed in that body, and not be left naked as an outcast (Rev. 3: 18). If, on the other hand, it was his lot to die before the Lord came, he wished for the full consummation of God's purpose. He had no desire to be a disembodied spirit, but he wished to pass through that state to his final spiritual body; just as a seed might say that it did not wish for the germinal death, but was ready to pass through that stage in order to reach its future as a new plant. Paul did not long for divestment, but for the superinvestment of immortality, the swallowing up of the carnal by the spiritual, as in the case of Enoch (Gen. 5: 24) and Elijah (2 Kings 2: 11). "The transition of figure from building to clothing is very easy, for our clothes are but a tighter house. One is a habit, the other a habitation" (*Whedon*). 5 **Now he that wrought us for this very thing is God, who gave unto us the earnest of the Spirit.** [God designed man for such superinvestment, and hence placed in him the longing or groaning for its accomplishment. As an infallible guarantee that the longing should be satisfied, he has given to the redeemed an earnest of the Spirit. Having given unto us of his own Spirit, it is a light thing that he should give us the spiritual body (Rom. 8: 32). **6 Being therefore always of good courage, and knowing that, whilst we are at home in the body, we are absent from the Lord 7 (for we walk by faith, not by sight); 8 we are of good courage, I say, and are willing rather to be absent from the body, and to be at home with the Lord.** [The soul has two homes, a bodily and a spiritual, and the latter is preferable; but the latter is not attained before the resurrection day. In the state between death and resurrection, of which Paul speaks in verse

194 SECOND EPISTLE TO THE CORINTHIANS

4, the spirit is with Christ, as we are here informed. Though Christ is with us now while we are in the flesh, yet we walk by faith and have no perception of him. After death we have a spiritual perception of his presence, as Paul's language indicates; but it is only at the resurrection, when we are fully incorporated in our spiritual body, that we shall see him as he is (1 John 3: 2), and know as we are known (1 Cor. 13: 12). The disembodied state, though inferior in happiness to the resurrection glory, is yet preferable to our present state. Though such a condition may be lower than the highest heaven, yet it is "home" and "with the Lord."] **9 Wherefore also we make it our aim, whether at home or absent, to be well-pleasing unto him. 10 For we must all be made manifest before the judgment-seat of Christ; that each one may receive the things** *done* **in the body, according to what he hath done, whether** *it be* **good or bad.** [Paul's aspirations caused no laxity as to duty. He tried to so live as to please Christ now, and also when summoned before him; *i. e.*, he strove to please Christ whether conscious of his presence or not, realizing that all his deeds would come to public and open manifestation and judgment. In thus outlining his own course, the apostle gave a salutary warning to his enemies that they should follow his example, and also gave them a tacit notice that, no matter how ill they might use him, they would still find him sustaining the conflict with untiring zeal.]

V.

RECONCILIATION, AND THE MINISTRY OF RECONCILIATION.

5: 11-21.

11 Knowing therefore the fear of the Lord, we persuade men, but we are made manifest unto God; and I hope that we are made manifest also in your consciences. [Knowing therefore what reason there is to fear displeasing God, we do not court his displeasure by abandoning our ministry because men misjudge and slander us, nor by letting our ministry lose its force and power through our indifference to the good opinion of men concerning us; but, on the contrary, we continue in our ministry, and patiently persuade our opponents of our sincerity and integrity when we assert (verse 9) that our sole ambition is to please God. But we do not need to persuade God in this matter, for our hearts are known and manifest to him, and I trust that they are also in like manner manifest to you by reason of this apology which you have caused me to make.] **12 We are not again commending ourselves unto you, but** *speak* **as giving you occasion** [literally a "starting-point," or, in warfare, "a base of operations"] **of glorying on our behalf, that ye may have wherewith to answer them that glory in appearance, and not in heart.** [In thus speaking of his manifest righteousness in the sight of God and the church, the language of Paul might be construed as boastful and self-commendatory. To prevent such a misconstruction he tells them plainly that his purpose is to draw a contrast between himself and his opponents, a contrast which Paul's friends in Corinth might use with telling effect when contending for the superiority of the apostle. Paul's opponents gloried in those things which were outward, or which made an external show, taking pride in their letters of recommendation, their personal knowledge of Christ in the flesh, their learning and eloquence, their intercourse with the original apostles, their Hebrew descent, circumcision, etc. Paul, on the contrary, gloried in the vital religion of the heart, in that moral and spiritual imitation of Christ which is well pleasing to God, and which delights in the thought that it is constantly manifest to God.] **13 For whether we are beside ourselves, it is unto God; or whether we are of sober mind, it is unto you.** [Paul could not appeal to the approval of his character in the sight of God without bringing to his own mind and the mind of his readers the striking difference between the manifestations of divine communion, inspiration, etc., **which** characterized his own life, and the dry, barren **formalism** which characterized the lives of his critics; yet he well knew that if his friends gloried in those things wherein his life touched upon the divine, his enemies would sneer at them as mere evidences of insanity and madness. To answer this sneer the apostle sets forth his whole life in its two grand divisions or forms of manifestation, viz.: his insanity and sanity. That which his enemies knew as the insane part of it was wholly devoted to God, and that which was generally recognized as the sane part of it was wholly devoted to the church, and at this time especially directed toward Corinth. Hence it appeared that in neither department of his life was there any room for self-seeking. His friends therefore could answer his enemies thus: "Viewed in one aspect, Paul's life is wholly devoted to the glory of God, and viewed in another it is utterly sacrificed for us and our salvation. It is evident, therefore, that having but these two ends in view, he can not be seeking self-exaltation." Paul's opponents looked upon his madness as commencing with his conversion, and in their eyes his ecstasies, visions, revelations, trances, inspiration and mystic intercourse with God and Christ were conclusive evidences that his mind was unbalanced. But the very nature of the phenomena showed a character void of all self-seeking. Paul's sanity consisted in his sound judgment, forbearance, tact, consideration, charity, etc., in the handling of the churches as is displayed in all his epistles. It is true that in this field the apostle maintains his dignity and authority, but in every instance where he does so, it is for the obvious purpose of directing and benefiting others, and not with any design to exalt himself.] **14 For the love of Christ constraineth us; because we thus judge, that one died for all, therefore all died; 15 and he died for all, that they that live should no longer live unto themselves, but unto him who for their sakes died and rose again.** [Paul's life was devoted to Christ, and to man for Christ's sake. When tempted to swerve from either of these services, Christ's love for him confined him within the limits of the life of sacrifice which he has described, and which he regarded as prescribed for him by the Lord. His reasons for regarding this life as prescribed for him grew out of his view of the death of Christ. He regarded the death of Christ as representative. As Christ had died as the head of the race, therefore all men had died with him to their sins, and so were obligated to lead self-sacrificing, unselfish, sinless lives for the sake of him who, on their behalf, had died and risen again. Compare Rom. 6: 1-11; Gal. 5: 4; 2: 19, 20; Col. 3: 3.] **16 Wherefore we henceforth know no man after the flesh: even though we have known Christ after the flesh, yet now we know** *him so* **no more. 17 Wherefore if any man is in Christ,** *he is* **a new creature: the old things are passed away; behold, they are become new.** [By his spiritual participation in the death and resurrection of Christ, Paul had become a regenerated man, and as such he refused to judge or look upon men after that carnal, superficial, unregenerate method which estimates them according to outward appearances, and not according to their inward spiritual life. In asserting this great principle he is reminded that before his conversion he had known and judged Christ after this carnal fashion. The allusion suggests that if he made a woeful mistake in thus doing, his enemies were even now following in his footsteps in thus judging him, a minister and servant of Jesus Christ. Christian men, being spiritual beings, are to be judged as such. The old standards of the law can not be applied to them; they are not to be accepted because they are children of Abraham, nor rejected because they are Gentiles. To them all things are become new, and they must judge and be judged by the new environment into which the providence of God has brought them.] **18 But all things are of God, who reconciled us to himself through Christ, and gave unto us the ministry of reconciliation; 19 to wit, that God was in Christ reconciling the world unto himself, not reckoning unto them their trespasses, and having committed unto us the word of reconciliation.** [Christ's love, I say, constrains me to sacrifice for men, and to persuade them when they grossly misconstrue me, and to seek reconciliation with them when they fight against me. For the whole dispensation under which I work is from God, and is an effort on his part to reconcile his human enemies unto himself. When I myself was such an enemy God reconciled me, and gave to me the work or ministry of reconciling others; so that I am obliged, both by a sense of duty and of gratitude, to proclaim to man that God sent Christ to reconcile the world to him through the forgiveness of those trespasses which made them fear and hate him; and that I may not fail in this sacred office I am likewise obliged to persuade men that this ministry of reconciliation is committed to me.] **20 We are ambassadors therefore on behalf of Christ, as though God were entreating by us: we beseech *you* on behalf of Christ, be ye reconciled to God. 21 Him who knew no sin he made *to be* sin on our behalf; that we might become the righteousness of God in him.** [Wherefore, I have no choice in the matter, but must meet enmity with persuasion and an effort at reconciliation; for if men attack me I am not a free and independent man, but an ambassador to Christ the Reconciler; and if they attack my ministry, lo, it also is not mine, but is Christ's ministry of reconciliation; so on Christ's behalf I am constrained to seek reconciliation, not with myself alone, but with God. And surely my appeal is not without weight, for it has the constraining power of the love of God—a love manifested in God's gift of his sinless Son, who was made sin for us that we might be reconciled to God by attaining the righteousness of God in him; *i. e.*, by virtue of our union with him as part of his mystical body.]

VI.

INTRODUCTION TO A WARNING, AND THE WARNING

6: 1-7: 1

1 And working together *with him* we entreat also that ye receive not the grace of God in vain 2 (for he saith, At an acceptable time I hearkened unto thee, And in a day of salvation did I succor thee: behold, now is the acceptable time; behold, now is the day of salvation) [The apostle here begins to give a warning which is fully set forth later (vs. 14-18). Before giving the warning he pauses to establish his character, influence and authority among them, that his warning may have weight. This establishment of his authority, etc., fills up the intervening space (vs. 3-13). These two verses of introduction will be considered together with the warning itself]: 3 giving no occasion of stumbling in anything, that our ministration be not blamed [The participle "giving" co-ordinates with "entreats" found in verse 1. To give force and effect to his entreaty, Paul conducted himself in the manner described in this and the following verses. It is a well-recognized fact that whenever blame attaches to a minister, his ministry will be weakened, if not neutralized. Without the confidence of the people the minister possesses little power, no matter how extraordinary his talent. Therefore, before proceeding to fully express the matter of his beseeching, the apostle pauses to fully set forth all the pains, cares, suffering, etc., which he had habitually undergone in order to make his beseeching effective]; 4 but in everything commending ourselves, as ministers of God, in much patience, in afflictions, in necessities, in distresses, 5 in stripes, in imprisonments, in tumults, in labors, in watchings, in fastings [Instead of weakening his ministry by making it blameworthy, Paul had striven to make it commendable by the patient endurance of all manner of trials. Had he shrunk from

enduring these trials, he would have been ill qualified to prescribe for others those rules of duty which called for self-sacrifice, one of which rules he is about to lay down for the Corinthians. Paul specifies three classes of sufferings which he endured, and each class contained three members. In the first three the idea of hindrance predominates, and in the second that of violent opposition, and in the third that of hardship. For a sample of Paul's afflictions see chap. 1: 4-11. For necessities arising from his poverty, etc., see Acts 20: 34, and compare with incidents in his later life; as, Phil. 4: 12 and 2 Tim. 4: 13. The word "distresses," which forms the climax of the first triplet, means "extreme pressure" and is used to describe one who is jammed in a corner, or so pressed upon by the multitude that he can not move: it is found at 4: 8. For the "stripes" see 11: 23-28. The only instance of imprisonment of which Luke tells us is found at Acts 16: 24. The imprisonments at Jerusalem, Cæsarea and Rome took place after this was written. As to the tumults, they were the normal incidents of Paul's daily life (Acts 13: 50; 14: 19; 26: 22; 17: 4, 5; 18: 12; 19: 28, 29; 21: 27-39; 22: 22, 23; 23: 9, 10; 27: 42, etc.). As to Paul's wasting labors, see ch. 11: 28; 1 Cor. 4: 12; 15: 10; Acts 20: 34; 1 Thess. 2: 9; 2 Thess. 3: 8; Rom. 16: 12. We may well imagine that so many tumults and such incessant labor would result in many sleepless nights or painful watchings (ch. 11: 27); but Paul also labored at night (Acts 20: 31; 1 Thess. 2: 9, etc.). The fastings mentioned were not voluntary, but indicate the unavoidable hunger which came upon him by reason of his incessant ministry. Having rehearsed the sufferings which he endured, the apostle next names six especial gifts or virtues which he manifested while thus enduring]; **6 in pureness** [he had lived a holy and chaste life], **in knowledge** [His sufferings had not perverted his understanding of the gospel, or of God's plan. As he had endured all temptations to self-indulgence, so had he likewise withstood all those whisperings of Satan which bade him make life easier by compromising the truth which he knew], **in longsuffering, in kindness** [If he had been loyal in the sight of God, in that he had abstained from self-indulgence **and** heresy, so he had been faithful toward men in patiently enduring their misconstructions and insults, and in constantly returning good for evil], **in the Holy Spirit, in love unfeigned** [If Paul's sufferings had given an appearance of weakness to his life, the Holy Spirit had given it unquestioned power and had crowned his ministry with success (1 Thess. 1: 5; Rom. 15: 18, 19). And if the Spirit had thus sanctioned his work by outward conquests, he had likewise sanctioned it by inward victories, so that Paul had risen to that love unfeigned which is the supreme gift of the Spirit (1 Cor. 8: 1; 13: 1-13; Rom. 12: 9-21; ch. 12: 15; 1 Pet. 1: 22; 2 Pet. 1: 5-8). From those traits and gifts which were more passive, Paul now turns to enumerate those which were more active], **7 in the word of truth, in the power of God** [If Paul had kept his private life in fit condition for the ministry, he had likewise demeaned himself publicly as a true apostle. If he had kept his heart loyal to the truth, he had likewise kept his tongue faithful to the proclamation of it. In exercising discipline he had manifested the fullness of the power of God which was in him—ch. 4: 7; 1 Cor. 2: 4, 5; 4: 19-21; Acts 13: 9-12]; **by the armor of righteousness on the right hand and on the left** [The armor of the right hand was offensive, and that of the left was defensive. As a true minister of Christ engaged in the Christian warfare, Paul knew how to strike so as to discipline all real offenders, and he also was well able to defend himself against the attacks of unchristian Jews, etc., and false brethren, who assailed his character as they had here at Corinth], **8 by glory and dishonor** [When present in such cities as Philippi, Thessalonica and Corinth, etc., Paul had been held in glory and honor by the converts of his ministry, but had been dishonored by heathens, Jews and Judaizing Christians], **by evil report and good report** [in his absence those who honored him spoke well of him, and those who dishonored him gave him an evil report]; **as deceivers, and *yet* true** [regarded by some as a deliberate cheat and a misleading impostor, yet approved of God and his own conscience as a true apostle]; **9 as unknown, and *yet* well known** [ignored and unrecognized by the rulers and the general public, yet well known by all those in any way interested in the gospel of Christ, either as friends or enemies]; **as dying, and behold, we live** [the life of the apostle was constantly exposed to death and just as constantly delivered and preserved]; **as chastened, and not killed** [Paul was being continually schooled and educated by suffering and yet the suffering was not more than he could bear—Ps. 118: 18; Heb. 12: 5-10]; **10 as sorrowful, yet always rejoicing** [having abundant sorrow as to this present life, yet boundless rejoicing in contemplation of the life to come]; **as poor, yet making many rich** [being penniless indeed in worldly goods, yet able to enrich all men with the knowledge of the grace of God, and the heavenly blessings and benefits resulting and to result from that grace]; **as having nothing, and** *yet* **possessing all things.** [As having sacrificed all things for Christ and his gospel (Phil. 3: 7, 8), and yet sensible of having lost nothing by the exchange, but of having made infinite gain thereby (Matt. 16: 25; 1 Cor. 3: 21, 22). Such had been the ministry of the apostle on behalf of the Corinthians, and therefore in the next three verses the apostle appeals to them to show to him an affection like that which he has bestowed upon them.] **11 Our mouth is open unto you, O Corinthians, our heart is enlarged. 12 Ye are not straitened in us, but ye are straitened in your own affections. 13 Now for a recompense in like kind (I speak as unto** *my* **children), be ye also enlarged.** [When Paul had written his former letter his heart had been narrowed by his suspicions as to the loyalty of the Corinthians, and he had spoken to them as with compressed and guarded lips, weighing not only his words, but mindful, as it were, of the tone in which he uttered them. But by their obedience to the instructions which he gave them his confidence in them had been restored, his heart had dilated to its former largeness and wealth of affection toward them, and his mouth had been set free to speak to them unreservedly and openly. If any strained or straitened relations existed between them, they arose from the hearts of the Corinthians themselves. Paul therefore beseeches them to recompense his love with their love,

THE WARNING

his largeheartedness with corresponding largeness of heart on their part, and he does this in the spirit and with the expectation which a father has when talking with his children. Thus, after the long parenthetical digression which began at verse 3, the apostle comes back to the subject-matter of verses 1 and 2. Having put himself in a proper position to give an admonition, and the Corinthians in the right attitude to receive it, he imparts the warning which he began to introduce in verse 1.] **14 Be not unequally yoked with unbelievers** [a figure drawn from the law—Deut. 22: 9-11]: **for what fellowship have righteousness and iniquity? or what communion hath light with darkness? 15 And what concord hath Christ with Belial?** [Literally, "worthlessness," "depravity." The term is here used as a synonym for Satan, who is the impersonation of impurity] **or what portion hath a believer with an unbeliever? 16 And what agreement hath a temple of God with idols? for we are a temple of the living God; even as God said** [Lev. 26: 12; Ex. 29: 45; Ezek. 27: 27; Jer. 31: 1], **I will dwell in them, and walk in them; and I will be their God, and they shall be my people.** [In the first epistle to the Corinthians the apostle had reasoned with the church, giving it instruction as to marriage ties between pagans and believers, and as to the social and other fellowships which tempted the Corinthians to take part in idol feasts. In all this his language had been careful and guarded, and he had recognized to the full every principle of Christian liberty involved in these questions. He now lays aside the argumentative reserve which characterized his first letter and tells them plainly that by thus going to the extreme limits of their liberty they are liable to make the grace of God in vain as to them. That life is a brief day of probation wherein they should not hazard their salvation. Then, by a series of short, terse questions he shows the utter folly, the inconsistency and incongruity of every form of alliance which entangles the children of God with the children of the devil. The world has not so improved, and Satan has not so repented, as to in any way nullify, or even weaken, the weight and applicability of this apostolic warning.] **17 Wherefore**

Come ye out from among them, and be ye separate, saith the Lord [Isa. 52: 11], And touch no unclean thing; And I will receive you, 18 And will be to you a Father, And ye shall be to me sons and daughters, saith the Lord Almighty. [Hos. 1: 10; Isa. 43: 6.]

VII. 1 Having therefore these promises, beloved, let us cleanse ourselves from all defilement of flesh and spirit, perfecting holiness in the fear of God. [By an appeal to the prophets the apostle shows how it was God's design that his people should avoid all fellowship with unrighteous people in their unrighteous practices. To stimulate them to obedience, God had given them the wonderful promise that he would adopt them as his children if they would obey him in these things. This promise of adoption had been renewed in the new covenant, and belonged to all Christians, and therefore it behooved Christians not to temporize with evil because of any vainglorious desire to display their liberty, lest they should thereby lose the real and eternal glory of being adopted sons and daughters of God.]

VII.

AN APPEAL TO BE ACCEPTED

7: 2-16.

[In this section the apostle appeals to the Corinthians to accept him as a true apostle and minister of Christ, and as persuasive to this end he sets forth his affection for them, his anxiety concerning them, and his joy at learning of their loyalty to him.] 2 Open your hearts to us: we wronged no man, we corrupted no man, we took advantage of no man. [Open your hearts and receive us into your love and confidence, for, despite all that our enemies have said about us, it must be apparent to you when you have sifted their accusations that they have proved nothing which should shake your confidence in us. We have replied to their accusations without in any way dealing unjustly by them, and they have failed to show that we have corrupted any one, either in morals or doctrine, or that we have in any way overreached anybody, or shown any mercenary spirit (1 Cor. 9: 1-6.) Compare Num. 16: 15; 1 Sam. 12: 3-5.] **3 I say it not to condemn** *you:* **for I have said before, that ye are in our hearts to die together and live together.** [I do not say these things as though I would complain of you that you are so ungrateful and unjust as to accuse me of them. I am merely defending myself and not condemning you. I have no desire to do the latter, for as I have before said, I love you so that I am ready to die with you or live with you. Compare 1 Thess. 2: 8; Phil. 1: 7, 20, 24; 2: 17, 18; also John 10: 11. The apostle mentions death first, because to him death seemed daily more probable than life. He would have loved to dwell among the Corinthians as James then dwelt with the church at Jerusalem, and afterwards John took up his abiding-place at Corinth, but his duties as apostle to the Gentiles made him a wanderer.] **4 Great is my boldness of speech toward you, great is my glorying on your behalf: I am filled with comfort, I overflow with joy in all our affliction.** [This verse tells of Paul's restored confidence in the Corinthians, and his consequent freedom of speech and joyfulness of heart. The next few verses show us that these changes were wrought in him by the report which he received from Titus concerning affairs at Corinth.] **5 For even when we were come into Macedonia our flesh had no relief, but** *we were* **afflicted on every side ; without** *were* **fightings, within** *were* **fears.** [The apostle here resumes the thread of his narrative begun at 2: 12, 13. For the connection see the comment on those verses. He here tells us that even after he came to Macedonia his burdens were increased rather than lightened ; for, in addition to the fears and anxieties which he felt concerning Corinth, he became the object of persecution. His condition, therefore, was less agreeable than at Troas, for there he had a full and free opportunity to preach the gospel.] **6 Nevertheless he that comforteth the lowly,** *even* **God, comforted us by the coming of Titus ; 7 and not by his coming only, but also by the comfort wherewith he** was comforted in you, while he told us your longing, your mourning, your zeal for me; so that I rejoiced yet more. [The apostle was not only refreshed by the presence of Titus, and the report which he brought, but he was more especially cheered by the visible satisfaction of Titus with regard to affairs at Corinth. Paul regarded the feeling of Titus as a more palpable proof of the improved state of things at Corinth than even the substance of the report which he brought. Thus the consolation felt by Titus became transferred to the heart of Paul, and the joyful manner in which Titus gave his report, as he told how the Corinthians longed to see the apostle, how they mourned over those things which they had done to displease him, and what zeal they showed to carry out his instructions, was more to Paul than the mere facts which he narrated. If Titus felt comfort or joy in narrating these facts, Paul felt more joy in hearing them thus narrated. Or we can take the phrase "yet more" as a comparison between his present joy and his previous sorrow. This latter construction fits better with what is said in the next two verses.] 8 For though I made you sorry with my epistle, I do not regret it: though I did regret *it* (for I see that that epistle made you sorry, though but for a season), 9 I now rejoice, not that ye were made sorry, but that ye were made sorry unto repentance; for ye were made sorry after a godly sort, that ye might suffer loss by us in nothing. [In his first epistle to the Corinthians Paul had sternly rebuked them. Though recognizing that the rebuke was well deserved, the apostle regretted that he had written so sternly and uncompromisingly, fearing lest his letter might not work the results which he wished, for speaking what is right does not always lead to happy results (John 6: 60-68). His words were calculated to cause them the sorrow of vexation or hurt vanity, or the sorrow of mortified pride, etc. But when he learned from Titus that it had caused them to sorrow as being culpable in the sight of God, and so caused them to repent as he desired, the apostle was glad that he had written as he had, for they had lost nothing by rea-

AN APPEAL TO BE ACCEPTED

son of his timidity or tenderheartedness. He had made them sorry but for a season, and could now make them glad by this second epistle which contained the consolation of his approval.] **10 For godly sorrow worketh repentance unto salvation,** *a repentance* **which bringeth no regret: but the sorrow of the world worketh death.** [Godly sorrow results in repentance, and repentance results in salvation, and this result is never to be regretted, either by those who attain it, or by those who have helped towards its attainment. While it is true that the sorrow of the world tends toward despair and suicide and so towards death, as is witnessed by the cases of Saul, Ahithophel and Judas, yet this is not the apostle's thought; he means that worldly sorrow tends toward that eternal death which is the antithesis of salvation. This becomes apparent when we consider that a worldly sorrow, arising because of and by means of the consequences of sin, tends to make the sinner worse instead of better, for it breeds in him a boldness, a malignant recklessness and a morbid despair which tend to paralyze all efforts toward reformation.] **11 For behold, this selfsame thing, that ye were made sorry after a godly sort, what earnest care it wrought in you, yea what clearing of yourselves, yea what indignation, yea what fear, yea what longing, yea what zeal, yea what avenging! In everything ye approved yourselves to be pure in the matter.** [This very selfsame incident is an example of godly sorrow worthy of your consideration. For you see in how many ways it brought forth the fruit of repentance in you. As to yourselves, it made you most careful to set yourselves right with God, and indignant with yourselves that you had been so lax in your discipline. As to me, it made you fearful that I would come with a rod as I had promised, and punish you, and after you had removed the cause for such punishment, you felt a longing for my presence. As to the offender, it roused you to aggressive action against him to punish him for having injured the cause of Christ. Thus, your sorrow worked a repentance which rested **not** until it had cleared your hands of all blame. The apostle here, of course, refers to the discipline of the incestuous person, which, as he has said, he made a test case of their obedience or willingness to repent under his instruction (chap. 2: 9). As to the phrase "this matter," it has been well said that Paul, in accordance with his usual manner, "speaks indefinitely of what is odious"—1 Thess. 4: 6.] **12 So although I wrote unto you** [for what he had written, see 1 Cor. 5: 1-5], *I wrote* **not for his cause that did the wrong** [*i. e.*, the incestuous son], **nor for his cause that suffered the wrong** [*i. e.*, the injured father], **but that your earnest care for us might be made manifest unto you in the sight of God.** [In writing to you to discipline the incestuous man, I was not moved by the small motive of setting to rights a difficulty between two parties, though one of them was clearly a wrongdoer, and the other obviously a sufferer by reason of his wrong-doing. My motive was much larger. I wished you to see that despite all the accusations brought against me to which you gave ear, you still show, by your own conduct, as you view it in the sight of God, that you know better than to disobey me.] **13 Therefore we have been comforted: and in our comfort we joyed the more exceedingly for the joy of Titus, because his spirit hath been refreshed by you all.** [Therefore, as we have said before, our anxiety has been removed, and we have been comforted when we have seen how you have obeyed us, and stood the test which we imposed upon you, and our joy has been greatly increased as we have seen the joy felt by Titus at your conduct.] **14 For if in anything I have gloried to him on your behalf, I was not put to shame; but as we spake all things to you in truth, so our glorying also which I made before Titus was found to be truth.** [Paul had evidently told Titus that he would find the Corinthians true and loyal, and ready to obey the apostle's letter. Had events proved otherwise, Paul would have been put to shame in the eyes of Titus. But as the apostle, despite the accusations of the Corinthians to the contrary (1: 15-17), had always spoken truth *to* them, so he had always been truthful in speaking to Titus *about* them. Paul's affection for the Corinthians had not caused him to overstep the limits of perfect accuracy while

AN APPEAL TO BE ACCEPTED

boasting of them to Titus.] **15 And his affection is more abundantly toward you, while he remembereth the obedience of you all, how with fear and trembling ye received him. 16 I rejoice that in everything I am of good courage concerning you.** [The affections which the Corinthians had awakened in the heart of Titus, who had come among them and had been received as Paul's messenger, greatly established the confidence of the apostle in that church, as he here tells them. Having thus led up to a well-grounded expression of confidence, Paul makes it a basis on which to rest the second division of his epistle—a division in which he appeals to them to fulfill their promises with regard to the collection for the poor at Jerusalem.]

PART SECOND.

8: 1-9: 15.

CONCERNING THE COLLECTION FOR THE JERUSALEM CHURCH.

I.

THE COLLECTION AND THE MESSENGERS IN CHARGE OF IT.

8: 1-24.

[In this section Paul exhorts the Corinthians to proceed with the collection for the poor of the Jerusalem church. For Paul's instructions in regard to this collection, and the reasons for it, see 1 Cor. 16: 1-3, and notes thereon.] **1 Moreover, brethren, we make known to you the grace of God which hath been given in the churches of Macedonia; 2 how that in much proof of affliction the abundance of their joy and their deep poverty abounded unto the riches of their liberality.** [The only Macedonian churches known to us were those at Philippi, Thessalonica and Berœa. The district of Macedonia had suffered in the three civil wars, and had been reduced to such poverty that Tiberius Cæsar, hearkening to their petitions, had lightened their taxes. But in addition to this general poverty, the churches had been made poor by persecution (2 Thess. 1: 4). This poverty put their Christian character to the proof, and Paul wishes the Corinthians to know, that they may be benefited by the example, how nobly the Macedonians endured the proof. Despite their afflictions they were so filled with the grace of God that their joy abounded and worked positively in combination with their abysmal poverty, which worked negatively to manifest the extreme riches of their liberality.] **3 For** according to their power, I bear witness, yea and beyond their power, *they gave* of their own accord, 4 beseeching us with much entreaty in regard of this grace and the fellowship in the ministering to the saints: 5 and *this*, not as we had hoped, but first they gave their own selves to the Lord, and to us through the will of God. [The apostle here sets forth the liberality of the Macedonians, and shows that of their own accord, and without any entreaty on his part, they gave, not only according to their means, but even beyond their means. When he, recognizing that they were giving beyond their means, sought to restrain them, they laid siege to him with persistent entreaty, both that they might be allowed to exercise the grace of liberality which God had put in their hearts, and that they might have fellowship in so worthy a work as ministering to the needs of God's people. The apostle, knowing their poverty, had hoped for but little from them, but they had exceeded all his expectations, for (and here was the secret of their liberality) they had surrendered their will to the will of God, so that before attempting to give their money they had first given themselves to the Lord, and to the apostle as the Lord's servant.] **6 Insomuch that we exhorted Titus, that as he had made a beginning before, so he would also complete in you this grace also.** [Inspired by the example of the Macedonians, Paul was moved to exhort Titus to return to Corinth, that having begun the work of gathering an offering from the church there, he might continue until the Corinthians made a liberal offering.] **7 But as ye abound in everything, *in* faith, and utterance, and knowledge, and *in* all earnestness, and *in* your love to us, *see* that ye abound in this grace also. 8 I speak not by way of commandment, but as proving through the earnestness of others the sincerity also of your love.** [Paul here speaks of liberality as a grace or gift of the Spirit. Paul testifies that the Corinthians abounded in spiritual gifts (1 Cor. 4: 7). He here reminds them of some of these prominent gifts, and exhorted them to add thereto the gift of liberality, and to make it con-

212 SECOND EPISTLE TO THE CORINTHIANS

spicuous among the other gifts by its perfection. He does not command them to give, for the very virtue or value of giving lies in its spontaneity, but, using the case of the Macedonians as an example or means of comparison, he measures or tests the love of the Corinthians by it.] **9 For ye know the grace of our Lord Jesus Christ, that, though he was rich, yet for your sakes he became poor, that ye through his poverty might become rich.** [In making liberality the test of love, Paul is reminded of that supreme love of Christ and the test which it endured. The grace of liberality in Jesus caused him to lay aside his glory, and those other attributes of his divinity which were not compatible with his being made flesh, and took upon him our poor and despised humanity, that he might enrich it with all that he had surrendered. The words here should be compared with Phil. 2: 5-11. What Christ gave up for us becomes to us a criterion for giving. The love which promoted such a sacrifice should constrain us to sacrifice for others.] **10 And herein I give *my* judgment: for this is expedient for you, who were the first to make a beginning a year ago, not only to do, but also to will.** [I do not, as I have said, command you to give, but I think that, having undertaken the work, you should complete your collection. If it was a mere matter of doing, I would command you, but, as it is a matter of willing, I can only advise you, therefore I do advise you to willingly give (ch. 9: 7). As Paul wrote soon after the beginning of the Jewish year, the phrase "a year ago" might mean only a few months. But the mention of this collection in Paul's first Epistle shows that the Corinthians had had it in mind for more than six months.] **11 But now complete the doing also; that as *there was* the readiness to will, so *there may be* the completion also out of your ability. 12 For if the readiness is there, *it is* acceptable according as *a man* hath, not according as *he* hath not.** [As you once had the willingness to give, let your will perfect itself in doing, and take up the collection according to your ability to give, for if a man is willing to give, God accepts the gift, not valuing it according to its magnitude, but according to the proportion which it bears to the means in the possession of the giver.] **13 For** *I say* **not** *this* **that others may be eased** *and* **ye distressed; 14 but by equality: your abundance** *being a supply* **at this present time for their want, that their abundance also may become** *a supply* **for your want; that there may be equality** [The apostle did not take money from the Corinthians for the purpose of impoverishing them and enriching the church at Jerusalem: his idea was that the abundance enjoyed by the Corinthians might be withdrawn from their side of the scales and placed in the Jerusalem side, so that the scales might balance—not a literal balancing, but such a one as would insure that those at Jerusalem would not suffer because of their poverty. And he did this with the expectation and understanding that whenever conditions were reversed, those at Jerusalem would donate their superfluity to the support of Corinth. That such equality is approved of God, was shown by the manner in which he meted out his manna, as appears by the citation in the next verse]: **15 as it is written** [Ex. 16: 17, 18], **He that** *gathered* **much had nothing over; and he that** *gathered* **little had no lack.** [In the gathering of the manna some of the Israelites were able to find more than the others, but when they came to measure what they gathered, God's providence so intervened and ordered that each found he had an omer. Now that which God effected by irresistible law under the old dispensation, he was now seeking to effect under the new dispensation through the gracious influence of brotherly love. Our differences in ability make it inevitable that some shall surpass others in the gathering of wealth; but as selfishness gives place to Christian love, the inequality in earthly possessions will become more even.] **16 But thanks be to God, who putteth the same earnest care for you into the heart of Titus. 17 For he accepted indeed our exhortation; but being himself very earnest, he went forth unto you of his own accord.** [The apostle thanks God that he had given to Titus the same desire to benefit the Corinthians which animated Paul himself, so that Titus not only accepted the apostle's exhortation to go back to Corinth and induce them to take up the collection, but was even ready of his own accord to undertake the work.] **18 And we have sent together with him the brother whose praise in the gospel** is *spread* **through all the churches** [Baynes, in his "Horæ Lucanæ," argues very conclusively that this was Luke. He was at Philippi about this time, and was among those who accompanied Paul from Macedonia (or perhaps Corinth) to Jerusalem (Acts 20: 2-6). The phrase "in the gospel" can hardly be taken as indicating that at this time Luke had written his Gospel, but the Gospel which he wrote is evidently not the work of a day. No doubt at this time Luke was so versed in the gospel history as to be fittingly described by the words here used by Paul]; **19 and not only so, but who was also appointed by the churches to travel with us in** *the matter of* **this grace, which is ministered by us to the glory of the Lord, and** *to show* **our readiness** [Paul is commending those whom he sent to gather the collections. Luke's primary commendation is his general character revealed in his love for the gospel facts; his further qualification is his appointment by the churches in Macedonia to assist in this very work. He had resided in Macedonia for some six years, or since Paul had first come to Philippi, and so was well known and fully trusted by the Macedonians. He was appointed that the glory of Christ might not be tarnished by any suspicion that the money was raised for selfish purposes, and that Paul's zeal to raise the money might not be regarded with evil surmises]: **20 avoiding this, that any man should blame us in** *the matter of* **this bounty which is ministered by us: 21 for we take thought for things honorable, not only in the sight of the Lord, but also in the sight of men.** [Paul welcomed the appointment of assistance in this work, for their co-operation lifted him above suspicion, which was according to his desire, for he wished not only to have a good character in the sight of God, but also a fair reputation among men.] **22 And we have sent with them our brother, whom we have many** times proved earnest in many things, but now much more earnest, by reason of the great confidence which *he hath* in you. [As to this third party, Alford well says, "Every possible person has been guessed." There is no means of determining who it was. Paul's words show that he had been often used by the apostle because of his earnestness, and that he was employed in this work because he evidently knew and had great confidence in the Corinthians.] 23 Whether *any inquire* about Titus, *he is* my partner and *my* fellow-worker to you-ward; or our brethren, *they are* the messengers of the churches, *they are* the glory of Christ. 24 Show ye therefore unto them in the face of the churches the proof of your love, and of our glorying on your behalf. [As a final commendation, and as one calculated to stop the mouths of all objectors, Paul describes Titus as a partner with himself in raising the contribution of Corinth, and he describes the other two who went with Titus as not only messengers of the churches in this behalf, but as men whose daily life glorified the Master whom they served. In view, therefore, of the fitness of those whom he sent to them, Paul asks the Corinthian church to raise the collection under their direction as an evidence of the general benevolence of their disposition, and as a proof that he spoke the truth when he boasted of their liberality.]

II.

EXHORTATION TO HAVE HIS BOASTING SUSTAINED.

9: 1-15.

1 For as touching the ministering to the saints, it is superfluous for me to write to you: 2 for I know your readiness, of which I glory on your behalf to them of Macedonia, that Achaia hath been prepared for a year past; and your zeal hath stirred up very many of them. [It is needless for me to urge upon you the fact that

it is a becoming thing in you to minister to the poor in the churches, for you have long since acknowledged the becomingness of the deed by pledging yourself to do it. And this readiness on your part I have used with great effect in Macedonia, for I told them how last year you consented to take this collection, so that many of them, feeling their tardiness in comparison with you, have been stirred to great activity and zeal in this matter.] **3 But I have sent the brethren** [Titus and the other two], **that our glorying on your behalf may not be made void in this respect; that, even as I said, ye may be prepared: 4 lest by any means, if there come with me any of Macedonia and find you unprepared, we (that we say not, ye) should be put to shame in this confidence.** [I have gloried or boasted concerning you in many respects, and have hitherto had to retract nothing which I said. That my glorying concerning your liberality may not prove an exception and require a retraction, I have sent these messengers that they might gather together the collection which you pledged, and perhaps began to take up last year. For if any Macedonians should come with me to Corinth and find the collection ungathered, I would be ashamed for having represented you as better than you were, and you would be ashamed of having been held up as a model for the emulation of those who were, in fact, better than you.] **5 I thought it necessary therefore to entreat the brethren, that they would go before unto you, and make up beforehand** [*i. e.*, before my coming] **your afore-promised bounty, that the same might be ready as a matter of bounty, and not of extortion.** [I sent these messengers on before me that they might stir you up to gather the collection before I came, that the offering might be seen to be your own free gift and not a veritable tax extorted from you by the fear of my displeasure and your shame at being exposed in your selfishness.] **6 But this** *I say*, **He that soweth sparingly shall reap also sparingly; and he that soweth bountifully shall reap also bountifully.** [The same law which pertains to the physical world pertains with equal effect in the moral

THE COLLECTION

and spiritual realm, so that those who are stingy and niggardly in giving to others, shall receive scantily of the blessings bestowed by God.] **7 Let each man *do* according as he hath purposed in his heart: not grudgingly** [literally, of sorrow], **or of necessity: for God loveth a cheerful giver.** [Let each man give as his own heart prompts him and not as improperly influenced by others. Let no one give as if half crying to part with his money, and let no one feel constrained to give from any motives of necessity, such as popular applause, or to keep up with his neighbors, or to be rid of the solicitations of some urgent collector. Such giving is valueless in the sight of God, who values gifts only as they are really and truly such, and in no way extortions. The spirit of extortion is sorrow, but that of giving is cheerfulness.] **8 And God is able to make all grace abound unto you; that ye, having always all sufficiency in everything, may abound unto every good work: 9 as it is written, He hath scattered abroad, he hath given to the poor; His righteousness abideth for ever.** [Ps. 112: 9. God is able to bestow every blessing, both temporal and spiritual, and so he can give blessings to those who dispense them, and thus enable them to abound in good works which they are performing. That this is true is shown by the Psalmist's description of the man who fears the Lord. Such a man is profuse in his liberality and his remembrance of the poor, and he is able to keep up his right-doing in giving, for the Lord continually supplies him with means to that end. We should, however, note that Paul's words here, like those at Ps. 91: 11, 12, which Satan quoted to the Lord in his temptation (Matt. 4: 6), are not to be so interpreted and applied as to tempt the Lord.] **10 And he that supplieth seed to the sower and bread for food, shall supply and multiply your seed for sowing, and increase the fruits of your righteousness** [and he that, in the economy of nature, makes returns to the sower, so that he not only has his seed again, but bread for food, shall in like manner in the domain of grace, supply and multiply the seeds of charity which you sow, so that you will not only be able to do again the deed of charity which you have done, but he will also bless all your other acts of righteousness by making them fruitful]: **11 ye being enriched in everything unto all liberality, which worketh through us thanksgiving to God.** [Thus, your liberality multiplies your means of liberality, and also works, through the agents which dispense it, thanksgiving to God from the poor in Jerusalem who receive it.] **12 For the ministration of this service not only filleth up the measure of the wants of the saints, but aboundeth also through many thanksgivings unto God; 13 seeing that through the proving *of you* by this ministration they glorify God for the obedience of your confession unto the gospel of Christ, and for the liberality of *your* contribution unto them, and unto all; 14 while they themselves also, with supplication on your behalf, long after you by reason of the exceeding grace of God in you.** [This ministry of yours, in giving to the poor at Jerusalem, not only fills up the measure of the wants of these people of God, but overflows that measure, for it results in many thanksgivings to God. And these results are evident, for by thus showing your liberality to the Jewish church at Jerusalem, you prove to it that you are indeed true and obedient to your confession of your faith in the gospel of Christ, and thus cause them to glorify God, as they also do for the liberality of your contribution unto them and (potentially) unto all. You cause them also to pray for you and long to see you face to face, that they may know those in whom God's grace abounds to so full a measure. It will be remembered that the church in Jerusalem, influenced by the prejudices of the Jews which surrounded it, and also by the sentiments and feelings which it inherited from its previous life, looked upon the church as planted by Paul, with eyes full of suspicion. They regarded these churches as lawless bodies, inimical to all that the Jews held as ancient or sacred. They were ready to believe any wild rumor which might start with regard to the unchristian character of the apostle's converts, and the reckless lawlessness of the apostle himself. The riot which arose soon after when

THE COLLECTION 219

Paul was found in the temple at Jerusalem aptly illustrates the attitude of the Jewish mind toward him and his work. Now the apostle felt confident that a liberal gift from his Gentile churches would bring about a better understanding, and would work wonderful changes in the thoughts of Jewish Christians. He felt that it would persuade the latter that his Gentile converts were truly obedient to the religion which they confessed, and that it would persuade them also that those who had overcome their prejudices sufficiently to give liberally to Jews would have no prejudices which would prevent them from giving liberally to other people. He was likewise confident that the Jewish Christians, seeing these things, would be fully persuaded of the genuine Christian grace of his converts, and therefore would not only pray for them, but even long for personal acquaintance and fellowship with them. How far the apostle was correct in this judgment we can not say; but he certainly seems to have been well received by the Christians at Jerusalem when he came as the representative of these Gentile churches. If the attitude of the unchristian Jewish mind toward him was still relentlessly bitter, it must be borne in mind that he took no collection for them, and that they were in no manner in his thought in this connection.] **15 Thanks be to God for his unspeakable gift.** [Of course, the Christ himself is God's great gift to man, but the personality of Christ is not in the trend of Paul's argument. The thought that fills his mind is that the Corinthians, by their liberality, are showing themselves truly changed and converted by the gospel of Christ, and that this gospel, modifying and softening the Jewish mind, is preparing it to step over the middle wall of partition, and receive the Gentiles as part of the family of God. For the unspeakable gift, therefore, of a gospel which works such blessed changes in the bigoted, stubborn and selfish hearts of men, Paul gives thanks. The thanksgiving, therefore, is proximately for the gospel and ultimately for Christ, the author of the gospel.]

PART THIRD.

10: 1-13: 14.

PAUL MEASURES OR COMPARES HIMSELF WITH HIS CHIEF OPPOSERS OR OTHER DETRACTORS.

I.

FOES, WEAPONS AND MEASUREMENTS.

10: 1-18.

[The two previous parts of this epistle have been mainly addressed to that portion of the congregation at Corinth which was loyal to the apostle. This third part, however, is especially addressed to his enemies, though he at times evidently speaks to his friends. The apostle in neither case formally indicated which party he was addressing, for he rightly assumed that each would wisely appropriate to itself the sentiments which properly belonged to it.] **1 Now I Paul myself entreat you by the meekness and gentleness of Christ, I who in your presence am lowly among you, but being absent am of good courage toward you: 2 yea, I beseech you, that I may not when present show courage with the confidence wherewith I count to be bold against some, who count of us as if we walked according to the flesh.** [Hitherto the apostle had associated Timothy as a joint author of this letter, but as he now prepares to deal with his enemies and matters personal to himself, he disengages himself from all entangling fellowships and steps forth alone to defend his name and influence. That there may be no doubt as to his purpose in thus standing alone, and that his enemies may understand the spirit in which he presents himself before them, he quotes their own belittling description of him: for they had described him as a coward who threatened and thundered when absent, but was meek and lowly enough when present. Accepting for the moment this false estimate of himself, he beseeches them by the meekness and gentleness of Christ (for Jesus ever preferred gentleness to severity) that they may so amend their conduct as to make their estimate of him true thus far; viz.: that at his coming he may indeed be permitted to show them gentleness, and may not, as he now confidently expected, be compelled to show his severity toward those who accused him of conducting himself as an unprincipled worldling.] **3 For though we walk in the flesh, we do not war according to the flesh 4 (for the weapons of our warfare are not of the flesh, but mighty before God to the casting down of strongholds); 5 casting down imaginations, and every high thing that is exalted against the knowledge of God, and bringing every thought into captivity to the obedience of Christ; 6 and being in readiness to avenge all disobedience, when your obedience shall be made full.** [For though we are indeed human, we do not contend after a human or worldly fashion (for our weapons are not slander, detraction, misrepresentation, etc., which are the methods employed by the world in overcoming opponents, but we use divine powers in our conflicts (1 Cor. 4: 19-21; 5: 5), powers which are mighty in the sight of God to tear down defenses), and which can cast down all false human reasonings, sophistries and vain deductions, and every like thing which men presumptuously rear in opposition to the word of God, and which can bring every rebellious thought into captivity, so that it shall obey Christ. With this power, therefore, I am ready to come to punish all the disobedient; but I pause that all who desire to repent may do so, and after the number of the obedient is made full I will punish the rebellious remnant that remain. In verse 4 Paul evidently alludes to the crow, a large military engine with a great claw to it, which was used to pull down the walls of castles, forts and other strongholds. Stanley thinks that Paul has in mind in this passage certain military operations which occurred in Cilicia, the province in which he was born. In the hills and mountains of that locality, certain bands of pirates and robbers entrenched themselves, and for awhile withstood the Roman arms. Cicero made some headway in suppressing them, and on his return was honored with a Roman triumph, but the final victory was achieved by Pompey the generation before Paul was born. Pompey made great use of the crow, for he pulled down one hundred and twenty fortresses. But the crow was then in as general use as the cannon is now, and a writer would hardly be thought to refer to Gettysburg if he happened to use cannonading as a figure of speech. However, Pompey's campaign is a useful bit of history, for it shows us how forceful the figure was which Paul employed.] **7 Ye look at the things that are before your face. If any man trusteth in himself that he is Christ's, let him consider this again with himself, that, even as he is Christ's, so also are we.** [You false teachers who oppose me view things very shallowly and superficially, for ye deem yourselves to be Christ's because ye came from Judæa, or perhaps have seen him, or been present with him during a large part of his ministry (Acts 1: 21, 22); and ye make bold to reject us as his because we seem to have been denied these privileges, failing to notice that our claims to be the Lord's are (at the least!) equal to yours. If they were apostles merely because they had seen the Lord, so also was Paul, and in addition he had, what they did not, a direct, official appointment from Christ (Acts 9: 15), a recognition from the twelve (Acts 15: 25), and a compact or arrangement with them regarding the division of their work —Gal. 2: 9.] **8 For though I should glory somewhat abundantly concerning our authority (which the Lord gave for building you up, and not for casting you down), I shall not be put to shame: 9 that I may not seem as if I would terrify you by my letters. 10 For, His letters, they say** [a general expression, equivalent to "it is said"], **are weighty and strong; but his bodily presence is weak, and his speech of no account.** [Now even if I boast most freely that my authority is greater than yours, my boasting will not bring shame upon me if you put me to the test. You will find that I am not terrible in letters alone, but also in my presence, and you will find how falsely you have spoken when you said that my letters were the only part of me calculated to cause fear. However, I shall regret to thus demonstrate my power against you, for God gave me this power to use rather in building you up than in tearing you down. The apostle thus draws a subtle contrast between himself and his adversaries, for they had delighted in destructive rather than constructive works.] **11 Let such a one reckon this, that, what we are in word by letters when we are absent, such** *are we* **also in deed when we are present. 12 For we are not bold to number or compare ourselves with certain of them that commend themselves: but they themselves, measuring themselves by themselves, and comparing themselves with themselves, are without understanding.** [Let all who thus accuse me of cowardice know assuredly that when I come my deeds will comport with the threatenings and warnings in my letters. I have in no way exaggerated my authority or power in my writing to you, for in this art of exaggerated self-praise or self-commendation I am not the equal of the false leaders in Corinth. In this art I am not so proficient that I can presume to measure myself with these Corinthian experts, for they, never looking outside their own narrow circle, but comparing themselves with each other, have swelled with an inflated sense of self-importance which would have long since been punctured so that it would have collapsed if they had brought themselves into comparison with the real apostles. Real worth can never speak so highly of itself as can conceited and unreasoning vanity. Those who compare themselves with Christ lose that self-exaltation which belongs to those who compare themselves only with men, hence they are too handicapped to enter into competition with any such in the matter of boasting.] **13 But we will not glory beyond** *our* **measure, but according to the measure of the province which God apportioned to us as a measure, to reach even unto you.** [Paul got no false idea of his own stature by measuring himself with other men;

but as the most apt measure for the point to be determined, viz.: his stature or capacity as a minister of the gospel, he chose the province or territory which God had assigned him as his field of operation. Though the whole world was his bishopric (Gal. 2: 7-9), yet he contents himself with saying it included Corinth. In the eyes of his opponents Corinth was the sum and center of all things, but in the larger life of Paul it was a mere dot in a limitless field of operations. See 11: 28.] **14 For we stretch not ourselves overmuch, as though we reached not unto you: for we came even as far as unto you in the gospel of Christ: 15 not glorying beyond *our* measure, *that is*, in other men's labors; but having hope that, as your faith groweth, we shall be magnified in you according to our province unto *further* abundance, 16 so as to preach the gospel even unto the parts beyond you, *and* not to glory in another's province in regard of things ready to our hand.** [Though God gave us so vast a bishopric, we indeed filled so much of it as to reach you. We were not so much smaller than this bishopric which God gave to us, that we had to stretch ourselves to cover it. To make a show of covering our territory we did not need to take possession of other men's labors and claim the fruits of their ministry, as though they wrought as our agents. If we had done this, we would indeed be glorying beyond our measure. But thus far (*i. e.*, as far as unto you) we have covered the province assigned to us, and we have a hope that as your faith groweth, and ye become subject to Christ through being subject to his true ministers, we ourselves shall grow and be magnified so that we shall more nearly attain to the magnitude of our great province. At present your vacillation and infidelity confine our labors to you. Having taken you as a fortress for Christ, we can not leave you assailed by Satan and half surrendered to him. When you are again established in the faith I expect to go on into Italy and into Spain, and do work in those parts of my province which lie far beyond you. It is no part of my plan or intention to take possession of some other man's labor and glory in it, as you false leaders have done by coming to Corinth and taking possession of the church which I left there ready to your hand.] **17 But he that glorieth, let him glory in the Lord.** [Paul here gives the rule of boasting as condensed from Jer. 9: 23, 24. Paul's enemies had not observed this rule; he had. In verse 5 he ascribed all his power to God, and in verse 13 he shows that, vast as his work was, it was far less than God demanded of him.] **18 For not he that commendeth himself is approved, but whom the Lord commendeth.** [The self-commendation of a man rests on no higher evidence than the testimony of his own lips, but the commendation of God is shown by the works which he enables those to do whom he approves.]

II.

APOLOGY FOR SELF-COMMENDATION, DENIAL OF CHARGES AND LAYING OF COUNTER CHARGES.

11: 1-15.

[While this third part of Paul's epistle is directed against his enemies, it is obvious that even these are, in his estimation, divided into two classes; *i.e.*, the leaders and the led. The apostle does not always keep these separate in his mind, yet we frequently find him, as in this section, appealing to those who were led, and denouncing those who led them.] **1 Would that ye could bear with me in a little foolishness: but indeed ye do bear with me. 2 For I am jealous over you with a godly jealousy: for I espoused you to one husband, that I might present you** *as* **a pure virgin to Christ. 3 But I fear, lest by any means, as the serpent beguiled Eve in his craftiness, your minds should be corrupted from the simplicity and the purity that is toward Christ. 4 For if he that cometh preacheth another Jesus, whom we did not preach,.or** *if* **ye receive a different spirit, which ye did not receive, or a different gospel, which ye did not accept, ye do well to**

bear with *him.* [These first four verses are introductory. The apostle, seeing the effect which the self-glorification of these false teachers has had upon certain of the Corinthians, determines, for a time, to adopt their tactics, descend to the foolishness of boasting, and thus overcome them on their own ground. Paul, in his consecration to Christ and forgetfulness of self, could not thus descend to the level of boasting, even though he merely related facts, without a sense of shame and a petition for consideration. When he considers the folly of the situation, it seems to him that the Corinthians could not put up with it, but when he remembers their affection for him, he is sure they will. He tells them that nothing but the strongest motives could induce him to thus belittle himself, but he found such a motive in his extreme jealousy for them on Christ's behalf. As the paranymph, or "bridegroom's friend" (John 3: 29), the one whose office it was to procure and arrange the marriage, he had espoused them to one husband, even Christ, and had so instructed and led them as to present them pure and spotless before the Lord at his coming. But now he feared that as the serpent led Eve into sin by his crafty wickedness, so these false teachers were corrupting the church at Corinth from that simplicity of doctrine and purity of life which they owed to Christ, their espoused husband. Now, if these false teachers (and Paul speaks of one of them as a sample of them all) had come professing to preach another Jesus and another religious spirit, and a different gospel from any that Paul preached, there might have been some excuse in giving them ι patient hearing. But such had not been the case. Professedly they were preaching the same Jesus, etc., that he did, and so the Corinthians were without excuse in permitting them to assail Paul. They had sold their apostle and had received nothing in exchange for him. With the next verse his boasting begins, but in a very mild and apologetic form.] **5 For I reckon that I am not a whit behind the very chiefest apostles.** [I can not think that you receive these rival teachers and professed apostles as so much superior to me, for I am not behind these super-apostolic apostles. Paul is not here comparing himself with the twelve, but with these spurious apostles at Corinth. Paul reveals his emotion by the use of that strange word which is translated "very chiefest." It means "out-and-out," "extra-super," "overmuch," a term he would have never applied to the twelve. It is as though he said, Though these men claim to be apostles a hundred times over, yet I can certainly take my place in the front ranks with *them*.] **6 But though *I be* rude in speech, yet *am I* not in knowledge; nay, in every way have we made *this* manifest unto you in all things.** [Paul admits that one criticism of him was true. He did indeed pay litttle regard to the laws of rhetoric, and scorned to weaken his thought by loading it with verbal ornament or the studied expressions which the schools regarded as eloquence. But though he was thus rude in speech, a very unimportant matter, he was not deficient in the all-important sphere of knowledge. The Corinthians had had every opportunity to test him in this particular, and he felt that the truth of his statement must be so manifest to them as to need no further proof.] **7 Or did I commit a sin in abasing myself that ye might be exalted, because I preached to you the gospel of God for nought?** [A second accusation which his enemies never wearied in presenting was that he had preached the gospel in Corinth without charge. They had said that he did this because he knew that he was not an apostle, and so was hindered by his conscience from taking the wages of an apostle—see 1 Cor. 9: 1-15 and notes. As Paul has already refuted this charge, he does not repeat the refutation; he merely asks them if he had committed a sin in so doing.] **8 I robbed other churches** [Paul again shows his emotion by the indignant hyperbole "robbed"], **taking wages *of them* that I might minister unto you; 9 and when I was present with you and was in want, I was not a burden on any man; for the brethren** [*i. e.*, Silas and Timothy, Acts 18: 5], **when they came from Macedonia, supplied the measure of my want; and in everything I kept myself from being burdensome unto you, and *so* will I keep *myself*.**

[Here the apostle relates the well-known history of his ministry at Corinth. The church at Philippi is the only one which we know of that contributed to his needs while in Corinth (Phil. 4: 15, 16). When his necessities had reached a crisis and he had come to want, he had not appealed to the Corinthians, but had endured until relieved by the coming of his friends from Macedonia. His enemies had slandered him as to this, hoping to drive him to receive wages that they might reduce his influence in this respect to the level of their own; but in this hope they would be disappointed, for he would continue to preach without compensation as he always had done.] **10 As the truth of Christ is in me, no man shall stop me of this glorying in the regions of Achaia. 11 Wherefore? because I love you not? God knoweth. 12 But what I do, that I will do, that I may cut off occasion from them that desire an occasion; that wherein they glory, they may be found even as we.** [The apostle is determined that whatever he may do elsewhere he will receive no compensation for any preaching in Achaia. Knowing that they would wish to know why he thus made an exception in their case, he raises the question himself, but does not answer it, because to do so frankly would have been to show the deficiencies of their entire character and nature. But that he does not thus except them because of any lack of love, is shown by his appeal to God, who knew his heart. Compare 6: 11-13; 7: 2; 12: 15. One motive for his conduct he will tell them, and that is that he may silence the tongues of those who seek an opportunity to detract him. Here the language of the apostle grows bitterly sarcastic. The false teachers had received wages from the beginning, yet he speaks of them as if they gloried in preaching the gospel for nothing and declares that he will do likewise that they may be found no better than he. In the next three verses Paul speaks with the most unreserved plainness, and, as Bengel observes, "calls a spade a spade."] **13 For such men are false apostles, deceitful workers, fashioning themselves into apostles of Christ.** [Thus he declares plainly that these men are not apostles, that they maintained their false position by imposture, and that they assumed the name and office of apostles, though never having been called to be such by Christ.] **14 And no marvel; for even Satan fashioneth himself into an angel of light. 15 It is no great thing therefore if his ministers also fashion themselves as ministers of righteousness; whose end shall be according to their works.** [The apostle says that no one need stand aghast at such awful presumption, for Satan himself sets an example in this respect and his ministers may be expected to follow it. Some think that Satan fashioned himself as an angel of light when he appeared before God as narrated in the Book of Job; others, that he did so when he appeared before Jesus to tempt him. It is not clear to what incident in the life of Satan Paul refers. In this age, as in all ages, these warning words of the apostle should be weighed and considered. As Jesus bade us beware of wolves in sheep's clothing, so Paul bids us beware of the emissaries of Satan, who come claiming to be leaders in religion. The servants of Satan do not hesitate to hold ecclesiastical offices, or occupy pulpits.

III.

A COMPARISON OF LABOR, SIGNS, ETC.

11: 16-12: 13

[In this section the apostle draws a comparison between himself and the false apostles, showing how he excelled them in labors, revelations, signs, etc.] **16 I say again** [having twice swerved from the distasteful task, Paul unwillingly resumes his apparent boasting], **Let no man think me foolish; but if ye *do*, yet as foolish receive me, that I also may glory a little. 17 That which I speak, I speak not after the Lord, but as in foolishness, in this confidence of glorying.** [Let no man think that I am foolish enough to boast wittingly of my own accord, but if any one does so think, let him, nevertheless, bear with me a little while in my boasting, since my adversaries have made it the order of the day. I am painfully conscious that the Spirit of God does not prompt to boasting, but I do so on my own responsibility, or according to my own confident folly, my so doing having been made a permissible necessity by your behavior toward me.] **18 Seeing that many glory after the flesh, I will glory also.** [I am about to follow the carnal example of the boasters, that I may defeat them with their own weapon.] **19 For ye bear with the foolish gladly, being wise** *yourselves*. **20 For ye bear with a man, if he bringeth you into bondage, if he devoureth you, if he taketh you** *captive*, **if he exalteth himself, if he smiteth you on the face. 21 I speak by way of disparagement, as though we had been weak. Yet whereinsoever any is bold (I speak in foolishness), I am bold also.** [You encourage me to talk foolishly, for it pleaseth you to indulge fools that ye may thereby flatter yourselves with a show of superiority, and by your recent conduct toward these, my rivals in boasting, you have shown to what lengths of patient endurance you will go in this matter, for you have permitted them to bring you into bondage to their authority and their false doctrine, to impoverish you by exorbitant exactions of wages, to treat you as their captives, and to exalt themselves over you as though they were your conquerors, and even to smite you as though you had become their slaves. If you bore with such strenuous boastfulness, you can bear with me in my weak foolishness. But I have indeed disparaged myself when I talked about my meekness, as I will now show you, for if any ever addressed bold words to you, you are now about to hear such from me also. And yet my words will all be foolishness, for all the things whereof I boast are really worthless as commendations to you in comparison with my being called of Christ as his apostle. The apostle speaks of the whole class of false apostles as if they were a single individual. Thus, after many preliminary apologies and explanations, Paul comes at last to his boast, not of his exploits or talents, as one might expect, but of his sufferings and humiliations, revelations and self-sacrifices.] **22 Are they Hebrews? so am I. Are they Israelites?**

A COMPARISON OF LABOR, SIGNS, ETC. 231

so am I. Are they the seed of Abraham? so am I.
[This verse shows clearly that Paul's enemies were Judaizing Jews. They had evidently boasted of their race, nationality, etc., to the disparagement of Paul. They probably urged that Paul was greatly inferior to them because he was born at Tarsus, was a Roman citizen, lived much like a Gentile, and did not abjectly obey the Jewish law. By their whisperings they no doubt laid the foundation for that calumny which was long after found formed against him; for "it would appear from Epiphanius," says Stanley, "that Judaizers went so far as to assert that he was altogether a Gentile by birth, and only adopted circumcision in order to marry the high priest's daughter." In answer to this rising cloud of slander, Paul asserts his racial, national, etc., equality with his enemies. He was a Hebrew, he belonged to the sacred nation and spoke the sacred language (Acts 22: 2); and an Israelite, he belonged to the theocracy, and being of the seed of Abraham, he was by birth an heir to the promises, and was not a proselyte nor descended from one.] **23 Are they ministers of Christ? (I speak as one beside himself) I more; in labors more abundantly** [1 Cor. 15: 10], **in prisons more abundantly, in stripes above measure, in deaths oft.** [1 Cor. 15: 31. On Jewish grounds Paul claimed equality, but as a minister of Christ, superiority. Knowing that his enemies would say that it accorded with his general insanity to thus assert his superiority, he ironically admits his madness in thus asserting that his ministerial labors exceeded those of his easy-living adversaries— theirs being in fact no labor at all, but rather an effort to steal the credit of his labors. This verse gives the general bodily distresses endured, while the next three tell of special cases. According to Acts, Paul had, up to this date, been imprisoned but once, and was afterwards imprisoned thrice. Clement of Rome, who wrote toward the close of the first century, says that Paul was imprisoned seven times. Paul's life for long periods was hourly exposed to death (Acts 9: 23; 13: 50; 14: 5, 6, 19; 17: 5, 13); but the best comment on this expression is the catalogue of sufferings which follow.] **24 Of the Jews five times re-**

ceived I forty *stripes* save one. [Deut. 25: 2. The law limited all beatings to forty stripes; but one stripe was omitted lest the law should be accidentally broken through careless counting. Such a scourging inflicted the agony of death, and generally resulted in it. Not one of these scourgings is mentioned in Acts.] **25 Thrice was I beaten with rods, once was I stoned, thrice I suffered shipwreck, a night and a day have I been in the deep** [The Romans punished by using the vine rods of the soldiers or the *fasces* of the lictors, and no law limited the number of strokes. Such beatings often caused death. Roman citizenship was presumed to protect from such punishment, but in his orations Cicero tells us that in the provinces the rights of citizenship were often set at nought in this respect. Luke tells of but one of these beatings (Acts 26: 22). The stoning took place at Lystra (Acts 14: 19). Luke tells in all of six sea voyages, but says nothing of the wreckings here mentioned. In referring to the twenty-four-hour struggle for life amidst the waves, Paul uses the present tense, showing that the horror of his situation was still vividly remembered]: **26** *in* **journeyings often,** *in* **perils of rivers,** *in* **perils of robbers,** *in* **perils from** *my* **countrymen,** *in* **perils from the Gentiles,** *in* **perils in the city,** *in* **perils in the wilderness,** *in* **perils in the sea,** *in* **perils among false brethren** [Disasters at sea remind Paul of similar trials by land, and the eightfold reiteration of "perils" emphasizes the fact that he was nowhere safe. Traveling in those days was both arduous and dangerous. The highways were infested with robbers and the streams were often without bridges, the mountain torrents were sudden and violent in their risings, and the science of navigation and the art of shipbuilding were each extremely crude. For perils from his own countrymen, see Acts 13: 45, 50; 14: 2, 5; 17: 5, 13; 18: 15; 19: 9; 21: 27. They even attempted to take his life a few weeks later as he was leaving Corinth (Acts 23). For perils from the Gentiles, see Acts 19: 30, 31. For his perils in the cities, see verse 32, and Acts 9: 24, 25, 29; 13: 50; 14: 5, 19; **16: 19;** 17: **5,** 13; 18: 12; 19: 23. Perils from false brethren

A COMPARISON OF LABOR, SIGNS, ETC. 233

were the most distressing of all, for they wounded the affections—Phil. 3: 18; Gal. 2: 4]; **27 *in* labor and travail, in watchings often, in hunger and thirst, in fastings often, in cold and nakedness.** [The apostle here tells how he labored until labor became a pain; how he sacrificed his sleep that he might teach, preach and pray (Acts 20: 31; 1 Thess. 3: 10); how his journeyings often took him where he suffered for water and was faint with hunger; how he often fasted for the good of the cause (Acts 13: 2, 3; 14: 23; 1 Cor. 9: 27); and how he was cold and insufficiently clad. The apostle makes no mention of the frequency of his hunger and thirst, etc., for the recurrency of these trials was beyond his control. He employs the word "often" when speaking of the watchings and fastings which were directly under his control, and which he might have avoided had he chosen to do so. Surely this catalogue of privations must have made the apostle's character stand in strong contrast to the self-indulgent spirit of his adversaries. From physical trials Paul now turns to those which were mental.] **28 Besides those things that are without, there is that which presseth upon me daily, anxiety for all the churches.** [Besides the things which I have already mentioned—trials which come from external circumstances—there are others which attack me daily; I mean the wranglings, disputes, backslidings and apostasies of all the churches which are constantly brought to my attention that I may instruct, arbitrate or discipline according as the cases may demand. This verse may also be taken to mean that there were trials other than those mentioned, which came upon Paul from without.] **29 Who is weak, and I am not weak? who is caused to stumble, and I burn not?** [In this verse Paul shows what the care of the churches meant to him. It was an excessive drain upon his sympathies. If any weak one suffered through the rash selfishness of a brother who abused his liberty by eating in an idol temple, Paul suffered with him as if he also were weak, and if any were caused to stumble, Paul made the case of such a one his own, and burned with indignation.] **30 If I must needs**

glory, I will glory of the things that concern my
weakness.] If my enemies force upon me the moral necessity of boasting, I will at least not boast of my exploits, but of
those things which others might regard as matters of shame.
Thus the apostle shows how impossible it was for him to really
boast after the fashion of a worldly mind.] **31 The God
and Father of the Lord Jesus, he who is blessed for
evermore knoweth that I lie not.** [This solemn asseveration is not to be restricted to the statements contained in the
next two verses, but applies to all he has said or is about to
say in this entire section. No doubt in the apostle's own mind
it was called forth by what he was about to say concerning his
revelations, his mind looking forward to what he intended to
say when he added the last item to his catalogue of sufferings.]
**32 In Damascus the governor under Aretas the king
guarded the city of the Damascenes in order to take
me: 33 and through a window was I let down in a
basket by the wall, and escaped his hands.** [In the
walled cities of the Orient, houses were often built against the
walls so that the windows projected over them. No doubt in
Paul's mind an apostle in a basket seemed the depth of humiliation. Aretas was king of Arabia from B. C. 7 to A. D. 40.
Damascus belonged to Rome, and it has puzzled some to find
it at this time under the control of the king of Arabia. But it
will be remembered that Aretas engaged in war with Herod,
because he dismissed the Arab's daughter and took his niece,
Herodias, for a wife. Aretas defeated Herod, and the Romans
took up the quarrel, and it seems likely that in the ensuing contest the city of Damascus fell, for a time, into the hands of the
Arabians.]

XII. **1 I must needs glory, though it is not expedient;. but I will come to visions and revelations
of the Lord.** [I feel constrained to go on with my boasting,
though I recognize that it is not expedient for me to do so since
it gives my enemies further material for detraction and vilifica-
tion. Yet I will speak of the visions which the Lord gave me
and the revelations which they brought me.] **2 I know a**

man in Christ, fourteen years ago (whether in the body, I know not; or whether out of the body, I know not; God knoweth), such a one caught up even to the third heaven. 3 And I know such a man (whether in the body, or apart from the body, I know not; God knoweth); 4 how that he was caught up into Paradise, and heard unspeakable words, which it is not lawful for man to utter. 5 On behalf of such a one will I glory: but on mine own behalf I will not glory, save in *my* weaknesses. [Here Paul speaks of an experience of his, but declines to name himself, or use the first person, lest he might be thought to be glorying in his own exaltation. He had been caught up into paradise, or the secret place of the Almighty. This he calls the third heaven, for in the Jewish estimation the air was the first heaven, the region of the sun, moon and stars was the second heaven. Somewhere beyond the stars was the abode of the Almighty. He was miraculously drawn up into heaven, but whether his whole personality went thither, or whether merely that part of him (his spiritual nature) which was suited to comprehend and enjoy heaven, he could not tell. While here he had heard words which it was not lawful for him to try to interpret by the insufficient and consequently misleading worth of earth. He tells this event, but it was an honor so much above his deserving that he avoids even such a method of telling it as might be construed to be boastful. If he gloried on his own behalf, it would still be in his weaknesses. As Paul wrote this epistle in A. D. 57, the deduction of fourteen years would bring us to A. D. 43, the season when Paul was in Antioch.] 6 For if I should desire to glory, I shall not be foolish; for I shall speak the truth: but I forbear, lest any man should account of me above that which he seeth me *to be*, or heareth from me. [Now, if I should desire to boast, I should not need to foolishly vaunt myself as to imaginary things, but I could confine myself to truth, and tell many wonderful experiences of visions exposed to my eyes and revelations imparted to my mind. But I forbear to proceed further, lest any man should think of me as more excellent than my conduct or my speech would indicate. This I do not want. I desire no exaggerated reverence, but seek only that goodwill and esteem which my conduct merits.] **7 And by reason of the exceeding greatness of the revelations, that I should not be exalted overmuch, there was given to me a thorn in the flesh, a messenger of Satan to buffet me, that I should not be exalted overmuch.** [From the earliest ages down men have indulged in wild speculation as to what Paul meant by his thorn in the flesh. See comment on 1: 10. The most plausible theory is that it was disfiguring and acute ophthalmia. Suffice it to say that it was some bodily infirmity which acted as a balance to Paul's mind, drawing his thoughts and attention to his earthly state, lest they should dwell too constantly in meditation upon the things which had been revealed to him.] **8 Concerning this thing I besought the Lord thrice** [Matt. 26: 44], **that it might depart from me. 9 And he hath said unto me, My grace is sufficient for thee: for** *my* **power is made perfect in weakness.** [Phil. 4: 13; 1 Cor. 2: 3-5.] **Most gladly therefore will I rather glory in my weaknesses, that the power of Christ may rest upon me.** [The prayer was not granted, but a compensation was made for denying it. How evident it must have been to the Corinthians, from the sufferings he so cheerfully endured, that he was the true messenger of Christ! Paul's use of the phrase "rest upon me" suggests the resting of the Spirit on the apostles at Pentecost—Acts 2: 3.] **10 Wherefore I take pleasure in weaknesses, in injuries, in necessities, in persecutions, in distresses, for Christ's sake: for when I am weak, then am I strong.** [God so orders it that the times of my weakness are the very hours when my strength is revealed, and thus each period of death is turned into a season of resurrection—4: 10.] **11 I am become foolish: ye compelled me; for I ought to have been commended of you: for in nothing was I behind the very chiefest apostles, though I am nothing.** [You, who should have spoken in my defense and commendation, by keeping silence have compelled me to boast, and to show that, nobody as I am, I am at least equal to these overmuch apostles.] **12 Truly the signs of an apostle were wrought among you in all patience, by signs and wonders and mighty works. 13 For what is there wherein ye were made inferior to the rest of the churches, except** *it be* **that I myself was not a burden to you? forgive me this wrong.** [And you are without excuse in thus compelling me to defend myself by proving my apostleship, for it was proved long since among you by the miracles which I wrought among you as signs and evidences of it (evidences which his enemies wholly lacked); and also by the patient spirit in which I wrought the miracles, for I have again and again forborne to use my power to crush my wicked opposers (1: 1-3; 1 Cor. 4: 21). And I so fully proved my apostleship among you, that you showed to no disadvantage whatever when compared with other churches founded by any others, for you had all the signs, gifts, graces, etc., which they had, unless it be that I myself did not aid my opposers in the good work of extorting wages from you—forgive me for thus wronging you! These last words, though ironical, are superbly dignified and pathetic. By his disinterested kindness to them, the apostle had favored them above all other churches—11: 8.]

IV.

THE THIRD VISIT. CONCLUSION.

12: 14-13: 14.

14 Behold, this is the third time I am ready to come to you; and I will not be a burden to you: for I seek not yours, but you: for the children ought not to lay up for the parents, but the parents for the children. [There has been much dispute as to whether Paul says that this is his third visit, or the third time he has *intended* to visit. Evidently it was to be his third visit. See 2: 1; 12: 21; 13: **1, 2.**

Knowing that if this letter moved them to repentance or shame, the Corinthians would wish him to accept some compensation for his services, and that if he did so his enemies would revive their slanders against him, and assert that his whole purpose in writing was to gratify his mercenary desires, Paul makes it easy to decline any such offer on their part by declining it now beforehand. He asserts that he will maintain himself without their support, as he has done on his two former visits, and lest they should resent this independence on his part, he declares that he is actuated thereto by an intense love for them—a love which seeks not their money for his benefit, but their souls for their own benefit. He affectionately, yet almost playfully, bases his conduct on that rule as to parents and children which, though it sometimes permits children to aid parents, obliges parents *always* to maintain children. He was their spiritual father (1 Cor. 4: 14, 15), and he claims the obligations of his parental relation as if they were much-coveted rights. Thus, as throughout the epistle, the thunders of the apostle have quickly subsided into the tender accents of the parent.] **15 And I will most gladly spend and be spent for your souls. If I love you more abundantly, am I loved the less? 16 But be it so, I did not myself burden you; but, being crafty, I caught you with guile.** [And as a doting parent I will gladly spend all that I have and all that I am for your soul's sake. Gladly, as it were, will I break the earthen vessel that its contents may be lavishly poured out upon you (4: 7; Mark 14: 3). And can it be possible that you will be so unnatural as to love me less in proportion as I love you the more? "But," say my detractors, "you *apparently* did not burden us; we concede this to be so; but you caught us with guile, for you have levied contributions, ostensibly for the poor in Jerusalem, but really to reimburse yourself for the wages which you feel to be due you, and about which you have been so noisily boasting."] **17 Did I take advantage of you by any one of them whom I have sent unto you? 18 I exhorted Titus, and I sent the brother with him. Did Titus take any advantage of you? walked we** not in the same spirit? *walked we* not in the same steps? [Now let us look at the facts and see where I used such guile. My detractors admit that I myself took nothing: then I must have taken it through the agency of others. If so, by whom? Titus and the brother who accompanied him were the only agents I sent. Did Titus thus cheat you in my behalf? Did he not, on the contrary, show you the same inner spirit of self-sacrifice which I displayed? Did he not outwardly follow my plans, exhorting you not to give it to him, or send it to me, but to lay it up in your own treasury weekly as I directed? See 1 Cor. 16: 1, 2. If Titus, as we have supposed, accompanied the messengers who bore Paul's first epistle to Corinth, he very naturally carried out the directions of that epistle. Who was then with him we do not know. Titus had not yet reached Corinth to undertake this work a *second* time as Paul directed (8: 6, 16, 17). Paul's actions were ever free from guile or covetousness—1 Thess. 2: 3-5.] **19 Ye think all this time that we are excusing ourselves unto you. In the sight of God speak we in Christ. But all things, beloved,** *are* **for your edifying. 20 For I fear, lest by any means, when I come, I should find you not such as I would, and should myself be found of you such as ye would not; lest by any means** *there should be* **strife** [1 Cor. 6: 7], **jealousy** [11: 19, 22], **wraths, factions** [1 Cor. 1: 11], **backbitings, whisperings, swellings** [1 Cor. 8: 1, 2], **tumults** [disorders]; **21 lest again when I come my God should humble me before you, and I should mourn for many of them that have sinned heretofore, and repented not of the uncleanness and fornication and lasciviousness which they committed.** [Doubtless all the while you have been reading or listening to my words you have been thinking that you are sitting in judgment on my case, and that I have been making my defense before you, anxiously hoping for a favorable verdict. Be not deceived. We can never be judged by you, but are divinely appointed a judge over you (Matt. 19: 28). My only object is to speak before God in Christ, that is, to acquaint you with the truth as it appears in God's sight, that you may be instructed and not left in harmful ignorance. For I fear that even yet after all this instruction you may not profit by it, so that when I come I may find you not obedient as I would have you, and that I may be found of you not gentle as you would have me to be. For I expect to find among you the very sins which I have reproved in these epistles, and which were there when I last visited you (2: 1). I will not spare you this time as I did then, but I shall exercise discipline, and therefore I fear that I shall mourn for many whom I shall be compelled to deliver over to Satan (1 Cor. 5: 5), because they still impenitently persist in their unchaste sins despite all my reproof.]

XIII. 1 This is the third time I am coming to you. At the mouth of two witnesses or three shall every word be established. [Deut. 19: 15.] **2 I have said beforehand, and I do say beforehand, as when I was present the second time, so now, being absent, to them that have sinned heretofore, and to all the rest, that, if I come again, I will not spare** [The apostle here declares that patience has reached its just limit. Twice he has been present and has forborne, but at the third coming he will handle them with rigorous discipline. He will not, however, proceed rashly, nor will he decide who is guilty by direct or immediate revelation, lest he be regarded as arrogating to himself the offices of both witness and judge. He will proceed by due legal form, and call witnesses, since they are to be had, and obviate the necessity of employing miraculous knowledge. Some argue from the context that Paul means to say that his three visits will be, as it were, three witnesses against them, or that his thrice-repeated threats are shown to be true by these repetitions. But such interpretations are fanciful. There may, however, be a parallelism in Paul's thought; thus: Let my three warnings, repeated at such long intervals, persuade you that my words will testify against me if I do not keep them by punishing you, for I have thrice said I would do this thing, viz.: when I first wrote, when I was present, and now, when

THE THIRD VISIT. CONCLUSION 241

I am writing again, that I would do this thing]; **3 seeing that ye seek a proof of Christ that speaketh in me; who to you-ward is not weak, but is powerful in you: 4 for he was crucified through weakness, yet he liveth through the power of God. For we also are weak in him, but we shall live with him through the power of God toward you.** [The apostle here gives the reason why he had so fully decided to discipline: they had tauntingly desired it. You ascribe, says he, weakness to the Christ who speaks in me, and strength to the Christ, who, according to their profession, speaks in these false apostles, and you would put me to the test. Their Christ, ye say, is the mighty Keeper of the Jewish law, while mine is the weak, crucified Christ. But you should remember that he has not been weak toward you, either in my ministry (12: 12), or in miracles and judgments (6: 7; 1 Cor. 2: 4, 5; 11: 30), or in the bestowal of gifts (1 Cor. 1: 7), for, though he did indeed manifest through the weakness of our humanity a mortal life susceptible to death by crucifixion (Phil. 2: 7, 8; 1 Cor. 1: 23; Heb. 2: 14); yet, *per contra*, through the power of God the Father working in him (Rom. 1: 4; 6: 4; Eph. 1: 20), he overcame this weakness and lives again. And by virtue of our union with him, we follow the pattern of his life in our dealings with you; for you who have beheld our physical weakness, infirmities, gentle forbearance, etc. (10: 10; 12: 5, 9, 10), and have, as it were, put our influence and power to death among you, shall behold also in me the same divine power of God effecting a resurrection of us because of our union with Christ, that we may exercise our rightful authority over you. We should note the direct assertion of inspiration, and the willingness to have it tested contained in verse 3.] **5 Try your own selves, whether ye are in the faith; prove your own selves. Or know ye not as to your own selves, that Jesus Christ is in you? unless indeed ye be reprobate. 6 But I hope that ye shall know that we are not reprobate.** [Ye who are so eager to put me to the test as to whether I am united with Christ, would exercise a **truer** wisdom if you tested your own selves to see whether you are in possession of that faith which should unite you with Christ—yea, test your own selves and do not foolishly wait for me to apply the rigors of my testing. Ye seek to know whether Christ is in me, but the obvious, immediate way of testing this is to see if I have been able to impart Christ to you. Or have you indeed lost all consciousness of Christ being in you, using you as his temple? Compare John 15: 4, 5; 1 John 3: 24; Gal. 2: 20; 4: 19; Eph. 3: 17; Col. 1: 27. Surely you have this consciousness which is the conclusive test of my ministry (3: 1-3; 1 Cor. 9: 2), unless indeed ye are proved to be no Christians at all, by the application of this test. But I hope that by my testing when I come, the true authority of Christ in me may be vindicated, and that, testing me, you may find me approved by the testing. Reprobate means that which fails to stand the test (Jer. 6: 30). It is evident to the casual observer that Paul uses the word in an entirely different sense from that horrible meaning read into it by Calvin.] **7 Now we pray to God that ye do no evil; not that we may appear approved, but that ye may do that which is honorable, though we be as reprobate. 8 For we can do nothing against the truth, but for the truth.** [While hoping or expecting to be vindicated, his prayer is of a different sort. We pray, says he, that you may be kept from evil, and thus escape the discipline. We do not thus pray for the sake of approving ourselves by showing our power to restrain you from evil (and thus our approval would result from our prayer), but we thus pray because of our earnest desire for your righteousness. We would have you do that which is honorable, even though you thereby deprive us of the opportunity of vindicating ourself, so that we shall still be looked upon by you as untrustworthy, and not capable of enduring tests. Compare with the like unselfishness at Rom. 9: 3. For our apostolic power is given to us to use, not against, but for, the truth. We are powerless against anything which is right and true. If ye, therefore, do the truth, you withdraw your demand for a test of us, and deprive us of this chance of vindicating ourselves by showing our power, and this we desire that you should do.] **9 For we rejoice, when**

THE THIRD VISIT. CONCLUSION 243

we are weak, and ye are strong: this we also pray for, even your perfecting. 10 For this cause I write these things while absent, that I may not when present deal sharply, according to the authority which the Lord gave me for building up, and not for casting down. [Here Paul amplifies the thought of verses 7 and 8. If the Corinthians are only perfected in strength, if they are mighty in faith and righteousness, he is content to be looked upon as weak by them; and therefore to spare himself the pains of disciplining them at his coming, he has taken the milder method of doing so by letter. For it indeed pained him to use divine power in tearing down a church, when that power was given him for the purpose of building up churches. In short, Paul was content that they should look upon him as no apostle at all, provided they could do so *without any injury to themselves*. He was zealous for his apostolic authority over them, because without his guiding power they would make shipwreck of the faith.] 11 **Finally, brethren, farewell.** [Literally, rejoice; a reverting to the purpose declared in 1: 24. Compare Phil. 4: 4.] **Be perfected** [Eph. 4: 13; Matt. 5: 48]; **be comforted** [1: 6; 7: 8-13; 1 Thess. 4: 18]; **be of the same mind** [1 Cor. 1: 10; Phil. 2: 2; 1 Pet. 3: 8; Rom. 12: 16, 18]; **live in peace** [Eph. 4: 3]: **and the God of love and peace shall be with you. 12 Salute one another with a holy kiss.** [Rom. 16: 16; 1 Cor. 16: 20; 1 Pet. 5: 14. See note on 1 Thess. 5: 6.] 13 **All the saints salute you.** [That is, all the saints with me in Macedonia.] 14 **The grace of the Lord Jesus Christ, and the love of God, and the communion of the Holy Spirit, be with you all.** [This is the full apostolic benediction. It contains three blessings respectively derived from the three divine sources. It occurs nowhere else in the Scripture. Coming, as it does, after this, the most severe of letters, it reminds one that the greatest showers of blessing often follow the fiercest flashes of lightning and the mightiest reverberations of thunder. Thus closes Paul's second epistle to the church at Corinth. It evidently furthered the good work set in motion by the first epistle and by Titus; for when Paul a little later wrote his letter to the Romans from Corinth, he was evidently in a calm and peaceful frame of mind. Also compare 10: 15, 16 and notes, with Rom. 15: 22-24. Moreover, the collection for Jerusalem was taken, and was apparently generous, for Paul accompanied them who bore it to Jerusalem. Compare 1 Cor. 16: 4 and note, with Rom. 16: 18; Acts 22: 4.]

EPISTLE TO THE GALATIANS.
INTRODUCTION.

This epistle, unlike the other church epistles of Paul, is addressed, not to a single congregation dwelling in a city, but to the churches of a district—"the Galatic Land." The Roman province of Galatia, lying in the central portion of Asia Minor, was larger than "the Galatic Land," for it included several other districts. The territory of the Galatians originally belonged to the Phrygians, but certain tribes of Gauls, as Frenchmen were then called, moved by their restless, conquest-loving spirit, and by the pressure of rival tribes at home, invaded to the southeastward and attempted to overrun Greece. Being repulsed at Delphi, they crossed the Bosphorus, and, after many conflicts, were finally content to confine themselves to this territory, which, as we see, eventually bore their name. This occurred about B. C. 279. In B. C. 189 they were conquered by the Romans, but were still permitted to retain their kings. In B. C. 25 their self-government was taken away and they became part of the Roman province which was also named for them. They were divided into three tribes, each occupying subdistricts, with the cities of Tavium, Pessinus and Ancyra (now Angora), as their respective capitals, which last was also capital of the whole Roman province of Galatia. Though speaking Greek, they also retained their language, so that Jerome leads us to believe that a Galatian and a Frenchman could have conversed together with ease as late as the fourth century A. D. Though a part of the Celtic race, which includes the French, Welsh, Irish and Scotch, they were Frenchmen, and their characteristics are described by Julius Cæsar, who says: "The infirmity of the Gauls is that they are fickle in their resolves and fond of change, and not to be trusted." And Thierry speaks of them thus: "Frank, impetuous, impressible, eminently intelligent, but at the same time extemely changeable, inconstant, fond of show, perpetually quarreling, the fruit of excessive vanity." Paul had planted churches among them and had revisited and confirmed these churches; but after his departure certain Judaizers had entered among them, and had persuaded them that becoming Jews was a condition precedent to their becoming Christians, and hence they could not be saved without circumcision. Being met by the teaching which the Galatians had learned from Paul, these Judaizers had felt the necessity of destroying Paul's influence. They undertook to do this by denying that he was an apostle, and asserting that he was, if anything, only an unfaithful messenger of the other apostles. The main purpose, therefore, of this epistle is to establish the fact that Christianity was a religion independent of Judaism, and that Paul was an apostle independent of the twelve. The date of the epistle can not be determined with accuracy, but it was evidently written sometime during the third missionary tour; for Paul had been twice in Galatia when he wrote it, having confirmed the Galatians on his second visit. Compare Acts 16: 6; 18: 23; Gal. 1: 9; 5: 21. It has been said that it was written from Ephesus, or Troas, or Macedonia, or Corinth. There are several internal evidences which cause us to prefer one or the other of the two places last named, and to place the date in A. D. 57, in the short interval between the writing of 2 Corinthians and Romans. The two Corinthian letters, with Romans and Galatians, if we may judge by their similarity, were all written at about the same period, and, in fact, the points of resemblance between these epistles are so many and so striking that to concede the authenticity of one, is to practically concede that of all. Hence all four epistles have been recognized as authentic even by Renan and Baur. For incidental similarities, such as the mentioning of Damascus and Titus, compare 2 Cor. 11: 32 and Gal. 1: 17; 2 Cor. 2: 7; 8: 12 and Gal. 2: 1-3. For verbal similarities, compare 2 Cor. 10: 1-11 and Gal. 4: 18, 20; 2 Cor. 12: 20, 21 and Gal. 4: 19-21; 2 Cor. 9: 6 and Gal. 6: 7; 2 Cor. 11: 2 and Gal. 4: 17; 2 Cor. 11: 20 and Gal. 5: 15. The relation between Galatians and Romans

INTRODUCTION

is argumentative, for Paul discussed the relations of the law and the gospel in each. The relation between 2 Corinthians and Galatians is personal, for Paul is defending himself against similar charges in each. For other relations between Galatians and Romans see Rom. 8: 14-17 and Gal. 4: 6, 7; Rom. 10: 5 and Gal. 3: 12; Rom. 4: 13, 14, 16 and Gal. 3: 14, 16, 29; Rom. 11: 31 and Gal. 3: 22. The epistle may be loosely divided into three sections of two chapters each, as follows: Part 1—chapters 1 and 2, Arguments sustaining Paul's gospel and apostolic office. Part 2—chapters 3 and 4, Justification is by faith in Christ and not by legalism as proved by Scripture. Part 3—chapters 5 and 6, Exhortations to steadfastness and faithfulness to Christian duty. The epistle has been in all ages the stronghold of evangelical Christianity in defending itself against ecclesiasticism and ritualism of all kinds. It was the favorite book of Martin Luther, who wrote three commentaries upon it. But Luther strained the words of Paul and drew from them such extreme conclusions that John Wesley regarded him as guilty of blasphemy. But the perversions of this precious epistle in no way militate against it or its proper use.

EPISTLE TO THE GALATIANS.
PART FIRST.
ARGUMENTS SUSTAINING PAUL'S GOSPEL AND APOSTOLIC OFFICE.

1: 1-2: 17.

I.

PAUL'S GOSPEL AND APOSTLESHIP DIVINELY DERIVED.

1: 1-24.

1 Paul, an apostle (not from men, neither through man, but through Jesus Christ, and God the Father, who raised him from the dead), 2 and all the brethren that are with me, unto the churches of Galatia [These two verses form not only the text of this first section, but also the keynote of the entire epistle. Without a moment's introduction, Paul passes at once to that which caused him to write, viz.: the challenge of his apostleship. If it was urged against him that he was but the faithless messenger of the other apostles, he replies by asserting, in the clearest, most forceful way, the nature of his apostleship. Both as to source and agency it was divine. The call to it came from God and not from men, and the call came through the agency of Jesus Christ, and not through the agency of any man. The election of Matthias throws light upon these words (Acts 1: 23-26), for if he was not called of the apostles, he was at least called through their agency. Paul's call, on the contrary, was from the lips of Jesus himself, and had in it no human mixture whatever. Why Paul speaks of the resurrection of Jesus is not clear. It has been thought that Paul could claim a call from God the Father, because the Father, by the resurrection of the Son, gave official countenance to the acts of the Son. Again it is thought

that Paul has in mind the fact that Jesus rose from the dead for our justification (Rom. 4: 25), and since justification by faith in Christ is the main theme of the epistle, he mentions the resurrection to pave the way for the introduction of that theme. But it seems more likely, from the context, that he has in mind the fact that his own call came *after* the resurrection of Jesus, and so the resurrection of Jesus was an essential element in the proof of his apostleship. Paul mentions the brethren who were with him. For a probable list of them see Acts 20: 4; 21: 16. Paul does not mention them by name, as he does in the epistles to the Thessalonians and Corinthians, because the letter is of a more personal nature than any of these others. But he does mention them to let the Galatians know that others sympathized with him in all that he wrote. The address implies that there were many churches in Galatia, yet to none of them does he attach any honorable title, for none of them does he offer the usual expression of thanksgiving, and to none of them does he speak the customary words of commendation and praise. This ominous silence on the part of the apostle constitutes a most telling rebuke]: **3 Grace to you and peace from God the Father, and our Lord Jesus Christ** [see 1 Cor. 1: 1 and note], **4 who gave himself for our sins, that he might deliver us out of this present evil world, according to the will of our God and Father: 5 to whom** *be* **the glory for ever and ever. Amen.** [The mention of the Lord Jesus Christ in the benediction, coupled with the thought which was uppermost in his mind, namely, that the Galatians were forsaking salvation through Jesus in the hope that they might obtain it through the law of Moses, leads Paul in these very opening sentences to fully set forth the atoning sacrifice of Christ, the deliverance through him, and the will of God, who ordered that atonement and deliverance should come in this way. Gratitude to Christ, who, owning his life, might have retained it, but freely gave it for us, and desire for deliverance from this present evil world, and respect for the sovereign will of God our Father, are three strong motives prompting us to be steadfast in the profession

of our Christian faith. To each of these motives Paul appeals. It is the apostle's habit, whenever he has occasion to make mention of the mercy of God, to break forth in expressions of thanksgiving (2 Cor. 9: 15; Eph. 3: 20), and he follows his custom here.]
6 I marvel that ye are so quickly removing from him that called you in the grace of Christ unto a different gospel [The word translated "marvel" conveys the idea of admiration rather than of wonder. Their fickleness was sufficiently striking to be brilliant. Since, if Paul wrote this letter from Corinth on his third missionary tour, it was three years since he had been with them, commentators have been tempted to choose some other date comporting better with "quickly," for three years is rather a long period. But Paul refers to *moral* speed. The Galatians were changing their position hastily and without due consideration. In doing this they were withdrawing from the God who called them (for "him" refers to God, and not to Paul—1: 15; 5: 8; Rom. 8: 30; 1 Cor. 1: 9; 1 Thess. 2: 12; 5: 24; 2 Tim. 1: 9) and from the grace, or liberty, peace, etc., of the kingdom into which they had been called, for what? for a new gospel which was not worthy of the name. There can be but one gospel; that there might be two, between which men might choose, is something which the apostle denies in the next verse];
7 which is not another *gospel*: **only there are some that trouble you, and would pervert the gospel of Christ.** [This verse defines the meaning of that which precedes, so as to correct the false impression that there might be two gospels, similar in some respects and equally effective. The folly of such a thought is ironically set forth at 2 Cor. 11: 4. There is, says the apostle, emphatically but one gospel, but there are some who would revolutionize you (the word "trouble" has this force) by perverting the gospel, making it an unholy, ineffectual compound of living truth and obsolete Jewish forms. His failure to name the leaders in this movement shows his contempt for them. They were parties unknown and deserving to remain unknown. One can not help wishing that modern churches would waken to the truth here

spoken by the apostle. There is and must ever be but one gospel. There is not a separate gospel suited to the prejudices or so-called "tastes" of each sect or denomination. There is but one gospel, and hence all church divisions result from perversions of that gospel, and all such secessions or revolutionary divisions are but the beguiling of Satan, drawing disciples from "the simplicity and purity that is toward Christ"—2 Cor. 11: 3.] **8 But though we, or an angel from heaven, should preach unto you any gospel other than that which we preached unto you, let him be anathema. 9 As we have said before, so say I now again, If any man preacheth unto you any gospel other than that which ye received, let him be anathema.** [Here the apostle supposes an impossibility, that he may thereby show that it is not possible to make any alterations in the gospel which God would sanction or accept. No man could make such alterations; no, not even an angel. Chrysostom suggests that these gospel perverters claim for their teaching the authority of the older apostles, Peter, James, John, etc., and interprets Paul thus: "Don't tell me of John, don't tell me of James. If one of the highest angels were to come, corrupting the truth originally preached, he must be rejected. . . . When the truth is in question, respect of persons is inadmissible." In this connection it is interesting to note that the Galatians had at first received Paul as an angel of light (Gal. 4: 14), and they were now probably so receiving these' perverters. Also we may observe that the words of angels would be valueless if spoken in an improper spirit (1 Cor. 13: 1), and lastly that the sayings of Jesus differ from the sayings of the law in this very respect, viz.: they are weightier than any words conveyed through the agency of angels (Heb. 1: 2; 2: 1-3). Upon all such perverters Paul pours out the anathema of God, devoting them to destruction. See 1 Cor. 16: 22. In later centuries the anathema became associated with excommunication, until the two words became convertible terms; but no such confusion of terms existed in Paul's day, and his words mean more even than severance from the church. Moreover, excommunication would not affect angels, since they are not members of our churches. Paul's language shows that at his last visit (Acts 18: 23) he had warned the Galatians against such Judaizers, and he now makes the warning more effectual by repetition. His reference to his former words suggests surprise that they should have so far forgotten them as to be misled despite them. The strong wording of this entire passage forms a solemn warning against the sin of corrupting the gospel. All offices, appearances and reputations to the contrary, whoso perverts the divine truth is an enemy to Christ, and rests under the curse of God. Compare Matt. 7: 22, 23. And who will presume to say how large or important a change must be to constitute a perversion? It is best, as Dean Howson observes, to understand Paul as "precluding any deviation of any kind from the original gospel."] **10 For am I now seeking the favor of men, or of God? or am I striving to please men? if I were still pleasing men, I should not be a servant of Christ.** [Paul's enemies accused him of being a time-serving, man-pleasing factionist, who, to gain for himself a large party of adherents, had allowed the Gentiles undue liberty, even receiving them into the fellowship of the church without subjecting them to the essential rite of circumcision, thus being content to let them rest in a low state of imperfection and perhaps even risk their salvation rather than alienate their affections by telling them unpalatable truths, or making unwelcome requirements. Paul therefore makes his present conduct an answer to all this. Neither in his present utterance or in his life since his conversion had he proved himself such a time-server. On the contrary, however, whenever a crisis arose requiring him to make a choice between pleasing man and God, he had spoken God's unpleasant truths freely, regardless of their effect on human friendship. Whatever he had done when he was a Pharisee to please priest or people, he was not continuing to do so now. He was no longer a Jew, a Pharisee, or a persecutor of Christians as he would be if he were pleasing men, but he was a servant of Christ; though being so involved being misunderstood, hated, slandered, persecuted and reviled.] **11 For I make known** to you, brethren [Paul's affection will crop out], **as touching the gospel which was preached by me, that it is not after man. 12 For neither did I receive it from man, nor was I taught it, but** *it came to me* **through revelation of Jesus Christ.** [I want you to understand that the gospel which I preach was in no sense my own invention or production, for it was of a nature not after man; *i. e.*, not such as man could design or devise. And the method by which I received it proves that it was not of a human origin, and hence also not of a human character; for I did not receive it from man, nor did I acquire it by the slow and progressive method of teaching, but it came to me through revelation of Jesus Christ. Jesus revealed himself to Paul on the way to Damascus and he was soon preaching the gospel in that city. Therefore Paul's revelations must have been received about the time of his conversion, and most probably during his sojourn in Arabia. As to exactly when they were received Paul himself is silent; but as to the manner, he declares that he received them from Jesus, so his gospel was from the same source as that of the other apostles. The rest of the chapter is taken up in proving the statements of these two verses.] **13 For ye have heard of my manner of life in time past in the Jews' religion, how that beyond measure I persecuted the church of God, and made havoc of it: 14 and I advanced in the Jews' religion beyond many of mine own age among my countrymen, being more exceedingly zealous for the traditions of my fathers.** [Paul's first proposition is that though it might be possible that he was taught the gospel by men, or that he might have attempted to originate it, it was certainly highly improbable; for his whole early life showed a strong antipathy and aversion to such teaching, and an intense love for that very form of teaching which was now being used to pervert the gospel. Of these very facts the Galatians themselves were in a manner witnesses; for they had doubtless heard the common report concerning them, and had also learned them from Paul himself at a time when they had no bearing on the question now discussed. Paul made no secret of his past life (1 Cor. 15: 9; 1 Tim. 1: 13; Acts 22: 4, 5; 26: 10, 11). Thus the story of his miraculous call, with which they were perfectly familiar, was evidently true. By "my fathers" Paul means his spiritual fathers, the Pharisees. He was zealous for the whole Jewish religion, as expounded by the Pharisees, with all its forms, rites, laws, etc., both divine and human.] **15 But when it was the good pleasure of God, who separated me, *even* from my mother's womb, and called me through his grace, 16 to reveal his Son in me, that I might preach him among the Gentiles; straightway I conferred not with flesh and blood** [anything mortal]: **17 neither went I up to Jerusalem to them that were apostles before me: but I went away into Arabia; and again I returned unto Damascus.** [Paul's conversion, being too well known to the Galatians to require restatement, is simply referred to in the phrases "called me," "returned to Damascus," etc. He appeals to that conversion to show that he was neither man's apostle nor even an apostle's apostle, but a true apostle of God. Moreover, even he himself had no part in the call, for he could in no way have fitted or qualified himself to be such, since God had called him to the place from birth, as he had done Moses, John the Baptist, Isaiah (Isa. 49: 1), and Jeremiah (Jer. 1: 5). His call to be an apostle was, therefore, due to the free grace of God and not because of anything which Paul was as a man, or held as derived from man. Moreover, in purpose the call was purely apostolic, for he was called to receive illumination, that, having received a revelation of Christ, he might be sent forth to enlighten the Gentiles with it. And this illumination was absolutely independent of any person or persons at Jerusalem, for he had received it in another land, and it was made wholly sufficient without any recourse to Jerusalem, as was clear from the fact that he had not turned to that city for more light, but had gone into Arabia, and, returning to Damascus, had entered upon his ministry (Acts 9: 19, 22; 26: 20). The sojourn in Arabia must have been brief. Paul's predestination to the office of an apostle is an entirely different thing from

predestination to salvation, for he nowhere claims the latter—
1 Cor. 9: 27.] **18 Then after three years I went up to Jerusalem to visit Cephas, and tarried with him fifteen days. 19 But other of the apostles saw I none, save James the Lord's brother. 20 Now touching the things which I write unto you, behold, before God, I lie not. 21 Then I came into the regions of Syria and Cilicia. 22 And I was still unknown by face unto the churches of Judaea which were in Christ: 23 but they only heard say, He that once persecuted us now preacheth the faith of which he once made havoc; 24 and they glorified God in me.** [The term "three years" may be taken to mean three full years, or one year and parts of two others. Assuming that Paul was converted in A. D. 37, the visit to Jerusalem took place somewhere between A. D. 38 and 40. Luke describes this same period as "many days" (Acts 9: 23). For a curious parallel see 1 Kings 2: 38, 39. Persecution drove Paul from Damascus (Acts 9: 22-25 ; 2 Cor. 11: 31, 32), and the desire to form the acquaintance of Peter led him to Jerusalem. The James whom he met was, as described, "the Lord's brother," and was neither James, the son of Zebedee, nor James, the son of Alphæus. In fact, he was not properly an apostle, but was called such probably because of his nearness to Jesus and his great influence. For further information concerning him, see " Fourfold Gospel," page 225. Paul's reasons for leaving Jerusalem are found at Acts 9: 29, 30 ; 22: 17-21. Cilicia was commonly coupled with Syria in popular phrase ; for, though part of Asia Minor, it was cut off from that district by the high ridge of Mt. Taurus, and so formed social and commercial affinities with Syria. The gist of Paul's argument is this: My gospel did not come to me from Jerusalem, for, 1. I was in no haste to go there. 2. I did not go there for the purpose of perfecting my knowledge of the gospel. 3. I was not there long enough to perfect such knowledge. 4. Leaving there, I was conscious of no deficiency of knowledge, but went at once to localities far distant, and was not personally known in the regions contiguous

to Jerusalem, as I must have been had I lingered in that city long enough to learn the gospel history. 5. But I was known to them by my repentance, and by works for which they praised God, which facts show that I was recognized by them as proficient in a gospel which I did not learn from them.]

II.

PAUL'S GOSPEL APOSTOLICALLY APPROVED. HIS EQUALITY WITH PETER.

2: 1-21.

[Paul, having shown that his gospel was independent of the powers at Jerusalem, proceeds to prove that it was fully endorsed by them, and so he was not a false apostle, as his enemies represented him to be.] 1 **Then after the space of fourteen years** [*i. e.*, after his conversion, or about A. D. 51] **I went up again to Jerusalem with Barnabas, taking Titus also with me.** [Paul omits his second visit to Jerusalem, which took place about A. D. 44 (Acts 11: 30; 12: 35). It is not needful to mention this visit, for it was a brief one, and made at a time when persecution raged there, and when James, the son of Zebedee, was beheaded, and Peter cast into prison. It was no time for conference, and had no bearing whatever on Paul's apostleship or gospel. The third visit (Acts 15: 1-35) had such bearings, and is therefore mentioned. Titus was among the "certain other" mentioned at Acts 15: 2. Titus was a Gentile convert, and Paul evidently took him with him that he might use him to test the question as to whether circumcision was required of such converts. If Paul wrote from Corinth, Titus was then with him, a living witness of Paul's success in this test case. At this council which Paul and Barnabas attended, a decree confirming the liberty of the Gentiles was issued. Some question has arisen as to why Paul did not cite the decree to prove the correctness of his position on the question of circumcision. Paley gives an elaborate number of reasons for his not doing so, none of which are

PAUL'S GOSPEL APPROVED

wholly satisfactory, but the real reason is very obvious. Paul could prove his apostleship easier than he could the decree, and the decree would settle only one or two questions, while the establishment of his apostleship would enable him to settle every question. Moreover, the Galatians had no doubt seen the decree and had it explained away—Acts 16: 4-6.] **2 And I went up by revelation: and I laid before them the gospel which I preach among the Gentiles but privately before them who were of repute, lest by any means I should be running, or had run, in vain.** [Paul went up to Jerusalem because he was outwardly appointed to do so by the church at Antioch (Acts 15: 2), and inwardly prompted to do so by the Lord. This revelation may have come to Paul through some prophet (Acts 13: 1, 2), but it was more likely by the guidance of the Holy Spirit (Acts 10: 17-19; 11: 12; 16: 6, 7), but the important point to note is, that as his gospel came from God, so also its sanctioning was brought about by God. Paul wisely consulted with the apostolic leaders (Acts 15: 4) before entering the council, lest, through some misunderstanding, he might encounter their opposition, and so have his work destroyed, for he recognized that if his labors were discountenanced at the fountain-head, all that he had done would be in vain. According to his characteristic use of metaphors, he describes his labors under the figure of the Grecian race.] **3 But not even Titus who was with me, being a Greek, was compelled to be circumcised: 4 and that because of the false brethren privily brought in, who came in privily to spy out our liberty which we have in Christ Jesus, that they might bring us into bondage: 5 to whom we gave place in the way of subjection, no, not for an hour; that the truth of the gospel might continue with you.** [But the sequel showed that I did not run in vain, for my voice and my authority were recognized in that council in the matter of Titus; and though certain Jews, who were members of the church and yet not Christians at all, but had entered the church to further Jewish interests, and who were even then present in the council as spies of the Jews to spy out our liberty which we have in Christ, that they might bring the church of Christ back into the bondage of the law—though these I say were present, demanding the circumcision of Titus, I did not yield to them at all, but saved the liberty of Titus, that the true liberty of the gospel might be preserved for you Gentiles. Paul after this circumcised Timothy, who was by birth entitled to circumcision. He did this because by so doing he would give Timothy larger influence in preaching to the Jews, and because the church at Jerusalem, having, after a full hearing, accepted one uncircumcised Christian, had once for all admitted that circumcision was not essential to Christianity. Had Paul yielded in the case of Titus, the precedent would have established the contrary rule.] **6 But from those who were reputed to be somewhat (whatsoever they were, it maketh no matter to me: God accepteth not man's person)—they, I say, who were of repute imparted nothing to me** [Having exposed the Judaists and set forth his triumph over them, and shown them to be no-what, he now turns to discuss those who by reason of their office, influence, etc., seem to be somewhat. Thus, he reaches the main question which the Galatians were asking, viz.: "What, Paul, was your final attitude toward the apostles, those great pillars of the church universal?" He recognizes that in the very putting of such a question they were, so far as he was concerned, exalting the Jerusalem apostles above their true height. He was himself a pillar of equal altitude, and no more to be measured by them than they by him. Though, says he, these men, buttressed by a multitude of followers and by their established official position, seemed indeed to be more important than a lone stranger such as I, yet God is not deceived by such seeming. He knew me to be an apostle as well as they; and they added no gospel fact or doctrine to my store, nor did they impart to me any new authority, or suggest any change in what I preached]: **7 but contrariwise, when they saw that I had been intrusted with the gospel of the uncircumcision, even as Peter with** *the gospel* **of the circumcision 8 (for he**

PAUL'S GOSPEL APPROVED

that wrought for Peter unto the apostleship of the circumcision wrought for me also unto the Gentiles); 9 and when they perceived the grace that was given unto me, James and Cephas and John, they who were reputed to be pillars, gave to me and Barnabas the right hands of fellowship, that we should go unto the Gentiles, and they unto the circumcision; 10 only *they would* that we should remember the poor; which very thing I was also zealous to do. [These men, as I say, in no way reproved or corrected me, but, on the contrary, when they saw, by the testimony of the Spirit, that I was sent to the Gentiles as Peter was sent to the Jews (for the Spirit, who gave Peter wisdom and knowledge and power when he worked among the Jews, gave me these same gifts for my work among the Gentiles), and when they also saw the manner in which the Spirit had fitted me for my work, they recognized that God had appointed to each of us a separate sphere of operations; so they agreed, these pillars, that I should preach to the Gentiles, and they should preach to the Jews, and our agreement was not a loose and tacit affair, but one to which we formally pledged ourselves by the giving of hands. The only requirement they made of me was that I should remember the poor in Judæa whenever persecution, etc., brought them into distress, and this I would have done without their request. James is mentioned before Peter because he was elder at Jerusalem, and because he appears to have acted as president of the council. (See Acts 15.) The Scripture knows nothing of the supremacy of Peter, as contended for by the Roman Catholics. As to this agreement formed between the apostles, we should note that it was not rigid. Paul, in his missionary journeys, invariably preached first to the Jews, and Peter did work at Antioch and elsewhere among the Gentiles, and was, according to the appointment of Christ, the first to open the door of the kingdom for the Gentiles (Matt. 16: 19; Acts 10; 15: 7). Moreover, we should note that while the greatest goodwill and cordiality and most perfect understanding existed between the leaders of these two great wings of the church, this concord did not extend to the wings themselves, for it was a part of Peter's grand division of the church which was causing Paul trouble in Galatia. As to collections for the poor, Paul had taken one such offering to Jerusalem even *before* the meeting of this council (Acts 11: 28-30), and was even now taking another such collection on a large scale (Rom 15: 26, 27; Acts 24: 16), of which facts the Galatians were not ignorant.] **11 But when Cephas came to Antioch, I resisted him to the face, because he stood condemned.** [There is no means of determining when this scene took place, but it was probably very soon after the council at Jerusalem. It forms the climax in Paul's argument, showing that he was not only the equal of Peter, but, at times, even his superior. It upsets the Romish doctrine of Peter's supremacy, and also shows that in his conduct he was not infallible; for in this instance he was not so much condemned by his fellow-apostle as he was, to use Paul's phrase, self-condemned—his conduct at one time reproving and convicting him for his conduct at another. Luther regards Paul as here drawing a contrast between his own conduct in withstanding Peter to his face, and these gospel perverters who were slandering him behind his back.] **12 For before that certain came from James, he ate with the Gentiles; but when they came, he drew back and separated himself, fearing them that were of the circumcision.** [The Jews regarded it as unlawful to have social intercourse with, or to eat with, Gentiles; but Peter's great vision, teaching the fact that God was no respecter of races or persons, bore especially on the social difference (Acts 10: 11-16). Peter, therefore, instructed by the vision, ate with the Gentiles, and defended his conduct in so doing (Acts 11: 3, 4, 12). He therefore knew perfectly what was right and lawful in the matter, but, fearing those who came from James, he played the coward, being, as Alford says, "ever the first to recognize, and the first to draw back from great truths." Peter, therefore, to avoid the censure of these Jerusalem critics, began to withdraw from the Gentiles, and finally to separate himself altogether. Such a withdrawal

PAUL'S GOSPEL APPROVED 261

would mean that Peter could not take the communion with the Gentiles. The "certain" is contemptuous, and corresponds to the "some" of 1:7. It is not likely that James gave these men any authority for what they did. See his words at Acts 15: 19, and those of the decree, Acts 15: 24. But James stood in high favor with the Jewish party, and hence, in his absence, would readily be quoted as sanctioning the teachings of that party.] **13 And the rest of the Jews dissembled likewise with him; insomuch that even Barnabas was carried away with their dissimulation.** [These Jews from Jerusalem appear to have swept in like an invading army, and were joined by Peter, and then by the rest of the Jewish Christians in Antioch, and lastly by even Barnabas, who had hitherto been Paul's colleague in defending the gospel liberties. Truly the situation was critical. Either the surrender of the Gentiles, or a division of the church, was sure to follow if these conditions continued. Paul calls the conduct of these men "dissimulation." They were pretending that they believed one principle, when, in reality, they believed the very opposite. Bishop Lightfoot suggests that the action of Barnabas at this time may have paved the way for the quarrel which soon after separated him from Paul.] **14 But when I saw that they walked not uprightly according to the truth of the gospel, I said unto Cephas before *them* all** [Antioch was the center and citadel of Gentile Christianity with all its privileges and liberties, and Antioch was being captured. It was time to act, and the whole fate of the church, humanly speaking, rested on one man, but that man was equal to the occasion. When leaders failed to walk according to the truth of the gospel, Paul was always heard from. He spoke here, and the church was saved. The open boldness of his unsparing rebuke, delivered before some great congregation, was a warning to these gospel-perverters of what he would do should he come to Galatia. Doubt exists as to where Paul's words to Peter end, but they seem to embrace the entire chapter], **If thou, being a Jew, livest as do the Gentiles, and not as do the Jews, how compellest thou the Gentiles**

18

to live as do the Jews? **15 We being Jews by nature, and not sinners of the Gentiles, 16 yet knowing that a man is not justified by the works of the law but through faith in Jesus Christ, even we believed on Christ Jesus, that we might be justified by faith in Christ, and not by the works of the law: because by the works of the law shall no flesh be justified.** [If thou, being a Jew to begin with, livest, as is shown by your past custom, like a Gentile, and not like the Jews, by what right do you demand, by your changed custom, that the Gentiles should live like Jews? For even you and I, both being born Jews, and both taking the best view of ourselves possible, and regarding ourselves after the most untempered and unwarranted pride and prejudice of our race as infinitely superior to the degraded heathen (as we were wont to call them), both in righteousness and acceptability to God, even we, I say, despite all this, were forced to see and acknowledge that a man is not justified by those works of the law in which we trusted, but through faith in Jesus Christ, so that we believed on Christ Jesus that we might obtain the justification that comes through him, rather than the vain and insufficient justification of the law, for the Scripture itself (Ps. 143: 2) says," By the works of the law shall no flesh be justified."] **17 But if, while we sought to be justified in Christ, we ourselves also were found sinners, is Christ a minister of sin? God forbid.** [But if we were forced by Christ's light to confess that we were sinners under the law, so that we turned our backs upon the law as a means of justification; and if we were now so disappointed and dissatisfied with the justification which we have obtained from Christ, that we in turn abandon him and seek to return to the law, what will be said of Christ? Will not all be compelled to say that, so far as we are concerned, he has proved himself not a minister to our justification, but rather a minister to our sense of sin? And is he indeed such a minister? God forbid the thought! We may regard Paul's reproof as closing here and look upon the rest of the chapter as an elaboration of the thought addressed to the Gala-

PAUL'S GOSPEL APPROVED

tians. But his address to them begins properly at 3: 1, so we prefer to take it as a continuation of the reproof, wherein Paul drops the plural for the singular that he may declare to Peter his *own* intentions in the matter.] **18 For if I build up again those things which I destroyed, I prove myself a transgressor. 19 For I through the law died unto the law, that I might live unto God. 20 I have been crucified with Christ; and it is no longer I that live, but Christ liveth in me: and that** *life* **which I now live in the flesh I live in faith,** *the faith* **which is in the Son of God, who loved me, and gave himself up for me.** [If, as I say, I follow your course, Peter, and abandon and seek to destroy the law because it does not justify me, and, failing to be justified anywhere else, I return to and again build up the law, I prove myself to be a hopeless, unjustified sinner. But I am no such self-convicted transgressor; for I, following my own course, was, by the agency of the law acting as my schoolmaster (3: 24), led to die to the law, thus utterly abandoning it, that I might live unto God (Rom. 7: 1-6). And seeking refuge from the law, I have identified myself with Christ, and in him I have died to the law, for I have been crucified with Christ; and thus it is no longer I, Paul, the law-condemned Jew, that lives, but Christ, the righteous, the justified, liveth in me. And that life I now live in the flesh is thus merged in and identified with Christ by faith—faith in the Son of God, who loved me and gave himself up for me, dying to fulfill the sentence of the law in my stead.] **21 I do not make void the grace of God: for if righteousness is through the law, then Christ died for nought.** [I do not, Peter, in following my course, make void the grace of God which gave us Christ. But your course does this very thing, for if a man can be righteous and obtain justification under the law, then the death of Christ is superfluous. Paul's rebuke to Peter is not only a complete climactic justification of his claims as an apostle, but forms also a most fitting introduction, both in matter and spirit, to his immediately following rebuke of the Galatians, who were, like Peter, returning to the law.]

PART SECOND.

BIBLE TEACHING AS TO FAITH.

3: 1-4: 31.

I.

JUSTIFICATION BY FAITH IN CHRIST BIBLICALLY VINDICATED.

3: 1-29.

1 O foolish Galatians, who did bewitch you, before whose eyes Jesus Christ was openly set forth crucified? [The Galatians were of well-known intellectual capacity, and their foolishness in not detecting the fallacious reasoning of the Judaizers was hard to understand. Their conduct was so inexplicable that it seemed as if some bewitching fascination like our modern animal magnetism had been made use of, and even this explanation was hardly sufficient, for Christ had been so clearly and forcibly preached unto them, that he had been, as it were, crucified in their very presence, and before their very eyes; so that they had only to look to him to find an antidote to the Satanic poison which was destroying them—Num. 21: 9.] **2 This only would I learn from you, Received ye the Spirit by the works of the law, or by the hearing of faith?** [Rom. 1: 5; 16: 26. I need ask you but one test question to utterly condemn your conduct. I will refer you to your own experience. When I came and labored among you, God approved and seconded my labor by imparting to you the miraculous powers (v. 5; Mark 16: 17; Heb. 2: 4) and spiritual graces (v. 14; 4: 5, 6; Eph. 1: 13) of the Spirit. Now, did ye receive the Spirit by these works of the law which these gospel perverters would have you perform, or did ye receive him by hearing and believing the gospel

JUSTIFICATION BY FAITH

which I preach? The Galatians could give but one answer to this question, and that answer decided the point between Paul and his opponents, and showed that God was with the apostle, and not with his enemies.] **3 Are ye so foolish? having begun in the Spirit, are ye now perfected in the flesh? 4 Did ye suffer so many things in vain? If it be indeed vain.** [Paul here reproves them in that they have begun their life in the manhood of the Spirit, with the attendant spiritual powers, liberties and graces, and were now seeking to advance or perfect that life by turning back to the childhood of the law with its fleshly forms, rites and ordinances. They were advancing backward! (See 4: 1-6.) He next reminds them of their sufferings, which were vain, since they might have escaped them altogether, had they begun by embracing Judaism, for the Jews were not being persecuted, but were the very parties who had stirred up the hostility of the Gentiles against all Christians. "If it be indeed vain," as translated in the text, expresses a hope that they may repent of their apostasy, and so not lose the reward of their sufferings (Matt. 5: 11, 12). But the phrase may be rendered "if indeed it is only in vain," which expresses a desire that the loss may be confined to the reward of their sufferings, and may not be extended to something further, as the loss of their salvation. Cook, Meyer, etc., prefer this latter meaning, but, though less commonplace and more forceful, it is also more strained.] **5 He therefore that supplieth to you the Spirit, and worketh miracles among you, doeth he it by the works of the law, or by the hearing of faith?** [According to the unvarying rule of Paul's writings, the pronoun "he" in this verse refers to God rather than to God's minister, though the latter reference might make the smoother reading. The idea is this: Does God, who works miracles among you (or perhaps in you—2: 8; Matt. 14: 2; Eph. 2: 2; Phil. 2: 13), do it as a result of your obedience to the law, or because you have heard the gospel and believed it? Verily, by your belief; and so your case is like Abraham's.] **6 Even as Abraham believed God, and it was reckoned unto him for righteousness.**

[Gen. 15: 6; Rom. 4: 3, 9, 21, 22.] **7 Know therefore that they that are of faith, the same are sons of Abraham.** [For by faith Abraham came into such relations with God that he attained righteousness and justification; and I want you to know that those who follow his spiritual example are his real or spiritual children, to the exclusion even of his fleshly children, made such by birth, or adopted, as ye seek to be, by circumcision. **8 And the scripture, foreseeing that God would justify the Gentiles by faith, preached the gospel beforehand unto Abraham,** *saying,* **In thee shall all the nations be blessed.** [Gen. 12: 3.] **9 So then they that are of faith are blessed with the faithful Abraham.** [The word for "Gentiles" and "nations" is the same; so Paul says that the Scripture, foreseeing that the Gentiles would be justified by faith, just as Abraham was, foretold to him this gospel of justification by saying, "In thee shall all the Gentiles be blessed." That is, the blessing of justification which is imparted to you, the father, shall attach to all the spiritual children which are potentially in you, and are hereafter to be, as it were, born out of you; even the Gentiles. Those, therefore, that are of faith, and not those who are children of Abraham after the flesh (for the Gentiles can never be such), are blessed with Abraham.] **10 For as many as are of the works of the law are under a curse: for it is written, Cursed is every one who continueth not in all things that are written in the book of the law, to do them.** [Deut. 27: 26. But if the Scripture declares positively that the blessing of justification comes by faith, it likewise declares negatively that it does not come by the law, for all failed to keep the law, and it says that all who thus fail rest under a curse, instead of a blessing.] **11 Now that no man is justified by the law before God, is evident: for, The righteous shall live by faith** [Hab. 2: 4; Rom. 1: 17]; **12 and the law is not of faith; but, He that doeth them shall live in them.** [Lev. 18: 5. Moreover, later prophecy bears out the earlier declaration made to Abraham, for it says that the righteous obtain life, or salvation, by faith, and this has no ref-

JUSTIFICATION BY FAITH

erence whatever to the law, for the law is not a system of faith, but an antithetical system of works, for the Scripture so defines it by a counter statement to the one I have quoted, which says that whoever keeps the precepts of the law shall live by them. Compare Rom. 11:6.] **13 Christ redeemed us from the curse of the law, having become a curse for us; for it is written, Cursed is every one that hangeth on a tree: 14 that upon the Gentiles might come the blessing of Abraham in Christ Jesus; that we might receive the promise of the Spirit through faith.** [Deut. 21:23. Compare Matt. 20:28; 1 Tim. 2:6; 1 Cor. 5:20; 7:23; Tit. 2:14, etc. That the Galatians may realize the full meaning of their foolishness, Paul shows them that the condemnation to which they were returning, was the very thing from which the death of Christ redeemed them; for the law brought a curse upon men, but Jesus had delivered from the curse by taking it unto himself, as the Scripture proves; for it called all cursed who were crucified. And Jesus removed this obstructing law and curse, that in himself he might bring Abraham's blessing of justification upon the Gentiles, that all might receive the fulfillment of God's promise, that promise which agreed to give the Spirit to all who rendered the obedience of faith—Acts 2: 38, 39.] **15 Brethren, I speak after the manner of men: Though it be but a man's covenant, yet when it hath been confirmed, no one maketh it void, or addeth thereto. 16 Now to Abraham were the promises spoken, and to his seed. He saith not, And to seeds, as of many; but as of one, And to thy seed, which is Christ.** [Gen. 13:15; 17:8.] **17 Now this I say: A covenant confirmed beforehand by God, the law, which came four hundred and thirty years after, doth not disannul, so as to make the promise of none effect. 18 For if the inheritance is of the law, it is no more of promise; but God hath granted it to Abraham by promise.** [Brethren, I wish to use an illustration taken from our daily business life, viz.: that of our usage concerning contracts or agreements. Now if, when a human contract has once been confirmed, it becomes so sacred that no man will presume to annul or change it without the consent of both parties, much more is a covenant of God's too sacred to be modified or tampered with. But God made such a ratified or confirmed contract or covenant with Abraham, for he spoke promises to · Abraham, and to his seed. Not in fact meaning to Abraham and all his posterity, but to Abraham and his spiritual posterity (for he used a word which may be so interpreted), for he did not use the plural "seeds," but the singular "seed," thereby referring especially to Christ as the head of the spiritual posterity. Now, I say therefore, that this covenant, having been confirmed before the law came, still holds good, and can not be annulled by the coming of the law, for the law, as you know, did not come until four hundred and thirty years after the covenant was confirmed. Now, to sum up what I have said, the promise, being given to the seed of Abraham, becomes to them an inheritance, and inheritances do not come from two parties, but from one; so, if the inheritance had been derived from the law, it could not have been derived from the promise also; but it was derived from the promise, since God thus gave it to Abraham. We lack space for the grammatical and chronological difficulties of this passage. Suffice it to say, "seed," being a collective noun, is capable of being applied to many; but it is also, as Paul says, capable of being applied to one, and none of his auditors would object at all to his thus applying it solely to Christ. Again, if the term of four hundred and thirty years is inaccurate, it is the number given in the Septuagint, which was then universally used. And, for argumentative purposes, was sufficiently correct as a round number.] **19 What then is the law? It was added because of transgressions, till the seed should come to whom the promise hath been made;** *and it was ordained through angels by the hand of a mediator.* **20 Now a mediator is not** *a mediator* **of one; but God is one.** [This verse has been interpreted in more than three hundred different ways.] **21 Is the law then against the promises of God? God forbid: for if there had been**

JUSTIFICATION BY FAITH

a law given which could make alive, verily righteousness would have been of the law. 22 But the scripture shut up all things under sin, that the promise by faith in Jesus Christ might be given to them that **believe.** [The apostle now undertakes to show the inferiority of the law to the gospel. For what purpose then, you ask, was the law? It was added by God for the purpose of revealing and manifesting to man his sinfulness, and was to exist only during the interim between the giving of the promise and the fulfillment of the promise by the coming of Christ (2: 18; Rom. 5: 13-20; 7: 7). It was not given directly by divine lips, as was the gospel, but through the intervention of angels (Deut. 33: 2; Heb. 2: 2); and it was not given personally, but through Moses, a mediator (Deut. 5: 5). Now, this mediatorship of Moses also argues the temporal nature of the law; for a mediator is no part of the personality of the one whom he represents: he is a different personality; but God is one personality, and can not, therefore, be properly represented by any other than himself. Such a mediatorship, therefore, must, in the very nature of the case, be but temporary. The men who represent God are mortal and pass away, but God is immutable and ever-abiding. His promises, therefore, stand on a different plane from anything which rests on human mediation. But some one will ask, if the law brings a curse, is it not antagonistic to the promises which bring a blessing? God forbid that we should think that the Almighty acts in so contrary a manner. There are two ways in which the law might antagonize the gospel. 1. If righteousness could have been obtained by it, it might have proved a rival way of life. But it is no such rival. 2. If it had destroyed life despite the gospel, it would have been contradictory to the gospel. But it merely shut men up as prisoners, doomed for their sins, that justification by faith in Jesus Christ might be given to all them that believe. Thus, instead of being antagonistic to the gospel, the law emphasized and revealed the blessedness of the gospel.]

23 But before faith came, we were kept in ward under the law, shut up unto the faith which should

afterwards be revealed. **24 So that the law is become our tutor *to bring us* unto Christ, that we might be justified by faith.** [In the first of these two verses, Paul enlarges the thought of verse 22, fully describing those subjects of the law as prisoners incarcerated in a fortress, and awaiting the coming of a deliverer. The next image is distinct from that of a fortress, yet very similar to it; for the pedagogue or tutor was usually a slave, whose duty it was to take charge of a boy from his childhood to his majority, shield him from physical and moral evil, accompany him in all his amusement, and, as it were, keep him as a prisoner at large, lest he should in any way injure himself. Now, the law was such a tutor to bring those under his care to a state of development fit for the society and fellowship of Christ, the spiritual father.] **25 But now that faith is come, we are no longer under a tutor. 26 For ye are all sons of God, through faith, in Christ Jesus.** [Faith, announcing justification from sin, is like a messenger of the father's announcing maturity and liberty to the son so long under the care of a tutor. From the time of this announcement the son ceases to be a minor, shut off from the father, and becomes the companion of the father. Paul plainly declares the literal meaning of his figurative language in v. 26. Fausset draws attention to the analogy between the illustration here and that formed by the history of Moses and Joshua. Moses, as a representative of the law, brought the people to the border of the land of liberty; but it was the privilege of Joshua, as a type of faith, to lead the people into the full enjoyment of that liberty.] **27 For as many of you as were baptized into Christ did put on Christ. 28 There can be neither Jew nor Greek, there can be neither bond nor free, there can be no male and female; for ye are all one *man* in Christ Jesus.** [Having declared that faith, that is to say, the gospel, brings us into sonship to God, Paul describes the particular step by which this is accomplished. That step is baptism, for by baptism we become part of the mystical body of Christ. We put on the personality of Christ in the sight of God, and so become, in an

JUSTIFICATION BY FAITH

individual sense, sons of God, but the individual sense is almost wholly lost in the collective, so that all those racial distinctions and all the fictitious distinctions of caste, and even the distinction of gender, which made a man look upon a woman with contempt, are lost sight of. Not only are all men and women new creatures in Christ Jesus, so that old things are passed away, but they are all part of one new organism, which in glory and importance obscures all former differences.] **29 And if ye are Christ's, then are ye Abraham's seed, heirs according to promise.** [The promise was given to Christ, the seed of Abraham, and if ye are Christ's, then are ye in him heirs of that promise. Thus Paul demonstrates that the gospel privileges are not obtained by the law, but by the gospel system of justification through faith, which gospel system was promised equally to all nations, and may be enjoyed by them all without any racial or less distinctions.]

II.

CHILDHOOD AND MANHOOD. SARAH AND HAGAR.

4: 1-31.

1 But I say that so long as the heir is a child, he differeth nothing from a bondservant though he is lord of all; 2 but is under guardians and stewards until the day appointed of the father. 3 So we also, when we were children, were held in bondage under the rudiments of the world: 4 but when the fulness of the time came, God sent forth his Son, born of a woman, born under the law, 5 that he might redeem them that were under the law, that we might receive the adoption of sons. [In this paragraph Paul resumes the metaphor begun at 3: 24; but from a slightly different point of view. There, law, or the tutor, was prominent; here, the son, or pupil, is the chief object of consideration. The point now illustrated is the reason why the bondage of the law preceded the liberty of the gospel. It was for purposes of development, similar to those by which youth is trained to manhood. The child in this instance is regarded as wholly subject to the terms of a will (though that of a living father, as appears later). Though the will provides that the son shall eventually be heir of all things, yet for the present he is so hampered, governed and restricted by the inflexible terms of the will that his condition differs, so far as comfort and freedom are concerned, in no respect from that of a bondservant, or slave. His person is under the care of guardians, and his estate is under the direction of stewards, and he can in no way expect to have his affairs bettered until the time has elapsed which is fixed by the will as the period of his subserviency, or minority. Thus, says the apostle, both Jews and Gentiles, as one common, congregate body, or heirs in God's sight, were held in bondage either to the law of Moses or some other form of law, which laws are collectively described as the rudiments of the world. But when the time arrived which was stipulated in the will for the termination of this period of tutelage, then God took the steps for the liberation of the ward (which steps were also outlined beforehand in the promise to Abraham, and referred to in the types of the will as recorded by Moses), and sent forth his Son to effect the liberation of the ward. At 3: 13 the apostle has already suggested that this liberation was to be effected by the son taking the place of the ward, etc. He shows, therefore, the steps by which the Son took upon him this wardship. He took upon him the nature of the ward by becoming flesh, being born of a woman (John 1: 14), and he assumed the state of the ward, for he was born under the law and thus came under the wardship. And his gracious purpose in all this was to redeem all those under ward and bring them to the estate of sons (2 Cor. 8: 9)—adopted sons.] **6 And because ye are sons, God sent forth the Spirit of his Son into our hearts, crying, Abba, Father. 7 So that thou art no longer a bondservant, but a son; and if a son, then an heir through God.** [And being made sons by the Son through the operation of faith (John 1: 12), the Spirit of Christ is bestowed upon us to bring us to blissful realization of our sonship, so that we may speak to God, calling him Abba, Father. Abba is the Syriac for father. The Syriac and Greek names are both used by Paul, probably that all the tender associations which, to either Jews or Greeks, clustered around the paternal name, might be, at the sound of the sacred word, transferred to God. Thus, by the blessed ministration of Christ, all who believed on him in Galatia passed from servitude and wardship to the estate of sons and heirs—Rom. 8: 17.] **8 Howbeit at that time, not knowing God, ye were in bondage to them that by nature are no gods: 9 but now that ye have come to know God, or rather to be known by God, how turn ye back again to the weak and beggarly rudiments, whereunto ye desire to be in bondage over again? 10 Ye observe days, and months, and seasons, and years. 11 I am afraid of you, lest by any means I have bestowed labor upon you in vain.** [This paragraph is addressed especially to the Gentile Christians. He reminds them that at the time of their wardship their condition differed from that of the Jews; for, having no true copy of the will or law, they were in the more severe bondage of idolatry. Having come from this low, degraded, poverty-stricken bondage into the joyous estate of sonship, where they knew and were known of God the Father, they should have been more impressed by the contrast even than were the Jews, and so should have been more reluctant to return to bondage again. They, therefore, had less excuse than the Jews, who had not been so far removed from God. The bondage is forcefully described, and the points of description are thus aptly defined by Johnson: "Weak, because they have no spiritual power to strengthen us; beggarly, because they have no rich promise like the gospel; rudiments, because they belong to a rudimentary condition, to an undeveloped state, to the childhood of the race." In proof of the unquestioned relapse of the Galatians, Paul cites their observance of days, etc., set apart by the terms of the bondage, or law. It is not stated whether these were Sabbaths and festivals of Judaism, or the ritual days of paganism, but as they were observed at the instance and through the urgency of the Judaizers, there can be little doubt that they were the former; and the Jewish calendar corresponds to Paul's list, for they had Sabbath days, and new moon festivals each month, the great feasts in their seasons, and Sabbatical years. This passage, and that in Colossians (Col. 2: 16), if taken together, show very clearly that the Christians are not required to keep the Jewish Sabbath, and Paul's closing words, expressing fear as to the results of his labors, is a forcible warning, indicating that salvation itself may be forfeited by a return to legalism.] **12 I beseech you, brethren, become as I am, for I also** *am become* **as ye** *are.* **Ye did me no wrong: 13 but ye know that because of an infirmity of the flesh I preached the gospel unto you the first time: 14 and that which was a temptation to you in my flesh ye despised not, nor rejected; but ye received me as an angel of God,** *even* **as Christ Jesus. 15 Where then is that gratulation of yourselves? for I bear you witness, that, if possible, ye would have plucked out your eyes and given them to me. 16 So then am I become your enemy, by telling you the truth?** [I beseech you, brethren, become as I am, and be not Jews; for I forsook Judaism and became simply a Christian, which made me, in the eyes of my brethren, a Gentile like you. Though I have spoken severely to you, it is for no personal reasons. Ye have done me no wrong. On the contrary, your actions have been very gracious, for you will remember (and here the apostle refers to facts that are nowhere recorded, but which we presume to run thus:) that my journeying was providentially delayed as I was passing through your land, by my sickness; and so it came about that I preached the gospel unto you; and though my sickness was of so revolting a nature that ye might well have yielded to the temptation to ridicule or despise me, and reject me because of it, ye did not; for, conversely, ye received me as if I had been an angel of light, or the Lord himself. What, then, has become of your self-gratulation that you felt at having a real apostle among you? for I bear you witness that you so honored me that you would have plucked out your very eyes for my sake. Am I then showing myself to be your enemy by telling you truly how foolishly you are conducting yourselves? This plucking out of the eyes for another was a proverbial expression, indicating extreme attachment, and we have so rendered it in the paraphrase. Many take this as an indication that Paul's thorn in the flesh was ophthalmia; see 2 Cor. 12: 7 and note; and this is not improbable, for, though the expression is proverbial, Paul does not here state it in proverbial form. The words "given them to me" suggest that he needed eyes, and these words are not essential to the proverb.] **17 They zealously seek you in no good way; nay, they desire to shut you out, that ye may seek them. 18 But it is good to be zealously sought in a good matter at all times, and not only when I am present with you.** [The Jews showed great zeal in proselyting (1: 14; Matt. 23: 15; Rom. 2: 10), and the apostle states that in this case their zeal exhibited itself in courting the Galatians in an unworthy manner, and, what was more serious, for an unrighteous purpose. They were zealous to exclude the Galatians from the church and kingdom of God, by showing them to be not rightly converted; that, feeling themselves forlorn and lost, the Galatians might seek the Judaizers for counsel and advice, and might thus come to look upon them as great shepherds and deliverers. As the apostle sees in imagination the Galatians seeking earnestly for the instruction of the Judaizers, he remembers how they had once sought him, whom they had now forsaken, so he adds: I find no fault with you for zealously courting them, but with the evil cause for which they have you seek them; for it is at all times good to be zealously sought as a teacher in a good cause, and so, for my cause's sake, you should thus seek me, not only when present, but when absent.] **19 My little children** [1 Tim. 1: 18; 2 Tim. 2: 1; 1 John 2: 1], **of whom I am again in travail until Christ be formed in you 20 but I could wish to be present with you now, and to change my tone; for I am perplexed about you.**

[My little children, for whom I endured spiritual travail to give you birth at the time of your conversion, and for whom I a second time endure travail, that the Christ life may be formed in you, so that you may live, and think, and glory in nothing but Christ.—Here the apostle breaks suddenly off and at once explains why he did so. If the Galatians had come to look upon him as an enemy, how ridiculous such affectionate language would sound to them! He did not, as he viewed them at a distance, and as they were pictured to him by report, feel free to use such tender speech; but still, trusting that matters were better than reported, he wished that he might be present, and, finding them indeed loyal, lay aside the perplexity which was now hampering him, and change his tone from rebuke and reserve to the accents of loving persuasion. No language could be devised that would more fully reveal the apostle's heart in all its contending emotions.] **21 Tell me, ye that desire to be under the law, do ye not hear the law? 22 For it is written** [Gen. 16:15; 21:2], **that Abraham had two sons, one by the handmaid, and one by the free woman. 23 Howbeit the** *son* **by the handmaid is born after the flesh; but the** *son* **by the freewoman** *is born* **through promise.** [Gen. 18:10, 14; 21:1, 2; Heb. 11:11; Rom. 4:13; 9:7-9.] **24 Which things contain an allegory: for these** *women* **are two covenants; one from mount Sinai, bearing children unto bondage, which is Hagar. 25 Now this Hagar is mount Sinai in Arabia and answereth to the Jerusalem that now is: for she is in bondage with her children. 26 But the Jerusalem that is above** [Phil. 3:20; Heb. 12:2; Rev. 3:12; 21:2] **is free, which is our mother. 27 For it is written** [Isa. 54:1; 51:2], **Rejoice, thou barren that bearest not; Break forth and cry, thou that travailest not: For more are the children of the desolate than of her that hath the husband. 28 Now we, brethren, as Isaac was, are children of promise. 29 But as then he that was born after the flesh persecuted him** *that was born* **after the Spirit, so also is it now.**

CHILDHOOD AND MANHOOD 277

30 Howbeit what saith the scripture? [Gen. 21: 10.] Cast out the handmaid and her son: for the son of the handmaid shall not inherit with the son of the freewoman. 31 Wherefore, brethren, we are not children of the handmaid, but of the freewoman. [Tell me, ye who are so eager to return to the law, do ye not note what the law itself says? Of itself it warns you not to do this thing, in that it tells you the story of Abraham's two sons, one of whom, Ishmael, was the son of the bondwoman, Hagar; and the other of whom, Isaac, was the son of the freewoman, Sarah. These sons, it tells you, were born differently. Ishmael, the slave-born, came into the world according to the usual course of nature; but Isaac, the freeborn, came through the promise of God, which held good even contrary to the laws of nature. Now, this history, though literally true, is, nevertheless, so designed as to contain an allegory; for these two women represent the two covenants which we have been discussing. Hagar represents the law, which came from Mt. Sinai, and which, like Hagar, bears slave-born children. Hagar, then, in earlier history, represents Mt. Sinai in Arabia with its covenant, and in later history she stands for Jerusalem, the successor to Mt. Sinai, for she, like Hagar, is in bondage; and all her children are, as to sin and the law, slave-born (John 8: 32-34). Leaving out the preliminary steps, Paul rushes at once to the comparison of the two cities, for the emissaries of Jerusalem were constantly disparaging him as not the equal of those who were the heads of the church there (2: 6, 7). Filling in all the steps, according to the analogy of the apostle's reasoning, the full allegory would run thus: Sarah, the freewoman, represents the gospel covenant, which, like Sarah, bears freeborn children according to God's promise, and she is now represented by the celestial Jerusalem, which, with her free children, is our mother. And the Scripture itself recognizes the order of these two covenants, showing how the law should be populous for a time, and then be excelled by the fecunditi of the gospel covenant, which seemed so long barren; for Isaiah foretells it in the words, "Rejoice, etc." As for a time Hagar

seemed to be the real wife, and as such to own the husband, so for centuries those of the old covenant seemed to be the real Bride and to own the Lord. Resuming the allegorical history and directly identifying the Christian with Isaac, Paul shows how the history continued to run parallel, for, as Ishmael persecuted Isaac, so the progeny of the law persecuted the children of the gospel. Then, prophetically conscious of God's design to continue the parallel to the end, he gives the final prophecy of the rejection of God's once chosen people, and closes with the incontrovertible conclusion that the Galatians are not children of the bondwoman, or law, but of the freewoman, or gospel. Thus Paul, knowing the passion of the Judaizers for allegorizing, meets them with their own weapon, and casts into this appropriate mold matter which he presents argumentatively and logically at Rom. 9: 6-9, and prophetically at Rom. 11: 15. The fact that Isaac and the gospel were both matters of promise, forestalled the Judaizers in any attempt to adjust the allegory so as to turn it against Paul. Moreover, the Jews themselves universally recognized the law as a practical bondage (Acts 15: 10; Matt. 23: 4), and the complaint against Paul was that he allowed too much liberty.]

PART THIRD.

EXHORTATIONS TO STEADFASTNESS IN FREEDOM AND TO FAITHFULNESS.

5: 1-6: 18.

I.

EXHORTATION TO MAINTAIN FREEDOM WITHOUT LICENSE, AND TO ABSTAIN FROM LEGALISM.

5: 1-26.

1 For freedom did Christ set us free: stand fast therefore, and be not entangled again in a yoke of bondage. [This verse continues the thought of the last chapter, and forms a connecting link between it and this section. It means that Christ made us free, not incidentally, but with the very design that we should cherish and enjoy our freedom, and we should therefore stand fast in it, and not return to bondage.] **2 Behold, I Paul say unto you, that, if ye receive circumcision, Christ will profit you nothing.** [By the use of an exclamation followed by his name, Paul calls attention to the sentence, or decree, which, as an apostle, he pronounces in the case. Though circumcision of itself might be nothing (v. 6; Acts 16: 3), yet if the Galatians looked to it, and through it to the covenant which it represented, for justification, or even their perfection in Christian grace, they forfeited all their rights in Christ. Though both covenants were of God, they could not be confused without disastrous results. Though a man's mortal and spiritual bodies may both be from God, the soul which has advanced to the spiritual body would forfeit its salvation by returning to the corrupt mortal body.] **3 Yea, I testify again to every man that receiveth of circum-**

cision, that he is a debtor to do the whole law. [The apostle here gives the reason for what he has said in the previous verse. Circumcision was, in its symbolic significance, an entrance into covenant relations with God under the terms of the old covenant, and as that covenant embraced not a part, but the whole law, the covenantee, or circumcised person, was obliged to observe the whole law, or forfeit his claims to life. Paul had probably fully explained this fact on one of his previous visits, and so he now reiterates it.] **4 Ye are severed from Christ, ye who would be justified by the law; ye are fallen away from grace.** [Therefore, in being circumcised for the purpose of being justified by the law ye have been guilty of a complete apostasy; there is no longer any justification for you, for you are not under the grace of Christ, but rest under the condemnation of the law.] **5 For we through the Spirit by faith wait for the hope of righteousness.** [That ye have fallen from grace is apparent by your contrast with us; for we true Christians, not trusting in carnal ordinances, but strengthened by the Spirit, wait for the fulfillment of the hope which righteousness by faith, instead of by law, insures to us.] **6 For in Christ Jesus neither circumcision availeth anything, nor uncircumcision; but faith working through love.** [It makes no difference in God's sight what a man has been, whether a circumcised Jew, or an uncircumcised Gentile. There is, in his sight, no merit in either condition. That which he values is a faith in his Son, Christ Jesus, which manifests itself in loving service to him.] **7 Ye were running well; who hindered you that ye should not obey the truth? 8 This persuasion** *came* **not of him that calleth you.** [The apostle again borrows a metaphor from the foot-race of the Grecian game. In their faith and love and works the Christians were running in a course obedient to the truth, but some one had broken up the race-course, and had persuaded them to desist from running. Who had done this? Paul does not answer, but states the important fact in the matter that whoever these persuaders were they were not the agents of the God who had

FREEDOM WITHOUT LICENSE 281

called them to enter the race. The term "hindered" is military and indicates the embarrassment of an army's progress by tearing down bridges, etc.] **9 A little leaven leaveneth the whole lump.** [Paul felt that by this time those who read his letter would be saying that he was censuring the whole church for a course of conduct pursued only by a small minority, but he quotes one of the proverbs of the New Testament (1 Cor. 5: 6) to show that the effect of minorities, if tolerated, becomes a menace to majorities.] **10 I have confidence to you-ward in the Lord, that ye will be none otherwise minded: but he that troubleth you shall bear his judgment, whosoever he be.** [The apostle here expresses his confidence that they will take the same view of the situation that he does, and avoid the contaminating influence of the minority by disciplining it or its ringleader, no matter who he may be.] **11 But I, brethren, if I still preach circumcision, why am I still persecuted? then hath the stumbling-block of the cross been done away.** [It is evident that in this verse Paul defends himself against the charge of having taught the necessity of circumcision by having circumcised Timothy. His answer is that false brethren might misconstrue his act for the purpose of founding false teaching upon it, but that the Jews, the real parties in interest, placed a truer construction upon the act, for they still continued to persecute him as an enemy to circumcision. If Paul had preached circumcision, the stumbling-block of the cross would have been done away. Paul taught that the whole Jewish system of ordinances perished at the cross, and that on the cross Jesus made the one and only atonement for sin. Such teaching was a stumbling-block to the Jews. Had Paul rejected the doctrine of the cross and preached circumcision, as these Judaizers contended that he did when they wished to countenance their errors with his authority, he would have been a hero among the Jews.] **12 I would that they that unsettle you would even go beyond circumcision.** [If those who trouble you insist on mutilating themselves, I wish they would go further and cut themselves entirely off from the church. Having fully established the liberty of the gospel, the apostle now turns to correct any false antinomian theories which might have arisen out of a misconception of his words. Liberty is permissible, but not license. The liberty of a son is infinitely larger than that of a ward, and yet the son is not wholly without restraint.] **13 For ye, brethren, were called for freedom; only *use* not your freedom for an occasion to the flesh, but through love be servants one to another. 14 For the whole law is fulfilled in one word, *even* in this: Thou shalt love thy neighbor as thyself. 15 But if ye bite and devour one another, take heed that ye be not consumed one of another.** [Do not think because you are free that you are therefore free to do evil. As a contrast to the spirit of liberty which is indeed yours, I counsel you to become servants one to another, not because the law commands you, but because love constrains you. For ye are indeed under the law of love, and that whole law is summed up in one sentence, which is this: " Thou shalt love thy neighbor as thyself." But if, instead of having the spirit of love, which becomes men, ye be animated with the spirit of wild beasts, which, in their hasty rancor, bite each other, and, in their settled, inveterate malice, gnaw at and devour each other, take heed that your conduct does not result in your being consumed one of another.] **16 But I say, Walk by the Spirit, and ye shall not fulfil the lust of the flesh. 17 For the flesh lusteth against the Spirit, and the Spirit against the flesh; for these are contrary the one to the other; that ye may not do the things that ye would.** [The Christian is under the guidance of the Spirit, and the Spirit continually prompts him to imitate the Father who has adopted him, and the Christ who has died for him. Now, any one who submits himself to the guidance of the Spirit, will not yield to those lusts of the flesh which he knows are displeasing to God. But he will be tempted to yield to those lusts, for there is an inner conflict forever waged within him in which the flesh contends with the Spirit, and the Spirit with the flesh, each desiring to constrain the man to fulfill its will. And thus it comes about that ye may not do things that ye would, for there are two wills within you, and one or other of them must be subdued and disappointed.] **18 But if ye are led by the Spirit, ye are not under the law.** [By as much as the Spirit triumphs within us, by that much are we freed from feeling the presence of the law. So long as we have two wills we are sensible of conflict, and so of the restraint of law, but when our nature is merged in the will of the Spirit, so that there is but one will within us, then we lose all consciousness of restraint. We attain to that true rule of liberty which Augustine condenses in the saying: "Love God, and do what you please." God himself leads the life of perfect righteousness, yet God can never be said to be under law. He knows no law but his own choice, but his choice is ever righteousness because of the perfect holiness of his character. So the Christian should strive to bring his own will into such perfect accord with the will of the Spirit that he does not feel the constraint of law resting upon him.] **19 Now the works of the flesh are manifest, which are** *these:* **fornication, uncleanness, lasciviousness, 20 idolatry, sorcery, enmities, strife, jealousies, wraths, factions, divisions, parties, 21 envyings, drunkenness, revellings, and such like; of which I forewarn you, even as I did forewarn you, that they who practice such things shall not inherit the kingdom of God.** [These sins are too well known to need analysis or comment. It is startling to find "factions, divisions, parties," in so black a list, and coupled with so clear a declaration that these sins exclude the perpetrator of them from the kingdom of God. Verily all professing Christians would do well to take heed to what the Bible designates as sins, and not trust too much to their own fallible sentiment and judgment in such matters.] **22 But the fruit of the Spirit is love, joy, peace, longsuffering, kindness, goodness, faithfulness, 23 meekness, self-control; against such there is no law.** [Contrast between light and darkness is no more definite and distinct than that between these two catalogues which represent carnal and spiritual desires. All those who do these works of God, find no law of God interfering with them in the exercise of their labors.] **24 And they that are of Christ Jesus have crucified the flesh with the passions and the lusts thereof.** [All those who have been baptized with Christ have been symbolically united with him in his crucifixion and death (Rom. 6: 2-6). In Christ, therefore, they have crucified the flesh with its passions, and so have consented to cut themselves off from the indulgence of the same.] **25 If we live by the Spirit, by the Spirit let us also walk. 26 Let us not become vainglorious, provoking one another, envying one another.** [If we have been born and live in the Spirit, let us manifest that fact by our daily life, abstaining from evil. The especial evils mentioned in the last verse were probably very common among the Galatians.]

II.

EXHORTATIONS TO MUTUAL HELPFULNESS. RIGHT AND WRONG GLORYING.

6: 1-18.

1 Brethren, even if a man be overtaken [literally, caught] **in any trespass, ye who are spiritual, restore** [a surgical term] **such a one in a spirit of gentleness; looking to thyself, lest thou also be tempted.** [Brethren, if a man be surprised, or caught unaware by temptation, and so fall into sin, ye who have not so done, but have walked according to the guidance of the Spirit, deal gently with such a sinner. Do not amputate him, as a piece of gangrene flesh, from the church body, but so handle him as to restore him. Also do not do this in a proud, Pharisaical spirit, but in the spirit of gentleness, bearing in mind that thou thyself art not beyond the reach of temptation.] **2 Bear ye one another's burdens** [Greek, *bara*, burden, or distresses], **and so fulfil the law of Christ. 3 For if a man thinketh himself to be**

something when he is nothing, he deceiveth himself.
4 But let each man prove his own work, and then
shall he have his glorying in regard of himself alone,
and not of his neighbor. 5 For each man shall bear
his own burden. [Greek, *phortion*, burden or responsibility.
Bear one another's burden of trial and suffering, those burdens
which come by reason of infirmity of the flesh, and so fulfill the
law of Christ, which bids us love one another (John 13: 34;
15: 12; 1 John 3: 23). For if a man think himself to be something, etc., *i. e.*, so good that he can not be tempted, or so
strong that he can not fall, or so perfect that he will never need
the patience and sympathy of his brethren, when in reality he
is nothing, *i. e.*, no better than other men, he deceives himself.
But let each man prove his own work instead of criticizing and
judging the work of others, and then shall he have glory in
himself alone, and not because he seems superior to his neighbor by comparison of his work with that of his neighbor. And
it behooves us to be concerned about our own work, and to
thus test it, for each one of us shall bear his own load of duty and
accountability, for which alone he shall be called to answer in
the judgment.] 6 But let him that is taught in the word
communicate unto him that teacheth in all good things.
[Let the one taught remunerate his teacher, bringing him pecuniary aid, honor, reverence and all other good things. The
financial support of teachers is elsewhere referred to (1 Tim.
5: 17). Failure to contribute funds to this good end, no doubt,
suggested what follows (compare 2 Cor. 9: 7, 8); but the paragraph is by no means to be confined to such failure, for the
language is too general.] 7 Be not deceived; God is not
mocked: for whatsoever a man soweth, that shall he
also reap. 8 For he that soweth unto his own flesh
shall of the flesh reap corruption; but he that soweth
unto the Spirit shall of the Spirit reap eternal life.
[God is not to be deceived by false appearances, and whoever
hopes to overreach him only deceives himself (2 Kings 5: 15-
27; Acts 5: 4, 5, 9). It is a broad law of God's (and he can
not be deceived about it) that whatever a man sows he shall

reap. As in the natural world he reaps grain for grain, so in the moral world, if he sows fleshly indulgence, he shall reap corruption, and so in the spiritual world, if he sows to the Spirit of God, he shall of the Spirit reap life everlasting.] **9 And let us not be weary in well-doing: for in due season we shall reap, if we faint not. 10 So then, as we have opportunity, let us work that which is good toward all men, and especially toward them that are of the household of the faith.** [And let us who are sowing in this latter manner not grow weary in the good work, for in due season we shall reap (Jas. 5: 7, 8) if we do not grow disheartened and quit. And because we are then sure to reap, let us sow our harvest of good deeds as often as we have opportunity to sow, and let us do good toward all men, especially toward all our brethren in God's household of believers.] **11 See with how large letters I write unto you with mine own hand.** [There is no indication that Paul had ever before written to the Galatians, and they were probably not familiar with his handwriting. To call attention, therefore, to the fact that the amanuensis has now turned over the stylus, or pen, to him, and that he is putting his own closing lines as an autograph to the Epistle, he bids them note the difference in the letters. They were much larger than those of the amanuensis. This large lettering is taken by some as an additional evidence that Paul's thorn in the flesh was defective eyesight.] **12 As many as desire to make a fair show in the flesh, they compel you to be circumcised; only that they may not be persecuted for the cross of Christ. 13 For not even they who receive circumcision do themselves keep the law; but they desire to have you circumcised, that they may glory in your flesh.** [In taking the pen in his own hand it was natural that he should show his earnestness in what he had dictated about circumcision and the Judaizers, tracing with his own fingers a line or two more on that subject. This, therefore, he does, telling them that all those who desire to make a fair show in the flesh, *i. e.*, to please men by complying with worldly demand, seek to compel them (the Galatians) to be circumcised. They did this for no zeal for circumcision, but in order to escape the persecution of their Jewish brethren for adherence to the doctrine of the cross. Moreover, these Judaizers who were thus urging circumcision did not do so from any zeal for the law, for they made no effort themselves to keep it, but they did it that they might boast to other strict and unconverted Jews how they were making Jews out of Gentile Christians. Thus their motives were not religious and holy, but base and selfish.] **14 But far be it from me to glory, save in the cross of our Lord Jesus Christ, through which the world hath been crucified unto me, and I unto the world.** [Let these glory if they will, in their wicked activity against the cross, but God forbid that I should glory save in that very cross against which they lift their hands, the cross by which the world has died to me, so that it no longer allures me with its false glories, or terrifies me with its frowns and threats; and by which I, in my turn, have died with Christ as to the world, so that I no longer enjoy or take part in its sinful lusts, and no longer rest under its sentence of condemnation.] **15 For neither is circumcision anything, nor uncircumcision, but a new creature.** [I glory in this cross of death from which I have been born again, a new creature in Christ, because, in this new dispensation of Christ's, former things have lost their value. As a Jew I once held myself superior to Gentiles, and despised them; and had I been of the Gentiles I would, no doubt, have looked at things from their standpoint, and so I should have looked with contempt upon the Jews; but in Christ I have died to all this worldly pride, for in his dispensation there is no advantage or profit in the circumcision which makes a Jew, or the lack of it which makes a Gentile. The whole profit lies in being born again from either of these states (John 3: 3) so as to become a child of grace, a recipient of justification, an heir of God.] **16 And as many as shall walk by this rule, peace** *be* **upon them, and mercy, and upon the Israel of God.** [Upon all who walk by the rule which I have just stated—the rule which rejects carnal ordinances, and accepts a regenerated life—upon them, even upon the Israel of God, be peace and mercy. The word translated "and" often means "even," and it has that force here, for it was Paul's constant contention that Christians were the true Israel of God, the *bone-fide* sons of Abraham.] **17 Henceforth let no man trouble me; for I bear branded on my body the marks of Jesus.** [We have here a figure taken from the life of a slave, who, in that day, was often branded with his master's name, so as to insure his recovery should he attempt to escape. Now, Paul had been troubled by the Judaizers, who asserted that he was teaching their doctrine, and was as they were (5: 10, 11). But this, in Paul's eyes, was an assertion that he was free from Christ (5: 4). Now, it troubled him to be thus accused of being no longer the servant of Christ, and, to silence such calumny, he appeals to the scars on his body, which showed that he was indeed the branded servant of Christ, and not a time-pleasing, persecution-evading (v. 12) servant of the world.] **18 The grace of our Lord Jesus Christ be with your spirit, brethren. Amen.** [The Epistle closes with a fraternal benediction, but the word of grace rests on the spirit of the Galatians, and not on their bodies. Blessing was to be found in rectitude of spirit, and not in fleshly righteousness ceremonially obtained through ordinances. We have no word of history which reveals to us the immediate effect of Paul's Epistle; but the fact that it was preserved argues that it was well received. Considering the vigor and power of it, it could not have been otherwise than effective. We may say, then, that it, with 2 Corinthians and Romans, were three blows which staggered Judaism, and restrained it, till smitten by the hand of God himself at the destruction of Jerusalem, A. D. 70, it ceased to trouble the church till its forms were again revived in the days of the great apostasy.]

EPISTLE TO THE ROMANS.

INTRODUCTION.

Paul had long wished to visit Rome, and to preach the gospel at this center and seat of earthly power and government. He wished to so dispose the church at Rome towards himself and his work that he might use it, in part at least, as a base for his operations in the regions of the far West (chap. 15: 24). But he had not been able as yet to visit Rome (chap. 1: 10-13); so, during his three months' stay in Corinth (Acts 20: 3), when he was gathering the offering for Judæa (chap. 15: 25, 26), apparently finding that Phœbe, a member of the near-by church at Cenchræa, the port of Corinth, was about to depart for Rome (chap. 16: 1, 2), he determined to improve the occasion by writing this Epistle, which would accomplish many of the purposes of a visit. The Epistle would forearm the disciples against the slanderous misrepresentations of his enemies, and would prepare them to be improved and benefited by his visit, for he still planned to visit them after going to Jerusalem (Acts 1: 21; 15: 23-28). The place, therefore, from which the Epistle was written, was Corinth; and the time, the early spring of A. D. 58; for it is a well-known fact that Paul left Corinth early enough to reach Jerusalem by Pentecost of that year (Acts 20: 16). The Epistle, then, was written when Paul was in the prime and vigor of his manhood, and when his activities in the ministry were most fully exercised, and when the new religion of Christ was assuming its supremacy over all known forms of worship. No wonder, therefore, that Paul produced on this occasion a letter which Coleridge has rightly described as "the most profound work in existence." As to the origin of the church to which he wrote, we have no data. It is evident from Paul's Epistle that, up to the time of writing it, he had never visited Rome, and this accords with the general trend of the Book of Acts, and the special statement of Acts 23: 11. Paul's silence as to Peter argues very strongly that that apostle also had not yet been in Rome—if he was ever there. Indeed, the silence of Scripture as to the origin of that church, if rightly considered, forbids the assumption that any of the apostles participated in the initial preaching at the great metropolis. Possibly pilgrims, converted at the ever memorable Pentecost, carried the gospel back with them, and sowed the first seed (Acts 2: 10). Or, those scattered by the persecutions which arose at the death of Stephen, and which raged subsequently in Judæa, may have eventually traveled as far as Rome, and preached the truth there. Or, more likely still, those who resorted to Rome in the ordinary way of travel or business may have founded this church, for it was afterwards filled with such sojourners, many of whom were Paul's friends, acquaintances and fellow-workers, as is shown by his salutations in the last chapter. But, however the church had started, it was now strong and influential and had a world-wide fame (chap. 1: 8). It is also apparent that while it contained, as did all the others, many Jews (chap. 16: 7, 11), the church was largely Gentile. This is obvious from the habitual tone of the Epistle (chaps. 1, 5, 6, 13, 14; 11: 13-24; 14: 1-15; 16: 3-27; and also from the narrative at Acts 28, especially verse 28). Had the Roman church been composed principally of Jews, the apostle to the Gentiles, while interested in it, would not likely have felt sufficiently responsible for it to have written to it when most of its members were strangers to him. His own words suggest so much (chap. 15: 14-16). Moreover, the teaching of the church would have been strongly Judaic if the Jews had preponderated; whereas it was unquestionably pronounced in its Pauline purity of doctrine (chap. 16: 17-20). While, therefore, this Epistle discusses the same general theme handled in the Epistle to the Galatians, it is didactic and not polemic in its style. Though Paul would not have written to strangers in the same tone that he employed in addressing his own erring, backsliding converts, yet he would certainly have employed a far different style than that which characterizes this Epistle, had Judaizers corrupted the church at Rome as they did those churches in

INTRODUCTION

Galatia and Corinth. The purpose of the Epistle, aside from that of preparing the church for his visit, is easily discovered. The Judaizing tendencies which had recently appeared in Corinth and Galatia were sure eventually to appear in other churches, perhaps ultimately in all, and the attitude assumed by a church already so influential and destined to increase in power was sure to carry great weight in deciding the controversy. Therefore, to set the church of Rome right as to the design and nature of the gospel was a work of supreme importance, and the great letter from the great apostle to the great church on the question of the hour would be read with interest and profit by the entire brotherhood. The purpose of the letter is to set forth, as Baur rightly expresses it, "both the relation of Judaism and heathenism to each other, and the relation of both to Christianity;" primarily, for the instruction of the Christians in Rome, and, secondarily, for the benefit of all the churches by the establishment of peace between their Jewish and Gentile elements, and, ultimately, for the enlightening of the kingdom of God in all ages. Paul's Jewish enemies had, as we have seen, already been busy in slandering and misrepresenting him even in churches which he had founded. They made the apostle feel the limitation of travel, and, no doubt, caused him to desire that he might multiply himself, so as to be in many places at once. Within a few days after this Epistle was written Paul began that journey wherein it was testified to him in every city he passed through that bonds and imprisonment awaited him in Jerusalem; so it is highly probable that he already had a prophetic premonition of his coming temporary inability to visit the churches and correct, by his presence, as at Corinth, the falsehood circulated in his absence. Therefore, to establish the churches in the truth, and to preserve his own salutary influence over them, how needful it was that he have an Epistle to speak for him in those coming days of confinement, and that his friends have in their possession his true preaching, that they might have "wherewith to answer them" who misrepresented him and his teaching. And of all Epistles, which could better serve his purpose than one addressed to the

Romans, who were at the center of all earthly influences? That the Epistle is authentic is conceded even by Baur. It was quoted by Clement of Rome before the end of the first century; and in the second century by Ignatius, Polycarp, Justin Martyr and Irenæus; and the Muratorian Fragment, A. D. 170, places it in the catalogue of Paul's Epistles. Its genuineness, too, is practically universally conceded, save that the Tubingen critics, with their usual zeal and eagerness to cast doubt upon any portion of the Scripture, have questioned the last two chapters, or rejected them. The reasons for doing this are not weighty. The chapters are called in question, not because they are omitted from any manuscripts now known, but from certain that are mentioned by the Fathers. But those who tell us of these mutilated copies (Tertullian, and especially Origen) also inform us that that arch-heretic, Marcion, was the offender who thus abbreviated them, and that he did so for the reason that he found in them passages which he wished to suppress because they conflicted with his own erroneous teaching. Surely the knife of Marcion should cast no more doubt over the Epistle of Paul than that of Jehoiakim did over the writings of Jeremiah. As a simple analysis of the book, we submit the following:

PART I. DOCTRINAL. *The universal need of righteousness satisfied by the gospel, as is shown by the manifold results emanating from gospel righteousness and justification* (1: 1-8: 39). SUBDIVISION A. *Introductory.* Salutation and personal explanation (1: 1-15). Righteousness by the gospel (1: 16, 17). SUBDIVISION B. *Universal need of righteousness.* Need of righteousness by the Gentiles (1: 18-32). Need of righteousness by the Jews (2: 1-29). Jewish privilege does not diminish guilt, and the Scriptures include both Jew and Gentile alike under sin (3: 1-20). SUBDIVISION C. *Universal need of righteousness satisfied by the gospel proclamation of righteousness by faith.* Neither Jew nor Greek can obtain righteousness otherwise than by the gospel (3: 21-31). The gospel method of justification, exemplified in the cases of Abraham and David, must be applied both to the legal and spiritual seed of Abraham (4: 1-25). SUBDIVISION D. *Results of Christ's life discussed, and shown to be capable of as limitless universality as the results of Adam's life.* Results of the justification wrought by Christ, viz.: peace, hope, love and reconciliation (5: 1-11). Adam, the trespasser unto death, contrasted with Christ, the righteous unto life (5: 12-21). SUBDIVISION E. *Sanctification of the believer required, and obtained in change of relationship by the gospel.* Justification is brought about by such a relation to Christ as creates an obligation to be dead to sin and alive to righteousness, as is symbolically shown by baptism (6: 1-14). Justification results in a change from service of law and sin, with death as a reward, to the service of grace and righteousness, with life as a reward (6: 15-22). Change of relationship from law to Christ illustrated (7: 1-6). The sense of bondage which comes through the relationship of the law prepares the soul to seek deliverance through relationship to Christ (7: 7-25). The new relationship to Christ changes the mind from carnal to spiritual, so that we escape condemnation and obtain life (8: 1-11). The new relationship to Christ results in adoption, the spirit of adoption, and that heirship for the revelation of which creation groans (8: 12-25). The new relationship results in the aid of the Spirit, and the blissful assurance of salvation, because it is divinely decreed (8: 26-39).

PART II. EXPLANATORY. *The doctrine of righteousness by faith reconciled to* · (:) *the promises made to Israel;* (2) *the election of that people, and* (3) *the faithfulness of God* (9: 1-11: 36). Mourning for Israel (9: 1-15). The rejection of Israel not inconsistent with God's promise, which has been kept to those to whom it was given (9: 6-13). The rejection of Israel not inconsistent with the justice of God (9: 14-18). God's absolute power asserted, his justice and mercy vindicated, and his course in rejecting the Jews not inconsistent with prophecy (9: 19-29). Gentiles following the law of faith contrasted with Jews following the law of works (9: 30-33). Jews responsible for their rejection, since they had an equal chance with the Gentiles of being accepted (10: 1-13). Righteousness comes by faith, and faith comes by that hearing as to which Jews and Gentiles had equal opportunity (10: 14-21). The casting-off of Israel not so complete as supposed, a remnant being saved by faith (11: 1-10). Salutary results of the temporary fall and future rise of Israel. Gentiles warned not to glory over Israel (11: 11-24). Jews and Gentiles having each passed through a like season of disobedience, a like mercy shall be shown to each (11: 25-32). Ascriptions of praise to God for his ways and judgment (11: 3-36).

PART III. HORTATORY. *Various duties enjoined, and mutual toleration enforced* (12: 1-14: 23). Self-dedication besought, and self-conceit discouraged (12: 1-8). A galaxy of virtues (12: 21). Concerning governments, love and approaching salvation (13: 1-14). Forbearance towards scruples, refraining from judging, sacrifice for others (14: 1-23).

PART IV. SUPPLEMENTARY. *Concluding exhortations and salutations* (15: 1-16: 27). Exhortations to mutual helpfulness. The Gentiles to glorify God (15: 1-13). The apostle's ministry and plans. Request for prayers (15: 14-33). Commendation of Phœbe. Salutations. Warnings against dissension and apostasy. Benediction (16: 1-25).

PART FIRST.

DOCTRINAL: THE UNIVERSAL NEED OF RIGHTEOUSNESS SATISFIED BY THE GOSPEL, AS IS SHOWN BY THE MANIFOLD RESULTS EMANATING FROM GOSPEL RIGHTEOUSNESS AND JUSTIFICATION.

1: 1-8: 3.

Subdivision A.

INTRODUCTORY.

1: 1-17.

I.

SALUTATION AND PERSONAL EXPLANATIONS.

1: 1-15.

1 Paul, a servant of Jesus Christ, called *to be* an apostle, separated unto the gospel of God, 2 which he promised afore through his prophets in the holy scriptures, 3 concerning his Son, who was born of the seed of David according to the flesh, 4 who was declared *to be* the Son of God with power, according to the spirit of holiness, by the resurrection from the dead; *even* Jesus Christ our Lord 5 through whom we received grace and apostleship, unto obedience of faith among all the nations, for his name's sake; 6 among whom are ye also, called *to be* Jesus Christ's: 7 to all that are in Rome, beloved of God, called *to be* saints: Grace to you and peace from God our Father and the Lord Jesus Christ. [The apostle opens his Epistle with one of his characteristic sentences: long and intricate, yet wonderful in its condensation and comprehensive-

ness; his style of expression being, as Tholuck says, "most aptly compared to a throng of waves, where, in ever loftier swell, one billow presses close upon the other." The opening here may be compared with that at Gal. 1: 1-5. Taken without its qualifying clauses, the sentence runs thus: "Paul to all that are at Rome: Grace to you and peace from God our Father and the Lord Jesus Christ." (Comp. Acts 23: 26.) This sentence the apostle enlarges by three series of statements which lead up to each other, and the items of which also introduce each other, thus forming a closely connected chain of thought. First, by statements about *himself*, which assert that he, Paul, is an apostle, separated from worldly occupations, and sent out to preach the *gospel* (Gal. 1: 15; Acts 9: 15; 22: 14, 15); second, by statements about the *gospel*, viz.: that it had its source of origin in God, that it was no innovation, being promised long beforehand through the prophets in the Holy Scriptures (comp. Acts 26: 22; see Mic. 4: 2; Isa. 40: 9; 52: 7; Nah. 1: 15); that it concerned *God's Son;* third, by statements about *God's Son*, viz.: that according to the flesh (*i. e.*, as to his human or fleshly nature) he was born (in the weakness of a child), and thus came into being as a descendant of David (which was required by prophecy—Ps. 89: 36; 132: 11, 12; Jer. 23: 5); that according to the spirit of purity or holiness (*i. e.*, as to his spiritual or divine nature, which, though a Sonship, was birthless, and hence did *not* come into being, but existed from the beginning) he was pointed out, declared or demonstrated to be the Son of God with power; which power manifested itself by triumphing over death in his resurrection (Ps. 7: 2; 16: 10. Comp. 2 Tim. 2: 8; Acts 12: 23, 30); and that the Son of God is *Jesus Christ our Lord.* Thus Paul's thought completes its circle, and comes back again to *himself* and his *apostleship*, and introduces the second series of statements, which are about himself and his apostleship in this gospel of the Son of God: First, that through this *Jesus Christ our Lord* he had received grace (*i. e.*, forgiveness, reconciliation, salvation, and all the other blessings which the gospel bestows), and the apostleship of which he has spoken; and that the aim of

PERSONAL EXPLANATIONS 297

that apostleship, or the purpose for which he was sent, is (1) to produce among all nations, *i. e.*, the *Gentiles*, that obedience to the will of God which results from faith, or belief, in Jesus Christ, and (2) to glorify or exalt the name of Jesus Christ by promoting this obedience, etc. (Acts 9: 15); (the majesty, dignity and authority of the apostleship are emphasized by the Lordship of him who gave it, by the world-wide scope of it and the glorious purpose of it); second, that his apostleship embraced those to whom he wrote, since they were also *Gentiles*, who had been called into this faith which made them Christ's. And here the second series leads to the third, and Paul now addresses the Roman Christians, to whom he writes, and states that they are: (1) the object of God's love, and (2) called to that obedience of faith which separates from sin and makes holy. Thus, step by step, Paul explains as to *what gospel* he is an apostle, as *to whom* his gospel relates, *from whom* he received his apostleship, for what *purpose* he had received it, what *right* it gave him to indite this letter, and *to whom* the letter was addressed. So much for the paragraph as a whole. Looking over its items, we may remark that: the term "servant" employed by Paul applied to all Christians generally (1 Cor. 7: 22; Eph. 6: 6); but the apostles loved to appropriate it, as expressing their entire devotion to Christ and his people, and lack of all official pride (Jas. 1: 1; 2 Pet. 1: 1; Jude 1; Rev. 1: 1). The phrase "spirit of holiness" is equivalent to Holy Spirit. It serves to show that Jesus had the same divine nature as the Holy Spirit, yet does not confuse the two personalities, so as to lose our Lord's identity. The resurrection of our Lord differed from all other resurrections in several important respects, each of which aided to reveal his divinity: (1) The prophets announced it beforehand (Ps. 16: 10, 11). (2) He himself announced it beforehand (Matt. 16: 21). (3) The power which raised him was not external to him, but within him (John 2: 19; 10: 17, 18). (4) It was a representative and all-inclusive resurrection (1 Cor. 15: 22). (5) It was not a temporary restoration, like the cases of Lazarus and others who returned once more to the grave, but an eternal triumph over death (6:

9; Rev. 1: 18). (6) It was the firstfruits of a like immortality for all those who, being part of the mystical body of Christ, shall be raised with him at the last day (1 Cor. 15: 23-26). Lard, in his comments on this paragraph, calls attention to the fact that *faith* and *belief* are absolutely synonymous, for the two words in our English Bible are represented by one single substantive in the Greek text, viz.: *pistis*, which is derived from the verb *pisteuoo*, which is uniformly translated "believe." An endless amount of theological discussion and mystical preaching would have been avoided if our translators had not given us two words where one would have sufficed. Having in his opening address shown that he had an *official* right to write to the church at Rome, the apostle next reveals to them that he has an additional right to do so because of his *interest* in them and *affection* for them, which is manifested by his thanksgivings, prayers, etc.] **8 First** [*i. e.*, before I proceed to other matters, I wish you to know that], **I thank my God through Jesus Christ for you all, that your faith is proclaimed throughout the whole world.** [Through the mediation of Christ (comp. Heb. 13: 15; 2 Pet. 2: 5; Col. 3: 17; Eph. 5: 20) Paul offers thanks on account of the Christians at Rome, because their faith had so openly and notoriously changed their lives from sin to righteousness that, wherever the apostle went, he found the churches in the whole Roman world, which then embraced western Asia, northern Africa and almost the whole of Europe, took notice of it. The apostle realized the incalculable good which would result from the proper enthronement of Christ in so important a center as Rome, and in view of its future effects on the world, its present influence over the church, its tendency to lighten and facilitate his own labors, and many like blessings and benefits, Paul thanks God that his enthronement had taken place in the loyal heart of those whom he addresses. He refers to the knowledge of believers, for the church was comparatively unknown to unbelievers, even in the city itself—Acts 28: 22.] **9 For God is my witness, whom I serve in my spirit in the gospel of his Son, how unceasingly I make mention of you, always in my pray-**

PERSONAL EXPLANATIONS

ers 10 making request, if by any means now at length I may be prospered by the will of God to come unto you. [Since he could call no other witness as to the substance or contents of his secret prayers, he reverently appeals to God to verify his words, that he had continually remembered the Romans in his petitions, and had requested that, having been so long denied it, the privilege of visiting the church at Rome might now at last be granted to him. Paul's appeals to God to verify his words are quite common (2 Cor. 1: 23; 11: 31; Gal. 1: 20, etc.). He describes God as one whom he serves not only outwardly but inwardly, publishing the gospel of his Son with hearty zeal, devotion and joy. He had traveled widely and constantly; his failure, therefore, to visit Rome might look like indifference, and his impending departure from Corinth, not toward Rome, which was now comparatively near, but in the opposite direction, might suggest that he was ashamed to appear or preach in the imperial city. The apostle replies to all this by simply stating, and asking God to verify the statement, that God had not yet prospered him in his plans or efforts to go to Rome.] **11 For I long to see you, that I may impart unto you some spiritual gift, to the end ye may be established; 12 that is, that I with you may be comforted in you, each of us by the other's faith, both yours and mine.** [Paul here sets forth the reason why he so earnestly desired to visit the church at Rome; it was because he wished to enjoy the blessedness both of giving and receiving. Spiritual gifts are those wrought by the Holy Spirit, and of these Paul had two kinds to bestow: 1, extraordinary or miraculous, and 2, ordinary, or those pertaining to the Christian graces. No doubt he had the bestowal of both of these gifts in mind, for no apostle had yet visited the church to bestow the former, and, from the list of gifts recorded at 12: 6-8, it appears that that of prophecy was the only miraculous one they possessed; and the context, especially verse 12, indicates that the latter, or ordinary gifts, were also in his thoughts. Because their faiths were essentially the same, Paul here acknowledges the ability of all disciples, even the humblest, to comfort, *i. e.*, to encourage and help him by a strengthening of his faith; because their steadfastness would react on him. Gifts, whether of a miraculous nature, or merely graces, tended to establish or strengthen the church.] **13 And I would not have you ignorant, brethren, that oftentimes I purposed to come unto you (and was hindered hitherto), that I might have some fruit in you also, even as in the rest of the Gentiles.** [He had desired to visit Rome that he might glorify Christ by making many converts in Rome (John 15: 8, 16), just as he had in other Gentile cities. "That," says Meyer, "by which Paul had been hitherto hindered, may be seen at 15: 22; consequently it was neither the devil (1 Thess. 2: 18), nor the Holy Spirit (Acts 16: 6). Grotius aptly observes: "The great needs of the localities in which Christ was unknown constrained him." But the word at 15: 22, and also at 1 Thess. 2: 18, is *egkoptoo*, and the word here, and at Acts 16: 6, is *kooluoo*, which, primarily, means *to forbid*, and implies the exercise of a superior will. The whole context here indicates that the divine will restrained Paul from going to Rome, and this in no way conflicts with the statement that the needs of the mission fields hindered him. God's will forbade, and the needs co-operated to restrain; just as in the instance in Acts, the Holy Spirit forbade to go any way save toward Europe, and the visionary cry from Europe drew onward. Two causes may conspire to produce one effect. Paul's entire will was subject to the will of Christ. As a free man he formed his plans and purposes, but he always altered them to suit the divine pleasure. **14 I am debtor both to Greeks and to Barbarians** [foreigners, those who did not speak the Greek language], **both to the wise and to the foolish. 15 So, as much as in me is, I am ready to preach the gospel to you also that are in Rome.** [Paul's knowledge of the good news, and his apostleship as to it, laid upon him the sacred obligation to tell it to all who had not heard it (1 Cor. 9: 16-19). His commission as apostle to the Gentiles sent him to both Greeks and Barbarians, the two classes into which the Gentiles were divided; and left him no right to discriminate between the cultured and the ignorant. Moved by a desire to pay this debt, he was ready, so far as the direction of his affairs lay in his own power of choice, to preach to the Romans, who held no mean place among the Gentiles.]

II.

RIGHTEOUSNESS BY THE GOSPEL.

1: 16, 17.

16 For I am not ashamed of the gospel: for it is the power of God unto salvation to every one that believeth; to the Jew first, and also to the Greek. 17 For therein is revealed a righteousness of God from faith unto faith: as it is written [Hab. 2: 4], But the righteous shall live by faith. [This paragraph has been rightly called the "Theme" of the Epistle, for all from 1: 19 to 11: 36 is but an expansion of this section. Since, therefore, its meaning determines the gist of the entire Epistle, it is not to be wondered at that commentators and theologians have made it a royal battleground. Limitations of space forbid us to even give an outline of these controversies. We content ourselves with the following paraphrase, which, we think, makes plain the apostle's meaning: I am ready to preach in your imperial city, for even there, where things of such magnitude transpire that all things else seem small by comparison, I should not be ashamed of the gospel. Among the Greeks, who prided themselves on their wisdom, my gospel was demonstrated to be the superior wisdom of God (1 Cor. 1: 30; 2: 7); and so I would come among you Romans, who compare all things with your imperial power, and I would show that I had no reason to be ashamed, for I would declare or publish unto you that gospel which is the power of God in the all-important and incomparable work of saving men, all of whom are lost in sin, and any of whom can be saved when he believes this gospel, whether he be one of God's chosen people, who have the first right to hear it, or a Gentile. It is God's power unto salvation, for it brings sinful men a righteousness which emanates from God, and which he

freely gives to believers, so that they are accounted righteous, and this righteousness, from first to last, is altogether bestowed upon faith, so that whatever righteousness a man has comes by faith, just as it was predicted in the Old Testament, for God there says: The man who is declared righteous lives by faith; *i. e.*, if his righteousness redeems him from sin and death and so entitles him to live, it does so because it is a righteousness obtained by faith.]

Subdivision B.
UNIVERSAL NEED OF RIGHTEOUSNESS.
1: 18-3: 20.

I.
NEED OF RIGHTEOUSNESS BY THE GENTILES.
1: 18-32.

18 For the wrath of God is revealed from heaven against all ungodliness and unrighteousness of men, who hinder the truth in unrighteousness ["For" is intended to introduce a direct proof as to the statement in verse 17, thus: The righteousness of God of which the apostle has been speaking is revealed to a man by his faith; *i. e.*, it is seen only by the believing, for all that others see revealed towards man's unrighteousness is wrath. In other words, only God's gospel reveals this righteousness, and it is addressed to and received by faith. God's other revelations seen in nature reveal no pardoning, justifying grace; but show, in the visitations of terrible judgments, retributions, punitive corrections, deaths, etc., that God pours out the fruits of his displeasure on the wickedness of men, whether it be sin against himself (ungodliness), or sin against the laws and precepts which he has given (unrighteousness), either sin being a stifling of the truth which they knew about God, by willful indulgences in unrighteousness. The apostle is here speaking of the Gentiles; he discusses the case of the Jews separately later on. The precepts, truth, etc., to which he refers are, therefore, not those found in the Old Testament Scriptures, which were known to the *Jews;* but those which were traditionally handed down by and among the *heathen* from the patriarchal days. "All the light," as Poole says, " which was left in man since the fall "] ; **19 because that which is known of God is manifest in them; for God manifested it unto them. 20 For the invisible things of him since the creation of the world are clearly seen, being perceived through the things that are made, *even* his everlasting power and divinity; that they may be without excuse** [and God reveals his wrath against them, because that which is known of God, *i. e.*, the general truths as to his nature and attributes, is manifested unto them ; for God himself so manifested it, causing his invisible attributes, even his power, divinity, etc., to be constantly and clearly revealed in the providential working of nature from the hour of creation's beginning, until now, that they may be without excuse for sin, and so justly punishable] : **21 because that, knowing God, they glorified him not as God, neither gave thanks ; but became vain in their reasonings, and their senseless heart was darkened.** [And they were without excuse, for when they knew God they did not worship him according to the knowledge which they had, nor did they praise him for his benefits; but they erred in their mind, thus making their whole inner man senseless and dark, not having the light of truth with which they started. The phrase, "vain in their reasonings," means that their corrupt lives corrupted their minds, for, as Tholuck observes, "religious and moral error is always the consequence of religious and moral perversity." As Calvin expresses it: "They quickly choked by their own depravity the seed of right knowledge before it grew to ripeness."] **22 Professing themselves to be wise, they became fools, 23 and changed the glory of the incorruptible God for the likeness of an image of corruptible man, and of birds, and four-footed beasts, and creeping things.** [Vaunting their wisdom, these wicked ones made fools of themselves, so that they exchanged the glory of the immortal God for the likeness of an image of mortal man, or even images of baser things, as birds, beasts and reptiles. The audacity of the attempt to reason God out of existence has invariably turned the brain of man (Ps. 53: 1), and the excess of self-conceit and vanity developed by such an undertaking has uniformly resulted in pitiable folly. In the case of the ancients it led to idolatry. Reiche contended that idolatry preceded monotheism, and that the better was developed out of the worse; but history sustains Paul in presenting idolatry as a decline from a purer form of worship. "For," says Meyer, "heathenism is not the primeval religion, from which man might gradually have risen to the true knowledge of the wisdom of God, but is, on the contrary, the result of a falling away from the known original revelation of the true God in his works." Paul does not say that they exchanged the "form" of God for that of an idol, for God is sensuously perceived as glory, or *shekinah*, rather than as form. Hence, Moses asked to see, not the form, but the glory of God (Ex. 33: 18-22). The Greeks and Romans preferred the human form as the model for their idols, but the Egyptians chose the baser, doubtless because, having been longer engaged in the practice of idolatry, their system was more fully developed in degradation. The ibis, the bull, the serpent and the crocodile of the Egyptians give us the complements of Paul's catalogue. Schaff sees in the phrase "likeness of an image" a double meaning, and interprets it thus: "The expression refers both to the grosser and the more refined forms of idolatry; common people saw in the idols the gods themselves; the cultivated heathen regarded them as symbolical representations."] **24 Wherefore God gave them up in the lusts of their hearts unto uncleanness, that their bodies should be dishonored among themselves: 25 for that they exchanged the truth of God for a lie, and worshipped and served the creature rather than the Creator, who is blessed for ever. Amen.** [Wherefore, finding them living in lust, God ceased to restrain or protect them from evil (Gen. 6: 3), and abandoned them to the uncleanness toward which their lust incited them, that they might dishonor their bodies among themselves to the limit of their lustfulness, as a punishment for dishonoring and abandoning him. He did this because they had exchanged the truth of God (which from the start they had hindered in unrighteousness, vs. 18), *i. e.*, the truth respecting God and his law and worship, for the sham of idolatry and the false worship pertaining thereto, and because they had given to the creature that inward reverence and outward service which was due to the Creator, thus preferring the creature to the Creator, who is blessed for ever. Amen. "'Blessed' is not the word signifying happy, rendered blessed in Matt. 5: 3-11 ; 1 Tim. 1: 11 ; 6: 15 ; but the word signifying praised, adored, extolled ; *i. e.*, worthy to be praised, etc. In the New Testament this word is applied to none but to God only ; though the cognate verb is used to express the good wishes and hearty prayers of one creature for another, as well as praise to God—comp. Heb. 11: 20, 21 ; Jas. 3: 9"—*Plumer.*] **26 For this cause God gave them up unto vile passions: for their women changed the natural use into that which is against nature: 27 and likewise also the men, leaving the natural use of the woman, burned in their lust one toward another, men with men working unseemliness, and receiving in themselves that recompense of their error which was due.** [In this horrible picture Paul shows in what way they dishonored themselves among themselves. The sin of sodomy was common among idolaters. The apostle tells us that this depth of depravity was a just punishment for their departure from God. Petronius, Suetonius, Martial, Seneca, Virgil, Juvenal, Lucian and other classic writers verify the statements of Paul. Some of their testimonies will be found in Macknight, Stuart and other larger commentaries.] **28 And even as they refused** [did not deem it worthy of their mind] **to have God in** *their* **knowledge, God gave them up unto a reprobate mind** [*i. e.*, minds rejected in turn by God as unworthy], **to do those things which are not fitting** [indecent, immoral]; **29 being filled with all unrighteousness, wickedness, covetousness** [inordinate desire to accumulate property regardless of the rights of others: a sin which is not condemned by the laws of any country on the globe, and which is the source of universal unrest in all nations], **maliciousness** [a readiness to commit crime without provocation, a chronic state of illwill and misanthropy]; **full of envy, murder, strife, deceit, malignity; whisperers** [talebearers, those who slander covertly, chiefly by insinuation—Prov. 16: 28], **30 backbiters** [outspoken slanderers], **hateful to God** [many contend that this should read "haters of God," since Paul is enumerating the vices of men, and not God's attitude toward them. Others, following the reading in the text, see in these words what Meyer calls "a resting-point in the disgraceful catalogue"— a place where Paul pauses to reveal God's moral indignation toward the crimes particularized. But Alford takes the words in a colloquial sense as describing the political informers of that period. "If," says he, "any crime was known more than another, as 'hated by the God,' it was that of informers, abandoned persons who circumvented and ruined others by a system of malignant espionage and false information," though he does not confine the term wholly to that class], **insolent, haughty, boastful** [these three words describe the various phases of self-exultation, which, a sin in all ages, was at that time indulged in to the extent of blasphemy, for Cicero, Juvenal and Horace all claim that virtue is from man himself, and not from God], **inventors of evil things** [inventors of new methods of evading laws, schemers who discover new ways by which to unjustly accumulate property, discoverers of new forms of sensuous, lustful gratification, etc.], **disobedient to parents, 31 without understanding** [those who have so long seared their consciences as to be unable to determine between right and wrong even in plain cases. The loss of moral understanding is very apparent among habitual liars, whose minds have become so accustomed to falsehood that they are no longer able to discern the truth so as to accurately state it], **covenant-breakers** [those who fail to keep their promises and agreements], **without natural affection** [those having an abnormal lack of love towards parents, children, kindred, etc.], **unmerciful: 32** who, knowing the ordinance of God, that they that practise such things are worthy of death, not only do the same, but also consent with them that practise them. [All were not guilty of all these sins, but each was guilty of some of them. Though many of these evils still exist in Christian lands, they do so *in spite of* Christianity; but then they existed *because of* idolatry. Lard observes that the Gentiles, starting with the knowledge of God, descended to the foolishness of idolatry. At this point God abandoned them, and they then began their second descent, and continued till they reached the very base and bottom of moral degradation, as indicated in the details given above. The Gentiles had traditions and laws, founded on original revelations, declaring these things sinful; and, though they knew that death resulted from sin, yet they not only defied God and persisted in their sins, but even failed to condemn them in others; yea, they encouraged each other to commit them. Such, then, was the helpless, hopeless state of the Gentiles. When they were justly condemned to death for unrighteousness, God revealed in his gospel a righteousness unto life that they might be saved.]

II.

NEED OF RIGHTEOUSNESS BY THE JEWS.

2: 1-29.

1 **Wherefore thou art without excuse, O man, whosoever thou art that judgest: for wherein thou judgest another, thou condemnest thyself; for thou that judgest dost practise the same thing.** [The apostle, it will be remembered, is proving the universal insufficiency of *human* righteousness, that he may show the universal need of a *revealed* righteousness. Having made good his case against one part of the human race—the Gentiles, he now proceeds to a like proof against the other part—the Jews. He does not name them as Jews at the start, for this would put them on the defensive, and made his task harder. He speaks to them first as individuals,

without any reference to race, for the Jew idolized his race, and would readily admit a defect in himself which he would have denied in his race. But Paul, by thus convicting each of sin in his own conscience, makes them all unwittingly concede sin in all, even though Jews. It was the well-known characteristic of the Jews to indulge in pharisaical judgment and condemnation of others (Matt. 7: 1 ; Luke 18: 14), especially the Gentiles (Acts 11: 3 ; Gal. 2: 15). The apostle knew, therefore, that his Jewish readers would be listening with gloating elation to this his castigation of the Gentiles, and so, even in this their moment of supreme self-complacency, he turns his lash upon them, boldly accusing them of having committed some of the things which they condemned, and, hence, of being in the same general state of unrighteousness, though, perhaps, on a somewhat less degraded plane. To condemn another for his sin is to admit that the sin in question leads to and justifies condemnation as to all who commit it, even including self. The thought of this verse is, as indicated by its opening "Wherefore," closely connected with the preceding chapter, and seems to form a climax, thus: The simple sinner is bad, the encourager of sin in others is worse, but the one who condemns sins in others, yet commits them himself, is absolutely defenseless and without excuse. Whitby has collected from Josephus the passages which show that Paul's arraignment of the Jews is amply justifiable.] **2 And we know that the judgment of God is according to truth against them that practise such things. 3 And reckonest thou this, O man, who judgest them that practise such things, and doest the same, that thou shalt escape the judgment of God?** [The argument may be paraphrased thus: Yielding to the force of argument, that like sin deserves like condemnation, even you, though most unwillingly, condemn yourself. How much more freely, therefore, will God condemn you (1 John 3: 20). And we know that you can not escape, for the judgment of God is according to truth; *i. e.*, without error or partiality against the doers of evil. And do you vainly imagine, O man, that when thine own moral sense

RIGHTEOUSNESS BY THE JEWS

is so outraged at evil that thou must needs condemn others for doing it, that thou, though doing the same evil thyself, shalt escape the judgment of God through any partiality on his part? Self-love, self-pity, self-justification, and kindred feeling, have, in all ages, caused men to err in applying the warnings of God to themselves. Among the Jews this error took the form of a doctrine. Finding themselves especially favored and privileged as children of Abraham, they expected to be judged upon different principles from those of truth, which would govern the judgment and condemnation of the rest of mankind. This false trust is briefly announced and rebuked by John the Baptist (Matt. 3: 7-9), and afterwards more clearly and fully defined in the Talmud in such expressions as these : " Every one circumcised has part in the kingdom to come." "All Israelites will have part in the world to come." "Abraham sits beside the gates of hell, and does not permit any wicked Israelite to go down to hell." The same error exists to-day in a modified form. Many expect to be saved because they are the children of wealth, culture, refinement; because they belong to a civilized people ; because their parents are godly ; or even, in some cases, because they belong to a certain lodge, or order.] **4 Or despisest thou the riches of his goodness and forbearance and longsuffering, not knowing that the goodness of God leadeth thee to repentance? 5 but after thy hardness and impenitent heart treasurest up for thyself wrath in the day of wrath and revelation of the righteous judgment of God ; 6 who will render to every man according to his works** [The apostle here touches upon a second error which is still common among men. It is, as Cook says, that "vague and undefined hope of impunity which they do not acknowledge even to themselves." God's present economy, which sends rain upon the just and the unjust, and which postpones the day of punishment to allow opportunity for repentance, leads untold numbers to the false conclusion that God is slack as to his judgment, and that he will ever be so. They mistake for indifference or weakness that longsuffering gràce of his which exercises patience, hoping that he may thereby lead men to repentance (2 Pet. 3: 9). Those who, by hardness of heart, steel themselves against repentance, thereby accumulate punishments which will be inflicted upon them in the day when God reveals that righteous judgment which has been so long withheld or suspended, for God is righteous, and he will render to every man in that day according to his works, after the following described manner]: **7 to them that by patience in well-doing seek for glory and honor and incorruption, eternal life: 8 but unto them that are factious, and obey not the truth, but obey unrighteousness,** *shall be* **wrath and indignation** [to those who, by steadfastly leading a life of work (which, as Olshausen observes, no man can do, according to Paul, save by faith in Christ), seek for glory (and the future state is one of unparalleled grandeur—John 17: 24; Rev. 21: 24), honor (and the future state is an honor; bestowed, though unmerited, as a reward—Matt. 25: 23, 40) and incorruption (which is also a prime distinction between the future and the present life—1 Cor. 15: 42), eternal life shall be given. But God's wrath and indignation shall be poured upon those who serve party and not God (and the Jews were continually doing this—Matt. 23: 15; Gal. 6: 12, 13), and obey not the truth (John 8: 31, 32), but obey unrighteousness], **9 tribulation and anguish, upon every soul of man that worketh evil, of the Jew first, and also of the Greek; 10 but glory and honor and peace to every man that worketh good, to the Jew first, and also to the Greek: 11 for there is no respect of persons with God.** [Paul here reiterates the two phases of God's judgment which he has just described. He does this to emphasize their *universality*—that they are upon every man, regardless of race. The punishment shall come upon Jew and Gentile alike; but the Jew, because of pre-eminence in privilege, shall have pre-eminence in suffering (Luke 12: 47, 48). The blessings also shall be received alike, but here also the Jew, having improved his privileges, and having more pounds to start with (Luke 19: 16-19), shall have pre-eminence in reward in as far as he has attained pre-eminence in life; for there is no unfair partiality or unjust favoritism with God. The man born in a Christian home stands to-day in the category then occupied by the Jew. He will be given greater reward or greater punishment according to his use or abuse of privilege.] **12 For as many as have sinned without the law** [Gentiles] **shall also perish without the law** [*i. e.*, without being judged by the expressed terms of the law]: **and as many as have sinned under the law** [the Jews] **shall be judged by the law** [*i. e.*, his conduct shall be weighed by the terms of it, and his punishment shall be according to its directions. Thus the Gentiles, having the lesser light of nature, and the Jews, having the greater light of revelation, were alike sinners. By his altars, sacrifices, etc., the Gentile showed that nature's law smote his conscience as truly as the clear, expressed letter of the Mosaic precept condemned the Jew. Thus both Jew and Gentile were condemned to perish; *i. e.*, to receive the opposite of salvation, as outlined in verse 7]; **13 for not the hearers of the law are just before God, but the doers of the law shall be justified** [Of course, the Jew had a great advantage over the Gentile in that he possessed the law—Paul himself concedes this (3: 1, 2); but this mere possession of the law, and this privilege of hearing and knowing the will of God, by no means justified the sinner. Jews and Gentiles alike had to seek justification through perfect obedience to their respective laws, and no one of either class had ever been able to render such obedience. The Jew had the advantage of the Gentile in that he had a clear knowledge of the Lord's will, and a fair warning of the dire consequences of disobedience. The Gentile, however, had advantages which offset those of the Jews, thus making the judgments of God wholly impartial. If the law which directed him was less clear, it was also less onerous. In a parenthesis the apostle now sets forth the nature of the law under which the Gentiles lived; he evidently does this that he may meet a supposed Jewish objection, as though some one said, "Since what you say applies to those who have a divine law given to them, it can not apply to the Gentiles, since they possess no law at all." It is to this anticipated objection that Paul replies]; **14 (for when Gentiles that have not the law do by nature the things of the law, these, not having the law, are the law unto themselves; 15 in that they show the work of the law written in their hearts, their conscience bearing witness therewith, and their thoughts one with another accusing or else excusing** *them*) [The meaning here may be quickly grasped in the following paraphrase: Jews and Gentiles are alike sinners, yet each had a chance to attain legal justification; the former by keeping an outwardly revealed law, the latter by obeying an inwardly revealed one. Now, the Gentiles have such a law, as appears from their general moral conduct; for when those who do not have the law of Moses, do, by their own inward, natural promptings, the things prescribed by the law of Moses, they are a law unto themselves, having in themselves the threefold workings of law, in that the guidance of their heart predisposes them to know the right, the testimony of their conscience bears witness with their heart that the right is preferable, and lastly, after the deed is done, their thoughts or inward reasonings accuse or excuse them according as their act has been wrong or right. These well-known psychological phenomena, observable among the Gentiles, are proof conclusive that they are not without law, with its power and privilege of justification. Therefore, all are not sinners because there is respect of persons with God, for all have the possibility of attaining justification]; **16 in the day when God shall judge the secrets of men, according to my gospel, by Jesus Christ.** [This verse relates to the thought interrupted by the parenthesis; *i. e.*, the thought of verse 13. Not hearers, but doers, shall be justified in the judgment-day, that day when God shall judge the secrets of men's lives and judge them, as my gospel further reveals, through Jesus Christ as Judge. The Jewish Scriptures revealed a judgment-day, and the thought was not unfamiliar to the Gentiles; but it remained for Paul's gospel to reveal the new truth that Jesus was to be the Judge. Paul started with the thought that, in judging another, a sinner condemned himself (v. 1: 3).

RIGHTEOUSNESS BY THE JEWS

Having discussed that thought and shown that it is applicable to the Jew, because God's judgments rest on moral and not on national or ceremonial ground, the apostle here resumes it once more, in connection with verse 13, that he may show that if the law of Moses did not shield from condemnation, neither would circumcision.] **17 But if thou bearest the name of a Jew, and restest upon the law, and gloriest in God, 18 and knowest his will, and approvest the things that are excellent, being instructed out of the law, 19 and art confident that thou thyself art a guide of the blind, a light of them that are in darkness, 20 a corrector of the foolish, a teacher of babes, having in the law the form of knowledge of the truth; 21 thou therefore that teacheth another, teachest thou not thyself?** [But if doers, and not hearers, are not justified, why do you put your confidence in mere hearing, and such things as are analogous to it? Since only the doers of the law are justified, why do you vainly trust that you will be acceptable because you bear the proud name of Jew (Gal. 2: 15; Phil. 3: 5; Rev. 2: 9), rather than the humble one of Gentile? Why do you rest confidently merely because you possess a better law than the Gentiles, because you glory in the worship of the true God (Deut. 4: 7), and in knowing his will (Ps. 147: 19, 20), and in being instructed so as to approve the more excellent things of the Jewish religion above the debauchery of idolatry? Of what avail are these things when God demands *doing* and not mere knowing? And of what profit is it to you if the law does give you such a correct knowledge of the truth that you are to the Gentiles, yea, even to their chief philosophers, as a guide to the blind, a light to the benighted, a wise man among fools, a skilled teacher among children? Of what avail or profit is it all if, with all this ability, you teach only others and fail to teach yourself? The apostle next shows, in detail, how truly the Jew had failed to profit by his knowledge, so as to become a doer of the law.] **thou that preachest a man should not steal, dost thou steal? 22 thou that sayest a man should not commit adultery, dost thou commit adultery? thou that ab-**

horrest idols, dost thou rob temples? **23 thou who gloriest in the law, through thy transgression of the law dishonorest thou God?** [These questions bring out the flagrant inconsistencies between Jewish preaching and practice. Teaching others not to steal, the Jew, though probably not often guilty of technical theft, was continually practically guilty of it in his business dealings, wherein, by the use of false weights, extortion, cheating, etc., he gathered money for which he had returned no just equivalent. Unchastity was also a besetting sin of the Jews, showing itself in the corrupt practice of permitting divorces without reasonable or righteous cause (Matt. 19: 8, 9). Some of the most celebrated Rabbis are, in the Talmud, charged with adultery. Paul's accusation, that the Jews robbed temples, has been a puzzle to many. This robbing of the temple, according to the context of his argument, must have been a species of idolatry, for he is charging the Jews with doing the very things which they condemned. They condemned stealing, and stole; they denounced adultery, and committed it; they abhorred idols, yet robbed the temples of them that they might worship them. Such is the clear meaning, according to the context. But we have no evidence that the Jews of Paul's day did such a thing. The charge is doubtless historic. The Jewish history, in which they gloried, showed that the fathers, in whom they had taken so much pride, had done this thing over and over again, and the same spirit was in their children, though more covertly concealed (comp. Matt. 23: 29-32). The last question sums up the Jewish misconduct: glorying in the law, as is shown in verses 17-20, they yet dishonored the God of the law by transgressing it, as is shown in this paragraph.] **24 For the name of God is blasphemed among the Gentiles because of you, even as it is written.** (Isa. 52: 5; Ezek. 36: 20-23.) By their conduct the Jews had fulfilled the words of Isaiah and the meaning of Ezekiel. The Gentiles, judging by the principle that a god may be known by his worshipers, had, by reason of the Jews, judged Jehovah to be of such a character that their judgment became a blasphemy. (See also Ezek. 16: 51-59.) Thus Paul took from the Jew a confidence of divine favor, which he had because he possessed the law. But the law was not the sole confidence of the Jew, for he had circumcision also, and he regarded this rite as a seal or conclusive evidence that he belonged to the people of God, being thereby separated by an infinite distance from all other people. He looked with scorn and contempt on the uncircumcised, even using the term as an odious epithet (Gen. 34: 14 ; Ex. 12: 48 ; 1 Sam. 17: 26 ; 2 Sam. 1: 20 ; Isa. 52: 1 ; Ezek. 28: 10.) The apostle, therefore, turns his fire so as to dislodge the Jew from this deceptive stronghold. He drives him from his hope and trust in circumcision.] **25 For circumcision indeed profiteth, if thou be a doer of the law : but if thou be a transgressor of the law, thy circumcision is become uncircumcision. 26 If therefore the uncircumcision keep the ordinances of the law, shall not his uncircumcision be reckoned for circumcision ?** [In verse 25 the apostle takes up the case of the Jew ; in verse 26 that of the Gentile. By circumcision the former entered into a covenant with God, and part of the terms of his covenant was an agreement to obey the law. Thus the law was superior to circumcision, so much so that it, as it were, disfranchised or expatriated an Israelite for disobedience, despite his circumcision. On the contrary, if an uncircumcised Gentile obeyed the law, then the law naturalized and received him into the spiritual theocracy, notwithstanding his lack of circumcision. The verses are not an argument, but a plain statement of the great truth that circumcision, though beneficial to the law-abiding, has no power to withstand the law when condemning the lawless. In short, the Jew and Gentile stood on equal footing, for, though the Jew had a better covenant (circumcision) and a better law, yet neither attained to salvation, for neither kept the law.] **27 and shall not the uncircumcision which is by nature, if it fulfil the law, judge thee, who with the letter and circumcision art a transgressor of the law ?** [The Gentile, remaining as he was by nature, uncircumcised, if he fulfilled the law, shall, in his turn, judge the Jew, who was so ready to judge him

(v. 1), who, with a written law and circumcision, was yet a transgressor. The judging referred to is probably the indirect judging of comparison. On the day of judgment, the Gentile, with his poor advantages, will condemn, by his superior conduct, the lawlessness of the Jew. Comp. Matt. 11: 21, 22; Luke 11: 31, 32.] **28 For he is not a Jew who is one outwardly; neither is that circumcision which is outward in the flesh: 29 but he is a Jew who is one inwardly; and circumcision is that of the heart, in the spirit not in the letter; whose praise is not of men, but of God.** [He is not a Jew in God's sight (though he is, of course, such in the sight of the world) who is simply one without; *i. e.*, by being properly born of Jewish parents, nor is that a circumcision in God's sight (though it is in the sight of the world) which is merely fleshly. But he is the real, divinely accepted Jew who is one within; *i. e.*, who has in him the spirit of Abraham and the fathers in whom God delighted (John 1: 47). His life may be hid from men, so that they may see nothing in him to praise, but it is praiseworthy in the sight of God, and circumcision is not that outward compliance with the letter of the law—literal circumcision—but that inward spiritual compliance with the true meaning of circumcision, the cutting off of all things that are impure and unholy, and that make the heart unworthy of an acceptance into the household of God.]

III.

JEWISH PRIVILEGE DOES NOT DIMINISH GUILT, AND THE SCRIPTURES INCLUDE BOTH JEW AND GENTILE ALIKE UNDER SIN.

3: 1-20.

1 What advantage then hath the Jew? or what is the profit of circumcision? [Paul's argument was well calculated to astonish the Jews. If some notable Christian should argue conclusively that the Christian and the infidel stood on an equal footing before God, his argument would not be more

JEWISH PRIVILEGE 317

startling to the church than was that of Paul to the Jews of his day. They naturally asked the two questions found in this first verse, so Paul places the questions before his readers that he may answer them.] 2 **Much every way: first of all, that they were entrusted with the oracles of God.** [To the circumcised Jew God had given the Scriptures. The law, the Psalms, the prophets were his, with all the revelations and promises therein contained. They revealed man's origin, his fall and his promised redemption; they also described the Redeemer who should come, and prepared men to receive him and to believe him. How unspeakable the advantage of the Jew in possessing such a record. But the Jew had not improved this advantage, and so we may regard him as asking the apostle this further question, "But, after all, the greatest part of us have not believed on this Jesus, and so what advantage were our oracles to us in reality?" The apostle now answers this objection.] 3 **For what if some were without faith? shall their want of faith make of none effect the faithfulness of God?** 4 **God forbid: yea, let God be found true, but every man a liar; as it is written** [Ps. 51:4], **That thou mightest be justified in thy words, And mightest prevail when thou comest into judgment.** [True, the Jew, by unbelief, had failed to *improve* his advantage in possessing the Scriptures; but that did not alter the fact that he had had the advantage. He had failed, but God had not failed. Had the unbelief of the Jew caused God to break his promises, then indeed might the advantage of the Jew have been questioned, for in that case it would have proven a vanishing quantity. But, on the contrary, God had kept faith, and so the advantage, though unimproved, had been an abiding quantity. And this accords with the holiness and sinlessness of God. He is ever blameless, and because he is so, he must ever be assumed to be so, even though such an assumption should involve the presumption that all men are false and untrue, as, indeed, they are in comparison with him: for David testified to the incomparable righteousness of God, that it was a righteousness which acquitted God of all unfaithfulness to his words, and which causes him to prevail whenever men call him to account or pass judgment upon him.] **5 But if our unrighteousness commendeth the righteousness of God, what shall we say? Is God unrighteous who visiteth with wrath? (I speak after the manner of men.)** [I am not expressing my own views, but those of the man who objects to the truth I am presenting.] **6 God forbid: for then how shall God judge the world? 7 But if the truth of God through my lie abounded unto his glory, why am I also still judged as a sinner? 8 and why not (as we are slanderously reported, and as some affirm that we say), Let us do evil, that good may come? whose condemnation is just.** [But some of you Jews, objecting to my argument, will say, "According to your statements, the unbelief and disobedience of us Jews, with reference to God's Scripture, drew out, displayed and magnified the faithfulness and goodness of God in fulfilling his Scripture. Therefore, since our unbelief, etc., added to the glory of God by commending his righteousness, is not God unjust to punish us for that unbelief, etc., since it works such praiseworthy results?" My answer is, God forbid that sin should become righteousness, for if sin ceases to be sinful, how shall God judge the world, since then there shall be no sin to be condemned or punished? You see, then, the absurdity of your question, since it is a practical denial of the divinely established fact that there is to be a day of judgment. Sin, though it may, by its contrast, display the righteousness of God, is nevertheless utterly without merit. As an illustration, my case is analogous to yours. You arraign me before the bar of Jewish opinion, even as you yourselves are arraigned before the bar of God; yet you would not permit me to use before you the very same argument which you are seeking to use before God. You Jews regard me as a sinner, and charge me with being untrue to the Jewish religion, and with being a false representative of it, in that I declare it to be fulfilled in the gospel. Now, my lie (as you consider it), in this respect, redounds to the glory of God by being a contrast to his truthfulness. But would you Jews

JEWISH PRIVILEGE

acquit me of the sin of heresy if I should make use of this your argument? And, again, if your reasoning is correct, why should I not, as certain, meaning to slander me, report that I do, and affirm that I say, Let us do evil that good may come? But those who avow such principles are justly condemned. Thus Paul showed that, in condemning him (though falsely), they condemn the very argument which they were seeking to affirm in verse 5.] **9 What then? are we [Jews] better than they?** [The Gentiles.] **No, in no wise: for we before laid to the charge both of Jews and Greeks, that they are all under sin** [Having met the effort of the Jew to make an exception in his case, as set forth in verse 5, the apostle now reaffirms his original charge of universal unrighteousness, in which both Jews and Greeks were involved. This charge he further proves by an elaborate chain of quotations, taken from the Old Testament, and chiefly from the Psalms] ; **10 as it is written, There is none righteous, no, not one; 11 There is none that understandeth, There is none that seeketh after God; 12 They have all turned aside, they are together become unprofitable; There is none that doeth good, no, not so much as one** [Ps. 14: 1-3 ; 53: 1-3] : **13 Their throat is an open sepulchre ; With their tongues they have used deceit** [Ps. 5: 9] : **The poison of asps is under their lips** [140: 3]: **14 Whose mouth is full of cursing and bitterness** [Ps. 10: 7] : **15 Their feet are swift to shed blood ; 16 Destruction and misery are in their ways; 17 And the way of peace have they not known** [Isa. 59: 7, 8] : **18 There is no fear of God before their eyes.** [Ps. 36: 1. The above quotations are placed in logical order. "The arrangement is such," says Meyer, "that testimony is adduced: first, for the *state* of sin generally (vs. 10-12); second, the *practice* of sin in word (vs. 13, 14) and deed (vs. 13-17); and third, the sinful *source* of the whole— v. 18."] **19 Now we know that what things soever the law saith, it speaketh to them that are under the law** [*i. e.*, to the Jews] ; **that every mouth may be stopped, and all the world may be brought under the judgment** of God: 20 because by the works of the law shall no flesh be justified in his sight; for through the law *cometh* the knowledge of sin. [Having, by his quotations from the Old Testament, shown that the Jew was sinful, the apostle sets forth the result of this sin. Does the law provide any remedy? Is the Jew right in hoping that it shall afford him immunity from his guilt? These questions have been for some time before the apostle, and they now come up for final answer. We, says he, universally accept the truth that when the law speaks, it speaks to those who are under it. If, therefore, it has no voice save condemnation—and it has no other—and if that voice is addressed particularly to the Jew—and it is—his state is no better than that of the Gentile; he is condemned; and the law thus speaks for this very purpose of silencing the vain, unwarranted confidence of the Jew, that he may see himself in the same condition as the Gentile, and brought, with the rest of the world, under the condemnation of God; and there can be no legal escape from this condemnation, because, by the works of the law, it is impossible for humanity, in its frailty, to justify itself in God's sight—nay, the law works a directly contrary result, for through it comes the knowledge and sense of sin, and not the sense of pardon or justification.]

Subdivision C.

THE UNIVERSAL NEED OF RIGHTEOUSNESS SATISFIED BY THE GOSPEL PROCLAMATION OF RIGHTEOUSNESS BY FAITH.

3: 21-4: 25.

I.

NEITHER JEW NOR GREEK CAN OBTAIN RIGHTEOUSNESS OTHERWISE THAN BY THE GOSPEL.

3: 21-31.

21 But now apart from the law a righteousness of God hath been manifested, being witnessed by the

RIGHTEOUSNESS BY THE GOSPEL   321

law and the prophets [Having shut up all under condemnation for sin under the law with its works, Paul turns now to point all to freedom and justification under the gospel with its grace. This section of the Epistle is, therefore, as Bengel observes, "the opening of a brighter scene." There was no justification under the Mosaic dispensation, says the apostle; but now, under the dispensation of Christ (v. 26; ch. 16: 26), a righteousness apart from or independent of the law, having God as its author, and proceeding from God, and long hid in the councils of God, has been at last manifested (ch. 16: 25, 26; I Tim. 3: 16). Having thus distinctly announced this new justification, Paul proceeds to give details, the first of which is a statement that it did not come unannounced or unheralded, for in their types, promises and prophecies (Gen. 15: 6; Hab. 2: 4) both the law and the prophets foretold that this righteousness would be revealed]; **22 even the righteousness of God through faith in Jesus Christ unto all them that believe; for there is no distinction; 23 for all have sinned, and fall short of the glory of God; 24 being justified freely by his grace through the redemption that is in Christ Jesus** [The apostle adds four additional details, viz.: 1. This justification is conditional, being obtained through faith in Jesus Christ. 2. It is bestowed upon Jew and Gentile without distinction, for both classes, having failed to attain that perfection of righteousness and character which is the glory of God, are equally condemned without it. 3. It is a free gift, bestowed by God's grace or favor. 4. It was obtained as a redemption by the giving of Jesus Christ as a ransom (I Cor. 6: 30). The last detail is further elaborated in what follows]: **25 whom God set forth** *to be* **a propitiation, through faith, in his blood, to show his righteousness because of the passing over of the sins done aforetime, in the forbearance of God; 26 for the showing,** *I say,* **of his righteousness at this present season: that he might himself be just, and the justifier of him that hath faith in Jesus.** [God set forth (or exhibited in his blood on the cross) Jesus Christ to be a propitiatory sacrifice (*i. e.*, a sacrifice which would justify God in pardoning sinners) for the benefit of those who, through faith in him, would present him to God as such. And God thus set him forth as a bloody sacrifice, that he might in him, show his righteousness (*i. e.*, his retributive justice, his hatred of sin, and firmness in punishing it), for this retributive justice of God had for a long time been obscured by his conduct towards sinners, for he had passed over, or left only partially punished, the sins done aforetime (*i. e.*, all sins committed before Christ's death), for he had neither fully forgiven nor fully punished them, but had passed them over, reserving the full punishment of them to inflict it upon Jesus when suffering upon the cross (Isa. 53: 4-6); that full forgiveness also might flow from the cross (John 1: 29; 1 John 1: 7; Rev. 1: 5; 7: 14), God forbearing to punish man because he anticipated this method of pardoning him. Thus God explained, or made clear, his former conduct, by setting forth, in these days, his crucified Son as a propitiatory sacrifice, that he might show himself, not just in condemning, but just and yet the justifier of him that hath faith in Jesus. Thus Paul makes it apparent that the sacrifices of the Old Testament were types, and because of them God showed forbearance, looking forward to Christ, the real propitiatory sacrifice, in whose sufferings on the cross God punished sin, that he might show mercy and grant pardon to the sinner. The propitiatory sacrifice of Christ could only take place with his free and full consent, for it would have else been unjust to punish one being for the sin of another.] **27 Where then is the glorying?** [2: 17, 23.] **It is excluded. By what manner of law? of works? Nay: but by a law of faith.** [In all that portion of this Epistle embraced between 2: 17–3: 20, Paul has been demolishing the boastful spirit of the Jew. As he ends his successful argument, he pauses now to ask, triumphantly, What is left of this boasting? If a man is saved not as a righteous person, but as a pardoned criminal, where is there room for boastfulness? There is none at all; it is excluded. But by what law or principle is it excluded? by that of works? No; for such a law tends to foster it; but

RIGHTEOUSNESS BY THE GOSPEL 323

by the law or principle of faith. The law of works, which says, "Do this if thou wouldst live," tended to develop a spirit of self-righteousness; but the law of faith, which says, "Believe on the Lord Jesus, and thou shalt be saved," silences all boasting.] **28 We reckon therefore that a man is justified by faith apart from the works of the law. 29 Or is God *the God* of Jews only? is he not *the God* of Gentiles also? Yea, of Gentiles also: 30 if so be that God is one, and he shall justify the circumcision by faith, and the uncircumcision through faith.** [Therefore, as the conclusion of the whole argument, we reckon that every man, be he Jew or Gentile, is justified by faith apart from the works of the law. If only those who kept the law of Moses could be justified, then only could Jews be justified, for they alone possessed this law, and it is addressed only to them. But this state of affairs would belie the character of God. Does he not create, feed and govern the Gentiles? and is he not then the God of the Gentiles? Or are there *two* Gods: one for the Jew and one for the Gentile? The question is absurd; there is but one God, and he is God both of the Jews and Gentiles, and as each race is alike wholly dependent upon him, he must deal impartially by each; and this he does, for he saves both Jew and Gentile in the same manner; *i. e.*, by faith. It may be well to note, in this connection, that Luther added the word "alone" to this verse, thus: "We reckon, therefore, that a man is justified by faith *alone*." In combating the error of Rome (that men are justified by works), Luther fell into another error, for repentance is as much a means of justification as faith, and there is no *merit* in either of them. The meritorious cause of our justification is the *atoning blood of Christ*, and by faith, repentance, baptism, etc., we appropriate the blood of Christ. These acts, on our part, do not make us *worthy* of justification, but they are the *conditions* fixed by Christ, on compliance with which he invests us with the benefits of his blood; *i. e.*, justifies us.] **31 Do we then make the law of none effect through faith? God forbid: nay, we establish the law.** [Does the conclusion, proved by my argument, make the law of none effect? God forbid: on the contrary, it establishes the law by clearing it of misunderstanding. It was given to show that no man could attain salvation by self-righteousness, and we establish it by showing that it accomplished the end for which it was framed. We have shown that it was of no service to justify men; but of great service to convict them of sin, and thus lead them to Christ for justification.]

II.

THE GOSPEL METHOD OF JUSTIFICATION, EXEMPLIFIED IN THE CASES OF ABRAHAM AND DAVID, MUST BE APPLIED BOTH TO THE LITERAL AND SPIRITUAL SEED OF ABRAHAM.

4: 1-25

1 What then shall we say that Abraham, our forefather, hath found according to the flesh? [The word "found" means "obtained" (Heb. 9: 12) or "got" (Luke 9: 12). Knowing that the Jew would resist and controvert his conclusion that the Jew would have to be justified by faith, just as the Gentile, Paul further confirms his conclusion by a test case. For the test he selects Abraham, the father of the race, and the earthly head of the theocracy. No more fitting individual could be chosen, for the nation had never claimed that it had risen higher than its head; therefore, whatever could be proved as to Abraham must be conceded to be true as to all. What, says Paul, in the light of our proposition, shall we say that Abraham, our forefather, hath obtained, by his fleshly nature, apart from the grace of God; *i. e.*, as a doer of the law (Gal. 3: 2, 3)? Surely, he obtained nothing whatever in this manner.] **2 For if Abraham was justified by works, he hath whereof to glory; but not toward God. 3 For what saith the scripture?** [Gen. 15: 6] **And Abraham believed God, and it was reckoned unto him for right-**

eousness. [Now, of course, Abraham was some way justified. If he was justified by works, as you Jews suppose, he has ground for glorying toward God, for he can claim his justification from God as a debt due to him; but we hear of no such glorying toward God, and hence he was not justified by works. On the contrary, we hear that he was justified by faith, for the Scripture says that he believed God and his belief was counted unto him for righteousness.] 4 **Now to him that worketh, the reward is not reckoned as of grace, but as of debt. 5 But to him that worketh not, but believeth on him that justifieth the ungodly, his faith is reckoned for righteousness.** [Let us illustrate our point by the case of a workman. If the workman does *all* he agreed to do, then his reward or hire is due him, not as a matter of grace or favor, but as a just debt. But if, on the contrary, the workman does not fulfill his agreement at all, but merely believes the promise of his employer that he shall nevertheless be paid, then the hire is not hire at all; it is a mere gift of grace and favor, and not a debt. Now, this latter is the position occupied by Abraham, and by every one that believeth on him that justifieth the ungodly, for their faith is reckoned unto them for the works of the law—those works of righteousness which they promised to do, but never performed. The sentence is very elliptical, the apostle mingling the illustration with its application, in the onrushing of his thought.] 6 **Even as David also pronounceth blessing upon the man, unto whom God reckoneth righteousness apart from works,** 7 *saying* [Ps. 32: 1, 2], **Blessed are they whose iniquities are forgiven, And whose sins are covered. 8 Blessed is the man to whom the Lord will not reckon sin.** [The quotation from David does not show a positive imputation of righteousness, but a negative one—a refusal to reckon the unrighteous. "It is implied," says Alford, "by Paul, that the remission of sin is equivalent to the imputation of righteousness, that there is no negative state of innocence, none intermediate between acceptance for righteousness and rejection for sin." This accords with the entire trend of Scripture, which recognizes but two great classes: those who shall stand upon the right, and those who shall pass to the left in the judgment. Paul has now concluded his first point in the test case of Abraham—he has shown that he was justified by faith, and that such a justification was recognized by David, and pronounced blessed. He now takes up the second point, and shows that if Abraham was not justified by the doing of the law, neither was he by the rite of circumcision. In this part of the argument it should be borne in mind that God declared Abraham justified by faith at least thirteen years *before* Abraham submitted to the rite of circumcision. Moreover, he unites Abraham with *all* the uncircumcised, and tries the case of all in Abraham.] **9 Is this blessing then pronounced upon the circumcision, or upon the uncircumcision also? for we say, To Abraham his faith was reckoned for righteousness. 10 How then was it reckoned? when he was in circumcision, or in uncircumcision? Not in circumcision, but in uncircumcision** [Do the words of David apply only to the Jews, the circumcised, or do they likewise apply also to the Gentiles, the uncircumcised? Surely they apply to the uncircumcised, for they describe the blessing which Abraham enjoyed before his circumcision. Of what use, then, was circumcision, and why did Abraham receive it?]: **11 and he received the sign of circumcision, a seal of the righteousness of the faith which he had while he was in uncircumcision: that he might be the father of all them that believe, though they be in uncircumcision, that righteousness might be reckoned unto them; 12 and the father of circumcision to them who not only are of the circumcision, but who also walk in the steps of that faith of our father Abraham which he had in uncircumcision.** [Now, circumcision was not given to Abraham to justify him, but as a seal, or token, that he had obtained righteousness by faith. Moreover, it was given to him that he might become the father of all believing Gentiles, God having agreed to make him the head or spiritual father of all those saved by Christ on condition of his being circumcised, and Abraham having been circumcised in order to obtain this exalted honor, and thirdly, that he might be the spiritual father of those who are not only circumcised like him, but walk in the steps of that faith of his of which circumcision was the seal. Thus circumcision was the seal that God had made Abraham the father of all who believe in God, and are justified by their belief, whether they belong to the Jews, who, in the earlier ages, had the better opportunity to believe, or to the Gentiles, who had that better opportunity in these latter ages.] **13 For not through the law was the promise to Abraham or to his seed that he should be heir of the world, but through the righteousness of faith.** [In this third division of his argument Paul shows that Abraham did not obtain the promise of heirship for himself and his seed through the agency of the law, but by reason of the righteousness reckoned to him because of his faith. Many promises were given to Abraham (Gen. 12: 7; 13: 14, 15; 15: 13; 17: 8; 22: 17), and Paul sums them all up in the phrase, "that he should be heir of the world." This phrase has been variously explained, but it obviously means that Abraham should inherit the world as his spiritual children, and that his children should inherit it also as their spiritual family or household. The heirship of Abraham in no way conflicts with that of Christ or God. Comp. 8: 17.] **14 For if they that are of the law are heirs, faith is made void, and the promise is made of none effect: 15 for the law worketh wrath; but where there is no law, neither is there transgression.** [Abraham had, by reason of his human nature, to be justified by his faith. If justification had to be earned, and men had to seek it by the works of the law, then faith—all the things which we hope for and believe in—would be made void.] **16 For this cause** *it is* **of faith, that** *it may be* **according to grace; to the end that the promise may be sure to all the seed; not to that only which is of the law, but to that also which is of the faith of Abraham, who is the father of us all 17 (as it is written** [Gen. 17: 5], **A father of many nations have I made thee) before him whom ye believed,** *even*

God, who giveth life to the dead, and calleth the things that are not, as though they were. 18 **Who in hope believe against hope, to the end that he might become a father of many nations, according to that which had been spoken, So shall thy seed be.** [Now, since a righteousness of law is unattainable by men, the inheritance was bestowed because of a righteousness of faith, that it might be a free gift, and that all the promises concerning it might be sure, to the entire household. Not only to that division of Abraham's spiritual children who are under the law (believing Jews), but also to that part who are only his children by reason of a like faith with him (believing Gentiles), for Abraham is the father of all believers, whether Jews or Gentiles; as it is written, "A father of many nations have I made thee." And Abraham was such a spiritual father in the estimate of God, who, in his omnipotence and omniscience, gives life to the dead (and, from a child-bearing standpoint, Abraham and Sarah were as good as dead), and speaks of unborn and as yet non-existent children as though they already had being. And God spoke thus to the man who, when nature withheld all reason to hope, still hoped for the purpose of obtaining from God the fulfillment of the promise that he should be the father of many nations, according to God's gracious assurance, when he bade Abraham look upon the stars, and said, "So shall thy seed be." The word "made," in verse 17, means to constitute or appoint. "This word," says Shedd, "denotes that the paternity spoken of was the result of a special arrangement or economy. It would not be used to denote the merely physical connection between father and son." Such a word is to be expected, for the promise was that Abraham was to be a spiritual, not a fleshly, father of many nations. Again, it is fittingly said that Abraham was such in God's sight, for it was God, and not man, who thus anticipated the future. Though Abraham and Sarah were long past the age of child-bearing, and though it was to be many centuries before Abraham would have spiritual children, begotten of the gospel among the Gentiles, yet God spoke of him as the father of many nations; foreknowing his own power and foreseeing his own workings, God meant both to make him a father in the near future, and to give him a spiritual seed among the Gentiles in the remote future.] **19 And without being weakened in faith he considered his own body now as good as dead (he being about a hundred years old), and the deadness of Sarah's womb; 20 yet, looking unto the promise of God, he wavered not through unbelief, but waxed strong through faith, giving glory to God, 21 and being fully assured that what he had promised, he was able also to perform.** [This paragraph explains the clause in verse 18, which sets forth how Abraham "in hope believed against hope." God promised Abraham a son, and though nature told him that it was now impossible for him to have a son, by reason of his own age, and the age of his wife, yet Abraham believed that (the promise of) God was more potent than (the laws of) nature, and in this belief he waxed strong, and glorified God above nature, being fully assured that God was able to perform all that he promised.] **22 Wherefore also it was reckoned unto him for righteousness.** [Abraham, like all others, could not honor God by rendering perfect obedience to his will, but he could honor him by being fully persuaded that he would keep his word, though to do so might seemingly involve an impossibility. It was this act of honoring God by belief which was reckoned unto Abraham for righteousness. Faith still thus honors God when it trusts that God can love a sinner and save him notwithstanding his lost condition. "The sinner," says Hodge, "honors God, in trusting his grace, as much as Abraham did in trusting his power."] **23 Now it was not written for his sake alone, that it was reckoned unto him; 24 but for our sake also, unto whom it shall be reckoned, who believe on him that raised Jesus our Lord from the dead, 25 who was delivered up for our trespasses, and was raised for our justification.** [Now, Moses, when he recorded the fact that Abraham was accounted righteous for his faith, did not do so for the sole purpose of giving Abraham the honor due him, but he also recorded the fact for our sakes also, unto whom a like righteousness shall be reckoned because we believe on God the Father that raised Jesus our Lord from the dead, even Jesus who was delivered up to die for our sins, and raised from the dead for our justification. This paragraph shows that our belief is very similar to that of Abraham. If Abraham believed that God could accomplish seemingly impossible things concerning his son Isaac, so we likewise believe that God accomplished, and will accomplish, seemingly impossible things through Jesus, who, according to the flesh, was also a son of Abraham. In both cases it is no mere abstract belief in God, but a concrete belief as to certain facts accomplished and to be accomplished by God. In verse 25 Paul presents the twofold nature of Christ's propitiatory work, for he was both sacrifice and priest. He offered himself and was delivered up as a sacrifice for our sins, and he was raised from the dead and ascended to heaven that he might, as High Priest, present his blood before the face of God in a heavenly sanctuary for our justification, thus completing his high-priestly duties or offices—Heb. 9: 11-28.]

Subdivision D.

RESULTS OF CHRIST'S LIFE DISCUSSED, AND SHOWN TO BE CAPABLE OF AS LIMITLESS UNIVERSALITY AS THE RESULTS OF ADAM'S LIFE.

5: 1-21.

I.

RESULTS OF THE JUSTIFICATION WROUGHT BY CHRIST, VIZ.: PEACE, HOPE, LOVE AND RECONCILIATION.

5: 1-11.

1 Being therefore justified by faith, we have peace with God through our Lord Jesus Christ; 2 through whom also we have had our access by faith into this

RESULTS OF THE JUSTIFICATION

grace wherein we stand; and we rejoice in hope of the glory of God. [Having fully established justification by faith as a fact beyond all controversy, the apostle now proceeds to display its fruits and benefits. Therefore, says he, being justified or accounted righteous because of our faith, we have, through the merits of Jesus Christ, obtained peace with God; that is to say, we have the friendship of God, and our disquieted conscience has grown tranquil in the assurance that God no longer regards us as enemies, to be subdued, or criminals, to be punished. And, through the merits of Christ, we have also entered, by faith, into this gracious state of covenant relationship, favor, fellowship and communion with God which is now accorded us, and by which we are now strengthened and established, and we have hope of that infinitely greater fellowship and communion which we shall enjoy when we stand at last in the revealed glory of God—John 17: 24; Rev. 21: 11; 22: 4, 5.] **3 And not only so, but we also rejoice in our tribulations: knowing that tribulation worketh stedfastness; 4 and stedfastness, approvedness; and approvedness, hope: 5 and hope putteth not to shame; because the love of God hath been shed abroad in our hearts through the Holy Spirit which was given unto us.** [But the joy of the believer is not confined to this expectation of future good; he rejoices also in present evils, even in tribulation, because tribulation develops in him those elements of character which make him useful here, and prepare him for heaven hereafter; for tribulation teaches him that patience or steadfastness which endures without flinching, and this steadfastness wakens in him a sense of divine approval, and the thought that God approves adds to his hope that he shall obtain the blessings of the future world, and this hope is not so fickle as to disappoint or mock him, but gives him triumphant certainty, because the love which God has towards him fills his heart, being inwardly manifested to him by the Holy Spirit, who is given to all believers—at the time of their regeneration.] **6 For while we were yet weak, in due season Christ died for the ungodly. 7 For scarcely for a righteous man** will one die: for peradventure for the good man some one would even dare to die. 8 But God commendeth his own love toward us, in that, while we were yet sinners, Christ died for us. 9 Much more then, being now justified by his blood, shall we be saved from the wrath *of God* through him. 10 For if, while we were enemies, we were reconciled to God through the death of his Son, much more, being reconciled, shall we be saved by his life; 11 and not only so, but we also rejoice in God through our Lord Jesus Christ, through whom we have now received the reconciliation. [We have here the external evidences or manifestations of that love of God which, shed abroad in the heart of the Christian, forms the basis of his hope. Before we were strengthened and established by covenant, justification, or any of the blessings of a state of grace (verse 2), yea, even while we were in that helpless weakness of sin which so incapacitated us as to render us incapable of goodness, Christ, at the time appointed by the Father as best for all (at the time when the disease of sin raging in the human race had reached its climax), died for our benefit, though we were then reckoned among the unknown and the ungodly. And how apparent was the love of this action on his part, for though men are reluctant and unwilling enough to die for a righteous, *i. e.*, a just or upright, man, and might, perhaps, be persuaded to die for a good, *i. e.*, a loving and a benevolent, man, yet God commends to us the love he bears towards us, in that we see that he gave Christ to die for us while we were not good, no, not even upright, but while we were sinners. And no wonder that such a love becomes to us a source of hope, for, viewing the situation as to our previous and present states, if he did this for us while in a sinful or unjustified state, much more will he now save us from wrath and deserved punishment, since we are now in a justified state, being cleansed of all our sins by the blood of Jesus. And viewing the situation as to Jesus, and his past and present power, if, by dying, he exercised such a power over our lives that he reconciled us to God, much more, being made amenable to his power by being thus reconciled, shall he be able, by the greater power of his life (for the living Christ is more powerful than a dead one), to keep us in the way of life, and ultimately save us. Thus we see that peace, and a covenant state, and joy triumphing over tribulations, and hope founded on the love of God, are all fruits of justification; but the apostle, in verse 11, adds one more: Not only, says he, do all these fruits result, but there is yet another, viz.: we rejoice in God. We no longer rejoice in rites, ceremonies, ancestries, or legal righteousness, or any such thing; on the contrary, we rejoice in God, approaching him through our Lord Jesus Christ, through whom God has also approached us, for through him we have now received this reconciliation which causes us to rejoice in God. In verse 6, instead of saying that Christ died for us, the apostle uses the abstract term "the ungodly." Had he used the pronoun "us," it might have confused the mind of his readers, for they might have applied it to themselves as Christians, "us" indicating the unity of church fellowship. But the term "ungodly" admits of no misconstruction; it describes the scattered, the unknown, the lost.]

II.

ADAM, THE TRESPASSER UNTO DEATH, CONTRASTED WITH CHRIST, THE RIGHTEOUS UNTO LIFE.

5: 12-21.

12 Therefore, as through one man sin entered into the world, and death through sin; and so death passed unto all men, for that all sin:—13 for until the law sin was in the world; but sin is not imputed when there is no law. 14 Nevertheless death reigned from Adam until Moses, even over them that had not sinned after the likeness of Adam's transgression, who is a figure of him that was to come. [The comparison opened in verse

12 is carried through various contrasts and correlations until it closes, as modified by the intervening verses, in verse 18. Adding to verse 12 the modifications which appear in verse 18, and skipping the intervening correlations, that we may get the connection, and have the central thought clearly before us, we would paraphrase thus: Now, since Christ is the source of justification and all its benefits, we submit to you a comparison between him and Adam, who is the source of condemnation and all its hardships, thus: As through the act of the one man, Adam, sin entered into the world, and as through this one sin death also entered, so that for this one sin the sentence of death passed upon us all, even so through the one act of the one, Christ (viz.: his suffering on the cross), the free gift of being accounted righteous came unto all men to justify them (*i. e.*, to release them from the sentence of death which came upon them by Adam's sin), that they might live. Such is the central thought of the remainder of this chapter. But we have anticipated the full comparison, and the reader must bear in mind, in the perusal of what follows, that Paul is working it out, and does not complete it until verse 18. With verse 13 Paul enters on a proof that all sinned in Adam, and incurred the death penalty by reason of his sin as their federal head, and not by reason of their own individual sins. To understand his argument, we must remember that God gave a law of life and death to Adam, and then refrained from giving any law like it until the days of Moses. The law of Moses was also one of life and death. It provided that those who kept it should live, and that those who failed to keep it should die. But as none kept it, it became a general law, involving all under it in the condemnation of death. It is clear, therefore, that Adam died for his own sin, and equally clear that those who lived under the Mosaic law might have died for their own sin as well as for Adam's sin. But for whose sin did those die who lived in the twenty-five centuries between Adam and Moses? Clearly they died for the sin committed by Adam, their head. Keeping these things before us, we follow Paul's reasoning thus: It is clear that men die because they sinned in Adam, their federal head,

and not because they committed sin in their individual capacity; for though it is true that the people living in the world from the days of Adam until the giving of the law committed sin, yet where there is no law condemning to death (and there was none such in those days) sin is not imputed so as to incur the sentence of death. Therefore, in this absence of law, the people of that day would have lived in spite of their own individual sins; nevertheless, death reigned from Adam until Moses, even over those who had not broken any law having a death penalty attached to it, as did Adam, who, in his representative capacity as head of the race, was a figure or a type of the coming Christ, who was also to be manifested as a representative head of the race. It may be noted here that some, by reason of their gross wickedness, may have been specially punished by death, as, for instance, those who were obliterated by the deluge, or those who were burned in the flames of Sodom, etc., and also it may be observed that murderers should suffer death for their sin (Gen. 9: 6). But there was no general law involving all in the death penalty, and such special instances in no way weakened Paul's argument, for these, indeed, died by special dispensation of providence, on account of their peculiar wickedness; but they would have died just the same, under the decree passed upon Adam, if they had never been guilty of this peculiar wickedness, just as all others died who were not thus guilty. In other words, individual guilt did not bring the death sentence, for it already rested on all; it only brought a sudden, summary and peculiar mode of death upon these particular sinners, so as to stamp them as abnormally wicked.] **15 But not as the trespass, so also** *is* **the free gift.** [Thus far Paul has told us that Adam is the source of sin, condemnation and death, and that he is a type of Christ. In this fifteenth verse he qualifies the relation of type and antitype by a statement that their resemblance does not hold good in all respects, for the sin of Adam is not like the free gift of Christ when he offered himself upon the cross. Not only do these two acts differ in their very essence, **one** being the perfection of self-indulgence, with power to kill, **and**

the other the perfection of self-sacrifice, with power to make
alive; but, as might be expected, there is a world-wide difference, both as to the results, and as to the range or scope, and
the certainty of the results. With these thoughts Paul now
concerns himself.] **For if by the trespass of the one the
many died, much more did the grace of God, and the
gift by the grace of the one man, Jesus Christ, abound
unto the many.** [If Adam's one act of sin brought death
upon the race, so that all men die because of his act, much
more did the goodness or favor of God and the gift of life
by the goodness or favor of one man, Jesus Christ, abound
unto the many. We are here informed that the result of the
sacrificial act of Christ fully reversed and nullified the effects
of the act of Adam, and that it did even much more. The
effect, in other words, had in all points as wide a range, and
in some points a much wider range, than that of Adam's act.
Without explaining how it is as wide-reaching as Adam's act,
the apostle presses on to tell in what respects the act of Christ
is wider. But, to avoid misunderstanding, we should pause to
see how Christ's act equaled and nullified Adam's act. Adam,
as progenitorial head of the race (1 Tim. 2: 13; 1 Cor. 11: 8),
involved, by his sin, all the race in natural death—death without any hope of a resurrection, much less of immortality.
Christ, as creative head of the race, by his righteousness
redeemed all from this natural death by accomplishing for all
the resurrection of the dead. So far, the act of Christ merely
cancels the act of Adam. If the act of Christ had had no
wider effectiveness than this, it would have been insufficient
for man's needs. It would doubtless have sufficed for infants,
and others whom immaturity and mental incapacity rendered
incapable of individual sin, but it would have fallen short of
the needs of those who, in addition to their sin in Adam, had
other sins of their own for which to answer. The hope of the
world lies, therefore, in the "much more" which Paul states.
Again, we should notice that if we had only Adam's sin to
answer for, then the teaching of this passage would establish
the doctrine of universal salvation, for Christ's act completely

counteracted Adam's act. But there are other sins beside that first one committed by Adam, and other punishments beside natural death. It is in its dealings with those that the range of Christ's act exceeds that of Adam, and it is here also that salvation becomes limited. The resurrection (which nullifies the effect of Adam's act), though a form of justification, *precedes* the hour of judgment, and hence can not be final justification, for the latter is the product of the judgment. Moreover, the resurrection which Christ effects, as federal creative head of the race, does not depend upon faith; for all, the believing and the unbelieving, the just and the unjust, have part in it. But the justification which comes *after* that resurrection depends upon other relations and provisions. In administering this final justification, Christ stands as the federal *regenerative* head (the headship which peculiarly pertains to the church, and not to the race—Eph. 1: 22, 23), and bestows it upon that part of the race which has been regenerated by faith. This headship, therefore, is conditional, and the salvation which depends upon it is not universal, but conditioned on faith. To illustrate by a figure, there are *two* doors which we must pass in order to inherit eternal life. The first is natural death. This door was closed for all by Adam, and opened for all by Christ. The second is the judgment. This door was closed for all having capacity to sin by their own individual sins, and opened by Christ for those who shall be justified through belief in him. Therefore, in teaching that Christ leads all through the first door, Paul has not taught universal salvation, for true, complete salvation lies beyond the second door. Justification from the sin of Adam is one thing, and final justification from our own sins is quite another.] **16 And not as through one that sinned, *so* is the gift: for the judgment *came* of one unto condemnation, but the free gift *came* of many trespasses unto justification.** [The apostle here makes mention of the main particular, wherein the effect of Christ's act has a wider range than the effect of Adam's act. It may be well to observe, at this point, that wherever the act of Christ is simply *equal* in range to that of Adam, the effect is unconditional; but wherever the range *exceeds* that of Adam, then it becomes conditional upon faith, and is only enjoyed by believers. Paul does not here pause to bring out this important detail, but it is abundantly set forth by him elsewhere, and by other New Testament writers, so that it is, of course, implied here. Moreover, says he, the sentence of condemnation which came through the one person, Adam, though it comprehended the whole human family, is not as wide-reaching as the free gift, or justification, which came through Christ, for the judgment came because of one sin; but the free gift of justification came as to many trespasses to pardon them. In other words, the bestowal of justification exceeded in quantity the bestowal of condemnation; for one condemnation was given for one sin, but the justification was bestowed many times because of many sins. If Christ's one act of sacrifice had simply counteracted the effects of the one sin of Adam, then there would have been equality; but it did much more, for it also effected the justification of the countless trespasses of believers who obtained pardon by reason of it. How great is the efficacy of our Lord's sacrificial act! If one single sin brought death upon the entire human family, how unspeakably awful is its power! Who can measure the destructive force and the eternal energy of a single sin? Who then can estimate the justifying power of the sacrifice of Christ, since it nullifies, for believers, the accumulative power of the incalculable numbers of sins committed by innumerable sinners, in all the untold moments of human lives, each sin of which carries a destructive force which no lapse of ages can exhaust? No wonder, then, that we are told that there is no "other name under heaven, that is given among men, wherein we must be saved." We should note also that Paul does not here say that the sacrifice of Christ justifies all mankind from their many trespasses. This would be Universalism. He merely contrasts the power of one sin with that greater power which nullifies the effect of many sins, and thus shows that the range of Christ's act exceeded that of Adam. To counteract Adam's one sin in a million of his descendants, is a narrower work than to counteract the more than a million sins committed by any mature sinner, much less the unthinkable number committed by millions of sinners.] **17 For if, by the trespass of the one, death reigned through the one; much more shall they that receive the abundance of grace and of the gift of righteousness reign in life through the one,** *even* **Jesus Christ.** [The apostle now undertakes to show wherein the results of Christ's act are more certain than those of Adam's act. By the use of "receive," which is active, and not passive, Paul makes it plain that the results of Christ's act, of which he now speaks, are conditioned upon an *acceptance* of the act on the part of mankind. For if, says he, by the trespass of one man, death reigned upon all, through the sin of one, much more surely (because of the nature of God the Father, and the august personality of his Son) shall they that accept and receive to themselves the abundance of grace offered through Christ, and the abundance of the gift of righteousness (or justification), reign in that ineffable future of life through one, even through Jesus Christ. The Son of God is a greater personage than Adam, and the positive power of his righteousness is greater than the negative power of Adam's sin; therefore, if Adam's act has insured, and still insures, the reign of death in the world, much more does Christ's act insure the reign of life in the future world. The word "abundance," found in this verse, is very significant. *All* shall have the *ordinary* grace and righteousness in Christ which result in the resurrection—gracious result, which equals and nullifies the ungracious workings of the sin of Adam; but *only those* who "receive" it by faith shall have that *surplus* or "abundance" of the act of Christ which exceeds the act of Adam, and results in a reign of life, not a mere resurrection.] **18 So then as through one trespass** *the judgment came* **unto all men to condemnation; even so through one act of righteousness** *the free gift came* **unto all men to justification of life.** [So then, says the apostle, in conclusion, if one act of sin brought sentence of condemnation unto death upon all, because all were in sinful Adam as their forefather, thus sharing his act; so also one act of righteousness (the sacrifice of the cross) brought unto all justification (or release from Adam's sentence of condemnation) unto life. Adam's sin brought natural death upon the whole human family, but nothing more. The punishment which we incur through Adam terminates at death. If men are punished *after* death, it is not because of Adam's, but because of their *own*, individual sins.] **19 For as through the one man's disobedience the many were made sinners, even so through the obedience of the one shall the many be made righteous.** [Verse 18 has spoken of the effects; viz.: condemnation and justification. This verse proves that these *effects* must come, for it sets forth the *causes*, sin and righteousness, which produce them, and shows where and how these causes came to exist, thus showing that Adam and Christ resemble each other in that one is the fountain of evil and the other the fountain of good; for, as the disobedience of one caused many (all) to be constituted sinners who had personally committed no sin, so the obedience of the other (Phil. 2:8) caused the many (all) to be constituted righteous as to Adam's sin (*i. e.*, sufficiently to be resurrected). It is evident that only in verses 16 and 17 does Paul suggest any of those larger results wherein the act of Christ exceeded those of the acts of Adam. It may seem strange to some that, having thus introduced the larger things of Christ, Paul should, in verses 18 and 19, return to those things wherein the acts of each were equal. But this is to be expected, for Paul is describing the resemblance of the two; and, of course, where one exceeds the other, the resemblance ceases. It is natural, therefore, that Paul should briefly dismiss these enlargements or "abundances" of Christ which exceed similarity, and return to that precise point, *the unity of the many in the one*, which constitutes between the two federal heads the relation of type and antitype. It was Paul's design to establish this oneness, "in order that," as Chrysostom observes, "when the Jew says to you, 'How by the well-doing of one, Christ, was the world saved?' you may be able to say to him, 'How by the disobedience of one, Adam, was the world condemned?'"] **20 And the law came in** besides, that the trespass might abound; but where sin abounded, grace did abound more exceedingly: 21 that, as sin reigned in death, even so might grace reign through righteousness unto eternal life through Jesus Christ our Lord. [All this reasoning almost wholly ignores the Mosaic law: where then did it come in? and how did it affect the situation? Thus: the law came in, in addition to sin and death, for the purpose of increasing sin, and also that sense of guilt which could not be very poignantly felt while men were dying on account of a prenatal sin committed by Adam. But when the law had thus made men conscious of the abundant and universal prevalence of sin, then the grace of God made itself even more abundant in longsuffering, in patience, in forbearance, etc., and especially in preparing the gospel; that as sin had reigned, and produced death, even so grace might reign through righteousness unto eternal life, through the ministry and sacrifice of our Lord Jesus Christ.]

Subdivision E.
SANCTIFICATION OF THE BELIEVER REQUIRED AND OBTAINED IN CHANGE OF RELATIONSHIP BY THE GOSPEL.

6: 1-8: 30.

I.

JUSTIFICATION IS BROUGHT ABOUT BY SUCH A RELATION TO CHRIST AS CREATES AN OBLIGATION TO BE DEAD TO SIN AND ALIVE TO RIGHTEOUSNESS, AS IS SYMBOLICALLY SHOWN BY BAPTISM.

6: 1-14.

1 What shall we say then? Shall we continue in sin, that grace may abound? 2 God forbid. We who died to sin, how shall we any longer live therein?

[Macknight says, truly, that the thought of this and the next chapter reverts to 3: 31, and is intended to refute the thought of that verse, as reintroduced by 5: 20, 21; viz.: that justification by faith renders the law useless, and encourages sin, that grace may abound. Paul refutes these thoughts, and asserts the contrary principle, that justification by faith establishes the law. What, says he, shall be inferred from what we have taught? It is true that God's favor abounds in proportion to sin, so as to always exceed it; but are the friends of Christ therefore justified in thinking they can live sinfully (Gal. 5: 13)? or are the Lord's enemies justified in asserting that we teach that men should do evil that good may come (3: 9)? or that we teach that Christians should continue to commit sin, as they did before their conversion, in order that they may increase the grace by increasing the sin (5: 20)? Not at all. Our gospel destroys sin: can it, therefore, give encouragement and vigor to it? We who, by baptism, have put away sin, so that we died to it, can we, nevertheless, accomplish the impossible by still living in it? The apostle, in asserting that baptism is a death to sin, does not speak literally, but uses a bold and appropriate figure, suggested by the inherent symbolism of the ordinance. Baptism is the consummation of repentance; and were repentance *perfect*, the immersion would result in such an abhorrence of sin, such a complete cessation of it, and such a love of righteousness as would bring about an actual death toward, or abolition of, sin, and the Lord designed and desires such a full transformation; but truth compels us to acknowledge that repentance, like all other human operations, is imperfect, and, therefore, in baptism we only die to sin in so far that righteousness becomes the rule of life, and sin the painful, mortifying, humiliating, heart-breaking exception.] **3 Are ye ignorant that all we who were baptized into Christ Jesus were baptized into his death? 4 We were buried therefore with him through baptism into death: that like as Christ was raised from the dead through the glory of the Father, so we also might walk in newness of life.** [The apostle's argument rests on the nature

JUSTIFICATION 343

of Christ's death, etc. Jesus died to take away our sins, to bear them for us, and rid us of them (John 1: 29; 1 Pet. 2: 24); but in order that he may do this for us, so that we may partake of the benefits of his death, it is necessary that he be our representative; *i. e.*, that we be in him, and in him *at the very time* when he thus gave himself unto death, so that his death becomes, representatively, our death. To aid us in conceiving the accomplishment of this unity with him in the act of death, the ordinance of baptism was instituted, so that, by it, we are not only baptized into him, but also into his death. One purpose, therefore, of baptism is to so unite us with him that, in him, we may die to sin and a life in a sinful kingdom of darkness, and rise to live again in righteousness in a sinless kingdom of light (7: 4; 8: 13; Gal. 2: 19, 20; 5: 24; 6: 14; Col. 2: 11-20). Such being the nature of the ordinance, it precludes the idea that a baptized person could continue to commit sin. You must therefore recognize, says the apostle, that in baptism you died with Christ unto sin, or are ye so ignorant of the meaning of that ordinance that you do not understand that it symbolizes your death to sin and your resurrection to righteousness? If you are thus ignorant, then know that all we who were immersed into Christ were immersed into his death. We were buried with him, through immersion, into death as to our sin: that like as Christ was raised from the dead, because the glory of the just and holy Father required it, so we also might walk or act in a new manner of life; *i. e.*, a sinless life. Thus baptism, which is a burial and resurrection performed in water, attests, in the strongest manner, the Christian's obligation to be sinless. Only the dead are buried. Brief as is the momentary burial of the immersed, it is, nevertheless, a seal of their death to sin, and hence of their cleansing from it (Acts 2: 38; 22: 16). Only the resurrected rise from the grave. Therefore, one who has not fully resolved to live as having died unto sin has no right to be lifted from the waters of baptism. If he is still dead in trespasses and sin, he should remain buried.]
5 For if we have become united with *him* **in the likeness of his death, we shall be also** *in the likeness* **of his**

resurrection [The apostle here meets the cavil of some objector who supposes that we might die to sin in baptism, and still be under no obligation to refrain from it after baptism. The answer is, that we can not be united to Christ in one part of the ordinance (the burial, or immersion), and severed from him in the other part (the resurrection, or emersion). If, says he, we have become united with Christ in that part of the ordinance wherein he died to destroy the power of sin, it is morally certain that we shall continue to be united with him in that other part, wherein he rose to lead a new life—a life no longer confined to earth and its sinful environment, but one far removed from the realm of wickedness in the courts of the Father. If, therefore, we died with him to sin, we must also rise with him to lead a new life in the (to us) new kingdom of God, which looks forward to the enjoyment of those very changes wrought in Christ by his ascension. Neither in dying nor living do we accomplish the actual in the ordinance. We are not actually united with Christ in death, but in an ordinance which resembles it. We do not actually die as to sin, as did Christ; but we do profess a *likeness* to his death. We do not rise, as did he, to a glorified life, but we strive to maintain a similitude, or likeness, to it. When at last, in a real death and resurrection, Christ actually unites us with himself, we shall indeed be dead to sin, and alive to righteousness; for there is no sin among the immortals, and there shall be no lack of perfection in those who have been changed into Christ's image]; **6 knowing this, that our old man was crucified with *him*, that the body of sin might be done away, that so we should no longer be in bondage to sin; 7 for he that hath died is justified from sin. 8 But if we died with Christ, we believe that we shall also live with him; 9 knowing that Christ being raised from the dead dieth no more; death no more hath dominion over him. 10 For the death that he died, he died unto sin once: but the life that he liveth, he liveth unto God. 11 Even so reckon ye also yourselves to be dead unto sin, but alive unto God in Christ Jesus.** [At this

JUSTIFICATION 345

point the apostle passes over from the symbolic union which is effected on our part by baptism, to the actual union effected on Christ's part by his real assumption of our humanity through his incarnation. Though, in baptism, we only symbolically died, yet we may be sure that the symbolism has actual truth and verity back of it, for we know that our sinful human nature, which we sought to bury in baptism, did really, actually, die in the person of Christ crucified, that the sin might be purged, and that it, being a slave to sin, might obtain actual, unqualified liberty; for who so dies pays the penalty of sin, and (if he can live again) obtains his freedom. But if we thus actually die in Christ, we believe that we shall also actually live with him (not a merely symbolically glorified life, such as this present, but an actually glorified existence in the future), for we were actually united with him in his passion, and we know that he rose triumphant from the grave, to die no more; and so, we being in him, did likewise, and the act was final (as to us), for Christ died to sin once (and we also in him), but the life that he liveth he liveth no longer in mortal flesh on earth among men, but he liveth it in the presence of and unto God (and we also in him). Since we know, therefore, that these grand verities underlie the symbolic profession which we make in baptism, we must exalt the actual above the symbolic, and indeed look upon ourselves as dead unto sin, but alive unto God in Christ Jesus, and not as mere dreamers following an idle, visionary symbol.] **12 Let not sin therefore reign in your mortal body, that ye should obey the lusts thereof: 13 neither present your members unto sin as instruments of unrighteousness; but present yourselves unto God, as alive from the dead, and your members as instruments of righteousness unto God. 14 For sin shall not have dominion over you: for ye are not under law, but under grace.** [Thus the apostle vindicates his teaching, and shows that it does not justify any indulgence in sin. The Christian is to live realizing that in the person of Christ he has already actually passed from death unto life, and that therefore it is incumbent upon him to lead, as far as his strength permits, a life of heavenly perfection. He is to remember that however hard his conflict with sin may be, yet sin is not to lord it over him in the end, so as to procure his final condemnation, for he is under a system of grace which shall procure his pardon in the hour of judgment, and not under a system of law which would, in that hour, most certainly condemn him.]

II.

JUSTIFICATION RESULTS IN A CHANGE FROM SERVICE OF LAW AND SIN, WITH DEATH AS A REWARD, TO THE SERVICE OF GRACE AND RIGHTEOUSNESS, WITH LIFE AS A REWARD.

6: 15-22.

15 What then? shall we sin, because we are not under law, but under grace? God forbid. [In the last section Paul showed that sin was not justified, even though it causes God's goodness to abound. In this section he shows that freedom from the law does not justify freedom in sinning. As usual, he presents the proposition, denies its validity, and expands his denial in what follows.] **16 Know ye not, that to whom ye present yourselves** *as* **servants unto obedience, his servants ye are whom ye obey; whether of sin unto death, or of obedience unto righteousness?** ["I take it for granted that ye know and believe" (*Stuart*) the principles, that no man can serve two masters (Matt. 6: 24), and that no matter what profession he makes to the contrary, a man is truly the servant of that master to whom he habitually and continually yields a slavish obedience (John 8: 34). These things which are true in the ordinary walks of life are equally true in spiritual matters, whether this obedience be rendered unto sin, which compensates with the wages of eternal death, or whether it be rendered unto God, so as to be rewarded with righteousness or justification (which is a prerequisite to eternal life). Thus it appears that, while we are not under law, we are under God; and hence under obligation to foster and preserve our relation to him as his servants, a relationship which is not lost by a single act of weakness, but which is lost if we continue in sin. "The apostle," says Scott, "demanded whether it might not be proved what master any one served by observing the constant tenor of any one's conduct. A person may do an occasional service for any one to whom he is not servant; but no doubt he is the servant of that man to whom he habitually yields and addicts himself, and in whose work he spends his time, and strength, and skill, and abilities, day after day, and year after year."] **17 But thanks be to God, that, whereas ye were servants of sin, ye became obedient from the heart to that form of teaching whereunto ye were delivered; 18 and being made free from sin, ye became servants of righteousness. 19 I speak after the manner of men because of the infirmity of your flesh: for as ye presented your members *as* servants to uncleanness and to iniquity unto iniquity, even so now present your members *as* servants to righteousnesss unto sanctification.** [But thanks be to God that these principles are not mere matters of speculation with you, but have been tested and applied by you in your actual experience, for whereas ye were once the slaves of sin, ye, of your own free will and heart's choice, changed your masters, and became, by your obedience to it, the servants of slaves of the principles set down in the Christian or gospel form of teaching whereunto (as is the custom when slaves are sold) ye were delivered for service. Now, I use this illustration of the transfer of slaves, which is taken from daily, secular affairs, not because it is a perfect and adequate representation of your change of relationship in passing from the world unto Christ, but because your fleshly nature clouds your understanding of spiritual ideas, and you therefore comprehend them better if clothed in an earthly or parabolic dress, even if the figure or illustration is defective. Christ is far from being a tyrannical master, and certainly cherishes no such feelings towards you as those which a slave-owner holds towards his slaves; yet the figure nevertheless aids you to comprehend the point which I am now discussing, for you can readily see that, as under the old slavery, you presented your members as servants to impurity and to lawlessness for the purpose of being lawless, so, under the new service, it behooves you to now present your members as servants to righteousness for the purpose of becoming sanctified or holy.] **20 For when ye were servants of sin, ye were free in regard of righteousness.** [Whole-hearted service to God is now no more than you, by your past conduct, recognized as reasonable. For when ye were servants of sin ye made no effort whatever to serve righteousness, or to have two masters. If ye rendered no double-minded, divided service to sin in the days of your unregeneracy, surely you ought now to render a whole-souled, single-minded service to righteousness in these your regenerate days.] **21 What fruit then had ye at that time in the things whereof ye are now ashamed? for the end of those things is death. 22 But now being made free from sin and become servants to God, ye have your fruit unto sanctification, and the end eternal life. 23 For the wages of sin is death; but the free gift of God is eternal life in Christ Jesus our Lord.** [If consistency demands that you serve God with your whole heart, so profit and advantage also urges you so to do; for what profit had you when you served sin? In this present you were reaping, in that service, the things at which you may now well blush with shame, since they were preparing you to reap in the future death as a final harvest. But now having been made free from the slavery of sin, and having become a servant of God, your present reward is the blessedness and joy of a clean life, and your future reward is life eternal. And this is obvious, for, following my figure of slaves, masters and wages to the end, the wages which men earn and receive from your former master, sin, is death; but the wages which you can not earn, or deserve, but which God freely gives you for serving him, is eternal life in Christ Jesus our Lord.]

III.

CHANGE OF RELATIONSHIP FROM LAW TO CHRIST ILLUSTRATED.

7: 1-6.

[In 6: 14 Paul laid down the principle that sin does not have dominion over Christians, because they are not under law, but under grace. The section which we have just closed discusses the first clause of this proposition under the figure of slavery, and shows that sin does not have dominion over us, for we have changed masters. This section discusses the second half of the proposition under the figure of marriage, and shows that we are not under the law, but under grace, for in Christ we have died as to our former husband (law), and been married to our new husband (grace).] **1 Or are ye ignorant, brethren (for I speak to men who know the law), that the law hath dominion over a man for so long time as he liveth? 2 For the woman that hath a husband is bound by law to the husband while he liveth; but if the husband die, she is discharged from the law of the husband.** [If, on the one hand, ye are, as I have shown, emancipated from the horrible tyranny of sin, that ye may serve righteousness, so, on the other hand, are ye likewise emancipated from the more sane and orderly, but still rigorous, dominion of law, whether given by Moses or otherwise, that ye may live under the mild and gentle sway of grace. And would any of you deny this latter proposition? Surely, in order to do so, you must be very crude in knowledge; but I can not think you are so crude, for I am writing to those who know something about law, and hence must at least know this elementary principle, that law rules the living, and not the dead. The apostle might have cited many cases where this principle is applied: for instance, no public duties, taxes, etc., are required of the dead; they are never indicted for their crimes, etc.; but he chooses one illustration which peculiarly fits his argument, for it throws light on this question of dominion, viz.: the release from the law of marriage which is accorded to both the parties to a matrimonial contract, when death releases one of them. In this connection, and before we enter upon Paul's argument, we should notice the principle to which he appeals, in order that we may not be confused by his application of it. It is the *party who dies* that is primarily released or freed from the law, and hence left free to contract a second marriage. The party who survives is, of course, likewise freed; but the freedom of the survivor is secondary, and derived from the freedom of the deceased, which has been attained by death. If the living only were free, and the deceased were bound by the marriage contract, the apostle would have nothing on which to base an illustration or found an argument.] **3 So then if, while the husband liveth, she be joined to another man, she shall be called an adulteress: but if the husband die, she is free from the law, so that she is no adulteress, though she be joined to another man.** [If such freedom is accorded to the survivor, an equal liberty must be accorded to the deceased. But this liberty can not be enjoyed by him unless, by some means, he be raised from the dead.] **4 Wherefore, my brethren, ye also were made dead to the law through the body of Christ; that ye should be joined to another, *even* to him who was raised from the dead, that we might bring forth fruit unto God.** [While the marriage lasts the husband (law) has headship and control over the wife (mankind). But death breaks the marriage bond, so that both parties are thereby at once released and made free to marry again. But the Christian occupies the position of the deceased party. He was united to Christ, being in the humanity of Christ; and being thus in Christ, he was, as it were, married to the law, for Christ was born even under law in its strict Mosaic form (Luke 2: 21-27; Gal. 4: 4); and lived subject to that law (Matt. 5: 17, 18); and died to the law in the death of the cross (Col. 2: 14). Now we, being united to Christ in all this, are, in him as our representative, also dead to the law (6: 6;

CHANGE OF RELATIONSHIP 351

Gal. 2: 19), that we might, as one freed by death from marriage to the law (Ezek. 16: 8-38; Jer. 2: 2; 3: 14), be at liberty to contract the second marriage with and to the risen Christ, that in this marriage it might be our privilege and obligation not to obey the law, but to bring forth fruit unto God. The Christian, enjoying a resurrection in Christ, derives untold benefit from a well-recognized legal principle. Ordinarily the liberty from law enjoyed by the dead is of no practical value to them; but the Christian rising, in Christ his representative, from the dead, is free from law and espoused to Christ.] **5 For when we were in the flesh, the sinful passions, which were through the law, wrought in our members to bring forth fruit unto death. 6 But now we have been discharged from the law, having died to that wherein we were held; so that we serve in newness of the spirit, and not in oldness of the letter.** [These verses set forth the change in state and habit which results from our change of husbands, or the different fruitage of our lives, as suggested in verse 4. As Christians, a different fruitage is expected from that which our lives bore under the law; for before we became Christians, when we were governed by our fleshly nature, the sinful passions—passions which prompted us to gratify them, and which led us to sin if we did gratify them, and which we discovered to be sinful by means of the light of the law—lusted and worked in our bodily members to bring forth the fruit of death: but now we are released from the dominion of our husband (the law), having severed the tie that bound us to him by dying in the person of Christ, our representative, so that now we serve God with our new, regenerated spirit (an inward power), and not in the old-fashioned manner, which was by obedience to a written precept (an external power).]

IV.

THE SENSE OF BONDAGE WHICH COMES THROUGH THE RELATIONSHIP OF THE LAW PREPARES THE SOUL TO SEEK DELIVERANCE THROUGH RELATIONSHIP TO CHRIST.

7: 7-25.

7 What shall we say then? Is the law sin? God forbid. Howbeit, I had not known sin, except through the law: for I had not known coveting, except the law had said [Ex. 20: 17; Deut. 5: 21], **Thou shalt not covet: 8 but sin, finding occasion, wrought in me through the commandment all manner of coveting: for apart from law sin *is* dead.** [Those following the apostle through the last section would be apt to have confused views concerning the law, which would lead them to ask, "If it is such a blessed thing to be free from the law, is not the law evil? If God took as much pains to emancipate us from the law as he did to free us from sin, are not the law and sin equally evil, and practically synonymous, so that we can truly say, The law is sin?" Not at all, is the prompt denial of the apostle; but there is an apparent ground for such a question, for the law is an occasion of sin, for sin is not sin where it is not *known* to be sin, and in the law lies that revelation or knowledge of sin which makes it sinful, so that I had not experienced the sense of sin except through the law. For example, I would not have known that inordinate desire for the property of others was a sin called coveting if the law had not defined it, and made it a desire after the forbidden, and hence a sinful desire, by saying, Thou shalt not covet. But when the law thus spake, then sin, finding in the utterance of the law an opportunity or occasion to assert itself, stirred me up to desire all those things which were forbidden by the law, and filled me with the sense of my sinfulness by reason of the revelation of the law; for without this

THE SENSE OF BONDAGE 353

revelation the sense of sin would have been dead in me. Without the law sin was not roused to life and consciousness.] **9 And I was alive apart from the law once: but when the commandment came, sin revived, and I died; 10 and the commandment, which** *was* **unto life, this I found** *to be* **unto death: 11 for sin, finding occasion, through the commandment beguiled me, and through it slew me. 12 So that the law is holy, and the commandment holy, and righteous, and good.** [In the days of his youth (and perhaps also even in his young manhood—Phil. 3: 6), Paul had that free, untroubled conscience which is enjoyed by the innocent, and felt that he lived, and was entitled to live, before God; but later, as to its fullest extent he grasped the meaning of the law, he found how vain was his confidence; and that he was really a condemned man in the sight of God, having no true life in him (6: 21-23), being dead in trespasses and sin. Thus the law which was ordained to give life, and had the promise of life attached to it (10: 5; Lev. 18: 5), he found, to his amazed surprise, to be to him, because of his sinfulness, only a means of death: for sin, finding in the law a golden opportunity to accomplish his ruin, deceived him into breaking the law, and, by thus drawing down upon him the curse of the violated law, slew him. It has been observed that sin, as here personified, occupies the place filled by Satan in literal life (Gen. 3: 14; 2 Cor. 11: 3). Again we should note how Satan, operating on the sinful nature of Paul, beguiled and deceived him into supposing that he could obtain righteousness and life by keeping the Mosaic law (Phil. 3: 4-7), and also into thinking that in persecuting Christians he was doing God service (Acts 26: 9), while in reality he was making himself the chief of sinners (1 Tim. 1: 15). So, clearing the law of this doubt which his own argument had raised, the apostle declares in conclusion that it is worthy of all the unquestioned respect and confidence which it had so long enjoyed as a holy, righteous and good institution of God.] **13 Did then that which is good become death unto me? God forbid. But sin, that it might be shown to be sin, by working death to me** through that which is good;—that through the commandment sin might become exceeding sinful. [Paul assumes an objection suggested by the word "good," as though some one said, "Good? do you mean to call that good which works death in you?" and Paul replies, Did this good law really work death in me? Not at all; sin (and not law) worked death in me. And God ordained it thus to expose sin by letting it show itself as something so detestable that it could turn even so good a thing as the law to so evil a purpose as to make it an instrument of death; that is to say, the commandment was not given to injure me, but that through it sin might show itself to be exceeding sinful. God, the righteous, causes evil to work for good (Gen. 50: 20; Rom. 8: 20); but sin, the sinful, causes the good to result in evil.] 14 **For we know that the law is spiritual: but I am carnal, sold under sin. 15 For that which I do I know not: for not what I would, that do I practise; but what I hate, that I do. 16 But if what I would not, that I do, I consent unto the law that it is good.** [But the law can not be sin, for it is spiritual; *i. e.*, it is of divine origin, contains divine principles, and is addressed to the divine in man; and if man were as he should be, there would be no fault found with the law. But, alas! we are not as we should be. The law indeed is spiritual, but I (speaking for myself, and also as fairly representative of all other Christians) am not wholly spiritual, but carnal, and sold unto sin; *i. e.*, I dwell in a fleshly body, but have all the weaknesses, passions and frailties that flesh is heir to, and am, consequently, so much the servant of sin that I am as one sold into permanent slavery unto it; so that as long as I am in the flesh I have no hope to be wholly free from it. So much is this the case—so much am I a slave to powers that control me—that I act as one distracted, not fully knowing nor being conscious of the thing that I do; for my actions and practise are not according to my own wishes, which follow the law; but, on the contrary, I do those things which I hate, and which are contrary to the law; my spiritual nature wishing to obey the spiritual law, but not being able, because blended with my flesh and weakened by it. But if I do the things contrary to the law, at the same time wishing to do as the law directs, I agree with the law that it is right, endorsing it by my wish, though failing to honor it in my conduct. My own consciousness, therefore, belies the accusation that the law is sin.] **17 So now it is no more I that do it, but sin which dwelleth in me.** [From what I have said it is apparent that it is not my spiritual or better self, uninfluenced by the flesh, which does the evil; but it is sin which dwells in my flesh that does it. If I were left to my spiritual self, uninfluenced by the flesh, I would do as the law requires; but sin excites and moves my fleshly nature, and thus prompts me to break the law. The apostle is not arguing for the purpose of showing that he is *not responsible* for his own conduct; the establishment of such a fact would have no bearing whatever on the question in hand. He is arguing that the law is good, and he seeks to prove this by showing that his better, regenerated, spiritual nature loves it, and strives to fulfill it, and never in any way rebels against it; and that any seeming rebellion found in him is due to his fleshly, sinful nature—that part of himself which he himself repudiates as vile and unworthy, and which he would fain disown.] **18 For I know that in me, that is, in my flesh, dwelleth no good thing: for to will is present with me, but to do that which is good *is* not. 19 For the good which I would I do not: but the evil which I would not, that I practise.** [I am not surprised that part of me rebels against God's law, for I know that in the fleshly part of my nature dwells no good thing. Sin dominates my flesh, so that none of the tendencies which come from that part of me incite to righteousness, and the contrast between the spiritual and fleshly parts of me makes me painfully conscious of this fact; for on the spiritual side my power to wish, and to will to do right, is uncurbed and unlimited, but when I come to use the fleshly part to execute my will, here I encounter trouble, and feel my limitation; for I find myself hindered by the flesh, and unable, because of it, to perform the right which I have willed and wished. Yea, it is not in willing, but in this matter of performance, that I fail to keep the law; for though I wish to do good I can not compass it, and though I do not wish to do evil my fleshly nature constrains me to it even against my wish.] **20 But if what I would not, that I do, it is no more I that do it, but sin which dwelleth in me. 21 I find then the law, that, to me who would do good, evil is present.** [So then, I say again that I, in my own conscience, endorse the goodness of the law, for my spiritual nature wishes to perform its dictates, and only fails to do so because overborne by my fleshly nature, which sin has such power to influence. I find it then to be the rule of life, regulating my conduct, that though I always want to do good, evil is ever present with me, because I am in the flesh, which is never without evil influences. The presence of the flesh is the presence of evil, and since I can not rid myself of the one, neither can I of the other.] **22 For I delight in the law of God after the inward man: 23 but I see a different law in my members, warring against the law of my mind, and bringing me into captivity under the law of sin which is in my members.** [And such a state of conflict is unavoidable; for, in my spiritual and intellectual nature, I not only approve, but actually delight in, the law of God, so that I eagerly and heartily wish to perform its requirements, that I may be righteous; but when it comes to performance, I find a law within my flesh operating its members, antagonistic to that law of God which my intellect approves, and warring against it, and sometimes overcoming my allegiance to it, and bringing me into captivity to the sinful law which influences my flesh.] **24 Wretched man that I am! who shall deliver me out of the body of this death? 25 I thank God through Jesus Christ our Lord. So then I of myself with the mind, indeed, serve the law of God; but with the flesh the law of sin.** [Wretched or toil-worn man that I am, living in a state of perpetual warfare, now struggling to maintain my freedom under God's law, and anon led captive in spite of myself, and brought under the hard service of sin; who shall deliver me from this scene of warfare, from this fleshly, sinful nature which is condemning me to eternal death? Through Jesus Christ our Lord I render thanksgiving unto God my Deliverer. So then, in conclusion, with my mind or higher faculties I serve always the revealed will of God, and when, occasionally, I serve the law of sin, I do so, not with my mind, but because of the influences of my fleshly nature. The whole passage shows the helplessness of man under any form of law. Law does not change his nature, and hence law can not save him from himself. But God, in his dispensation of grace, provides for the change of man's nature, so that the sinful in him shall be eliminated, and his spiritual, regenerate nature shall be left free to serve God in righteousness.]

V.

THE NEW RELATIONSHIP TO CHRIST CHANGES THE MIND FROM CARNAL TO SPIRITUAL, SO THAT WE ESCAPE CONDEMNATION AND OBTAIN LIFE.

8: 1-11.

[This chapter describes, as Meyer says, "the happy condition of a man in Christ," and is, as Tholuck observes, "the climax of this Epistle."] **1 There is therefore now no condemnation to them that are in Christ Jesus. 2 For the law of the Spirit of life in Christ Jesus made me free from the law of sin and of death.** [From all that I have written, it is a just conclusion that, under Christ, we are so fully justified from sin that those who are in him shall stand uncondemned at the last judgment, since there is now no ground for their condemnation. For the gospel, or law, given by the Holy Spirit, who is the spirit of life, has made me free from law (whether given by Moses or otherwise) which produces sin and death. Laws which can not be obeyed result in sin, and sin ends in death.] **3 For what the law could not do, in that it was weak through the flesh, God, sending his own Son in the likeness of sinful flesh and for sin,** condemned sin in the flesh: 4 that the ordinance of the law might be fulfilled in us, who walk not after the flesh, but after the Spirit. [For what the law could not possibly do (viz.: condemn sin in the flesh, so as to destroy it and free us from it), because the flesh through which it operated was too weak, God, by sending his own Son in the likeness of sinful flesh, and for sin, did; that is to say, he condemned sin in the flesh, that justification from the law might be accomplished in us who walk not according to the flesh, but according to the Spirit. Though the law was designed to condemn and banish sin, and was in itself a perfect means of deliverance from sin and death to those who kept it, it was really, because of the sinful weakness of the human race, to which it was given, no means of deliverance at all, but a source of complete and perfect condemnation. Hence, some other deliverance became necessary. God provided this other means of salvation by sending his Son to die for man, and man's sin. That he might do this, God sent his Son to become a fleshly human being, to be incarnate in the same kind of flesh as that belonging to the rest of sinful mankind, thus fully sharing their nature. He sent him in this manner for the purpose of dying, to remove all the sin of the flesh he bore thus representatively, no matter by whom committed. Jesus, by his sinless life, lived in the flesh, as the Son of man, resisted, conquered, condemned, sentenced, and destroyed the power of sin in the flesh. Thus God sent his Son as a conqueror of sin, and as an offering for sin, that the ordinance of the law, which we fail to fulfill, might, by him who bore our flesh, and was our federal head and representative, be fulfilled in us who walk not according to the outward, fleshly nature, which lusts to do wrong, but after the inward, spiritual nature, which desires to do right.] **5 For they that are after the flesh mind the things of the flesh; but they that are after the Spirit the things of the Spirit.** [For they that live carnal lives indulge the lustful, evil desires of the flesh; but they that live after the Spirit set their minds on those heavenly things of the present and future which are revealed to man by the Spirit. Those who daily strive to lead

NEW RELATIONSHIP TO CHRIST

the latter life may hopefully look to God to forgive their shortcoming and temporary failure.] **6 For the mind of the flesh is death ; but the mind of the Spirit is life and peace** [Those who give themselves up to carnality, so that their minds take that general view of the affairs of life, shall reap death; but those who cultivate the thoughts and ideals of the Spirit, so that His mind governs the view of life, shall find great peace in their present lives, and hereafter life everlasting]: **7 because the mind of the flesh is enmity against God; for it is not subject to the law of God, neither indeed can it be: 8 and they that are in the flesh cannot please God. 9 But ye are not in the flesh but in the Spirit, if so be that the Spirit of God dwelleth in you. But if any man hath not the Spirit of Christ, he is none of his. 10 And if Christ is in you, the body is dead because of sin; but the spirit is life because of righteousness.** [That the fleshly mind leads to death is obvious, for the mind of the flesh is opposed to the God of life, since it is not only not subject to him, but can not become subject to him: so they that cherish it can not please him. The mind of man must be changed from carnal to spiritual, and he must cease to serve the flesh before he can serve God. But ye Roman Christians are not carnally, but spiritually minded, if indeed ye are truly regenerate, so that the Spirit of God dwells in you. If ye have not the Holy Spirit who proceeds from Christ, ye are not regenerate, ye are not his. And though Christ dwells in you (representatively by means of his Spirit), your body is doomed to natural death (and hence is to be accounted as already dead) because of (Adam's) sin; yet your spirit lives because it is justified and accounted righteous (by reason of Christ).] **11 But if the Spirit of him that raised up Jesus from the dead dwelleth in you, he that raised up Christ Jesus from the dead shall give life also to your mortal bodies through his Spirit that dwelleth in you.** [Moreover, if the Spirit of the Father (*i. e.*, the Holy Spirit) who raised up Jesus from the dead dwells in you, then he that raised up Christ Jesus from the dead shall also make alive your mortal bodies through his Holy Spirit that dwelleth in you; *i. e.*, if God employs the same agency, we may expect the same results, and hence we may look for him to raise us from the dead by the indwelling Holy Spirit, just as he raised Christ from the dead by that same indwelling Spirit.]

VI.

THE NEW RELATIONSHIP TO CHRIST RESULTS IN ADOPTION, THE SPIRIT OF ADOPTION, AND THAT HEIRSHIP FOR WHICH CREATION GROANS.

8: 12-25.

12 So then, brethren, we are debtors, not to the flesh, to live after the flesh: 13 for if ye live after the flesh, ye must die; but if by the Spirit ye put to death the deeds of the body, ye shall live. [So then, brethren, because of the relation which we sustain to Christ, and because of the opposite effects of living fleshly and spiritual lives, we, though free from the law, are under no obligation to be lawless, and to live after the flesh: for if ye so live ye must pay the penalty of such a course by dying; but if, by the exercise of your will, and the aid of the Holy Spirit, ye put an end to the sinful practices of your fleshly nature, ye shall live. The testimony of Christian experience is that the aid of the Holy Spirit, though real and effectual, is not so obtrusive as to enable the one aided to take sensible notice of it. To all appearance and sensation the victory over flesh is entirely the Christian's own, and he recognizes the aid of the Spirit, not because his burdens are sensibly lightened, but because of the fact that in his efforts to do right he now succeeds where lately he failed. The success, moreover, though habitual, is not invariable, for invariable victory over temptation breeds self-consciousness and self-righteousness, and other sins perhaps more dangerous than the ordinary lusts of the flesh.] **14 For as many as**

are led by the Spirit of God, these are the sons of God. [To mortify the flesh is to be led of the Spirit, and to be led of the Spirit is to be a son of God; for, though all in the church claim this sonship, the claim is only demonstrated to be genuine in the case of those who are led of the Spirit. The Spirit leads both externally and internally. Externally, the Spirit supplies the gospel truth as set forth in the New Testament, and the rules and precepts therein found are for the instruction and guidance of God's children. Internally, the Spirit aids by ministering strength and comfort to the disciple in his effort to conform to the revealed truth and will of God.] **15 For ye received not the spirit of bondage again unto fear; but ye received the spirit of adoption, whereby we cry, Abba, Father.** [That ye are the sons of God is apparent, as I say, because of the Spirit which leads and animates you, and which changes your own spirit. For, in your unsaved, unregenerate state you had a spirit of bondage, leading you to fear God, and his wrath; but when ye were baptized, and became regenerate, ye received a different spirit; viz.: the spirit of adoption or sonship, which dispels fear, and causes you, with confident gladness, to approach and address God as your Abba (which is, being interpreted, Father).] **16 The Spirit himself beareth witness with our spirit, that we are children of God: 17 and if children, then heirs; heirs of God, and joint-heirs with Christ; if so be that we suffer with *him*, that we may be also glorified with *him*.** [In interpreting this passage we should remember that Paul is speaking to those already converted. Hence, in these and in the preceding verses, he is not telling them how to *become* children of God, but how to *continue* such. Now, it is true that the Spirit lays down the terms by which we may become Christians, and if we obey these terms, then both the Holy Spirit and our own spirits testify that we are sons of God. But since Paul is not addressing converts, such an interpretation would be wide of his thought, which is this: If the Holy Spirit indeed leads us in a conflict with sin and a steady effort towards righteousness, and if we submit to be thus led, then the Holy Spirit unites with our spirit to testify that we are God's children. The testimony is, of course, *self-directed; i. e.*, the testimony is for the purpose of assuring and confirming our own faith. If we are *led*, we know it, and so our own spirit testifies to us. If we are led *in the godly, spiritual path*, it can be none other than the Holy Spirit who leads; and so, in the very act of leading, the Spirit testifies to us. And, lastly, if we are *led*, and if we *follow*, this union of our spirit and God's Spirit in joint action proves us children of God; for our co-operation with God in this paternal government of his shows us accepted of him as his children. But we can not be children in this one respect of government without being children also in the other respect of heirship. We are, therefore, God's heirs, joint-heirs with his only begotten Son, provided that we are truly led of the Spirit as he was, which we may readily test, for the Spirit led him through suffering to glory, and should lead us by the same pathway, if we are to enjoy somewhat of the same glory.] **18 For I reckon that the sufferings of this present time are not worthy to be compared with the glory which shall be revealed to us-ward. 19 For the earnest expectation of the creation waiteth for the revealing of the sons of God.** [Though the life in the spirit may involve us in sufferings, yet we are encouraged to bear them; for the sufferings are merely for the present time, and are insignificant when compared with the glory toward which they lead, which shall be revealed in us, and upon us, at the time of our resurrection. And this glory must indeed be as large as we imagine, for even creation itself waits in eager expectancy for this coming day, when the redeemed in Christ shall be revealed and manifested before all to be indeed the children of God. There is much argument as to what Paul means by "creation." From the context, we take it that he means the earth and all the life upon it except humanity.] **20 For the creation was subjected to vanity, not of its own will, but by reason of him who subjected it, in hope 21 that the creation itself also shall be delivered from the bondage of corruption into the liberty**

THE SPIRIT OF ADOPTION 363

of the glory of the children of God. **22 For we know that the whole creation groaneth and travaileth in pain together until now.** [And creation thus waits; for at and by reason of the fall of man, it became subject to frailty; *i. e.*, it also fell from its original design and purpose, and became abortive, diminutive, imperfect, and subject to premature decay. And this it did not do of its own accord, but because the will of God ordered that it should be thus altered (Gen. 3: 17, 18); not leaving it, however, without hope that it also should so far share in the redemption of the sons of God as not only to be delivered from the bondage of being corruptible, to which God subjected it, but also to be transferred to the liberty which results from or accompanies the revelation or glorification of the sons of God. And this hopeful waiting is evident, for we Christians know that God designs to make all things new (2 Pet. 3: 13; Rev. 21: 1, 5), and also that the whole creation so shares man's deterioration and degradation that with him it groans, and has, as it were, the pains of childbirth, even to this hour. The figure of childbirth is appropriate, since nature wishes to reproduce herself in a new, fresh and better form, corresponding to that which she had before the fall of man.] **23 And not only so, but ourselves also, who have the first-fruits of the Spirit, even we ourselves groan within ourselves, waiting for *our* adoption, *to wit*, the redemption of our body.** [And not only do we recognize this vast, unuttered longing of nature, but we find similar groanings even within ourselves, though occupying a much more privileged and advantageous position than nature, having, in the firstfruits of the Spirit, an earnest or inspiring foretaste of the good things to come, and yet, despite our advantage, so exceedingly desirable is the glory yet to be revealed, that even we ourselves groan within ourselves because of those parts wherein we are nearest akin to the material creation, waiting for the time to come when we shall be openly revealed as the adopted children of God, by those changes which culminate in that transformation brought about by the resurrection—when our mortal, corruptible, weak, dishonored, natural body shall be transfigured into the immortal, incorruptible, powerful, glorified, spiritual body, thus accomplishing the redemption of the body.] **24 For in hope were we saved: but hope that is seen is not hope: for who hopeth for that which he seeth? 25 But if we hope for that which we see not,** *then* **do we with patience wait for it.** [We groan, I say, waiting for this future blessing. For when we were converted and saved from the world, we were not so saved that all salvation includes was bestowed upon us; but we were saved unto a salvation which even yet exists largely in hope. If it were otherwise, we would now see the things which we still hope for. But when hope is attained it ceases to be hope, for hope applies only to the unattained, not to the attained. But if our full salvation is not yet seen or attained, then should we patiently wait for its attainment, which will be accomplished when we are at last revealed as God's children.]

VII.

THE NEW RELATIONSHIP RESULTS IN THE AID OF THE SPIRIT, AND IN BLISSFUL ASSURANCE OF SALVATION, BECAUSE IT IS DIVINELY DECREED.

8: 26-39.

26 And in like manner the Spirit also helpeth our infirmity: for we know not how to pray as we ought; but the Spirit himself maketh intercession for *us* **with groanings which cannot be uttered** [And not only are we encouraged by the sympathetic groaning of creation, and our well-grounded hopes to wait patiently for deliverance and glorification, but we are also in like manner aided in doing so by the ministration of the Holy Spirit, who helps us in our weakness, especially in obtaining the strength, patience, etc., necessary to enable us to endure faithfully until the hour of our deliverance arrives. And we require such help, for, left to ourselves, we would fail to ask for these things which we need, and would spend our time and strength asking for those things which we do not need; for we are not wise enough to pray for the things which, considering our real, present weakness, we ought to pray for. But the Spirit knows these needful things, and he affords a remedy for our weakness by himself interceding for us, not praying independently, or apart from us, but moving and exalting us in our prayer, and stirring within us sighings, longings, aspirations and soulful yearnings for those things which are our real needs, but which are so poorly understood by us that we can not adequately express them in words] ; **27 and he that searcheth the hearts knoweth what is the mind of the Spirit, because he maketh intercession for the saints according to** *the will of* **God.** [Though we, in our ignorance, do not know how to express these inward groanings, or yearnings, and though the Holy Spirit, in his operations within us, can not so lead or train us as to make us able to give them articulate utterance, yet God, who searcheth the heart, or that inner man where the Spirit dwells, knows what it is that the Spirit has in mind; *i. e.*, what the Spirit is prompting us to desire, because the Spirit pleads for the saints according to the will of God, asking those things which accord with the plans, purposes and desires of God. "In short," says Beet, "our own yearnings, resulting as they do from the presence of the Spirit, are themselves a pledge of their own realization." The remainder of the chapter gives the third ground of encouragement, which is briefly this: the Christian has nothing to fear (outside of himself), for nothing can defeat the plan or purpose which God cherishes toward him, and nothing can separate him from the love of God.] **28 And we know that to them that love God all things work together for good,** *even* **to them that are called according to** *his* **purpose.** [In addition to the encouragements already mentioned, there is this: We know (partly by experience, but primarily by revelation) that all these present ills, hardships, adversities, afflictions, etc., are so overruled of God as to be made to combine to produce the permanent and eternal advantage and welfare of those who love God, even, I say, to those who love God, or who may otherwise be described as those that are called according to his purpose. "All things" evidently refers to all that class of events which threaten to result in evil. The phrase evidently is not to be pressed, for it can hardly include sin or any other thing which injures the soul. The apostle himself, in verses 35-39, fully describes what he means by "all things." "The love of believers for God," says Lange, "is not the ground of their confidence, but the sign and security that they were first loved of God." The gospel reveals God's purpose to redeem, justify and glorify those who believe in Jesus. Those who accept this gospel through belief in Jesus are truly called of God according to the purpose for which he extended the call. Paul does not regard unbelievers as thus called, as the context shows, for the other descriptive clause which he here applies to the "called" (viz.: "those who love God") would not be applicable to unbelievers. Therefore the two clauses taken together show that Paul is simply speaking of Christians, or those who have heard the gospel, and have accepted it, and have been saved by it. All such know assuredly that God will direct the events of life so that they shall result in good to those called according to his purpose; for his purpose is of such import, such magnitude, such eternal fixedness and perennial vitality, etc., as to be a guarantee that God will permit no temporal accidentals to thwart it.] **29 For whom he foreknew, he also foreordained *to be* conformed to the image of his Son, that he might be the firstborn among many brethren: 30 and whom he foreordained, them he also called: and whom he called, them he also justified: and whom he justified, them he also glorified.** [The keyword which opens the hidden meaning of these two verses is the word *purpose*, found in verse 28. Before man was created God foresaw his fall, and designed the gospel for his redemption; this fact is well attested by Scripture (16: 25, 26; 1 Cor. 2: 7; Eph. 1: 8; 3: 9; Col. 1: 25, 26). In those times eternal, man, the gospel, justification, etc., existed only in the *purpose* of God; and it is of these times and conditions that the apostle speaks, showing how God foreknew that a certain class yet to be born would accept of a salvation yet to be provided through the terms of a gospel yet to be made actual. As to this class he foreordained, or foredecreed, that they should, after the resurrection, bear the image or likeness of his Son, that the Son might have the preeminence of being the firstborn (from the dead) among many brethren. And this class, whom in his *purpose* he thus foreordained, them likewise in his purpose he also called justified and glorified by successive steps, not actually, but in his purpose. Thus the apostle is speaking not of *actual* decrees, calls, justifications, etc., on the part of God, but of such as existing only in divine contemplation and purpose. So, also, he is not speaking of actual, called, etc., persons, but imaginary, ideal persons, who existed as yet only as a class in the councils or purposes of the Almighty; and Paul's design is not to show the foreordination of any individuals, but to substantiate the assurance of verse 28, by emphasizing the far-reaching purposes of God, which will not suffer afflictions, hardships, or any of the trivialities of time, to frustrate him in working out his eternal plans. That he is not speaking of actualities is shown by the last term in his sequence, viz.: "glorified." Since the apostle is speaking of what transpired in the councils of the Almighty prior to the creation of man, he properly uses the past tense: "glorified;" but if he were speaking of actuality, he would be compelled to use the future tense, to accord with conditions as stated in verse 18, where he clearly recognizes the glorification of man as a future event for which he waits. Thus it is apparent that the foreordination set forth in these two verses is purely hypothetical.] **31 What then shall we say to these things? If God *is* for us, who *is* against us?** [What conclusion, then, are we warranted in drawing from this definite and eternal purpose of God? If he be thus for us, are we not right in saying that all things shall work together for our good, for what is there that can work otherwise in successful opposition to God?] **32 He that spared not his own Son, but delivered him up for us all, how shall he not also with** him freely give us all things? [This verse is an answer, and more than an answer, to the question just asked. In it the negative and positive sides of God's actions are suggested, but not fully developed. The full thought may be thus expressed: To bring for his redeemed good out of all things may entail many sacrifices on the part of God—sacrifices which he might well regret to make on account of love for the thing sacrificed, and others which he might well withhold for lack of love towards the parties for whom the sacrifice is made. But what God has already done in accomplishing his eternal purpose is a guarantee that he will continue to do whatever more may be required. If he spared not his own Son, he will not halt at making any other sacrifice; neither value nor preciousness can cause him to withhold what we need. Again, our unworthiness and insignificance form no obstacle to the outpouring of his most marvelous gifts; for if God delivered up his own Son for us (while we were yet sinners), will he not now even more willingly and freely, to the gift of his Son, add all other gifts which lead to or consummate our glorification? In short, nothing but our own act of apostasy can cause us to fail of our inheritance.] **33 Who shall lay anything to the charge of God's elect? It is God that justifieth; 34 who is he that condemneth? It is Christ Jesus that died, yea rather, that was raised from the dead, who is at the right hand of God, who also maketh intercession for us.** ["But, Paul," says some doubting heart, "surely there are ten thousand things which will come to light to do us harm in the all-revealing hour of the judgment. It can not be that all these things shall then work us good." The apostle replies that these things will, at that time, certainly work us no evil, for in that august hour when all of all nations shall be called to give account before the throne of Christ the Judge, who is it that shall lay any charge against those whom the Father has chosen because of their faith in Christ and obedience to him? How could any one presume to attempt any such thing? or what difference would it make if he did attempt it? for it is the Father himself who speaks to the contrary, declaring that

THE AID OF THE SPIRIT 369

the sins of those who believe on Jesus are forgiven, and that they are justified in Jesus. Thus Christians shall be safe during the hearing; but when the hearing is closed, and the fate of each rests in the hands of the Judge, then shall they be equally safe as to the final sentence. Who shall condemn them? There is but one who has the power to do this, and that one is the Judge; and the Judge is none other than Christ Jesus, who died to expiate our sins, lest they should condemn us; who was raised for our justification; who was enthroned at the right hand of God to rule for our sakes, and to judge us; and who even now pleads as our intercessor against our condemnation. Surely the past and present attitudes of Christ towards us guarantee his future conduct, and confirm us in the confidence that he, the unchangeable, will acquit us in that hour, and save us from the condemnation against which he has made such ample preparation and provision. So far as the Father is concerned, the cause of man is settled and sealed, for he has committed judgment to the Son. Whatever contingency there is, lies, therefore, in the bosom of the Son. He has made the sacrifice, and accomplished the work necessary to acquit man at the judgment; but as his decree and sentence are not yet spoken, it is, of course, contingent. Will he change his mind, and condemn man? The apostle answers this question by asking another.] **35 Who shall separate us from the love of Christ? shall tribulation, or anguish, or persecution, or famine, or nakedness, or peril, or sword?** [The thought of verse 28, which has not been out of the apostle's mind since he introduced it, here comes once more squarely to the front. Shall any of the hardships of our present life so work evil as to cause Christ to change his present feeling toward us, or his future purpose to justify us? Can we who know his love ask such a question? Can anything in the whole catalogue of hardships work such results? Though in our day the sufferings may vary somewhat from the items given by the apostle, yet they raise the same doubts—produce in us the same effects. It is natural to man to look upon the sufferings of the Christian life as a contradiction to the scheme of grace.

According to our earthly conceptions, a journey which is to *end* in glorification should continually rise toward it, so that pleasures, joys, honors, etc., should increase daily. When, instead of such a program, we meet with tribulation, anguish, nakedness, etc., it looks to us as if God were leading us the wrong way—the way that would end in degradation and death, rather than glorification and life. The answer to such thoughts is found in this argument of the apostle. God makes any road lead to good and glorification, and especially those roads which seem to run in the opposite direction; so that we may regard those things which appear to argue his hatred and neglect as, on the contrary, the strongest evidences of his love and care. And this, adds the apostle, is no new truth, for it has been the experience of God's people in the past, as the Scripture testifies.] **36 Even as it is written, For thy sake we are killed all the day long; We were accounted as sheep for the slaughter.** [Ps. 44: 22. This Psalm is supposed to have been written during the Babylonish captivity, and that it is a correct description of the state of the Jew in that day, we may readily conceive from details given in Daniel and Esther. But the Psalm was also prophetic. As the Jew suffered because of the peculiar religion which God had bestowed upon him, so also did the Christian; and in both cases the enemies of the revealed religions looked upon the worshipers as people who were to be killed as a matter of course, without compunction or pity, just as sheep are slain for sacrifice or for the market.] **37 Nay, in all these things we are more than conquerors through him that loved us.** [But though we be in tribulation, and be slain like sheep, yet in all these things we not only gain the conquest, so that we survive them, but we come out more than victors, for we are crowned over them with immortality and eternal life. But this victory is achieved not of ourselves, but because of the love of Christ, who, by his death, won for us these better things. The phrase "more than conquerors" is a single word in the Greek, and means, literally, "over-conquerors." Some see in this a peculiar kind of victory. "This is a new order of victory," says Chrysostom, "to conquer by means of our adversaries." "The adversaries," says Chillingsworth, "are not only overcome and disarmed, but they are brought over to our faction; they war on our side." If such a meaning may be properly put upon this word, then the idea here is beautifully harmonious and consonant with the thought expressed in verse 28, which shows that God indeed causes things which seem to be inimical to serve our interests and further our blessedness.] **38 For I am persuaded that neither death, nor life, nor angels, nor principalities, nor things present, nor things to come, nor powers, 39 nor height, nor depth, nor any other creature, shall be able to separate us from the love of God, which is in Christ Jesus our Lord.** [From the various grounds of assurance which he has enumerated in this chapter, Paul gives it as his own personal, final conviction that (apart from the disciple's own will) nothing can separate him from God's love as displayed in the gift of Christ to die for man's redemption, and to reign for man's glorification. To illustrate the wide range of possible antagonism which may arise to oppose man's glorification, he submits a wonderful list of things having such inherent vastness and grandeur that they can not be defined without diminution and loss. If we should attempt to explain him, we would say that neither terrestrial existence, with its phases of life and death; nor celestial existence, reaching from angels to unknown altitudes of rulership; nor time, present or future; nor any other imaginable power; nor space, heavenward or hellward; nor any other form of creation, visible or invisible, known or unknown, can effect a separation between God and those objects of his love whom he has redeemed in Christ. As to the whole passage, the words of Erasmus are a characteristic comment. "Cicero," says he, "never said anything more eloquent." It is far more easy for us all to grasp the rhetorical and superficial beauty of this marvelous passage, which soars to the extreme altitude of divine inspiration, than to appreciate, even in the slightest or most remote degree, the excellencies of the sublime and eternal verities which it seeks to bring home to our consciences. The love of God is so little comprehended by our sinful and finite natures, that expositions of it are to us as descriptions of color are to the blind, or as explanations of melody and harmony are to the deaf. We, as they, admire the verbiage and the skill of him who has dazed our understanding, and are hardly conscious how far we fall short of truly following the conceptions which the writer sought to convey to our spirits.]*

---

* NOTE.—At this point the work on Romans was discontinued on the 16th of July, 1908. Since then (in October, 1911) Bro. McGarvey went to his rest and reward. Now, June 15, 1914, I resume work alone, and shall miss him. He was to me a considerate editor, a genial companion, a most thoughtful and faithful friend. Soon after the work was discontinued I received from him a much-prized letter, containing these words: "You have written a commentary which will compare favorably with any."

Encouraged in part by so frank a commendation from so competent an authority, I did not destroy my analysis of the Book of Romans; but (though it is very similar to that found in the Introduction) I filed it away, believing that if his judgment were correct, the merits of the work would some day call for its completion. Now, after five years and eleven months, the analysis comes forth from its dusty pigeon-hole and the work is resumed; but he is not here to rejoice with me. How inspiring the thought that he is where the pleasures unknown abound, and where such joys as I would share with him are as dust and weightless motes upon the balances!

CINCINNATI, O., June 15, 1914.   PHILIP Y. PENDLETON.

PART SECOND.

EXPLANATORY: THE DOCTRINE OF RIGHTEOUSNESS BY FAITH RECONCILED AS TO (1) THE PROMISES MADE TO ISRAEL; (2) THE ELECTION AND COVENANTS OF THAT PEOPLE; (3) THE SCRIPTURES; (4) THE FAITHFULNESS OF GOD.

9:1-11:36.

I.

SINCE HIS DOCTRINE RESULTS IN THE CONDEMNATION OF ISRAEL, PAUL SHOWS THAT THIS RESULT IS CONTRARY TO HIS PERSONAL BIAS, OR WISH

9:1-5.

[In Part I. of his Epistle (chaps. 1-8) Paul presented the great doctrine that righteousness and salvation are obtained through faith in Jesus Christ. But the unbelief of the Jews excluded them generally from this salvation, yet "salvation is from the Jews" (John 4:22). The doctrine, and the situation engendered by it, raised before the minds of Paul's readers several great questions, such as these: How could Scripture, which promised blessings to the Jews, be fulfilled in a gospel which gave blessings to Gentiles to the exclusion of Jews? The covenants to Abraham guaranteed blessings to his seed, how, then, could the gospel be the fulfillment of these covenants when it brought blessing and salvation to the Gentiles, and rejection and damnation to the Jews, the seed of

Abraham? It is for the purpose of answering these and kindred questions which naturally arose out of the doctrine of the first part of his work, that this second part was written. As these questions arose out of the history of Israel, Paul naturally reviews that history, so Tholuck calls this second part of his work "a historical corollary." The apostle's effort is to show that the gospel of Christ, while it conflicts with the false doctrinal deductions which the Jews drew from their history, agrees perfectly with all correct deductions from that history.] **I say the truth in Christ** [This is not an oath. Some modern, and most of the earlier, commentators suppose it is; but they forget that Deut. 6:13 is repealed at Matt. 5:33-37. If it were an oath, we would, in the absence of any verb of swearing, have the Greek preposition *pros* ("by") with the genitive, but instead we have *en* ("in") with the dative. His asseveration is, however, as solemn and binding as an oath, and is designed to give vehement emphasis to his words—comp. 2 Cor. 2:17: as though he said, "I speak the truth, for Christ is true, and I am a member in Christ, and he himself, therefore, speaks through me—comp. Gal. 2:20; Phil. 1:21], **I lie not** [Such a coupling of the positive and negative for purposes of emphasis is common to Scripture. See Deut. 33:6; Isa. 38:1; John 1:20], **my conscience bearing witness with me in the Holy Spirit** [my conscience, though enlightened, guided and made more than naturally sensitive and accurate by the indwelling of the Holy Spirit, still testifies that in this I am wholly and unequivocally truthful], **2 that I have great sorrow and unceasing pain in my heart.** [Paul, in the depth of his passion, does not deliberately state the cause of his grief, but leaves it to be implied. His grief was that the gospel had resulted in the rejection of his own people, the Jews. He had closed the first part of his Epistle in a triumphant outburst of praise at the glorious salvation wrought by the gospel of belief in Christ, but ere praise has died on his lips, this minor wail of anguish opens the second part of his Epistle because Israel does not participate in this glad salvation. "The grief for his nation and people," says Poole, "he expresseth, 1. By the greatness of it; it was such as a woman hath in travail; so the word imports. 2. By the continuance of it; it was *continual,* or without intermission. 3. By the seat of it; it was in his *heart,* and not outward in his face." And why does Paul asseverate so strongly that he feels such grief? 1. Because only himself and God (and God had to do with him through Christ and the Holy Spirit) knew the hidden secrets of his bosom. 2. Because without some such asseveration the Jews would hardly believe him in this respect. Even Christian Jews looked upon his racial loyalty with suspicion (Acts 21:20, 21); what wonder, then, if unbelieving Jews regarded him as the most virulent enemy of their race (Acts 28:17-19), and believed him capable of corrupting any Scripture to their injury, of inventing any doctrine to their prejudice, of perverting any truth into a lie to work them harm? (See 2 Cor. 6:8; 1:17; 2:17; 4:1, 2; 7:2, etc.) In their estimation Paul was easily capable of giving birth to this doctrine of salvation by faith for no other end than the joy of pronouncing their damnation for their unbelief. Yea, they could readily believe that his joy expressed at Rom. 8:31-39 was more due to the fact that Israel was shut out from salvation, than that there was salvation. To thoroughly appreciate the full bitterness of the Jewish mistrust and hatred toward Paul we must remember the constancy with which for years they persecuted him, and that very soon after the writing of this Epistle they occasioned his long imprisonment in Rome, and relentlessly persisted in their accusations against him till they became the immediate cause of his martyrdom. Therefore, in expressing his sorrow over the rejection of Israel, Paul pledges his truthfulness in Christ for whom he had suffered the loss of all things, and in the Holy Spirit who was wont to strike down all lying Ananiases (Acts 5:3-5), for it

was necessary, before another word be said, that
every Jew should know that Paul's doctrine was not
his own, that it did not arise in his mind because of
any spleen, malice, hostility, illwill, or even mild distaste for the Jewish people. On the contrary, his personal bias was against the doctrine which he taught;
and none knew this so well as the Christ with whom
the doctrine arose, and the Holy Spirit who inspired
Paul to teach it.] 3 **For I could wish** [Literally, "I
was wishing." Some therefore regard Paul as referring to his attitude to Christ while he was persecuting
the church in the days before his conversion. But
Paul is asserting his *present* love toward Israel, and
his *past* conduct proved nothing whatever as to it.
The tense here is the imperfect indicative, and is
correctly translated "I could wish," for it indicates
arrested, incomplete action, a something never finished; and it therefore often stands for the conjunctive.
This potential or conditional force of the imperfect
is, as Alford remarks, "no new discovery, but common enough in every schoolboy's reading." Paul
means to say that he never actually formed this wish,
but could conceive of himself as going to the length
of forming it, if admissible—if it were merely a question of love toward his countrymen, and no obstacle
intervened] **that I myself were anathema from Christ
for my brethren's sake** [The root idea of anathema
is anything cut or torn off, anything separated or
shut up. In the Old Testament the inanimate thing
devoted or anathematized was stored up, while the
animate thing was killed (Lev. 27:26-29). Compare
the anathemas of Jericho and Achan (Josh. 6:16;
7:15, 22-26). But the New Testament prefers that
use of the word which indicates spiritual punishment;
viz., exclusion, banishment, as in the case of one resting under a ban (Gal. 1:8. 9; 1 Cor. 12:3; 16:22), for
Paul certainly ordered no one to be physically put to
death. The idea of banishment is, in this case, made
even more apparent by the addition of the words "from
Christ." Paul therefore means to say, "I may, indeed,

CONDEMNATION OF ISRAEL 377

be regarded as an enemy of my people, delighting in their being excluded from salvation by their rejection of the gospel (as they indeed are—Gal. 1:8, 9; 5:4); but so far am I from doing this that I could, were it permissible, wish for their sakes that I might so exchange places with them that I might be cut off from Christ, and be lost, that they might be joined to him and be saved. For their sakes I could go into eternal perdition to keep them from going there." Men of prudent self-interest and cold, speculative deliberation regard Paul's words as so unreasonable that they would pervert them in order to alter their meaning. They forget that Judah offered to become a slave in Benjamin's stead (Gen. 44:18-34); that David wished he had died for Absalom (2 Sam. 18:33), and that the petition of Moses exceeded this unexpressed wish of the apostle (Ex. 32:32). They are blind to the great truth that in instances like this "the foolishness of God" (even operating spiritually in men of God) "is wiser than men" (1 Cor. 1:25). No man can be a propitiation for the souls of other men. Only the Christ can offer himself as a vicarious sacrifice for the lives of others so as to become in their stead a curse (Gal. 3:13), abandoned of God (Mark 15:34). But surely the true servant of Christ may so far partake of the Spirit of his Master as to have moments of exalted spiritual grace wherein he could wish, were it permissible, to make the Christlike sacrifice. (Comp. 2 Cor. 12:15; Phil. 2:17; 1 Thess. 2:8; 1 John 3:16.) In this instance we may conceive of Paul as ardently contemplating such a wish, for: 1. He had prophetic insight into the age-long and almost universal casting off of the Jews, and their consequent sorrows and distresses, all of which moved him to unusual compassion. 2. He had also spiritual insight into the torments of the damned, which would stir him to superhuman efforts on behalf of his people. 3. He could conceive of the superior honor to Christ if received by the millions of Israel instead of the one, Paul. 4. He could deem it a sweeter joy to

Christ to give salvation unto the many, rather than merely unto the one, Paul. 5. He could contrast the joys his exchange might give to the many with the single sorrow of damnation meted out to himself alone, and could therefore feel some satisfaction in contemplating such a sacrifice for such a purpose. (Comp. Heb. 12:2.) 6. Finally, just before this he has asserted the possibility of one *dying* for a *righteous* or *good man* (Rom. 5:7). If such a thing is possible, might not Paul be excused if he felt ready, not only to die, but even to suffer *eternal exclusion from Christ,* if his act could avail to save a whole covenanted people, so *worthy* and so *loved of God,* as Israel was shown to be by those honors and favors bestowed upon it, which he proceeds at once to enumerate? Under all the circumstances, therefore, it is apparent that such strong words and deep emotions are to be expected from one who loved as did Paul. For further evidences of his love toward churches and individuals, see 1 Cor. 1:4; Phil. 1:3, 4; Eph. 1:16; 1 Thess. 1:2; Philem. 4; 2 Tim. 1:3, 4; 2 Cor. 11:28, 29], **my kinsmen according to the flesh** [And here we have the first impulse for the strong expression of passion just uttered. In the Jew an ardent family affection, blending with an intense national pride, combine to form a patriotism unparalleled in its fervor and devotion]: **4 who are Israelites** [The first distinction of the chosen people was their descent from and right to the name "Israel": a name won by Jacob when, wrestling, he so prevailed with God that he was called Israel, or prince of God (Gen. 32:28), and also won for himself the unique honor of having *all* his descendants bear his name, and be accepted as God's covenant people]; **whose is the adoption** [*i. e.,* the Sonship. Israel is always represented as the Lord's *son* or first-born, in contradistinction to the Gentiles, who are his creatures—Ex. 4:22, 23; 19:5; Deut. 7:6; 14:1; Isa. 1:2; Jer. 31:9; Hos. 11:1; Mal. 1:6], **and the glory** [The glory of having God manifested visibly as their friend and protector. This glory was called the Shekinah and appeared in the pillar of cloud by day and fire by night (Ex. 13:21, 22), and rested on Mt. Sinai (Ex. 24:16) and on the tabernacle (Ex. 29:43), and in the tabernacle (Ex. 40:34-38; Lev. 9:23, 24), and enlightened the face of Moses (Ex. 34:29-35; 2 Cor. 3:7-18), and filled Solomon's temple (1 Kings 8:10, 11), and is thought to have abode between the cherubim, over the mercy-seat of the ark of the covenant (Ex. 25:22; 29:43, 44; Heb. 9:5), whence it is also thought that the ark itself is once called "the glory of Israel"—1 Sam. 4: 21], **and the covenants** [Especially the Messianic and promised-land covenants given to Abraham, Isaac and Jacob, to which may be added the covenants with Aaron (Ex. 29:9) and Phinehas (Num. 25:10-13), and those made with Israel on the plains of Moab (Deut. 29, 30) and at Shechem (Josh 24:25), and the throne covenant with David (2 Sam. 7:12-17], **and the giving of the law** [It was given at Mt. Sinai directly from the person of God himself, and its retention in Israel was a notable mark of distinction between them and all other people, for it placed them under the divine government, as the peculiar heritage of Jehovah], **and the service of God** [The order of praise and worship in tabernacle and temple under charge of Levites and priests and explained at length in the Epistle to the Hebrews. "The grandest ritual," says Plumer, "ever known on earth, with its priests, altars, sacrifices, feasts, and splendid temple"], **and the promises** [The term "promise" is about the same as "covenant" (Acts 2:39; Rom. 15:8; Gal. 3:16; Eph. 2:12; Heb. 11:17). If there is any distinction to be drawn between the two words, covenant is the larger, including threatenings as well as assurances of grace. In the promises the threatenings are omitted, and the details of the good are enlarged]; **5 whose are the fathers** [At Hebrews 11 we have the list of the chief of these fathers. They were Israel's pride and inspiration. "The heroes of a people," says Godet, "are regarded as its most precious treasure."

The three pre-eminent "fathers" were Abraham, Isaac and Jacob—Ex. 3:6, 13, 15; 4:5; Matt. 22:32; Acts 3:13; 7:32], **and of whom** [*i. e.*, of or descended from the fathers] **is Christ as concerning the flesh** [Paul's enumeration of Israel's endowments ends in this as the climax of all their glories when coupled with the statement as to the divine nature of this Christ. But to this climax Israel failed to attain. They accepted neither the humanity nor divinity of Christ, hence Paul's grief], **who is over all, God blessed for ever. Amen.** [These words have quite a history. None of the so-called Ante-Nicene Fathers (theologians who wrote prior to A. D. 325) ever thought of contorting them from their plain reference to Christ. Even among later writers, but two—Diodorus of Tarsus (bishop in A. D. 378; died in 394) and Theodore of Mopseustia (A. D. 350-429)—ever questioned their reference to Christ. Then came Erasmus (A. D. 1465-1536). This fertile genius seems to have exerted all his ingenuity on this passage, for, by changing the punctuation, he made it read four different ways, two of which have attracted some notice. The first of these reads thus: "Of whom is Christ as concerning the flesh, who is over all. Blessed be God for ever. Amen." This effort to cut off the last clause and make a benediction of it is open to several objections; we note two. 1. It is too abrupt. 2. It is not grammatical if taken as a benediction, for to be in correct form *eulogetos* ("blessed") should precede *Theos* ("God"), but, instead, it follows it, as in narrative form (Rom. 1:25; 2 Cor. 11:31), which it is. The second reading makes the whole passage a benediction, thus: "Of whom is Christ concerning the flesh. Blessed for ever be God, who is over all. Amen." To this reading it may be properly objected: 1. That a benediction is contrary to the apostle's mood and thought. He is mourning over the rejection of Israel. Though he does recount the endowments of Israel, why should he burst forth in ecstatic benediction when all these endowments only brought the heavier condemnation because of Israel's unbelief? 2. Why should he leave his analysis of Christ unfinished (compare the finished, similar analysis at Rom. 1:3, 4) to wind up in a benediction, when he might have finished his analysis and thereby laid, in a finished climax, a better basis for a benediction? 3. Again, the *eulogetos* still follows the *Theos*, when it should precede it to form a benediction, as it does above twenty times in Scripture (Luke 1:68; 2 Cor. 1:3; Eph. 1:3; 1 Pet. 1:3, etc.). 4. The *ho oon*, "who is," stands naturally as in apposition to the preceding subject, *ho Christos*, "the Christ," and if by any unusual construction it has been meant to be taken in apposition to *Theos*, "God," it is hardly conceivable that we should have had the participle *oon*, "is" (literally "being"), which under such a construction is superfluous and awkward. This untenable reading would soon have been forgotten, but, unfortunately, Meyer has given respectability to it by a long argument in its favor; in which he insists that the reading, "Christ . . . who is over all, God blessed for ever," is contrary to the invariable teaching of Paul, who always recognizes the subordination of the Son to the Father and who does this by *never* calling the Son "God"; always reserving that title for the Father. It is true that Paul recognizes this subordination, and generally does it in the way indicated, but he does it as to Christ *the unit; i. e.,* Christ the united compound of God and man. But Paul is here resolving that compound into its two elements; viz., Christ, man-descended after the flesh; and Christ, God after the Spirit. Now, when thus resolved into his elements, the divine in Christ is not described as subordinate to the Father, nor is the full measure of deity withheld from him. On the contrary, John and Paul (whom Meyer conceives of as disagreeing as to the Christ's subordination) agree perfectly in this, only Paul is even clearer and more explicit in his statement. John begins with our Lord before his divinity became compounded with humanity, and calls him the Word. "In the beginning," says he, "was the Word, and the Word was with God, and the Word was God" (John 1:1). Surely there is no subordination indicated by John in treating of the *separate* divine nature of our Lord. Then he tells of the compounding of that divine nature with the human nature. "And the Word," says he, "became flesh, and dwelt among us" (John 1:14). Here, then, is that compounding of divinity and humanity which we call Jesus, and this Jesus is, according to John, subordinate to the Father. On this important point John lets the God-man speak for himself. "The Father," says Jesus, "is greater than I" (John 14:28). Now let us compare this teaching with the doctrine of Paul. "Have this mind in you," says he, "which was also in Christ Jesus: who, existing in the form of God" (that is, when he was what John calls the Word; when he was not as yet compounded with humanity), "counted not the being on an equality with God" (here Paul is more explicit than John in asserting our Lord's unsubordinate condition before he became incarnate) "a thing to be grasped, but he emptied himself, taking the form of a servant, being made in the likeness of men" (equivalent to John's "the Word became flesh," after which follows the statement of subordination; viz.); "and being found in fashion as a man, he humbled himself, becoming obedient *even* unto death, yea, the death of the cross," etc. (Phil. 2:5-11). To one, therefore, who carefully compares these passages, it is apparent that according to apostolic doctrine Jesus, the unit, is subordinate to the Father, but when Jesus is separated by analysis into his component parts, his divine nature is God, and equal with God (Col. 2:9). At Rom. 1:3, 4 this divine nature is called "Son of God"; here it is called "God over all, blessed for ever." So Meyer's contention against the reading of the text is not well taken. The natural reading refers the words to Christ, and there is good Scriptural reason why this should be done, for all things here said of Christ rest on

Scriptural authority; for (1) he is called God (Isa. 9:6; John 1:1; Phil. 2:5-11; John 20:28; Tit. 1:3; 2:13; 3:4, 6; Col. 2:9. Comp. 1 Tim. 2:5 with Acts 20:28, and the "my church" of Matt. 16:18). (2) The term *eulogetos* may be fittingly applied to him, for it is even applied to mere men by the LXX. (Deut. 7:14; Ruth 2:20; 1 Sam. 15:13), and is no stronger than the term "glory" (2 Pet. 3:18; Heb. 13:21; 2 Tim. 4:18). (3) Christ himself claims to be "over all" (John 3:31; Matt. 28:28), and it is abundantly asserted that such is the case (Phil. 2:6-11; Eph. 1:20-23; Rom. 10:12; Acts 10:36). So complete is his dominion that Paul deems it needful to expressly state that the Father is not made subordinate (1 Cor. 15:25-28). The whole passage, as Gifford well says, constitutes "a noble protest against the indignity cast upon him (Christ) by the unbelief of the Jews."

II.

THE REJECTION OF ISRAEL NOT INCONSISTENT WITH GOD'S PROMISE OR ELECTION—HIS PROMISE HAS BEEN KEPT TO THOSE TO WHOM IT WAS GIVEN.

9:6-13.

6 But it is not as though the word of God hath come to nought. [Or, as Fritsche translates, "The matter, however, is not so as that the word of God had come to nought." Paul is answering the reasoning of the Jew which runs thus: "You speak of God's covenants and promises given to the fathers and enlarged in the Scriptures, yet you say the Jew has failed to receive the blessings guaranteed to him by God in those covenants and promises. If such is the case, then you must admit that the word of God has failed of fulfillment." Paul begins his answer by denying the failure of the word of God, and proceeds to prove his denial. But his argument is not rigidly polemic; it is rather a heart-to-heart discussion of well-known historic facts which show that God's present enactments, rulings and executions harmonize perfectly with those of the past, which, too, have been heartily and unanimously approved by the Jews. "No," is then Paul's answer, "the word of God has not come to nought in Israel's rejection, for it (in the Old Testament), as you well know and approve, taught and worked out in precedent and example the same principles and same distinctions which are to-day affecting the rejection of Israel." God has not changed, nor has his word failed: it was Israel which had changed and failed.] **For they are not all Israel, that are of Israel** [The Jews would never have regarded Paul's teaching as subversive of the promises or word of God if they had not misconstrued the promises. They read them thus: "The promises guarantee salvation to all Jews, and the Jews alone are to be saved." Paul begins his argument by denying the correctness of their construction of God's word. "The word of God has not failed," says he, "because God has cast off a part of Israel (the fleshly part represented by the Jews), for God's word is kept as long as he keeps covenant with the other part (the spiritual part, represented by the Christians, principally Gentiles), for you are wrong in thinking that all the descendants of Jacob are reckoned by God as Israelites, or covenant people, and also wrong in supposing that Israel has only fleshly children, and no spiritual children." This argument apparently concedes for the moment that God's covenant was to give Israel salvation, which was not really the case. God's covenant was to provide the sacrifice in his Son, which would *afford the means of salvation,* conditioned on faith and obedience]: **7 neither, because they are Abraham's seed, are they all children: but** [as God said to Abraham—Gen. 21:12], **In Isaac shall thy seed be**

GOD'S PROMISE KEPT

called. [*I. e.*, the children of Isaac alone shall be known distinctively as thy children, the heirs of thy covenant. Here, again, Paul attacks a second false construction which the Jews placed upon the promises. They said: "We must all be saved because we have Abraham for our father (Matt. 3:9). If God does not save us, he breaks his word with Abraham." "Here again ye err," says Paul, "for at the very start when Abraham had but two sons, God rejected one of them, casting Ishmael off, and choosing Isaac; and later when Abraham had many sons God still refused all but Isaac, saying, The sons of yours which I shall call mine shall descend from Isaac alone."] **8 That is, it is not the children of the flesh** [of Abraham] **that are** [reckoned or accounted as] **children of God; but the children of the promise are reckoned for a seed.** [Are accounted the children of God through Abraham. Fleshly descent from Abraham, of itself and without more—*i. e.*, without promise—never availed for any spiritual blessing (Gal. 4:23). "This," says Trapp, "profiteth them no more than it did Dives, that Abraham called him son" (Luke 16:25). So flesh avails neither then nor now, but *promise*. Paul proceeds to show that Isaac was a son of promise, and whatever covenants or promises availed for his children came to them because they, through him, became symbolically sons of promise, Isaac typifying Christ, the real son of promise given to Abraham (Gal. 3:16), and Isaac's posterity typifying the real children of promise, the regenerated sons of God begotten unto Christ through the gospel (Gal. 4:28; John 1:12, 13). So as Abraham had a fleshly seed according to the first promise, "In Isaac shall thy seed be called," these being Jews; so he had a spiritual seed according to the second promise, "In thee and in thy seed shall all the nations [Gentiles; but not excluding Jews] of the earth be blessed," these being Gentiles. Hence, if the two promises were each kept with the two parties to whom they were severally given, the word of God was not broken, and his promise had not failed.

But such was indeed the case, for God kept his word with the fleshly seed, fulfilling to them the fleshly promise that Christ should be born of their stock (John 4:22; Gal. 3:16), and to the spiritual seed he was fulfilling the spiritual promise granting them eternal life through that faith in Christ which made them spiritual children of Abraham, the father of the faithful (Gal. 3:7-14). So it was not two promises to one seed, but two promises to two seeds, and each promise was kept of God to each promisee. And why, says Paul, do we call Isaac the son of promise? Because he was not born according to the natural law of the flesh, his mother being past bearing, but contrary to nature and by reason of the divine power, working to fulfill the promise of God, which promise is as follows] 9 **For this is a word of promise** [this is the saying or promise that brought Isaac into being, and made him a child of promise and not of natural birth —Gen. 18:10], **According to this season** [Godet translates, "Next year at the moment when this same time (this same epoch) will return"] **will I come** [to fulfill my promise], **and Sarah shall have a son.** [This fixing of the definite time (an exact year from the date of the promise) when the child of promise should be born, is extremely significant. Ishmael was alive when this promise was given. But what Jew would have justified him in urging a claim as against the promised Isaac? Later, in the days of Daniel, a time limit was set for Christ, the greater Son of promise, by which it is made sure that he would begin his ministry in A. D. 26. If Ishmael had no reason or right to complain that he and his offspring (though he was established as a son) were stood aside for Isaac and his offspring, what right had Isaac in his turn to complain if God set a date when he and his offspring (though established son as was Ishmael) should in like manner be stood aside for the greater Son of promise, the Christ and his offspring? God fixed the dates in each case, and the dates in Dan. 9:24, 25 are equally explicit with Gen. 17:21. The

GOD'S PROMISE KEPT 387

Christ, "the anointed one, the prince," was to appear at the end of sixty-nine weeks of years, or in A. D. 26, and at the full end of the seventy weeks, or eight years later, in A. D. 34, the time "decreed upon thy [Daniel's] people" came to an end.* The Holy Spirit that year emphasized the rejection of fleshly Israel and the acceptance of the children of promise (believers in Christ, his spiritual offspring) by withdrawing from the Jews and appearing upon the household of Cornelius, the firstfruits of the Gentiles (Acts 10). God gave Ishmael only one year's warning, and no especial call to repent, or opportunity to save himself in any way. But through Daniel, Israel had five hundred years of warning, and was invited of Christ and of all his apostles (even being invariably invited *first*, by Paul the apostle to the Gentiles) to become joint children of promise with the Gentiles; a joint relationship wherein they were bound by every circumstance to obtain and hold the pre-eminence. Surely, then, the word of God had not failed as to them, but they had failed as to it.] **10 And not only so** [Not only is Ishmael rejected for the promised Isaac, but even Isaac's seed, his two sons Esau and Jacob, are made the subject of choice by God, showing that even the seed of the children of promise may be so sifted that part may be received and part re-

---

* The count in Daniel runs thus: each seven weeks includes a jubilee, and hence numbers fifty years. Seventy weeks therefore equal, with their jubilees, five hundred years. The last of these weeks includes its jubilee, and so has eight years. The count ostensibly begins when the decree is issued to rebuild Jerusalem, or with the year 537 B. C., but in fact the seventy years mentioned at Dan. 9:2 are first deducted, making the count begin 467 B. C.

The law of couplets requires this reduction. Moreover, these years are deducted for sabbath years which the Jews *would not keep* while the seventy weeks or five hundred years immediately after the captivity were passing; just as God exacted a like seventy years in Babylonian captivity for sabbatical years which the Jews *did not keep* during a like seventy-week or five-hundred-year period just previous to the captivity (2 Chron. 36:20, 21; Ezek. 20:23, 24; Jer. 25:11, 12).

The actual count, then, begins 467 B. C., or with the jubilee of deliverance under Queen Esther.

Deducting sixty-nine weeks, or four hundred and ninety-two years, from this date, gives us A. D. 25-26—a year embracing parts of two of our years, for the Jewish year began in October; and the full seventy weeks, or five hundred years, gives us A. D. 33-34.

Therefore Messiah's week, or the last eight of the five hundred years, ran from October, A. D. 25, to October, A. D. 34.

jected, for God indeed did this, accepting Jacob and rejecting Esau]; **but Rebecca also having conceived by one, *even* by our father Isaac** [Now, it might be objected by the Jew (unjustly in view of the fact that four of the tribes of Israel were descended from bondwomen) that his case was not parallel to that of Ishmael, for Ishmael was the son of a bondwoman (an Egyptian), and was of a mocking, spiteful disposition (Gen. 21:9). Ishmael's rejection, therefore, was justifiable, while the exclusion of the Jew by Paul's so-called gospel was utterly unwarranted. To this Paul makes answer by citing the cases of Jacob and Esau. They had one father, Isaac the child of promise; and one mother, Rebecca the well beloved, approved of God; they were begotten at one conception, and were twins of one birth, yet God exercised his right to choose between them, and no Jew had ever questioned this, his right of choice. Yea, the unbounded freedom of choice was even more clearly manifest in other details which Paul enumerates]—11 **for *the children* being not yet born, neither having done anything good** [as might be supposed of Jacob] **or bad** [as might be presumed of Esau], **that the purpose of God according to election** [choosing] **might stand** [might be made apparent and be fully and finally confirmed], **not of works, but of him that calleth** [not a choosing enforced on God by the irresistible, meritorious claims of man, in keeping the law of works, human and divine; but a free choosing on God's part manifested in his calling those who suit his purpose], **12 it was said unto her, The elder shall serve** ["Servitude," says Trapp, "came in with a curse, and figureth reprobation—Gen. 9:25; John 8:34, 35; Gal. 4:30"] **the younger.** [*I. e.*, Esau shall serve Jacob. It is evident from these words that Jacob and Esau do not figure personally, but as the heads of elect and non-elect nations, for personally Esau never served Jacob. On the contrary, he lived the life of a prince or petty king, while Jacob was a hireling, and Jacob feared Esau as the man of power.

GOD'S PROMISE KEPT 389

But the nation sprung of the elder son did serve the nation descended from the younger. "History," says Alford, "records several subjugations of Edom by the kings of Judah; first by David (2 Sam. 8:14) ;—under Joram they rebelled (2 Kings 8:20), but were defeated by Amaziah (2 Kings 14:7), and Elath taken from them by Uzziah (2 Kings 14:22); under Ahaz they were again free, and troubled Judah (2 Chron. 28:16, 17; comp. 2 Kings 16:6, 7,—and continued free as prophesied in Gen. 27:40, till the time of John Hyrcanus, who (Jos. Antt. 13:9, 1) reduced them finally, so that thenceforward they were incorporated among the Jews."] **13 Even as it is written** [Mal. 1:2, 3], **Jacob I loved, but Esau I hated.** [Expositors of Calvinistic bias insist upon the full, literal meaning of "hatred" in this passage; but Hodge, whose leaning that way is so decided that he can see no more injustice in eternal than in temporal election (he apparently never weighed the words of our Saviour at Luke 16:25; 12:48, and kindred passages which show that temporal favors which are indeed bestowed arbitrarily are taken into account to form the basis of just judgment in the bestowal of eternal favors), is nevertheless too fair-minded an exegete to be misled here. He says: "It is evident that in this case the word *hate* means *to love less, to regard and treat with less favor.* Thus, in Gen. 29:33, Leah says she was hated by her husband; while in the preceding verse the same idea is expressed by saying, 'Jacob loved Rachel more than Leah' (Matt. 8:24; Luke 14:26). 'If a man come to me and hate not his father and mother, etc.' (John 12:25)." As this ninth of Romans is the stronghold of Calvinism, the arsenal of that disappearing remnant who believe in eternal foreordination according to the absolute decree of the sovereign will of God, we feel that a word ought to be said about the doctrinal trend of its sections. We therefore submit a few points. 1. It is rather odd that this chapter should be used to prove salvation by election when, so far as it bears on election at all, it is wholly an effort to justify God in casting off an elect people (Jews) and choosing a non-elect people (Gentiles). If, therefore, the chapter as a whole teaches anything as to arbitrary election, it is plainly this, that those who depend upon God to show partiality in electing some and condemning others, will either be disappointed as were the Jews, or surprised as were the Gentiles, for election will never work out as they suppose. For, after showing favor to Abraham's seed for nineteen hundred years, God adjusted the balances, and, turning from Jews to Gentiles, made the first last, and the last first; the elect, non-elect; and the non-elect, elect. And now, the non-elect, having enjoyed the favors and privileges for a like term of nineteen hundred years, are now being called to account, and will, in their turn, be cut off. But if they are, it will be wholly their own fault, just as the rejection nineteen hundred years ago was by Israel's fault, and not by arbitrary decree of God. 2. Moreover, Paul is not discussing salvation, or foreordination as to eternity. There is not one word on that subject in the entire ninth chapter. The apostle is introducing no new doctrine, no unheard-of and strange enormity like Calvinism. "The difficulty," as Olshausen aptly puts it, "and obscurity of the whole section before us are diminished when we reflect that it by no means contains anything peculiar; since the same ideas which so startle us in reading it, are also expressed throughout the whole of the Old as well as the New Testament. It is only their conciseness, their bold and powerful utterance, that lends them, as it were, an unprecedented appearance here." The apostle is speaking of the bestowal of temporal advantages and benefits, and is showing that these, even when relating to Messianic privileges, are bestowed according to God's free will—they have to be! They are like other earthly benefits or privileges; for instance, the distinction as to new-born souls. It is God alone who must determine how each shall enter the world, whether as of the white, brown, red, black or yellow race, whether among the rich or poor. So also, rising a step higher, whether a soul shall have a perfect or a defective brain to think with, and whether it shall enter a Christian or a pagan home. Now, as God gave a promise to Eve, the same law of necessity made it compulsory that he choose arbitrarily what household should be the repository of that promise and thus perpetuate a lively expectation of its fulfillment. God therefore first chose the Chaldees among the nations, then, as second choice, he elected Abraham among the Chaldees; third, he chose Isaac from Abraham's seed, and, fourth, Jacob from Isaac's offspring. Up to this time there was a marked *separation,* both spiritual and geographical, between the elect and the non-elect, so that there was no confusion in anybody's mind as to the inherent exclusiveness of election. But with Jacob a change came. His sons all dwell together, and during his lifetime till his last sickness no election was announced as to them until on his deathbed Jacob gave Judah the pre-eminence (Gen. 49:8-12). But Moses passes over this pre-eminence (Deut. 33:7) and there was no segregation of Judah. In fact, other tribes seem to have overshadowed Judah in importance, notably that of Levi, all of whom were set apart as Levites for God's service, and of which tribe also came Moses the lawgiver and Aaron the father of the priesthood. Moreover, many of the great judges came from other tribes, and the house of Benjamin furnished the first king. This community of interest, this privilege of enjoying the appurtenances and collaterals of election, should have taught Israel that the *blessing promised* was greater, wider and more gracious than the mere privilege of being the repository of that blessing, but, instead, it begot in them the mistaken idea that all the twelve tribes were elect. So, indeed, they were as to possessing the land, but they were not elect as to being repositories of the Messianic promise, which honor was first limited to Judah (1 Chron. 5:2) and afterwards to the house of David (2 Sam. 7:12; Mic. 5:2; John 7:42). Now, this is what Paul is discussing. With him it is a question of fixing a promise so that men may watch for its fulfillment in a certain race and family—a promise which, when fulfilled, brings blessings and benefits not confined to any race or family, but open and free to all who accept them, and denied to all who refuse and reject them, yea, even to the very race and family which have been the age-long repositories of the promise. And the point of Paul's whole argument is this: As God was absolutely free to choose who should be the repositories of the promise, so is he absolutely free to fix the terms by which men shall enjoy the blessings promised, even if those terms (because of rebellion against them on the part of the repositories) work out the failure of the repositories to enjoy the blessings so long held by them in the form of unfulfilled promise. And what has all this to do with electing infants to eternal damnation? No more than the election which makes one child black and the other white, when both are born the same moment. In short, *no temporal election, no matter how blessed, includes salvation to the elect or necessitates damnation upon the non-elect,* for it is apparent to all that the election of the Gentiles as repositories of Christian truth does not save half of them, and the rejection of the Jews from this holy office damns none of them. Salvation is accorded the Jew who believes as freely as it is to the Gentile, and the unbelieving Gentile is damned with the unbelieving Jew, and rests under heavier condemnation because he sins against greater temporal privileges and advantages. In either case the temporal advantage or disadvantage will be duly considered in forming a just judgment (Luke 12:48). 3. It should be noted that Paul proves God's right at any time to limit his promise. Thus the blessing to Abraham's seed was first "nakedly and generally expressed," as Chalmers puts it. Then it was limited to one son, Isaac. Again it was limited to Isaac's son, Jacob. Therefore, as God established his right of limiting the promise to those whom he chose in the inner circle of the promise, so he could in the gospel age limit the promise to spiritual to the exclusion of fleshly seed. This is not just what he did, but this is what he established his right to do, for if he could disinherit Ishmael after he had apparently obtained vested rights, and if he disinherited Esau before he was born, there was no limit to his right to disinherit, providing only that he kept within the promise and chose some one of Abraham's seed, or the seed of some one of his descendants to whom a like covenant was given. Compare his offer to make Moses the head of a new people (Ex. 32:10), which he was free to do, not having confirmed the rights in Judah pronounced by Jacob (Gen. 49:8-12).

III.

REJECTION OF ISRAEL NOT INCONSISTENT WITH THE JUSTICE OF GOD.

9:14-18.

14 What shall we say then? [The apostle makes frequent use of the semi-dialogue. Five times already in this Epistle he has asked this question (3:5; 4:1; 6:1; 7:7; 8:31). He begins with this question which calls out an objection in the form of a question, to which he replies with an indignant denial, which he backs up by a full and detailed answer, or explanation. The question called out is] **Is there unrighteousness with God?** [The indignant denial is as usual] **God forbid.** [Poole calls this "Paul's repeated note of detestation." He uses it fourteen times. It expresses indignant, pious horror. Literally it is, "Let it not be;" but as this form of expression was too tame for our English ancestry who have ever held God's name in that light reverence which makes free use of it for emphasis, we find it translated "God forbid" by Wyclif, Coverdale, Tyndale, Cranmer, the Genevan, etc. But the use of God's name, being needless, is inexcusable. The import, then, of verse 14 runs thus: If God chooses arbitrarily, is he not unjust? and does he not thereby do violence to his moral character, his holiness? The apostle's answer is unique; for it is merely a quotation from Scripture. His argument, therefore, rests upon a double assumption; first, that God is truly represented in the Scripture, and, second, the Scripture everywhere represents him as just, holy and perfect. Paul's objector, in this case, would be a Jew, and any Jew would accept both these assumptions as axiomatic. If, therefore, Paul's Scripture quotation shows that God's power of choice is absolutely free, then the apostle by it has likewise shown that God's arbitrary choices are nevertheless just and holy, and objection to them as unjust is not well founded. The arbitrary choice of a sinful heart is sinful, but the arbitrary choice of the Sinless is likewise sinless, just and holy partaking of his nature who chooses.] **15 For he saith to Moses** [Ex. 33:19. Surely if the Scripture generally was final authority to the Jew, that part of it would be least questioned wherein God is the speaker and Moses the reporter], **I will have mercy on whom I have mercy** [God chooses both the occasion and the object of mercy, and it is not regulated by anything external to him. That which is bestowed upon the meritorious and deserving is not *pure* mercy; for, as Shakespeare expresses it, "The quality of mercy is not strained"], **and I will have compassion on whom I have compassion.** [Compassion is a stronger term than mercy; it is mercy with the heart in it. The words quoted were spoken to Moses when he requested to see God, and his request was in part granted. In expounding Ex. 33:19, Keil and Delitzsch speak thus: "These words, though only connected with the previous clause by the copulative *vav,* are to be understood in a causal sense as expressing the reason why Moses' request was granted, that it was an act of unconditional grace and compassion on the part of God, to which no man,

REJECTION NOT INCONSISTENT 395

not even Moses, could lay any just claim." This interpretation is strengthened by the Old Testament reading, which runs thus: "I will be gracious to whom I will be gracious, and will show mercy on whom I will show mercy," for the act was one of grace rather than of compassion. Let us remember that Paul is here addressing a hypothetical Jewish objector. The Jew, influenced by false reasoning on his law, held a theory that man's conduct regulated God's and that man took the initiative and that God's actions were merely responsive. Such might, in some measure, have been the case had any man ever kept the law; but as things actually stood, to the subversion of all such things, it was evident from Scripture that Moses, the great lawgiver, himself had never been able to *merit* a favor at God's hands, but, on the contrary, God granted that to him as a matter of *gracious mercy* which he could never claim as a matter of right; viz., not eternal life with God, but the mere momentary glimpse of the passing of God's glory. Surely, with such a precedent before him, the rational, thoughtful Jew, whether of Paul's day or of our own, could and can have small hope of gaining heaven by the works of the law. Since it is true that Abraham obtained favor by faith and Moses received it solely by grace, who shall win it by merit under the law?] **16 So then** [With these words Paul introduces the answer to the question in verse 14, as inferred or deduced from the citation in verse 15; as though he said, "As a conclusion from what I have cited, it is proven that as to the obtaining of God's favor"] **it is not** [the accomplishment] **of him that willeth** [of him that wants it], **nor of him that runneth** [of him that ardently strives, or offers works for it, as a runner does for his prize], **but of God that hath mercy.** [Many expositors, following Theophylact, refer this "willing" to Isaac, who sought to bless Esau against God's choice in Jacob, and refer the running to that of Esau, who ran to get the venison. But that running of Esau was too *literal;* it lacked in that moral effort Godward which Paul's argument implies. Others, as Meyer, Godet, etc., confine the willing and running to Moses, but this, too, is objectionable, as too narrow a base for so broad a principle. Paul includes Abraham, Isaac, Ishmael, Jacob, Esau, Moses, and all like them. No man is chosen of God because *he* chooses or strives to be chosen till God has *first* chosen him (John 15:16-19). The *first* choice rests in the will of God. If God did not call *all* (John 3:16; Tit. 2:11; Rev. 22:17) and choose all who respond by sincerely wishing and striving to be chosen, the dark side of Calvinism might indeed be true. Originally there was no curb to the freedom of God in dealing with fallen man save the unspeakable mercy and goodness of God. Justice at that time afforded no curb; for man was a sinner without means of propitiation or atonement, and stood condemned by justice. The verbal form "runneth," though it comes in abruptly, is not of special, but of general, reference ("him" being equivalent to "any one"), and indicates strenuous moral effect toward God, or salvation. (Ps. 119:32). It is part of the old and familiar figure wherein life is regarded as a race or "course," moral effort being a "running" therein (see comment, Rom. 9:31, 32). This figure is so well known that it is customarily introduced thus abruptly (Acts 13:25; 20:24; 2 Tim. 4:6, 7). The use of the verb "to run" is as common as the noun "course," and is also brought in abruptly, as needing no gloss (Gal. 2:2; 5:7; Phil. 2:16; Heb. 12:1. Comp. Phil. 3:11-14 and 1 Cor. 9:24-26, where the apostle elaborates the figure). These very references to Paul's use of this figure afford abundant proof that *after* God chooses us (and he has now chosen us all, for he would not that any should perish, but that all men be saved, and come unto the knowledge of the truth—2 Pet. 3:9; 1 Tim. 2:4; Rom. 2:4; Tit. 2:11: Ezek. 18:23, 32; 33:11), *then* everything depends upon our "willing" (Luke 13:34; Acts 13:46) and "running," for we ourselves having obtained of God's free will and grace a calling and election, must of ourselves make that calling and election sure (2 Pet. 1:10, 11); yea, we must work out our own salvation with fear and trembling and the aid of God (Phil. 2:12), and must so "run" that we may obtain. Paul is here proving the unfettered freedom of the Almighty *before* he gave the gospel. A freedom which permitted him to give it when, how, where and to whom he chose, save as he had gradually limited himself, slightly, from time to time, by his promises. This freedom permitted him at last to give such a gospel that the self-righteous Jews saw fit to reject it and become castaways. Paul in all his argument says never a word about God's limitations *in* the gospel *after* the gospel was given; for they have nothing to do with his argument which relates to God's freedom *when preparing* the gospel and *before* the gospel was given. Failure to note this simple, obvious distinction has brought forth that abortive system of inexorable logic called Calvinism, which has gone near to attribute both the sins of man and the iniquities of the devil to God himself. God *was* free, but in his goodness he chose to provide salvation to those who would accept it on his conditions. Thus the Lord, being free, chose to be bound by his covenants and promises, even as the Lord Jesus, being rich, chose to be poor (2 Cor. 8:9). Paul proves God's *past* freedom; no one save the Jew of his day ever denied it; but to say that Paul establishes a *present* freedom and absolute sovereignty in God, which robs man of his freedom to do right, or wrong; repent, or continue in sin; accept Christ, or reject him, etc., is to dynamite the gospel, and blast to shivers the entire rock of New Testament Scripture. Calvinism denies to God the possibility of making a covenant, or giving a promise, for each of these is a forfeiture of freedom, a limitation of liberty. According to Calvinism, God is absolutely free; according to the Scripture, he is free save where he has pledged himself to man in the gospel.] **17 For the scripture** [Paul is still answering the question at verse 14 by Scripture citation] **saith unto Pharaoh** [We have had election choosing between Ishmael and Isaac, and Esau and Jacob: we now have it choosing between a third pair, Moses and Pharaoh. In the first case God *blessed both* Isaac and Ishmael with promises (Gen. 17:20; 21:13, 18, 20); in the second case he blessed Jacob and *withheld* his promise from Esau; in the third case he granted favor to Moses, and *meted out punishment* to Pharaoh. Thus there is a marked *progress* in reprobation in the three non-elect characters, which is suggestive, since Israel was *thrice* given over to a reprobate mind, and each punishment was more intense. First, all were rejected in the wilderness, but *all* their children were permitted to enter the promised land—time, forty years; second, all were rejected at the carrying away into Babylon, and only a small body were permitted to return—time, seventy years; third, the race as a race was rejected in Paul's day and only a remnant will, even at the end, be restored (Isa. 10:22, 23; 1:9)—time, about nineteen hundred years], **For this very purpose did I raise thee up** [caused thee to occupy a time and place which made thee conspicuous in sacred history], **that I might show in thee my power, and that my name might be published abroad in all the earth.** [For the publishing of God's name, see Ex. 15:14-16; Josh. 2:9, 10; 9:9. The dispersion of the Jews and the spread of Christianity have kept God's name glorified in the history of Pharaoh to this day. Paul is still establishing by Scripture God's freedom of choice. He chose the unborn in preference to the born; he chose between unborn twins; he chose between the shepherd Moses and Pharaoh the king. In this last choice Moses was chosen as an object of mercy, and Pharaoh as a creature of wrath, but his latter choice in no way violates even man's sense of justice. Instead of raising up a weak and timid owner of the Hebrew slaves, God exalted Pharaoh, the stubborn, the fearless. And who would question God's right to do this? Having put Pharaoh in power, God so managed the contest with him that his stubbornness was fully developed and made manifest, and in overcoming his power and stubbornness through the weakness of Moses, God showed his power. The transaction is very complex. God starts by stating the determined nature of Pharaoh (Ex. 3:19) and follows the statement with the thrice repeated promise, "I will harden his heart" (Ex. 4:21; 7:3; 14:4. Comp. 14:17). Once Jehovah says, "I have hardened his heart" (Ex. 10:1). Thrice it is said that his "heart was hardened as Jehovah had spoken" (Ex. 7:13; 8:19; 9:35). Once it reads that his "heart was hardened, and he hearkened not unto them; as Jehovah had spoken" (Ex. 7:22). Five times we read that "Jehovah hardened" his heart (Ex. 9:12; 10:20; 10:27; 11:10; 14:8). Thus thirteen times (with Ex. 8:15, fourteen times) Pharaoh's hardness of heart is said to be the act of God. (Comp. Deut. 2:30; Josh. 11:20; Isa. 63:17; John 12:40; 9:39; Mark 4:12.) Inexorably so? By no means: God would have gotten honor had he relented before matters reached extremes. Hence Pharaoh is called upon to repent (Ex. 10:3), and several times he is near repenting, and might have done so had not God been too ready to show mercy (Ex. 8:28; 9:27; 10:24). So there was sin in Pharaoh. We read that his "heart is stubborn" (Ex. 7:14); "was stubborn" (Ex. 9:7). "Pharaoh hardened his heart, and hearkened not unto them, as Jehovah had spoken" (Ex. 8:15). "Pharaoh hardened his heart" (Ex. 8:32; 1 Sam. 6:6). "Pharaoh sinned yet more, and hardened his heart" (Ex. 9:34). As the hardening was the joint work of Pharaoh and God, and as Pharaoh sinned in hardening his heart, God's part in the hardening was not an absolute, overmastering act. It was not even a persuasive act, as in cases of conversion. God hardened Pharaoh's heart by providing *opportunity* and *occasion,* as the narrative shows, and Pharaoh did the rest by improving the opportunity in the service of the devil. The same act of patience, forbearance and mercy which softens one heart, hardens another by delaying punishment, as we may see every day. The same sunshine that quickens the live seed, rots the dead one. The Jews approved God's course toward Pharaoh, but resented the same treatment when turned upon themselves, ignoring the natural law that like causes produce like effects. God found Pharaoh hard and used him for his glory negatively. He found Israel hard and made the same negative use of them, causing the gospel to succeed without them, thus provoking them to jealousy —Rom. 10:19.] **18 So then [see verse 16] he hath mercy on whom he will, and whom he will he hardeneth.** [This does not mean that God arbitrarily chooses the worst people upon whom to shower his mercies, and chooses those who are trying hard to serve him and hardens them that he may punish them. The point is that, in the absence of any promise or other self-imposed limitation, God is free to choose whom he will for what he will. As applicable to Paul's argument, it means that God's freedom of choice is not bound by man's judgment or estimation, for he may prefer the publican to the Pharisee (Luke 18:9-14) and may choose rather to be known as the friend of sinners than the companion of the rulers and chief priests, and he may elect the hedge-row Gentile to the exclusion of invited but indifferent Jews (Luke 14:23, 24). God is bound by his nature to choose justly and righteously, but all history shows that man can not depend upon his sin-debased judgment when he attempts to specify what or whom God approves or rejects. Here we must be guided wholly by his word, and must also be prayerfully careful not to wrest it. In short, it is safer to say that God chooses absolutely, than to say that God chooses according to my judgment, for human judgment must rarely square with the divine mind. Had the Jew accepted Paul's proposition, he might centuries ago have seen the obvious fact that God has chosen the Gentiles and rejected him; but, persisting in his erroneous theory that God's judgment and choice must follow his own petty notions and whims, he is blind to that liberty of God's of which the apostle wrote, and naturally—

> "For, Och! mankind are unco weak,
> An' little to be trusted;
> If *self* the wavering balance shake,
> It's rarely right adjusted!"]

IV.

GOD'S ABSOLUTE POWER ASSERTED—HIS JUSTICE VINDICATED AND ALSO HIS COURSE IN REJECTING THE UNBELIEVING JEWS AND ACCEPTING THE BELIEVING GENTILES.

9: 19-29.

19 Thou wilt say then unto me, Why doth he still find fault? [That God actually and always *does find fault* with sinners is a fact never to be overlooked, and is also a fact which shows beyond all question or peradventure that God abhors evil and takes no positive steps toward its production. Even in the case cited by Paul, where God hardened Pharaoh's heart, the act of God was *permissive,* for else how could the Lord expostulate with Pharaoh for a rebellious spirit for which God himself was responsible? (Ex. 9: 17; 10: 3, 4.) Again, let us consider the case in point. If God hardened Israel by positive act, why did his representative and "express image" weep over Jerusalem? and why was the Book of Romans written?] **For who withstandeth his will?** [Since Paul is still justifying God in formulating a gospel which results in the condemnation of Jews and the saving of Gentiles, this objector is naturally either a Jew or some one speaking from the Jewish standpoint. This fact is made more apparent in the subsequent verses, **for in them the apostle appropriately answers the Jew**

out of his Jewish Scriptures. The objection runs
thus: But, Paul, if God shows mercy to whom he will,
and if he hardens whom he will, then it is he who has
hardened us Jews in unbelief against the gospel.
Why, then, does he still find fault with us, since he
himself, according to your argument, has excluded
us from blessedness, and made us unfit for mercy?
This reply implies three things: 1. God, not the Jew,
was at fault. 2. The Jew was ill used of God, in being deprived of blessing through hardening. 3. The
rewards of saints and sinners should be equal, since
each did God's will absolutely in the several fields of
good and evil where God had elected each to work.
To each of these three implications the apostle replies
with lightning-like brevity: 1. It is impious, O man,
to so argue in self-justification as to compromise the
good name of God. 2. It is folly for the thing formed
to complain against him that formed it. 3. Rewards
and destinies need not be equal, since, for instance,
the potter out of the same lump forms vessels for different destinies, whether of honor or dishonor. But
it must be borne in mind that in the last of these
three brief answers the apostle aims rather, as Alford
says, "at striking dumb the objector by a statement of
God's indubitable right, against which it does not become us men to murmur, than at unfolding to us the
actual state of the case." Let us now consider the
three answers in detail.] **20 Nay but** [One word
in Greek; viz., the particle *menounge*. "This particle
is," says Hodge, "often used in replies, and is partly
concessive and partly corrective, as in Luke 11:28,
where it is rendered, *yea, rather;* in Rom. 10:18, *yes,
verily.* It may here, as elsewhere, have an ironical
force. Sometimes it is strongly affirmative, as in Phil.
3:8, and at others introduces, as here, a strong nega-
tion or repudiation of what has been said." "I do not
examine the intrinsic verity of what you allege, but,
be that as it may, this much is certain, that you are
not in a position to dispute with God"—*Godet*], **O
man** ["Man" stands at the beginning and "God" at

the end of the clause to emphasize the contrast. Man, thou feeble morsel of sinful dust, wilt thou wrangle with God!], **who art thou that repliest against God?** ["That chattest and wordest it with him" (*Trapp*). "Repliest" signifies an answer to an answer. It suggests, to those familiar with legal parlance, the declaration and answer, the replication and rejoinder, the rebutter and surrebutter to the limits both of human impudence and divine patience. Before answering the objection, Paul, therefore, felt it necessary to rebuke the impious presumption of the objector. It is permissible to fathom and understand what God reveals about himself, but it is not allowable for us, out of our *own* sense of justice, arrogantly and confidently to fix and formulate what principles must guide God in his judging. To do this is to incur the censure meted out to Job (Job 38-41). "No man," says Haldane, "has a right to bring God to trial." Man's understanding is not adequate to such a task.] **Shall the thing formed say to him that formed it, Why didst thou make me thus?** [In the Greek the form of the question indicates that a negative answer is expected. The question is not a quotation, but rather "an echo" of Isa. 29:16 and 45:9. "Formed" implies, not creation, but subsequent ethical moulding. God does not create us evil, but we are born into a world which, if not resisted, will form us thus. This is the *actual* work of God in the case. If we find ourselves formed after the pattern of evil, can we, in the light of all that he has done in the gospel, censure God for our life-result? Being insensate, the wood can not quarrel with the carpenter, nor the iron with the smith. Being sensate, and knowing the grace of God, and his own free will, man also is silent, and can render no complaint. The free will of man is an offset to the insensibility of the wood and iron, and makes their cases equal, or, legally speaking, "on all fours." Inanimate material can not complain of malformation, for it lacks understanding of the facts; but man, having understanding, likewise can not complain, for the malformation was his own free choice. Speaking mathematically, the "free will" cancels the "lack of understanding," and leaves the animate and the inanimate equal, and therefore alike silent as to the results of the processes of moulding.] **21 Or** [This word presents a dilemma, thus: Either the clay (thing formed) has no right to question, or the potter has no right to dictate. In the Greek the form of the question indicates the affirmative answer: "The potter has a right to dictate"] **hath not the potter a right over the clay, from the same lump to make one part a vessel unto honor, and another** [part of the lump a vessel] **unto dishonor?** [God is the potter, the human race is the clay, and the vessels are nations. Being under obligations to none, for all, having fallen into sin, had thereby forfeited his regard and care as Creator, God, for the good of all, made election that the Jewish nation should be a vessel of honor (Acts 13:17) to hold the truth (2 Cor. 4:7; Rom. 3:1, 2), the covenants and the progenital line through which came the Messiah. Later he chose the Egyptians as a vessel of dishonor, to be punished for their abuse of the covenant people, and the murder of their little ones. In Paul's day he was choosing Gentiles (Europeans) as vessels of honor to hold the knowledge of the gospel. This choosing and forming is to the prejudice of no man's salvation, for *all* are invited in matters pertaining to eternal life, and each temporal election is for the eternal benefit of all. Potter's clay and potter's vessels are used to indicate *national* weakness (Dan 2: 41-44; Lam. 4:2; Isa. 41:25; Ps. 2:9; Rev. 2:26, 27) and *national* dependence (Isa. 64:8-12) and *national* punishment (Jer. 19:1, 10-13; Isa. 30:14). It is a *national* figure (Ecclus. 33:10-12), yet it recognizes national free will (Jer. 18:1-12). In the single instance where it is used *individually*, it is employed by Paul in a passage very similar to this, yet clearly recognizing the power of *human* vessels to change destinies by the exercise of free will (2 Tim. 2:20, 21). But no individual vessel is one of honor till cleansed by blood

GOD'S ABSOLUTE POWER ASSERTED 405

(Heb. 9:21, 22; Acts 9:15; 22:14-16), and who will say that a vessel cleansed in Christ's blood is one of dishonor? And we are cleansed or not according to our own free choice.] **22 What if** [With these words Paul introduces his real answer to the question asked in verse 19. The full idea runs thus: "I have answered your impudent question by an assertion of the absolute right of God, which you can not deny (Prov. 26:5; Ps. 18:26). *But what will you say if,* etc." If the absolute abstract right of God puts man to silence, how much more must he be silent before the actual, applied mercy and grace of God which forbears to use the right because of his longsuffering pity toward the impenitent, and his forgiving leniency toward the repentant. Paul asserts the absolute right of God, but denies that he applies it. Herein he differs from Calvinism, which insists that he applies it] **God, willing to show his wrath, and to make his power known, endured with much longsuffering vessels of wrath fitted unto destruction** [And now, O man, how silent must you be if it appears that God, although willing to show his displeasure against wickedness, and ready to show his power to crush its designs, nevertheless endured with much longsuffering evil men whose conduct had already fitted them for, or made them worthy of, destruction. Paul has already told us that the longsuffering of God is exercised to induce repentance, though its abuse may incidentally increase both wrath and punishment (Rom. 2:4-11). It is not affirmed that *God* "fitted" these evil ones for destruction. "And," says Barnes, "there is an evident design in *not* affirming it, and a distinction made between them and the vessels of mercy which ought to be regarded. In relation to the latter it is expressly *affirmed* that *God* fitted or *prepared* them for glory. (See vs. 23.) 'Which HE had afore prepared unto glory.' The same distinction is remarkably striking in the account of the last judgment in Matt. 25:34-41. To the righteous, Christ will say, 'Come, ye blessed of my Father, inherit the kingdom prepared for you,' etc. To the wicked, 'Depart from me, ye cursed, into everlasting fire, prepared FOR THE DEVIL AND HIS ANGELS;' not said to have been originally prepared *for them.* It is clear, therefore, that God intends to keep the great truth in view, that *he* prepares his people by *direct agency* for heaven; but that he exerts no such *agency* in preparing the wicked for destruction." No potter, either divine or human, ever made vessels just to destroy them. But any potter, finding a vessel suited to a dishonorable use, may so use it, and may afterwards destroy it. How the Jews "fitted" themselves for destruction is told elsewhere by the apostle—1 Thess. 2:15, 16]: **23 and** [A copula of thoughts, rather than of clauses: God spared the wicked because of longsuffering mercy to them, *and* because they could be used to aid him in making known the riches of his glory upon vessels of mercy. Without attempting to show that God's patience with the godless aids him to win the godly, we will let it suffice to say that God spares the wicked for the sake of the righteous, lest the hasty uprooting of the former might jeopardize the safety of the latter—Matt. 13:28-30] **that** [he showed longsuffering to the wicked, in order that] **he might make known the riches of his glory** [God's glory is his holiness, his perfection; "riches," as Bengel observes, "of goodness, grace, mercy, wisdom, omnipotence"] **upon vessels of mercy, which he afore prepared unto glory** [It is much disputed whether the "glory" here mentioned is the temporal honor of being a church militant, a covenant people, a temple of the Spirit (Eph. 2:22), a new dispensation of grace supplanting that of the law (glories won by the Gentiles, and lost by the Jews), or whether it refers to the glory of the land celestial, and the bliss of heaven. The context favors the latter view, for "glory" is the antithesis of "destruction" in the parallel clause, and destruction can refer to nothing temporal. By comparing the two parallel clauses, Gifford deduces the following: "We see (1) that St. Paul is here speaking, not of election or predestination, but of an actual preparation and purgation undergone by vessels of mercy to fit them for glory, before God *'makes known the riches of his glory upon them.'* Compare 2 Tim. 2: 20, 21, a passage which evidently looks back on this. (2) We observe that this preparation, unlike that by which *'vessels of wrath'* are *'fitted for destruction,'* is ascribed directly and exclusively to God as its author, being wholly brought about by his providence and prevenient grace. The idea of *fitness,* akin to that of desert, is ascribed only to the vessels of wrath. The vessels of mercy God has made *ready* for glory, but there is no idea of merit involved"], **24 *even* us, whom he also called, not from the Jews only, but also from the Gentiles?** [The apostle ends his question with a clear specification of who the vessels of mercy are. They are those called impartially from both Jews and Gentiles. "In calling to salvation," says Lard, "God is equally merciful to all. He sends to all the same Christ, the same gospel; on them he spends the same influences, and to them presents the same incentives to duty. But beyond this he strictly discriminates in bestowing mercy. He bestows it on those only that obey his Son. On the rest he will one day pour out his wrath." We may add, that toward those who accept his call he is equally impartial in preparing for glory, giving them the same remission of sins, the same gift of the Holy Spirit, the same promises, etc. But the impartiality which the apostle emphasizes is that which gave no preference to the Jew.] **25 As he saith also in Hosea** [Paul does not seek to prove his question about God's grace to the wicked which he exercises instead of his right to immediate punishment —that needs no proof. That God wishes to save all, and hath no pleasure in the damnation of any, has always been Scripturally plain. What he now seeks to prove is his last assertion about impartiality. He has shown out of the Scriptures that God has elected between the apparently elect; he now wishes to also show, out of the same Scriptures, that he has elected the apparently non-elect—viz., the Gentiles—and that the apparently elect, or Jews, are all to be rejected save a remnant. The first quotation is a compilation of Hos. 2:23 and 1:10. The translation is from the Hebrew, modified by the LXX., and by Paul, but not so as to affect the meaning. It reads thus:], I will call that my people, which was not my people; And her beloved, that was not beloved. 26 And it shall be [shall come to pass], *that* in the place where it was said unto them, Ye are not my people, There shall they be called sons of the living God. [These verses originally apply to the to-be-returned-and-reinstated ten tribes, after the devastation and deportation inflicted by the Assyrians. To illustrate the stages in the rejection of Israel, Hosea was to take a wife and name his daughter by her Lo-ruhamah, which means, "that hath not obtained mercy" (1 Pet. 2:10), which Paul translates "not beloved"; and the son by her he was to name Lo-ammi; *i. e.*, "not my people." This symbolic action is followed by the prophecy (not yet fulfilled) that the day should come when "Lo-ruhamah" would be changed to "Ruhamah," "that which hath obtained mercy" or "beloved"; and "Lo-ammi" would be changed to "Ammi," "my people." Some expositors have been at a loss to see how Paul could find in this prophecy concerning *Israel* a prediction relating to the call of the *Gentiles*. But the prophecy and the facts should make the matter plain. By calling them "not my people," God, through Hosea, reduced the ten tribes to the status of Gentiles, who were likewise rejected and cast off. Paul therefore reasons that if the restoration of the ten tribes would be the same as calling the Gentiles, the prophecy indicates the call of Gentiles. All this is borne out by the facts in the case. The "lost tribes" are to-day so completely Gentile, that, without special revelation from God, their call must be the same as calling Gentiles. The word "place" (vs. 26) is significant. The land of the Gentiles, where the ten tribes are dispersed and rejected, and are become as Gentiles, is to be the place of their reinstatement and acceptance, and this acceptance

GOD'S ABSOLUTE POWER ASSERTED 409

shall resound among the Gentiles. This *publishing* on the part of the Gentiles is a strong indication of their *interest,* hence of their like conversion. Having shown by Hosea that the "no-people" or non-elect Gentiles are clearly marked *in Scripture,* as called and chosen, Paul now turns to Isaiah to show that of the elect, or Jewish people, only a remnant shall be saved. And this fact is the source of that grief which Paul mentions at the beginning of the chapter.] **27 And Isaiah crieth** [in deep feeling, excessive passion—John 1:15; 7:28, 37; 12:44; Matt. 27:46] **concerning Israel, If the number of the children of Israel be as the sand of the sea** [thus Isaiah minishes the promise given to Abraham (Gen. 22:17) and quoted by Hosea—Hos. 1:10], **it is the remnant that shall be saved: 28 for the Lord will execute *his* word upon the earth, finishing it and cutting it short.** [Isa. 10:22, 23. This prophecy, like that of Hosea, refers to the return of the ten tribes in the latter days, and is therefore an unfulfilled prophecy, save as it had a preliminary and minor literal fulfillment in the destruction of Jerusalem, a few years after Paul wrote this Epistle, which was the climax of rejection for the generation to which Paul wrote, and the full establishment of that age-long rejection of the majority which pertains unto this day. Daniel, dealing with its spiritual fulfillment, foretold that the labors of the Christ "confirming the covenant" with Israel would only last a week—a jubilee week having in it *eight* years, or from A. D. 26 to A. D. 34 (Dan. 9:27). How small the remnant gathered then! In the centuries since how small the ingathering! And, alas! now that we have come to the "latter days" and the last gathering, and the final literal and spiritual fulfillment of the prophecy, it gives us assurance of no more than a mere remnant still! Verse 28, as given in full by Isaiah, is thus happily paraphrased by Riddle, "He (the Lord) is finishing and cutting short the word (making it a fact by rapid accomplishment) in righteousness, for a cut-short word (one rapidly accomplished) will the Lord

make (execute, render actual) upon the earth." When
we consider that the Lord reckons a thousand years
as but a day, how short was the spiritual privilege of
the eight years' exclusive ministry of Jesus and his
apostles! and how brief was the forty years' (A. D.
30-70) temporal privilege between the crucifixion and
the destruction of Jerusalem! Isaiah's word shows us
that the final fulfillment will be also a brief season, a
cut-short word, doubtless a repetition of Daniel's
week.] **29 And, as Isaiah hath said before** [This may
mean, Isaiah has said this before me, so that I need
not prophesy myself, but may appropriate his word,
or, as earlier expositors (Erasmus, Calvin, Grotius,
etc.) render it, Isaiah spoke the words which I am
about to quote earlier than those which I have already
quoted, the latter being Isa. 10:22, 23, and the former
being at Isa. 1:9. Since the apostle is proving his
case by the Scripture and not resting it upon *his own
authority*, the former reading seems out of place. It
would be somewhat trite in Paul to state that Isaiah
wrote before him! It is objected that the latter
rendering states an unimportant fact. What difference can it make which saying came first or last?
But it is not so much the *order* as the *repetition* of
the saying that the apostle has in mind. Isaiah did
not see some moment of national disaster in a
single vision, and so cry out. He saw this destruction of all save a remnant in the very *first vision* of
his book, and it is the oft-repeated burden and refrain
of a large portion of his prophecies], **Except the Lord
of Sabaoth** [Hebrew for "hosts"] **had left us a seed**
[for replanting], **We had become as Sodom, and had
been made like unto Gomorrah.** [Like "cities of
which now," as Chalmers observes, "no vestige is
found, and of whose people the descendants are altogether lost in the history or our species." (Comp. Jer.
50:40,) In contrast with these, the Jews, though
few in number, have ever been found in the kingdom
of God. Since the section just finished is the stronghold of Calvinism, we should not leave it without not-

GOD'S ABSOLUTE POWER ASSERTED 411

ing that Simon Peter warns us not to put false construction upon it. He says: "Wherefore, beloved, seeing that ye look for these things" (a new heaven and a new earth), "give diligence that ye may be found in peace, without spot and blameless in his [God's] sight, and account that the longsuffering of our Lord is salvation; even as our beloved brother Paul also, according to the wisdom given to him, wrote unto you; as also in all his epistles, speaking in them of these things; wherein are some things hard to be understood, which the ignorant and unstedfast wrest, as *they do* also the other scriptures, unto their own destruction. Ye therefore, beloved, knowing these things beforehand, beware lest, being carried away with the error of the wicked, ye fall from your own stedfastness" (2 Pet. 3: 14-17). Now, Paul uses the word "longsuffering" ten times. Seven times he speaks of the longsuffering of men. Once he speaks of the longsuffering of Christ extended to him personally and individually as chief of sinners. Twice (Rom. 2: 4-11; 9: 19-29) he fills the measure of Peter's statement, and writes that men should "account that the longsuffering of our Lord is salvation." As the first of these passages (Rom. 2: 4-11) has never been in dispute, it follows either that *all* have wrested it, or that *none* have wrested it, so that in either case its history does not comply with Peter's description. The passage before us, then, is the one which the ignorant and unsteadfast have wrested, and that so seriously that it has *compassed their destruction*. In further support of this identification, note (1) that this passage was, as we have seen, addressed to the *Jews,* and it therefore answers to the "wrote unto *you*" of Peter's letter, which was also addressed to *Jews*; (2) while "the longsuffering of God," etc., is not prominent in *all* Paul's Epistles, as we have just shown, the *doctrine of election,* which is the stumbling-block here, is a common topic with the apostle. Since, then, Peter warns us against wresting this section, let us see who wrests it. According to Peter, it is those who get a soul-destroying doctrine out of it, and such is Calvinism. It is those who derive from it a doctrine which palsies their effort, so that, believing themselves impelled by inexorable will and sovereign, immutable decree, they hold they can do nothing either to please or displease God, and therefore cease to "give diligence that they may be found in peace, without spot and blameless in his sight," and cease to "account that the longsuffering of our Lord is salvation," and thus, "being carried away with the error of the wicked" that human effort is of no avail, they cease to make any, and so "fall from their own stedfastness." Surely with so plain a warning from so trustworthy a source we are foolish indeed if we wrest this Scripture so as to make it contradict the doctrines of human free will and responsibility so plainly taught in other Scriptures.

V.

THE GRAND CONCLUSION AND ITS EXPLANATIONS

9:30-11:36.

Subdivision A.

THE CONCLUSION OF THE ARGUMENT REACHED; NAMELY, GENTILES JUSTIFIED BY FOLLOWING GOD'S LAW OF FAITH, WHILE JEWS, FOLLOWING THEIR OWN LAW OF WORKS, ARE CONDEMNED.

9:30-33.

30 What shall we say then? ["Shall we raise objection, as at verse 14, or shall we at last rest in a correct conclusion? Let us, from the Scriptures and facts adduced, reach a sound conclusion." Paul's conclusion, briefly stated, is this: God's sovereign will has elected that men shall be saved by belief in his Son. The Gentiles (apparently least apt and prepared) have, as a class, yielded to God's will, and are being saved. The Jews (apparently most apt and prepared) have, as a class, resisted God's will, and are being lost.] **That the Gentiles, who followed not after righteousness, attained to righteousness, even the righteousness which is of faith** [The righteousness which the apostle has in mind is that which leads to justification before God. Righteousness is the means, justification the end, so that the word as here used *includes* the idea of justification. Now, the Gentiles were not without desire for moral righteousness. The Greeks entertained lofty ideals of it, and the Romans, following the legalistic bent of their nature, plodded after it in their systems of law and government; but as Gentiles they had no knowledge of a God calling them to strict account in a final judgment, and demanding full justification. Hence they were not seeking it. But when the revelation of God and his demand for justification, and his graciously provided means for obtaining it, all burst upon their spiritual vision, they at once accepted the revelation in its entirety; being conscious that they had no righteousness of their own; being, indeed, filled with its opposite (Rom. 1:18; Eph. 2:2, 3). "Faith," the leading and initiatory part of the conditions of justification, is, by a form of synecdoche, employed to designate the whole of the conditions, so Bloomfield justly observes: "Faith in Christ implies a full acceptance of his gospel, and an obedience to all its requisitions, whether of belief or practice"]: **31 but Israel, following after a law of righteousness, did not arrive at *that* law.** [Israel was not seeking justification. Their search was rather for a *law* that would produce in them a righteousness *meriting* justification. This craving arose from a proud, self-sufficient spirit, and God answered it by giving the law of Moses, for the express purpose of revealing their universal sinful weakness and insufficiency (Acts 15:10; Gal. 2:16), and need of a Saviour (Rom. 7:24, 25); wherefore Paul describes the law as "our tutor to bring us unto Christ, that we might be justified by faith" (Gal. 3: 24). Realizing the impossible task of attaining justifying righteousness by the law of Moses, the Jew began adulterating that law by traditions; but even the law thus modified gave small delusive hope, and the cry was still, "What shall I do to inherit eternal life?" (Luke 10:25; 18:18). But to this solemn and awful question there were but *two* answers: (1) Keep the law of Moses (Matt. 19:17; Rom. 10:5; Gal. 3:12), and when the Jew answered, "I can not," then (2) the "Follow me" of Christ (Matt. 19:21). Since no man could keep the law of Moses, all men were and are shut in by God to the *one law of salvation through faith in Christ*. No wonder, then, that the Jew, seeking relief by Moses, or by a *third* law, failed to find any law that satisfied his soul or operated with God. Godet calls this success of the uninterested Gentile, and failure of the Jew who made the search of righteousness his daily business, "the most poignant irony in the whole of history"; yet the cases of the two parties are not wholly antithetical, as Paul clearly shows, by the use of the word "righteousness" instead of "justification." If both parties had sought justification, the Jew would have no doubt been the first to find it. But the object of the Jewish search was a *law* which would give life, yet preserve his pride and self-conceit, and his search was therefore for an impossibility. The Master himself discloses the difference in heart between the Jew and the Gentile in the parable of the Pharisee and the publican (Luke 18:9-14). The humble spirit of the Gentile accepted righteousness as the gift of the humble Christ, but the proud Jew could not so demean himself as to place himself under obligations so lofty to One so lowly. Let us note that the words "follow after" and "attain" are *agonistic*; that is to say, they are technical words describing the running after the prize, and the grasping of it, as used in the Olympic games. Their presence here at the end of the argument shows that the "willeth" and "runneth" of verse 16 also have the *agonistic* force which we gave to them in interpreting that verse. Paul's conclusion explains the willing and running. It is folly to will and run *contrary* to the law and will of Him who, as supreme Sovereign, has laid down the immutable rules of the great race or game of life. The prize is the free gift of the King: there is no *merit* in running that can win it, when the running is *random* and contrary to rule, as the Jews suppose. There is no *merit* in running that can give a *legal* right to it, even when the running is according to *rule,* but there is in him who runs a *moral fitness and aptness* for the prize which makes it his, according to the will of him who called him to so run for it.] **32 Wherefore?** [Why, then, did the Jews fail to find any law of life? Answer: Because there is but *one* such law, and they sought *another.*] **Because they sought it not by faith, but as it were by works.** [In interpreting, we have contrasted the law of works with what *we* have called "the law of faith," but the apostle does not use this latter term: with him life it attained by "faith," though he treats it as a working principle in that he contrasts it with the other active principle, or law of works. In this verse, however, he drops the abstract altogether, and places the concrete "faith" and "works" in vivid opposition. It is not so much a question of law against law, and principle against principle; it is one of faith which appropriates the perfect righteousness of Christ, and of Jewish works which, scorning the garment of the purity of God, revealed in his Son, still clings to the filthy rags of self-righteousness, self-sufficiency, Phariseeism, etc.— Phil. 3:4-14.] **They stumbled at the stone of stumbling** [The language here still follows the metaphor of the race-course. The Jew, running with his eye on an imaginary, non-existing, phantom goal, and blind as to the real goal, stumbles over it and falls. The picture presented by the apostle suggests the sad truth that the Jew has run far enough and fast enough to win, but, as he has rejected the terms and rules of the race, his efforts are not counted by the Lord of the race. Christ was placed of God as a goal, and not as a stumbling-block; as a Saviour, not as a source of condemnation; but he is indeed either man's salvation or his ruin—Matt. 21:42-45]; **33 even as it is written** [The passage about to be quoted is a compound of the Hebrew at Isa. 8:14 and the LXX. at Isa. 28:16. The first reads thus, "But he shall be . . . for a stone of stumbling and for a rock of offence to both the houses of Israel," and the second, "Behold, I lay in Zion for a foundation . . . he that believeth shall not be in haste." The reader can see how the apostle, for brevity, has blended them; quoting only such part of each as suited his purpose], **Behold, I lay in Zion** [Jerusalem, the capital city of my people] **a stone of stumbling and a rock of offence: And he that believeth on him shall not be put to shame.** [Why the LXX. substituted "not be put to shame," for "not be in haste," is not clear, though the meaning of the latter phrase is near kin to the former, conveying the idea of fleeing away in confusion. Shame, however, is a very appropriate word here, for it was the chief cause of Christ's rejection by the Jews: they were ashamed of him (Mark 8:38; Luke 9:26; Rom. 1:16; 2 Tim. 1:8). The apostle is justified by New Testament authority in regarding both these Scriptures as Messianic prophecies (1 Pet. 2:6-8; Matt. 21:42; Acts 4:11. Comp. Ps. 118:22; 1 Cor. 3:11; Eph. 2:20); but it adds greatly to the weight of his argument to know that the Jews also conceded them to be such. "Neither of these passages," says Olshausen, "relates to the Messiah in its immediate connection, but they had been typically applied to him as early as the Chaldean and Rabbinical paraphrases, and Paul with propriety so applies them. The Old Testament is one great prophecy of Christ." And Tholuck says: "Jarchi and Kimchi also testify that it (Isa.

28:16) was explained of the Messias." And our Lord was a stone of stumbling! As Moule exclaims: "Was ever prophecy more profoundly verified in event?" If he spake plainly, they were offended; and if he spake in parables, they were equally angered. If he healed, they took offense; and if he forbore healing, and refused to give a sign, they were likewise dissatisfied. If he came to the feast, they sought his life; and if he stayed away, they were busy searching for him. Nothing that he did pleased them, nothing that he forbore to do won him any favor. His whole ministry developed an ever-increasing distaste for his person, and animosity toward his claims. As a final word on this great chapter, let us note that God's foreordination rejected the Jew by presenting a gospel which appealed to sinners, and was offensive to that worst class of sinners, the self-righteous. God sent his Son as Physician to the sick, and those who supposed themselves well, died of their maladies according to a reasonable, rational and equitable plan—but also a foreordained plan. This conclusion of the ninth chapter will be fully discussed in the tenth.

Subdivision B.

FIVE EXPLANATIONS OF THE GRAND CONCLUSION, AND ASCRIPTIONS OF PRAISE.

10:1—11:36.

I.

FIRST EXPLANATION—JEWS RESPONSIBLE FOR THEIR REJECTION, SINCE THEY HAD AN EQUAL CHANCE WITH THE GENTILES OF BEING ACCEPTED.

10:1-13.

Brethren [Seven times in this Epistle Paul thus addresses the brethren at Rome generally (Rom. 1:13; 8:12; 11:25; 12:1; 15:14, 30; 16:17). Twice he thus addresses the *Christian Jews* (Rom. 7:1, 4), and this "brethren" is evidently a third time they are especially spoken to. So thought Chrysostom, Bengel, Pool, Alford, Barnes, Hodge, etc. "Dropping now," says Bengel, "the severity of the preceding discussion, he kindly styles them brethren"], **my heart's desire** [literally, "my heart's *eudokia*, or *good pleasure*, or *good will*" (Luke 2:14; Eph. 1:5-9; Phil. 1:15; 2:13). At Matt. 11:26, and Luke 10:21, it is translated *"well pleasing"*; at 2 Thess. 1:11, the literal "fulfil every *good pleasure* of goodness" is translated, "fulfil every *desire* of goodness." *Eudokia* does not mean *desire*, but we have no English word which better translates Paul's use of it. Stuart conveys the idea fairly in a paraphrase "the benevolent and kind desire"] **and my supplication to God is for them** [the Israelites], **that they may be saved.** [Those who tell our faults and foretell their punishment usually appear to us to be our enemies. Paul described the sin and rejection of Israel so clearly that many of them would be apt to think that he prayed for their punishment. This did him gross wrong. Every time the Evangelist denounces sin from love toward the sinner. (Comp. Gal. 4:16.) As to the apostle's prayer, it showed that his conception of foreordination was not Calvinistic. It would be of no avail to pray against God's irrevocable decree; but it was very well worth while to pray against Jewish stubbornness in unbelief, trusting to the measureless resources of God to find a remedy. So the remark of Bengel is pertinent, "Paul would not have prayed, had they been utterly reprobates." Paul's prayer being in the Spirit (Rom. 9:1) was a pledge that no fixed decree prevented God from forgiving, if Israel would only repent and seek forgiveness.] **2 For I bear them witness that they have a zeal for God, but not according to knowledge.** ["For" introduces Paul's reason for having hope in his prayer. Had Israel been sodden in sin, or stupefied in indifference, he would have had less heart to pray. But they were ardently religious, though ignorantly so, for, had they possessed a true knowledge of their law, it would have led them to Christ, and had they understood their prophets, they would have recognized that Jesus was the Christ (Gal. 3: 24; Luke 24:25-27; Rev. 19:10). But the chief ignorance of which Paul complained was their failure to see that there is no other way to justification and salvation save by faith in Christ Jesus. As to their zeal, which in the centuries wore out the vital energy of the Greek, and amazed the stolidity of the Roman, till in the siege of Jerusalem it dashed itself to atoms against the impregnable iron of the legionaries, no tongue nor pen can describe it. Of this zeal, Paul was a fitting witness, for before conversion he shared it as a persecutor, and after conversion he endured it as a martyr (Phil. 3:6; 2 Cor. 11:24; Acts 21:

20-31; 22:4). But misguided zeal miscarries like a misdirected letter, and the value of the contents does not mend the address. "It is better," says Augustine, "to go limping in the right way, than to run with all our might out of the way." Their lack of knowledge, being due to their own stubborn refusal to either hear or see, was inexcusable.] **3 For being ignorant of God's righteousness** [Here Paul shows wherein they lacked knowledge. "For they," says Scott, "not knowing the perfect justice of the divine character, law and government; and the nature of that righteousness which God has provided for the justification of sinners consistently with his own glory"—Rom. 3:26], **and seeking to establish their own** [Refusing to "put on Christ" (Gal. 3:27), they clothed themselves with a garment of their own spinning, which they, like all other worms, spun from their own filthy inwards. Or, to suit the figure more nearly to the language of the apostle, refusing to accept Christ as the Rock for life-building, they reared their crumbling structure on their own sandy, unstable nature, and as fast as the wind, rain and flood of temptation undermined their work, they set about rebuilding and *re-establishing* it, oblivious of the results of that supreme, unavertable, ever-impending storm, the last judgment—Matt. 7:24-27], **they did not subject themselves to the righteousness of God.** ["Subject" is the keyword here. The best comment on this passage is found at John 8:31-36. Those who admit themselves bondservants of sin find it no hardship to enter the free service of Christ, but those whose pride and self-sufficiency and self-righteousness make them self-worshipers, can bring themselves to submit to no one. By use of the phrase "righteousness of God," Paul indicts them of rebellion against the Father and his plan of salvation, rather than of rebellion against the person of the Christ, who is the sum and substance of the Father's plan— the concrete righteousness whereby we are saved.] **4 For** [With this word the apostle gives further evidence of the ignorance of the Jews. He has shown that they did not know that they could not *merit* eternal life by good works; he now proceeds to show that they did not know that the law itself, which was the sole basis on which they rested their hopes of justification by the merit of works, was now a nonentity, a thing of the past; having been fulfilled, abolished and brought to an absolute and unqualified *end* by Christ. The Jews, therefore, are proven ignorant, for] **Christ is the end of the law unto righteousness to every one that believeth.** [The apostle places the enlightenment of believers in contrast with the lack of knowledge of the Jews. All believers understand (not only that Christ is the end or *aim* or *purpose* for which the law was given, and that he also ended or *fulfilled* it, but) that Christ, by providing the gospel, put an end to the law—killed it. The apostle does not mean that the law only dies to a man when he believes in Christ, else it *would still live,* as to unbelieving Jews: "to every one that believeth," therefore, expresses a contrast in *enlightenment,* and not in *state* or *condition.* The new covenant or testament, which is the gospel, made the first testament old (Heb. 8:13). That is to say, the new or last will revokes and makes null and void all former wills, and no one can make good his claim to an inheritance by pleading ignorance of the New Will, for the Old Will is abrogated whether he chooses to know it or not. As the word "end" has many meanings, such as aim, object, purpose, fulfillment, etc., expositors construe Paul's words many ways, but the literal meaning, an *end—i. e.,* a termination— best suits the context. "Of two contrary things," says Godet, "when one appears, the other must take and end." "Christ is the end of the law, as 'death,' saith Demosthenes, 'is the end of life'" (*Gifford*). The Lord does not operate two antagonistic dispensations and covenants at one time. To make evident the fact that the gospel terminates the law, the apostle now shows the inherent antagonism between the

two; one of them promising life to those obedient
to law, the other promising salvation to the one
being obedient to or openly confessing his faith.
And so there is an antagonism between the gospel
and the law.] **5 For Moses [the lawgiver] writeth
that the man that doeth the righteousness which is
of the law shall live thereby.** [Lev. 18:5. (Comp.
Neh. 9:29; Ezek. 20:11, 13, 21; Luke 16:27-29;
Gal. 3:12.) The context indicates that the life promised is merely the possession of the land of Canaan
(Lev. 18:26-29); but Tholuck observes that "among
the later Jews, we find the notion widely diffused that
the blessings promised likewise involve those of
eternal life. Orkelos translates: 'Whosoever keeps
these commandments, shall thereby live in the life
eternal.' And in the Targums of the Pseudo-Jonathan, Moses' words are rendered: 'Whosoever fulfils
the commandments shall thereby live in the life
eternal, and his portion shall be with the righteous.' "
Paul evidently construes it as being a promise of
eternal life. (Comp. Luke 18:18-20.) But no man
could keep the law. Was, then, the promise of God
ironical? By no means. The law taught humble
men the need of grace and a gospel, and for all such
God had foreordained a gospel and an atoning
Christ. But to the proud, the self-righteous, the
Pharisaical who would *merit* heaven rejecting grace
and the gospel, the promise was ironical, for "doeth
. . . live," implies that whoso fails, dies (Deut. 27:
26; Gal. 3:10; Jas. 2:10). There was, then, righteousness by the law, and such as had it were ripe
for the gospel which it foreshadowed, especially in
its continual sacrificial deaths for sin; but there was
no *self*-righteousness by the law, and those who
strove for it invariably rejected Christ. Those seeking life by law supplemented by grace found in Jesus
that fullness of grace which redeemed from law, but
those seeking life by law without grace, failed and
were hardened—Rom. 11:5-7.] **6 But** [marking the
irreconcilable contrast and antagonism between the

new gospel and the old law] **the righteousness which is of faith saith thus** [we would here expect Christ to speak, as the antithesis of Moses in verse 5. But if Jesus had been made spokesman, Paul would have been limited to a quotation of the exact words of the Master. It, therefore, suited his purpose better to personify Righteousness-which-is-of-faith, or the gospel, and let it speak for itself. Compare his personifications of Faith and Law at Gal. 3:23-25. By doing this, he (Paul) could, in this his final summary of the gospel's sufficiency and applicability to the needs of men, employ words similar to those in which Moses in his final summary of the law, spake of its sufficiency and applicability (Deut. 30:11-14). Thus on a similar occasion, and with a similar theme, Paul speaks words similar to those of Moses; so varying them, however, as to bring into vivid contrast the *differences* between the law and the gospel —between that which typified and foreshadowed, and that which in its superlative superiority fulfilled, terminated and forever abolished. Moses said of the law: "For this commandment which I command thee this day, it is not too hard for thee, neither is it far off. It is not in heaven, that thou shouldest say, Who shall go up for us to heaven, and bring it unto us, and make us to hear it, that we may do it? Neither is it beyond the sea, that thou shouldest say, Who shall go over the sea for us, and bring it unto us, and make us to hear it, that we may do it? But the word is very nigh unto thee, in thy mouth, and in thy heart, that thou mayest do it." His meaning is, first, that the law is not so hard but that a man who makes right use of it may please God in it (this was true of the law till the gospel abolished it); second, the law was the fully prepared gift of God, and, being possessed by the Jews, they neither had to scale the heavens to get false gods to give a law to them, nor did they have to cross the sea (a dangerous and rarely attempted task among those of Moses' day) to get unknown, remote and inaccessible nations of men to bring a law to them. They were required to perform no impractical, semi-miraculous feat to secure the law—it was theirs already by gift of God, and that so fully and utterly that, instead of being locked in the holy seclusion of the sanctuary, it was their common property, found in their mouths (daily talk) and hearts (worshipful, reverential meditation—Ex. 13:9; Josh. 1:8; Ps. 37:30, 31; 1:2; 119:14-16). Such was the law as described by Moses. In contrast with it Paul lets the gospel describe itself thus], **Say not in thy heart, Who shall ascend into heaven?** (that is, to bring Christ down:) **7 or, Who shall descend into the abyss?** [Hades, the abode of the dead—Luke 8:31; Rev. 17:8; 20:1; Ps. 139:8] **(that is, to bring Christ up from the dead.) 8 But what saith it?** [Here Paul interrupts the gospel with a question. If the word of life is not in these places (heaven and Hades), where, then, is it? Where does the gospel say it is? He now resumes the gospel's personification, and lets it answer the question.] **The word is nigh thee, in thy mouth, and in thy heart** [Here end the words spoken by the gospel. Their import is similar to that of the second meaning of Moses' words found above. The gospel is the fully prepared gift of God (John 3:16), and, being once accepted and possessed by the believer, he is not called upon to scale the heavens to procure a Christ and bring him down to see the needs of man and devise a gospel (for the Word has already become incarnate, and has dwelt among us—John 1:14—and seeing what sacrifice was needed for man's forgiveness and cleansing, he has provided it—Heb. 10:3-9); neither is it demanded of him that he descend into the abyss (Hades, the abode of the dead) to find there a Christ who has died for our sins, and to raise thence a Christ whose resurrection shall be for our justification (for God has already provided the Christ who died for our sins—1 Cor. 15:3; Isa. 53:5, 6; Rom. 3:25; 5:6; 8:32; 2 Cor. 5:21; Gal. 1:4;

1 Pet. 2:24; 3:18—thus making an end of sins, and making reconciliation for iniquity—Dan. 9:24—and who also was raised for our justification—Rom. 4:24, 25; 1 Cor. 15:17; 1 Pet. 1:21—thus bringing in everlasting righteousness—Dan. 9:24). Thus far the apostle's argument runs thus: As the sources whence a law might be found were questions about which the Jew needed not to trouble himself, since God provided it; so the sources whence a Christ-gospel might be procured were also questions about which the Christian need feel no care, for the all-sufficient wisdom and might of God which provided the law had likewise perfected and supplied the gospel, so that men need only to accept it by faith. In either case His was the provision and theirs the acceptance; and what the apostle makes particularly emphatic was that the *gospel was as easily accepted as the law,* for it, too, could be familiarly discussed with the lips and meditated upon with the heart, being as *nigh* as the law. Nearness represents influence, power over us; remoteness, the lack of it (Rom. 7:18, 21). As the words of Moses were spoken about the *type* of the gospel (the law), they were of course prophetically applicable to the Christ who is the sum of the gospel, and likewise the living embodiment of the law. But to make plain their prophetic import, Paul gave them a *personal* application to Christ, and changed the search among the distant living (where law might be found) to search among the farther distant dead (where Christ must be found to have been in order to give life). Thus Paul's variations from Moses constitute what Luther calls "a holy and lovely *play* of God's Spirit in the Lord's word"]: **that is, the word of faith, which we preach** [At this point the apostle begins again to speak for himself and his fellow-ministers, and shows that the "word" of which Moses spoke is the gospel or "word of faith" preached by Christians. He also shows that the words "mouth" and "heart," as used by Moses, have prophetic reference to the gospel terms of salvation]:

9 because [the gospel (and Moses) speak of the mouth and heart, because] **if thou shalt confess with thy mouth Jesus *as* Lord, and shalt believe in thy heart that God raised him from the dead, thou shalt be saved** [Moses emphasized the *nearness* of the law. The Jew was to keep it near (accept it), for, as a far-off, neglected thing, it would be of no avail. As an accepted rule, loved and talked over daily, it would be effective unto righteousness. Jeremiah, foretelling the days when a new law would be more effective than the old, declared that the promise of Jehovah was: "I will put my law in their inward parts, and in their hearts will I write it." Thus it would become *nearer* than when written externally upon stone. When this new law came, Jesus indicated the fulfillment of Jeremiah's word by saying, "The kingdom of God is within you" (Jer. 31:33; Luke 17:20). Therefore, when Paul quotes Moses' words about that *nearness* of the law which makes it effective, he takes occasion to describe how the gospel or "word of faith" is made effective unto righteousness by the believer's full consent to the will of God that it be near him, making it an inward nearness by confession with the mouth and belief in the heart. In short, the gospel is not righteousness unto life until it is accepted, and the prescribed method by which it is to be accepted is faith leading to confession, followed by obedience of faith, beginning with baptism, which symbolically unites us with our Lord in his death and resurrection. But Paul makes no reference to the ordinance, laying stress on the central truth of Christianity which the ordinance shows forth; namely, God raised Jesus from the dead. The zealous lover of first principles might expect Paul to make the *Christhood* of Jesus the object of belief (Matt. 16:16). But that is already taken care of by the apostle in the brief summary: "Confess with thy mouth Jesus *as* Lord." The truth is, the resurrection is the *demonstration* of that proposition: "Jesus is the Christ, the Son of

JEWS RESPONSIBLE FOR REJECTION 427

the living God." "Jesus" means "Saviour," and the resurrection proves or demonstrates his ability to save from death and the grave (1 Cor. 15:12-19; 1 Pet. 1:3-5; 2 Cor. 4:14). Jesus is Christ; that is, God's anointed Prophet, Priest and King over all men; for such is the meaning of "Christ." Now, the resurrection proves that Jesus was a teacher of truth, for God honors no liars with a resurrection like that of Jesus; it proves that he is an acceptable High Priest, for had not his offering for sin canceled the guilt of sin, he had appeared no more in the land of the living (Matt. 5:26), but he was raised to complete his priestly work for our justification (see note on Rom. 4:25, p. 336, and Acts 13: 37-39); it demonstrated that he was the King, for by his resurrection he led captivity captive (Eph. 4:8) and received the gift of universal power (Matt. 28:18; Acts 2:23-36; 13:34-37; 17:31; Phil. 2:8-11; Eph. 1:19-23); and, finally, it declared him to be the Son of God with power (Rom. 1:4; Acts 13:32, 33): **10 for with the heart man believeth unto righteousness; and with the mouth confession is made unto salvation.** ["The seat of faith," says Calvin, "is not in the brain, but in the heart. Yet I would not contend about the part of the body in which faith is located: but as the word *heart* is often taken for a serious and sincere feeling, I would say that faith is a firm and effectual confidence, and not a bare notion only." The belief must be such as to incite to love (1 Cor. 13:1, 2) and the obedience of faith (Jas. 2:14-26). The faith of the heart introduces the sinner into that state of righteousness which in this present world reconciles him to God. The continual profession of that faith by word and deed works out his salvation, which ushers him into the glory of the world to come. Salvation relates to the life to come (Rom. 13:11). When attained it delivers us from the dominion of the devil, which is the bondage of sin; from the power of death, which is the wages of sin, and from eternal torment, which

is the punishment of sin. Such is salvation negatively
defined, but only the redeemed know what it is
positively, for flesh can neither inherit it (1 Cor.
15:50) nor utter it—2 Cor. 12:1-5.] **11 For the
scripture saith** [Again Paul appeals to the Scripture
to show that what he is telling the Jews has all
been prophetically announced in their own Scriptures. Thus he slays their law with its own sword],
**Whosoever believeth on him shall not be put to
shame.** [A passage already quoted at Rom. 9:33;
but Paul changes "he" into "whosoever," thus emphasizing the *universality* of the verse, for God's
universal mercy to believers is his theme, and we
shall find him amplifying and proving it in the next
two verses. "Shame" has especial reference to the
judgment-day. By faith we learn to so live that
God ceases to be ashamed of us (Heb. 11:6-16). By
faith also we are brought into such union with Christ
that he also no longer feels ashamed to recognize
us (Heb. 2:10, 11). But if we glory in sin which is
our shame (Phil. 3:18, 19), walking nakedly in our
shame (Rev. 16:15), and refusing the gift of the
garment of Christ's righteousness (Rev. 3:18), being
ashamed of it and him; in that day he also will be
ashamed of us (Mark 8:38; Luke 9:26), and great
then will be our shame in the sight of all God's hosts,
and marked will be the contrast between us and the
believers who are not ashamed—1 John 2:28.] **12
For** [The Scripture uses such universal language
about our being freed from shame by justification,
because] **there is no distinction between Jew and
Greek: for the same *Lord* is Lord of all, and is rich
unto all that call upon him** [Paul here announces the
same truth which Peter discovered when he said:
"Of a truth I perceive that God is no respecter of
persons" (Acts 10:34). As the Jews were for several
centuries under the dominion of the Greeks, and as
the cultured of the Romans, their later masters, also
spoke Greek, the term *Greek* became to them a
synonym for *Gentile,* for they had more dealing with

JEWS RESPONSIBLE FOR REJECTION 429

Greeks than with any other people. Now, as there is but one God, the Jews and Greeks were compelled to receive blessings from that same God, and as the Jew and Greek stood in equal need of salvation, God offered the same salvation to each upon the same free terms and each had equal ability to accept the terms (Eph. 2:11-22). Thus God showed the riches of his favor to all, and so rich is God in his mercy and providences toward salvation, that no multitude can exhaust them; therefore the Jew had no reason to envy or begrudge the Gentiles their call, since it in no way impoverished him. But this breaking down of distinctions was, nevertheless, very offensive to the Jew]: **13 for** [and this lack of distinction on God's part is further proved by Scripture, *for* it saith], **Whosoever shall call upon the name** [*i. e.,* person—Prov. 18:10; Ps. 18:2, 3] **of the Lord shall be saved.** [Joel 2:32. This passage is quoted by Simon Peter at Acts 2:21. In place of "Lord," Joel has the word "Jehovah," which latter term the Jews regard as describing God the Father. The application of this word to Christ by Paul (and it is so applied to Christ, as the next verse shows) is proof of our Lord's divinity. "There is," says Alford, "hardly a stronger proof, or one more irrefragable by those who deny the Godhead of our blessed Lord, of the unhesitating application to Him by the apostle of the name and attributes of Jehovah." (Comp. 1 Cor. 1:2.) It is evident that the mere crying out, "Lord, Lord!" is of no avail (Matt. 7:21-23). One must call upon Jesus as he directs, and must worshipfully accept him as the Son and Revelation of God. "The language," says Johnson, "wherever used, implies coming to the Lord and calling upon him in his appointed way. (Comp. Acts 22:16; 2:21; Gen. 12:8.)" Having thus demonstrated the *gratuitous* and *universal* nature of the gospel, the apostle prepares us for his next paragraph, which presents the thought of *extension*. That which God has made free and for all should be published and offered to all. How unreasonable, therefore, the hatred which the Jews bore toward Paul for being apostle to the Gentiles!

II.

SECOND EXPLANATION OF THE GRAND CONCLUSION—THE UNIVERSALITY OF THE GOSPEL DEMANDS ITS WORLD-WIDE EXTENSION—BUT THIS UNIVERSALITY IS LIMITED BY HUMAN REJECTION.

10:14-21.

[Since the apostle's thought in this section is obscurely connected, the line of argument has been found difficult to follow. It will aid us, therefore, at the start to get his purpose clearly in view. He has shown that the gospel is universal. But in giving a universal blessing God would of course see to it that it was universally published and propagated. This, God had earnestly attempted to do, but his efforts had largely been frustrated so far as Israel was concerned. But this was Israel's fault, and therefore that people were utterly without excuse (1) for not becoming part of the universality which God contemplated and attempted; (2) for not fully understanding this universality and rejoicing in it; nay, for so *misunderstanding* it, despite full Scripture warning, as to be made jealous by it, so as to spurn it and reject it.] **14 How then shall they call on him in whom they have not believed?** [The form of the Greek question demands the answer, "They can not." Though the question presents a psychological impossibility, Paul is not thinking of psychology, but of his two quotations from Scripture; viz., verse 11, which (as interpreted by verse 9) conditions salvation on belief, and verse 13, which conditions it on

UNIVERSALITY OF THE GOSPEL 431

invocation or calling on the name of the Lord. He has twice coupled these two conditions in the "belief" and "confession" of verses 9 and 10; and now he couples them a third time in the question before us, which is a strong way of asserting there can be no acceptable calling without believing. Since, then, salvation, the all in all of man's hopes—salvation which God desired should be universal—depends upon acceptable calling or invocation, and since acceptable calling in its turn depends upon belief, whatever steps are necessary to produce universal invocation and belief should by all means be taken on the part of God and his evangelists, and should likewise by all means be universally accepted by man. What these steps are the apostle proceeds to enumerate] **and how shall they believe in him whom they have not heard?** [Hearing is the next step. We can believe nothing till we have first heard it. But in the apostle's thought our belief is not directed toward an *abstraction,* but toward Jesus, a *person.* We are to hear him, and believe him, and believe on him. As we can not meet him face to face, we must believe on him as he presents himself to us by his commissioned agents (Luke 10:16; John 13:20; 1 Thess. 4:8; Eph. 2:17; 4:19, 20; 1 John 4:5, 6), called preachers (1 Tim. 2:7; Mark 16:15). Therefore the next question reads] **and how shall they hear without a preacher?** [and the Jews hated Paul for being one!] **15 and how shall they preach, except they be sent?** [Sending is the last step as we reason *backward,* but the first as we look *forward toward* salvation; for, as Gifford observes, "Paul argues back from effect to cause," so that, turning his series around, it will read, Sending, preaching, hearing, believing, turning to or calling upon God, salvation (Acts 8:4-39). In these days of missions we have grown so familiar with the *gospel* that the idea of *sending* has become fairly limited to the transportation of the missionary; when, therefore, we enlarge Paul's *sending* till it includes the idea of a *divine commission* or command to go, we feel that we have achieved his conception. But the thought of the apostle is wider still. With him the *sending* finds its full meaning in that unction of God which provides the messenger with a *divine message,* a message of *good news* which only the lips of God can speak, a message which he could gather from no other source, and without which all *going* would be vanity, a mere running without tidings. Compare Paul's vindication of the heavenly origin of his message (Gal. 1:11-24). To understand the relevancy of the quotation with which the apostle closes the sentence, let us remember that while this is an argument, it is also, by reason of the matter argued, a hymn of praise, a love-song, a jubilation, an ecstasy of joy. How could it be otherwise? Now, at Rom. 8:28-30 the apostle presents the heaven-forged links of the unbreakable chain of God's holy and gracious *purpose* to glorify man. Having presented that chain, he devotes the remainder of the chapter (31-39) to an elaboration of the joyful confidence which wells up within him at its contemplation, for a heart of flesh could not do otherwise. So here the apostle has presented the links of the corresponding chain— the chain of *means* whereby the *purpose* is effected or consummated, so that man is saved or glorified; and that chain ends, as Paul inversely counts its links, in the unspeakable honor of being a messenger of God, sent to bear the gospel of Christ to a dying world. Could the apostle pass this by and stick to his argument? (Comp. Eph. 3:7-12; Acts 26:17, 18; Rom. 15:15, 16; Gal. 1:15, 16.) Nay, if he did so, would it not weaken his argument? For, while the passage at Rom. 8:31-39, and the quotation here about "beautiful feet," may not fit in *syllogistically,* they have unspeakable power *suggestively;* for the first pictures that peace of God that passes all understanding, which the Jew was rejecting; and this second depicts the glorious ministry of God's mercy to the lost and life to the dying, which the Jew was missing by his

UNIVERSALITY OF THE GOSPEL 433

proud unbelief.* Let us note in passing how Paul's argument emphasizes Christ unto the unbelievers. "All this," says Plumer, "relates to Christ, Jehovah. The prayer is to him or through him; the faith is in him; the report respects him; the heralds are his messengers; the sum of all they proclaim relates to his person, work, offices and grace; he is himself the chiefest among ten thousand and altogether lovely." With this introduction we are ready for the quota-

---

* To avoid incumbering Paul's argument we have given the briefest possible interpretation of "sending," 'ut as sending is the bottom of the heavenly ladder the top of which reaches unto salvation, it should be fully understood. The first sending was by the Father, and of this sending Jesus was both messenger and message. The next sending was that of the twelve and the seventy, a sending which culminated in the great commission (Matt. 28 19; Mark 16: 15, 16; Luke 24: 47; Acts 1: 8). The first of these sendings was perfect as to sender, message and messenger (John 3: 34). The second was perfect as to sender and message, but weak as to the messengers The third sending was by the Holy Spirit and the church at Antioch (Acts 13: 2, 3). In this sending the message was practically perfect, but the church participated in the sending, so that the sender and the messengers were imperfect. A little later the message itself became corrupted and imperfect, and from that day to this the weakness of the gospel plan has been at this bottom rung of the great ladder; and the weakness is threefold, being in the sender, the sent and the thing sent. In Paul's day the weakness of the sending churches was the thing to be deplored. *For this the Jew was chiefly to blame, for had he appreciated the honor and privilege and answered to the call of Christ*, the world could easily have been evangelized by him, for he had synagogues and organized groups of worshipers, and a popular hearing in nearly every city on the habitable globe; but, instead of becoming a help, he, with all his accessories, became a hindrance. For the weakness of evangelism man, *and especially Israel*, was to blame, for God's part was perfect, being wrought in Christ. Moreover, the commision of Christ was full, sufficient and final. *But the Jew, to whom message, messenger and commission first came, had been a visionless, cold, unappreciative and defective messenger from the beginning.* It required a miracle to get Peter to carry the message to the Gentile Cornelius (Acts 10), and even then his Christian brethren found fault (Acts 11), and accepted as an unwelcome but inevitable decree of God, that which should have inspired them to shout for joy. No wonder, then, the Spirit of God ceased to struggle with the Jerusalem church in this matter, and withdrew to Antioch, making it the missionary center of the world. As ordaining and sending were, even in Paul's day, well-nigh wholly in the hands of the church, so that even Paul himself was a church-sent man (Acts 13: 2, 3), it is hardly likely that Paul's words here are lacking in reference to this fact, for (1) the Jew was extremely culpable in failing to further the sending of the gospel; (2) the Roman church generally needed admonition along this line, for the apostle was looking to them to aid him as Christ's messenger, or missionary, to Spain (Rom. 15: 22-29). Finally, the weakness of Christ's coworkers, the *senders*, was the problem in Paul's day, and it is still the problem, just as Jesus covertly prophesied when he said, "Pray ye therefore," etc. (Luke 10: 2); for our prayer though directed to God, must be answered by man, tor he is *de facto* the sender (or, more properly, the NON-SENDER) of laborers into the harvest. The world could be evangelized in a single generation if men would only send the gospel to its peoples, but they lack that vision of the feet beautiful which thrilled the mighty soul of the lion of Benjamin, the apostle to the Gentiles.

tion] **even as it is written, How beautiful are the feet of them that bring glad tidings of good things!** [Isa. 52:7. Paul quotes enough to suggest the full passage, which reads thus: "How beautiful upon the mountains are the feet of him that bringeth good tidings, that publisheth peace, that bringeth good tidings of good, that publisheth salvation, that saith unto Zion, Thy God reigneth!" Paul quotes this exuberant, throbbing joy of Israel's prophet which expressed his own feelings, as a sharp contrast to the sullen, malignant, vindictive spirit of those to whom he prophesied. How acceptable was Paul and how glorious his world-wide message as visioned to the evangelical Isaiah! How despisable was Paul, and how abhorrent his message, to the Israel of the gospel age! The contrast suggests that some one erred: which was it? Were the prophet and apostle indulging in a sinful joy? or were the Jews playing the fool of all fools in excluding themselves from it? Though the citation from Isaiah has a primary reference to the restoration of the Jews from the land of exile, yet it is unquestionably Messianic, for that very restoration from exile "derived all its value," as Hodge observes, "from being introductory to that most glorious deliverance to be effected by the Redeemer." "That return," says Alford, "has regard to a more glorious one under the future Redeemer." Besides, the prophet has been talking of Messianic times, when "the glory of Jehovah shall be revealed, and all flesh shall see it together" (Isa. 40:5). "Jewish expositors," says Tholuck, "no less apply to the Messias almost the whole of the chapter (Isa. 52), besides the quotation. (See Wetstein, *ad h. l.*)." The law was to end in the gospel, and Israel was to be the apostles of this joyful development, but failed through blindness as to the personality of the Messiah (a suffering sacrifice for sin, and not a great conqueror and temporal ruler); through ignorance as to the nature of the gospel (salvation by faith, and not by the accident of Abrahamic descent); through a bigoted nar-

UNIVERSALITY OF THE GOSPEL

rowness which took offense at the gospel's universality (a universality which offered salvation to Jew and Gentile on equal terms, and was devoid of all partiality). Thus it happened that Paul ran, and Israel forebore. Finally, as to the words of Isaiah, let us compare them with 2 Sam. 18:26: "And the king said, He also bringeth tidings. And the watchman said, I think the running of the foremost is like the running of Ahimaaz the son of Zadok. And the king said, He is a good man and cometh with good tidings." Here we see that *men* were *known* by their running, and their *tidings known* by their character. With these facts before us, the imagery of Isaiah becomes complete. Jerusalem, the daughter of Zion, bereft of all her children by the Babylonians, sits in sackcloth, covered with the dust of mourning and bowed with grief as though drawn down with chains about her neck. Suddenly the phantom watchmen on her desolated walls see her Ahimaaz—her good man that cometh with good tidings!—tidings of the return of all her lost children! Far off upon the mountains the swift glint of the white feet tell of that speed of the heart which urges to the limit of human endurance. With such a message what place is there for weariness! All the long miles that lie behind are forgotten, and as the goal comes in view the wings of the soul possess the feet, and the pace increases with each step as the runner presses toward the mark or prize of his heart's desires! Ah, how beautiful upon the mountains are the feet of him that bringeth good tidings! Sing! watchmen, for ye shall see face to face how Jehovah returned to Zion to glorify and comfort it with his presence. Awake, awake, O Zion! Shake off thy dust, loose thyself from the bonds of thy neck, and put on thy beautiful garments, O Jerusalem, for the messenger of salvation is at thy very gates, and how beautiful is his approach! He tells of thy children who are coming! coming! journeying homeward behind him! No wonder that with this imagery before him Paul clung to the figure of the runner to the very end (Phil. 3: 12-14; 2 Tim. 4:7). No wonder, either, that he could not forbear adding this quotation as the climax of his argument, that, having reared a granite mountain, he might cap it with the glorifying coronet of sunshine upon snow, thus making his argument as persuasive by its glory as it was convincing by its power. No wonder that he discerned the Messianic meaning of Isaiah's message, patent even to uninspired eyes. Having thus completed the circle of his argument from the message to the universality of the message, thence to the extension of it, and thence again to the means of extension, and finally back to the message itself as glorified in the vision of the prophet, the apostle is ready once more to grapple the Jew and show his inexcusable sin in rejecting the message. However, before discussing what follows it is well to note that its connection of ideas is uncertain, so much so that Stuart justly complains of not having found a single commentator who gives him satisfaction respecting it. The connection is not stated, and is therefore difficult. To solve the problem we must find the unspoken thought in the mind of the apostle, and we think it is this. The glorious chain of God's *purpose* to glorify men (Rom. 8:28-30) and this equally glorious chain of *means* to that end, *ought* to make the gospel as universal as God designed it to be; but, nevertheless, so great is man's sinful perversity, such is not the case; and the Scripture so foretold it, and, in foretelling, explained it, and exposed the reason. Hence he continues] **16 But they did not all hearken to** [*Hupakouoo:* a word derived from the verb *akouoo*, which is translated "heard," and "hear" in verse 14. It means to *hear attentively, to give heed to, to obey*] **the glad tidings. For Isaiah saith** [predicted], **Lord, who hath believed our report?** [*Akoe;* also a word derived from *akouoo* of verse 14, meaning *the thing that is caused to be heard*] **17 So** [as I said, and, as you see, Isaiah corroborates] **belief cometh of** [is

UNIVERSALITY OF THE GOSPEL

born of, or grows out of] **hearing, and hearing by** [by reason of, because of] **the word** [saying, behest, command. See Luke 5:5; Heb. 11:3; 1:3] **of Christ.** [And so, briefly paraphrasing the apostle's thought, it runs thus: Can God's glorious purpose and inimitable means fail to accomplish the universal glorification of man? Assuredly they can, for Isaiah so predicted. To accomplish universal salvation there must be a universal *heed-hearing*. But Isaiah complained, "Lord, who hath believed that which we have caused them to hear?" meaning that very few gave a heed-hearing. So we see from Isaiah that it is precisely as I said (vs. 14, 15); namely, that belief comes of hearing, and hearing is caused by the command or commission of Christ, as is made apparent by the fact that Isaiah reports back to Christ (whom he calls Lord) that men have not heard what Christ sent, or commissioned, him to tell them. How culpable, then, was Israel as foreseen in the visions of Isaiah and as literally seen by the eyes of Paul! A message commanded by Christ the Lord! How could they be excused for not giving it a heed-hearing, an obedience? Only in two ways: first, by showing that they had never heard it; second, by proving that they were misled by their Scriptures so that they could not recognize it as coming from their Lord— and the point where they would assert and attempt to prove the misleading was this very one now mooted; namely, *universality*, for the Jew regarded the reception of the Gentile as contrary to all that God had ever revealed, or caused to be written down. Therefore the apostle takes these two excuses in order, and exposes their emptiness.] **18 But I say** [To give my cornered Jewish objector every chance to escape from his obvious culpability, I ask in his behalf this question], **Did they not hear?** [This question demands a negative answer—a denial of the "not heard," and is therefore an emphatic way of asserting that they had heard. "They" is unlimited, *all* had heard it, so the Jew could never plead lack of hearing as an excuse for rejecting the gospel. Having thus asserted his position in the question, he proceeds to prove it in the answer] **Yea, verily** [*Menounge*. See note on Rom. 9:20, p. 402.], **Their sound** [Ps. 19:4. "The Psalmist," says Clark, "has *kavvam*, their *line*, which the LXX., and the apostle who quotes from them, render *phthoggos, sound.*" *Line* means *string, harpstring*, a *tone*, a *chord*, and then, metonymically, *sound*] **went out into all the earth, And their words unto the ends of the world.** [It was Alford who, in this connection, discovered "that Psalm 19 is *a comparison of the sun, and glory of the heavens,* with the *word of God*. As far as verse 6 the glories of nature are described: then the great subject is taken up, and the parallelism carried out to the end. So that the apostle has not, as alleged in nearly all the commentators, merely accommodated the text allegorically, but *taken it in its context,* and followed the comparison of the Psalm." The light of the knowledge of God had hitherto been confined to the narrow space of Palestine, but the light of the gospel had now passed beyond these boundaries, and had begun to be as world-illuminating as the celestial orbs, and in doing this it had only fulfilled the words of David. God had done his part as thoroughly in grace as it had been done in nature, and no Jew could excuse himself at the expense of God's good name. "There is not," says Godet, expressing the sentiments of Paul, born of the memories of his own ministry, "a synagogue which has not been filled with it, not a Jew in the world who can justly plead ignorance on the subject." "When the vast multitude converted at Pentecost," says Johnson, "were scattered to their homes, they carried the gospel into all parts of the civilized world." (Comp. Tit. 2:11; Col. 1:6, 23.) This bestowal of natural light and bounty universally was more than a suggestion that God intended to bestow spiritual light and grace upon all. (Comp. Acts 14:17.) "As he spake," says Calvin, "to the Gentiles by the voice of the heavens, he showed by this prelude that he designed to make himself known at length to them also." "It was," says Hengstenberg, "a pledge of their participation in the clearer, higher revelation."] **19 But I say** [Again I ask a question to give my Jewish objector the benefit of every loophole of escape. See verse 18], **Did Israel not know?** [This question also requires a negative answer, and thus, being like the preceding question, the negative of a negative, it amounts to a strong affirmative. Assuredly Israel knew. But knew what? Why, the fact just asserted, to wit, that the gospel should sound out to all, both Jew and Gentile, as freely as light and sunshine, according to the world-wide commission or command of Christ. Did this fact take Israel by surprise? Was the issuing of a world-wide commission a thing untaught in their Scriptures, allowing them to plead ignorance of it? Had Paul cited the promise to Abraham, "In thee shall all the families of the earth be blessed" (Gen. 12:3), then the Jew would have claimed that this promise must be fulfilled *by their all becoming Jews* (Acts 15:1). But he begins with Moses, the first writer of Scripture, and cites a passage which precludes the idea of blessing by absorption or amalgamation, for it is plainly blessing in rivalry and opposition.] **First Moses saith** ["First in the prophetic line" (*De Wette*). First in point of time and place, as Isaiah was near the last. His two citations therefore suggest the entire trend of Scripture, from beginning to end. Compare the "said before" of Rom. 9:29], **I will provoke you to jealousy with that which is no nation, With a nation void of understanding will I anger you.** [The passage cited is Deut. 32:21. The Jews had moved God to jealousy by their "no-gods" (idols), and had provoked him to anger by their vanities; he therefore prophetically announces that he will provoke them to like jealousy and anger by adopting in their stead a "no-people," a foolish nation. A "no-people" describes a nation which has no covenant relation with God, and hence is not recognized as his people. A "foolish nation" describes one made wise by no revelation. The weight of the citation was greatly increased by the name of Moses attached to it, and by the remoteness of the period when uttered. Many utterances of the prophets sounded harsh and hostile, but no one had ever doubted the loyal friendship of Moses to Israel; yet Moses said this even in his day.] **20 And Isaiah is very bold** ["What Moses insinuates, Isaiah cries out boldly and plainly" (*Bengel*). And Isaiah is the favorite prophet of the Jewish people to this day!], **and saith, I was found of them that sought me not; I became manifest unto them that asked not of me.** [Isa. 65:1. (Comp. Isa. 49:1-9; 52:15; 54:5; 66:3-5, 18-21.) They sought me not until I first sought them, and they asked not of me until I made myself known and invited them to offer their petitions. Such is the full meaning in the light of gospel facts. "That the calling of the Gentiles," says Brown, "was meant by these words of the prophet, is manifest from what immediately follows. 'I said, Behold me, behold me, unto a nation that was not called by my name.'" Thus God's design to call another people besides the Jews was so plainly revealed in Scripture that Israel was without excuse for not knowing it. "Nothing," says Lard, "is more inexplicable than their blindness, unless it be their persistence in it." Normally we would say that if God was found of strangers, much more would he be found of his own people. But the ignorance and corruption of the Gentiles constituted a darkness more easily dissipated by the light of the gospel, than the proud obduracy and abnormal self-righteousness of the Jews. The universal preaching of the gospel made this quickly manifest, and, as Paul shows us, Isaiah foretold it.] **21 But as to Israel he saith** [Isa. 65:2], **All the day long did I spread out of my hands unto a disobedient and gainsaying people.** [Here Isaiah presents the full contrast between the Gentiles and Jews. Commentators gener-

UNIVERSALITY OF THE GOSPEL   441

ally regard the spread-out hands as picturing those of a parent extended toward a wayward or prodigal child; but we have no such usage in Scripture. As Plumer observes: "When Paul stretched out his hand, he beckoned to the people that he might cause silence and secure attention (Acts 21:40). Sometimes stretching out the hand is for rescue and deliverance (Deut. 26:8). Sometimes it is to offer and bestow benefits (Isa. 26:10, 11). Sometimes it is the gesture of threatening, chastening, displaying of powers in miracles (Deut. 4:34). Sometimes it points the way in which we should walk or run. No gesture is more natural than this. Again, stretching out the hand is the posture of earnest address and imploring supplication." This last is evidently the sense in which it is here used. "All the day long" may refer to the entire length of the Mosaic dispensation, but it has here especial reference to the time of Christ and his apostles, and their exclusive ministry to the lost sheep of the house of Israel; for at no other time was God's supplication with Israel so marked, and at no other season was the rejection of the Lord so personal, so vehement, so bitter and cruel; all the Gospels are full of it, and the rejection of the Son was the rejection of the Father (John 14:7-9; 2 John 9; John 5:23; 1 John 5:7). Moreover, compare the "this day" of Luke 19:42. "Gainsaying" is added to the Hebrew by the LXX. Pool aptly says: "They were disobedient in heart and gainsaying with their tongues, contrary to those two gracious qualifications mentioned at verses 9 and 10, belief in the heart and confession of the mouth. Their gainsaying answers to "repliest" of Rom. 9:20. For examples of this sin on their part, see Mark 15:8-15; Acts 3:13, 14; 7:51-57; 13:45, 50; 14:2, 19; 17:5; 17:13; 18:12. "Gainsaying," says Godet, "characterizes the hair-splittings and sophisms whereby the Israelites seek to justify their persevering refusal to return to God." As we glance back over the ninth and tenth chapters, they reveal clearly how Israel, zealous for religious monopoly and their exclusive rights under the law, hardened their hearts and rejected the gospel, though grace followed them to the ends of the earth with the offer of salvation. Surely it was their own wickedness, and no arbitrary, cold decree absolute, which excluded them from salvation; and it is equally certain that the Being whom Jesus called Father, and who sent our Lord as a world's Saviour, will never rest or desist until the dark picture of a lost Israel is transformed and transfigured with the glory of the heavenly light by the ultimate inbringing of all Israel, to be, with the purged Gentiles, one kingdom of God upon earth.

III.

THIRD EXPLANATION OF THE GRAND CONCLUSION—THE CASTING OFF OF ISRAEL IS BUT PARTIAL, AN ELECT REMNANT BEING SAVED BY FAITH.

11:1-10.

[In the tenth chapter Paul's argument for gospel universality only required him to show by Scripture that the Gentiles were to be received independently; *i. e.*, without first becoming Jews. But the Scripture which best established this fact also proved a larger, greater fact; viz., that the reception of the Gentiles would so move the Jews to anger and jealousy that they would, as a people, reject the gospel, and thereby cease to be a covenant people, and become a cast-off, rejected nation. This fact is so clearly and emphatically proved that it might be thought that, as Tholuck puts it, "the whole nation, conjointly and severally, had, by some special judgment of God, been shut out from the Messiah's kingdom." The denial of this false inference is the burden of the

AN ELECT REMNANT SAVED

section now before us. In this section he will show that the casting off of Israel is not total, but partial: in the next section he will show that it is not *final,* but *temporary.*] **XI. 1 I say then** [Again, as in verses 18 and 19 of the previous chapter, Paul, for the benefit of the Jewish objector, draws a false inference from what has been said, that he may face it and correct it], **Did God cast off his people?** [Apparently, yes; but really, no. He had only rejected the unbelieving who first rejected him. True, these constituted almost the entire nation; but it was not God's act that rejected them; it was what they themselves did in rejecting God in the person of his Son that fixed their fate. Israel as believing was as welcome and acceptable as ever. So *God* has not rejected them. "The very title *his people,*" says Bengel, "contains the reason for denying it." Comp. 1 Sam. 12:22.) God had promised not to forsake his people (Ps. 94:14). He kept the promise with those who did not utterly forsake him, but as to the rest, the majority, Jesus foretold that the kingdom should be taken from them (Matt. 21:41-43). Comp. Matt. 22:7; Luke 21:24.] **God forbid.** [A formal denial to be followed by double proof.] **For I also am an Israelite** [De Wette, Meyer and Gifford construe this as equal to: I am too good a Jew, too patriotic, to say such a thing. As if Scripture were warped and twisted to suit the whims and to avoid offending the political prejudices of its writers! If Paul was governed by his personal feelings, he ceased to be a true prophet. Had he followed his feelings, instead of revealed truth, he would have avoided the necessity for writing the sad lines at Rom. 9:1-3. The true meaning is this: God has not cast away *en masse,* and without discrimination or distinction, the totality of his ancient people, for I myself am a living denial of such a conclusion; or, as Eubank interprets it, such a concession would exclude the writer himself (as to whose Christianity no Jew has ever had any doubts). "Had it been," says Chrysostom, "God's intention to reject that nation, he never would have selected from it the individual [Paul] to whom he was about to entrust [had already entrusted] the entire work of preaching and the concerns of the whole globe, and all the mysteries and the whole economy of the church"], **of the seed of Abraham** ["A Jew by nurture and nation" (*Burkitt*). Not a proselyte, nor the son of a proselyte, but a lineal descendant from Abraham. Compare his words at Acts 22:28], **of the tribe of Benjamin.** [Comp. Phil. 3:5. Though the apostle had reason to be proud of his tribe as furnishing the first king in Saul (1 Sam. 9:16) and the last Biblical queen in Esther (Esth. 2:17), yet that is not the reason for mentioning Benjamin here. He is showing that God had not cast off the Theocracy, and he mentions himself as of Benjamin, which was second only to Judah *in theocratic honor.* On the revolt of the ten tribes it constituted with Judah the surviving Theocracy (1 Kings 12:21), and after the captivity it returned with Judah and again helped to form the core or kernel of the Jewish nation (Ezra 4:1; 10:9). The apostle was no Jew by mere family tradition (Ezra 2:61-63; Neh. 7:63-65), nor was he of the ten tribes of outcasts, but he was duly registered as of the inner circle, and therefore his acceptance proved the point desired.] **2 God did not cast off his people which he foreknew.** [Here is the second proof that God did not cast off his people. It is in the nature of an axiom, a statement which is so palpably true that it needs no corroboration. God's foreknowledge can not fail, therefore that nation which in the eternity before the world he knew to be his own nation, can not ultimately fail to become his nation. "Of all the peoples of the earth," says Godet, "one only was [published and openly designated as] chosen and known beforehand, by an act of divine foreknowledge and love, as the people whose history would be identified with the realization of salvation. In all others salvation is the affair of *individuals,* but here the notion of salvation is attached to the *nation* itself; not that the liberty of individuals is in the least compromised by the collective designation. The Israelites contemporary with Jesus might reject him; an indefinite series of generations may for ages perpetuate this fact of national unbelief. God is under no pressure; time can stretch out as long as he pleases. He will add, if need be, ages to ages, until there come at length the generation disposed to open their eyes and freely welcome their Messiah. God foreknew this nation as believing and saved, and sooner or later they can not fail to be both." Comp. Acts 15:15-18; Isa. 45:17; 59:20; Jer. 31:31, 34; Ezek. 34:22; 37:23; 39:25; Rom. 11:26.] **Or know ye not what the scripture saith of Elijah?** [Literally, *in Elijah*. Anciently Scripture and other writings were not divided into chapters and verses, but into sections. These among the Jews were called *Parashah*. Instead of being numbered, they had titles to them, describing the contents. Thus it came to pass that any one wishing to refer to a passage of Scripture would quote enough of the *Parashah's* title to identify it. So Paul here quotes words found "in [the *Parashah* about] Elijah"; viz., 1 Kings 19:10-18. Comp. Mark 12:26; Luke 20:37] **how he pleadeth with God against Israel: 3 Lord, they have killed thy prophets, they have digged down thine altars; and I am left alone, and they seek my life.** [Against these two proofs adduced by the apostle it might be objected that if God was not rejecting his people he must be *receiving them,* but you, Paul, practically admit that this is not the case, for, were it so, why can you point only to your *single self* as accepted? Surely your very proofs are against you. To this objection Paul presents a third proof —*i. e.,* the case of Elijah—and his argument, paraphrased, runs thus: You err in supposing that I alone am accepted, and this I will prove by the case of Elijah, who, prophet of prophets though he was, erred in so judging by appearances as to think that he alone remained acceptable. The law required that the nation use the *one* altar which stood in front of the sanctuary in Jerusalem (Lev. 17:8, 9; Deut. 12:1-14). But the Rabbins say (see Lightfoot and Whitby *ad h. l.*) that when the ten tribes revolted, and their kings forbade them to go up to Jerusalem to worship, then this law ceased as to them, and the Lord permitted them to build other altars and sacrifice on them as at the beginning (Gen. 12:7, 8; 13:4, 18; 22:9; 26:25; 33:20; 35:1-7; 46:1), and as they did before worship was centered at Jerusalem (1 Sam. 7:9, 17; 9:13; 11:15; 16:2, 3). That this is so is proved by the conduct of Elijah, who reconstructed the Lord's altar on Mt. Carmel (which these apostates of whom he speaks had thrown down) and offered sacrifice thereon, and the Lord publicly sanctioned and approved the altar by sending fire from heaven (1 Kings 18:30-39). The altars were to be made of earth and unhewn stone (Ex. 20:24, 25), hence it was proper to speak of *digging* them down.] **4 But what saith the answer of God unto him? I have left for myself seven thousand men, who have not bowed the knee to Baal.** [Jezebel and Ahab, in their zeal for the Phœnician god, Baal, had apparently exterminated the worship of the true God. At least, Elijah was deceived into so thinking. But the answer of God corrected his mistake. Paul inserts the words "for myself." "*I. e.,*" says Meyer, "to myself as my property, and for my service, in contrast to the idolatrous abomination," or service of idols. The feminine article *te* is inserted before Baal, and this has greatly puzzled expositors, for the LXX. have the masculine article. It has been explained in various ways; Erasmus and others by supposing a feminine noun such as *eikoni* (image) to be understood; Estius, etc., by supposing *stele* (statue) to be supplied, or, as Lightfoot and Alford think, *damalei* (calf); or, according to Reiche, that there was a female Baal; or, as Wetstein and Olshausen, that Baal was androgynous (an hermaphrodite); or, as

AN ELECT REMNANT SAVED 447

Gesenius and Tholuck, that the feminine was used of idols in contempt; or, as Fritsche, Ewald and Barmby, that Paul may have happened upon a copy of the LXX. which gave the feminine instead of the masculine. Of the above we prefer to supply *damalei*, calf, following the reasoning of Lightfoot. Baal was both a specific name for the Phœnician god, and also a common name for idols, hence the plural, Baalim. Of idols at the time referred to, Israel had two of great prominence: 1. The idol to the Phœnician god Baal, whose image was a bull. 2. The golden calves set up by Jeroboam, at Bethel and Dan. Now, it would avail nothing if Israel rejected one of these idols, yet worshiped the other, as in the case of Jehu, who rooted out the Phœnician, but accepted the calf of Jeroboam. But *calf Baal* would be an inclusive expression, striking at *both* forms of idolatry. (Comp. also 1 Kings 19:18 with Hos. 13:2.) Moreover, the Phœnician worship was but recently re-established and had received a terrific blow at the hand of Elijah, while Jeroboam's calves were old and popular, hence we find in Tobit the expression, "And all the tribes that revolted together, sacrificed to the calf Baal" (literally, *te Baal, te damalei; to Baal, to the calf*— Tob. 1:5). Here we have an instance where the word *damalei* is actually supplied, and that by a Hebrew writer, and "where," as Alford adds, "the golden calves of the ten tribes seem to be identified with Baal, and were a curious addition in [the manuscript] *Aleph* refers expressly to their establishment by Jeroboam.] **5 Even so then at this present time also there is a remnant according to the election of grace.** [Resuming the argument. "As at the time of the great deflection in Elijah's day there seemed to him to be but one, yet God had reserved to himself seven thousand, so now in this time of falling away, you who judge by outward appearance will judge just as poorly. You may think derisively that I am the sole representative of the election of which I speak, but, scattered and dispersed as they are, there are vastly

more than you dream (comp. Acts 21:20); for the
unchangeable God always reserves to himself a remnant, whom he has chosen as his own." "One thing
indeed," says Godet, "follows from the election of
grace applied to the whole of Israel; not the salvation
of such or such individuals, but the indestructible
existence of a believing remnant at all periods of
their history, even in the most disastrous crises of
unbelief, as at the time of the ministry of Elijah, or
of the coming of Jesus Christ. The idea contained in
the words, 'according to the election of grace,' is
therefore this: In virtue of the election of Israel as
the salvation-people, God has not left them in our
day without a faithful remnant, any more than he did
in the kingdom of the ten tribes at the period when
a far grosser heathenism was triumphant." In the
eternal purpose of God the election of the salvation-class preceded any human act, but it does not therefore follow that it preceded a *presumptive, supposititious* act. The same wisdom which foresaw the
election also foresaw the *compliance* of the elect
individual *with the terms and conditions of election.*
This must be so, for in the outworking of the *eternal
purpose* in the realms of the *actual,* man *must* first
comply with the conditions of election before he becomes one of the elect; for, as Lard wisely says,
"election or choosing, in the case of the redeemed,
does not precede obedience, and therefore is neither
the cause of it nor reason for it. On the contrary,
obedience precedes election, and is both the condition
of it and reason for it. Obedience is man's own free
act, to which he is never moved by any prior election
of God. Choosing, on the other hand, is God's free
act, prompted by favor and conditioned on obedience.
This obedience, it is true, he seeks to elicit by the
proper motives; but to this he is led solely by love of
man, and never by previous choice. True Scriptural
election, therefore, is a simple, intelligible thing, when
suffered to remain unperplexed by the subtleties of
schoolmen." As the open reference to Elijah con-

tains a covert one to Ahab and his Israel, Chrysostom bids us "reflect on the apostle's skill, and how, in proving the proposition before him, he secretly augments the charge against the Jews. For the object he had in view, in bringing forward the whole of that testimony, was to manifest their ingratitude, and to show that of old they had been what they were now."] **6 But if it is by grace, it is no more of works: otherwise grace is no more grace.** [With these words, Paul explains the last clause of the preceding verse—viz., "the election of grace"—and thereby shows that he means them in their full sense, and abides by that meaning. Alford paraphrases his meaning thus: "And let us remember, when we say an election *of grace,* how much those words imply; viz., nothing short of the entire exclusion of all human *work* from the question. Let these two terms [grace and work] be regarded as and kept distinct from one another, and do not let us attempt to mix them and so destroy the meaning of each." He means that grace and works are absolutely antithetical and mutually exclusive. Paul is talking about *works of the law,* not about the *gospel terms or conditions of salvation.* These terms are faith, repentance and baptism, and complying with them made, and still makes, anybody one of the elect. But does this compliance fulfill any part, parcel or portion of the Mosaic law? Assuredly not. On the contrary, it is seeking salvation by another way. Moreover, the one complying with these conditions is *immediately* one of the elect. Has he, then, in any way *merited* election, or is it wholly of *grace?"* Even granting that there is *some work* in complying with these conditions, could any one so lack brains as to be confused into thinking that the work *weighs anything* as a meritorious basis on which to demand election to that unspeakable gift, eternal life? But do not the works of a Christian life count as merit toward election? Assuredly not; for they are wrought *after* the election has taken place. In short, almost like Jacob, we are elected at the moment of our birth from the water, when we are spiritual babes in Christ (John 3:5; Tit. 3:5), "neither having done anything good or bad, that the purpose of God," etc. (Rom. 9:11). Complying with the gospel conditions of election is mere spiritual birth, and what merit hath an infant though its struggles aid in its parturition? We are by the process of conversion brought no further than the condition of babes in Christ (1 Cor. 3:1-3; Heb. 5: 11-14; 1 Pet. 2:2), and our birth-throes are without merit, though essential to our further continuance in life. There is, therefore, nothing in the gospel conditions which conflict with the doctrine of election by grace, nor do they mix works with grace.] **7 What then?** [What results from the facts just stated? If God only acknowledges covenant relations with a remnant, and with them only by grace, surely you expect me to make some statement as to the status of the bulk of Israel. My statement is this:] **That which Israel** [the bulk or main body of the nation] **seeketh for, that he obtained not; but the election obtained it, and the rest were hardened** [The search spoken of is that with which we are already familiar; viz., the endeavor to obtain justification before God. All Israel sought this treasure. Those seeking it by the works of the law (the vast majority of the nation) failed to find it, but the remnant, seeking it by faith in Christ, found themselves chosen of God or elected to it. "The Jew, he says, fights against himself. Although seeking righteousness, he does not choose to accept it" (*Chrysostom*). If he could not find it by his own impossible road of self-righteousness and self-sufficiency, he would have none of it, though the apostle showed how easily it might be obtained by pointing out those who made it theirs by receiving it as a free gift from God through faith in Christ. But for those despising this rich gift, God had another gift, even that of hardening, which means the depriving of any organ of its natural sensibility. The calloused finger loses the sense of touch; the

AN ELECT REMNANT SAVED

cataractous eye no longer sees clearly; the hardened mind loses its discernment between things good and bad, and readily believes a specious lie (2 Thess. 2: 9-12); the hardened heart becomes obdurate like that of Pharaoh's, and is not touched or softened by appeals to pity, mercy, etc. We have seen, in the case of Pharaoh, that the hardness was the joint act of God and Pharaoh. The same is shown to be the case of the Jews, for Paul here attributes it to God, while it is elsewhere charged against the Jews themselves (Matt. 13:14, 15). Of course God's part is always merely permissive, and Satan is the active agent. "God," says Lard, "never yet hardened any man to keep him from doing right, or in order to lead him to do wrong. He is not the author of sin. He may permit other agencies, as Satan and the wickedness of men, to harden them, but he himself never does it"]: **8 according as it is written** [Isa. 29:10; Ezek. 12:2; Deut. 29:4], **God gave them a spirit of stupor, eyes that they should not see, and ears that they should not hear, unto this very day.** [As the passage quoted is a combination of Isaiah and Deuteronomy, and is found in part also in Ezekiel, it suggests that the spirit of stupor, deafness and blindness characterized the course of Israel from beginning to end; and it was therefore to be guarded against as a chronic sin. *Katanuxis* (stupor) may be derived from *katanussoo* (*Fritsche, Meyer*), which means to *prick* or *sting*, and hence, as in bites of reptiles, etc., to *cause stupefaction;* or it may come from *katanuzoo* (*Volkmar*), which means *to bend the head in order to sleep, to fall asleep.* It is used in Ps. 60:3, where it is translated "wine of staggering," though Hammond contends that the passage refers to the stupefying wine given to them who were to be put to death. It means, then, that condition of stupor, or intellectual numbness, which is almost wholly insensate; for the term "spirit" means a pervading tendency. "Such expressions," says Gifford, "as *'the spirit of heaviness'* (Isa. 61:3), *'a spirit of meekness'* (1 Cor. 4:21), 'the spirit of bondage' (Rom. 8:15), show that *'spirit'* is used for the pervading tendency and tone of mind, the special character of which is denoted by the genitive which follows."] **9 And David saith, Let their table be made a snare, and a trap, And a stumblingblock, and a recompense unto them** [Ps. 69:22, 23. the word "trap" is added from Ps. 35:8. Theodoret says that Psalm 69 "is a prediction of the sufferings of Christ, and the final destruction of the Jews on that account." That which is presented in the form of a wish is, therefore, really a prophecy. Let the food on their table be as the bait to the snare and the trap, and the stumbling-block over which the tempted creature falls to lame itself. Let that which they think a source of pleasure and life become an enticement to pain and death. Dropping the figure, the words mean that the very religion of the Old Dispensation, to which the Jew looked for spiritual joy and sustenance, should become to him a sorrow and a fatal famine, so that this very blessing became to him a curse. The word "recompense" denotes a punishment for an evil deed; its presence here shows that the evil which came upon the Jews was caused by their own fault and sin, and not by *absolute decree*]: **10 Let their eyes be darkened, that they may not see, And bow thou down their back always.**] This verse is usually construed to picture the political servitude and spiritual bondage of Israel after the fall of Jerusalem. No doubt it has reference to conditions ushered in by that event, but it pictures the dimness and decrepitude of *old age*—a blind eye, and a back beyond straightening. The Jews were to partake of the nature of the old, worn-out dispensation to which they clung (Matt. 9:16, 17; Heb. 8:13). God's people can not grow old, they renew their youth like the eagle's (Ps. 103:5), but a people which ceases to be his, falls into decay. J. A. Alexander's comment on Ps. 69:22 deserves note. He says: "The imprecations in this verse, and those following it, are revolting only when considered as the expressions

AN ELECT REMNANT SAVED

of malignant selfishness. If uttered by God, they shock no reader's sensibilities; nor should they when considered as the language of an ideal person, representing the whole class of righteous sufferers, and particularly Him who, though he prayed for his murderers while dying (Luke 23:34), had before applied the words of this very passage to the unbelieving Jews (Matt. 23:38), as Paul did afterward."

IV.

FOURTH EXPLANATION OF THE GRAND CONCLUSION—SALUTARY RESULTS OF THE TEMPORAL FALL AND FUTURE RISE OF ISRAEL—GENTILES WARNED NOT TO GLORY OVER ISRAEL.

11:11-24.

11 I say then, Did they stumble that they might fall? [Fall (*piptoo*) is a much stronger word than stumble, and the contrast between the two words makes the former emphatic. To fall means to be killed, and is in Greek, as in English, applied to those slain in battle. (*Homer*, Il. 8:475; 11:84.) As emphasized, then, it means to become "utterly irrevocable" (*Clark*); "*irrevocable ruin,* in opposition to that which is *temporary*" (*Hodge*); "to fall forever, finally" (*Pool*); "perish forever" (*Meyer*); "so as utterly to fall" (*Stuart*). Paul is arguing as to God's intention. Therefore, according to his established custom, he asks a question that he may guard against a false conclusion, and the form of the question, as usual, demands a negative answer, for the false conclusion is to be denied. From the foreseen "stumbling" of Israel (Rom. 9:33; 11:9), and from the "hardening" (v. 7), it *might* be concluded that God sent a stumbling-block Saviour, a Messiah in an unwelcome form, and an unpalatable gospel-salvation with the intent and purpose of working Israel's downfall and ruin—his final, irrevocable fall. Did God bring about or cause a stumbling of the Jews of Christ's day, that all future generations might fall, or be cast off forever? Such is the question, and the answer is] **God forbid** [This general denial is followed by a threefold explanation: (1) The fall of Israel was permitted because spiritually profitable to the Gentiles (11); (2) the rising again of Israel will be for the greater spiritual profit to the Gentiles (12-15); (3) the fall of Israel is only temporary—they shall rise again—26]: **but** [introducing the real purpose or design of Israel's fall] **by their fall** [*paraptoma,* from the verb *parapiptoo,* which means to sideslip, to fall away, to fall. Hence *paraptoma* means fall, trespass (*Alford*), lapse (*Stuart*), slip (*Green*), false step (*Godet*), offence (*Gifford*), fault, sin. It is best translated here by the word "offence"] **salvation *is come* unto the Gentiles, to provoke them to jealousy.** [Emulation is a better translation than jealousy. Their offence was their unbelief, which caused God to put them away, and this putting away greatly facilitated the success of the gospel among the Gentiles. So great was the pride and exclusiveness of the Jews, and such was their blind loyalty to their race, ritual, temple, law, etc., that even the most thoroughly converted and indoctrinated Christians among them, such as the very apostles themselves (Paul alone excepted), never manifested any enthusiasm in preaching the gospel to the Gentiles. It took a miracle to constrain Peter to do such a thing (Acts 10), and, after having done so, his Christian brethren demanded an explanation and apology for his intercourse with Gentiles (Acts 11), and later, instead of yielding to his apostolic leadership, they were so stubborn in their aversion to the free admission of Gentiles into the church, that the fear of them triumphed and caused Peter to conform to their views (Gal. 2:11-14; for further evidence of their bigotry, see Acts 15:1, 2; 21:17-24). Their opposition to Paul only ceased with his life. With such a spirit among Jewish Christians, two things were sure to happen if they retained their pre-eminence in the church, and continued to dominate its policy. (1) There would be but little preaching supplied to the Gentiles, since pride and enmity made the Jews unwilling to serve them (1 Thess. 2:15, 16); (2) such gospel as was preached to the Gentiles would be woefully corrupted and perverted by Judaistic teaching and practice (Gal. 1:6-9; 3:1-3; 6:12-14), for "Israel," as Lange observes, "did not desire the Gentiles, under the most favorable circumstances, to participate in the Messianic salvation, except as proselytes of the Jews," since they took more pride and joy in converting men to Moses than in winning them to Christ. Thus by their zeal for the law they would imperil the Gentiles' liberty in Christ (Gal. 4:9, 21-5:1), so that Christianity could scarce escape becoming merely a new patch on an old garment, even as the Master forewarned (Matt. 9:16), in which secondary capacity it could never so save the Gentile as to convert the world. Hence to save the wine Jesus cast aside the old Jewish bottle, and stored the gracious gospel fluid in the new Gentile wine-skin (Matt. 9:17). And he not only cast off the Jewish people as unworthy of that pre-eminence in the church which was naturally theirs, but he even stood aside the eleven apostles as too hopelessly narrow-minded for Gentile evangelism, and committed the whole of this colossal ministry to the one man, Paul (Acts 9:15; 22:21; 26:17, 18; Rom. 1:5; 11:13; 15:16; Gal. 1:15, 16; Eph. 3:7, 8; 1 Tim. 2:7; 2 Tim. 1:11; especially Gal. 2:7-9). And even in his case we note how the prompt "offence," or unbelief, of the Jews enabled him to preach "to the Jew first," yet speedily left him free and unfettered to push the work among the Gentiles (Acts 13:45-48; 28:28). So the "offence" and consequent casting off of Israel did facilitate the conversion of the Gentiles. Israel, as a reluctant, sluggish, half-converted hindrance, was thrust from the doorway, that the Gentiles might enter freely and fully into the kingdom (Luke 11:52; Matt. 23:13). Salvation of the Gentiles was the *proximate* purpose accomplished, and still being accomplished, by the rejection of the Jews: the salvation of the Jews themselves was the *remote* purpose of the rejection, and it is largely future, even yet. It is to be brought about by a spirit of emulation. "Seeing," says Godet, "all the blessings of the kingdom, pardon, justification, the Holy Spirit, adoption, shed down abundantly on the Gentile nations through faith in Him whom they had rejected, how can they help saying at length: These things are ours? And how can they help opening their eyes and recognizing that Jesus is the Messiah, since in him the works predicted of the Messiah are accomplished? How shall the elder son, seeing his younger brother seated and celebrating the feast at his father's table, fail to ask that he may re-enter the paternal home and come to sit down side by side with his brother, after throwing himself into the arms of the common father?" A blessed result indeed, but long delayed by the carnal, half-converted state of the Gentile church, as witnessed by the Roman Catholicism which is Sardis (Rev. 3:1) and Protestantism which is sectarianism (1 Cor. 3:1-5), a Philadelphia church lapsing into Laodicean indifference—Rev. 3:14-19.] **12 Now if their fall** [*paraptoma*] **is the riches of the world, and their loss** [*hettema,* that loss or diminution which an army suffers by defeat, also moral loss, impoverishment, to be defeated, to be reduced, or made inferior. "A reduction in one aspect to a race of scattered exiles, in another to a mere remnant of 'Israelites indeed' "—*Moule*] **the riches of the Gentiles; how much more their fulness?** [*Pleroma,* the full number, the whole body, the totality. To emphasize the situation and impress it upon his readers, Paul makes use of the Hebrew parallelism, presenting two clauses which express substantially the same thing. If there be any difference, we would say that "world" indicates sinners, and "Gentiles" the uncovenanted races. If paraphrased thus, it would read, Now, if the sin or offence of godly Israel enriched the ungodly, sinful world, and if the loss or spiritual impoverishment and numerical diminution of the covenanted people enriched and multiplied the covenanted among the hitherto uncovenanted people, how much more would both the sinful world and its uncovenanted inhabitants have been blessed every way, had Israel been of the right spirit, so as to have received enrichment instead of being cast off and diminished. Because Israel had a proud, narrow. inimical spirit (1 Thess. 2:15, 16), its depletion worked blessing to the world and the Gentiles; but if Israel had yielded to Christ so as to be transformed like that persecuting Saul who became Paul, the apostle to the Gentiles, who can measure the fullness of blessing which would have come to the inhabitants of the earth by the enlargement, enrichment and full spiritual endowment of every son of Abraham dispersed through the world! With millions of Pauls in all lands throughout all generations, we should have measured our heavenward progress by milestones instead of inches. "Goodness," says Thomas Aquinas, "is more capable of bearing blessing than is evil; but the evil of the Jews brought great blessing to the Gentiles; therefore much more should their goodness bring greater blessing to the world."] **13 But** [A note of correction. At Rom. 7:1, 4 Paul began to address the Jews, and all that he has said since then has had specific reference to that people. Since verse 11, however, the thought has gradually passed to the Gentiles and now Paul openly notes that he is speaking to them, lest any should think he was still speaking to Jews about Jews] **I speak to you that are Gentiles.** [Much that the apostle has said might be misconstrued by the Gentiles so as to minister to their pride. The apostle therefore addresses them personally, and prepares the way for an admonition against vainglory in themselves and a contemptuous spirit against the Jews.] Inasmuch then as I am an apostle of Gentiles, I glorify my ministry; 14 if by any means I may provoke to jealousy *them that are* my flesh [my kindred: the Jews], **and may save** [do the human part of saving] **some of them.** [Finding myself set apart by Christ to minister to Gentiles instead of Jews, I perform my task with a double zest, for (I not only rejoice to save Gentiles, but) it is a means (also) of saving some of Israel by provoking them to an honorable and generous emulation even now; since the mass of them will be won that way in the end, as indicated above. And, moreover, I do this in fullest love and goodwill to you Gentiles, for I foresee what incalculable blessings the conversion of the Jews will bring to you.] **15 For if the casting away of them *is* the reconciling of the world, what *shall* the receiving of them be, but life from the dead?** [Again we have a passage wherein "the apostle," as Meyer expresses it, "argues from the happy effect of the worse cause, to the happier effect of the better cause." If a curse, so to speak, brought a blessing, what would not a blessing bring? If the casting away of Israel in Paul's day resulted in the beginning of the times of the Gentiles, and the turning of them from idols and imaginary deities to seek after the true God as part of a theocratic family wherein converted Jew and Gentile are reconciled to each other and to God (see Eph. 2:11-22 for a full description of this double reconciliation), what would the receiving again of the vast body of unconverted Jews at the end of the times of the Gentiles (vs. 25, 26) be but a veritable life from the dead, an unprecedented, semi-miraculous revival? Theophylact, Augustine, Melanchthon, Calvin, Beza, Bucer, Turretin, Philippi, Bengel, Auberlen, Clark, Macknight, Plumer, Brown, Lard, Gifford, Moule, Riddle, etc., view this as a great spiritual resurrection, a revival of grace accompanying the conversion of the whole world. Others, as Origen, Chrysostom, the earlier commentators generally, Ruckert, Meyer, De Wette, etc., look upon it as a literal, bodily resurrection, while Olshausen, Lange and Alford consider it as a combination of spiritual and bodily resurrections. The first of these positions is most tenable. "This," says Barnes, "is an instance of the peculiar, glowing and vigorous manner of the apostle Paul. His mind catches at the thought of what *may be* produced by the recovery of the Jews, and no ordinary language would convey his idea. He had already exhausted the usual forms of speech by saying that even their rejection had *reconciled* the world, and that it was the *riches* of the Gentiles. To say that their *recovery*—a striking and momentous event; an event so much better fitted to produce important results—would be attended by the conversion of the world, would be insipid and tame. He uses, therefore, a most bold and striking figure. The resurrection of the dead was an image of the most vast and wonderful event that could take place." Some of those who view this as a literal resurrection, do so from a lack of clear conception as to the order of the dispensations. They look upon the conversion of the Jews as taking place at the very end of the world, and hence *synchronous* with the final resurrection. They do not know that the Jewish dispensation, or age, gave place to the present one, which is called "the times of the Gentiles" (Luke 21:24), and that this dispensation will give place to a third, known as the millennium or age of a thousand years (Rev. 20:1-6). The Jewish dispensation ended with the death of Christ, and the Gentile dispensation will end when the gospel is preached unto all nations (Matt. 24:14). Its end, as Paul shows us at verses 25 and 26, will also be synchronous with the conversion of the Jews. Failure to grasp these important facts has led to much general confusion, and to gross mistakes in the interpretation and application of prophecies, for many Biblical references to the end of the Gentile dispensation, or age, have been erroneously referred to the end of the world, or end of the ages. The last age,

or millennium, will be the triumph of the kingdom of
God, the thousand-year reign of the saints on earth,
and it will begin with the conversion of the world
under the leadership of the Jews, and this is the event
which Paul fittingly describes as "life from the dead."
The millennium will be as a resurrection to the Jews
(Ezek. 37), for they will return to their own land
(Ezek. 37:11-14, 21, 25) and revive their national life
as a united people (Ezek. 37:22). It will be as a
resurrection of primitive, apostolic Christianity to the
Gentiles, for the deadness of the "last days" of their
dispensation (2 Tim. 3:1-9; 4:3, 4), with its Catholic
Sardis and its Protestant Laodicea (Rev. 3:1-6, 14-
22), will give place to the new life of the new age,
wherein the "first love" of the Ephesian, or first,
church will be revived (Rev. 2:4, 5), and the martyr
spirit of Smyrna, its successor, will again come forth
(Rev. 2:10), and the devil will be chained and the
saints will reign (Rev. 20:1-6). This spiritual resurrection of the last age is called the "first resurrection," for it is like, and it is followed by, the *real*
or *literal* resurrection which winds it up, and begins
the heavenly age, or eternity with God. Ezekiel tells
what the last age will do to the *Jews,* Paul what it
will be to the *Gentiles,* and John what it will mean to
them *both.* As to Paul's description Pool thus writes:
"The conversion of the Jewish people and nation will
strengthen the things that are languishing and like to
die in the Christian church. It will confirm the faith
of the Gentiles, and reconcile their differences in
religion, and occasion a more thorough reformation
amongst them: there will be a much more happy and
flourishing estate of the church, even such as shall be
in the end of the world, at the resurrection of the
dead." All this, as Paul boldly asserts, will result
from the blessed power of Jewish leadership, as in
the beginning. "The light," says Godet, "which converted Jews bring to the church, and the power of
life which they have sometimes awakened in it, are
the pledge of that spiritual renovation which will be

produced in Gentile Christendom by their entrance *en masse*. Do we not feel that in our present condition there is something, and that much, wanting to us that the promises of the gospel may be realized in all their fullness; that there is, as it were, a mysterious hindrance to the efficacy of preaching, a debility inherent in our spiritual life, a lack of joy and force which contrasts strangely with the joyful outbursts of prophets and psalmists; that, in fine, the feast in the father's house is not complete . . . why? because it can not be so, so long as the family is not entirely reconstituted by the return of the elder son. Then shall come the Pentecost of the last times, the latter rain." Against the above view that Paul speaks of a spiritual resurrection it is weakly urged that it *assumes* a future falling away of the Gentiles, and a lapse on their part into spiritual death, and that the apostle gives no intimation of such a declension by them. But it is right to assume such a declension, for Paul most clearly intimates it; for (1) all the remainder of this section is a discussion of how the Jews brought their dispensation to an end, and a warning to the Gentiles not to follow their example and have their dispensation end in a like manner. (2) In verse 25 he speaks of the fullness or completeness of the Gentiles. But, according to the divine method, this dispensation of the Gentiles could not reach completeness and be done away with *until* it became corrupt and worthless. God does not cast off till iniquity is full and failure complete (Gen. 6:13; 15:16; Matt. 23:29-33). Moreover, some five years before this, in the second Epistle that ever came from his pen, Paul had foretold this declension in the church, and had described it as even then "working," though restrained (2 Thess. 2:3-12). The assumption on which this view of a spiritual resurrection rests is both contextual and natural. Finally, as to this being a literal body resurrection, we must of course admit that an all-powerful God can begin the millennium that way if he chooses, but to suppose

that the literally resurrected dead shall mingle and
dwell with the rest of humanity for a thousand years,
or throughout an entire dispensation, savors of fanaticism. Even Jesus kept aloof during his forty days
of waiting before his ascension. A healthy mind can
not long retain such an idea, nor can we think that
Paul would introduce so marvelous and abnormal a
social condition without in some measure elaborating
it. As against a literal, physical resurrection Hodge
argues strongly. We give a sentence or two: "Not
only in Scriptures, but also in profane literature, the
transition from a state of depression and misery, to
one of prosperity, is expressed by the natural figure
of passing from death to life. The Old Testament
prophets represented the glorious condition of the
Theocracy, consequent on the coming of Christ, in
contrast with its previous condition, as a rising from
the dead. . . . Nowhere else in Scripture is the
literal resurrection expressed by the words 'life from
the dead.' Had Paul intended a reference to the
resurrection, no reason can be assigned why he did
not employ the established and familiar words 'resurrection from the dead.' If he meant the resurrection,
why did he not say so? Why use a general phrase,
which is elsewhere used to express another idea?
Besides this, it is not according to the analogy of
Scripture, that the resurrection of the dead, and the
change of those who shall then be alive (1 Cor. 15:
51; 1 Thess. 4:14-18), are to be immediate, consequent on the conversion of the Jews. The resurrection is not to occur until 'the end.' A new state of
things, a new mode of existence, is to be then introduced. Flesh and blood—*i. e.*, our bodies as now
organized—can not inherit the kingdom of God."
For a full discussion of the spiritual nature of the
resurrection, from the pen of A. Campbell, see his
articles on the second coming of the Lord, in the
Millennial Harbinger. We shall never know how dead
our liquor-licensing, sectarian, wealth-worshiping,
stock-gambling, religio-fad-loving, political, war-

waging Christendom has been until the spirit of the early church rises from the dead to form the new age; then it will be at once apparent to all what Paul meant by this bold figure, "life from the dead." But the glorious prospect here presented rests on the supposition that the Jews *en masse* shall be converted. As that is a supposition which many expositors even in our day regard with doubt, the apostle first shows its Scriptural and natural reasonableness, and then plainly and unequivocally predicts it. He presents its reasonableness thus] **16 And if the firstfruit is holy, so is the lump: and if the root is holy, so are the branches.** [Another parallelism. The apostle demonstrates the same truth, first, from the standpoint of the law of God in the Bible (firstfruit and lump); second, from the law of God in nature (root and tree). As the harvest or raw material of the Jew was regarded as unclean, or ceremonially unholy, and not to be eaten till it was cleansed by the waving of a first-portion, or firstfruit, of it as a heave-offering before the Lord (Lev. 23:9-14; Ex. 34:26); so the meal or prepared material was likewise prescribed until a portion of the first dough was offered as a heave-offering. This offered "firstfruit," or, better, "first-portion" (*aparche*), made the whole lump (*phurama*) from which it was taken holy, and thus sanctified all the future meal, of which it was the representative or symbol, so that it could now be used by the owner (Num. 15:19-21; Neh. 10:37). The apostle, then, means that as the patriarchs, Abraham, Isaac and Jacob (called fathers in verse 28), the firstfruit by the revealed law, and the root by the natural law, were holy, so all their descendants as lump and tree were likewise holy. But holiness has two distinct meanings: (1) Purity, moral and spiritual perfection, absolute righteousness—a holiness unto salvation; (2) that which is consecrated or set apart for divine use—a holiness short of salvation. The second meaning is the one intended here. The Jews, being out of Christ, are certainly not holy or righteous unto salvation, Paul being witness; but they have what Gifford styles "this legal and relative holiness of that which has been consecrated to God." In this respect they are still "the holy people" (Dan. 12:7), "the chosen people" (Dan. 11:15), preserved from fusion with the Gentiles, and ultimately to be restored to their original pre-eminence as leaders in the worship of Jehovah. In short, then, there is no divinely erected barrier rendering them irrevocably unholy, and preventing their conversion. On the contrary, they are pre-eminently susceptible to conversion both by law divine and natural, and only their persistent unbelief prevents their Christianization.] **17 But if some of the branches were broken off, and thou [O Gentile believer], being a wild olive, wast grafted in among them, and didst become partaker with them of the root of the fatness of the olive tree** [Some commentators, recognizing that Christianity is a distinct thing from Judaism, have been unduly frightened at the manner in which the apostle here *blends* them as one tree. This has led them to forsake the obvious meaning of the apostle's words, in an endeavor to contort them so as to keep distinct the Christian and Jewish bodies. Some of these, therefore, regard Christ as the tree, and others regard it as representing the Christian church. But such exegesis violates the text, for the Jewish unbelievers are pictured as branches "broken off." Now, they could neither be broken off from Christ nor the church, for they were *never joined to either*. The tree is the Theocracy (Jer. 11:16; Hos. 14:6; Ezek. 17:3; Zech 11:2). In a sense it is one continuous tree, for it bears to God the continuous relation of being his peculiar people, but in another sense it is, as the apostle here presents it, an entirely different tree, for *all* the branches which were formerly accepted on the basis of natural Abrahamic descent were broken off, and *all* the branches, whether Jew or Gentile, which had the new requirement of faith in Christ, were grafted in. Surely, then, th⁓

SALUTARY RESULTS

tree is distinct enough as presented in its two conditions. Yet is it the same Theocracy, with the same patriarchal root and developed from the same basic covenants and promises (Heb. 11:39, 40; Eph. 2:11-22). Christianity is not Judaism, and no pen ever taught this truth more clearly than Paul's. Yet Christianity is a development of the old Theocracy, and is still a Theocracy, a kingdom of God, and this is plainly taught; for the Christian, be he Jew or Gentile, is still a spiritual son of Abraham (Rom. 4:16; Gal. 3:7, 29; 4:28), a member of the true Israel; the true Jew. Now, the Christian Jew, having already an organic connection with the Theocracy, is viewed by Paul as simply *remaining* in it. And here is the point where the confusion arises. If he became regenerate (John 3:1-6), and, dropping the carnal tie of the old, received the spiritual tie of the new (John 8:37-44), he indeed remained in the theocratic tree, but in it *as transformed at Pentecost*. If the Jew did not undergo this change, he was broken off and cast aside (Matt. 8:11, 12). Thus the apostle makes it clear that the Jew, as a Jew, and without spiritual change through faith in Christ, did not *remain* in *any* divinely accepted Theocracy. But as God originally contemplated the tree, every Jew was to develop into a Christian, in which case the tree would have been indeed continuous. Jewish unbelief frustrated the divine harmony and made it necessary for the apostle himself to here and elsewhere emphasize the difference between the old and new Theocracies. "The Gentiles are called a wild olive because God had not cultivated them as he did the Jews, who, on that account, are called (v. 24) the good or garden olives. . . . The juice of the olive is called 'fatness,' because from its fruit, which is formed by that juice, oil is expressed" (*Macknight*). "The oleaster, or wild olive," says Parens, "has the same form as the olive, but lacks its generous sap and fruits."]; **18 glory not over the branches: but if thou gloriest** [remember], **it is not thou that bearest the root, but** the root thee. [Pride *goeth* before destruction, and a haughty spirit before a fall" (Prov. 16:18). Religious pride had proved the undoing of the Jews. It made them despise and reject an unregal Messiah; it caused them to spurn a gospel preached to the poor; it moved them to reject a salvation in which the unclean Gentile might freely share. As Paul opens before his Gentile readers the high estate into which they had come, he anticipates the religious pride which the contemplation of their good fortune was so soon to beget in them, hence he at once sounds the timely note of warning. As to the Jew they had no reason to boast, for they were debtor to him, not he to them, for "salvation is from the Jew" (John 4:22). As to themselves they could not speak proudly, for the depression of the Jew was due to God's severity, and the exaltation of the Gentile was due to his goodness. The Gentile church was incorporated into a previously existing Jewish church, and their new Theocracy had its root in the old, so that in neither case were these privileges original, but wholly secondary and derived from the Jews. Moreover, "such presumption toward the branches," says Tholuck, "could not be without presumption toward the root." Would that the Gentiles, who to-day boast of their Christianity and despise the Jew from whence it was derived, could comprehend the folly of their course. How great is the sin of Christendom! "In its pride," says Godet, "it tramples underfoot the very nation of that grace which has made it what it is. It moves on, therefore, to a judgment of rejection like that of Israel, but which shall not have to soften it a promise [of final restoration] like that which accompanied the fall of the Jews."] **19 Thou wilt say then, Branches were broken off, that I might be grafted in.** [The apostle here puts in the mouth of a representative Gentile the cause or justification of the pride. Was it not ground for self-esteem and self-gratulation when God cast off his covenanted people to receive strangers?

—Eph. 2:19.] 20 **Well** [A form of partial and often ironical assent: equal to, very true, grant it, etc. It was not strictly true that God had cast off the Jew to make room for the Gentile, for there was room for both. The marriage supper shows the truth very clearly. The refusal of the Jew was the reason why he was cast off, not because there was lack of room, or partial favor on God's part, or superior merit on the part of the Gentiles—Luke 14:15-24]; **by their unbelief they were broken off, and thou standest by thy faith** [not merit]. **Be not highminded, but fear: 21 for if God spared not the natural branches, neither will he spare thee.** [Faith justified no boast, yet faith constituted the only divinely recognized distinction in the Gentiles' favor, in estimating between the Gentile Christian and the cast-off Jew. All the past history of the Jew stood in his favor; therefore the Gentile has vastly more reason to fear than had the Jew; for if natural branches fell through false pride which induced unbelief, how much more likely the adopted branches were to be cut off. Again, he had more reason for fear than for pride; for being on trial as the Jews had been, he was succumbing to the same sin of self-righteous pride, and more liable to suffer the same rejection. Paul now presents the even-balanced equality of Jew and Gentile if weighed in the scales of *merit* instead of the new scales of grace-toward-faith.] **22 Behold then the goodness and severity of God: toward them** [the Jews] **that fell, severity** [for lack of faith, not want of merit]; **but toward thee** [O Gentile], **God's goodness** [kindness not won by thy merit, else it were justice, not goodness; but goodness toward thee by reason of thy faith: a goodness which will be continued to thee], **if thou continue** [by faith, and the works thereof, to keep thyself] **in his goodness: otherwise thou also** [even as was the Jew for like reasons before thee] **shalt be cut off.** [From the theocratic tree. Severity and goodness, as used here, are merely relative. They do not express the *true* condition, but merely the state of affairs as viewed by those who still clung to the idea of legal justification and salvation by merit. To those holding such views it seemed severe indeed that the *better man* should be cut off for lack of faith, and a strange act of goodness that the *worse* should be received by reason of it and given opportunity to become fruitful; but the seeming severity vanishes and only the goodness remains when we reflect that according to the righteous judgment of God it was *impossible that either of them* should be received any other way. The apostle's next purpose is to present a further argument against Gentile pride; viz., the final restoration of the Jewish people and the restitution of all their original privileges and rights. This prophetic fact is revealed as a possibility in the next two verses, and established fully as a decreed event in the next section.] **23 And they** [the unbelieving mass of Israel] **also** [together with you], **if they continue not in their unbelief** [for it is not a question of any comparative lack of legal merit on their part], **shall be grafted in: for God is able to graft them in again.** [There is no insuperable reason why they can not be grafted in, and that blessed event will take place whenever the unbelief which has caused their severance shall cease. In Paul's day individual Jews were being grafted in (the "some" of verse 14); but in the glad future of which the apostle here speaks, the nation (or the "all Israel" of verse 26) shall be grafted in. However, the word "able" suggests the extreme difficulty of overcoming the obdurate unbelief of Israel. It is a task for God's almightiness, but, though difficult, yet, as verse 24 shows, most natural, after all.] **24 For if thou wast cut out of that which is by nature a wild olive tree, and wast grafted contrary to nature into a good olive tree; how much more shall these, which are the natural branches, be grafted into their own olive tree?** [Here we are referred to nature for the point emphasized in the apostle's lesson, that we may see that the present system of grace, as operating under the terms of conversion established as the basis of theocratic life in the New Testament, operates in *double* contradiction to nature. For (1) grafting is unnatural; (2) grafting bad to good is unnatural; for in nature the engraft always changes the juice of the stalk to its own nature, so as to still bear its own fruit. Hence the superior is always grafted into the inferior. But in grace this rule is so changed and operated so "contrary to nature," that the sap, passing into the tame, natural, superior Jewish branches, yielded corrupt fruit, so that they had to be severed; while the same sap, passing into the wild, grafted, inferior Gentile branches, communicated its fatness to them, so that they yielded good fruit. But as it is an accepted axiomatic premise that even God works more readily, regularly and satisfactorily along the lines of the natural than he does along those of the supernatural and miraculous, so it is unquestionably reasonable to suppose that if the Jew will consent to be grafted in by *belief,* the sap of his own tree will work more readily for him than it did in Paul's day for the Gentiles, or wild olive branches which were not of the tree save by the grafting, or union, of *belief.* "For," says Chrysostom, "if faith can achieve that which is contrary to nature, much more can it achieve what is according to it." By age-long, hereditary and educational qualifications the Jew has acquired a natural affinity for, and a pre-established harmony with, all that has come to the world through the promises to Abraham, and in fulfillment of the words of the prophets. In short, the conversion of the Jew of our day is a vastly more reasonable expectation than the conversion of the Gentiles which actually took place in Paul's day. Let no man, therefore, doubt Paul's prediction of the ultimate conversion of the Jews. "If God," says Stuart, "had mercy on the Gentiles, who were outcasts from his favor and strangers to the covenant of his promise, shall he not have mercy on the people whom he has always distinguished as being peculiarly his own, by the bestowment of many important privileges and advantages upon them?"

V.

FIFTH EXPLANATION OF THE GRAND CONCLUSION—GENTILES AND JEWS HAVING EACH PASSED THROUGH A LIKE SEASON OF DISOBEDIENCE, A LIKE MERCY SHALL BE SHOWN TO EACH.

11:25-32.

["The future conversion of Israel," says Gifford, "having been proved to be both possible and probable, is now shown to be the subject of direct revelation."] **25 For I would not, brethren, have you ignorant** [This form of expression is used by the apostle to indicate a most important communication to which he wishes his readers to give special attention, as something strange and contrary to their expectation (Rom. 1:13; 1 Cor. 10:1; 12:1; 2 Cor. 1:8; 1 Thess. 4:13)—in this case, a revelation from God] **of this mystery** [The word *musterion* is used twenty-seven times in the New Testament. As digested and classified by Tholuck, it has three meanings; thus: 1. Such matters of fact as are inaccessible to human reason, and can only be known through revelation (Rom. 16:25; 1 Cor. 2:7-10; Eph. 1:9; 3:4; 6:19; Col. 1:26; etc.). 2. Such matters as are patent facts, but the process of which can not be entirely taken in by the reason (1 Cor. 14:2; 13:2; Eph. 5:32; 1 Tim. 3:9, 16). 3. That which is no mystery in itself, but by its figurative import (Matt. 13:11; Rev. 1:20; 17:5; 2 Thess. 2:7). The first is the meaning here. Paul is about to communicate a revelation which was given of God, and could never have been divined by any process of the human intellect. As the conversion of the Gentiles was so unthinkable that it had to be made known to the Jew by revelation (Eph. 3:1-6; Acts 10, 11), so here the conversion of the Jew was so unbelievable that it also had to be made known to the Gentile by revelation], **lest ye be wise in your own conceits** [This revelation of the conversion and ultimate elevation of Israel to his former position of leadership comes to Paul, and is imparted by him to the Gentiles, to prevent them from following their own vain and mistaken opinions as to the relative theocratic positions of Jews and Gentiles, by which they would flatteringly deceive themselves into thinking too well of themselves as occupying permanently Israel's ancient post of honor, and too ill of Israel as thrust out and cast off forever. The reversal of the Jews and Gentiles in fortune and honor was but a temporary affair. It is significant that this publication of a revelation, and accompanying rebuke of the opposing self-conceit of human opinion and judgment, should be addressed to the Church of Rome! The more one ponders it, the more portentous it becomes], **that a hardening in part hath befallen Israel** [Here is the first term of the threefold revelation. Calvin and others connect "in part" with "hardening," so that the meaning is that a partial hardening has befallen Israel. But hardening, as mentioned at 9:18 or 11:7, is not qualified as partial. "In part" is properly connected with "Israel." A portion of Israel is hardened. This agrees with the entire context, which tells of a remnant saved (11:5), and the rest or larger portion fallen (11:12), cast away (11:15), and hardened. So "in part" stands for "the rest" of 11:7, and in contrast to the "some" of 11:17. The bulk of the Jewish nation, persistently and rebelliously refusing to believe in Christ, had, as their punishment, a dulling of their perceptions and a deadening of their sensibilities sent upon them. We can understand this punishment better if we compare it with its counterpart which befell the Gentiles. As they dishonored the form or body of God by presuming to make degrading, beast-shaped images of it, so God gave them up to degrade their own bodies (1:23, 24). As they preferred lies to truth in things pertaining to God, he gave them up to prefer lying, deceptive, unnatural uses of themselves, to the true and natural uses (1:25-27). As they refused to have a right mind about God, he gave them up to a reprobate mind (1:28-32). So here, in his parallel treatment of the Jew, he found them steeling their hearts against his love (John 3:16) and against the drawing power of the cross (John 8:28; 12:32), and he gave them up to the hardness which they chose and desired. Now follows the second term of the revelation which makes known how long this hardness should endure; viz.], **until the fulness of the Gentiles be come in** [The hardness of the Jews shall cease, and the veil which blinds their eyes shall fall (1 Cor. 3:14, 15), when the number of saved which God has allotted to be gathered during the Gentile dispensation (or "times of the Gentiles"—Luke 21:24) has been made complete, and has "come in," to the theocratic olive-tree. In other words, as the Gentiles were "given up" (1:23, 25, 28) during the entire period of the Jewish dispensation, so the Jews are to be "hardened" during the entire period of the Gentile dispensation. The millennium, or final dispensation, which is to follow this present Gentile dispensation, will be given into the hands of Jew and Gentile jointly, and will be as life from the dead to both parties, because of the glorious season of revival which shall characterize it almost to its end. "Fulness of the Gentiles" is, therefore, "not the general conversion of the world to Christ, as many take it," says Brown; "for this would seem to contradict the latter part of this chapter, and throw the national recovery of Israel too far into the future: besides, in verse 15, the apostle

MERCY SHALL BE SHOWN   473

seems to speak of the receiving of Israel, not as following, but as contributing largely to bring about, the general conversion of the world—but, until the Gentiles have had their *full* time [as possessors] of the visible church all to themselves while the Jews are out, which the Jews had till the Gentiles were brought in. See Luke 21:24." And this brings us to the conditions, or developments, which succeed the hardening, or the third term of the mystery or revelation which Paul is here making known; viz.]; **26 and so** [that is, in this way; namely, by abiding till this determinate time] **all Israel** [the national totality, the portion hardened; a round-number expression, allowing liberty to any small remnant which may possibly still persist in unbelief] **shall be saved** [Shall be Christianized by overcoming their unbelief. And this revelation, fully detailed by Paul, had already been adumbrated or partially published in the prophets, as follows] : **even as it is written, There shall come out of Zion the Deliverer; He shall turn away ungodliness from Jacob** [Isa. 59:20f] : **27 And this is my covenant** [lit. *the* covenant from me] **unto them, When I shall take away their sins.** [Isa. 27: 9. (Comp. Jer. 31:31-34.) Verse 26 is quoted from the LXX., but Paul changes "come in favor of Zion" to read, "come out of Zion," following a phrase found at Ps. 14:7. None can say why he made this change, but it prevents confusion as to the first and second advent. Christ's second advent will be out of heaven, not out of Zion. Bengel calls attention to the fact that as Paul in Romans 3 combines Isaiah 59 and Psalm 14, to prove the sinfulness of mankind, especially of the Jews, so he here seems to combine the same two parts of Scripture to prove the salvation of Israel from sin. Moreover, as in chapter 9 he lets Isaiah describe Israel as reduced to a remnant (9: 27-29), so he here appeals to the same inspired penman as the foreteller of the salvation of all Israel. Christ the Deliverer had already come, so that part of the prophecy had been fulfilled, but the future effects of the gospel were yet to accomplish the salvation of the Jews as a nation in two ways: (1) By turning them from their ungodly infidelity; (2) by forgiving their sins. Jewish unbelief will not be removed by any change *in* the gospel: it is complete and unalterable. The changes which will work upon the Jews will be those wrought in the world *by* the gospel. "And this is the covenant from me," etc., signifies, My covenant unto them shall be executed and completed on my part when I forgive their sins. To the Jews, therefore, there was, on God's part, in Paul's day, a present attitude of rejection manifesting itself in hardening, and a future attitude of acceptance sometime to manifest itself in forgiveness, and these attitudes are thus described] **28 As touching the gospel, they** [the unbelieving Israelites] **are** [regarded by God as] **enemies for your sake** [that their fall might enrich you. See verse 12]: **but as touching the election, they are beloved for the fathers' sake.** [Or on account of the fathers. The call, or election, of Israel gave them national, hereditary rights (of which salvation was not an essential part; it being eternally designed to be an *individual,* not a *national,* matter) that were to last to the end of the world (Lev. 26:40-45); but which provided for, or anticipated, that break, interim or hiatus known as "the times of the Gentiles." During all the years of the Gentile dispensation God cast off his people and regarded them as enemies in every field of vision where they came in conflict with or interfered with the Christians, or New Covenant, Gentile people. Yet, notwithstanding, in all other respects they have been and will be loved and cared for by God, on account of his own love for the fathers, and his eternal covenants with them. This mixture of present enmity and future benevolence characterizes God's attitude toward every unrepentant sinner who is to become a future saint. So long as he abides in sin he is an enemy, yet loved for the sake of the Lord Jesus. The condition of the Jew is therefore well defined. His ancestral covenants have no value unto salvation, but they are invaluable as an assurance that he shall be continued as a people until he accepts the gospel which is the covenant unto salvation.] **29 For the gifts and the calling of God are not repented of.** [A corollary growing out of the axiom that the all-wise God makes no mistakes and consequently knows no repentance (Num. 23:19; Ezek. 24:14; 1 Sam. 15:29). Repentance and regret imply miscalculation (Jas. 1:17). The term "gifts" is of very wide application. God gave to the Jew certain spiritual endowments and moral aptitudes fitting him for religious leadership; God also gave to him manifold promises and covenants, and the general rights of the elder brother or first-born (Luke 15:25-32), including priority in all spiritual matters (Acts 1:8; 3:25, 26; 13:46; Rom. 1:16; 2:9, 10; 1 Pet. 4:17). The calling is closely related to the gifts, for the Jews were called to be God's peculiar people (Deut. 7:6; Ps. 135:4), and were thereby called upon to discharge all the duties and obligations belonging to their station and arising out of their endowments (Luke 20:9-18); and likewise called to enjoy all the blessings and privileges of their stewardship, if found faithful in it (Luke 12:35-48). Now, God has not changed his purpose as to either gifts or calling. The Jew's rights are temporarily suspended during the Gentile dispensation. They have never been withdrawn, and will be restored whenever the Jew becomes a believer. As pledge of the permanent nature of Jewish precedence, the twelve gates of the Eternal City bear the names of the twelve tribes of Israel (Rev. 21:12), and the twelve foundations thereof bear the names of the twelve Jewish apostles—Rev. 21:14.] **30 For as ye** [Gentiles] **in time past were disobedient to God** [Rom. 1:16-32; Acts 17:30], **but now have obtained mercy by their** [the Jews'] **disobedience** [v. 15], **31 even so have these** [the Jews] **also now been disobedient, that by the mercy shown to you they also** may now obtain mercy. [How the Gentile received blessing by reason of the casting off of the Jew has already been explained at verse 15. As the Gentile went through a season of disobedience, from which he was saved by severity shown to the Jew, so the Jew was to have a like season of disobedience, from which he in turn is to be eventually saved by God's mercy to the Gentiles. Some construe the "mercy" to mean that the Gentiles are to have a continuous, ever-increasing spiritual prosperity until finally the very excess of the flood of it sweeps Israel into belief, and therefore into the kingdom. But such a construction plainly denies the New Testament prophecies which speak of a "falling away" (2 Thess. 2:3) in "the last days" (2 Tim. 3:1-9), and do not accord with the effects of gospel preaching as announced by Christ (Matt. 24:14). The meaning is that God's mercy to the Gentiles in Paul's day preserved the gospel in the world for the ultimate blessing of the Jews, and God's continued mercy to the Gentiles through the centuries, and even through the latter days of their acute apostasy, will still keep the gospel till the Jews are ready to accept it. God's mercy to the evil, Gentile earthen vessel preserves the truth wherein lies salvation, and will continue to preserve it till the Jew drinks of the water of life which it conserves (2 Cor. 4:7). In short, the cases are reversed. The Jewish dispensation ended in a breakdown, but not until the Gentiles became receptacles of the truth. Mercy was shown to the Jew till this Gentile belief was assured. So the Gentile dispensation shall likewise terminate in failure, but not until Jewish belief is assured. We are even now obtaining mercy waiting for the consummation of that part of God's plan. As God once spared the Jew till his blessings were transferred without loss to the Gentiles, so will he now spare the Gentile till the truth now stored in him has time to pass safely to the Jew. And as surely as he shifted his Spirit and mercies from Jew to Gentile, just so surely will he in turn shift back and re-endow the Jew. The apostle is here giving his whole attention to the acts of God, and omits for the time all reference to that human agency which paved the way for the divine action. However, it is indicated in the word "mercy." The change in either case was in justice long overdue before it came.] **32 For God hath shut up all unto disobedience, that he might have mercy upon all.** [The verb "shut up" is, as Barnes observes, "properly used in reference to those who are shut up in prison, or to those in a city who are shut up by a besieging army (1 Macc. 5:5; 6:18; 11:65; 15:25; Josh. 6:1; Isa. 45:1). It is used in the New Testament of *fish* taken in a net (Luke 5:6)." It here means that God has rendered it impossible for any man, either Jew or Gentile, to save himself by his own merit. For some two thousand years the Gentiles sinned against God as revealed in nature, and broke his unwritten law found in their own consciences (Rom. 1:19, 20; 2:14-16), their sin being known generally as idolatry. And now, for about an equal length of time, the Jews have sinned against God as revealed in Christ, and have broken his written law as found in the Old Testament, their sin being practically the same as that of the Gentiles, though called infidelity. Thus God shut each class up under a hopeless condemnation of disobedience as in a jail, that he might extend a general pardon to each, and save each by his grace and not by human merit. "All" is used in the general sense, and does not signify universal salvation irrespective of belief in Christ (Gal. 3:22). It is used here to show that, in shifting from Gentile to Jew, God will act in no arbitrary or partial spirit. He will not reject any of either class who live worthily. It means that hereafter each class shall be equally favored in preaching and all other gospel privileges. "The emphasis," says Calvin, "in this verse is on the word MERCY. It signifies that God is under obligation to no one, and therefore that all are saved by grace, because all are equally ruined."

VI.

CONCLUDING ASCRIPTIONS OF PRAISE TO GOD FOR HIS JUDGMENTS, WAYS AND RICHES.

11:33-36.

[Guided by the revelations imparted by the Holy Spirit, the apostle has made known many profound and blessed mysteries, and has satisfactorily answered many critical and perplexing questions, and has traced for his readers the course of the two branches of the human family, the Jew and the Gentile, from their beginning in the distant past, in a condition of unity, through the period of their separation by reason of the call of the Jews into a Theocracy, followed by a continuation of the separation, by the call of the Gentiles into a Theocracy, on into the future when both are to be again brought together in unity (Matt. 15:24; John 10:16). "Never," says Godet, "was survey more vast taken of the divine plan of the world's history." As the apostle surveyed it all, beheld its wisdom and grace, its justice and symmetry, he bursts forth in the ascriptions of praise which follow.] **33 O the depth of the riches both of the wisdom and the knowledge of God!** [We prefer the marginal reading, "O the depth of the riches and wisdom and knowledge," etc. Either of the readings is perfectly grammatical. It is objected against the marginal reading that the reading in the text is "simpler and more natural" (*Dwight*); that the context following says nothing about riches (*Brown*); that the notion of riches is too diverse in kind to be co-ordinated with knowledge and wisdom (*Godet*). To these it may be added (as suggested by Meyer) that the style of the apostle usually follows that of the text. Compare "riches of his grace" (Eph. 1:7; 2:7; Phil. 4:19). Nevertheless, depth of riches and wisdom and knowledge is the best reading here, for riches, as we have just seen, imply, with reference to God, his wealth of grace, or some kindred virtue; as, goodness, forbearance, longsuffering, etc. (Rom. 2:4; 10:12; Eph. 2:4). Now, in this instance the *mercy* of God was the thrice-repeated and last idea (in the Greek, the last *word*) dropping from the apostle's pen (see vs. 31, 32), and it is these riches of mercy and grace that move him to praise, and that give birth to the section before us. Moreover, these riches are the burden of what has gone before. See 9:23 for "riches of glory upon vessels of mercy," and 10:12 for "rich unto all," and 8:35-39 for a description of the saints' wealth in God's love. As, therefore, the mercy or lovingkindness of God is uppermost in the apostle's thoughts, and as it is the main inspiration for all human praise (Ps. 107, 118, 136), it is hard to conceive that Paul would turn from it in silence, and burst forth in raptures over God's wisdom and knowledge, for the wisdom and knowledge of God stir us to highest raptures only as we see them expended in merciful lovingkindness. "Depth" is a common Greek expression for inexhaustible fullness or superabundance. It is so used by Sophocles, Æschylus, Pindar and Plato (see references in Gifford). It is so used here, though, as employed by Bible writers, it generally means that which is so vast or intricate as to be incomprehensible to the common mind (Ps. 36:6; 1 Cor. 2:10; Rev. 2:24). The superabundance of God's knowledge has been made apparent in this Epistle. It, as Plumer describes it, "is his perfect intelligence of all that ever is, ever was, or ever shall be, and of all that could now be, or could heretofore have been, or could hereafter be on any conceivable supposition." It enables God to grant perfect free will to man, and still foresee his every act, and empowers him to combine men of free will in endless social, political and commercial complications, and yet foresee results arising from myriads of combined free agencies, thus enabling him to discern the effects upon the Gentiles wrought by the rejection of the Jews, and the results, proximate and ultimate, wrought upon the Jew by the acceptance and rejection of the Gentiles. Such are samples of the knowledge of God exhibited in Romans. The wisdom of God enables him to design the best purposes, the most blessed and happy results, the most perfect and satisfactory ends, while his knowledge empowers him to choose the best means, employ the best methods or modes of procedure, devise the best plans, select the most perfect instruments, etc., for accomplishing of those holy and benevolent purposes. In short, the wisdom of God foresees the desired end, and his knowledge causes all things to work together for the accomplishment of it. Refraining, for the moment, from describing the riches of God, the apostle proceeds to give a parallel setting forth of the excellency of God's wisdom and knowledge, thus:] **how unsearchable are his judgments, and his ways past tracing out!** [Job 5:9; 11:7] **34 For who hath known the mind of the Lord? or who hath been his counsellor?** [Isa. 40:13; Jer. 23:18. "Judgments" and "mind" have reference to God's wisdom; "ways" and "counsellor" look toward his knowledge. Knowledge precedes wisdom. It gathers the facts and ascertains the truths and perceives their meaning, and then wisdom enters with its powers of ratiocination and traces the relations of truth to truth and fact to fact, and invents procedures, devises methods, constructs processes, etc., and utilizes the raw material of knowledge to effect ends, accomplish purposes and achieve results. Therefore, as Gifford observes, "knowledge" is *theoretical,* "wisdom" is *practical,* and while "knowledge" is purely *intellectual,* "wisdom" is also *moral,* and for that reason is both the most perfect of mental gifts (*Aristotle,* Nic. Eth. 6:10) and the queen of all virtues (*Cicero,* 'de Off.' 1:43)." God's knowledge foresees all the evil desires, designs, intentions and actions of men and demons, of the devil and his angels; and his wisdom expends itself in transforming all these opposing powers and forces into so many means and aids for the accomplishment of his own holy designs and beneficent purposes. Exercising his wisdom, God judges or decrees, or determines or purposes in his mind, what is best to be done, or to be brought to pass, and these designs or purposes are wholly hidden from man save as God reveals them. We see his moves upon the chessboard of events, but the *motives* back of the moves lie hidden in a depth of wisdom too profound for man to fathom. "Ways" is derived from the word for "footsteps," and "tracing" is a metaphor borrowed from the chase, where the dog, scenting the footstep, follows the trail, or "way," the game has taken. The means which God chooses leave no track, and they can not be run down and taken captive by the mind of man. Nor does God seek information or ask counsel of man. He is a ruler without a cabinet, a sovereign without a privy council, a king without a parliament. His knowledge needs no augmentation. He accepts no derived information, and borrows no knowledge, but draws all from his own boundless resources. If we can not divine the *purpose* of his chessboard moves as chosen by his wisdom, neither can we even guess their *effects* which his knowledge foresees, for he produces unexpected results from contrary causes, so that he makes the Gentiles rich by Jewish poverty, and yet richer by Jewish riches. His wisdom sought the salvation of Jew and Gentile, yet his knowledge foresaw that racial antipathy would keep them from working together till ripened in character; so he worked with each separately. As each sought to establish the sufficiency of his own self-righteousness, he let them each try it, one with natural and the other with revealed law. To each he gave a season of covenant relation and a season of rejection, and in the end he will unite the two and have mercy on both. Such is the coworking of God's wisdom and knowledge.

The scheme is outlined in the parable of the prodigal son, the prodigal being the Gentile and the Jew the elder brother, not yet reconciled to the Father, but still offended at his kindness to the outcast. When the elder brother is reconciled, the story will be complete.] **35 or who hath first given to him, and it shall be recompensed unto him again?** [Job 41:11. This question emphasizes the riches of God, introduced at verse 33. The riches mentioned are those of mercy and grace. If we can not exchange gifts with God along the most *material* lines, as here indicated, how shall we purchase his mercy, buy up his love, or merit his salvation? The moralist, whether Jew or Gentile, can place God under no obligation whatever, for naught can be given to him who justly claims all things (Ex. 19:5; Deut. 10:14; Ps. 24:1; 50:12). "Do we not," says Trapp, "owe him all that we have and are, and can a man merit by paying his debts?" (Luke 17:10). God gives all and to all, and he receives from none. Behold his grace! He freely publishes his unknowable knowledge, that the simplest may profit by his omniscience; he fully reveals his unsearchable wisdom, that the feeblest may co-operate with his omnipotence; and he lovingly gives his unmeritable gifts, that the poorest may enjoy his riches forever! Oh that men might know their riches in him, their folly, their weakness, their poverty without him!—Rev. 3:17, 18.] **36 For of him, and through him, and unto him, are all things.** [Summary statement of the all-comprehensive riches of God. 1. God, in the beginning or past, is the author, origin and creative source of all existence. He is the efficient original cause from whence all came (hence his perfect knowledge). 2. God, in the middle or present, is the sustaining, supporting means of all existence. He is the continuous cause by which all things are upheld. By ruling and overruling all forces, he is the preserving governor and the providential director of creation in its course toward to-morrow (hence his unerring wisdom). 3.

God, in the end or future, is the ultimate purpose or end of all existence. He is the final cause for which creation was and is and will be; for all things move to consummate his purposes, fulfill his pleasure and satisfy his love. They shall glorify him and be glorified by him (hence his riches: he is all in all— 1 Cor. 15:28.] To him *be* the glory for ever. Amen. [Thus with the customary benediction (Gal. 1:5; 2 Tim. 4:18; Heb. 13:21; 1 Pet. 5:11) and the formal "Amen," the apostle closes the doctrinal division of his Epistle.]

PART THIRD.

HORTATORY APPLICATION — VARIOUS PHASES OF THE FAITH-LIFE OF THE BELIEVER IN CHRIST.

12:1—14:23.

I.

BASIS OF THE FAITH-LIFE DEFINED—IT IS SACRIFICIAL AND SANCTIFIED.

12:1, 2.

[The theme of this great Epistle is that "the righteous shall live by faith" (1:17), and its grand conclusion is that those who seek life this way find it, and all who seek it in other ways fail (9:30-33). But the popular way of seeking it was by obeying the precepts of the great moral or Mosaic law. If, then, Paul's letter overthrows all trust in morality, of what use is morality? And what bearing has his doctrine on *life?* May one live as he pleases and still be saved by his faith? Such are the questions which have ever arisen in men's minds on first acquaintance with this merciful and gracious doctrine. The carnal mind's first impulse on hearing the publication of grace is to abuse grace (6:1. Comp. Jas. 2:14-26). Anticipating the questionings and tendencies of the weak and sinful natures of his readers, Paul proceeds to first define the life of faith (12:1, 2). It is a sanctified, sacrificial life. He then illustrates the workings of this sanctified life in the two grand spheres of its activities, the spiritual kingdom of God or the church (12:3-8) and the civil kingdom of the world (12:9-21). But the faith-life is not defined didactically, but in an impassioned, hortatory manner, for Paul is not content that his hearers should know theoretically what it is; he wishes them to have experimental knowledge of it, to actually *live* it. In fact, it has been for the purpose of making the exhortation of this section that all the previous chapters have been written, for no Bible doctrine is a barren speculation, but a life-root, developed that it may bear fruit in the lives of those who read it. And here is the hortatory definition of the faith-life.] **XII. 1 I beseech you therefore, brethren, by the mercies of God, to present your bodies a living sacrifice, holy, acceptable to God, *which is* your spiritual** [more correctly, "logical"] **service.** [I entreat you, brethren, in the light of all that I have written you about this faith-life, making as the motive or ground of my appeal to you these mercies of God* which purchased for you the privilege of this life by the death of his Son (3:23, 24), which pardoned your iniquities that you might receive it (3:25, 26), which cast out his chosen people that your access to it might not be hindered (11:12), etc., etc., that you continuously consecrate your lives to God as living thank and peace offerings, keeping them ever holy and acceptable to God, which is the service you should logically render in the light of the truth presented to you and comprehended by you. The word "mercies" here used (*oiktermos*) is a stronger word than that (*eleos*) used in verbal form in the eleventh chapter, expressing the tenderest compassion. God's main mercies in the gospel are of that sort. If we are not saved by works, why is sacrifice demanded? The answer was plain to the Jew. Of the four sacrifices demanded by the law, two were offered *before* propitiation and *to obtain it*. These were the *sin* and *trespass* offerings. Christ, who is our propitiation, offered these expiatory sacrifices for believers, so that they are pardoned, justi-

---
* "He who is rightly affected by God's mercy enters into the whole will of God" (*Bengel*).

fied and saved not by their own merit, no matter
what their sacrifice, but are redeemed by his purchase in the offering of his priceless blood, and saved
by his merit as acknowledged by the Father. If the
Jewish program of sacrifices had stopped here, there
would have been no Biblical symbolism showing that
Christians are called upon to do anything in a sacrificial way. But there were two other sacrifices
offered *after* propitiation and expiation. These were
the burnt-offering, offered as an act of worship daily
and also on occasions of joy and thanksgiving (2
Chron. 29: 31, 32), and the peace-offerings, which
spoke of restored fellowship and communion with
God. Now, the faith-life was exempted from the
expiatory or *sin* and *trespass* offerings by the cross
of Christ, but it was *not* relieved of the *burnt* and
peace offerings, the former of which required that
the entire carcass of the victim be consumed in the
flame (Ex. 29: 38-42; Num. 28: 3-8) as a symbol of the
entire consecration of the offerer or devotee to the
service of God, for the life of the offering stood for
his own life.* Here, then, is the true basis or foundation principle on which the faith-life rests. Here is
the supreme fundamental law which must govern its
every action. Though the *purposes and motives* of
its sacrifice may be changed so that expiation gives
place to thanksgiving and communion, yet it is still
essentially and intrinsically a consecrated, sacrificial
life, and is as far removed from antinomianism as it
was when under the Mosaic law. The force of this
marvelous instruction is not weakened, but rather
strengthened, by being couched in hortatory form.
Let us note, in passing, the continuousness of sac-

---

* "The sincere worshiper, whether Jew or Gentile, saw in the sacrifice which he presented on the altar a symbol of his own self-devotion.
This symbolic purpose determined the choice of the proper material
for an altar-sacrifice: it must represent the offerer's *life*. For this
reason, in all the chief sacrifices, it must be itself a *living* creature:
and in every case, without exception, it must be the offerer's own lawful
property, the fruit of his *life-work*, and also fit, as food, *for the support of his life*. In presenting such a sacrifice the worshiper was presenting *a portion of his own life* as a symbol of the whole" (*Gifford*).

rifice implied by the term "living." The animal sacrifice was over and ended when its body was consumed. If perfect and accepted as without blemish, then (Deut. 15:21; 17:1; Lev. 1:3, 10; 3:1; 22:20; Mal. 1:8), it had passed all danger or possibility of future rejection at God's hands. But not so the Christian's sacrifice. In presenting himself he is to "reckon himself dead unto sin, but alive unto God in Christ Jesus" (6:11-13). For the Christian's dying leads at once to his being alive (6:2; 7:4; Gal. 2:19, 20; Col. 2:20; 3:5-10; 1 Pet. 2:5), and therefore, as Bengel says, "it is an abomination to offer a dead carcass." The Christian, therefore, as a living, never-to-be-recalled sacrifice, is required to keep up and perpetuate his holiness and acceptability, as "an odor of a sweet smell" (Eph. 5:2; Phil. 4:18; Lev. 1:9), lest he become a castaway. For this reason Paul lays emphasis on the "body," as the *corpus* or substance of the sacrifice, for our fleshly nature is spoken of in Scripture as the seat of sin, which is to be transformed into a temple for the indwelling of the Holy Spirit (1 Cor. 6:19, 20). Moreover, this direct reference to the body corrects the heresy that the faith-life is purely mental or spiritual, and devoid of bodily sacrifice or works (Gal. 5:13; Jas. 2:14-26). "How," asks Chrysostom, "can the body become a sacrifice? Let the eye look on no evil, and it is a sacrifice. Let the tongue utter nothing base, and it is an offering. Let the hand work no sin, and it is a holocaust. But more, this suffices not, but, besides, we must actively exert ourselves for good; the hand giving alms, the mouth blessing them that curse us, the ear ever at leisure for listening to God." Moreover, the sacrifice of the body includes that of mind, soul and spirit, for "bodily sacrifice is an ethical act" (*Meyer*). The comment of Barnes on this verse is very practical. "Men," says he, "are not to invent services; or to make crosses; or seek persecutions and trials; or provoke opposition." Romish and Mohammedan pilgrimages, Catholic and Oriental penances, thorn-beds, juggernauts, flagellations, and man-made ordinances of sacrifice, are worthless (Col. 2:20-23). Moreover, the designs of many to wait till sickness or old age overtakes them before presenting their sacrifice are … d, for such conduct is analogous to pres…… aimed and halt and blind to God. Fina…… elsewhere, and so it is indeed true tha… …istian's sacrifice is a "spiritual [*pneumatike*] service" (Phil. 3:3; 1 Pet. 2:5; cf. John 4:24), but the apostle has here conveyed that idea in the word "living," and he does not repeat the thought. Hence he does not say *pneumatiken* service, but *logiken* service, or, literally, *logical* or *rational* service. *Logiken* links itself with "therefore" at the opening of the sentence. Therefore your logical service (the one rationally expected of you by reason of the truths revealed in this Epistle, especially chapter 6) is to present your bodies, etc. In short, the very purpose for which the apostle wrote this Epistle was to convince his readers that they must render this service, and this exhortation enforces that conclusion.] **2 And be not fashioned according to this world** [or, literally, "age"]: **but be ye transformed by the renewing of your mind, that ye may prove what is the good and acceptable and perfect will of God.** [Here the apostle shows in general terms by what manner of life the demanded sacrifice is rendered or accomplished. To each soul there was presented then, as now, two models for character-building, the standards of the world-life and the Christ-life, the first represented by the imperative *suschematizesthai*, which means to imitate the pose or attitude of any one, to conform to the outward appearance or fashion of any one. The demands of the world require no more than an outward, superficial conformity to its ways and customs. As these ways and customs are the natural actions and methods of the unregenerate life, the sacrifice-resenting, fleshly nature of the Christian has no difficulty in conforming to them, if given rein and permission. Attainment to the Christ-life is, however, represented by the imperative

BASIS OF THE FAITH-LIFE 489

metamorphousthai, which demands that complete and fundamental inner change which fulfills and accomplishes regeneration, and which, in turn, is accomplished by the renewing of the mind. The natural mind, weakened, trammeled, confused and darkened by sin and Satan, can neither fully discern nor adequately appreciate the Christ model, so as to metamorphose the life to its standards. But in the regenerated man the mind once fleshly (Col. 2:18; Rom. 7:23), but now renewed by Christ (2 Cor. 5:17; Eph. 4:21-24) and the Holy Spirit (Tit. 3:5), and strengthened to apprehend by the Holy Spirit (Eph. 3:16-19), is able to so discern and love the Christ model as to be gradually metamorphosed into his image (Phil. 3:8-16). With this recovered capacity to discern and appreciate the life which God wills us to live, as exemplified in the incarnation of his Son, we are exhorted by the apostle to set about exploring, investigating, proving or testing the excellence of the will of God in selecting such a pattern for us, that we may have experimental knowledge that his will was devised in goodness toward us, that its choice for us is really well pleasing and acceptable to us; as our minds have become enlightened to truly understand it, and that considered in all ways its purposes and ends for us are the perfection of grace and benevolence, leaving nothing more to be asked or even dreamed of by us. Thus the renewed mind tests by experience the will of God, and knows it to be indeed the will of the Holy One of Israel (John 7:17), to be admired, followed and reduced to life. It remains to be shown how the word "age" comes to be translated "world." The Jews divided time into two divisions; viz., *before* the Messiah, and *after* the advent of the Messiah. The former they called "this age"; the latter, "the age to come." Thus the term "this age" became associated with those evils, vanities and Satanic workings which the Christian now calls "this world." Both terms are used by Jesus (Matt. 12:32. Comp. Heb. 6:5), and the expression "this age" is commonly used *after* the advent of Jesus to describe the moral and spiritual conditions which then and still oppose Christ and the age which he is developing (Matt. 13:22; Luke 16:8; 20:34; 1 Cor. 1:20; 2:6; 2 Cor. 4:4; Gal. 1:4; Eph. 6:12; 2 Tim. 4:10; Tit. 2:12).

II.

THE FAITH-LIFE OPERATING IN CHURCH AFFAIRS IN HUMILITY.

12:3-8.

[Having defined the faith-life as sacrificial and sanctified, the apostle next points out the principal virtues which it must manifest in the several spheres of its activities. The first sphere is the church, and the first virtue enjoined therein is humility.] **3 For I say** ["For" is epexigetical; *i. e.,* it introduces matter which further explains or elucidates the nature of the required living sacrifice; viz., that the Christian must humble himself. "I say" is mildly imperative], **through** [by right or authority of] **the grace** [the apostleship in Christ—1:5; 15:15, 16; Eph. 3:7, 8] **that was given me, to every man that is among you** [As apostle to the Gentiles, Paul divided his duties into evangelistic and didactic. In discharge of the former he founded churches, and in fulfillment of the latter we find him here instructing a church which he did not found. He addresses his instruction to each member without exception, and though his words in this section are more particularly meant for the more gifted, they also have the man with one talent in mind, and make allowance for no drones in the hive. "Among you" means "in your community" —*Meyer*], **not to think of himself more highly than he ought to think; but so to think as to think soberly** [It is evident that Paul anticipated a spirit of presumption among the Christians at Rome, by reason of their spiritual gifts, like that which he rebuked at Corinth (1 Cor. 12 and 14). It is well known that for the guidance, edification, etc., of the church, and for the converting of the world, spiritual gifts abounded among Christians in that age, and many of these were markedly supernatural or miraculous. These latter were well calculated to excite a false pride in the vainglorious pagans, so recently converted to Christ. As such pride is contrary to the spirit of Christ, and prompts the one yielding to it to save his life for the ends of ambition, rather than to offer it as a living sacrifice on the altar of service, Paul first sets himself to correct it, by commanding each to give to himself that sober, fair self-inspection which will correct overestimates of self and underestimates of one's neighbor], **according as God hath dealt to each man a measure of faith.** [Here was another check to pride. Sober thought would remind the proud and puffed up that the miraculous gifts were not of their *own acquiring,* but were *gifts* of God, and were therefore matters for gratitude rather than for vainglory (comp. 1 Cor. 4:6, 7; 12:11); stewardships to be carefully and conscientiously administered for the benefit of the church and not for selfish display and aggrandizement. "Measure of faith" is an expositor's puzzle. As saving faith is belief in testimony, it is the product of a man's own action, and God does not deal it out, or give it to any one. If he did, how could he consistently condemn men for the lack of it (Mark 16:16), or how could he exhort men to believe (John 20:27)? But even those whose theological errors permit them to look upon faith as a gift, are still in a quandary, for Paul is evidently talking about measure of gifts, and not measure of saving faith, and the passage parallels 1 Cor. 12:11; Eph. 4:7. Barnes says that faith here means religion. Hodge, hitting nearer truth, says that faith is used metonymically for its effects; viz., the various graces or gifts mentioned: *"that which is confided* to any, and equivalent to *gift*." Brown declares that it is "the receptive faculty of the renewed soul, the capacity to take gifts." Godet assigns it "the capacity assigned to each man in the domain of faith." These, and many similar passages which might be quoted, show that expositors are forced to recognize that faith here is employed in a very unusual sense, which is near akin to miraculous gifts. Now, as sound exegesis compels us to distinguish between the natural, perpetual gift of the Holy Spirit, bestowed upon every penitent believer at his baptism, and that miraculous gift which descended on the apostles at Pentecost and on the house of Cornelius, which passed away in the apostolic age; so we would here distinguish between natural, saving faith which is the possession of each Christian to this present hour, and miraculous faith, or faith which had power to work miracles, which was unquestionably dealt out as here described, so that different miraculous powers were displayed by different Christians. It was of this faith that Jesus spoke at Matt. 17:20; Luke 17:6, for had he meant the saving faith now possessed by us, it is evident that none of us possess a mustard-seed measure of it. This special, divinely bestowed (comp. Luke 17:5), miraculous faith also vanished with the apostolic age.] **4 For** [also epexigetical. See verse 3] **even as we have many members in one body, and all the members have not the same office: 5 so we, who are many, are one body in Christ, and severally members one of another.** [As God gives to each member of the human body its several function for the good of the whole body, so he distributed the miraculous gifts of the Spirit to the different members of the Roman church for the good of the whole church. The gifts were intended to be held in common, so that each member should contribute to the needs of all the others, and in return receive from all the others in mutual helpfulness and interdependence. Difference in office or function, therefore, was not a matter for pride or boasting, for the gift was held in trust for

HUMILITY

service, and was a gift to the *whole body,* through the individual member. There is no room for comparison or pride between the related members of one living organism. This comparison of the relationship of Christians to the mutual dependence of the members of the human body is a favorite one with Paul, and he elaborates it at 1 Cor. 12:4-31 and Eph. 4:1-16. See also Eph. 4:25; 5:30.] **6 And having gifts differing according to the grace that was given to us, whether prophecy, *let us prophesy* according to the proportion of our faith** [It would be as unreasonable and unwise to give all Christians the same gift as it would be to give all the members of the body the same function. Since, then, the gifts had to differ, and since God dealt them out, each member was to exercise humbly and contentedly that gift which God had portioned out to him, whether, compared with others, proportionately large or small, important or unimportant, for should the ear stubbornly refuse to hear, and set up a determined effort to smell or to see, it would produce anarchy in the body. Let each Christian, therefore, retain the place and station and discharge the work which God has designated as his by the proportion of faith, a miracle-working power, assigned to him. The power of Christ, operating through the Holy Spirit, awoke in Christians talents and endowments unexampled in the world's history. The greatest of these were bestowed upon the apostles. The next in order of importance were the gifts bestowed upon the prophet (1 Cor. 12:28; 14:29-32, 39). His gift was that inspiration of the Holy Spirit which enabled him to proclaim the divine truth, and make known the will and purpose of God, etc., whether as to past, present or future events. His work was supplementary to that of the apostles, and was greatly needed in the days when the New Testament was but partly written, and when even what was written was not yet diffused among the churches. Eventually the prophet ceased (1 Cor. 13:8, 9) and the Scripture took his place. In his day he was as the mouth of

God (Ex. 7:1; 4:16; Jer. 15:19; Deut. 18:18); he delivered a divine message at first-hand (Ezek. 2:7-10; 3:4-11; Luke 7:26-29) and was inspired of God—1 Pet. 1:10-12; Acts 2:2-4; 2 Pet. 1:19-21]; 7 or ministry, *let us give ourselves* to our ministry; or he that teacheth, to his teaching [Most of the spiritual gifts of Paul's day were either wholly supernatural or shaded into the miraculous, and, as miracles have ceased, it becomes hard for us to-day to accurately define gifts which have passed away. "Ministry" (*diakonia*) is derived from the Greek word for deacon, and probably described such services as deacons (Phil. 1:1; Rom. 16:1) then rendered. The order, "apostles, prophets, teachers, miracles, then gifts of healings, helps, governments" (1 Cor. 12:28), compared with the order here—viz., prophecy, ministry, teaching, exhorting, giving—suggests that miracles of healing may have been part of the ministry (comp. 1 Pet. 4:11), as well as caring for the poor, serving tables, etc. (Acts 6:1-6; 1 Tim. 3:8-13). Teaching was probably much the same as that of to-day, only the teacher had to remember the verbal instruction of the apostles and prophets (2 Thess. 2:15; 2 Tim. 1:13; 2:2; 3:10, 14) until the same was reduced to writing as we now have it in the Scriptures]; 8 or he that exhorteth, to his exhorting: he that giveth, *let him do it* with liberality [Exhortation is addressed to the feeling as teaching is to the understanding. It is used to stir or excite people, whether of the church or not, to do their duty. As endowed or spiritually gifted Christians of that day spoke with tongues (1 Cor. 12 and 14), both the teacher and the exhorter would be properly classed as among the workers of miracles. After mentioning the exhorter, Paul drops the word "or" (*eite*), and thus seems to make a distinction between the workers of miracles whom he has been admonishing, and the class of workers who follow, who evidently had no miraculous power whatever. "Liberality" (*haplotes*) signifies "the disposition not to turn back on oneself; and it is obvious that

HUMILITY

from this first meaning there may follow either that of *generosity,* when a man gives without letting himself be arrested by any selfish calculation; or that of *simplicity,* when he gives without his left hand knowing what his right hand does—that is to say, without any vain going back on himself, and without any air of haughtiness" (*Godet*). The word may be correctly translated objectively "liberality" (2 Cor. 8: 2; 9:11; 9:13; Jas. 1:5); but, used subjectively and more naturally, it signifies singleness of purpose, simplicity, sincerity (Matt. 6:22; Luke 11:34; 2 Cor. 1:12; 11:3; Eph. 6:5; Col. 3:22). The latter meaning is clearly indicated here by the context,* for Paul is rebuking ostentation (comp. Matt. 6:1-4) and enforcing humility, sober self-thought, subjective investigation, simplicity. The giving was to be with honesty of aim, without ulterior or personal or selfish motive]; **he that ruleth, with diligence; he that showeth mercy, with cheerfulness.** [Whether they ruled as elders and deacons in the church, or as parents at home (1 Tim. 3:3-5, 12), they were to do so with a spirit of zealous attention to the work entrusted to them, not with a vainglorious desire to lord it, or to exalt or enrich themselves (1 Thess. 5:12, 13; 1 Tim. 3:4, 5, 12; 5:17; 1 Pet. 5:1-4). Showing mercy is probably best defined at Matt. 25: 35, 36. Paul here directs that these acts be performed with cheerfulness. The context shows that he means inward joy, not outward simulation of it; for the whole passage is subjective, not objective.

---

* We are decidedly averse to criticizing or correcting the text of the English Revised Version, not wishing to breed suspicious unrest in the minds of its readers. But we can not but feel that occasionally the translators yield to the strong temptation to choose the English word which can be understood at once without the aid of the commentator, whether it conveys the shade of meaning desired by the Scripture writer or not. (Compare note on "spiritual," Rom. 12:1.) In such cases we have pointed out the looseness of the translators. "Give much!" is the urgent cry of this age, and it is thoroughly Scriptural; but the Spirit, speaking through Paul, also said, "Give in simplicity"—*i. e.,* in *meekness*—and the command must not be lost sight of, simply to effect an easy translation. Perhaps this age needs the latter command more than the former; for, as Caryl observes, "you must rather bring your graces to the touchstone, to try their truth, than to the balance, to weigh their measure."

(Comp. 2 Cor. 9:7.) Cheer, like love, must be without hypocrisy, for the one showing mercy has the better end of the blessing (Acts 20:35). The purpose of the entire passage is to enforce the spirit of contented humility upon Christians in all their actions, lest those having superior gifts be thereby betrayed into pride and self-exaltation, and those having inferior gifts be seduced by envy to fall into bitterness of spirit or idleness. "In the school of Christ," says Leighton, "the first lesson of all is, *self-denial and humility;* yea, it is written above the door, as the rule of entry or admission, 'Learn of me, for I am meek and lowly in heart.'"

III.

THE FAITH-LIFE OPERATING IN CHURCH AND SOCIAL AFFAIRS IN LOVE AND OTHER HEAVENLY VIRTUES.

12:9-21.

[In the last section we were told that spiritual and remarkable gifts are to be exercised in humility. This section deals with the ordinary and natural gifts, and is therefore addressed to the whole church. It shows that these ordinary, natural gifts or faculties are to be employed in harmony with the other Christian graces and virtues, the principal or basic one of which is LOVE. Therefore we may roughly subdivide the section as follows: 1. The faith-life showing love to the friendly or Christian (9-16). 2. The faith-life showing love to the unfriendly or unchristian—17-21.] **9 Let love be without hypocrisy.** [The apostle opens this section with a call for pure, genuine love, for it is the common or fundamental element of all the virtues of which he is about to write. This love must be unfeigned (2 Cor. 6:6; 1 Pet. 1:22; 1 John 3:18). The heart must really

LOVE AND OTHER VIRTUES

feel that measure of affection to which the conduct bears testimony. The Christian must not bear himself "like Judas to Christ, or Joab to Abner: a kiss and a stab"—*Johnson.*] **Abhor** [literally, "abhorring"] **that which is evil; cleave** [literally, "cleaving"] **to that which is good.** [The participles relate grammatically to "love" as their subject, and explain the two main ways in which an unfeigned love is required to operate. Love is not up to the required standard unless it abhors evil and cleaves to (literally, glues itself to) that which is good. "What a lofty tone of moral principle and feeling is here inculcated! It is not, Abstain from the one and do the other; nor, Turn away from the one and draw to the other; but, Abhor the one and cling with deepest sympathy to the other" (*Brown*). Objectively it must hate evil even in the character of a loved one, and not fall into Eli's sin (1 Sam. 3:13); and it must cling to the good, even in an enemy, and rejoice to increase it. Otherwise love is mere selfishness. "There are," says Lard, "many Christians, and among them many preachers, who oppose evil, it is true, but they do it so faintly as virtually to countenance it. They will not publicly endorse evil; but they will rather go quietly home, or get out of its way, and leave it to riot unrebuked. They do not abhor it. . . . These men are not obeying Paul." Subjectively the Christian's love will make him abhor in himself all retaliatory and revengeful promptings, all injurious and malicious mental suggestions against his enemy, and will hug to his heart every kind and generous and benevolent impulse, whether entertained toward an enemy or a friend. This general love toward all is next specialized, and love toward members in the church is thus described.] **10 In love of the brethren be tenderly affectioned one to another; in honor preferring one another** ["tenderly affectioned" is a word compounded of *philos*, loving, and *stergos*, which is from *stergeoo*, to feel natural affection, as an animal for its offspring, a parent for its child, a near relative

for his close kin. Its use here indicates that the
church tie should rival that of the family. Christians
should love each other "as natural brethren, and
more. More close are the ties of the heart than of
the body. We are brethren in Adam according to
the flesh, in and by Christ according to the Spirit"
(*Trapp*). "Preferring" means going before; hence
guiding, setting an example. In matters of giving
reverence, respect, and causing people to be held
high in public estimation, Christians are to strive to
outdo each other. The idea is that each should be
more eager to confer honors than to obtain them.
"Nothing," says Chrysostom, "tends so much to
make friends as endeavoring to overcome one's neighbor in doing him honor." "The Talmudists," according to Bengel, "say, Whoever knows that his neighbor has been accustomed to salute him, should anticipate his salutation"]; **11 in diligence not slothful;
fervent in spirit; serving the Lord** [These three
commands refer more especially to the *outward* life
of the Christian. In all matters of employment,
whether religious or secular, be active and energetic
(Eccl. 9:10), let your activities be vital with enthusiasm ("fervent" means seething, boiling; hence stirring), for life-service is Christ-service; the manifestation of love toward him (Col. 3:22-24). "Ever
considering," says Clark, "that his eye is upon you,
and that you are accountable to him for all that you
do, and that you should do everything so as to please
him. In order to do this there must be *simplicity* in
the INTENTION, and *purity* in the AFFECTION." "To be
cold and careless in God's service disparages his
excellency," says Burkitt]; **12 rejoicing in hope;
patient in tribulation; continuing stedfastly in prayer**
[In this triplet the apostle directs the manner in
which the Christian life is to *inwardly* manifest its
love toward God. The hopes of his begetting which
make bright the future are to fill it with joy; the
chastisements of his sending which make heavy the
present are to be endured with loyal, unmurmuring

LOVE AND OTHER VIRTUES 499

patience, as from him (Heb. 12:3-11), and both hope and patience are to be augmented and sustained by prayer which grants us the consolation of his presence. Persecutions added greatly to the afflictions of the church in Paul's day, and it was often beyond expectation that the Christian should rejoice in his present circumstances, but he could always be cheered by hope. "By patience," says Burkitt, "we possess ourselves; by hope we possess God; by prayer we are enabled to possess both"]; **13 communicating to the necessities of the saints; given to hospitality.** ["Communicating" (*koinoonountes*) means, literally, to be or act as a partner. Sometimes it means to receive (15:27; 1 Pet. 4:13; 1 Tim. 5:22). Here, as in Gal. 6:6, it means to bestow. The wants and needs of God's people are to be ours to the extent of our ability. This precept is obeyed by very few. "The scanty manner," says Lard, "in which the rich disciples of the present day share the wants of the poor, is a sham. From their thousands they dole out dimes; and from storehouses full, mete out handfuls. . . . Such precepts as the present will, in the day of eternity, prove the fatal reef on which many a saintly bark has stranded." "Hospitality" (*philoxenia*) means, literally, "love for strangers." It is often found in Biblical precept and example (Gen. 19:1, 2; Job 31:16, 17; Matt. 10:40, 42; 25:43; Luke 10:7; 11:5; 1 Tim. 5:10; Tit. 1:8; 1 Pet. 4:9; Heb. 13:2). In apostolic days the lack of hotels made hospitality imperative, and the journeys, missions and exiles of Christians gave the churches constant opportunities to exercise this grace. "Given" (*diookontes*) means to pursue. It is translated "follow after" (9:30, 31; 14:19). The idea is that Christ's disciple is not to passively wait till hospitality is unavoidable, but he is to be aggressively hospitable, seeking opportunity to entertain strangers. Hospitality is not to be limited to Christians, and Biblical hospitality is not to be confused with that so-called hospitality which bestows lavish entertainment upon

congenial spirits from a general love of conviviality
and good fellowship, and a desire for reputation as
a generous host. Biblical hospitality is born of a
desire to help the poor, especially the godly poor—
Luke 1:53; 14:12-14.] **14 Bless them that persecute
you; bless, and curse not.** ["Thus," says Johnson,
"did Christ on the cross, and the martyred Stephen."
The apostle here drops into the imperative because
quoting from the Sermon on the Mount (Matt. 5:
44: Luke 6:28). We would expect to find this command classified among duties to persons entirely
outside the church, but the apostle's life reminds us
that cursings were apt to come from those inside as
well as from those without (2 Cor. 11:26). "This
doubling of the exhortation (bless) shows both the
difficulty of the duty, how contrary it is to corrupt
nature, and also the constancy of the duty; we must
ever bless, and never curse" (*Burkitt*). Love must
win this battle for our untrue brother's sake.] **15
Rejoice with them that rejoice** [1 Cor. 12:26]; **weep
with them that weep.** ["One might think," says
Chrysostom, "it was no difficult task to rejoice with
others. But it is harder than to weep with them. For
that is done even by the natural man when he be-
holds a friend in distress. There is need of grace,
however, to enable us, not merely to abstain from
envying, but even with all our hearts to rejoice at
the good fortune of a friend." Love is to bind us
to God's people in full sympathy, both in their prosperity and adversity.] **16 Be of the same mind one
toward another.** [A general repetition of the special
command just given. Enter into the mind or feeling
of your brother, whether in joy or sorrow. In the
mental and sentimental sphere keep the Golden Rule
with him.] **Set not your mind on high things, but
condescend to things that are lowly.** [Luke 12:15.
This injunction also has loving concord for its object.
Class distinctions, high positions, situations, social
eminence, etc., are to be avoided as tending to sever
your sympathies, interests and desires from your

LOVE AND OTHER VIRTUES

humble brethren. "The greatest enemy to concord is pride" (*Tholuck*). Christ was meek, and we should be like the Master. Avoid such things as lead one "to flatter the great, to court the rich, and be servile to the mighty" (*Plumer*). It is a question whether we should here read "lowly things," or "lowly people." Either reading is correct, and commentators are about equally divided on the point. Meyer, who favors the neuter, reads: "Yielding to that which is humble, to the claims and tasks which are presented to you by the humbler relations of life." He illustrates by Paul's following the trade of tentmaker. Against this, Gifford says: "The adjective *tapeinos* (lowly) is used in the New Testament frequently of persons, never of things. It is better, therefore, to follow the same usage here, and understand it of lowly persons as in the Authorized Version." But Paul doubtless used the adjective in its fullest sense, combining both persons and things, making it, as it were, a double command; for he wished his readers to do all things needful to keep them in brotherly accord. If we keep in touch with the lowly, we must yield ourselves to be interested in their lowly affairs; and if we keep our hearts warm toward humble things, we will find ourselves in sympathy with humble people. So even if the command be made single, it will either way affect the double result of a double command, and without the double result either command would be insufficient. "Honor all your fellow-Christians, and that alike," says Chalmers, "on the ground of their common and exalted prospects. When on this high level, do not plume yourselves on the insignificant distinctions of your superior wealth or superior earthly consideration of whatever sort." Moreover, let your condescension be invisible; let it be so hid in love that no one, not even yourself, is conscious of its presence, for condescension without love is as spittle without healing —John 9:6.] **Be not wise in your own conceits.** [Prov. 7:3. Setting our hearts on high things as our proper sphere, and despising lowly things as unworthy of our lofty notice, begets in us a false idea of our own importance and wisdom, and a conceited spirit full of pride and vanity. This is the besetting sin of those having large mental endowment —those whom the world counts wise. The culmination of this self-conceit is that spirit which even cavils at God's precepts, and lightly criticizes and rejects his revelation. The proper spirit before God is childlike, teachable (Matt. 18:1-4; Mark 10:15), and it is better to be wise in the sight of the all-wise God than to be a Solomon in your own foolish estimation. As conceit grows, love ebbs, and all loveless life is profitless (1 Cor. 13:1, 2). We now approach a sphere of duties relating to forbearance in persecution, and life-relations outside the church.] **17 Render to no man evil for evil.** [Quoted from the Sermon on the Mount (Matt. 5:38-48). The precept bids us reject the *lex talionis,* and live contrary to it: it commands us to eschew both the spirit and practice of vindictiveness. "The heathen," says Burkitt, "reckoned revenge as a part of justice," but the Christian must look on justice as subservient to love.] **Take thought for things honorable in the sight of all men.** [Prov. 3:4, LXX. Give no cause for suspicion or offense, but disarm all enmity by open, fair-minded dealing. Let your light shine (Matt. 5:16). Let men note what company you keep (Acts 4:13). "Not letting habits, talk, expenses," says Moule, "drift into inconsistency; watching with open and considerate eyes against what others may fairly think to be unchristian in you. Here is no counsel of cowardice, no recommendation of slavery to a public opinion which may be altogether wrong. It is a precept of loyal jealousy for the heavenly Master's honor. His servant is to be nobly indifferent to the world's thought and word when he is sure that God and the world antagonize. But he is to be sensitively attentive to the world's observation where the world, more or less acquainted with the Christian precept or principle, and more or less conscious of its truth and right, is watching maliciously, or it may be wistfully, to see if it governs the Christian's practice. In view of this, the man will never be content even with the satisfaction of his own conscience; he will set himself, not only to do right, but to be seen to do it. He will not only be true to a monetary trust, for example; he will take care that the proofs of his fidelity shall be open. He will not only mean well toward others; he will take care that his manner and bearing, his dealings and intercourse shall unmistakably breathe the Christian air."] **18 If it be possible, as much as in you lieth, be at peace with all men.** [It takes *two* to live at peace. So far as the Christian is concerned, the rule of peace is absolute. He must stir up no needless opposition, he must avoid every act likely to give offense, he must harbor no resentment. But, so far as the other party is concerned, the rule is conditional, for no one knew better than Paul, out of life's bitter experiences, that the most sacrificial efforts to keep the peace may be frustrated by the acts of enemies whom no consideration can pacify, no concession quiet. For an event after this writing see Acts 21:26, 27. Our own conduct is in our power; our neighbor's, not. Here, too, love must do its best.] **19 Avenge not yourselves, beloved, but give place unto the wrath *of God:* for it is written, Vengeance belongeth unto me; I will recompense, saith the Lord.** [The quotation is from Deut. 32:35. We may look upon verse 17 as designed to check hasty, personal retaliation, or as relating to injuries of a more personal nature. The avenging of this verse savors more of a judicial punishment—a punishment which one's calm judgment, unbefogged by passion and unbiased by the sense of wrong, might haply mete out as absolutely just and unqualifiedly deserved. But even under such circumstances the Christian is to leave the culprit in God's hands, for the Lord claims exclusive jurisdiction in the case, and promises to give the just recompense. We bar God's judgments by attempting to anticipate them, and we also call down his tremendous sentence upon ourselves for the small satisfaction of executing our puny sentence upon one whom he would in time deal with if we were only patient. The wrath to which we must give place is evidently neither our own nor our enemy's, but God's (as appears by the context. Comp. Prov. 20:22; 24:29). Waiting persuades us to forgiveness, for when we reflect on the severity and lasting nature of God's punishment, we partake of his desire to show grace and grant pardon. But how just are the awards of his throne! His mind is clouded by no passion, biased by no prejudice, deceived by no false appearances, misled by no lying testimony, warped by no illwill. And when his judgment is formed, grace guides its course, mercy mollifies its execution, and, as far as righteousness permits, the love of a Father who pities his feeble, earth-born children transforms it into a blessing. Nevertheless, it is a judgment of God, and not of man, and the majesty of God is upheld in it. God-revealed religion bids us thus wait upon this judgment of God, but man-made religion speaks otherwise. "Mahomet's laws," says Trapp, "run thus: Avenge yourselves of your enemies; rather do wrong than take wrong; kill the infidels, etc." In giving this command Paul uses the term "beloved." "By this title," says Bengel, "he soothes the angry." "The more difficult the duty, the more affectionately does the apostle address his readers with this word"— *Tholuck.*] **20 But** [instead of avenging] **if thine enemy hunger, feed him; if he thirst, give him to drink: for in so doing thou shalt heap coals of fire upon his head.** [Quoted from Prov. 25:21, 22 LXX., where the words, "And Jehovah will reward thee," are added. Simply to forbear from avenging is only half a victory. The full conquest is to return good for evil (Luke 6:27-30). In feeding enemies we are like God, who daily feeds sinners, and the conduct of God is our law (Matt. 5:44-48). Heaping coals of fire is a figure derived from the crucible, where they were heaped upon the hard metal till it softened and melted. Kindness is not utterly lost on beasts, but with man it ought always to prevail, for it heaps coals upon the head, or seat of intelligence, filling the mind with the vehement pangs and pains of conscience, the torments of shame, remorse and self-reproach. The most effectual way of subduing an enemy is by the unbearable punishment of unfailing kindness—it is God's way. "The logic of kindness," says Johnson, "is more powerful than the logic of argument." The same thought is now repeated by the apostle without a figure.] **21 Be not overcome of evil, but overcome evil with good.** [Evil is the weak weapon of the sinner; goodness, the puissant, all-conquering blade of the saint. What shame, then, if the saint lose in the unequal conflict! "Thus David overcame Saul" (*Trapp*). "In revenge," says Basil, "he is the loser who is the victor." When evil leads us to do evil, then are we overcome of evil. When we meet evil with good, we have at least overcome the evil in ourselves, if not in our enemy.

IV.

THE FAITH-LIFE DISCHARGING CIVIL DUTIES, AND RECOGNIZING THE DIVINE ORDINATION OF GOVERNMENTS.

13:1-7.

[Paul, having shown how the faith-life offers itself as a daily sacrifice of love in spiritual and social spheres, now gives an outline of the sacrifice of self which it is to make in civil and business affairs. This he does in two sections, the first of which sets forth the Christian's relationship to government (1-7), and the second his civil relations to men, business, etc., under government (8-10.) As in spiritual

matters he was to first limit himself by humility
(12:1-8) and then give himself in love (12:9-21), so
he is here to limit himself by submission to the
state (1-7), and then give himself in love to his
fellow-citizens (8-10). But conditions at Rome made
this instruction as to the Christian's duty to be
loyal and submissive to government particularly op-
portune, for (1) the Jew believed that, as a citizen
of the Theocracy, it was at least derogatory to his
character, if not an act of treason toward God, to
acknowledge allegiance to any earthly government
(Deut. 17:15). This belief had already fomented
that unrest in Palestine (Acts 5:36, 37; Josep. Antt.
8:1:1) which ten years later broke out in rebellion,
and necessitated the destruction of Jerusalem. This
unrest had already resulted in banishment of Jews
and Christians from Rome about seven years before,
in A. D. 51 (Acts 18:2; Suet. "Claudius" c. 25; Dio
Cassius 60:6). This unrest was sure to permeate
the church (*Ewald*), for a considerable percentage of
the churches, the world over, were Jews, and this
influence in the church was great. There is nothing
in Acts 28 to contradict the idea that there were Jews
enough in the Roman church to have influence in it
(*contra*, see Weiss and Alford). (2) The world generally looked upon the Christians as a mere Jewish
sect, and the suspicions of disloyalty which attached
to the Jews would readily attach to the Christians
(*Calvin*). History confirms this. Nero had no difficulty in turning suspicion against them. How circumspectly, then, should they have walked. (3)
Moreover, many Christians entertained notions similar
to the Jews. They belonged to the new Theocracy,
and held that loyalty to Christ absolved them from
all allegiance to earthly government. Rome, as the
center of the world-power, at once inspired and
hindered the false dreams of well-intentioned but
deceived disciples. History proves that the world-
power of the Roman capital seduced Christians into
attempting to form of Christ's kingdom a temporal

world-power like that of the Cæsars—viz., the Roman Catholic hierarchy—and Paul tells us that this evil influence was already at work, though hindered, in his day (2 Thess. 2:6-12). (4) On general principles, the atrocities so soon to be perpetrated by· Nero were apt to put revolutionary and even anarchistic ideas in the heads of the most staid and sober. Nero's persecutions began about a year after this Epistle was written (*Tholuck*). These conditions made Paul's words timely indeed, but they are not, however, to be regarded as savoring of the temporary. His words are abiding and eternal truth, and contain fundamental and organic instruction for all ages.] **XIII. 1 Let every soul** [all humanity, whether in the church or not] **be in subjection to the higher powers** [Be subject to all civil powers—power higher than that of the common citizen, whether monarchic, oligarchal or republican. This injunction includes both persons and offices, and asserts that there is no *inherent* and *essential* conflict between the claims of God and those of the state. One can render, and must render, what is due to each—Matt. 22:21]: **for there is no power but of God; and the *powers* that be are ordained of God.** [Having asserted and commanded duty toward the state, the apostle next states the ground or reason of that duty, the justification of his command, in two heads: (1) Abstractly considered, governments are of divine origin; (2) concretely considered, God has ordained the present system of government, and has chosen the officers now in power; not directly, according to the exploded notion of the divine right of kings, but indirectly by the workings of governmental principles which God sanctions, by the operations of general providences of his ordering. Thus the government in force and the ruler in power in any country at any given time are, *de facto*, God-appointed. The apostle's first statement, that governments, viewed in general and abstractly, are ordained of God, is readily accepted as true; but this latter concrete statement, that each particular govern-

ment and governor is also of divine appointment, is harder to receive. The reason is that God's providences working evil to the evil, as well as good to the good, often place evil men in power as a cure to the evil in man which helped to place them there.]
2 Therefore he that resisteth the power, withstandeth the ordinance of God [This is the enunciation of the general principle without any accompanying exceptions. Pressed to its limits, this precept would prevent any revolution from succeeding, for the leader of the revolution could never be permitted of God to rule, as his rulership would then be countenanced by God as of his ordaining, and thus, in countenancing and ordaining *both opposing governments,* God would be divided against himself. The principle and its exceptions would best be understood by comparing the life of a government with that of a man. Each life is an emanation from God, and therefore each is protected by the general, fundamental law, "Thou shalt not kill." But this law in each case presumes that each life, whether governmental or individual, will so comply with the precepts and purposes of God, and so fulfill the ends for which it was created, as *to deserve to live.* If it does things worthy of death, it shall be put to death (Gen. 9:6). Paul, therefore, in laying down the rule, has in mind the age-long principle which, in our common law, finds expression in the maxim, "The king [government] can do no wrong." Only the most obvious, evident breach of this maxim can justify revolution. Each life must, as it were, be rigidly protected from lynch law, and must be given the calm deliberation of a judicial trial. When this is not the case, the one who assails the individual life becomes a murderer, and the one who attempts the life of the state "resists the ordinance of God." Every revolt, for a time, shakes public confidence in a divine institution, so there must be no resistance until the demand for it becomes practically unavoidable; otherwise we incur the resentment of God, for our conduct has

tended toward anarchy and confusion. We should therefore exhaust legitimate expedients, such as protests, political reactions, etc., before we resort to revolutionary extremes] : **and they that withstand shall receive to themselves judgment.** [Commentators, unable to define the preceding precept, and regarding it as ostensibly a prohibition of all revolution, or practically to that effect, have consoled themselves by limiting "judgment" to the punishments which the state inflicts, thus arriving at the conclusion that rebels have a right to rebel if they are willing to suffer the temporal punishment attendant on failure. But the context forbids this mollifying modification. If we resist the *ordinance of God,* we shall undoubtedly taste the *judgment of God,* and rightly, too, for what terrific misery, poverty, suffering and loss of life attend on revolution! Shall not God award justice to those who lightly and for personal ambitions fill the world with such horrors?] **3 For rulers are not a terror to the good work, but to the evil.** ["For" explains why the punishment comes upon the rebel. It is because government exists to promote the good and suppress the evil (1 Tim. 2:1, 2; 1 Pet. 2:13-17). If it does otherwise, "it," as Burkitt sagely remarks, "was not ordained for that end." A good man may suffer through misunderstanding, the machination of evil men, or even maladministration, but he can never suffer *as* a good man. Even Nero punished Christians *as* evil-doers (2 Tim. 2:9). History presents no instance where any government set itself to put down righteousness and exalt evil *as such;* though there are myriads of cases where human ignorance, prejudice and bigotry mistook the wrong for the right, and made havoc of the good, supposing it to be evil. Paul himself, as an executive of the Jewish Government, had been party to such an error (Acts 8:3; 9:1, 2; 1 Tim. 1:13). Intentional punishment of the good and countenancing of the evil would be governmental insanity and suicide. When it becomes apparent to the populace that the government has fallen into this state of aberrance, revolution is inevitable; but till the information becomes general, the individual must submit, for slight mistakes do not justify momentous changes and vast social upheavals, and peace for the many may well be purchased at the discomfiture of the few. But if armed or physical resistance is forbidden, *moral* resistance is strictly and unequivocally enjoined. The government must exact nothing contrary to or inconsistent with Christian duty. If it does, we must obey God rather than men (Acts 4:18-20; 5:28, 29); for under no circumstance can God's children be justified in doing wrong (Matt. 10:28; Rom. 3:8). Allegiance ceases when the law of the land seeks to subvert the law of God; and Paul teaches nothing to the contrary. As the martyr Polycarp said to the governor who bade him denounce Christ, and swear by the fortunes of Cæsar: "We are taught to give honor to princes and potentates, but such honor as is not contrary to God's religion." "It was the student of Paul," says Moule, "who, alone before the great Diet, uttering no denunciation, temperate and respectful in his whole bearing, was yet found immovable by pope and emperor: *'I can not otherwise; so help me God.'*"] **And wouldest thou have no fear of the power? do that which is good, and thou shalt have praise from the same** [comp. 1 Pet. 2:14]: **4 for he is a minister of God to thee for good.** [The law-abiding have no fear of the laws, and have just reason to expect the recognition and consideration which are the rightful dues of honesty and probity. "Commendations by magistrates," says Lange, "in opposition to punishments, were common even in ancient times." "When Paul wrote these things," says Grotius, "rage did not riot against the Christians at Rome." Seneca and Burrhus were still in power, and good men were the objects of governmental protection. "How much to be regretted it is," observes Lard, "that rulers do not more generally recognize the fact here stated by the

CIVIL DUTIES

apostle. Instead of this, however, they appear seldom even to dream that they are placed in office merely as God's servants. Rather, they seem to think that they are placed there solely for their own benefit. The fear of God is often not before their eyes, nor yet the good of the people a tithe as much as their own. Too frequently they serve merely self, with no regard for God, and but little for any one else. Such rulers serve not God, but Satan."] **But if thou do that which is evil, be afraid; for he beareth not the sword in vain: for he is a minister of God, an avenger for wrath to him that doeth evil.** [As we understand it, the idea which the apostle is seeking to convey is that duties to God and duties to the state are parallel, rather than antagonistic. If the Christian is true to his religion, he need fear neither the state nor God, for God rules, generally speaking, in and through the state, as well as in his providences. If, on the other hand, we do evil, we have reason to fear both God and the state, for the state is merely one of the forms of God's administration. The Romans made much of the sword as symbol of the power of life and death. Her magistrates and officers, holding the power of capital punishment, caused the sword (and the ax) to be borne before them in their public processions. Thus Paul declares that the office-holder is a servant of God to foster the good by praise and commendation, and to suppress the evil as an avenger appointed to inflict wrath—*i. e.*, punishment—upon it.] **5 Wherefore** [because of all that has been said—vs. 1-4] **ye must needs be in subjection, not only because of the wrath, but also for conscience' sake.** [1 Pet. 2: 13. The Christian has a double incentive for keeping the civil law; for if he resists the government he will not only be punished, but he will sin against God; thus both fear and conscience move him to obedience.] **6 For** [epexigetic, introducing a detail or illustrative fact proving the principle] **for this cause ye pay tribute also** [*i. e.*, among other acts of submission]; **for**

they [the recipients of the taxes] **are ministers of God's service, attending continually upon this very thing.** [*I. e.,* acting continually as servants of God in his civil administrations. The apostle cites the conduct of subjects in the payment of taxes, for no matter what theories the Jews or the Judaistic Christians might have as to the rights of government to his allegiance, he never failed to pay his taxes, being moved thereby by the very influences here named by the apostle; viz., fear and conscience. He feared the penal consequences of refusing to pay, and he conscientiously felt that the government deserved some compensation for maintaining peace and order, especially since, as Paul notes, they made this their business, gave their whole time to it, and made no other provision for their livelihood than their salaries as public functionaries, all of which is implied in "attending continuously," etc. Christians in our age have well-nigh universally forgotten that the tax assessor and the tax collector are ministers of God, and many evade making true returns with as little compunction as they would were the tax officials the servants of the devil. This sin has become so universal that it is well-nigh regarded as a virtue.] **7 Render to all** [civil officials] **their dues: tribute to whom tribute is due; custom to whom custom; fear to whom fear; honor to whom honor.** [Kypke points out the distinction between tribute and custom. The former means direct taxes; poll, real and personal; custom refers to tolls, imports, indirect taxes on goods and merchandise, known to us in the familiar tariffs on imports and exports. In Paul's time they appear to have been principally on imported goods, and were levied at the gates of the city at the time of entry (Matt. 9:9). As the Christian paid his taxes, so he was to go on discharging his other duties, fearing those in authority as those whom God placed over him, and honoring all those in governmental position because the officers are part of God's ordained plan, and those who hold them have been placed there by

CIVIL DUTIES

his general providence. Some hundred years later Paul's words about taxes were being strictly obeyed, for Tertullian, representing that time, says that what the Romans lost by the Christians refusing to bestow gifts on the idolatrous temples, they gained by their conscientious payment of taxes (Apolog. 42, Vol. I., p. 494).

V.

THE FAITH-LIFE OPERATING IN ALL CIVIL AND SOCIAL AFFAIRS IN LOVE, AND RECOGNIZING THE JUST RIGHTS OF OTHERS.

13:8-10.

[Having shown that the Christian must recognize the rights of those *above* him ("the higher powers"), the apostle now proceeds to enjoin upon him the recognition of the just rights of his fellow-beings who are all *about* him. If the state has a right to demand dutiful conduct of him, his neighbors, fellow-citizens, and the human race generally, may likewise exact of him the ministrations of love.] **8 Owe no man anything, save to love one another** [The indebtedness here meant includes, but is not confined to, pecuniary obligations. The precept does not prohibit the contraction of a debt, but it constrains us to be prepared to pay it when due. "Owe no tax, no custom, no fear, no honor, and pay all their dues" (*Lard*). The obligation to give the gospel to those that have it not is one of the Christian's greatest debts (1:14, 15). Love also is, as Bengel observes, "an eternal debt." "This," says Trapp, "is that *desperate debt* that a man can not discharge himself of; but must be ever paying, and yet ever owing. As we say of thanks, 'Thanks must be given, and yet held as still due:' so must this debt of love." Moreover, it is an ever-increasing debt, for it is like the payment of interest; only in this case each payment of interest is such an exercise and turning over of the principal as tends to its increase, thereby enlarging in a kind of arithmetical progression the payments of interest]: **for he that loveth his neighbor hath fulfilled the law.** ["The perfect *pepleroken* (*hath fulfilled*) denotes that in the one act of loving there is virtually contained the fulfillment of all the duties prescribed by the law. For a man does not offend or kill, or calumniate or rob, those whom he loves. Such is the idea developed in the two following verses"—*Godet*.] **9 For this** [Paul here begins the statement of a first premise, and in the eleventh verse, with the words "and this," he begins the statement of a second premise. The first premise is that the Christian (or faith) life, freed from the complications and onerous burden of the multitudinous laws of the Jewish (or law) life, is governed by the principle underlying all these laws most happily reduced to a simple commandment; viz., "Love thy neighbor as thyself" (9, 10). The second premise is that salvation, which is so dimly suggested to the Jewish (or law) life as to be no incentive at all to good deeds, is clearly and distinctly promised to the Christian (or faith) life, and is comprehended by it to be as rapidly and as surely approaching as the dawning day. From these two premises the conclusion is drawn that we should lead the faith-life becomingly, by putting on Christ. If we supply the word "reason" after each "this," the meaning will be clear. Surely the simplicity of the Christian life, and the sureness and exceeding greatness of the salvation which is its reward, are sufficient reasons for our leading it becomingly], **Thou shalt not commit adultery, Thou shalt not kill, Thou shalt not steal, Thou shalt not covet, and if there be any other commandment, it is summed up in this word, namely, Thou shalt love thy neighbor as thyself.** [The Ten Commandments are divided into two divisions of four and six. The first four relate to duties to God, and are taken no notice of here, for they do not pertain to justice to our fellowman, and hence are outside the sphere of Paul's present argument. The second division, or second table of the Ten Commandments, contains six precepts which relate to man's duty to his fellows: four of them are given here, and two relating to honoring parents and bearing false witness are omitted (Ex. 20:12-17). Though not named, they are included in the phrase "any other commandment." The order, too, is not that given in the Hebrew Bible, but follows one of the versions of the LXX. The order in which the commands are here given is likewise found at Mark 10:19; Luke 18:20; Jas. 2:11, and also in Philo, and Clement of Alexandria. It is surmised that the LXX. changed the order because of some of their traditions. Many commands as to conduct towards neighbors are summed up by Moses in this love commandment in a manner somewhat similar to Paul's (Lev. 19:9-18; comp. Matt. 19:19; 22:39, 40; Gal. 5:14, 22, 23). The last of the ten forbids covetousness, a passion which presents almost as broad and powerful an impulse for the breaking of all the commandments as love does for keeping them, for the love of money alone is a root of all evil (1 Tim. 6:10), though it is but one phase of covetousness. The truth is that covetousness gives wider scope to self-love than any other passion, and self-love is the motive which leads to all breaches of law. Love of neighbor is the opposite motive, counteracting all lawlessness, and tending to the manifestation of the perfect life. But we have no perfect example of this ideal, altruistic love save in the Christ himself. *Plesion* means *near, close by:* with the article it means "neighbor"; *i. e., the near by*. We readily acknowledge the one who is *permanently* and *literally* near by as our neighbor; but Christ taught us that the one who is *temporarily* near is also a neighbor (Luke 10:30-37), and so likewise are those who are *constructively* near; that is, those with whom modern means of communication have made us acquainted,

so that, knowing their needs, we are thereby
prompted to sympathize and impelled to help—Acts
16:9, 10.] **10 Love worketh no ill to his neighbor: love
therefore is the fulfilment of the law.** [All divine law,
whether of Moses and the prophets, of Christ or the
apostles, is fulfilled by love, for those things that law
requires are the natural, normal acts of a loving heart.
"Love," says Leibnitz, "is that which finds its felicity
in another's good." Another has defined it thus: "Love
is holiness, spelt short." How easily, then, will it keep
all precepts, whether toward man or God! "The expression implies more than a simple performance of the precepts of the law; true love does more than this: it adds
a completeness to the performance. It reaches those
lesser courtesies and sympathies which can not be
digested into a code or reduced to rule. To the bare
framework of law, which is as the bones and sinews,
it adds the flesh which fills it, and the life which
actuates it" (*Webster and Wilkinson*). "Nor is it
possible to find for human life, amid all the intricate
mazes of conduct, any other principle that should be
at once as simple, as powerful and as profound"
(*Sanday*). "How many schemes would it crush. It
would silence the voice of the slanderer; it would
stay the plans of the seducer and the adulterer; it
would put an end to cheating and fraud, and all
schemes of dishonest gain. The gambler desires the
property of his neighbor without any compensation,
and thus works *ill* to him. The dealer in *lotteries*
desires property for which he has never toiled, and
which must be obtained at the expense and loss of
others. And there are many *employments* all whose
tendency is to work *ill* to a neighbor. This is preeminently true of the traffic *in ardent spirits*"
(*Barnes*). Love is the spirit of gracious addition, while
covetousness, theft, etc., are the spirits of subtraction.
Love emanates from God, whose name is Love, but
selfishness is of the devil, who asserts himself even
against God. Love, therefore, is the basis of all godlike action, the motive power for every noble deed.

VI.

THE FAITH-LIFE FINDS ITS MOTIVES FOR ALL THESE DUTIES IN THE EVER-IMPENDING COMING OF THE LORD.

13: 11-14.

[At Rom. 12: 1, 2 Paul began this hortatory division of his Epistle by reminding his readers of the *past mercies* of God, making of those blessings which lay *behind* them a strong motive, impelling them by every sense of gratitude to go forward in the Christian life. He here closes his exhortation with an appeal to the *future rewards* of God, summed up in that endless and glorious day of salvation which lay *before* them, attracting them by every sense of heavenly aspiration to continue on in the faith-life. Thus the spiritual forces of memory and hope are made use of by the apostle to push and pull his readers heavenward.] **11 And this** [see note at verse 9 above], **knowing the season, that already it is time for you to awake out of sleep** ["The imagery seems to be taken originally from our Lord's discourse concerning his coming (Matt. 24: 42; Mark 13: 33; Luke 21: 28-38), where several points of similarity to our verses 11-14 occur" (*Alford*). For other uses of the imagery, see 1 Cor. 15: 34; Eph. 5: 14; 1 Thess. 5: 6-8; Matt. 25: 1-13. Sleep is a figurative expression denoting that moral inattention, indifference and carelessness which permits sin. Out of this torpor the Christian is evermore striving to rouse himself, and into it the worldling is as constantly seeking to resign himself, that conscience, fear, and other awakening influences, may not disturb him. To be fully aroused is to be keenly and thoroughly conscious of all spiritual facts and responsibilities, all truths and possibilities. Some need to make the effort to come back to consciousness; all need to keep up their efforts to prevent the return of drowsiness. The warning here is addressed to Christians. "Whiles the crocodile sleepeth with open mouth," says Trapp, "the Indian rat gets into his stomach, and eateth through his entrails. Whiles Ishbosheth slept upon his bed at noon, Baanah and Rechab took away his head. Security ushereth in destruction. Go forth and shake yourselves as Samson did when the Philistines were upon him; lest Satan serve you for your souls, as Captain Drake did the Spaniard at Tamapasa in the West Indies for his treasure; he found him sleeping securely upon the shore, and by him thirteen bars of silver to the value of forty thousand ducats, which he commanded to be carried away, not so much as waking the man. Or lest Christ himself deal by us as Epimonidas did by the watchman whom he found asleep: he thrust him through with his sword; and being blamed for so severe a fact, he replied, 'I left him as I found him'"]: **for now is salvation nearer to us than when we *first* believed.** [Paul meant that his readers were nearer that state of final blessedness which we call salvation than they were when they were converted. The thought that each day takes from us forever an opportunity of service, and that it also brings us that much nearer the time of accounting, is a most powerful incentive to action; "one of the most awakening exhortations," says Plumer, "that can be presented. The Judge standeth before the door. Eternity is at hand." (Comp. Heb. 10:25.) In and of itself "nearer" does not necessarily imply that Paul expected the speedy approach of Christ; but the context, full of suggestion of a day about to dawn, does imply *close* nearness. In fact, the need of the *immediate* awakening suggested by "already it is time," lies as much in the rapidity as in the certainty of Christ's coming: a coming so rapid that the interval had appreciably diminished since Paul's readers had entered on the new life. Now, the second coming of Christ may be viewed under two aspects; *i. e.*, either as **racial or individual. In either case it is speedy, but**

MOTIVES FOR THESE DUTIES

the comparative speed, or the proportion of speed, is measured far differently, for the centuries of the life of the race are long compared with the brief span of life apportioned to each individual. Viewed racially, the long night of heathenish darkness was drawing to a close. The day began to dawn when Christ was born. An increase of light came when he gathered his first disciples, and now the full light, and consequently the salvation accompanying the second coming of the Christ, was spiritually (rather than temporarily) nearer than when believers first began to gather to the Master. While such a construction is well suited to the large ideas of Christ's coming, we yet prefer the more personal construction which limits the range of view to the individual. For the members of the church at Rome the day began to dawn at the hour of their conversion, and since then the advancing years had brought them nearer their salvation. There is, moreover, no direct mention of the Lord's coming; but it is clearly implied. This implication, however, suits the idea of the individual Christian's entrance into the Lord's presence by death as readily as does the Lord's approach to all in the hour of final judgment. To be absent from the body is to be present with the Lord (2 Cor. 5:8; Phil. 1:23). We naturally look upon death as a *going* on our part; but may it not likewise be truly a *coming* on the part of Christ? (See John 14:3; Luke 12:37.) Surely to the individual Christian salvation speedily grows nearer after conversion, and this night period of sin and sorrow soon gives place to the day of salvation, the state of eternal blessedness and peace and joy unending, and the brevity of the individual life is far more of a stimulus than the brevity of the race life. The commands of our Saviour to watch for his coming are a constant tonic if viewed as addressed to the individual, but they lose in power if viewed from the standpoint of the race. There are many apparently unfulfilled prophecies which delay our expectation that he will come for final judgment in the next year or two at least, but there is nothing, prophetic or otherwise, which justifies any one in feeling assured that he may not come for us *individually* before nightfall. "Stir up yourselves, therefore," says Trapp, "and strain toward the mark. There is a Greek word (*nuosta*) signifying the end of the race, which is derived of a word that signifieth to spur or prick forward. Surely as they that run their horses for a wager spur hardest at the race's end, therefore, since our salvation is nearer now than ever it was, we should run faster now than ever we did. When a cart is in a quagmire, if the horses feel it coming they pull the harder; so must we, now that full deliverance is hard at hand. Rivers run more speedily and forcibly, when they come near the sea, than they did at the spring: the sun shineth most amiably toward the going down. 'It is even high time for you and me,' said old Zanchius to his friend Sturmius, who was elder than he, 'to hasten to heaven; as knowing that we shall be with Christ, which is far, far better.'"] **12 The night is far spent, and the day is at hand: let us therefore cast off the works of darkness, and let us put on the armor of light.** [In this figure "night" stands for the Christian's earthly life, which is constantly being shortened and quickly becomes "far spent." "Day" stands for eternity, that unending day which is swiftly approaching. The passing of the night calls for a cessation of sleep; the dawning of the day demands ever-increasing wakefulness and activity. The Christian's former, unregenerate habits are called "works of darkness," not only because righteousness is emblematically viewed as "white," and sin as "black," but because sin is ashamed of light and consequent exposure (Job 24:13-17; John 3:19-21). Moreover, they are pictured here as a foul nightdress to be " cast off" as a repulsive thing (Eph. 4: 22; Col. 2:11; 3:8, 9; 1 Pet. 2:1), and in their place the Christian is to don the works of righteousness, or all the duties of his new life (Eph. 4:23, 24; Rom. 6: 4; 2 Cor. 5:17; Gal. 6:15; Col. 3:10), as defensive

MOTIVES FOR THESE DUTIES

armor against temptations, and offensive weapons for an aggressive campaign against the powers of evil, and as the fitting harness in which to report to Christ for present service, the proper garb in which to have him find us should he come suddenly and without warning, for we are his soldiers, and on duty. Some five years before this Paul wrote in similar strains to the Thessalonians, emphasizing the escape from darkness and mentioning the armor (1 Thess. 5: 4-8), and about four years after this we find him again using this figurative language in addressing the Ephesians, mentioning the darkness, and emphasizing the armor —Eph. 6: 11-18.] **13 Let us walk becomingly, as in the day** [*i. e.*, as if the day of salvation and the presence of God (Rev. 21: 3) were already here]; **not in revelling and drunkenness, not in chambering and wantonness, not in strife and jealousy.** [Here are three couplets of vices. The first pair relate to intemperance in eating and drinking (Luke 21: 34). The "revel" (*komos*) was a drunken carousal; it usually burst forth and paraded the streets, filling the night air with noisy songs, and annoying pedestrians with its buffoonery. Being a favorite entertainment among the devotees of Bacchus, the Romans were accustomed to it from their youth up, and found it hard to resist the old-time fun and frolic once so acceptable. The second pair described the varied forms of sexual lust, libertinism, lascivious dalliance, etc. "Chambering" means literally lying abed. It describes the more definite, and "wantonness" the more general, acts of lewdness and abandoned sensuality. The third pair portray the various forms of venomous and hateful feelings leading to discord, open rupture and brutal violence—feelings the very opposite of love of which the apostle has been discoursing. While these vices may be found singly, they normally go in pairs, and also naturally fall into the order here given. Beginning with revelry in the early evening, how many a poor, sinful youth has passed thence to drunkenness, and thence in turn to sexual uncleanness, and thence once more to strife and passion with his fellows, till, when the night was passed and morning broke, he was found either a murderer or murdered, to the disgrace of his friends and the broken-hearted sorrow of his kindred. Plain speech was needful in Paul's day: alas that it should be so badly needed still!] **14 But put ye on the Lord Jesus Christ** [Kypke's researches reveal the fact that this bold figure of speech, so little used by us, was very familiar to the writers who were read by those of Paul's day. If a man chose any hero or teacher as an example for his life, or as an object for his imitation, he was said to "put on" that hero or teacher. Chrysostom says it was a common figure. Thus Dionysius Halicarnassus says of Appius and the other decemvirs: "They were no longer the servants of Tarquin, but they clothed themselves with him." Lucian speaks of one "having put on Pythagoras," meaning that to the fullest extent he accepted the great mathematician as his teacher and guide. Some centuries after Paul, Eusebius says of the sons of Constantine, "They put on their father." "The mode of speech itself," says Clark, "is taken from the custom of *stage players:* they assumed the *name* and *garments* of the person whose *character* they were to act, and endeavored as closely as possible to imitate him in their spirit, words and actions." The initial step by which we put on Christ is by being baptized into him. This great truth Paul had revealed only a few months before he wrote to the Romans (Gal 3:27). Only after the inward change wrought by being born of the water and of the Spirit (John 3:5; Eph. 5:26; Tit. 3:5) are we capable of making the vesture of our outward conduct such that men may see Him and not ourselves in our daily life (Rom. 6:1-11; 2 Cor. 3:2, 3; Eph. 4:24; Col. 2:11-3:10). He becomes to us, then, the wedding garment which guarantees our acceptability to God (Matt. 22:11), and causes us to cast aside our garment of legal righteousness as a filthy rag—Phil. 3:6-11], **and make not provision for** the flesh, to *fulfil* the lusts *thereof.* [We are allowed to make reasonable provision for the just needs of the flesh (Matt. 6:33; Eph. 5:29; 1 Cor. 11:34; 1 Tim. 5:23), but our provision must, as it were, go on tiptoe, and be exercised with extreme caution, so as not to waken in us those slumbering dogs of lust which, if aroused, will tear our spiritual life to pieces. Pool aptly says of our fleshly life, "Sustain it we may, but pamper it we may not." Fulfilling the lusts of the flesh was the main object of life in pagan Rome.

VII.

THE FAITH-LIFE OPERATING IN MUTUAL FORBEARANCE BETWEEN CHRISTIANS, AS UNTO THE LORD.

14:1-15:13.

[The apostle begins this section with "but," thus marking its connection with the preceding paragraph as setting forth matter in the nature of an exception thereto. He has been exhorting his readers to armed activity and vigilance in the cause of righteousness, and he now enters his caveat lest they should turn this needful and virtuous aggressiveness into a sinful belligerency, so that the strong should devour the weak. The Christian is indeed called upon to wage constant warfare with sin, but as to all things of an immoral or indifferent nature he must suppress this martial spirit and show courteous and affectionate forbearance when dealing with the scruples of those whose consciences are by nature or education legalistic and puritanic. And the weak must show a like mutual consideration toward the liberties of the strong. This section is, as Lard remarks, "pre-eminently a chapter as to duties in regard to things indifferent in themselves." For things not indifferent there is another rule (Gal. 1:6-10; 2). This section is also subordinately connected with the preceding paragraph by continuous reference to the second coming of Christ. (See vs. 4, 10-12.) Verses 1-12 are addressed both to the strong and the weak; verses 13-23 and 1 are addressed to the strong alone, and verses 2-13 are addressed both to the strong and the weak.] **XIV. 1 But him that is weak in faith receive** [a strong word. See Acts 28:2; Rom. 15:7; Philem. 15-17] **ye, yet not for decision of scruples.** [Do not by your reception, which ought to be to him a blessing, bring him into the misery of unrest by discussions and contentions which can end only in vain reasonings and valueless conclusions. Do not discuss his doubts and pompously and condescendingly insinuate that he is a fool for having them. The Jew and the Gentile have stood in contrast throughout this book and they are here still in this passage, and it is therefore not necessary to hunt, as does Eichhorn for Pythagorean or other scrupulous Gentiles. The Jew with his qualms sufficiently answers all the calls of the context. Educated under the narrowing, restricting influences of the law, he could not readily and at once comprehend the liberty of the gospel; hence he was weak in comparison with the Gentile who was unhampered by legalistic conceptions of meats, days, etc. (Gal. 5:1-15; Col. 2:10-23; 1 Tim. 4:1-8). He is said to be "weak in the faith" because his judgment, still bound and tethered by silly scruples and obsolete laws, failed to assert that strength which the liberty of the new faith allowed it. Thus the Jewish conscience still shuddered at acts which the Gentile Christian regarded as wholly innocent and permissible; but, since its "failings leaned to virtue's side," and were usually capable of correction if patiently handled, it was to be treated with consideration and affectionate kindness. In fact, the apostle, for "is weak," uses a participle and not an adjective, thus indicating that the weakness is not inherent and permanent, but only a temporary defect, liable to be self-corrected at any moment.] **2 One man hath faith** [believes he has the liberty or right] **to eat all things: but he that is weak eateth herbs.** [We are familiar with the universal Jewish scruples with regard to swine's flesh and meat offered to idols; but there were some who refined their diet to far greater extremes—to the "mint, anise and cummin" standard. A sect called Therapeutæ had a regimen thus described by Philo: "Wine is not introduced . . . and the table bears nothing which has blood, but there is placed upon it bread food, and salt for seasoning, to which also hyssop is sometimes added as an extra sauce for those who are delicate in their eating." However, the abstinence here mentioned was most widely practiced by all scattered Jews. Knowing that any meat bought in Gentile markets was open to question and liable to be unclean, they, being unable to purchase clean meat as prepared by Jewish butchers, abstained from *all* meat and ate only those things (classed as herbs by the apostle) which they could trace from natural growth to use on their tables. (See Dan. 1; Tobit 1: 10, 11.) Josephus' "Life," Sec. 3, mentions certain priests who fed solely on figs and dates.] **3 Let not him that eateth set at nought him that eateth not; and let not him that eateth not judge him that eateth: for God hath received him.** [Eating or not eating was, with Paul, a matter of indifference; but uncharitable conduct toward a Christian brother was not a matter of indifference—it was sin. Hence the apostle interferes, not by way of counsel, but by unequivocal commandment, strictly forbidding the strong to look with disdainful eye upon the temerity of the weak, contemptuously despising him as the victim of narrow prejudice and baseless superstition; and with equal strictures charging the weak not to commit the sin of censorious judgment by ignorantly confounding liberty with license and thus unjustly condemning the strong as libertines and heretics, unscrupulous and irreverent. In modern times controversy over meat sacrificed to idols is unknown, but the principle still applies as to instrumental music, missionary societies, etc. Such matters of indifference are not to be injected into the terms of salvation, or set up as tests of fellowship. As to them there is to be neither contempt on the one part, nor judgment on the other. Baptism, however, is not a matter of indifference, being as much a divinely established term in the plan of salvation as faith itself (Mark 16:16). "It is a notable fact," observes Lard, "that the weak are always more exacting and sensitive than the strong, as well as more ready than they to press their grievances to extremes."] **4 Who art thou that judgest the servant of another? to his own lord he standeth or falleth. Yea, he shall be made to stand; for the Lord hath power to make him stand.** [We must avoid the sacrilegious presumption which condemns where God hath not condemned. Whether our brother in Christ stands in favor, so that his daily life and service are accepted of God, or whether he falls from grace, so that his labors are rejected, is a matter for the Master, and does not pertain to us servants. (Comp. 1 Cor. 10:12; 16:13; 1 Thess. 3:8; Rom. 8:33, 34; 11:22.) A kindly, affectionate concern is commendable, but a censorious condemnation is forbidden. Moreover, the latter is useless and idle, for it is the duty of each disciple to please his Master, not his fellow-servant, and the Master is able to justify and will justify without consulting human accusers (chap. 8:33), or paying respect to man-made technicalities about indifferent things. Christ's ability to justify extends to even positive, inexcusable sin (chap. 3:26; John 8:11). If we could only learn that the consciences of others, though different, are as active and as exacting as our own, we would judge less and love more. Acting by contrary rule, if we find that any man's conscience varies from our own, we straightway conclude that he has no conscience at all, and hence is a proper subject for our condemnation, a culprit well within the bounds of our jurisdiction.] **5 One man esteemeth one day above another: another esteemeth every day *alike*.** [Jewish Chris-

MUTUAL FORBEARANCE

tians generally continued to reverence and observe the sabbath, new moons and festival days commanded by the law of Moses, but which are no part of the Christian system (Gal. 4:10; Col. 2:15, 16); while the Gentile Christian regarded all days as equally holy, and to be spent in the fear and service of God.] **Let each man be fully assured in his own mind.** [About indifferent matters God has given no command, hence each must follow his own judgment and conscience, and none is required to adjust his conduct to satisfy the conscience, much less the scruples of another, though he must show charity and forbearance toward his brother's conscience.] **6 He that regardeth the day, regardeth it unto the Lord: and he that eateth, eateth unto the Lord, for he giveth God thanks; and he that eateth not, unto the Lord he eateth not, and giveth God thanks.** [The conduct of each was equally commendable, as the object of each was the same; that is, to serve God. The one who rested and the one who labored each sought to please God in his act. One gave thanks for meat and all, and the other gave thanks for all, less meat. "This so remarkable saying of the apostle furnishes us," says Godet, "with the true means of deciding all those questions of casuistry which so often arise in Christian life, and cause the believer so much embarrassment. May I allow myself this or that pleasure? Yes, if I can enjoy it to the Lord, and while giving him thanks for it; no, if I can not receive it as a gift from his hand, and bless him for it. This mode of solution respects at once the rights of the Lord and those of individual liberty." The passage indicates that grace before meals was the universal practice of Christians in Paul's day. It probably rested on the habit of Jesus—Luke 9:16; 22:17-19; 24:30-35.] **7 For none of us liveth to himself, and none dieth to himself. 8 For whether we live, we live unto the Lord; or whether we die, we die unto the Lord: whether we live therefore, or die, we are the Lord's.** [As we are Christ's by right of redemption and purchase (Acts

20:28; 1 Cor. 6:19, 20; 7:23; 1 Pet. 1:18, 19), we are not our own, but the rights of Christ overshadow all our individual rights, whether exercised in asserting our liberty or indulging our spirit of censoriousness. To live to self is forbidden; we must live with a view to our Lord and his interest in others. Whether, therefore, a man regard any particular act, food or pleasure as a thing permissible—a thing wherein he may, figuratively speaking, *live;* or whether he regards it as an affair wherein he must deny himself, and so, figuratively, *die,* in either case he must take more than himself into account, for he must include the Lord and others. Comp. 2 Cor. 5:15; Rom. 12:1; Phil. 1:21-24; 2 Cor. 5:6-9.] **9 For to this end Christ died and lived *again,* that he might be Lord of both the dead and the living.** [We are here told to what lengths Christ went to obtain the important right to rule over us in both spheres of being, or as *literally* living and dead. A right so dearly bought is not readily abandoned, and, moreover, if Christ rules over us in the literal, his rule also, of course, governs us in all lesser or figurative realms. He became purchaser of us by death (Acts 20:28), and ruler by his resurrection—Acts 2:30-36; 17:31; Rom. 1:4.] **10 But thou [O weak one], why dost thou judge thy brother? or thou again [O strong one], why dost thou set at nought thy brother? for we shall all stand before the judgment-seat of God.** [The fact that each is so great a sinner that Christ must needs die for him, should prevent the one from judging and the other from despising. Since Christ, having died, is able to justify whom he will, what folly is it to attempt to usurp Christ's office so as to condemn any who trust in him! The believer is not even judged of Christ, but is called into judgment that he may be justified—2 Cor. 5:10; Rom. 8:33.] **11 For it is written** [and hence was an already established doctrine, and not one just now promulgated by Paul], **As I live, saith the Lord, to me every knee shall bow, And every tongue shall confess to God.**

MUTUAL FORBEARANCE

[The quotation gives the sense of Isa. 45:23. Comp. Phil. 2:10, 11.] **12 So then each one of us shall give account of himself to God.** [God judges all, hence it is superfluous for the Christian to judge any. Why gather stones of condemnation and judgment when, after all, Jesus renders us powerless to throw them? (John 8:7.) Since, then, our judgments are futile and worthless, affecting no one but ourselves, let us refrain from them, and cultivate charity, remembering the rule which metes unto us as we measure to others (Matt. 7:1, 2). We should be glad that we escape the responsibility of judging, since Jesus himself expressed no eagerness to assume the burden. Comp. John 5:22, 27, 30, 45; 3:17-19; 8:15, 16; 12:47; Luke 12:13, 14.] **13 Let us not therefore judge one another any more: but judge** [decide] **ye this rather, that no man put a stumblingblock in his brother's way, or an occasion of falling.** [This warning is addressed both to the weak and to the strong. Each censorious judgment tempts the strong to a reactionary and excessive assertion of liberty, and each despising of the weak tends to decrease his faith in the power of God and the influence of the Holy Spirit to regenerate and sanctify men. Hence each is warned to show charity, and thus avoid placing stumbling-blocks in his brother's way. At this point Paul ceases to address both parties, and turns his remarks exclusively to the strong, since the weak have less control over their actions than the strong, and hence are mercifully spared the imposition of burdens too heavy for their strength.] **14 I know, and am persuaded in the Lord Jesus** [I am convinced in my apostolic capacity, as enlightened by the Holy Spirit sent of the Lord Jesus (John 14:26; 16:13-15). Paul's teachings in this entire section are contrary to his education and prejudice as a Jew. He is speaking as one freed and enlightened in Christ], **that nothing is unclean of itself: save that to him who accounteth anything to be unclean, to him it is unclean.** [See Matt. 15:11; Mark 7:18; Acts 10:14-28; 1 Tim. 4:4. In the gospel all ceremonial uncleanness is abolished, so that no food is any longer unclean, but if a man acts contrary to his conscience, he defiles it: hence food, clean of itself, may work sad havoc in his spiritual nature who eats contrary to his conscience—1 Cor. 8:7-13.] **15 For if because of meat thy brother is grieved, thou walkest no longer in love.** ["For" looks back to verse 13. Recklessness as to the welfare or safety of others is not loving. "Grieved" may express either a lapse into Judaism on the part of the weak because of the apparent worldliness of the strong, or it may indicate that the weak, tempted by the conduct of the strong, do things which are contrary to conscience, and hence come to grief (Matt. 27:3-5). It is likely that the latter danger was most prominent to the apostle's mind. (Comp. v. 20, and 1 Cor. 8:10.) The context, containing the words "destroy" and "overthrow" (v. 20), shows that the grief is more than mere fraternal disappointment at another's laxity.] **Destroy not with thy meat him for whom Christ died.** [This is the strongest possible appeal. What pleasure of liberty can be so sweet as to justify us in destroying our brother's life, and frustrating the agony and sacrifice of the Master in his behalf? Shall we set a higher value on our meat than Christ did on his divine life? How shall we look our Lord in the face if we have wantonly done such a thing!] **16 Let not then your good be evil spoken of** [Do not so use your liberty—the good you enjoy—as to provoke blame or censure, for by so doing you lose your power to influence others for good, whether they be weak or strong. A bad name has no power in God's kingdom—1 Tim. 3:7; Matt. 5:16; Acts 22:22]: **17 for the kingdom of God is not eating and drinking, but righteousness and peace and joy in the Holy Spirit. 18 For he that herein serveth Christ is well-pleasing to God, and approved of men. 19 So then let us follow after things which make for peace, and things whereby we may edify one another.** [Humanly prescribed and wholly external ordinances neither

MUTUAL FORBEARANCE

usher us into the kingdom nor increase its power within us, nor does the failure to observe them exclude us from it. Its blessings are not linked to sumptuary liberties, but are found in graces socially applied; in righteousness toward God; justice toward our neighbor; peace, or concord and harmony, with all; joy, or expressions of loving happiness prompted in us by the Holy Spirit, the source of all grace: these are the things which work the advance and glorification of the kingdom both within us and about us. These, then, are the habits of life which please both God who reads the heart, and man who looks upon the outward conduct, and, moreover, build up the kingdom.] **20 Overthrow not for meat's sake the work of God. All things indeed are clean; howbeit it is evil for that man who eateth with offence. 21 It is good not to eat flesh, nor to drink wine, nor *to do anything* whereby thy brother stumbleth.** [Do not for a trifling indulgence destroy a man, the noblest work and likeness of God. Look not at your act alone, but consider also its consequences. True, indeed, that your weak brother, in following your example, will not be harmed by the food itself, yet he will surely do evil if he offends his conscience in eating. Therefore your proper course is abstinence that your brother may not be tempted. Though Paul's reference is to the contamination of the wine of idolatry, yet the principle applies equally well to the wine of intemperance.] **22 The faith which thou hast, have thou to thyself before God.** [The faith or conviction of liberty which thou hast need not be abandoned; but it should be held or preserved in the heart before God, and should not be vauntingly paraded in the sight of the weak.] **Happy is he that judgeth not himself in that which he approveth. 23 But he that doubteth is condemned if he eat, because *he eateth* not of faith; and whatsoever is not of faith is sin.** [The apostle here presents the contrast between the strong and the weak. The former is blest indeed in that he has liberty without the sense of inward disapproval, while the other, not sure of his ground, plunges recklessly on, and, acting contrary to his convictions, and hence to that respect and reverence which is due to God, sins. His eating is sinful because not of faith (faith is here used in the abstract sense, and means grounded, undoubting conviction that God approves), for whatever is done without such settled conviction is sinful recklessness, and must not be done at all, for to act contrary to the will of God is to destroy his work in us. *Diakrenesthai*, translated "doubteth," means to be divided into two persons, one of whom says "yes," and the other "no." In the case of the weak the flesh says "yes," and conscience cries "no."] **XV. 1. Now** ["Now" is progressive; it means, "to proceed with the matter in hand"] **we** [It is a characteristic of Paul's to identify himself with those on whom he lays especial burdens] **that are strong ought** [1 Cor. 9:19-22. Strength in the gospel always brings upon its owner the obligation and command to serve (Gal. 6:2), and the one who would truly serve must eliminate his self-conceit and arrogance] **to bear the infirmities of the weak, and not to please ourselves. 2 Let each one of us please his neighbor for that which is good, unto edifying. 3 For Christ also pleased not himself** [The strong ought to give way to the weak because strength can yield better than weakness, since in so doing it in no way violates conscience and because this forbearance tends to build up the weak and make them strong. But this rule applies, of course, only to matters that are indifferent; in things that are erroneous or wrong we have no choice or discretion, but must stand for the right as God would have us. The only objection that the strong can urge against yielding to the weak is that to do so involves them in great sacrifice. In answer to this argument Paul sets forth the example of Christ. How can he that is self-pleasing, and that shrinks from sacrifice, make claim to be the disciple and follower of the One whose life was the supreme self-sacrifice of the annals of all time? Had Christ pleased himself hell itself might well shudder at the consequences]; **but, as it is written** [Ps. 69:9], **The reproaches of them that reproached thee fell upon me.** [When Christ bore the heavy burden of our reproaches and disgrace—our sin, and its consequences—can we not, as his disciples, cheerfully bear each other's light foibles and infirmities? We must not only be unselfishly fair; we must be self-denyingly generous, if we would be Christlike.] **4 For whatsoever things were written aforetime were written for our learning, that through patience and through comfort of the scriptures we might have hope. 5 Now the God of patience and of comfort grant you to be of the same mind one with another according to Christ Jesus** [I cite the Scripture as written for the instruction of the unborn church, for all Scripture, as it outlines what Christ would do sacrificially, also establishes what we should do as imitators of him. It also affords us, in our perusal of it, patience and hope in the doing, for God, the original source back of all Scripture, will not fail in administering aid and comfort to you in your effort toward that spirit of unity and concord which is according to Christ; *i. e.*, according to his desire, will, commandment and example]: **6 that with one accord ye may with one mouth glorify the God and Father of our Lord Jesus Christ.** [Beautiful picture! When in concord the whole church as a harmonious choir renders praise to God, the Father of our Lord, as one mouth! And how this will glorify our Saviour, Christ, showing the perfection of his work in us! Unanimity of inward feeling can not but result in harmony of outward expression, whether in doctrine, worship or praise.] **7 Wherefore receive ye one another, even as Christ also received you, to the glory of God.** [Against the trifling, selfish enjoyment of personal liberty, the apostle sets the supreme end and joy of life; viz., the glorification of God (Matt. 22:36-38; John 4:34). As Christ, suppressing all selfish promptings to assert his own rights and liberties, and ignoring all distinctions in his favor, however pronounced or impossible (Phil. 2:5-8), received us in all loving compassion to affect that glory; so also should we mutually receive one another in full love and fellowship to that end, excluding all unworthy selfishness, and all social, national or racial antipathies. Unity glorifies God, as the amity of a household reflects honor on its head.] **8 For** ["for" introduces the explanation as to how Christ's coming and ministry was for the purpose of glorifying God by receiving each party, Jew or Gentile] **I say that Christ hath been made a minister of the circumcision for the truth of God, that he might confirm the promises *given* unto the fathers, 9 and that the Gentiles might glorify God for his mercy** [In order that he might vindicate the veracity of God in confirming and in keeping the promises of the covenant given unto the fathers, Abraham, Isaac and Jacob: (now these covenant promises contained blessings for the Gentiles—Gen. 22:18; these blessings thus coming to them through the circumcision people and covenant—John 4:22; therefore Christ became the minister of the circumcision for the sake of the Gentiles also, that the Gentiles might also be received) and that they might glorify God for his mercy. If Christ, then, the Lord and Master, was a minister (Matt. 20:27, 28) unto each for purposes of unity and concord (Eph. 2:11-22), with what lowly humility should his servants receive and serve each other to effect these results]; **as it is written, Therefore will I give praise unto thee among the Gentiles, And sing unto thy name.** ["Sing" (*psalloo*) means, literally, "strike the harp to thy name." This quotation argues that the use of that instrument, as a means of divine praise, is innocent and permissible.] **10 And again he saith, Rejoice, ye Gentiles, with his people. 11 And again, Praise the Lord, all ye Gentiles; And let all the peoples praise him. 12 And again, Isaiah saith, There shall be the root of Jesse, And he that ariseth to rule over the Gentiles; On**

MUTUAL FORBEARANCE

him shall the Gentiles hope. [The quotations found in verses 9-12 are presented to confirm Paul's teaching that it was God's original, eternal purpose to include the Gentiles in Israel, the passages forming a parenthesis elucidating the idea of verse 7; viz., "even as Christ received you." The first passage is from Ps. 18:49, and introduces David as confessing and praising as theocratic King under God not apart from, but among, the Gentiles. In the second, taken from Deut. 32:43, Moses exhorts the Gentiles to rejoice in God together with all his people, or Israel. The third, from Ps. 117:1, repeats the thought of the second; while the last, from Isa. 11:10, is a definite announcement of the reign of Messiah as the root of Jesse, or head of the Davidic dynasty (and hence Jewish) over the Gentiles also, and that not as a foreign oppressor, but as a hope-fulfilling native king. The great prophetic fact forecast in all these quotations is a coming day of joint praise for Jew and Gentile. What a consolation and what an aid toward patience these Scripture quotations must have been to Paul, in his work as apostle to the Gentiles! (See v. 4.) The trend of the argument toward his apostolic ministry forms a transition leading to the epistolary conclusion which follows the benediction of the thirteenth verse.] **13 Now the God of hope fill you with all joy and peace in believing, that ye may abound in hope, in the power of the Holy Spirit.** [The apostle concludes the hortatory part of his letter with this solemn petition for his readers' welfare. Note what beautiful names for God are derived from the attributes which he inspires. "God of hope," "God of patience" (v. 5), "God of peace"— v. 33.]

PART FOURTH

EPISTOLARY CONCLUSION, CONTAINING PLANS, REQUESTS, EXPLANATIONS, COMMENDATIONS, SALUTATIONS. ETC.

Rom. 15:14—16:27.

The apostle, having finished his didactic and doctrinal instruction, turns to renew the personal tone with which his letter opened. He presents: (1) An apology for the liberty taken in so plainly admonishing them, reminding them of his office as apostle to the Gentiles which laid such a duty upon him (15:14-16; comp. 1:14, 15). (2) An explanation concerning his labors and his failure to visit them (15: 17-24; comp. 1:11-13). (3) A statement of his present and future plans, and a request for prayer (15:25-33). (4) Commendations and salutations (16: 1-24; comp. 1:7). (5) Doxology (16:25-27; comp. 1:1, 2).

I.

THE APOSTLE'S MINISTRY AND PLANS—A REQUEST FOR PRAYERS.

15:14-33.

14 And I myself also am persuaded of you [as to you], my brethren, that ye yourselves are full of goodness, filled with all knowledge, able also to admonish one another. [These Roman Christians were by no means "babes in Christ," yet even men, and that the best instructed, need apostolic preaching. But Paul's confidence in their understanding is shown in the quality of this letter which he wrote to them.

Compare a contrary feeling in his letter to the Corinthians (1 Cor. 2:6; 3:1-3), and in milder form the Epistle to the Hebrews (Heb. 6:11, 12). Moreover, the list of names of church leaders contained in this epistolary conclusion proves the efficiency of this Roman church, its goodness, and its ability to impart knowledge and admonition.] **15 But I write the more boldly unto you in some measure, as putting you again in remembrance** [Thus suggesting that the matter of his Epistle was not wholly new to them: comp. 2 Pet. 1:12, 13], **because of the grace** [*i. e.,* apostleship: comp. 1:5; 12:3; Gal. 2:9; Eph. 3:7-11] **that was given me of God, 16 that I should be a minister of Christ Jesus unto the Gentiles** [I have not carefully weighed my words as a stranger should, but have used some measure of boldness because it is my duty to so speak as your apostle commissioned by God's grace. "As though he said, 'I did not snatch the honor for myself, nor rush upon it first, but God laid this upon me, and that by way of grace, not a setting apart a worthy person to this office. Be not therefore offended, for it is not I that rise up against you, but God that has laid this upon me'"—*Chrysostom*], **ministering** [Greek, "ministering in sacrifice." He speaks in metaphor, assuming to himself the office of priest] **the gospel of God, that the offering up of the Gentiles might be made acceptable, being sanctified by the Holy Spirit.** [Christians are nowhere in the New Testament spoken of as literal priests, yet the idea of priestly sacrifice is forcefully used in a figurative way. (Comp. Rom. 12:1; Phil. 2:17.) Paul here speaks of himself metaphorically as a priest, not of the Levitical order with its material temple and tangible altar, but as pertaining to the gospel with its spiritual cleansing in Christ. As priests offered many offerings at the great festivals, so Paul, as apostle to the Gentiles, came before God in the festal hour or time of the glad tidings or the gospel of salvation, with the multitudinous offering of the myriads of the Gentiles. As carnal offerings were first cleansed by water before being offered, so these Gentiles, as victims of grace, were first made acceptable offerings by being cleansed by the outpouring of the Holy Spirit, after which they offered themselves as daily sacrifices. Compare his metaphor to that used by Isaiah in describing the final gathering of Israel (Isa. 66:19, 20). At Rom. 12:1 the apostle began by exhorting members of the Roman church to offer themselves as living sacrifices. He then proceeded to elaborate the things wherein self-sacrifice was demanded of them. Now in the verse before us he presents himself as a priest presiding officially over their sacrifice and presenting it to God, which was, figuratively speaking, his duty as apostle to the Gentiles.] **17 I have therefore my glorying in Christ Jesus in things pertaining to God.** ["Therefore" refers back to verse 15. I have therefore a right to address you boldly in things pertaining to God, for I am not contemptible in such matters, being able to glory, not in myself, but in reference to Christ Jesus in that I am called by him to be his apostle. My boldness in glorying, therefore, is not in myself, but in my apostleship and its resultant spiritual duties and powers. Compare 2 Cor. 12:1-13; Col. 1:25-29.] **18 For I will not dare to speak of any things save those which Christ wrought through me, for the obedience of the Gentiles, by word and deed, 19 in the power of signs and wonders, in the power of the Holy Spirit; so that from Jerusalem, and round about even unto Illyricum, I have fully preached the gospel of Christ** [I, as I have intimated, would not dare to glory in anything that I find in myself, but I glory in the manifest powers of the Holy Spirit, both in speech and miracle which have been mine by reason of my apostolic office, and which have enabled me to convincingly preach the gospel, not in any limited field, but far and wide in that great curve of the earth which begins at Jerusalem in the east and ends at Illyricum in the west.

"Chrysostom observeth," says Trapp, "that Plato came three times to Sicily to convert Dionysius the tyrant to philosophy, and could not. But Paul set a great compass, converted many souls, planted many churches: and why? Christ sat upon him as one of his white horses, and went forth conquering and to conquer (Rev. 6:2)." Paul began preaching at Damascus, but took a second start at Jerusalem under special commission to the Gentiles (Acts 9:19, 20, 27-29; Gal. 1:17, 18; Acts 22:17-21). Acts makes no direct mention of Paul's labors in Illyricum. However, the Romans incorporated Illyricum as part of Macedonia, and hence the journey thither may be included in the trip described at Acts 20:1, 2. Note the calm, sane way in which Paul speaks of his miraculous powers as a trust from Christ and a seal of his apostleship, both being mere accessories to that all-important task, the preaching of the gospel]; **20 yea** [yes, so full was the spiritual power imparted to me that I thought it an honor and recognition due to my office and to those powers to use them only on the hard, unbroken soil of utterly unenlightened paganism], **making it my aim so to preach the gospel, not where Christ was *already* named, that I might not build upon another man's foundation** [Had Paul done otherwise he would have used his supreme powers as though they were secondary, and he would have been choosing the easy tasks, leaving to others those harder undertakings for which Christ was hourly fitting and equipping him (1 Cor. 3:10; Eph. 2:20; 2 Cor. 10:12-16). It ill becomes a ten-talent man to seek a one-talent position. The pressing needs of the field also forbade the waste of time in resowing. Had Paul's example been followed, what needless overlapping of missionary effort might have been avoided. Sectarianism has caused and committed this sin, and it has been especially reprehensible where it has been done to foster points of difference which are matters of indifference, as is the case where factions of the same sect compete in the same field]; 21 but [on the contrary, I preach as following the program outlined by the prophet], **as it is written** [Isa. 52:15], **They shall see, to whom no tidings of him came, And they who have not heard shall understand.** [This verse, which speaks of the original enlightening of the Gentiles, might well appeal to the one commissioned to be their apostle, inciting him to be ever the first to rush to their relief.] **22 Wherefore also I was hindered these many times from coming to you: 23 but now, having no more any place** [territory where Christ is not known] **in these regions, and having these many years a longing to come unto you** [Because of the many benighted places in the unevangelized east, I have hitherto been held back from visiting you, but now the work here being finished, leaving me free, I find the very principle which once detained me in the east now impels me to seek those of the west, thus permitting me to visit you in passing (comp. chap. 1:11; 1 Thess. 3:6; 2 Cor. 7:7-11; Phil. 1:8), and I purpose to so do. As Rome was a place already founded in Christ, Paul's principle limited his stay there to a mere visit, but as it was the center of all influence in his Gentile field, it was fitting that it rest under his instruction. To compass this instruction Paul wrote this Epistle], **24 whensoever I go unto Spain** [We have no contemporary record stating that Paul visited Spain in his lifetime, but his noble wish was in large measure gratified, for he visited Spain in later centuries by his Epistles, which wrought so mightily that the Inquisition could only stamp out his influence by stamping out all the influenced] **(for I hope to see you in my journey, and to be brought on my way thitherward by you, if first in some measure I shall have been satisfied with your company)** ["Brought on;" *proempthenai* means primarily "to accompany, to go with." (See its use at Acts 15:3; 20:38; 21:5; 1 Cor. 16:6; 2 Cor. 1:16.) Paul thus delicately suggests, but does not deliberately ask, pecuniary and other aid to his journey.

He also makes it plain that his stay will be merely a visit—a tarrying to satisfy his hungry desire for their fellowship. But the counsels of God decreed that Paul's stay should be lengthened greatly (Acts 28:30) so as to let his influence over the Gentiles radiate from the great Gentile center, and so as to fully gratify his longings for a fellowship which was as loyal and as loving as any that ever refreshed his soul—Acts 28:14, 15]—**25 but now, *I say*, I go unto Jerusalem, ministering unto the saints.** [Despite the earnestness of my desire to see you just at present, I can not come, for duty calls me to Jerusalem. Verses 31 and 32 show that Paul anticipated danger and trouble at Jerusalem, but joy and rest at Rome. His anticipations were, however, partly mistaken, for he found rest while a prisoner at Cæsarea perhaps more than at Rome (Acts 24:23). Thus it often happens that along the dark road toward duty we find the sunniest spots in life.] **26 For it hath been the good pleasure of Macedonia and Achaia to make a certain contribution for the poor among the saints that are at Jeursalem.** [It was quite natural that there should be many Christians in Jerusalem, for Palestine was filled with poor, and it was to that class that the gospel was especially preached (Luke 7:22), and it was among that class that it was everywhere successful (1 Cor. 1:26-29). But it is also likely that these poor, being converted, lost their employment because of their faith, for such petty persecution has been common in all ages (Jas. 2: 4-7; Gal. 2:10; 1 Pet. 4:15, 16). But, unhappily, these cruel distinctions, when made by Jews against Jewish Christians, did not cause the latter to affiliate with Gentile Christians. On the contrary, Jerusalem became the center of a vast and practically worldwide enmity cherished by Jewish against Gentile Christians, by reason of racial and educational prejudice. To break down this prejudice and hatred, that the partition wall might be removed between Jew and Gentile, Paul conceived the idea of inducing the

Gentile Christians to send an offering to the poor Jewish Christians at Jerusalem (1 Cor. 16:1-3), hoping thereby to make each faction think more kindly of the other. In this he partly succeeded (2 Cor. 9:12-15). The Bible accounts of this collection lead us to think that it was quite large. See Acts 19:21; 24:17; 2 Cor. 8:1-9:15.] **27 Yea, it hath been their good pleasure** [The apostle twice notes the free-will or "good pleasure" nature of this offering. It dropped as the ripe fruit of the orchard; it was not squeezed as cider in the mill]; **and their debtors they are.** [The Gentiles are indebted to the Jews, and hence their offering is but a proper expression of gratitude.] **For if the Gentiles have been made partakers of their spiritual things, they owe it to them also to minister unto them in carnal things.** [Salvation is from the Jews (John 4:22). If, therefore, the Gentiles received eternal and heavenly treasure from the Jews, how small a matter was it that they make return of temporal and earthly treasure to such benefactors. The Gentile still owes this debt to the Jewish race, for of it came the Christ and the Scriptures. The law here announced might well be remembered by many rich congregations in dealing with their ministers in questions of salary, vacations, etc. (Comp. Luke 16:9.) By mentioning this offering, Paul sowed good seed in the heart of the Roman church—seed promising a harvest of liberality.] **28 When therefore I have accomplished this, and have sealed to them this fruit, I will go on by you unto Spain.** ["Seal" is a figurative expression for "deliver safely." Compare its use at 2 Kings 22:4, where it is translated "sum"; *i. e.*, count out. Our English word "consign" is a similar figure. Paul wished to complete a good work for them: to insure to them the benefit of a noble deed fully accomplished.] **29 And I know that, when I come unto you, I shall come in the fulness of the blessing of Christ.** [Paul had no doubt about the favorable conditions in the Roman church, nor about his

PAUL'S MINISTRY AND PLANS 543

kindly reception by the Christians at Rome. He felt that they would so receive him that he would be able to greatly enrich them in instruction and in all other spiritual blessings. "Beyond these blessings," says Lard, "he had nothing to bestow, nor they anything to ask." Far other were his presentiments as to Jerusalem, as he immediately shows us. For a like expectation of an evil reception, see 2 Cor. 1:23; 12:14, 20, 21; 13:1, 2.] **30 Now I beseech you, brethren, by our Lord Jesus Christ, and by the love of the Spirit, that ye strive together with me in your prayers to God for me** [Paul appeals to no natural love such as is provoked by environment, propinquity, social or fleshly ties, but to a love induced by the Spirit of God toward one whose face they had never seen. As Christ has power over you, and the Spirit prompts love within you, pray with me and for me. The word "strive" suggests the force of opposing spiritual powers which resist the accomplishment of the things prayed for, and the necessity of ardent prayer to overcome it. The prayer was granted, but by other means than those praying anticipated. With Paul position raised no presumption: neither visions, revelations, miraculous gifts, inspiration nor apostleship lifted him above praying for their prayers. "Spiritual beggary," says Trapp, "is the hardest and richest of all trades. Learn with Paul to beg prayer with all earnestness. 'Pray for me, I say; pray for me, I say,' quoth Father Latimer. 'Pray for me, pray for me, for God's sake pray for me,' said blessed Bradford"]; **31 that I may be delivered from them that are disobedient in Judæa, and *that* my ministration** [offering] **which *I have* for Jerusalem may be acceptable to the saints; 32 that I may come unto you in joy through the will of God, and together with you find rest. 33 Now the God of peace be with you all. Amen.** [The prayer is fourfold. (1) Personal safety. (2) A successful mission with the offering. (3) Divine permission to reach Rome. (4) Joyful rest in Rome. The prayer designates as "saints" those thousands of believers whose prejudice against Paul amounted to hatred. (Acts 21:20, 21). As to these Paul asks prayer that they may duly appreciate the offering which the Gentiles have made them, and that they may be properly softened and broadened by it. This prayer, as we have seen (v. 26), was answered. He describes as "disobedient" those Jews who were beyond all hope of conversion. Paul was already filled with dark forebodings and painful presentiments as to these latter, and like feelings were soon expressed by others (see Acts 20:22, 23; 21:4-14); yet God, who restrains the wrath of men (Ps. 76:10), caused the very illwill of these disobedient to provide for Paul the long rest at Cæsarea and the free journey to Rome, attended with no greater hardship than usually accompanied his travels. Here, too, prayer was answered. He closes with his prayer for them, which is, as Lard remarks, "the sum of all prayers, the embodiment of all good wishes."

II.

COMMENDATION OF PHŒBE—SALUTATIONS—WARNINGS AGAINST DISSENSIONS AND APOSTASY —BENEDICTION.

16:1-27

[This chapter is mostly taken up with salutations or greetings sent to individuals, groups of individuals, and to small bodies of people which met separately, yet composed jointly the church at Rome. Aquila and Priscilla are known to us. The rest are practically unknown, hence their names are passed by us without comment.] 1 **I commend unto you Phœbe** [It is generally admitted that Phœbe alone was the bearer of this letter to the Romans. (Comp. Col. 4:

7; Eph. 6:21.) Had there been others with her, they would doubtless have been also commended] **our sister** [our fellow-Christian], **who is a servant** [Literally, a "deaconess." For deacons, see Acts 6: 1-6; Phil. 1:1, etc. The word "deaconess" is found only here; but this single reference with commendation stamps the office with apostolic sanction and approval, though the attempt to revive the office in our modern churches has not as yet met with any marked success. Pliny, in his letter to Trajan (A. D. 107-111), mentions deaconesses, saying that he extorted information from "two old women who were called *ministræ.*" The Latin *minister* (feminine, *ministræ*) is the equivalent of the Greek *diakonos*, or deacon] **of the church that is at Cenchreæ** [This city was the port of Corinth on the Saronic Gulf, opening out to the Ægean Sea. It was nine miles east of Corinth, and was important because of its harbor and the great fortress which commanded the isthmus uniting northern and southern Greece. From this port Paul sailed for Syria after his second missionary journey, and may have at that time paused long enough to sow the seed from which the church at that point sprang]: **2 that ye receive her in the Lord** [*i. e.,* as Christians should receive a Christian], **worthily of the saints, and that ye assist her in whatsoever matter she may have need of you** [what Phœbe's business was is unknown]: **for she herself also hath been a helper of many, and of mine own self.** [In the Greek there is a play upon words here: "Help her, for she is a helper." She probably helped the apostle during his stay in Cenchreæ—Acts 18: 18.] **3 Salute Prisca** [The diminutive of this name is Priscilla. Compare Jane and Jennie, Drusa and Drusilla] **and Aquila** [Paul met these two at Corinth in A. D. 53, and they sailed with him from thence to Syria (Acts 18:1-18; 1 Cor. 16:19). Again, two years later they were with him at Ephesus—Acts 19] **my fellow-workers in Christ Jesus** [It is probable that as he sent two before him into Macedonia

(Acts 19:22), so these two were now in Rome preparing the field for his coming (comp. Luke 10:1) and ready to aid him with information as to its condition and needs and in other ways when he accomplished his declared purpose to visit that metropolis (Acts 19:21). But Paul's visit was delayed beyond expectation—more than two years (Acts 24:27). Confident of their unchanging loyalty, Paul salutes them first of all and as fellow-workers in the present tense, not as those who "labored" in the past—comp. v. 12], **4 who for my life laid down their own necks** [As Paul's chief danger lay in Ephesus (1 Cor. 15:32), it was evidently there that Aquila and Priscilla risked their lives for him, though no specific account is given us of any such service, or of other dangers than the great riot—Acts 19:23-41]; **unto whom not only I give thanks, but also all the churches of the Gentiles** [being grateful to the pair for aiding in saving so precious a life as that of their apostle, their light in gospel truth, the bulwark guarding their liberties against Jewish aggression]: **5 and salute the church that is in their house.** [That portion of the church that has its usual place of meeting in their house. (Comp. 1 Cor. 16:19; Acts 12:12; 18:7; Col. 4:15; Philem. 2.) Church buildings did not then exist in Rome.] **Salute Epænetus my beloved, who is the firstfruits of Asia unto Christ.** [Of Epænetus and the rest of these Christians nothing is known. "But thus it is on earth," as Lard remarks. "Single short sentences tell the story of those who have prepared its inhabitants for eternal life, while huge tomes are insufficient to record the exploits of those who have often turned it into a slaughter-house." By "Asia" Paul means proconsular Asia, that province in the southwest corner of Asia Minor of which Ephesus was the capital.] **6 Salute Mary, who bestowed much labor on you. 7 Salute Andronicus and Junias, my kinsmen** [my fellow-countrymen —Jews—Rom. 9:3], **and my fellow-prisoners** [When or where we do not know. Scripture tells of four

COMMENDATION, SALUTATIONS, ETC. 547

imprisonments of Paul, but Clement of Rome enumerates seven. There may have been even more—2 Cor. 11:23], **who are of note among the apostles, who also have been in Christ before me.** [Meaning that these were converted to Christ before he was— early enough to be well known to the apostles and to be honored by them before that body was scattered by persecution, it being slow to depart from Jerusalem—Acts 8:1; 12:1-3.] **8 Salute Ampliatus my beloved in the Lord. 9 Salute Urbanus our fellow-worker in Christ, and Stachys my beloved. 10 Salute Apelles the approved in Christ. Salute them that are of the *household* of** Aristobulus. [A Roman "household" included all in service from the noblest retainer to the meanest slave. This was probably the younger Aristobulus of the Herodian family. See Jos. Antt. 20:1, 2.] **11 Salute Herodion my kinsman. Salute them of the *household* of Narcissus, that are in the Lord.** [This is probably Narcissus the rich freedman and favorite of Cæsar's, whose household would therefore be compounded with Cæsar's. (Comp. Phil. 4:22.) He died A. D. 54, or some three years before Paul wrote this Epistle. For references as to Narcissus, see Tac. Ann. 11:29, *seq.*; 12:57; 13:1; Suet. Claud. 28. "Bishop Lightfoot argues very plausibly that most of those here greeted by Paul were Nero's servants, once in Greece, especially Philippi, and now called to Rome, whence they later sent back greetings to Philippi (Phil. 4:22). An imperial burial-ground at Rome bears names like most of these, and the parties there buried lived in Paul's day"—*Moule.*] **12 Salute Tryphæna and Tryphosa, who labor in the Lord. Salute Persis the beloved, who labored much in the Lord. 13 Salute Rufus the chosen in the Lord, and his mother and mine.** [We know nothing certain of these. Paul had evidently spent time in the home of Rufus, and had received motherly care at that time, which he now gracefully acknowledges, reckoning that if the woman of the home was Rufus' mother by nature, she was also his by service and affection (Matt. 19:29). Possibly this Rufus may have been Simon's son (Mark 15: 21), and Paul may have lived with them while a youthful student in Jerusalem (Acts 22:3). The tradition that Mark wrote his Gospel while at Rome adds to the plausibility that both he and Paul refer to the same Rufus.] **14 Salute Asyncritus, Phlegon, Hermes, Patrobas, Hermas, and the brethren that are with them.** ["With them" indicates another section of the church meeting in the homes of these men. Comp. vs. 5, 15.] **15 Salute Philologus and Julia, Nereus and his sister, and Olympas, and all the saints that are with them.** [These apostolic salutations are addressed to twenty-five individuals. Not a large group for one as widely known as Paul in a city as large as Rome, yet when we consider the limited circulation of news and the meager means of communication afforded in that day, it shows the deep affection of the apostle that he knew the whereabouts of so many of his brethren. Note also the women workers named in this small group. It was evidently only to Corinth, and not to Rome, that Paul wrote, "Let your women keep silence"—1 Cor. 14:34; comp. Phil. 4:3.] **16 Salute one another with a holy kiss.** [Osculatory salutation has always been common in the East (2 Sam. 20:9; Luke 7:45; Matt. 26:49). It early became an established practice among the Jews, from whence it passed to the apostolic church (1 Cor. 16:20; 2 Cor. 13:12; 1 Thess. 5:26; 1 Pet. 5:14). It is still retained in the Greek Church, in which the men thus salute men, and women, women. Paul is not teaching the Roman church a new custom, but is purifying an old one, insisting that the salutation be holy and void of all such dissimulation as characterized the kiss of Judas (Matt. 26:49). His precept still applies to all our salutations, no matter what their form.] **All the churches of Christ salute you.** [Having ended his own salutation, Paul adds those of the Gentile churches which he had just been visiting in collecting the offering (ch. 15:

26). These salutations indicate that the apostle talked much about his letter before he wrote it. Possibly he was drafting it as he journeyed. And it also shows that the church at the great metropolis, the center of government and civilization, was an object of interest and esteem to all. Comp. ch. 1:8.] **17 Now I beseech you, brethren, mark them that are causing the divisions** [in Corinth, Galatia, etc.] **and occasions of stumbling, contrary to the doctrine which ye learned** [from the brethren to whom I have sent salutations and others of their fellowship]: **and turn away from them.** [In an unregenerate world the gospel produces division (Matt. 10:34-37), but these divisions are along the cleavage line between good and evil. We are not responsible for these divisions; nay, we would sin if we shrank from causing them. "But," says Lard, "where we, by our own errors of teaching or conduct, produce divisions among the children of God, we sin against Christ. Nor is it a less offense to countenance or defend divisions, than it is to cause them. They must be utterly disfavored by the Christian. He is not at liberty even to feel indifferent toward them. He must actively oppose them where they exist, and actively endeavor to prevent them where they do not exist." It is against division in the church, then, that Paul warns his readers. Having named and saluted those whose doctrine he sanctioned and approved, he warns the church at once to be on the lookout for any who might oppose them, and seek to divide the church now united under them. The opening to the Epistle to the Philippians (written four or five years later) shows what these heretics afterwards did at Rome (Phil. 1:15-18; 3:2, 3, 17-19). Their appearance at Antioch, in Galatia and at Corinth made Paul sure that they would also invade Rome. Those whom Paul commended could, out of their own observation and experience, tell the Roman church what evil these pernicious Judaizers had done (Acts 15:1 *seq.*; Gal. 1:6 *seq.*; 3:1 *seq.*; Col. 2:8-23; 2

Cor. 11:13 *seq.*). At the time of Paul's writing the orthodox leaders appear to have been able to keep the church in unity.] **18 For they that are such serve not our Lord Christ, but their own belly** ["Belly" is meant to express all the appetites of the carnal life. The heretics here referred to, being mediocre and insufficient teachers in the true faith, resorted to the artifice of stirring up factions for the purpose of obtaining therefrom physical and pecuniary support. (Comp. Phil. 3:19.) Their breed is not extinct. There are many who shine as heretics who would pass their lives in obscurity if they were orthodox, and there are also many who amass fortunes preaching lies who would live at a poor, starving rate if they preached the truth. But nothing better can be expected of the devotees of the belly]; **and by their smooth and fair speech they beguile the hearts of the innocent.** [They succeeded, not by the inherent power of what they taught, but by the insidious manner in which they taught it. "Truth," says Trapp, "persuadeth by teaching, it doth not teach by persuading." It has always been a characteristic of truth that it comes to us in plain and simple garb, rugged, unadorned (Matt. 11:20; Acts 4:13; 1 Cor. 1:21-31; 2:1-16; 2 Cor. 3:12, 13; 10:10; 11:6; Jas. 3:17), and its rival, error, sits in the seat of the mighty, speaks with all subtilty and charms with rhetoric and oratorical display—Acts 8:9; 13:10; 12:21-23; 1 Cor. 8:1, 2; 1 Tim. 6:3-5; 2 Tim. 3:7, 8.] **19 For your obedience is come abroad unto all men. I rejoice therefore over you: but I would have you wise unto that which is good, and simple unto that which is evil.** [I warn you, for your obedience and docility, being so notorious, will sooner or later draw them to seek you as an enticing spoil. The apostle rejoiced in their simplicity, yet urges them to be careful in whom they placed their trust. (Comp. Matt. 10:16; John 10: 4, 5; 1 Cor. 14:20; 2 Cor. 11:3.) If the church could only attain the paradoxical state of being simple toward Christ, and wise toward those who pervert his word, sectarianism, with its divisions, would be at an end.] **20 And the God of peace shall bruise Satan under your feet shortly.** [Bruise is equivalent to "crush." (See Gen. 3:15; 2 Cor. 11:12-15.) If the Roman Christians hearkened to the apostle as to these open, material, visible enemies, they would quickly gain a victory over the supreme spiritual and invisible leader who inspired them. Thus the God of peace (not of division) would triumph over the prince of all strife. Life's battle is brief, and the Christian soldier who is steadfast soon gains the victory and is honorably discharged.] **The grace of our Lord Jesus Christ be with you.** [The apostle ends the personal section of his salutations with a blessing, after which he presents in another division the salutations of other friends.] **21 Timothy** [Acts 16:1-4; 2 Cor. 1:1, and Epistles to Timothy] **my fellow-worker saluteth you; and Lucius** [Acts 13:1 (?)] **and Jason** [Acts 17:5, 6, 7, 9 (?)] **and Sosipater** [Acts 20:4 (?)], **my kinsmen.** [If Paul's colaborers were known personally to churches to which he addressed Epistles, he evidently inserted their names with his own at the beginning of the Epistle (see 1 and 2 Corinthians, Philippians, Colossians, 1 and 2 Thessalonians); but where they were only known by reputation, he appears to have merely subjoined their salutations as he has done here.] **22 I Tertius, who write the epistle, salute you in the Lord.** [Paul habitually used amanuenses (Gal. 6:11; Col. 4:18; 2 Thess. 3:17). Tertius, the penman of this Epistle, and known to us only here, shows to us by his salutation that he was no mere hireling in this service.] **23 Gaius my host, and of the whole church, saluteth you.** [Very likely the Gaius of 1 Cor. 1:14. The name is found elsewhere (Acts 19:29; 20:4; 3 John 1). This Gaius evidently entertained Paul at the time the Epistle was written, and at least occasionally, probably to hear Paul preach, the many sections of the entire Corinthian church met at his house. It must have been a capacious home—Acts 18:8-11.] **Erastus** [possibly the person mentioned at Acts 19:22 and 2 Tim. 4:20] **the treasurer of the city saluteth you, and Quartus the brother.** [Here end the salutations, and there follows the most condensed yet most comprehensive benediction ever penned.] **25 Now to him that is able to establish you** [*i. e.*, to the one who has given you an eternal foundation for your life (Matt. 7:24-27) and is able to build you as enduring material thereon (1 Cor. 3:10-17). Comp. ch. 1:11] **according to my gospel and the preaching of Jesus Christ** [Establish you according to, or in conformity with, the terms, conditions, means, grace and power found in that gospel which was revealed to me personally (Rom. 2:16; Gal. 1:11-17), even the heavenly truth contained in the preaching of Jesus Christ, who is the core and heart of that gospel. (Comp. ch. 1:3; 2:16; 10:8-12; Gal. 1:6-8.) Paul's gospel did not differ from that committed to the twelve, but he calls it specifically "my gospel" because it was delivered to him in lessons where he was the sole pupil (Gal. 1:12), and because his spiritual discernment, coupled with his special commission as apostle to the Gentiles, enabled him to see clearly two things in the gospel which were but faintly comprehended by the others; viz., that gospel salvation is wholly gratuitous and is not partly gratuitous and partly a matter of purchase by obedience to the Mosaic law (Gal. 5:1-12); that it is universal to all who are obedient unto the faith, and is in no sense confined to the Jews or their proselytes—Gal. 3:26-29], **according to the revelation of the mystery which hath been kept in silence through times eternal** [Establish you by the gospel and preaching which accords with or is true to the revelation or unveiling of the great mystery or secret; *i. e.*, the divine purpose of God to save the world by the sacrifice of his Son—a secret of times eternal (2 Tim. 1:9; Tit. 1:2), known only to the Father, and therefore capable of no revelation till his voice broke silence as to it. Comp. Matt. 24:36; Mark 13:32; 1 Pet. 1:12; Acts 1:7], **26 but now is manifested, and by the scriptures of the prophets, according to the commandment of the eternal God, is made known unto all the nations unto obedience of faith** [Comp. Col. 1:26; 4:4; Gal. 1:12, 16; 1 Cor. 2:10. "Manifested . . . made known." These two words express the two phases of revelation. Christ himself was the manifestation (Luke 2:30-32; John 1:14-18; 2:11; Heb. 1:3), the Light of the world (John 1:4-9; John 8:12); but this manifestation is introduced, interpreted, explained, "made known" by the Scriptures of the Old and New Testament writers or prophets, the former with their types, shadows and forecasts (Luke 24:25-27; Gal. 4:21-31; Col. 2:16, 17; Heb. 8:5; 9:9; 10:1-9), the latter with their gospel sermons and doctrinal epistles (1 Cor. 15:1; Gal. 1:11; 1 John 1:1-3). And these Scriptures were written for that purpose, not at the motion, option or choice of the writers, but by order and command of God himself (Deut. 5:22; Jer. 36:27, 28; 2 Pet. 1:20, 21; 1 Cor. 2:13; 2 Tim. 3:16), that men might know, and, knowing, might believe and obey, the gospel in its conditions and be saved thereby. Thus the apostle assures us that the Father, who gave us the Christ, gave us also correct biographies as to his incarnation, miracles, life, death, resurrection and coronation; that the God who gave us a gospel also insured to us the preservation of it in an efficient and effective form in the record which he commanded; that the Lord who gave us a church has also provided for the perpetual safeguarding of its plans, specifications and model as designed in his holy mountain (Heb. 8:5), preserving them forever in those Chronicles of his kingdom which we call the Bible. Common sense should tell us this, even if Paul had kept silence. How could we attribute infinite wisdom to a God who sacrificed his Son to make a gospel and then neglected to preserve that gospel that it might be used for the purposes for which it was prepared at so much cost? Moreover, this passage shows that God himself, back of the human penman, wrote the Bible; for he, and not they—no, not even the angels (1 Pet. 1:10, 12)—knew the secret which these Scriptures were revealing. Yea, he wrote it for the universal instruction of the unborn church in matters which no human wisdom could discover for itself. Therefore, whoso strikes at the Old Testament would destroy the foundation of the New, would annul what God has commanded, obliterate what God has revealed, and rob the dying world of the gospel, the salvation and the Christ which God has given. The one who attempts to do this thing (God be praised, he can not succeed save for a brief season—Rev. 11:3-12) would destroy God's means of life, and would leave the world, "all nations," with their teeming but helpless millions to perish without hope, setting his wisdom against that of "the only Wise." Such an one rivals the devil, both in unfeeling heartlessness and in supreme presumption]: **27 to the only wise God, through Jesus Christ, to whom be the glory for ever. Amen.** [Owing to difference in Greek and English construction, the long sentence beginning with verse 25 is grammatically incomplete as rendered in English. If, however, the "to whom" of the last phrase be changed to read "to him," the sense is complete and plain. "To him that is able . . . to him be the glory." The whole passage, then, is an ascription of praise, with reasons for it injected in the form of a parenthesis. It is an implied prayer for the safety of the Roman church expressed in the form of a burst of confident praise to him in whom that safety lay. Of this benediction Gifford thus writes: "Comparing it with the introduction in chapter 1, we find in both the same fundamental thoughts of the Epistle: 'the power of God unto salvation' (1:16), the gospel entrusted to Paul for the Gentiles (1:5), the testimony of the prophets (1:2), the 'obedience of the faith' (1:5), the acceptance of all nations (1:5, 14-16)—all these thoughts are here gathered up into one harmonious burst of 'wonder, love and praise.'" Thus the conclusion of the Epistle swings back to the beginning, so that the whole instruction assumes the form of the circle, symbol of its divine perfection, its unending authority,

www.ingramcontent.com/pod-product-compliance
Lightning Source LLC
Chambersburg PA
CBHW052110010526
44111CB00036B/1606